650

Simulation

of Discrete Stochastic Systems

Simulation
of Discrete Stochastic Systems

Herbert Maisel

Associate Professor of Computer Science
Director, Computation Center
Georgetown University

Giuliano Gnugnoli

Assistant Professor of Computer Science
Systems Analyst, Computation Center
Georgetown University

SRA Science Research Associates, Inc.
Chicago, Palo Alto, Toronto, Henley-on-Thames, Sydney
A Subsidiary of IBM

To Scott and Ray with the hope that this book helps to make their world a better one — H.M.
To my parents Amedeo and Neutra — G.G.

The authors and publisher wish to express their gratitude for the gracious consent of the authors and publishers of the following materials that were excerpted for inclusion in this volume:

Definition on p. 8: By permission. From *Webster's Seventh New Collegiate Dictionary* © 1971 by G. & C. Merriam Co., Publishers of the Merriam-Webster Dictionaries.

Figure 1.1 and parts of Section 1.5 from *Introduction to Electronic Digital Computers* by Herbert Maisel. Copyright 1969, McGraw-Hill Book Company. Used by permission of McGraw-Hill Book Company.

Forms and results of the Social Security Administration district office simulation study used by permission of Jacob A. Williams, Director, SSA Operations Research Staff.

Tables A.2, A.3, and A.4 excerpted from *Biometrika Tables for Statisticians*, edited by E. S. Pearson and H. O. Hartley (New York: Cambridge University Press, 1954). By permission of E. S. Pearson for the Biometrika Trustees.

Table A.5 excerpted from an article by Leo Goodman in the *Psychological Bulletin* 51 (1954), pp. 160–68. By permission of the American Psychological Association and L. A. Goodman.

Table A.6 excerpted from a table by Eisenhart and Swed in the *Annals of Mathematical Statistics* 14 (1943). By permission of The Institute of Mathematical Statistics.

Table A.7 excerpted from *A Million Random Digits with 100,000 Normal Deviates* (New York: Free Press, 1955). By permission of The Rand Corporation.

Table A.8 excerpted from tables by C. E. Van Orstand in the *Memoirs of the National Academy of Sciences* 14 (1921).

Tables in Appendix C: Reprinted by permission from *GPSS/360 User's Manual* (IBM Systems Reference Library Form H20–0326). © by International Business Machines Corporation.

Contents

Preface   xi

Part One   Introduction   1

1   Simulations, Systems, and Models   3

1.1	Introduction	3
1.2	Definition of Simulation	4
1.3	Advantages and Disadvantages of Simulation	4
1.4	The Electronic Digital Computer	7
1.5	Definition of a System	8
1.6	Discrete and Continuous Systems	12
1.7	Stochastic and Deterministic Systems	13
1.8	Models of Systems	14
1.9	Critical-Event and Time-Slice Models	15
1.10	Man-Machine Simulations	15
1.11	Variables in Simulations	16
1.12	How Simulations Are Used	17
1.13	A General Outline of a Computer Simulation	19
1.14	Supplementary Reading	21

2   General Procedure   23

2.1	Introduction	23
2.2	Overall View of the Procedure	24
2.3	The Preliminary Analysis	24
2.4	Problem Formulation	25
2.5	First Models	26
2.6	Data Collection	27
2.7	Data Processing and Analysis	30
2.8	The Control Group	33
2.9	Validation and Refinement of the Models	33
2.10	The Simulation Team	35
2.11	Summary of the Procedure	37
2.12	Supplementary Reading	38

Part Two   Statistical Tools   39

3   Statistical Distributions   41

    3.1   Background   41
    3.2   Discrete Densities and
          Distributions   45
    3.3   Continuous Densities and
          Distributions   46
    3.4   Moments   47
    3.5   The Binomial Distribution   48
    3.6   The Poisson Distribution   49

    3.7   The Uniform Distribution   50
    3.8   The Normal Distribution   51
    3.9   The Exponential Distribution   52
    3.10 Empirical Distributions   54
    3.11 Distributions Used in Making
          Statistical Tests   58
    3.12 Supplementary Reading   60
    Problems   61

4   Statistical Tests   67

    4.1   Background   67
    4.2   The Framework   68
    4.3   The Procedure   69
    4.4   The t Test   71
    4.5   The F Test   75
    4.6   Testing the Poisson Parameter   76

    4.7   The Kolmogorov-Smirnov Test   77
    4.8   The Runs Test   79
    4.9   The Mann-Whitney U Test   81
    4.10 The Chi Square Test   82
    4.11 Supplementary Reading   85
    Problems   86

5   Regression   89

    5.1   Background   89
    5.2   The Framework   90
    5.3   Fitting a Straight Line   92
    5.4   Multiple Linear Regression (MLR) 95
    5.5   Selecting the Best MLR   97

    5.6   Analysis of the Residuals   102
    5.7   Nonlinear Regression   103
    5.8   Regression and Validity   105
    5.9   Supplementary Reading   108
    Problems   108

6   The Analysis of Variance   113

    6.1   Background   113
    6.2   The Framework   114
    6.3   Underlying Assumptions and
          Factorial Designs   115
    6.4   The One-Way Classification   116
    6.5   The Two-Way Classification   118
    6.6 2^n Designs   123
    6.7   The Analysis of Variance and
          Validity   124

    6.8   Sensitivity Analysis   124
    6.9   Error Reduction: Analysis of
          Covariance   125
    6.10 Concluding Remarks   126
    6.11 Supplementary Reading   127
    Problems   127

Part Three   Random Number
              Generation   133

7   Generating Uniformly Distributed
    Numbers   135

    7.1   Introduction   135
    7.2   Testing Sequences of Random
          Numbers   137
    7.3   Congruential Methods   140
    7.4   Additive Congruential Generators 142
    7.5   Other Generators of
          Pseudorandom Numbers   143

    7.6   The GPSS Random Number
          Generator   144
    7.7   Supplementary Reading   145
    Problems   146

8   Generating Random Numbers with
    Nonuniform Distributions   149

    8.1   Introduction   149
    8.2   The Inverse Transformation   150
    8.3   The Rejection Method   152
    8.4   The Composition, or Mixture,
          Method   153
    8.5   Generating Normally Distributed
          Numbers   153
    8.6   Generating Exponentially
          Distributed Numbers   154

    8.7   Generating Binomially and
          Geometrically Distributed
          Numbers   155
    8.8   Generating Poisson Distributed
          Numbers   155
    8.9   Generating Numbers with
          Empirical Distributions   156
    Problems   157

Part Four   The Computer and
             Simulation   159

9   Simulation Programming and
    Languages   161

    9.1   Introduction   161
    9.2   The Example   162
    9.3   Review of Simulation Terminology 162
    9.4   Time   163
    9.5   Arrivals   164
    9.6   FORTRAN   166
    9.7   Queues   169
    9.8   Queues and List Processing   170
    9.9   PL/I   173
    9.10 Statistics   180

    9.11 SIMSCRIPT: Basic Concepts   183
    9.12 SIMSCRIPT: Language Elements 188
    9.13 SIMSCRIPT: An Example   194
    9.14 GPSS: Basic Concepts   198
    9.15 GPSS: Language Elements   200
    9.16 GPSS: An Example   203
    9.17 General Remarks on
          Simulation Languages   205
    9.18 Supplementary Reading   208

10   GPSS: An Introduction   211

10.1   Introduction   211
10.2   GPSS: Review of Basic Concepts   212
10.3   A GPSS Program   213
10.4   Movement, Events, and
       the Passage of Time   218
10.5   Block Type Symbols and Formats   219
10.6   The GENERATE, ADVANCE,
       TRANSFER, and TERMINATE
       Blocks   223
10.7   Facilities and Facility-Oriented
       Blocks   225
10.8   Storages and Storage-Oriented
       Blocks   227

10.9   Queues and Queue-Oriented
       Blocks   228
10.10 GPSS Control Cards   230
10.11 GPSS Input Deck Format   232
10.12 Utilization Statistics:
       The Cumulative Time Integral   233
10.13 Storage, Facility, and Queue
       Statistics   235
10.14 A Second Example   238
10.15 Debugging   243
10.16 Supplementary Reading   247
Problems   247

11   Additional GPSS Features   253

11.1   Introduction   253
11.2   Standard Numerical Attributes   254
11.3   Transaction Parameters   255
11.4   Indirect Addressing and
       Indirect Specification   257
11.5   Savevalues   258
11.6   Initializing and Redefining
       Savevalues   262
11.7   Frequency Distribution Tables   263
11.8   Standard Table Output   266
11.9   Random Numbers   267
11.10 Representing Densities and
       Distributions   269

11.11 Variables   273
11.12 An Example   275
11.13 The TEST Block   280
11.14 User Chains   281
11.15 The PRINT Block   284
11.16 Special Output   285
11.17 Graphic Output   292
11.18 The Bank Branch Simulation   297
Problems   311
Term Projects   312

12   Simulation of Computer Systems   317

12.1   The Objectives   317
12.2   Level of Detail   318
12.3   The Job Generator   319
12.4   Synthetic Job Streams   320
12.5   The Processor and Main Storage   322

12.6   Simulation of Input/Output   323
12.7   Simulation of a Batch System:
       An Example   324
12.8   Simulation of a
       Multiprogrammed System   328

Part Five   A Case Study   343

13   Planning, Design, and the Field
     Study   345

13.1   The Need for a Simulation   345
13.2   Management's Questions   346
13.3   Review of the Literature   347
13.4   Designing the Field Study   348
13.5   Preliminary Design of the
       Simulation   349

13.6   Further Study Design   350
13.7   Preparation for the Study   351
13.8   Conduct of the Study   352
13.9   Analysis of Results   354
13.10 Effects on Modeling Activities   356
13.11 Supplementary Reading   357

14   Model Development   359

14.1   Introduction   359
14.2   Simulating Arrivals   360
14.3   Simulating Interview Lengths:
       The *Gamma* Distribution   364
14.4   Converting Frequencies to
       Densities   366

14.5   Development of the Preprocessor   366
14.6   Assigning Work to Claims
       Representatives   370

15   The District Office Network
     Simulation   375

15.1   Introduction   375
15.2   Overall Structure   376
15.3   How the Simulation Is Used   380
15.4   The Preprocessor   382
15.5   The GPSS District Office
       Simulation   384

15.6   The Postprocessor   386
15.7   Debugging the Simulation   388
15.8   Validity   388
15.9   An Application   390

Appendix A   Miscellaneous Statistical
             Tables   395

Table A.1   The Standard Normal
            Density and Distribution   396
Table A.2   Critical Values of the
            t Distribution   397
Table A.3   Critical Values of the *Chi*
            Square Distribution   398
Table A.4   Critical Values of the
            F Distribution   399
Table A.5   Critical Values for the
            Kolmogorov-Smirnov Test   403

Table A.6   Critical Values for the
            Runs Test   404
Table A.7   500 Five-Digit Random
            Numbers   405
Table A.8   The Exponential and
            Negative Exponential
            Functions   406

Appendix B   Computer Programs   407

Program B.1   The Exact Mean and Variance of *Chi* Square When Expectations are Small   408

Program B.2   Test for Normality with Provision for Standardization of Variables   413

Program B.3   Linear Regression in Two Variables   414

Program B.4   Nonlinear Least Squares   417

Program B.5   Generation of Random Numbers   426

Appendix C   GPSS Characteristics   435

C.1   GPSS/360 Block Definition Cards   436

C.2   GPSS/360 Entity Definition Cards   442

C.3   GPSS/360 Control Cards   443

C.4   GPSS/360 Program Errors   444

C.5   GPSS/360 Block Types Not Discussed in the Text   452

C.6   Description of GPSS V   453

Bibliography   455

Index   460

Preface

GENERAL OBJECTIVES   This book is intended to serve both as a text for a senior-year or graduate course and as a reference for professionals engaged in simulation activities. It is not a handbook on simulation, although some of the discussion of statistical methods follows the approach associated with a good handbook. However, we hope that the professional will find it useful to refer repeatedly to this book as he works on developing a simulation.

We believe that this book would serve as an excellent text for Course A4 (Systems Simulation) listed in the ACM recommendations for an undergraduate curriculum in computer science (*Communications of the Association for Computing Machinery* 11, No. 3, March 1968). A similar course is listed in the recommendations for an undergraduate program in computational mathematics, prepared by the Committee on the Undergraduate Program in Mathematics, the CUPM. (A report on these recommendations, dated May 1971, is available from the Mathematical Association of America.) This book also could serve as a text for part of Course CMI (Computational Models and Problem Solving) listed in the CUPM recommendations.

Throughout the book, special emphasis has been placed on two very important topics that are covered inadequately in existing texts: validity and the connection between statistical methodology and the development of a simulation. A simulation cannot be useful unless it is valid; it cannot be valid unless considerations of validity enter into every aspect of the development of the simulation. Repeated use of a variety of statistical techniques is necessary in the development of almost every simulation of a stochastic system.

Other important features of the book include (1) a description of the algorithmic process present in simulation programs and an illustration of how this algorithm is implemented in different programming languages [Chapter 9]; (2) a discussion of more advanced GPSS features [Chapter 11]; (3) a discussion of the simulation of computer systems [Chapter 12]; and (4) the case study [Chapters 13–15].

GPSS is the only programming language discussed in detail because (1) it is widely available; (2) it is designed specifically for application to simulation problems; and (3) both its use and description enhance and illustrate the discussion of simulation techniques. GPSS differs from most simulation languages in that it is oriented toward the logical description of the system being simulated, rather than toward a sequence of commands to be executed.

Other programming languages can be used in simulation. A survey of these languages and a brief introduction to them is given in Chapter 9.

This book discusses the simulation of discrete stochastic systems on an electronic digital computer. Other important kinds of simulations are discussed in Chapter 1; references are provided there to discussions of these other kinds of simulations.

Most chapters conclude with a section containing suggestions for further reading; all references are grouped together in a comprehensive bibliography at the end of the book. Key words and phrases are *italicized* in the context in which they are defined, and **bold type** is used in the index for the corresponding page references. This style of definition has been chosen deliberately in preference to a glossary, because glossary definitions all too often prove incomplete, inadequate, and misleading without accompanying discussion and examples.

Several term projects are recommended at the end of Chapter 11. If term projects are to be assigned (and we strongly recommend them), the assignments should be made at the beginning of the second semester for a two-semester course or at the beginning of a one-semester course. The location of the projects in this book indicates only that the student will not be able to complete them until he has mastered the material in Chapters 1 through 11. However, he will need to begin work on the project long before Chapter 11 is completed.

OUTLINE   The book is divided into five major parts. Part One delineates the scope of the book, defines some of the more important terms used in simulations, describes a simulation in rather broad terms, and outlines the procedure for developing a simulation. Chapter 1 concentrates on the first three of these objectives and Chapter 2 on the final objective.

Part Two covers a variety of statistical topics that are needed in simulations. The goals of this part are (1) to review basic statistical concepts, (2) to provide a summary of a few of the most important statistical techniques used in simulation, and (3) to guide the reader to further references. Because some previous experience in statistics is considered a prerequisite for this book, the basic concepts are merely reviewed and are not treated comprehensively. Because entire books have been written about the subject matter of each of the chapters in this section, we obviously can cover only a few statistical techniques here. The bibliography and the sections on supplementary reading at the end of each chapter will guide the reader to books and other writings on the subjects that are discussed. The discussion in each chapter is intended to guide the reader through the extensive and growing body of literature on these statistical topics. The major statistical topics covered in Part Two are statistical distributions (Chapter 3), parametric and non-parametric tests (Chapter 4), regression techniques (Chapter 5), and the design and analysis of simulation experiments (Chapter 6).

Part Three discusses the generation of pseudorandom numbers. Prescribed stochastic behavior is introduced in a simulation by means of such random numbers. Although the subject is covered reasonably thoroughly, the objective is to make the reader familiar with the techniques of random number generation, rather than to make him an expert on the subject.

Part Four discusses programming languages for use in a simulation and discusses the simulation of a computer system. Chapter 9 contains an overview of the programming languages used in simulations. Chapter 10 and 11 contain a detailed description of one of these languages, GPSS. Chapter 12 discusses the simulation of computer systems, a topic that is of interest in its own right and that also serves to illustrate many of the concepts and techniques introduced in earlier chapters.

In Part Five, the techniques, tools, and knowledge developed in earlier chapters are brought to bear on a specific simulation application. Examples are used throughout the book to illustrate definitions and to provide practice in procedures, but it isn't until Part Five that it all is "put together" in a description of the simulation of the Social Security district office network. We consider this detailed case study to be an essential part of the book.

There also are three important sets of appendices. Appendix A gives standard statistical tables that are useful in carrying out the statistical analyses associated with the development of a simulation. Appendix B contains descriptions of FORTRAN programs developed by the authors and their associates at the Georgetown University Computation Center. These programs are useful in carrying out some of the statistical analyses; they are listed here because they are not readily available from other sources. Several other useful programs (that are readily available from other sources) are cited in the text. Finally, Appendix C provides some detailed information about GPSS characteristics.

POSSIBLE COURSE CONTENT   This book is intended as a text for a two-semester course for students who have completed both a first course in statistics and a first course in computer science. Students with both an extensive background in statistical methodology and a first course in computers might be able to complete the course in one semester. For such a one-semester course, only Parts One, Three, and Five would be covered in full. Because it may be impossible to cover even these three parts fully in one semester, we recommend the following further reductions in the material offered:

Student Background Includes	Course Length (semesters)	Chapters To Be Covered
A first course in statistics and a first course in computers	2	All
An extensive background in statistical methodology and a first course in computers	1 (with difficulty)	1, 2, 7, 9, 10, 12–15
An extensive background in statistical methodology and a first course in computers	1	1, 2, 7, 9, 10, 14, 15

ACKNOWLEDGEMENTS   The authors are deeply indebted to Jacob Williams and Barbara Haskins of the operations research staff of the Social Security Administration for their help and cooperation in the development of the district office case study. Most of the programs used in the simulation of the district office network were written by John Fraser of the Social Security Administration. The publisher thanks Peter D'Anna, Public Affairs Officer of the Social Security Administration in San Francisco, for his cooperation and assistance in obtaining the photographs used in this book.

Finally, we wish to express our appreciation to Jay Nunamaker for providing the programs on random number generation (Program B.5 in Appendix B), to both Jay Nunamaker and Doug Seeley for their very helpful suggestions, to Sonja Harper for her efficient clerical assistance, and to our wives Millie and Liz who consoled us, helped us, and lost many weekends in order that this work might be completed.

Herbert Maisel
Giuliano Gnugnoli

The photographs that appear at the beginning of each chapter were taken by Ken Graves at the San Francisco district office of the Social Security Administration. This photo essay illustrates the reality that is being simulated in the major case study discussed in this book.

Part One

INTRODUCTION

Here we define some of the more important terms used in simulations and give a rather broad description of a procedure that may be used to develop a simulation of a discrete stochastic system on an electronic digital computer. This procedure has evolved from the experiences of one of the authors in working on development of several simulations of this kind. There certainly are other workable approaches, but nearly all of these approaches are more-or-less similar to the one outlined here.

CHAPTER 1 Simulations,
Systems, and Models

CHAPTER 2 General Procedure

1

Simulations, Systems, and Models

1.1 INTRODUCTION   Simulation is a technique of growing importance in many fields, both theoretical and applied. As the title indicates, this book discusses only one of several kinds of simulations. It is important to characterize the kind of simulation to be discussed—and, by implication, the kinds of simulations that are not discussed. Much of this first chapter is devoted to a survey of concepts and terms that will help to establish this characterization: simulation, system, digital computer, discrete system, stochastic system, variable, critical-event and time-slice models, etc. The chapter also considers the advantages and disadvantages of simulation and concludes with a brief description of how a simulation is used and of how it works.

1.2 Definition of Simulation

In general usage, simulation is defined as an act or process that gives the appearance or effect of some part of reality—a counterfeit, a feigning. Maisel (1969, p. 111) has suggested that the purpose of simulation is "to attain the essence without the reality." Such definitions are too broad. A more operational definition is given by Naylor et al. (1966, p. 3): "simulation is a numerical technique for conducting experiments on a digital computer, which involves certain types of mathematical and logical models that describe the behavior of a business or economic system (or some component thereof) over extended periods of time." Except for the restriction to business or economic systems and the specification of "extended" periods of time, it is a good working definition for our purposes. Social, biological, physical, and chemical systems also are simulated, and the duration of the time period depends upon the type of system being simulated and upon the kind of applications to be made. Of course, simulations may be carried out on an analog computer or with pencil and paper, but the simulations to be discussed in this book are those that are carried out on a digital computer (see Section 1.4). With the modifications suggested above, the working definition for our purposes in this book is the following:

Simulation is a numerical technique for conducting experiments on a digital computer; this technique involves certain types of mathematical and logical models that describe the behavior of business, economic, social, biological, physical, or chemical systems (or some component thereof) over periods of time.

1.3 Advantages and Disadvantages of Simulation

Increasing speed and decreasing cost of electronic computers—as well as development of programming languages particularly suitable for simulations— have resulted in a dramatic increase in the number of computer simulations in recent years. The growth in simulation activity is reflected in the literature of fields such as engineering, computer science, operations research, statistics, economics, and business administration. For example, a survey article on simulation appeared in the *Communications of the Association for Computing Machinery* (Teichroew and Lubin 1966), and engineering applications of simulation are emphasized in the periodical *Simulation Magazine*. Papers on simulation are common at national meetings of the relevant professional societies. A series of Annual Conferences on the Applications of Simulation recently has been established under the joint sponsorship of several professional societies. This increase in simulation activity is a result of the discovery that—for many applications—the advantages of simulation outweigh the disadvantages (see Table 1.1).

Attempts to represent or to model the natural world certainly are not novel. Such attempts were being made at the beginning of recorded history. Most early models were descriptive, but quantitative and predictive models of astronomical processes were developed very early. Attempts to build models stemmed from innate human curiosity about the world or from a need to understand and to control natural processes. A model provides a simplified analogy for a natural phenomenon. The model may be easier to understand; it may provide insight into the origins and effects of the process; it may facilitate experimental manipulation (of the model if not of the natural phenomenon). Much of scientific activity in the natural and life sciences has involved development and manipulation of such models. The use of explicit models in the social sciences is a more recent development, and business administrators only now are beginning to see the advantages in this attack on a problem.

A simulation (as defined above) is a particular kind of model of a real system. The major advantage of a simulation is that it permits study of the real system without actual modification of that system in any way. For many real systems, major experimentation involves very high risks. Changes of policy in a business enterprise, changes of law in a social system, changes of policy in an economic system, new strategies and tactics in combat, new treaties in international relations—such modifications may lead to very desirable results, or they may lead to catastrophe. How is the administrator to know which changes can be attempted? He can look to past experience; he can call upon expert opinion; he can implement changes on a limited basis. All of these things have been and will continue to be done. But if the system is simulated on a computer, the results of various modifications can be observed in the simulation without modifying the real system in any way. Alternative modifications can be tried and their consequences studied in a systematic and controlled way. Of course, other kinds of models also can be used to make predictions about the behavior of real systems. But for complex systems of the kinds mentioned, the simulation on a

TABLE 1.1 Summary of Advantages and Disadvantages of Computer Simulations

Advantages	Disadvantages
Permits controlled experimentation with: (a) consideration of many factors; (b) manipulation of many individual units; (c) ability to consider alternative policies; and (d) little or no disturbance of the actual system	Very costly Uses scarce and expensive resources Requires fast, high capacity computers Takes a long time to develop May hide critical assumptions May require extensive field studies
Effective training tool	
Provides operational insight	
May dispel operational myths	
May make middle management more effective	

digital computer is unequalled in its ability to provide realistic models of system behavior at a reasonable investment of time and money.

Simulation has other advantages. As a process is studied in preparation for a simulation, previously unrecognized relationships or deficiencies often are revealed. These discoveries may lead to immediate alterations and improvements in the process. Simulations also have many uses as training tools, and a number of simulations have been developed for this specific purpose. Finally, computer simulations permit the study of a broad range of problems and the asking of extremely complex questions. The computer can manipulate elaborate descriptive and mathematical models that consider a great number of factors, provide for complex interrelationships, and deal simultaneously with a large number of individual units.

Of course, the powerful advantages of computer simulations are offset to some extent by certain disadvantages. These include dollar cost, the use of scarce resources, and the long wait before an operational simulation is developed.

Simulations of large-scale real systems are expensive. Development of a simulation requires many high-priced specialists, time on large and expensive computers, and extensive studies of operating elements. For example, the development of a simulation of land combat (Maisel et al. 1963) involved an estimated 30 man-years of modeling talent, 30 man-years of effort by highly trained military officers, and about 40 man-years of computer programming effort. Development of this simulation also required about 3,000 hours of time on an expensive computer system. A useful simulation was not obtained until two and one-half years after development was begun. The overall cost of this effort was about 3 million dollars. As another example, consider a simulation of the district office network of the social security system, developed in the period 1967 through 1971 (Haskins 1969). This simulation required much less effort in modeling and computer programming, but a field study of the system involved 10 man-years of effort. About 2,500 hours of time on high speed computers was used in development of the simulation.

Computer simulations also have a more subtle disadvantage: the simulation exists only as a series of computer programs. As a result, management cannot "see" how the simulation actually operates. It is easy to overlook hidden limitations on the result, such as assumptions underlying the modeling effort and the compromises that had to be made "to get the simulation on the computer." Management often accepts the results without sufficient challenge, largely because there is something inherently reassuring about outputs from a complex mechanism, especially a computer. It always is advisable to obtain a "seat-of-the-pants" guess from an expert whenever possible. If there is a sizable difference between this guess and the result of the simulation, the simulation group must be challenged to explain the difference. There is a complementary advantage in this checking process. The expert may get better insight into the system through work with the simulation. Some myths about the system may be dispelled.

1.4 The Electronic Digital Computer

Useful and effective simulations can be implemented with equipment such as an analog computer or even a pencil and paper. Manual business and war games are examples of pencil-and-paper simulations. Training devices for pilots and astronauts are examples of simulations that use an analog computer. However, only a digital computer can handle the enormous number of calculations and extent of record keeping needed for a realistic simulation of subtle, complex relationships among many factors and involving many individual units.

Because this book will deal only with simulations using electronic digital computers, we shall summarize briefly here the distinctions between electronic and nonelectronic computers and between digital and analog computers. A more detailed description of the computer programming languages (the *computer software*) for simulations is given in Part Four.

More than 2,500 years ago, men began using various computational aids to assist in the tedious task of carrying out arithmetic calculations. Probably the first such aid significantly to enhance man's computational skills was the abacus. In the hands of a skilled operator, this device rivals the modern electro-mechanical desk calculator in speed of operation. In fact, it was not until the 1940s—with development of the electronic computer—that another significant improvement in computational speed and reliability was achieved. The components of an electronic computer—the vacuum tube and, later, the transistor—can be changed from one state to another so rapidly and reliably that these devices have led to improvements of several orders of magnitude. Computer technology already has reached the point where the speed of light is a limiting factor that must be considered. The time required for computer operations now is measured in *nanoseconds* (billionths of a second). An electronic pulse, moving at the speed of light, travels about 1 foot in a nanosecond. Thus, the distance that the pulse must move within the computer is a significant factor in computer-design considerations.

The electronic computer is very reliable. A modern computer can operate for days, weeks, or even months without failure. Further, the computer is so designed that any failure usually is detected before it affects the result. A failure in the computer hardware may result in lost time, but it seldom causes errors in the computational output. However, software is becoming an increasingly important component of the computer system, and software failures are far more likely to cause errors in output before they are detected. Even the possibility of time loss through hardware failure is greatly reduced by redundancy, particularly in auxiliary storage equipment such as magnetic tape drives or disk drives. This redundancy often allows work to be processed even though one of these units is inoperable.

The electronic computer is used for most complex simulations because of its ability to carry out extensive sequences of calculations quickly and reliably. But the computer used in most simulations not only is electronic; it also is digital. A digital computer records information in the form of a sequence of digits—in other words, as a number. With suitable codes, a sequence of digits also can represent alphabetic information and special characters, so that the range of information that can be processed on a digital computer is virtually unlimited. With longer and longer codes, the representation can be made very precise. Most computers in use today can record at least 16 or 17 decimal digits, giving a precision of one part in 10^{16} or 10^{17}. Thus, the digital computer can handle a wide variety of problems and, by means of suitable modification in its software, can process very different problems at different times (in rapid succession if this is necessary). Because of its versatility and precision, the digital computer has more widespread application than does the analog computer.

The *analog computer* represents information by means of some physical analogy. The slide rule is a nonelectronic analog computer in which numbers are represented by proportional distances along the scales. In electronic analog computers, quantities are represented by proportional voltages, currents, and resistances. The analog computer is less precise and less versatile than the digital computer, but it is somewhat faster and easier to use in certain applications. It has widespread use in certain kinds of simulations, particularly in devices that simulate such things as airplane and space flight or control equipment. It is possible that the analog computer could be used fruitfully in other kinds of simulations. However, the widespread availability of the general-purpose digital computer and the increasing pool of personnel experienced in its use probably will cause a further trend away from the use of analog computers in simulations. The discussion in this book will be limited to simulations using digital computers. Gordon (1969, pp. 29–47) discusses the place of analog computers in simulation, and McLeod (1968) gives several examples of their use.

1.5 Definition of a System

Webster's Collegiate Dictionary (1967, p. 895) defines a system as "a regularly interacting or interdependent group of items forming a unified whole." Gordon (1969, p. 1) gives an almost identical definition: "an aggregation or assemblage of objects joined in some regular interaction or interdependence." For our purposes, we will use a more specific and operational definition:

A *system* is a collection of regularly interacting or interdependent components (such as machines, people, information, and communications), acting as a unit in carrying out an implicitly or explicitly defined mission.

As an example of a system, consider a calculating unit with the following components: a desk calculator, its operator, a pad of paper, and a pencil. There are regular interactions among these components: the operator reads from the pad, presses buttons on the calculator, reads the output of the calculator, and uses the pencil to make notes on the pad. The components of this system might form a *subsystem* of a more complex system. For example, a statistical laboratory could be considered as made up of sixteen such subsystems and an instructor. In this case, the calculator operators in the subsystems are called students in the larger system. Other components, such as a blackboard and chalk, may be involved in the larger system. The mission of the calculator subsystem may be explicitly defined in the assignments of the instructor. The mission of the statistical laboratory may not be defined explicitly anywhere (except perhaps in the college catalog), but a mission is implicitly defined by its activities. Similar calculator subsystems might be found within the system of a business office, with missions defined explicitly by job descriptions or daily assignments.

As an example of a complex system with many subsystems, we will describe in some detail a district office of the social security system. This example will be used to illustrate a number of points throughout the book. The Social Security Administration has several hundred district offices in the United States and Puerto Rico. These offices are the principal points of contact between the public and the Social Security Administration. At these offices, social security account numbers are assigned, requests (*claims*) for retirement or disability benefits are submitted, and questions are answered.

District offices come in a variety of sizes and shapes. The largest, called *class-A offices*, are located in metropolitan centers. The smallest, *class-E offices*, are located in rural or small urban areas. Intermediate sized offices — classes B, C, and D, from largest to smallest — are found in a wide variety of locations.

Figure 1.1 shows the layout of a typical class-C or class-D office, with the path that a visitor might follow through the office shown by solid lines. The processing of the claim that he might submit is indicated by dashed lines. There are several categories of employees in the office, including the manager (**M** in Figure 1.1), assistant manager (**AM**), administrative clerk (**AC**), claims representatives (**CR**), field representatives (**FR**), service representatives (**SR**), claims-development clerical personnal (**CDC**), the receptionist (**R**), and clearance-service clerical personnel who work in the clearance-service unit (**CSU**).

The manager and assistant manager share the supervisory and policy-making activities of the office; they also make frequent public appearances to disperse information about the social security program. Field representatives also make public appearances from time to time. The administrative clerk assists with administrative details in the activities of the manager and assistant manager.

Responsibility for taking and developing a claim rests with the claims representatives (in the district office) and the field representatives (outside the office). Field representatives also have desks in the office, and occasionally they assist the claims representatives by conducting interviews or reviewing evidence in the office. The service representatives and claims-development clerical personnel also assist the claims representative. Service representatives handle telephone contacts, answer questions about the status of claims or about delays in benefits, and evaluate routine evidence. The claims-development clerical

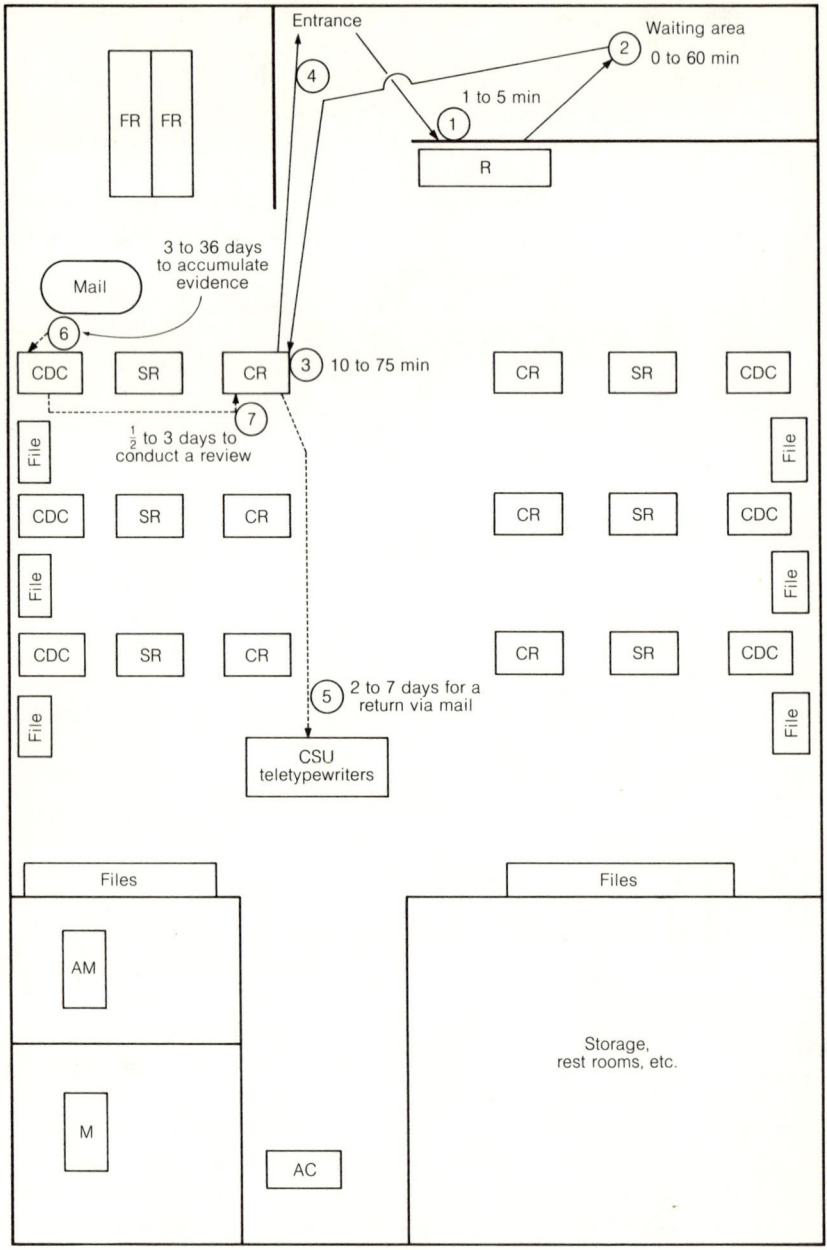

FIG. 1.1 Floor Plan of Social Security District Office (*scale, approximately* 1 *inch* = 10 *feet*), Showing Flow of Activities

personnel gather the evidence, prepare routine requests for additional material, and forward the evidence to the claims representative for evaluation.

The receptionist is the first person contacted by a visitor to the office. In most offices, the receptionist will issue account numbers and will answer simple questions, but she will refer a visitor to a claims representative or a service representative for interviews regarding the submission of a claim, the development of a claim already being processed, or delays or changes in benefit checks. The clearance-service unit prepares requests for earnings reports. These requests are transmitted by teletypewriter to the headquarters of the Social Security Administration.

Note the path of a typical claimant on his first visit to the district office (Figure 1.1). On entering the office, the visitor speaks to the receptionist (**1**), who determines the purpose of his visit. If the receptionist cannot satisfy the visitor, she determines whom he should see and, if that person is busy, asks the visitor to wait (**2**). If he wishes to submit a claim, he is interviewed by a claims representative (**3**) and then leaves the office (**4**). During the course of the interview, the visitor has become a *claimant* by filing a claim, which now must be processed. A folder is created by a clerical employee at the conclusion of the interview. All records relating to this claim will be stored in this folder.

A request for the record of the claimant's earnings is processed at the clearance-service unit (**5**) and is forwarded to headquarters by teletypewriter. When the earnings report arrives by mail from headquarters, a claims-development clerical employee (**6**) enters it in the folder established for the claim, along with other information gathered to permit evaluation of the claim. When sufficient evidence is in the folder, the clerical employee turns the whole file over to the claims representative for evaluation (**7**). This evaluation often results in further correspondence between the claimant, the district office, and headquarters. The new information arriving by mail is entered in the folder (**6**), and the folder again is forwarded to the claims representative for evaluation (**7**). Steps **6** and **7** may be repeated several times, until the claims representative is satisfied that the evidence in the folder is sufficient to permit him to make a decision about the claim.

In many district offices (such as the one shown in Figure 1.1), each claim is handled from submission through development and evaluation by a single team, composed of one claims representative, one service representative, and one claims-development clerical employee. The receptionist decides which team will be given the initial interview on the basis of account numbers or of the first letter of the visitor's surname. In some other district offices, there are separate pools of claims representatives, service representatives, and claims-development clerical employees. When work is to be done on a particular claim, it is given to the first person available in the appropriate pool, regardless of who first processed the claim or whether the employee in the pool has ever worked on this particular claim before.

Figure 1.1 also indicates the range of times required in visitor stations **1** to **3** and in steps **5** to **7** of processing the claim. For example, it takes from 2 to 7 days to get an earnings report from headquarters (**5**) and from 3 to 36 days to accumulate the evidence associated with a claim (**6**).

It is clear that this district office is a system. Its interacting elements include such things as personnel, office space, equipment, communication lines, and file folders. For analysis, it will be convenient to view the office as a collection of subsystems, each of which is centered around a group of employees. One subsystem is centered around the receptionist. Others are centered around each claims representative and his team or around each pool of a particular personnel category (depending upon the office organization). Still another subsystem is centered around the manager and assistant manager, and another around the clearance-service unit employees. (We have chosen to ignore other possible subsystems that are involved less directly in the processing of claims. For example, there is a subsystem centered around the janitorial employees who keep the premises clean, and another around the repairmen who come in occasionally to service the office equipment. Although the office could not function very well without these subsystems, we assume that they need not be studied in order to understand the system that interests us. Notice how easy it is for assumptions to slip undetected into the early stages of a simulation study.)

The activities of the district office system can be described by gathering descriptions of the activities of its subsystems. For the most part, a simulation of this system would be composed of models (and corresponding computer programs) for the way that each of the subsystems interacts with other subsystems and with the visitors and claims that pass through the office (the office workload). The nature of these interactions was outlined in the preceding paragraphs. The development of a simulation of this system is described in Chapters 13 through 15, with some examples of the models and computer programs used to represent these interactions.

1.6 Discrete and Continuous Systems

A system may be regarded as continuous or discrete, depending upon the way that it changes from one state to another. The distinction can best be seen by considering the values that can be taken on by the variables that characterize the state of the system. *Continuous systems* include variables that can take on any real value in a prescribed interval or intervals. *Discrete systems* include variables that can take on only particular values from among a finite (but possibly very large) set of alternatives. Both the statistical laboratory and the social security district office are discrete systems. The system changes from one distinct state to another as activities occur in a series of individual steps. For example, the operator of the desk calculator in the laboratory is engaged in a series of discrete activities. He presses a series of buttons, then makes marks on the paper, then reads from the paper or listens to the instructor, and so on. At any given moment, his state can be specified by a variable indicating which of these particular activities he is engaged in. In the district office, the trail of the claimant through the office is divided into a series of discrete actions: the claimant enters the door, speaks to the receptionist, waits, is interviewed, and leaves. His status at any moment could be indicated by a variable with a finite number of alternative values. Similarly, the status of the receptionist could be indicated by a variable whose discrete values show that she is either speaking with a visitor, handling a phone call, processing forms, waiting with nothing to do, out for lunch, or on vacation.

As an example of a continuous system, consider an airplane in flight. The power of the engines, the direction and speed of the wind, the positions of the control surfaces, and the position and velocity of the airplane all are continuous variables that take on a continuous series of values. Another continuous system is the solar system, with the planets, moons, sun, and other bodies moving smoothly and continuously. Simulation of continuous systems often involves systems of differential equations, which are handled conveniently on analog computers. Gordon (1969) discusses the simulation of continuous systems. This book deals only with discrete systems.

It could be argued that almost every system is continuous in reality. For example, the activities of a desk-calculator operator could be represented by describing the position of his hands in space-time coordinates. We choose not to do this because the model would become unnecessarily complicated, and because the positions of the operator's hands are of importance to us only insofar as they relate to the fact that he is operating the calculator or is writing on the scratchpad. Similarly, any continuous system could be represented by a discrete model. The flight of an airplane could be described with a series of discrete steps such as taking off, cruising between landmarks, and landing. Such a model might be useful for a study of air traffic. However, if the simulation is designed for evaluation of the flight characteristics of the airplane or for training of pilots, this discrete model would be unsatisfactory because too much information about the flight would be lost. Thus it should be clear that the simulation team decides in each case whether a discrete or a continuous model is most appropriate to serve the purposes of the simulation. In most cases it is easy to make this decision.

1.7 Stochastic and Deterministic Systems

A system may be regarded either as deterministic or stochastic, depending upon the causal relationship between input and output. The output of a *deterministic system* can be predicted completely if the input and the initial state of the system are known. That is, for a particular state of the system, a given input always leads to the same output. However, a *stochastic system* in a given state may respond to a given input with any one among a range or distribution (see Chapter 3) of outputs. For a stochastic system—given the input and the state of the system—it is possible to predict only the range within which the output will fall and the frequency with which various particular outputs will be obtained over many repetitions of the observation. It is impossible to predict the particular output of a single observation of the system.

An example of a deterministic system is a typewriter, which always responds with a particular output to a given input on its keyboard. An example of a stochastic system is a roulette wheel. In most systems, some elements are stochastic and others are deterministic. In such cases—because the output of the total system usually is affected by the stochastic elements—the system as a whole is treated stochastically.

It may be argued that systems are treated stochastically only because knowledge of the system is incomplete. If everything were known about the mechanism of the roulette wheel, the air currents around it, the gravitational field, and the exact input given by the operator as he tossed the ball and spun the wheel, the output might be predicted uniquely. This argument is of philosophical interest, but it is operationally unimportant because it would be senseless and hopeless even to attempt to determine the state and inputs of the system so precisely. The stochastic approximation—if indeed it is an approximation—is a useful and necessary one. In order to avoid unnecessary and expensive detail in models and programs, it often is useful to make a stochastic approximation even when a deterministic model might be possible.

This book deals with the simulation of stochastic systems. Obviously, such simulations are based upon statistical theory and methodology, and the more important statistical tools for simulations are summarized in Part Two. Introduction of stochastic behavior in a computer simulation requires the use of random number generators, which are discussed in Part Three.

1.8 Models of Systems

The preparation of models is an integral part of the development of a computer simulation. There are many kinds of models: physical, verbal-descriptive, flow-chart, mathematical, and computer. In many cases, a given system may best be modeled by a combination of these types. Each of these kinds of models has a place in the computer simulation of a discrete stochastic system. The computer model is, in fact, the simulation. That is, the set of programs (running on a digital computer) that model a discrete stochastic system is the objective of the efforts discussed in this book. The other models may contribute to the realization of this objective. Although physical models are less useful in simulations of discrete systems than they are in simulations of continuous systems, a mockup of an office or of a manufacturing plant has been used in simulation development. In various places throughout this book, flowchart, verbal-descriptive, mathematical, and computer models are used.

The authors know of no effective handbook for developing models. One of the most extensive discussions of model construction currently available is that given by Martin (1968). In this book, we present examples of model building in the hope that the process may be learned by analogy.

1.9 Critical-Event and Time-Slice Models

A discrete stochastic system ordinarily is modeled using either a critical-event or a time-slice approach. In the *critical-event* approach, the system is viewed as proceeding from one event to another until a prescribed sequence of events is completed. In the *time-slice* approach, the system is viewed as changing in all of its aspects over time; its status is updated, usually in fixed time increments, until a prescribed amount of time has elapsed.

For example, the operations of the district office might be viewed by either approach. In the critical-event approach, the office is viewed as a sequence of servers or processors acting on customers and claims. Each event is a step in the office's interaction with its customers and claims. A chain of events begins with the arrival of a visitor. This event leads to an interaction with the receptionist. The visitor's progress through the office is viewed as a chain of events, with each event leading to the generation of a following event. One event in this chain may be the generation of a claim, which in turn progresses through the office in a chain of events. Elapsed time between events simply is noted along the way. In the time-slice approach, the office is observed at fixed intervals of time. At each observation, the status of all elements in the model — visitors, servers, claims, and so on — is appropriately modified to reflect the activities that occurred during the preceding time interval.

In most cases, it is easiest to produce models and programs based upon the critical-event approach. However, this approach may not be easily applicable to complex systems in which many events are occurring simultaneously.

1.10 Man-Machine Simulations

The simulations discussed in this book may include a human component in their execution. Decision processes of management personnel or military officers proved difficult to model in some simulations. In simulating other systems, the training of future decision makers was a major objective of the simulation. In such cases, activities (almost always the making of decisions) by human components were integrated into the series of computer programs that simulate all other aspects of the system. Such simulations often are called *games* and the human components are called *players*. Examples of such simulation games include war games (Maisel et al. 1963) and business games (Naylor et al. 1966, pp. 205–215).

1.11 Variables in Simulations

In models of systems, either physical analogies or names are used to represent corresponding features of the real world. Computer models use names (*variables*) for this purpose. The variables used in a simulation can be classified according to several criteria.

Endogenous variables are those that denote characteristics internal to the system, whereas *exogenous* variables denote characteristics external to the system (in the system environment). For example, consider a variable used to denote the status of a particular claims representative in a simulation of a district office. We will call the claims representative Mr. A and will denote his status by the variable SCRA. This variable will have the value of 1 if Mr. A is conducting an interview, 2 if he is talking on the telephone, 3 if he is busy with paperwork (for example, evaluating evidence on a claim), 4 if he is idle but unavailable for interviewing (for example, if he is out for lunch), and 0 if he is idle and available for interviewing. Clearly, SCRA is a discrete variable that can take one of only five distinct values. SCRA is an endogenous variable because it helps to describe an aspect of the district office itself and because its value at any given time is determined by factors internal to the simulation. Another variable, SVISX, might be used to denote the status of a particular visitor, Mr. X. SVISX will have the value of 1 if Mr. X has come to ask a question, 2 if he has come to file a claim, 3 if he has come to get an account number, and 4 if he has come for further interviews about a claim already being processed. SVISX also is a discrete variable, but it is an exogenous variable because its value is determined by factors external to the simulation. Other exogenous variables might be used to describe the population levels and the socioeconomic status of the area serviced by the office or to denote the extent of nearby parking and public transportation facilities. Such variables may be used in the simulation to produce visitor arrival patterns or the distribution of the various kinds of claims submitted to the office.

Another criterion for classification of variables is based on the kind of features that the variable denotes. Variables used as names for the components of a system and its workload are called *entities*. Variables used to denote such things as employees, visitors, claimants, and claims in a district office are entities. Variables used to denote characteristics of these entities are called *attributes*. An entity is entirely characterized by its attributes. The claims representative, Mr. A, might be denoted in the simulation by a variable CRA, which would be an entity. The variable SCRA is an attribute of CRA, denoting the status of CRA. Other attributes might denote his years of experience, his civil service grade, or his current workload. Entities engage in *activities*, which may in some cases be represented by variables. More commonly, the activities are denoted by particular values assigned to an attribute variable. For example, the current activity of Mr. A is denoted by the current value of the attribute SCRA. Table 1.2 lists a few systems, with examples of an entity, an attribute, and an activity associated with each of them.

The use of a status attribute to indicate an activity is particularly useful for those entities that denote components performing services or modifying products. Often it is not necessary in the simulation to describe exactly what they are doing (their activity), but it is sufficient merely to specify whether they are available for new assignments or unavailable. Even when some detail is needed, a few different states may suffice. For example, there is no need in the district office simulation to distinguish among the many different activities that might be indicated by assigning the value 4 to SCRA. We do not care whether Mr. A is eating lunch, taking a coffee break, nursing a hangover, or on leave. All that matters is the fact that he is neither interviewing a claimant, working on a claim, nor available for a new interview.

Some authors use the terms entity, attribute, and activity to refer only to the features of the real system that is being simulated. We prefer to associate these terms with the variables used in the simulation to denote the real world features. For convenience, and where ambiguity will not result, we sometimes will use these terms to denote the real world features as well.

1.12 How Simulations Are Used

The flowchart of Figure 1.2 describes the way a simulation is used. In this book, we have followed the ANSI recommendations for the construction of flowcharts. These recommendations are listed in Appendix B of Maisel (1969).

In Figure 1.2, we assume that a simulation has been developed and is available for use. Its use is triggered by the need to solve a problem or to answer

TABLE 1.2   Examples of Entities, Attributes, and Activities

System	Entity	Attribute	Activity
Statistical laboratory	Student	Course, section	Operating desk calculator
District office	Claim	Type (*e.g.*, disability or retirement)	Being developed by a claims representative
Manufacturing plant	Lathe	Model, type	In transit to repair shop
Electronic digital computer	Card reader	Model, type	Reading cards

a question. If it is determined that use of the simulation is appropriate in this case, it then is necessary to choose a set of runs, select appropriate inputs for those runs, and establish an analytic procedure for evaluating the simulation. We use the term *simulation run* or simply *run* to refer to a single execution of the set of programs that constitute the simulation. It is important to note that effective use of a simulation requires a great deal of planning and analysis before the

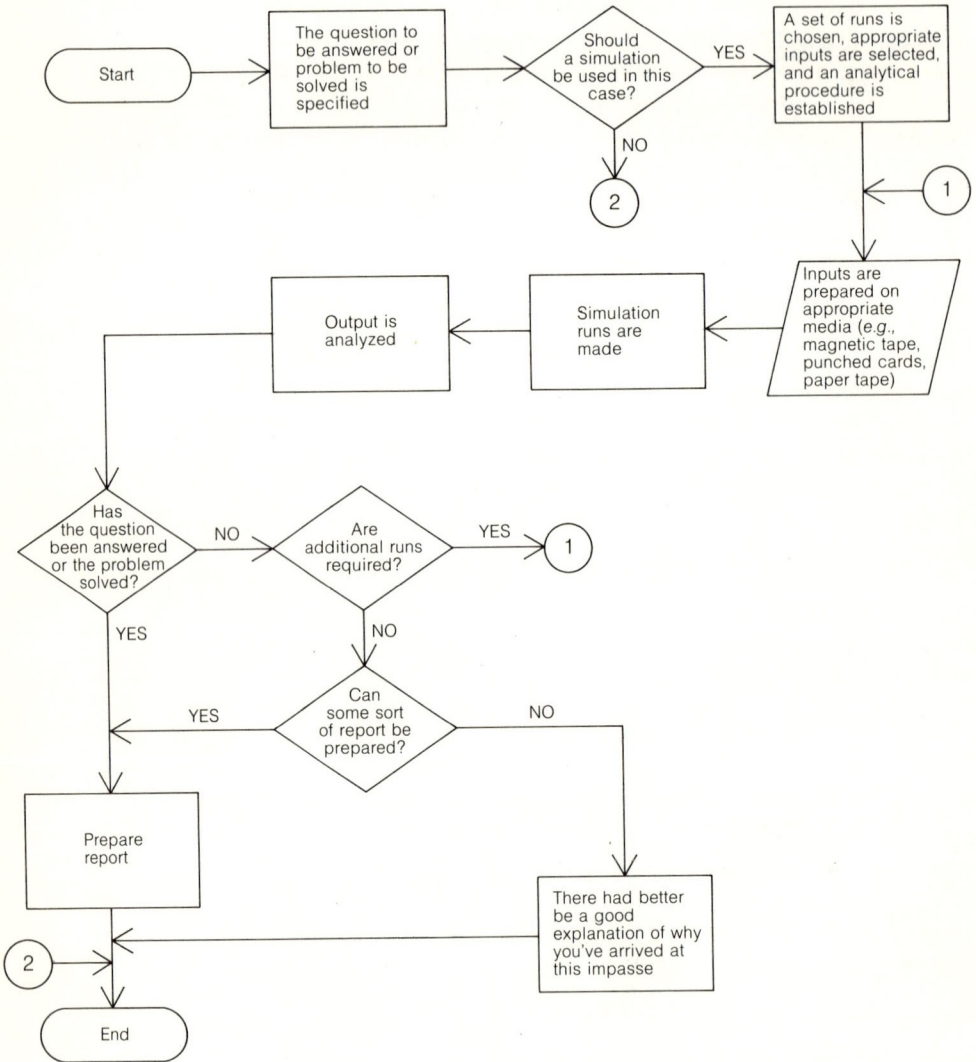

FIG. 1.2   The Use of a Simulation

first run is made. If this preparation is neglected, the whole procedure is much more likely to lead to the impasse indicated by the box in the lower right corner. In other words, after all of the simulation runs that could be made have been made, the problem will remain unsolved or the question will remain un-answered.

In some cases, a simulation — particularly a game — may be called into use to train personnel rather than to solve a problem or answer a question. In such a case, the choice of runs and inputs probably is well established. The reports generated at the close of the simulation will deal with the training objectives, not with the artificial problem or question created for the simulation runs. In short, use of a simulation for training purposes is more straightforward than is use of a simulation for problem solving. In this section we will say no more about the use of simulations for training.

As indicated by connector **1** in Figure 1.2, it often is necessary to make additional runs in order to reach a satisfactory conclusion. In fact, in most important applications of a simulation, this process will be repeated several times. Each repetition produces a more satisfactory answer to the original question. Often it is not easy to decide whether the question has, in fact, been answered satisfactorily. In part, this decision involves a statistical problem: how reliable are the results? what confidence should we have in them? In part, it is a difficult management decision, involving lots of intuitive judgment about the relation between the simulation results and the question or problem.

Figure 1.2 does not show one important alternative step in the process. If the question is not answered satisfactorily, the simulation may not be equal to the task. In such a case, the programs must be revised before new runs are made, if the question is to be answered. Program revision may involve a great deal of effort. It is not wise for the users of the simulation to undertake this revision, even if they have the necessary resources. Modifications of the simulation always should be carefully controlled and coordinated with the group that developed the simulation.

The final product of a simulation should be a written report. It is essential that each use of the simulation be documented by such a report. A verbal report on a small or an extremely important question might be given first, but ulti-mately it should be documented by a full written report. Only a written report can convey the result effectively, with all its limitations and implications. Furthermore, the series of written reports on the use of a simulation provide a very useful data base for a study of the validity of the simulation (see Chapter 2).

1.13 A General Outline of a Computer Simulation

Figure 1.3 gives a general outline of the way in which a simulation functions. In some stages, the way a simulation functions depends on whether the time-slice approach (dashed path) or the critical-event approach (solid path) is used. In

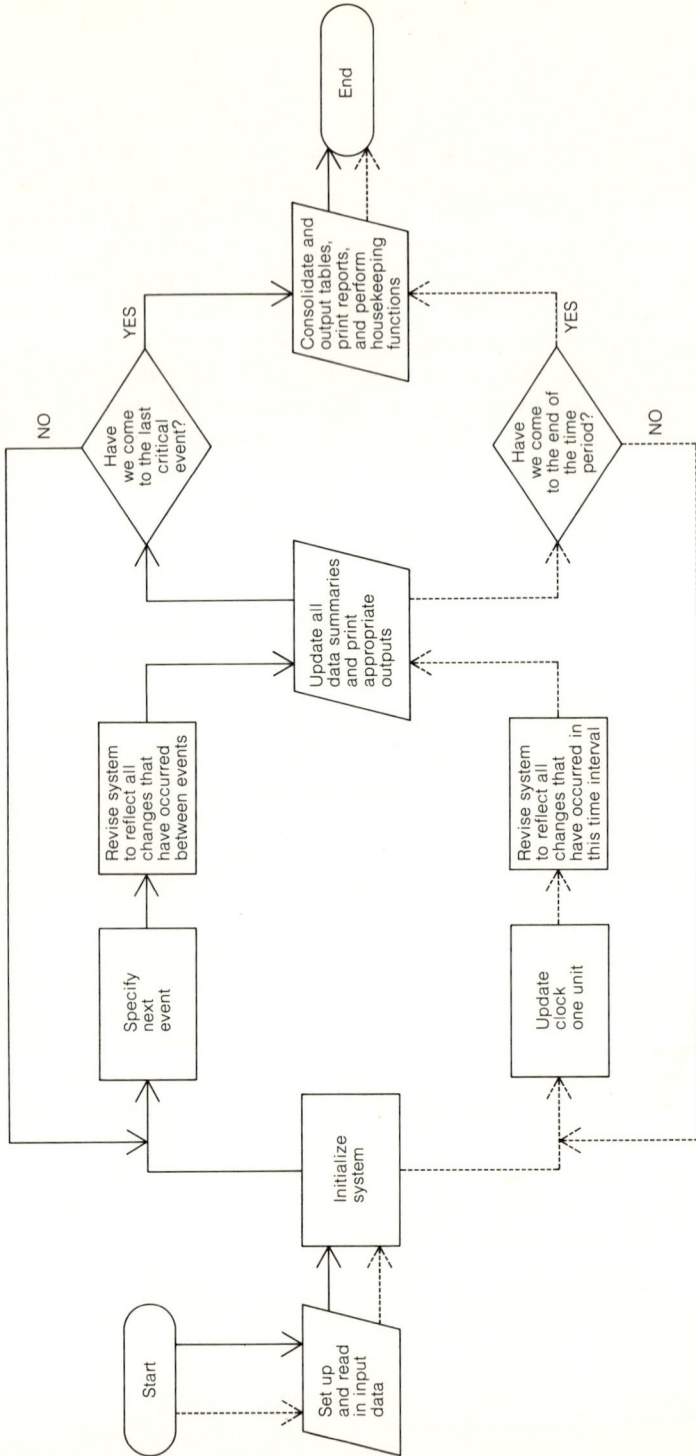

FIG. 1.3 How a Simulation Functions: A General Outline

other stages, the two approaches are the same. With either approach, the system first must be *initialized*: entities must be established, attributes assigned appropriate initial values, and activities specified. Inputs must be set up on the appropriate computer-compatible media, ready to be used by the programs. In many simulation runs, the appropriate initial state will be a *start-up* condition. The start-up condition of a system is that in which it just begins to function: for example, the state of a district office when it opens for business, or that of a statistical laboratory when the class first comes in. However, it usually is best to design a simulation so that it can be initialized in other states as well.

For both approaches, the basic mechanism of the central part of Figure 1.3 is to look ahead (in time or in events), to update all data appropriately, to keep tables of results as needed, to make the appropriate outputs, and then either to conclude the modeling of the system or to go through the whole sequence again. Even when the modeling is concluded, the simulation run is not. Tables must be consolidated and printed, reports generated, and other housekeeping activities must be completed. These housekeeping activities include such things as recording information about the random number generator, checking the values assigned to various attributes to see if these are compatible with the values they were expected to have at the end of the run, and building up data sets to be used in checking the validity of the simulation. This end of the process—the need for rules to stop the modeling and for the generation of tables and reports—is much the same for both approaches.

The case study discussed in Part Five provides a more detailed view of the development, function, and use of simulations.

1.14 Supplementary Reading

We would like first to call the reader's attention to two general-purpose bibliographies on simulation. International Business Machines Corporation (1966) lists and indexes 948 papers, articles, and books published from 1960 through 1964. Unfortunately, this comprehensive bibliography is dated, but a more recent bibliography might be available through local IBM representatives. More recent bibliographies are available from other sources, but this one is exceptionally well cross-indexed. Naylor (1969a) lists about 450 publications, indexed only by subject, and covers publications through 1968.

Chorafas (1965) gives several good case studies that include some nice examples of systems and models. The well-written book by Gordon (1969) includes an especially good discussion of systems and models in its early chapters. The reader who wishes some historical perspective will find a brief history of simulation in the introductory material of Martin (1968). Although the writing is uneven, the book by Naylor et al. (1966) includes a discussion of the advantages and disadvantages of simulation in its introductory chapter and lists some of the ways in which a simulation may be useful for testing policies.

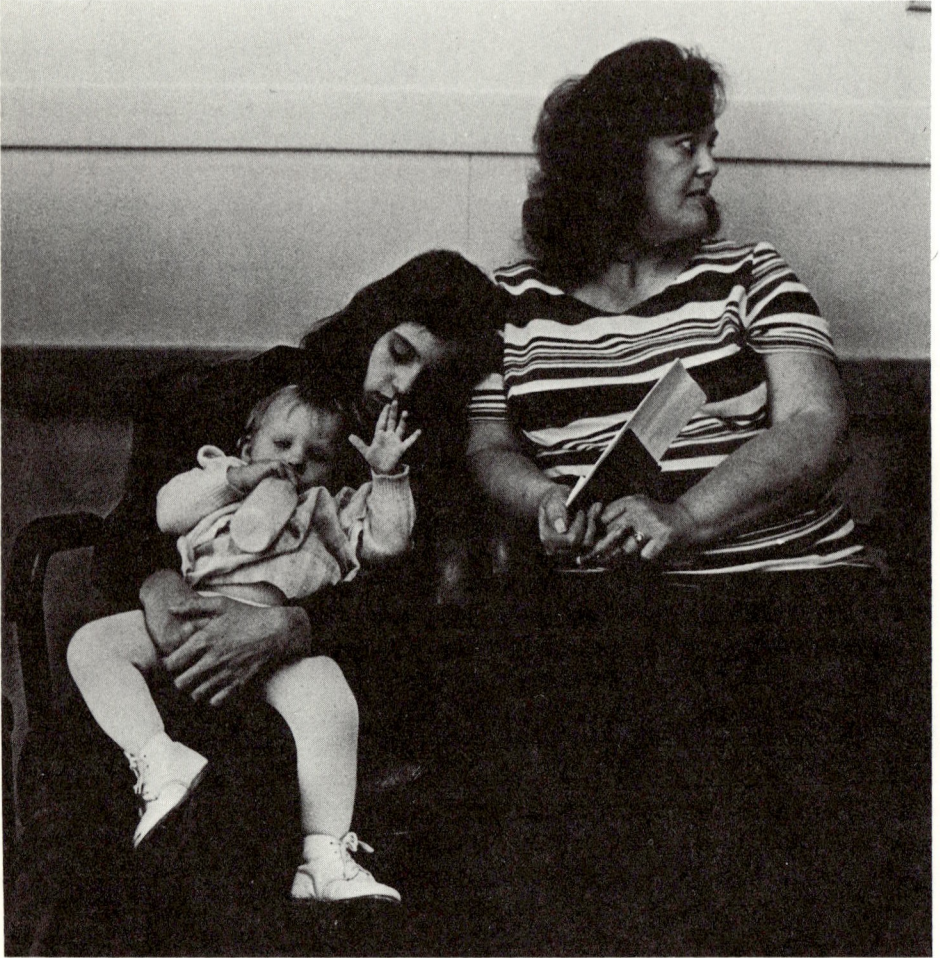

2

General Procedure

2.1 INTRODUCTION   The remainder of this book is devoted to a discussion of the development of computer simulations of discrete stochastic systems. This chapter outlines a procedure for developing such a simulation; subsequent chapters provide additional detail.

The procedure outlined here is lengthy, complex, and expensive to implement. Substantial simplification may be desirable, particularly if the system to be simulated is relatively uncomplicated or if it already has been extensively studied. However, development of a simulation often leads to the discovery that a system believed to be uncomplicated actually is quite complex. Also, if a simulation of a "much studied" system is needed, it is probable that the system is "much studied, but little understood." For these reasons, it always is safest to follow the full procedure outlined here.

2.2 Overall View of the Procedure

Development of a computer simulation involves six major steps: (1) a preliminary analysis to determine if a simulation is worth developing; (2) formulation of the problem; (3) collection and analysis of pertinent information; (4) model construction; (5) computer programming; and (6) validation. In most cases, the first two steps should be completed before anything else is done. Steps 3 through 6 are carried out in overlapping times, as dictated by the particular circumstances. A major factor in successful simulation development is the control of these overlapping activities to obtain a unified result. The implications and control of time overlap in these activities are discussed near the end of the chapter. Each of the next few sections of this chapter is devoted to a brief discussion of one of the development steps outlined above.

2.3 The Preliminary Analysis

A simulation uses up a lot of time, money, and other resources. Before undertaking a simulation, a preliminary analysis should be undertaken to be sure the simulation is worth this investment. All too often, the development of a simulation begins when a manager mentions computer simulations to an operations research analyst or other staff member. The manager casually wonders whether this impressive modern tool might be of some use to the company. Taking this hint, the staff evolves a formal request for budget to develop a simulation—perhaps inventing a problem primarily to justify the study. Over the next few years, management learns that an innocent suggestion can be quite costly.

Expensive but fruitless simulation studies usually can be avoided if the staff member begins with a careful preliminary analysis. First, he should spend some time reviewing records, talking with middle management and other employees involved in the system to be simulated, and observing the system in operation. His objective is to obtain rough answers to the following questions: (1) What is the system really like? and (2) How much do we already know about it?

The next step in the preliminary analysis requires rough estimates of the resources that will be needed to simulate the system and a description—in some detail—of the ways that the simulation will be used. In short, the analyst—on the basis of his preliminary information about the system—makes the best possible guess at the costs and the benefits of the simulation study. If the simulation appears to be worthwhile, the analyst can move on to the next step of formulating the problem. If it does not, the development of a simulation should be nipped in the bud. In either case, the staff member at this point will need to contact higher level management, either to ask their help in formulating the problem or to explain to them why a simulation should not be attempted.

2.4 Problem Formulation

The essence of problem formulation is the detailed specification of the applications to be made of the simulation. It is impossible to develop a simulation that could be used for every purpose. Even the real system is not that versatile. A computer simulation must be designed to accommodate a set of specific applications. Because the simulation usually is intended to provide information for management, the best source for ideas on specific applications is management itself, at all levels.

Begin by describing computer simulations and their possible uses. Then ask each manager to answer the following questions: (1) If a simulation of this system were available today, what questions would you want it to help answer? (2) What questions can you anticipate having this tool help you answer in the next 2 or 3 years? (3) What questions can you anticipate having this tool help you answer in the next 4 to 7 years?

Management will set down some vaguely worded, imprecise questions. These must be analyzed and rewritten — if possible, with management's assistance. Management personnel are notoriously short of time. They will not formulate questions — much less help you to rework them — if they can avoid it. Don't let them off the hook. The simulation is their tool and you will be on the spot later if it fails to answer the questions they're too busy to formulate now. If it is impossible to get management's help in reworking the questions, at least insist that they examine and approve the reformulated questions.

The reworked questions form the basis for the specifications of the simulation. You must decide which questions the simulation will be able to help answer and which it will not. At this stage, you also will develop lists of the entities, attributes, and activities to be included in the simulation. This list should include the name and definition of each variable and its relations to other variables. (With this list of variables, modeling has begun.)

Among the questions submitted by management, those relating to optimization will require the greatest reworking effort. This reworking is very important, both to give management increased insight into their system and to provide necessary input for the modeling effort. The choice of suitable measures of system effectiveness is very much a part of the formulation of the problem. In most cases, management (usually middle-level management) already will have developed some measure of effectiveness. Often these measures prove unsuitable or incomplete for the simulation development. The two examples that follow help to demonstrate the problem and to show how reworking can clarify the measures.

During development of a simulation of land combat (Maisel et al. 1963), high-ranking officers were briefed on the nature of computer simulations and then were asked what questions they would use the simulation to help answer. One response included the question, How should I restructure the infantry division to make it more effective in combat? Because high-level management in this case already had set aside enough time to permit discussion during the first briefing, it was relatively easy to get the help of the officers in making this question more precise. After considerable discussion, the question was reformulated: What is the most effective mix of artillery and armored units in battalion-size engagements in flat, open terrain? The analyst then pointed out that the reworked question still lacked a measure of effectiveness. Unfortunately, the briefing was adjourned at this point, and no further contact could be made with this particular officer. After a considerable effort, military officers that were part of the simulation development team established about half a dozen different useful measures of effectiveness for this situation. Each of these measures had some effect on the set of variables used in the models and on the way that they were used.

In another case, the system to be simulated was the operation of an electronic digital computer. The management of an academic computer facility was concerned about the best operating system (the computer programs that maintain smooth job flow, call up other programs for use in processing jobs, and keep accounting records). The original question was, Which of the three operating systems supplied by the manufacturer would be best? After some discussion, the question was reworked into this form: Given the distribution of work expected at the facility in the next three years, would OS/PCP, OS/MFT, or DOS (three of several operating systems available with the IBM System/360 family of computers) be the best operating system for our use? It then became necessary to find a precise definition of the phrase "the best operating system for our use." Several related definitions were found to be useful.

2.5 First Models

After an adequate set of questions has been formulated (or applications for the simulation have been specified in some other way), the first modeling effort should begin. A preliminary idea of the nature of the system was obtained in the preliminary analysis. Now it is necessary to revise and refine that outline with a full knowledge of the specific applications to be made of the simulation. The preliminary list of variables drawn up during problem formulation should be revised and expanded. The new list of variables (entities, attributes, and activities) should include the following information: (1) a precise definition of each variable, including units of measurement if appropriate; (2) for an entity, the subsystem in which it appears; (3) for an attribute, the entities with which it is associated; and (4) for an activity, the entities and/or attributes associated with it.

Table 2.1 is an excerpt from the list of variables associated with the modeling of a social security district office.

The list of variables must be supplemented by a description of the relationships among the variables. A *flowchart*—which is a step-by-step description of a system with each step enclosed in a box—provides a convenient way to describe such relationships. The boxes of the flowchart are connected by arrows that indicate the sequence of the steps. The shape of each box helps to characterize the kind of processing that takes place in that step. Flowcharts are used widely in computer programming (see Maisel 1969, Chapter 6; and Bohl 1971). They combine the precision of a step-by-step description with the convenience and clarity of a diagram. Figure 2.1 is a section of a flowchart of district office operations relating to the initial actions of a visitor entering the office.

2.6 Data Collection

The three major sources of data are system records, expert opinion, and field studies. In many cases, records of system inputs, performance, and outputs are

TABLE 2.1   Abbreviated List of Variables Used in Simulation of District Office

Symbol	Type	Definition	Related Variables and Comments
SR1	Entity	The first service representative. Service representatives handle telephone calls, answer questions about the status of claims, and evaluate routine evidence.	One of several members of the first claims-handling team; the other members are CR1 and CDC1.
SR2	Entity	The second service representative.	Other team members are CR2 and CDC2.
CSSA1	Entity	A type-1 claim; that is, a claim for retirement benefits.	Attributes include such things as date submitted, evidence associated with this claim, and the status of this evidence.
DOB	Attribute	The established date of birth of the claimant. Given as month, day, year.	An attribute of nearly all claims; it is one of the pieces of evidence.
QCR	Entity	The length of the queue of visitors waiting to speak with a claims representative; measured in number of visitors.	This variable may be associated with individual claims representatives (if so, there would be distinct variables QCR1, QCR2, etc.) or with a pool of all claims representatives, depending on the service policies of the office.

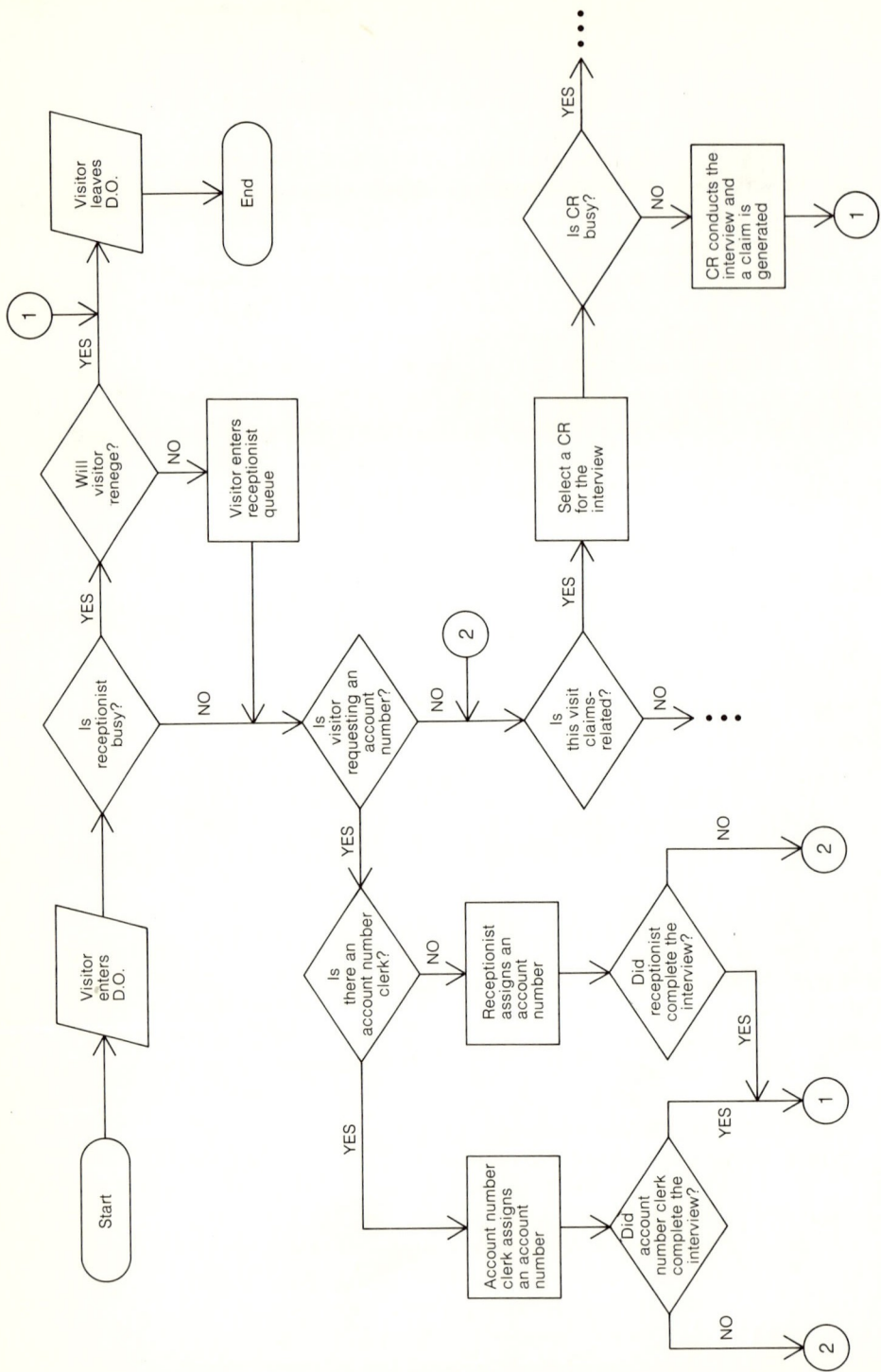

FIG. 2.1   Flowchart Fragment Showing Activities of Visitor Arriving at District Office (D.O.)

available. Accounting records of day-to-day operations often are most accurate but least readily available. If the records are maintained and updated on a computer, assistance of expert programmers may be needed to extract the required information from the records. Reports to management are more readily available but often are less accurate. Lower levels of management sometimes bias their reports to higher management by using inappropriate measures of effectiveness or by screening data. Historical records probably are the most readily available source of data—after the dust is wiped away—but they tend to be lacking in detail. Even with these limitations, system records usually are the most useful source of data.

Expert opinion frequently is subjective and lacking in detail, but in most cases it is the least expensive and handiest source of data. Carefully designed and worded surveys of expert opinion may provide more objective data. Muller (1962) and Hansen et al. (1953) give helpful information on opinion survey design. More detailed data may be obtained in some cases by interviewing the experts.

After effective use of both system records and expert opinion, the data still may contain gaps that require studies of the system itself. Such field studies are expensive and time-consuming. They should be attempted only after all other sources of data have been exhausted. Before a field study begins, many preliminary activities must be carried out: (1) designing a statistically valid study; (2) developing forms for recording information; (3) requisitioning and training study personnel; (4) scheduling study activities; (5) developing control mechanisms to assure valid study results; and (6) for extensive studies, conducting a small pilot study to check on the planned approach.

Effective statistical design is very important. Valid conclusions can be drawn about a whole system by observing only part of it, but proper sample survey techniques must be used. For example, in the field study of the social security district office network, a sample of 44 offices from more than 800 offices in the network was used. Muller (1962) and Hansen et al. (1953) also give helpful information on the design of field surveys.

Forms for recording data must be developed well before the study begins. In some organizations, prior approval is needed for the introduction of new forms.

Personnel requirements must be estimated and training programs instituted where necessary. Ineffective personnel conducting a study can make its results useless.

The scheduling of study activities requires attention both to the principles of good study design and to the best interests of the field installations. If seasonal fluctuations are expected, the system should be observed both in the busy and in the slack season in order to measure the magnitude of these effects. Any restrictions imposed by the field installations must be respected. Management may object to the potential disruption caused by field-study activities planned for certain times. In most cases, the final schedule is a compromise between the times requested by the study team and the times permitted by management and field personnel.

The study plan should include control observations. Every attempt should be made to detect possible biases in the results. For example, field personnel may perform differently when they are being observed. Certain reports, such as performance summaries, may be used to check on and correct for this "observer effect" or other biases. Reports or other system records can indicate whether the field-study results for a given office at a given time are typical of normal system operation. In the study of the district office network, each of the 44 offices was observed during a one-week period from Thursday through Wednesday. The district offices make regular weekly summary reports that cover this same Thursday-through-Wednesday period. Reports for the preceding week, the week of the study, and the succeeding week in the office being studied, and for the same three weeks in a similar office not included in the study sample, were examined as control data for the field study.

A limited pilot study may be useful to acclimate both field and study personnel to the data-gathering techniques and to reveal any flaws in the study procedures or forms so that these may be corrected before the main study begins. The pilot project should be very brief. Its purpose is to test the plans for the study, not to obtain useful data.

2.7 Data Processing and Analysis

In most simulation studies, a very large amount of data will be collected in the effort to quantify the models. The computer is an effective tool for the structuring, recording, and analysis of these data, and we assume that a computer will be used for these purposes. After data sources have been identified and data collection is underway, the data must be recorded, converted to computer-compatible form, processed, and analyzed.

Standard forms for recording data must be designed carefully. Unambiguous labels should be associated with each datum entry; items on the form should be sequenced in the order that will be used as entries are made; sufficient space should be allowed for the digits, comments, or other information that might be recorded; and forms should be available in quantities sufficient to avoid unnecessary delays or use of makeshift forms.

The conversion of data to computer-compatible form can be both frustrating and time consuming. The keypunch still is used most often for this purpose, but optical scanners and keyboard-to-magnetic-tape devices are becoming more and more common. A *keypunch* is a typewriter-like device that enters a character in one column of a punchcard as a single key is depressed. Often it is used in conjunction with a *verifier*, which is a device much like a keypunch except that it uses a previously punched card as input and signals an error if the operator strikes a key that does not correspond to the information already punched on the card. An *optical scanner* can accept certain special hand-marked records as inputs and convert the data directly into computer inputs. *Keyboard-to-tape devices* are very similar to typewriters in operation, but their output is a magnetic tape with the appropriate entries.

Choice among these and other computer input/output devices will depend upon the form of the data collected and upon the equipment available. An optical scanner usually is the most desirable data-conversion device. If it is to be used, a forms-design specialist should be consulted before deciding on the data-recording and -conversion procedure. Such a specialist may be able to develop a satisfactory form for use with the scanner, thereby eliminating all keypunching and verifying. The specialist is needed because such forms actually are a great deal more versatile than they may appear to the nonexpert. Figure 2.2 shows a form used in making an application for insurance. Data are entered directly on this form as they are gathered, and the optical scanner then automatically converts the data for computer processing. It is obvious that special training would be needed to teach the proper use of this form. However, with expert help in planning the form, it is possible to minimize the amount of training needed to obtain reliable data.

If the keypunching approach is to be used for data conversion, the columns in each punchcard must be allocated systematically to the items to be entered. Keypunchers must be briefed on this allocation and on the forms from which they will be punching. If a large volume of data is to be converted, verifiers should be used. If a volume on the order of thousands of cards is to be punched, it is essential to use quality control procedures to limit the error rate in the card entries. Juran (1962) describes such procedures. It is futile to attempt to check all entries. In processing a very large number of cards, the error rate after checking may be almost the same as the rate before checking.

It almost always is necessary to structure the data in fields, records, and files, particularly if a large volume of data is to be processed. A *field* denotes a single piece of information, such as a social security number or the address of a district office. A *record* denotes the set of all such pieces of information (fields) that pertain to a single unit. For example, all attributes and other descriptions associated with a single entity would constitute a record. A *file* is a complete collection of one class of records. For example, in the simulation of the district office network, the employee file contains the collection of all employee records, and the claims file contains the collection of all claims records. Such structuring prepares the data for effective processing and manipulation. It is possible to purchase software that simplifies the task of setting up and manipulating files.

Analysis of the data usually requires access to a library of statistical programs. In most computer installations, a library of such programs is already available. If not, it can be obtained from other users or from the computer manufacturer. In some cases it may be necessary to write new statistical pro-

ANY LIFE INSURANCE COMPANY

INDUSTRIAL APPLICATION

DATE OF POLICY	POLICY NUMBER

1. Your FULL NAME (Print)

(FULL FIRST NAME)   (MIDDLE INITIAL)   (LAST NAME)

2. RESIDENCE (Print) NO.   STREET   R.F.D. / FLOOR / APT. / FRONT / REAR

CITY OR TOWN   ZONE   STATE

3. Place of Birth   (STATE)   4. DATE OF BIRTH   5. AGE LAST Birthday

MONTH DAY YEAR   ....Years

6.
Married   Widowed   Single

7. What is your height and weight? ....ft. ....ins. ....lbs.

8. Do you now have insurance with the ANY LIFE INSURANCE COMPANY.?

YES   NO

IF YES, WHICH?

$250 $500 $750 $1000

9. POLICY APPLIED FOR   FACE AMOUNT PURCHASED

(a) PLAN

$25 $50 $75

WL75   E60   E85

$100 $250 $500

WL65   30E   E80

$750 $1000

IOPL   20E   E65

I5PL   20PL   30PL

10. (a) OCCUPATION, Job title, and nature of work performed.
If job title appears below check mark it otherwise complete Questions 10 a, b, c, on back.

(a) Job title   (b) Name of Present Employer   (c) Business address

HOUSEWIFE   STUDENT   CLERK   UNEMPLOYED

11. PREMIUM PAYABLE

MONTHLY   QUARTERLY   SEMI-ANNUAL   ANNUAL

12. CLASSIFICATION

STANDARD   RATING 1   RATING 3   OTHER SPECIFY ON BACK

A G E		1	2	3	4	TENS	5	6	7	8	9	
	0	1	2	3	4	UNITS	5	6	7	8	9	
H E I G H T			2	3	4		5	6	7			FEET
	0	1	2	3	4		5	6	7			INCHES
	8	9	10	11			1/4	1/2	3/4			
W E I G H T	0	1	2	3	4	100'S						POUNDS
	0	1	2	3	4	10'S	5	6	7	8	9	
	0	1	2	3	4	UNITS	5	6	7	8	9	

P O L I C Y										
N U M B E R	0	1	2	3	4	5	6	7	8	9

13. BENEFICIARY (Print FULL NAME)   AGE

14. RELATIONSHIP OF BENEFICIARY

WIFE   HUSBAND   MOTHER   FATHER   SON

DAUGHTER   CHILD   BROTHER   SISTER

COUSIN   NIECE   NEPHEW   OTHER SPECIFY ON BACK

15. Have you in the past five years consulted a doctor for a serious disease, ailment, or disability, other than a common cold, virus or minor bone fracture and such consultation resulted in treatment which exceeded a period of one week ?

YES   NO

16. Have you any physical defect or impairment of health ?

YES   NO

If yes, explain on back.

17. Within the last five years have you been declined, postponed, or offered a policy other than applied for by this or any other company?

YES   NO

If yes, explain on back.

18. Does applicant reside in same state in which district office is located?

YES   NO

				OCCUPATION CODE					
0	1	2	3	4	5	6	7	8	9

19. REPORT OF FIELD REPRESENTATIVE
Have you checked above application to make sure all items and questions are answered ?   YES   NO

Do you certify that all information contained on this REPORT OF FIELD REPRESENTATIVE is a true and correct copy of information which appears on application?

YES   NO

SIGNATURE OF FIELD REPRESENTATIVE ....

20. I hereby request that any DIVIDENDS payable under the policy applied for shall be applied to the purchase of PAID UP ADDITIONS TO THE SUM INSURED UNTIL AND UNLESS ANY OTHER OPTION SHALL BE SELECTED IN ACCORDANCE WITH THE TERMS OF THE POLICY.

The foregoing statements and answers are true and complete and it is agreed that: (1) these statements and answers shall form the basis of the contract of insurance if one is issued; (2) no agent or any other person, except the President, or Secretary of the Company, has power on behalf of the Company (a) to make, modify or discharge any contract of insurance or (b) to bind the Company by making any promises respecting any benefits under any policy issued hereunder; (3) the Company will incur no liability by reason of this application except as may be provided in a Conditional Receipt given on and bearing the same date as this application, until a policy has been delivered and the full first premium has been paid to the Company.

Amount paid in advance on account of   Dated at ....this .... day of ....

First Premium $ ....   Signature of Applicant ....

which does ...... does not ...... represent full first premium   Signature of Witness ....

H90007

FIG. 2.2   Example of Form Used to Prepare Inputs for Optical Scanner

grams to deal with unusual situations. We say more about this in Part Two and provide some computer programs.

2.8 The Control Group

Further development of the simulation involves a repeated series of model revisions, program revisions, and simulation runs. The runs reveal flaws that may require additional data gathering or processing, but certainly will require remodeling and reprogramming. In such reworking, the emphasis is on improved validity, but efficiency also must be considered. Before discussing the reworking itself, we must emphasize the importance of controlling this stage of development.

Unless careful control is exercised, it soon becomes nearly impossible to find out just which version of the simulation is embodied in the current set of computer programs. *A computer simulation exists only in the set of computer programs.* The models are only steps along the path of development. Although the models may provide useful descriptions of the system, only the computer programs give the full operational description of the simulation. A deliberate effort is needed to maintain control over the content of these programs.

One technique involves establishment of a *control group*—a staff that is responsible for overall supervision of simulation development. (More is said about this group and other members of the simulation team in Section 2.10.) Among other duties, the control group should set aside or mark each version of the set of programs as they are developed. The most recent of these versions is designated as the current version of the computer simulation. The program decks and listings are stored in a safe place, where the programming staff cannot tinker with them. Descriptions of the models and flowcharts of the programs for each version also should be prepared, marked, and safely locked away. Each of the marked versions should be suitable for use in applications. The control group determines which, if any, new modifications should be adopted as the new marked version. It also determines when to call a halt to further development of the simulation.

2.9 Validation and Refinement of the Models

The *validity* of a simulation is a measure of the extent to which it satisfies its design objectives. Notice that we did not say that a simulation is valid if it precisely matches the real system. This goal is an impractical one. Because a valid simulation is valid only with respect to the specified applications, it may be erroneous to use it to satisfy applications for which it was not designed.

The assurance of validity is a difficult task. Figure 2.3 indicates three of the ways in which validity is assured. Validity may be built into the simulation (central channel); it may be assured through use of expert reaction to computer

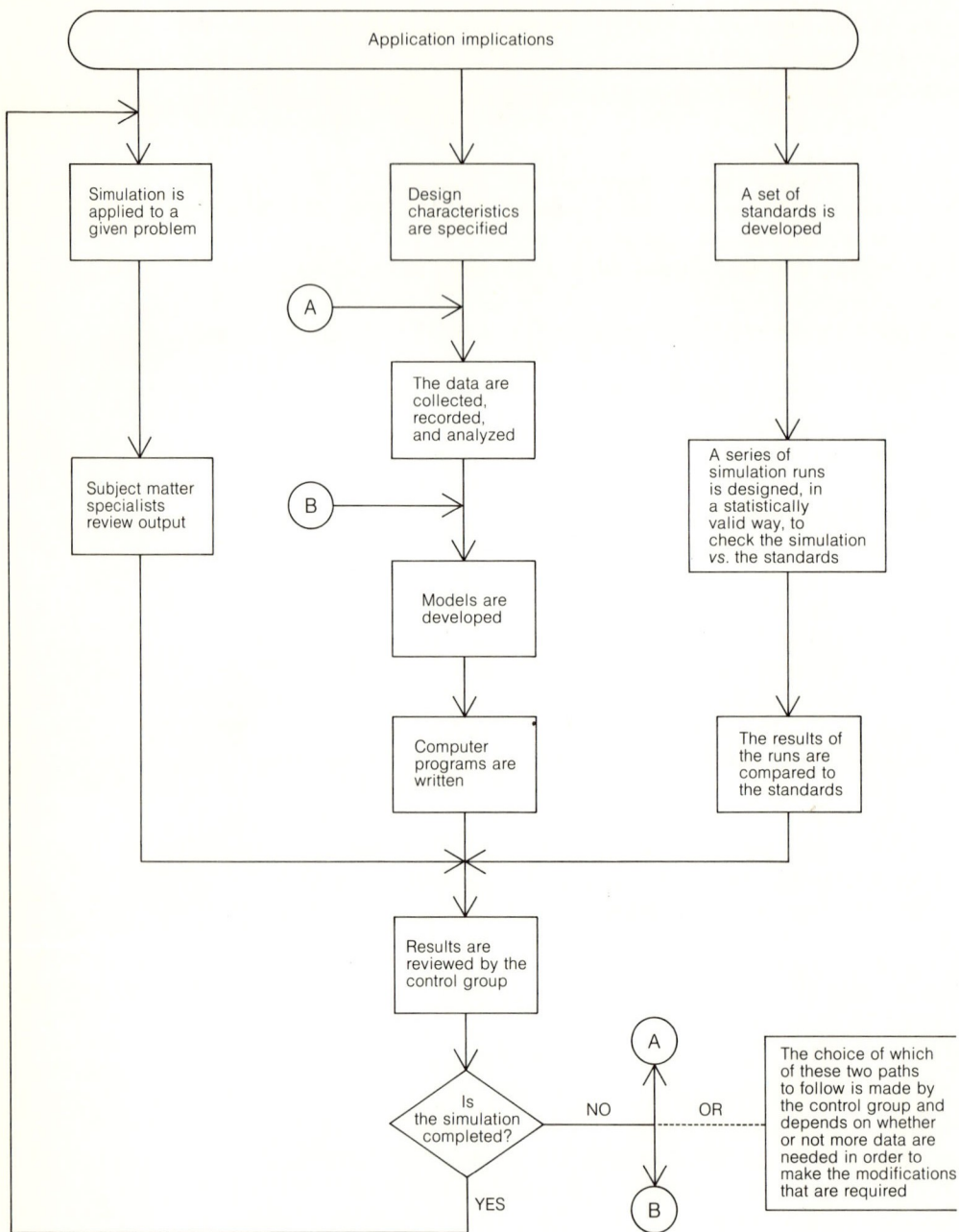

FIG. 2.3 Establishing the Validity of a Computer Simulation

runs (left-hand channel); and it may be assured by comparing run results with standards (right-hand channel). All three approaches are based upon consideration of the applications. The primary route for assuring validity is a conscientious development effort that keeps the applications firmly in mind.

Validity can be improved by using models that are parametric in so far as possible. *Parameters* in a simulation are variables that denote the state of the environment and the underlying characteristics of a system. Use of parameters rather than constants wherever possible makes it easier to modify the system characteristics and the relation of the system to its environment and thus to increase the validity of the simulation during development.

The reactions of experts to computer outputs from simulation runs can be helpful in pinpointing doubtful results. The control group should screen the expert reactions and determine whether system modification is needed. The control group also should decide which modifications in the models and programs should be made to adjust the outputs appropriately.

The third check for validity involves comparison of simulation run outputs with a standard. This approach can be used only if a standard is available. Historical information (data on performance of the real system under known conditions) probably is the best source for a standard. Statistical techniques must be used to determine whether differences between output of the runs and the standard data could be due to chance fluctuations. However—because simulations sometimes have tens, even hundreds, of independent variables and many dependent variables—present statistical methodology can be used for this task only in an awkward, piecemeal fashion. Therefore, in most cases, comparisons with standards are used to modify parts of the model rather than to make overall conclusions about the validity of the simulation.

In simulating large, complex systems, all three approaches to validity probably will be used. All will lead to the same result: a series of modifications in the models and the programs, bringing the simulation closer to its design objectives.

2.10 The Simulation Team

Development of a computer simulation of a complex system requires the services of a variety of skilled professional personnel: statisticians, operations research analysts, subject-matter specialists, computer programmers, and systems analysts. For most effective use, these personnel must be grouped into teams. In early stages, only operations analysts and subject-matter specialists may be required. Expert statistical help will be needed later as the need arises for sample survey designs and for data-gathering and -analysis techniques. Programmers and systems analysts will be required when the first rough models are being converted into computer programs. Systems analysts are needed because a computer simulation is a complex and lengthy set of programs. It often taxes the limits of computer-system speeds and capacities, and novel system approaches may be required.

The overall simulation team may include all of these experts, with each subgroup joining the team as it is needed during development. For more complex projects, separate teams may be established to model different aspects of the system. A control group must be set up to coordinate modeling efforts, to model the interrelationships among the separate teams, to develop the computer program that controls the flow and action of the different components, and to mark the developmental stages of the simulation (Section 2.8). The control group is a team of personnel with the same skills as those in the other teams. However, the subject-matter specialist and operations research analyst on the control team also must be effective administrators; the statistician must be conversant with many areas of statistics; and the systems analyst must have superior skills in administration and systems analysis.

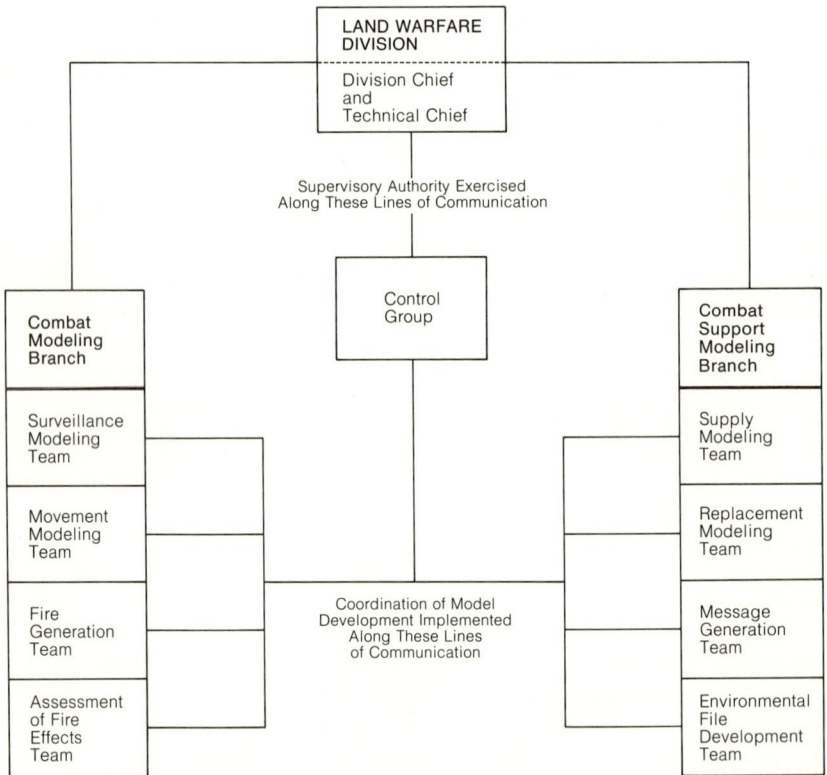

FIG. 2.4 Outline of Organizational Structure Used in Development of Computer Simulation of Land Combat

Figure 2.4 outlines the organizational structure used in developing a computer simulation of land combat (Maisel et al. 1963). The division and branch chiefs were subject-matter specialists (military officers), assisted by civilian employees who supervised the technical staff of the division or branch. Division and branch chiefs exercised line supervision over the team members and prepared performance evaluations and recommendations for promotions or pay increases. Day-to-day activities of the teams were reviewed and modified by the control group. Some teams were composed of two or three people; others had as many as four or five. Programming personnel were assigned to teams in a loose association and frequently were moved from team to team according to current needs for programming assistance. This loose assignment of programmers permitted effective use of this particularly scarce resource.

Obviously, the exact structure of the simulation team will be determined both by the needs of the project and by the structure of the larger organization of which the team is a part. However, this structure should be worked out and clearly specified before the team begins working, in order to avoid confusion, conflicts, and inefficiency.

2.11 Summary of the Procedure

Table 2.2 summarizes the tasks involved in development of a simulation. The tasks are classified according to the stage of the development (by columns) and the principal personnel requirements in carrying out the tasks (by rows).

TABLE 2.2   Summary of Tasks Involved in Simulation Development

Stage of Development	Personnel Required		
	Management and Subject-Matter Specialists	Operations Analysts and Statisticians	Computer Programmers and Systems Analysts
Planning and Preparation	Set of questions. Statement of objectives.	List of parameters. Set of test problems. Specifications for conforming with objectives.	Error-checking programs. Specifications for program de-bugging.
Modeling	Expert opinion. Historical data.	Field studies. Mathematical models and algorithms.	Computer programs.
Validation and Application	Continuing review of "good sense" of results.	Design of validation and application runs. Model revisions.	Reprogramming.

2.12 Supplementary Reading

It should be clear by now that flowcharts are very useful tools at all stages of development of a computer simulation. They are useful not only in building models of the system and planning computer programs, but also in describing other systems such as the simulation team itself. A familiarity with techniques for design and construction of flowcharts is essential for work on simulations. Leeds and Weinberg (1961, pp. 66–98) provide one of the best discussions of flowcharting. Miller et al. (1960) discuss in a delightful manner the application of information-processing models, including flowcharts, to many areas of psychology. Just to prove that the topic is indeed extensive, we might mention that entire books on flowcharting have been written by Bohl (1971) and Schriber (1970).

Martin (1968, Chapters 4, 7, and 8) outlines another approach to developing a simulation, with particular emphasis on model development but little discussion of the place of the computer. Naylor et al. (1966, Chapter 2) suggest another approach to simulation development, again tending to neglect the contribution of the computer.

Glock (1967) gives a comprehensive review of the design and use of survey techniques in social science research. Separate articles are devoted to the design and use of the survey in each of the following fields: sociology, political science, psychology, economics, sociocultural anthropology, education, social work, and public health.

Part Two

STATISTICAL TOOLS

Statistical methodology is used at nearly every stage in the development of a simulation. Statistical distributions are used both in the introduction of stochastic behavior in the simulation and for the statistical tests that must be made. Nonparametric tests, which can be carried out with a minimal number of assumptions about the system, are needed during simulation development, when many tests must be made but little is yet known about the behavior of the variables. Regression techniques are essential in order to determine empirically the relations among variables used in the simulation model. Finally, carefully designed experiments must be used to validate and to apply the simulation. Analysis of variance and related methodologies are important in experimental design. Within the limits of this book, it is impossible to cover all the details of these essential statistical tools, or even to do more than mention other useful techniques. Therefore the references suggested in these chapters are of great importance for a full understanding of the statistical tools needed in simulation development.

CHAPTER 3   Statistical Distributions

CHAPTER 4   Statistical Tests

CHAPTER 5   Regression

CHAPTER 6   The Analysis of Variance

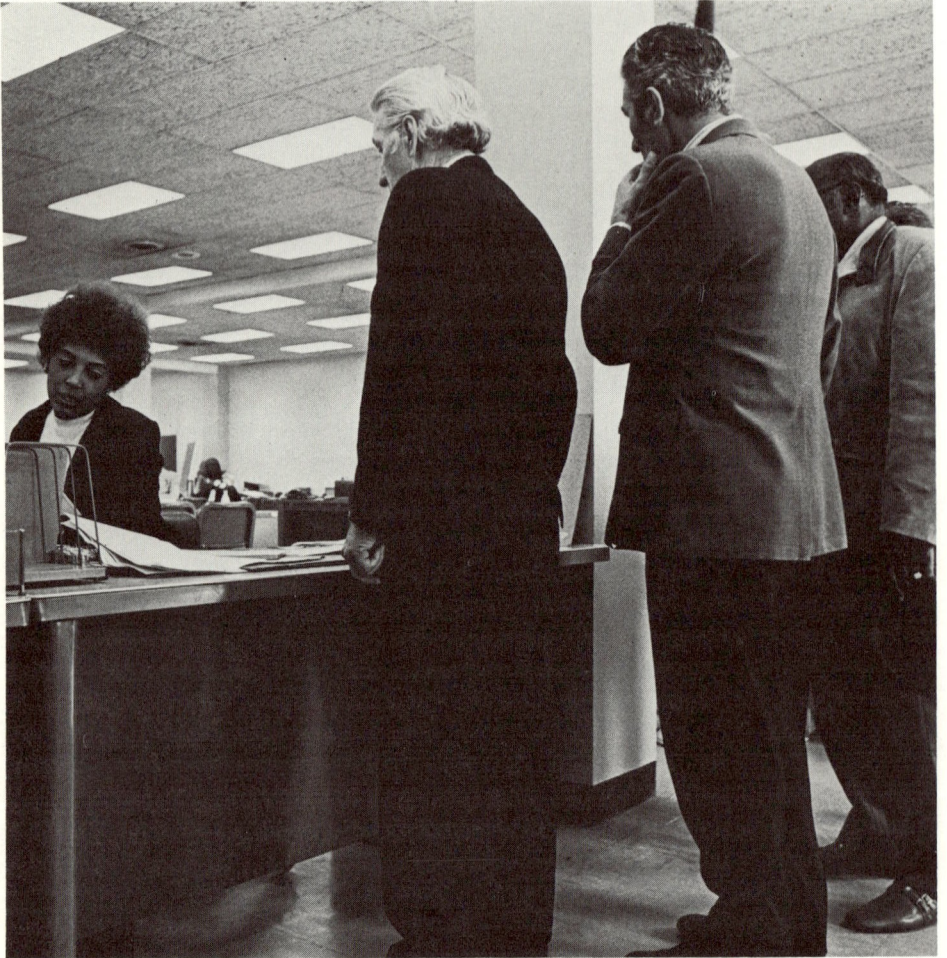

3

Statistical Distributions

3.1 BACKGROUND   A stochastic system, in a given state and with a given set of inputs, may produce any one among a whole range of outputs (Section 1.7). In addition, the exogenous variables and other inputs of the system may be stochastic. Thus, in a simulation of a discrete stochastic system, many of the inputs and the outputs will be represented by distributions of values rather than by single numbers.

In this chapter we define the term *distribution* (as it is used in probability and statistics), discuss some of the more important theoretical distributions encountered in simulations, and discuss the treatment of those distributions that cannot be characterized in mathematical terms. Distributions based only upon actual observations (and not related to one of the theoretical, mathematical distributions) are called *empirical distributions*.

First, we must review some basic concepts of probability. Cramer (1955) gives a more elaborate discussion of these concepts and of the whole subject of statistical distributions.

As Cramer notes, the general objective of probability theory is to provide a mathematical model suitable for the description and interpretation of a certain class of observed phenomena. The phenomena that we have called stochastic belong to this class. Some basic concepts of probability theory must be defined carefully, because they form the groundwork for the mathematical treatment of stochastic systems.

In many fields of activity — including the physical and social sciences, government, and business — the result of an activity appears to contain a certain amount of intrinsic variability. That is, repeated observations of an event under apparently identical conditions do not always yield the same outcome. In such a case, we say that we are dealing with random observations, or with a *random event*. In general, the set of possible outcomes for a random event can be established a priori.

Consider an event that has four possible outcomes (call them A, B, C, and D). The set of possible outcomes for a random event is called the *sample space* and is denoted by S. The sample space for this event is the set of four outcomes: A, B, C, and D. If the event is repeatedly observed (say, n times), each outcome will be observed a certain number of times. These numbers are called the *absolute frequencies* for each outcome and are denoted by f. For example, suppose that in 100 repeated observations ($n = 100$), outcome A is observed to occur 31 times, outcome B 17 times, outcome C 28 times, and outcome D 24 times. Then the absolute frequency (f) of outcome A is 31, that of outcome B is 17, and so on. Note that the sum of the absolute frequencies over all of S must be equal to n. (The outcomes must be defined in such a way that one and only one outcome is possible for each repetition of the event, and all possible outcomes must be anticipated. In other words, the outcomes are mutually exclusive and exhaustive.)

If each absolute frequency is divided by n, we obtain the *relative frequencies* (f/n) of the outcomes. For example, the relative frequency of outcome A is 31/100, or 0.31. Note that the sum of the relative frequencies over all of S must be equal to 1.

For many types of random observations, the relative frequency of a particular outcome is fairly stable for large values of n. In other words, as n is made larger and larger, the relative frequency of a particular outcome will tend to approach a constant value. Phenomena that behave in this way are said to demonstrate *statistical regularity*. We shall assume that all stochastic events encountered in the systems to be simulated are statistically regular in this sense.

If we now take the view that an observed relative frequency is an empirical measurement of some underlying characteristic of the event, then we may postulate the existence of a probability (say, P) associated with the occurrence of the outcome A among the set of outcomes (S) that can occur in a given set of observations. If the event is statistically regular, then we may expect that the observed relative frequency (f/n) will approximately equal P for large values of n.

As an example, consider the throw of a single die. The sample space (S) contains six possible outcomes: A, the face with one dot is uppermost; B, the face with two dots is uppermost; C, the face with three dots is uppermost; D, the face with four dots is uppermost; E, the face with five dots is uppermost; and F, the face with six dots is uppermost. Suppose that a series of 50 throws of the die yields the following series of outcomes: AEBBD FACAB CFFEA EFCCA FDECC BFCDA FECBA EBFCD DDBCA CDFEE. For this series of observations, n is 50, and the absolute and relative frequencies of the outcomes are those shown in Table 3.1.

If the die is unbiased, we expect the probabilities of the various outcomes to be equal. Therefore, the probability of each outcome should be 1/6, or about 0.167. Is this set of observations consistent with the assumption that the die is unbiased? This question is typical of those encountered in the study of stochastic systems, and it is discussed in Chapter 4.

As another example, consider observations of the time (measured in minutes) between arrivals at a social security district office during the period from 9:00 A.M. through 5:00 P.M. Table 3.2 lists the series of such interarrival times observed at one office on a particular day. Let A represent the outcome that 0 minutes elapsed between arrivals, B that one minute elapsed, and so on. Table 3.3 summarizes the absolute and relative frequencies associated with this set of observations. The righthand column shows the cumulative relative frequency for each outcome (the sum of its relative frequency and the relative frequencies of

TABLE 3.1 Outcomes of a Series of Throws of a Die

Outcome	Absolute Frequency (f)	Relative Frequency (f/n)
A	8	0.16
B	7	0.14
C	11	0.22
D	7	0.14
E	8	0.16
F	9	0.18
Total	$n = 50$	1.00

TABLE 3.2 Interarrival Times (*in Minutes*) Observed at a District Office

0,	2,	1,	6,	20,	8,	3,	3,	3,	2,	3,	1,	13,	0,
2,	0,	0,	2,	5,	1,	2,	2,	1,	1,	1,	9,	9,	2,
1,	0,	2,	4,	1,	19,	2,	0,	3,	1,	7,	2,	5,	6,
4,	0,	5,	9,	1,	5,	6,	0,	1,	0,	2,	1,	15,	9,
2,	0,	4,	5,	4,	5,	4,	2,	1,	3,	0,	4,	6,	3,
11,	4,	12,	0,	0,	5,	1,	1,	3,	3,	3,	3,	1,	6,
8,	12,	9,	3,	6,	1,	4,	5,	3,	0,	3,	7,	1,	1,
7,	0,	2,	3,	1,	1,	6,	1,	1,	0,	7,	0,	2,	0,
0,	6,	2,	0,	0,	14,	22,	18,	6,	5.				

TABLE 3.3 Frequencies of Interarrival Times at a District Office

Event		Frequency		
Label	Minutes Elapsed	Absolute (*f*)	Relative (*f*/*n*)	Cumulative Relative
A	0	21	0.172	0.172
B	1	23	0.189	0.361
C	2	16	0.131	0.492
D	3	15	0.123	0.615
E	4	8	0.066	0.680
F	5	9	0.074	0.754
G	6	9	0.074	0.828
H	7	4	0.033	0.861
I	8	2	0.016	0.877
J	9	5	0.041	0.918
K	10	0	0.000	0.918
L	11	1	0.008	0.926
M	12	2	0.016	0.943
N	13	1	0.008	0.951
O	14	1	0.008	0.959
P	15	1	0.008	0.967
Q	16	0	0.000	0.967
R	17	0	0.000	0.967
S	18	1	0.008	0.975
T	19	1	0.008	0.984
U	20	1	0.008	0.992
V	21	0	0.000	0.992
W	22	1	0.008	1.000
		n = 122		

all the outcomes above it in the table). This set of data is examined further in later sections of this chapter. Figure 3.1 shows the same results in a graphical form.

3.2 Discrete Densities and Distributions

In order to treat a random event mathematically, it is convenient to define a frequency function, or *density function*, which will associate the proper probability with each possible outcome. Empirically, the probability of an outcome is measured by the relative frequency of that outcome. Therefore, an empirical density function associates relative frequencies with outcomes.

As an example, consider the throw of the die. If the die is assumed to be unbiased, the theoretical density function, $f(x)$, can be written in this form:

$$f(x) = 1/6, \text{ for } x = 1, 2, 3, 4, 5, \text{ and } 6, \tag{3.1}$$

where x denotes the event that x dots appear on the uppermost face of the die.

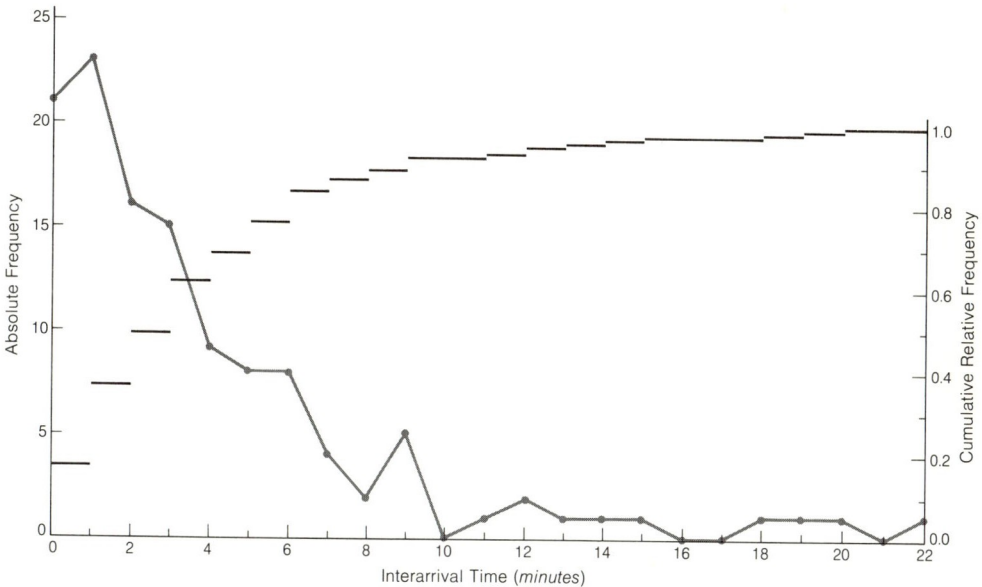

FIG. 3.1 Plots of the Frequencies from Table 3.3 (Interarrival Times)

An empirical density function can be obtained from the data in Table 3.1:

$$f(x) = \begin{cases} 0.16, & \text{if } x = 1 \\ 0.14, & \text{if } x = 2 \\ 0.22, & \text{if } x = 3 \\ 0.14, & \text{if } x = 4 \\ 0.16, & \text{if } x = 5 \\ 0.18, & \text{if } x = 6 \end{cases} \tag{3.2}$$

Note that the first density function is a theoretical one based on the assumption that each face has an equal chance of appearing uppermost, whereas the second one is the actual relative frequencies observed in one series of throws in a specific experimental situation (a particular die, thrower, surface, method of throwing, and so on).

Another useful function is the cumulative distribution, or *distribution function*, $F(x)$, which denotes the probability that the random variable x takes on a value less than or equal to x. From this definition it is clear that the value of $F(x)$ for a given value of x can be derived by accumulating values of $f(x)$ for all values of x less than or equal to the value being considered. In the empirical distribution function for the die throws, $F(1) = f(1) = 0.16$, $F(2) = f(1) + f(2) = 0.16 + 0.14 = 0.30$, and so on. It also should be clear that, if a is the smallest value of x and b is the largest, then $F(x) = 0$ for all $x < a$, and $F(x) = 1$ for all $x \geq b$.

The cumulative relative frequencies listed in Table 3.3 and plotted in Figure 3.1 are values of the distribution function for the interarrival data. The steplike appearance of the plot is typical of the appearance of plots of discrete distributions. Both the die throw and the interarrival time are discrete functions, because x may take only certain discrete values. In other words, only a finite number of distinct outcomes are possible. If x may take on any of a continuous series of values, the function is said to be continuous.

3.3 Continuous Densities and Distributions

The interarrival times at the district office were recorded to the next lowest minute. The actual pattern of arrival times was continuous, because the interarrival time need not be an integral number of minutes; it could be any real value greater than or equal to zero (and less than the total number of minutes that the office was open). The times in Table 3.2 were converted to integers by a process of "rounding off." Assume that the rounding-off was done by eliminating any fractional part of a minute; in other words, by rounding off to the next lowest whole minute.

From Table 3.3, we see that $f(4) = 0.066$. In fact, this represents the relative frequency of observations for which $4 \leq x < 5$. This serves to estimate the density function.[1] Similarly, $F(4) = 0.680$ represents the relative frequency of observations for which $x < 5$. If the interarrival time is considered to be a continuous variable, the frequencies in Table 3.3 no longer can be regarded as exact values for the empirical density and distribution functions. However, these values do provide an estimate of the values for these functions.[2]

Figure 3.1 could be made more accurate by shifting some of the plotted values. For example, the absolute frequency associated with a 0-minute interval actually applies to all times in the range $0 \leq x < 1$. Therefore, this value might better be plotted at the center of this interval, above an interarrival time of $1/2$ minute. Similar shifts in other points for both curves can be made, and the continuous functions then can be approximated by drawing the lines as continuous curves rather than step functions.

3.4 Moments

Various measures associated with statistical distributions can provide insight into some of the more important characteristics of the distributions. The most important of these measures are the moments of a distribution. In general, the nth *moment* of a discrete distribution with a random variable x (that takes on the values $x_1, x_2, x_3, \ldots$, with associated probabilities $p_1, p_2, p_3, \ldots$) is given by

$$\sum_{i=1}^{\infty} x_i^n p_i. \tag{3.3}$$

For a continuous distribution, the nth moment is given by

$$\int_{-\infty}^{\infty} x^n f(x) dx. \tag{3.4}$$

The first moment ($n = 1$) is called the *mean*. The mean usually is denoted by the Greek letter μ and is used to indicate the central tendency or location of the distribution.

Moments also may be taken about some constant value, say c. In this case, the nth moments about c for a discrete distribution are given by

$$\sum_{i=1}^{\infty} (x_i - c)^n p_i. \tag{3.5}$$

---

[1]More specifically, the next-to-the-last column of Table 3.3 gives the empirical probability that the interarrival time is between $n - 1$ and n minutes. In general, the density at $x - a/2$ — in other words, the value of $f(x - a/2)$ — can be estimated from $[F(x) - F(x - a)]/a$ for small values of a. In the example, the smallest value of a that can be used is 1, and $f(x - 1/2) = F(x) - F(x - 1)$ is used.

[2]In dealing with continuous data of this kind, it is assumed that the probability of getting an interarrival time of exactly 5 minutes is zero. Thus, we can say that $F(4)$ represents the relative frequency of observations for which $x \leq 5$.

For a continuous distribution, the nth moments about c are given by

$$\int_{-\infty}^{\infty} (x-c)^n f(x)\, dx. \tag{3.6}$$

Moments about the mean ($c = \mu$) are called *central moments*. The second central moment is called the *variance* and is used as a measure of dispersion. The square root of the variance is called the *standard deviation*. The third central moment is used to measure *skewness*, or the degree of asymmetry of the density function. More specifically, if μ_i is used to denote the ith central moment, then skewness commonly is measured by the quantity $\mu_3/(\mu_2)^{3/2}$ — that is, the third central moment divided by the cube of the standard deviation. The fourth central moment is used to indicate the "peakedness," or *kurtosis*, of a density function. A commonly used measure is μ_4/μ_2^2.

Cramer (1955, pp. 71–86) gives a more extensive discussion of moments and measures of location, skewness, and kurtosis.

The next few sections describe a few discrete and continuous distributions that are useful in simulation development. The chapter ends with a discussion of the discrete, empirical distribution — the distribution most widely encountered in simulation.

3.5 The Binomial Distribution

The *binomial distribution* is a discrete density function that results from n trials of an experiment with only two possible outcomes. In such a case, if the probability associated with one outcome is p, then the probability associated with the other outcome is $1 - p$. Let us denote the first outcome by $x = 1$ and the second outcome by $x = 0$.

In n trials, the result $x = 1$ can occur any integral number of times from 0 to n. In other words, the possible values for the absolute frequency of the event $x = 1$ are $0, 1, 2, \ldots, n$ in a series of n trials. The probability of observing an absolute frequency of exactly i in n trials is given by the expression:

$$p_i = \binom{n}{i} p^i (1-p)^{n-i}, \text{ where}$$

$$\binom{n}{i} = \frac{n!}{i!(n-i)!} = \frac{n(n-1)(n-2)\,\cdots\,(2)(1)}{i(i-1)\,\cdots\,(2)(1)(n-i)(n-i-1)\,\cdots\,(2)(1)}. \tag{3.7}$$

The mean of this distribution is np, and the standard deviation is $\sqrt{np(1-p)}$. Other measures of this distribution include $\mu_3 = np(1-p)(1-2p)$ and $\mu_4 = 3n^2 p^2 (1-p)^2 + np(1-p)\,[1 - 6p(1-p)]$. Therefore, the measures of skewness and kurtosis, respectively, associated with the binomial distribution are

$$\frac{\mu_3}{(\mu_2)^{3/2}} = \frac{1 - 2p}{\sqrt{np(1 - p)}},\tag{3.8}$$

and

$$\frac{\mu_4}{\mu_2^2} = \frac{[1 - 6p(1 - p)]}{np(1 - p)}.\tag{3.9}$$

Tables of the distribution function for various values of n and p are useful if it is necessary to deal extensively with the binomial distribution. The table prepared by the U.S. Ordnance Corps (1952) is one of the best for this purpose, but it is not readily available. National Bureau of Standards (1964) provides less extensive but still useful tables.

In simulations, the binomial density often is encountered when dealing with phenomena that are either present or absent, or with variables that take on values such as "yes" or "no." For example, in simulating a horse race, it may be necessary to denote the presence or absence of blinders on a horse. In modeling the workflow in a district office (Figure 1.1), it may be useful to establish a variable that assumes the value "yes" if a claims representative is available for an interview or the value "no" if he is unavailable.

Statistical tests involving binomial variables often are made as part of an analysis of variance, because the binomial variable may be only one of many that can affect a result, and its effect may be dependent on the values of some other variables. The analysis of variance permits valid statistical tests to be made under such conditions (see Chapter 6).

3.6 The Poisson Distribution

The Poisson distribution is another discrete distribution of importance in system simulation. In the binomial distribution, if p is very small and n is very large, then p_i is approximately equal to $(\lambda^i e^{-\lambda})/i!$, where $\lambda = np$. In fact, if p is allowed to approach zero and n to approach infinity in such a way that np is held constant, then p_i exactly equals the quantity shown for integral values of $i \geq 0$. Because this distribution is a limiting case of the binomial distribution for very small values of p, it is appropriate for characterizing the probability of rare events in a large number of trials. Both the mean and the variance are equal to λ.

The Poisson distribution has proven to be widely applicable. Because traffic problems arise frequently in simulations, we describe here one example of the application of this distribution to characterize telephone traffic. Suppose that the occurrence of telephone calls between two stations is distributed randomly in time. In other words, the probability that a call is made in any time interval of a given length is equal to the probability of a call being made in any other interval of the same length. With certain additional assumptions, it can be shown that the number of calls occurring between time 0 and time t

has a Poisson distribution. More specifically, if $p_i(t)$ is used to denote the probability of i calls occurring in the time interval 0 to t, then

$$p_i(t) = \frac{(\lambda t)^i}{i!} e^{-\lambda t}. \qquad (3.10)$$

In this case, λ can be interpreted as the intensity (rate) of incoming traffic and $1/\lambda$ as the mean time between consecutive calls (the mean interarrival time). Cramer (1955, pp. 104–107) gives a more detailed mathematical derivation of the properties of the Poisson distribution. Feller (1957, pp. 97–99, 142–145, 149–154, 177–178) discusses several other interesting examples of the use of this distribution.

3.7 The Uniform Distribution

Next we discuss one of the simplest continuous distributions. It is of some importance in simulations because of its central role in the generation of random numbers. For this rectangular distribution, or *uniform distribution*, the density function is

$$f(x) = \begin{cases} \dfrac{1}{b-a}, & \text{for } a < x \le b, \\ 0, & \text{for } x \le a \text{ and } x > b. \end{cases} \qquad (3.11)$$

In this distribution, all values of x in the range from a to b occur with equal probability, but values outside this range never occur. The corresponding distribution function is

$$F(x) = \begin{cases} 0, & \text{for } x \le a, \\ \dfrac{x-a}{b-a}, & \text{for } a < x \le b, \\ 1, & \text{for } x > b. \end{cases} \qquad (3.12)$$

The uniform density and distribution functions are plotted in Figure 3.2.

The *standard uniform distribution,* with $a = 0$ and $b = 1$, represents the case where any value of x between 0 and 1 is as likely as any other value within that range, while values less than 0 or greater than 1 never occur. The distribution function has the form, $F(x) = x$, for $0 \le x \le 1$. Thus, the probability is α that $x \le \alpha$ (for $0 \le \alpha \le 1$). This simple relationship makes it relatively easy to generate sets of numbers that have a standard uniform distribution; this topic is discussed more fully in connection with random number generation (Chapter 7).

For any uniformly distributed variable x, a simple transformation — namely, $y = (x - a)/(b - a)$ — results in a new variable y with the standardized uniform distribution. The uniform distribution has a mean of $(b + a)/2$ and a variance of $(b - a)^2/12$. Thus, the standard uniform distribution has a mean of $1/2$ and a variance of $1/12$.

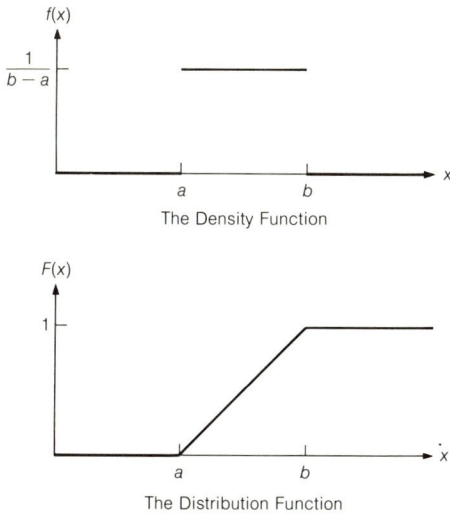

The Density Function

The Distribution Function

FIG. 3.2   The Uniform Distribution

3.8 The Normal Distribution

The *normal distribution* is one of the most important and most frequently encountered continuous distributions. Its density function is

$$f(x) = \frac{1}{\sigma \sqrt{2\pi}} e^{-(x-\mu)^2/2\sigma^2}. \tag{3.13}$$

The corresponding distribution function cannot be expressed in closed form,
but both the density and the distribution function have been tabulated extensively. National Bureau of Standards (1964) gives tables of the normal distribution; an abbreviated table is included in Appendix A of this book, because of
its usefulness in making statistical tests. The normal density and distribution
functions are plotted in Figure 3.3.

The normal distribution has mean μ and variance σ^2. The *standardized
normal distribution* has a mean of 0 and variance of 1; therefore, the standardized
normal density function is

$$f(x) = \frac{1}{\sqrt{2\pi}} e^{-x^2/2}. \tag{3.14}$$

For a normally distributed variable x, the transformed variable $z = (x - \mu)/\sigma$
(where μ is the mean and σ the standard deviation of the original distribution)
has the standardized normal distribution.

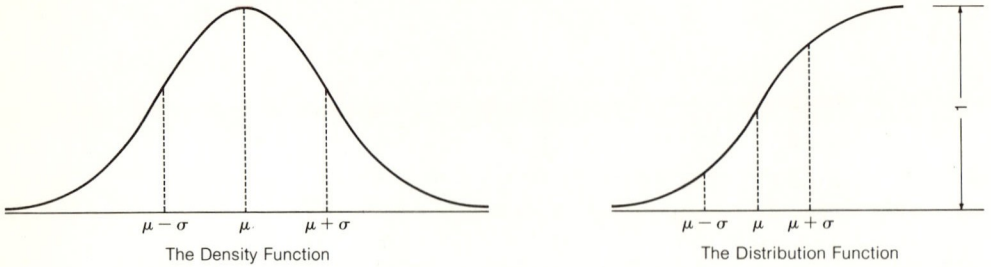

The Density Function   The Distribution Function

FIG. 3.3   The Normal Distribution

The notation $N(x;\mu,\sigma)$ or more succinctly $N(\mu,\sigma)$ commonly is used to indicate a normal distribution with mean μ and standard deviation σ. For example, the standardized normal distribution is represented as $N(0,1)$. For any normally distributed variable x, if $z = (x - \mu)/\sigma$, then $N(z;0,1)$.

The *central limit theorem* states that (under some rather general conditions) the sum of n independently and identically distributed random variables tends to be normally distributed as n approaches infinity. Roughly stated, this theorem means that variables resulting from the combination of many separate effects tend to be normally distributed. For this reason, the normal distribution is encountered frequently in simulations. For a more detailed discussion of the central limit theorem, see Cramer (1946, Chapters 17 and 28).

The third central moment (in fact, every odd central moment) of the normal distribution is zero; thus, the measure of skewness is zero. The fourth central moment is $3\sigma^4$; thus, the measure of kurtosis is 3.

Chapter 4 includes an example of normally distributed data, a discussion of the use of the normal distribution in statistical tests, and a computer program used to determine whether it is reasonable to assume that a given set of data is normally distributed.

3.9 The Exponential Distribution

The exponential distribution may be regarded as the continuous analog of the discrete Poisson distribution. The Poisson distribution was appropriate for the telephone line example discussed in Section 3.6. As might be expected, the exponential distribution is useful in characterizing waiting lines or arrival patterns that are inherently continuous.

The exponential density function is

$$f(x) = \frac{e^{-x/\sigma}}{\sigma}, \qquad \text{for } 0 \leq x. \tag{3.15}$$

The corresponding distribution function is

$$F(x) = 1 - e^{-x/\sigma}. \qquad (3.16)$$

The mean and variance are σ and σ^2, respectively.

Consider the data on interarrival times at a social security district office (Table 3.3 and Figure 3.1). Let us now assume that the observed data actually are approximations to an underlying continuous distribution. With the corrections for rounding-off (Section 3.3) and combinations of intervals to get at least five arrivals in each interval (except the last one), the distribution of interarrival times can be restated in the form of Table 3.4. The theoretical cumulative distribution given in the next-to-the-last column of Table 3.4 is an exponential distribution with $\sigma = 122/23 = 5.304$ (the average number of arrivals per minute). This theoretical cumulative distribution is plotted with the empirical one in Figure 3.4. The theoretical distribution falls consistently below the empirical one, but the curves do seem to be of similar shape. A better value of σ can be estimated by the method of least squares. In this method, the value of σ is chosen to minimize the sums of the squares of the vertical differences between the points on the empirical distribution and the corresponding points on the theoretical distribution. (The procedure used in this method is discussed in Chapter 5, and a computer program is given there for implementing the procedure.) The least squares method yields an estimated value of 4.329 for σ, and the theoretical cumulative distribution given in the last column of the table is derived from this value. This distribution clearly fits the empirical data better

TABLE 3.4   Summary of Distributions Associated with Interarrival Times

Time Interval (minutes)		Number of Arrivals in Interval	Empirical Cumulative Distribution	Theoretical Cumulative Distributions	
Lower Bound	Upper Bound			$\sigma = 5.304$	$\sigma = 4.329$
0	1	21	0.172	0.172	0.206
1	2	23	0.361	0.314	0.370
2	3	16	0.492	0.432	0.500
3	4	15	0.615	0.530	0.603
4	5	8	0.680	0.611	0.685
5	6	9	0.754	0.678	0.750
6	7	9	0.828	0.733	0.802
7	9	6	0.877	0.817	0.875
9	12	6	0.926	0.896	0.937
12	16	5	0.967	0.951	0.975
16	23	4	1.000	0.987	0.995

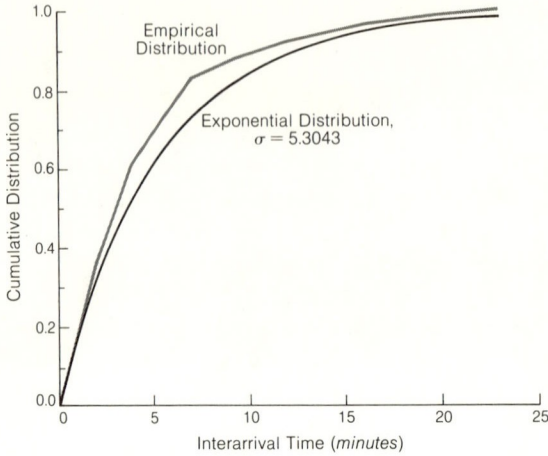

FIG. 3.4   Empirical and Theoretical Cumulative Distributions of the Interarrival Times in Table 3.4

than did the first one. The relatively poor fit obtained with the first estimate of σ is discussed further in the next section. In the next chapter, we discuss a statistical technique used to answer the question, Is it reasonable to assume that the actual pattern of interarrival times follows an exponential distribution?

3.10 Empirical Distributions

Statistical distributions are encountered in three different stages of simulation development: (1) in summarizing data obtained from field studies or system records; (2) in constructing models for systems or subsystems directly from theoretical considerations, and (3) in making statistical tests. In this section we discuss the first context: the use of statistical distributions to summarize empirical data.

The flowchart of Figure 3.5 outlines a procedure to be followed in processing an empirical distribution. Two major questions must be answered while executing this procedure: (1) Is the purpose of the procedure merely to summarize the data in a succinct fashion, or is it to obtain a characterization that will give new insight into the system, or is it to produce a distribution for use in one or more models of the system? and (2) Does the theoretical distribution fit the empirical data reasonably well? Techniques needed to answer the second question are discussed in Chapter 4. The first question should be easily answered in most applications.

As Figure 3.5 indicates, the first steps in dealing with the set of data are to tabulate and plot them, and then to calculate some of the moments (particularly

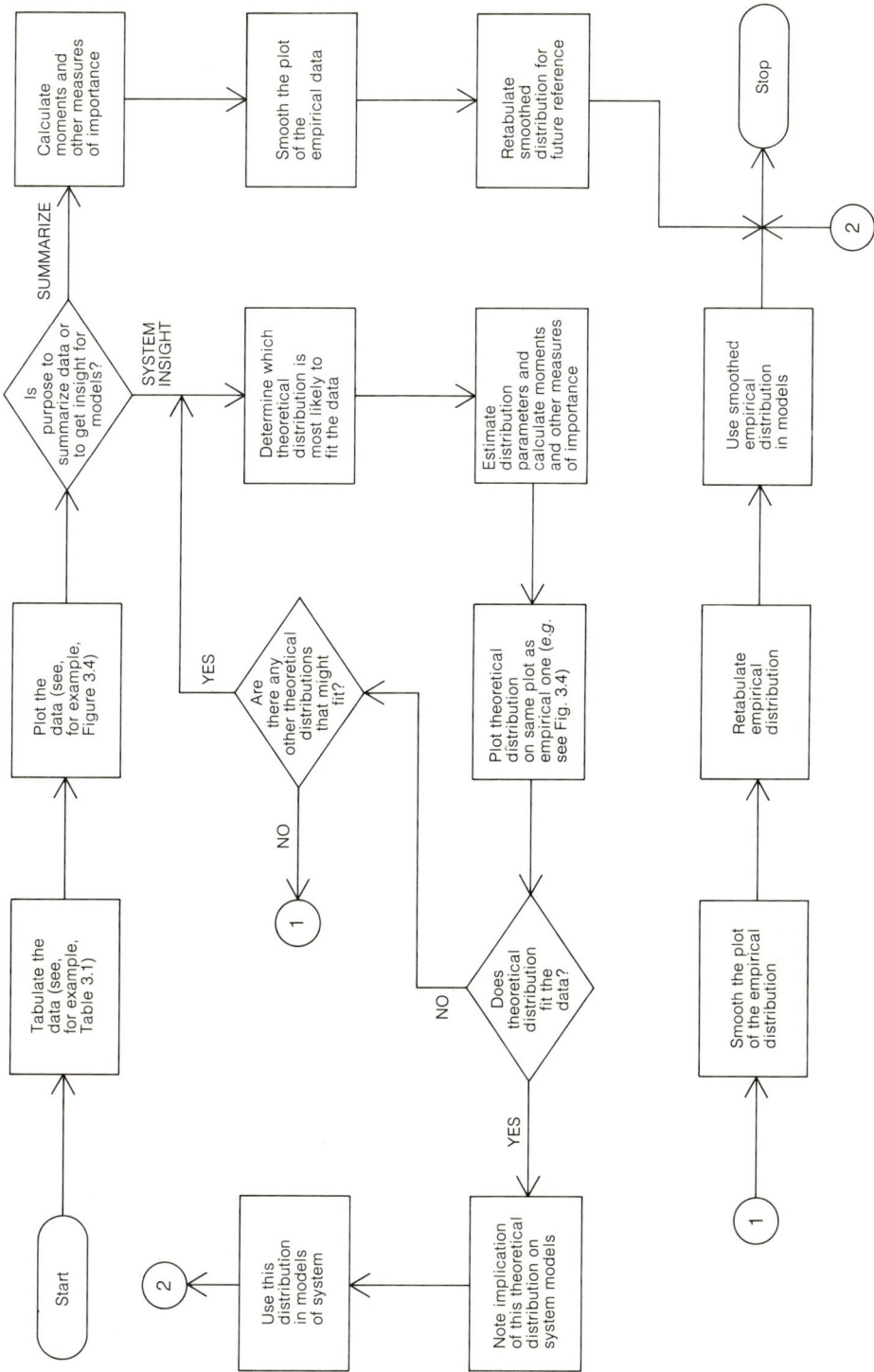

FIG. 3.5 Outline of a Procedure for Processing an Empirical Distribution

the mean and the variance) and other parameters associated with the distribution. If the data were collected in order to gain insight into the real system or in order to develop system models, then the next step is to choose the theoretical distribution that may be assumed to characterize these data best. (The flowchart suggests that this choice be made before the moments and other parameters are calculated. In practice, the sequence of these two steps will vary. At times the moments will be calculated first, and at other times a guess will be made about the underlying distribution before any calculations are made.) Before discussing the other steps to be followed in these cases, let us consider the steps to be taken if the purpose of the procedure is merely to summarize the empirical data. In this case, the data should be smoothed and the smoothed result should be tabulated. It might be appropriate simply to smooth the plot by eye (or to use french curves or mechanical splines to achieve a more polished result, but still one that is essentially "smoothed by eye"). If greater objectivity and accuracy is desired, spline functions may be used to smooth the data (see Greville 1967). The table of smoothed data serves to summarize the empirical results in a convenient form and thus completes the procedure for this case.

Let us return to the problem of choosing a theoretical distribution in the other cases. The references cited in earlier sections of this chapter may be useful aids in making this choice. In addition, Martin (1968, pp. 295–305) gives typical plots of various distributions that can be compared to the empirical plot. Johnson and Leone (1964, Vol. 1, Chapters 4 and 5) give a comprehensive description of distributions. Most important of all, however, is a knowledge of the phenomenon being studied. Is its nature discrete or continuous? Does it arise from a waiting-line or arrival pattern? Does it characterize the failure of equipment? Is it the result of a combination of many separate effects? Answers to such questions are needed in order to make an intelligent guess about the most appropriate theoretical distribution to fit the data. After a type of distribution is chosen, the distribution parameters are estimated, and a goodness-of-fit test is made of the assumption that this particular theoretical distribution fits the data. If the theoretical distribution does not fit, another might be tried, or it might be necessary to settle for use of the smoothed empirical distribution in the models. The GPSS programming language accommodates this approach very well (see Chapter 11).

Returning to the interarrival data considered in Section 3.9, let us see what further steps may be taken in studying the distribution. The data already have been plotted, an estimate of σ has been calculated for a theoretical exponential distribution, the theoretical and empirical distributions have been compared, and a new estimate of σ has been calculated by the least squares method (see Table 3.4 and Figure 3.4). The first estimate of σ produced a theoretical distribution that indicated a lower frequency of short interarrival times than actually observed, even though the estimate was based upon the mean of the empirical distribution. Can we find an explanation for this discrepancy? The choice of the exponential distribution was based upon the assumption that there is an equal probability of arrival for time intervals of equal length. Perhaps this assumption does not hold. For example, there may be busy and slow periods during the day, producing clusters of short interarrival times during some parts of the day and clusters of long interarrival times during other parts. Because the interarrival times in Table 3.2 are recorded in the order in which they occurred, we can test this explanation (see Chapter 4).

Another explanation might be based upon a closer study of the way in which the data were recorded. Each arrival time was recorded by a time-stamp clock that recorded time in minutes, advancing the recorded time by one minute at the end of each 60-second period. Thus, the data collected already represent a discrete approximation of the continuous distribution of actual interarrival times. If the successive arrival times were stamped as, say, 2:06 and 2:09, the interarrival time was calculated to be 3 minutes. However, the time stamp of 2:06 actually might represent any time from 2:06:00 through 2:06:59+ (where the last number indicates seconds), and the time stamp of 2:09 might represent any time from 2:09:00 through 2:09:59+. Thus the actual interarrival time could have been as short as 2 minutes or as long as 4 minutes. In general, a recorded interarrival time of n minutes actually may represent a real interarrival time of anywhere between $n - 1$ and $n + 1$ minutes. (The case where $n = 0$ is an exception, because negative interarrival times are impossible.) Does this approximation in the recording technique affect the empirical distribution?

Assume that the arrivals in the periods from 2:06 to nearly 2:07 and from 2:09 to nearly 2:10 are uniformly distributed. Then, the interarrival time distribution will be the difference between two uniformly distributed random variables with equal ranges. Such a difference has a *triangular distribution* with mean equal to the difference of the two means and variance equal to the sum of the two variances (Figure 3.6). In this case, the triangular distribution has a mean of 3 and a variance of 1/6. In the original empirical distribution, all

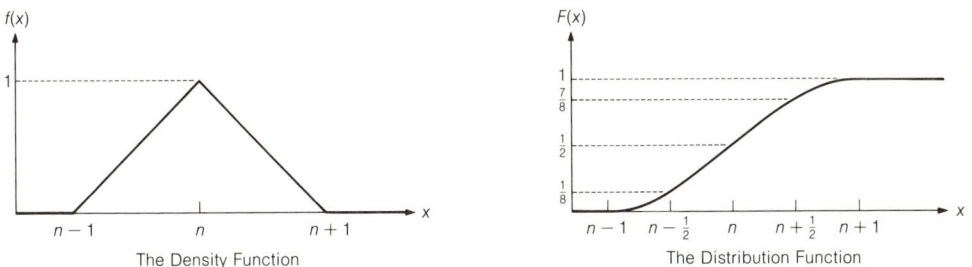

FIG. 3.6   The Triangular Density and Distribution Functions Used to Adjust Interarrival Times

of the interarrival times calculated as *n* minutes were assigned to the interval *n* through *n* + 1 minutes. It now is clear that one-half of those times should have been assigned to the interval *n* − 1 through *n* minutes. This adjustment of the data produces the revised empirical density and cumulative distribution functions listed in Table 3.5. However, this distribution differs even more than did the original one from the theoretical exponential distribution with $\sigma = 5.403$. The least squares estimate of σ for the revised empirical distribution is 3.788, and a theoretical function based on this value is included in Table 3.5. This distribution could be used to generate customer arrivals in district office models, but further discussion of this problem in Part Five leads to a still better way to generate the arrivals. Actual generation of arrivals from a chosen distribution is discussed in Part Three. The interarrival-times example illustrates the kind of adjustment needed when a continuous distribution is approximated by a discrete one. Ehrenfeld and Littauer (1964, p. 195) briefly discuss the adjustments needed when a discrete distribution is approximated by a continuous one.

3.11 Distributions Used in Making Statistical Tests

This section very briefly discusses three distributions that are important in making statistical tests. These distributions are tabulated in Appendix A.

Student's t distribution is used primarily to test differences in means of two samples selected from normally distributed populations. (It is named for a pseudonym — Student — used by the statistician W. S. Gossett.) The density function of this distribution is

TABLE 3.5   Revised Empirical and Theoretical Distributions for Interarrival Data

Time Interval (*minutes*)		Adjusted Number of Arrivals in Interval	Empirical Cumulative Distribution	Theoretical Cumulative Distribution $(\sigma = 3.788)$
Lower Bound	Upper Bound			
0	1	32.5	0.266	0.232
1	2	19.5	0.426	0.410
2	3	15.5	0.553	0.547
3	4	11.5	0.648	0.652
4	5	8.5	0.717	0.732
5	6	9.0	0.791	0.795
6	7	6.5	0.844	0.842
7	9	6.5	0.898	0.907
9	12	4.5	0.934	0.958
12	16	4.0	0.967	0.985
16	23	4.0	1.000	0.998

$$f(t) = \frac{\Gamma\left(\frac{n+1}{2}\right)}{\sqrt{n\pi}\ \Gamma\left(\frac{n}{2}\right)\left(1 + \frac{t^2}{n}\right)^{(n+1)/2}}, \quad \text{for } -\infty < t < \infty, \qquad (3.17)$$

where n is a parameter that ordinarily takes on integer values, $\Gamma(n+1) = \int_0^\infty e^{-x}\, x^{n-1}\, dx = n\,\Gamma(n)$, and $\Gamma(1/2) = \sqrt{\pi} = 1.77245385.\ \ldots$

The t distribution has a mean of 0 and a variance of $n/(n-2)$. The only parameter in this distribution is n, and—as is the case in many distributions used for statistical tests—this parameter is called "the degrees of freedom." A Student's t density function with $n = 4$ is plotted in Figure 3.7. A standardized normal distribution is plotted on the same coordinates to illustrate the similarity of these distributions.

The chi square distribution is used in goodness-of-fit tests and in certain other nonparametric tests. Its density function is

$$f(x) = \frac{x^{(n/2)-1}\, e^{-x/2}}{\Gamma(n/2) 2^{n/2}}, \quad \text{for } 0 \leq x < \infty. \qquad (3.18)$$

For the chi square distribution, the mean is n (the degrees of freedom), and the variance is $2n$. Chi square density functions for several values of n are plotted in Figure 3.8.

The F distribution is used primarily to test differences (actually, ratios) of variances between two samples from normally distributed populations. Its

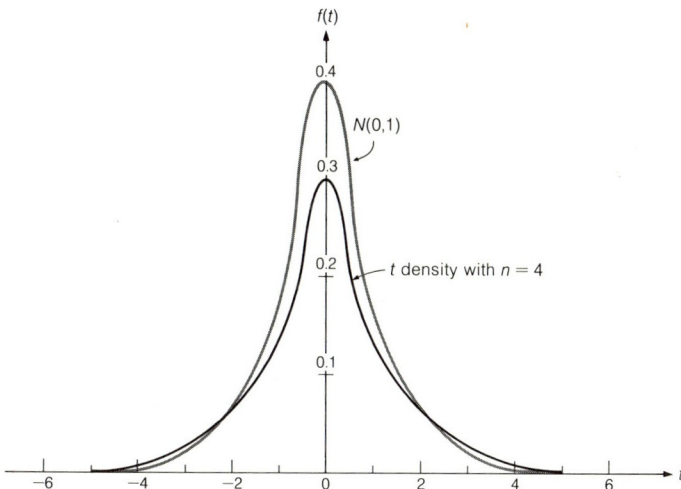

FIG. 3.7   Plot of the t Density with $n = 4$ (black line) and Plot of the Standardized Normal Density (gray line)

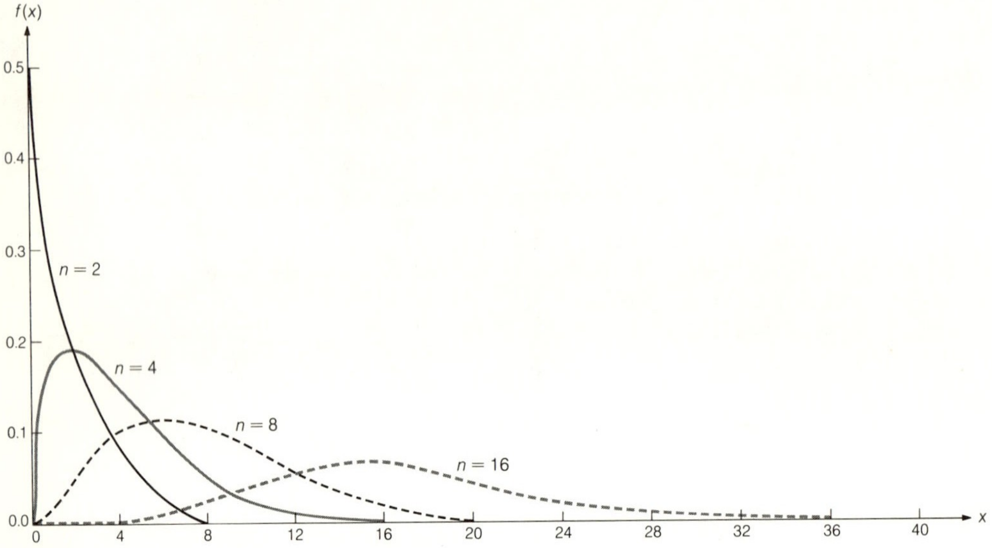

FIG. 3.8 Plot of the *Chi* Square Densities with $n = 2, 4, 8,$ and 16

density function has two parameters, one associated with each of the two variances involved in forming the F-ratio. Using m to denote the degrees of freedom associated with the variance in the numerator of the ratio and n to denote the degrees of freedom associated with the variance in the denominator, the density function is

$$f(F) = \frac{\Gamma\left[(m+n)/2\right]}{\Gamma(m/2)\,\Gamma(n/2)}\, m^{m/2}\, n^{n/2}\, F^{(m/2)-1}\,(m+nF)^{-(m+n)/2},$$

$$\text{for } 0 \le F < \infty. \qquad (3.19)$$

The mean of the F distribution is $m/(n-2)$, and the variance is $[m^2(n+2)]/[m(n-2)(n-4)]$.

3.12 Supplementary Reading

Almost every introductory book on probability contains one or more chapters on distributions. The references mentioned here were chosen either because they contain an exceptionally lucid description of some topics discussed in this chapter, or because they discuss one or more topics of potential interest that are not covered in this book.

Freund (1962, pp. 61–188) covers the subject of probability distributions in a lucid manner. The concluding sections of his third chapter contain a good definition of and introduction to the subject of multivariate distributions (probability distributions in more than one random variable). Feller (1957) already has been mentioned as a source for additional examples of the distributions discussed in this chapter. For a more elaborate and rigorous discussion of the central limit theorem, see Chapter 10 of Feller (1957) and Chapter 8, Section 4 of Feller (1966). Chapters 5 and 6 of the latter work contain a rigorous and comprehensive discussion of the general subject of distributions.

Martin (1968) also has been cited earlier, but we should like to call attention again to Appendix E (pp. 295–305), which contains definitions and plots of more than a dozen distribution functions. We also remind you of the two-volume work by Johnson and Leone (1964). Chapters 4 and 5 of the first volume contain a useful and comprehensive description of some of the most important distributions encountered in simulation work. Among the distributions not covered in this book but described by Johnson and Leone are the hypergeometric, the multinomial, the negative binomial, and the Weibull distributions. The same volume contains a good discussion (pp. 139–143) of the procedure for fitting a distribution to empirical data.

Beyer (1966) may be the handiest source for a variety of statistical tables. However, some of the tables (for example, those for the binomial distribution) are less comprehensive than may be needed, and others (for example, those for the exponential distributions) do not provide small enough increments for the arguments.

PROBLEMS

3.1 Estimate the probability that a random variable with each of the following distributions will fall in the range of the mean $\pm$ one standard deviation:
   (a) binomial, with $p = 0.5$ and $n = 5$;
   (b) binomial, with $p = 0.1$ and $n = 5$;
   (c) binomial, with $p = 0.5$ and $n = 20$;
   (d) Poisson, with $\lambda = 1$;
   (e) standard uniform;
   (f) $N(0,1)$;
   (g) $N(20,20)$;
   (h) exponential, with $\sigma = 1$; and
   (i) exponential, with $\sigma = 0.1$.

3.2 Verify by integration:
   (a) that the mean of a uniform distribution is $(a + b)/2$;
   (b) that the variance of a uniform distribution is $(b - a)^2/12$; and
   (c) that the mean of an exponential distribution is σ.

3.3 Using the table in Appendix A, plot the following normal density functions on a single set of coordinates: $N(0,1)$, $N(0,0.5)$, and $N(0,0.1)$.

3.4   Table 3.6 contains data on arrivals at a social security district office, as observed in a one-week field study (see Section 2.6). Calculate and plot on a single set of coordinates the cumulative distributions for each day and for the week.

TABLE 3.6   Distribution of Arrival Times During One Week
at a District Office

Time Interval		Absolute Frequencies of Arrivals					
Lower Bound	Upper Bound	Thursday	Friday	Monday	Tuesday	Wednesday	Total for Week
8:45	9:00	0	2	4	1	4	11
9:00	9:15	21	15	43	16	13	108
9:15	9:30	17	18	22	13	12	82
9:30	9:45	20	16	22	15	24	97
9:45	10:00	17	16	30	14	16	93
10:00	10:15	18	8	29	17	27	99
10:15	10:30	24	15	28	22	22	111
10:30	10:45	24	15	28	25	16	108
10:45	11:00	19	16	23	21	16	95
11:00	11:15	17	21	25	26	21	110
11:15	11:30	22	11	25	19	13	90
11:30	11:45	18	22	17	25	15	97
11:45	12:00	15	11	17	21	11	75
12:00	12:15	15	10	19	19	16	79
12:15	12:30	11	11	17	17	7	63
12:30	12:45	15	15	16	11	10	67
12:45	1:00	14	9	17	21	11	72
1:00	1:15	18	19	17	20	16	90
1:15	1:30	17	14	29	20	16	96
1:30	1:45	25	17	19	25	27	113
1:45	2:00	26	13	21	18	12	90
2:00	2:15	11	15	22	26	14	88
2:15	2:30	11	13	17	22	15	78
2:30	2:45	16	11	18	18	19	82
2:45	3:00	25	12	16	13	8	74
3:00	3:15	18	12	20	13	10	73
3:15	3:30	17	7	14	16	8	62
3:30	3:45	15	8	14	9	12	58
3:45	4:00	15	10	20	14	8	67
4:00	4:15	9	6	13	9	15	52
4:15	4:30	8	7	6	7	6	34
4:30	4:45	2	6	11	4	5	28
4:45	5:00	3	2	5	2	1	13
After 5:00		54	0	0	0	0	54
Total		577	403	644	539	446	2609

3.5 Table 3.7 summarizes weekly totals of arrival data for eleven class-B offices in the social security district office field study. Calculate and plot the cumulative distribution for each of these eleven offices. (Put three or four plots on each set of coordinates.) Calculate and plot the cumulative distribution for all offices combined.

TABLE 3.7 Distribution of Arrival Times During One Week at Eleven Class-B District Offices

Time Interval		Absolute Frequency of Arrivals for Each Office*										
Lower Bound	Upper Bound	NH	FL	AL	CH	CA	EP	FT	KC	LR	SL	SF	Total
8:00	8:15	0	0	0	0	0	0	0	0	5	0	0	5
8:15	8:30	0	5	0	0	4	4	0	0	1	0	4	18
8:30	8:45	0	11	4	7	16	7	0	16	19	0	47	127
8:45	9:00	3	19	21	9	11	18	51	5	20	19	21	197
9:00	9:15	29	31	18	20	18	24	25	20	16	23	22	246
9:15	9:30	28	46	20	12	25	34	22	12	24	17	28	268
9:30	9:45	29	32	26	24	26	23	25	12	22	24	32	275
9:45	10:00	26	45	37	26	28	26	33	21	25	27	29	323
10:00	10:15	24	28	34	23	22	24	45	23	30	33	33	319
10:15	10:30	35	47	36	29	31	28	31	13	33	24	35	342
10:30	10:45	31	40	33	23	35	37	42	24	22	27	39	353
10:45	11:00	37	42	30	22	25	30	39	16	27	29	23	320
11:00	11:15	34	53	20	30	32	22	43	25	21	30	37	347
11:15	11:30	26	37	26	23	29	20	26	19	18	34	30	288
11:30	11:45	31	50	25	22	24	28	21	17	21	32	43	314
11:45	12:00	29	35	32	14	26	14	35	13	18	19	23	258
12:00	12:15	30	29	19	21	22	12	21	9	23	30	31	247
12:15	12:30	23	28	13	10	29	17	24	14	21	27	24	230
12:30	12:45	21	38	23	18	26	28	16	6	20	28	29	253
12:45	1:00	23	40	27	14	18	14	36	24	20	35	13	264
1:00	1:15	28	36	28	12	21	23	27	17	20	27	29	268
1:15	1:30	30	35	31	16	27	27	39	27	28	44	25	319
1:30	1:45	35	38	22	23	18	18	25	17	26	27	30	279
1:45	2:00	28	46	17	15	25	22	33	17	17	32	35	287
2:00	2:15	20	42	28	25	29	25	42	15	20	33	34	313
2:15	2:30	22	41	29	20	27	22	34	19	22	30	42	308
2:30	2:45	22	39	17	14	17	19	33	12	23	39	21	256
2:45	3:00	39	38	16	10	15	23	25	13	18	40	32	269

TABLE 3.7—*Continued*

Time Interval		Absolute Frequency of Arrivals for Each Office*											
Lower Bound	Upper Bound	NH	FL	AL	CH	CA	EP	FT	KC	LR	SL	SF	Total
3:00	3:15	18	30	21	14	12	19	33	14	11	27	24	223
3:15	3:30	19	29	21	15	21	15	41	14	23	34	20	252
3:30	3:45	21	30	20	14	11	11	32	22	13	22	20	216
3:45	4:00	22	19	16	11	18	14	36	10	6	34	18	204
4:00	4:15	20	26	17	13	16	13	27	13	13	32	10	200
4:15	4:30	17	26	15	9	9	6	24	6	16	26	6	160
4:30	4:45	15	9	17	4	5	9	20	2	7	25	1	114
4:45	5:00	5	6	12	3	2	6	6	2	3	1	1	47
After 5:00		28	66	0	10	27	49	18	23	6	0	28	255
Total		848	1212	761	575	747	731	1030	532	678	931	919	8964

*Location of offices: NH = New Haven; FL = Flushing; AL = Alexandria; CH = Chester; CA = Chattanooga; EP = Elwood Park; FT = Flint; KC = Kansas City; LR = Little Rock; SL = Salt Lake City; SF = San Francisco. All are Class-B district offices of the social security network.

4

Statistical Tests

4.1 BACKGROUND   Many inferences about a stochastic system must be made from the available data. Collection of data about the system and statistical tests of these data may provide answers for questions such as (1) Are the interarrival times at a movie ticket booth exponentially distributed? (2) Is the average service time at a class-A district office the same as that at a class-D district office? or (3) Do customers prefer to use certain checkout stations in a supermarket? A wide variety of statistical tests is available; only a few of the more important ones are discussed in this chapter, with references to more extensive discussions of the topic in the literature.

4.2 The Framework

The point of view used in making a statistical test is not unlike that found in a jury trial. Much as the innocence of a defendant is assumed and then tested against the available evidence, an hypothesis about the system is assumed and then tested against the available data. For example, the questions in Section 4.1 might lead to hypotheses such as (1) Interarrival times at a movie ticket booth are exponentially distributed; (2) The average service time at class-A district offices is the same as that at class-D offices; and (3) If the queues at all checkout stations are of the same length, each checkout station has an equal probability of being chosen by the next customer. The data then are examined to determine whether or not the hypothesis is tenable. Before making the test, strict specifications are set for the conditions that must be met if the hypothesis is to be considered tenable.

We may distinguish four possible outcomes of this hypothesis-testing procedure: (1) the hypothesis actually is true, but the test leads to its rejection as untenable; (2) the hypothesis actually is true, and the test leads to its acceptance; (3) the hypothesis actually is false, and the test leads to its rejection; or (4) the hypothesis actually is false, but the test leads to its acceptance as valid. Obviously, outcomes 2 and 3 are desirable, and the specifications for the statistical test should be designed to maximize the probability of these outcomes. Outcome 1 is called a *type I error*, and outcome 4 is called a *type II error*; the test should be designed to minimize the probability of these outcomes. However, in most cases, the probabilities of the two types of errors can be simultaneously reduced only by increasing the number of observations used in the test. Therefore, some compromise must be made in the test specifications; certain levels of probability for type I and type II errors are accepted in order to permit the test to be made with a reasonable number of observations.

The size of the type I error (denoted by α) is the probability that (in many repetitions of a test with certain specifications for hypothesis tenability) a valid hypothesis will be rejected. The quantity $1 - \alpha$ is called the *level of significance* of the test. Specifications commonly are designed to ensure that $\alpha \leq 0.05$, but this is an arbitrary value, and larger type I errors might be accepted in particular situations.

The size of the type II error (denoted by β) is related to the degree of falsity of the hypothesis being tested. For example, suppose that in one real system, the actual difference between average service times at class-A and class-D district offices is 1 minute. In a second real system, the difference in average service times is 20 minutes. Obviously, with a particular statistical test, the false hypothesis that the average service times are the same is more likely to be accepted in the case of the first real system than in the case of the second. Thus, when a size is specified for the type II error, the degree of difference associated with this error must also be specified. The quantity $1 - \beta$ is called the *power of the test*.

For a given statistical test (with fixed sample size and fixed α), we can calculate β and the power $(1 - \beta)$ corresponding to various assumed levels for the extent of falsity of the hypothesis. This relation—with the extent of falsity as the abscissa, and the power as the ordinate—is called the *power curve* of the test. Consider, for example, a test of the hypothesis that two means are equal. If the real difference between the means is very near zero, the probability that the hypothesis will be accepted (the type II error) is very near $1 - \alpha$; thus, the power of the test is nearly $1 - (1 - \alpha) = \alpha$. As the real difference between the means increases, the power increases and approaches one as the difference gets very large. Thus, a typical power curve is S-shaped, and it rises from coordinates near $(0, \alpha)$ to coordinates of (a large value, almost 1).

The more that is known about a phenomenon, the smaller α and β can be made. In this context, "knowing more" almost always means taking a larger sample—that is, making more observations. However, there are times when a more clever test design—using variance reduction techniques—is as effective as taking additional samples (see Section 4.4). In this chapter, we generally assume that a test is fully characterized by α, β, and the sample size (n). Table 4.1 summarizes this framework for consideration of statistical tests.

4.3 The Procedure

The procedure used in making a statistical test involves four steps: (1) determine which test to use; (2) select the error levels (α and β, including for the

TABLE 4.1   The Framework for Making Statistical Tests

Test Result	State of Real World	
	Hypothesis Is False	Hypothesis Is True
Hypothesis rejected as invalid	Valid conclusion	Invalid conclusion, associated with type I error
Hypothesis accepted as valid	Invalid conclusion, associated with type II error	Valid conclusion

Type of Error	Size	Definition of Size	Quantity ($1 - Size$)
Type I	α	Probability that an hypothesis is rejected when it actually is true.	$(1 - \alpha)$ is called the "level of significance" of the test.
Type II	β	Probability that an hypothesis is accepted when it actually is false. The extent to which the hypothesis is false must be specified.	$(1 - \beta)$ is called the "power" of the test.

latter the extent to which the hypothesis may be false), sample size (n), and sampling procedure; (3) obtain the observations (data); and (4) carry out the statistical test. All too often, steps 1 and 2 are ignored, and data are obtained before the test has been chosen and the error levels have been fixed. Such careless procedure often leads to unsatisfactory results.

The choice of a test to be used will depend upon what is known about the distribution of the population from which the sample is drawn. The choice of a statistical test also depends upon the availability of tests suitable for use with this distribution. If the distribution is insufficiently known, or if the distribution is known but no suitable test for it is available, *nonparametric tests* (also called distribution-free tests) should be used. Parametric tests should be used whenever possible, because they generally can be expected to give a smaller β for fixed α and n—in other words, they are more powerful. Three parametric and four nonparametric tests are discussed in this chapter (Table 4.2). Johnson and Leone (1964, Vol. 1, Chapters 7 and 8) discuss many more parametric tests, and Siegel (1956) describes many other nonparametric tests.

After the test is chosen, it is important to fix α, to decide upon a suitable degree of difference (extent of falsity), to fix β, and finally to select an appropriate sample size. (An example of this step of the procedure for use of the t test is given in the next section.) It often happens that small values of α and β are selected at first; these values then prove to require too large a sample size,

TABLE 4.2   The Statistical Tests Discussed in This Chapter

Test Name	Type	Can Be Used to Test
t test	Parametric	Differences in levels of two samples from a normal distribution with unknown variances and differences in regression coefficients
F test	Parametric	Dispersions of two samples from a normal population; or levels of several samples from normal populations with equal variances
Poisson parameter test	Parametric	Difference between Poisson parameter and a prescribed constant
Kolmogorov-Smirnov test	Nonparametric	Goodness of fit to any cumulative distribution
Mann-Whitney U test	Nonparametric	Differences in distributions of two samples from any populations (this test is particularly sensitive to differences in levels)
Runs test	Nonparametric	Patterns in a sequence of observations from any distribution
Chi square test	Nonparametric	Goodness of fit to any density function

so a compromise among the values of α, β, and n must be made. Some approaches to this compromise involve consideration of the cost consequences of the test, usually in terms of a loss function. The statistical test is viewed as a step in a decision process, and the parameters of the test are so chosen as to optimize the cost consequences of the decision. Ehrenfeld and Littauer (1964, Chapters 6 and 7) and Goode (1962) discuss this cost-consequences approach to the compromise, and Maisel (1966) gives an example of its use. However, this very sophisticated approach seldom is used in the statistical tests made during simulation development, because usually it is impossible to estimate the cost consequences of the choices of α and β.

The gathering and processing of observations require careful preparation, planning, and execution (see Sections 2.6 and 2.7). In addition to the considerations discussed in the earlier sections, there is one aspect of this activity that is particularly relevant to tests of hypotheses. In most cases, an hypothesis about a whole population is to be tested against data about a sample drawn from that population. Generic questions about district offices, ticket booths, or checkout stations are to be answered on the basis of observations of certain offices, booths, or stations made at certain times. The statistical framework permits precise statements to be made about errors, levels of significance, and the power of a test. However, an assumption about the sampling methods underlies the mathematical development that justifies these precise statements: it must be assumed that the observations are based on a *random sample* from the total population. In other words, the sampling procedure must guarantee that each element in the population has the same chance of being included in the sample. Often—particularly in field studies—true randomness must be compromised in order to accommodate the restrictions imposed on the data-gathering process. Special precautions (such as controls) are needed to ensure that these compromises do not invalidate the conclusions of the test. (In Section 2.6, we describe the kinds of restrictions that might be imposed on a field study and give an example of a set of controls used in the district office field study.)

If the earlier steps in the procedure are executed correctly, the actual statistical test is easy to carry out. The only serious difficulty encountered in most cases is the computational burden, which may be particularly heavy for complicated tests or for tests involving large numbers of observations. Access to a computer facility and to its library of statistical programs usually will eliminate this difficulty. A few special-purpose programs that may be missing from the typical facility library are described in Appendix B.

4.4 The t Test

The t test can be used in deciding whether to accept or to reject a frequently occurring type of hypothesis: that two normally distributed populations have equal means. Samples are drawn from each of the two populations, and a series of calculations are made to determine whether or not the hypothesis is tenable. Before describing the actual test procedure, some background concepts will be clarified and the test-designing procedure described.

Implied in the hypothesis (that the means of the two populations are equal) is a kind of symmetry in the treatment of the two populations. If either population has a larger mean than the other, the hypothesis will be rejected. If the means are equal, it will be accepted. Another form of hypothesis sometimes is encountered: for example, the hypothesis that the mean of population A is smaller than the mean of population B. In cases such as this one, the treatment of the two populations is not symmetrical. This hypothesis will be accepted if the mean of population A is smaller than that of population B, but it will be rejected *either* if the mean of population B is smaller than that of population A, *or* if the two means are equal. Tests of the symmetrical form of hypotheses are called *two-tailed tests,* whereas tests of the unsymmetrical form are called *one-tailed tests.* The hypothesis must be examined carefully to determine which kind of test is appropriate.

The design of a t test involves the choice of α, specification of a difference in means, and choice of β. Next, the sample sizes needed to assure these error levels are calculated and, if possible, samples of these sizes are collected. As an example, consider a problem that might arise during development of a simulation of activities at a busy oil port. (The conditions specified are realistic for a port such as Subic Bay in the Philippine Islands, but the specific data used are hypothetical.) Study of the system reveals that the length of time required to remove oil from a tanker is a function of several variables, one of which is the actual (as opposed to the nominal) load of oil in the tanker. In this particular port, nearly every tanker has a capacity of 12,000 tons of oil. There are two major kinds of tankers: those operated by oil firms, and those operated by the Navy under a special leasing arrangement. The data indicates that the difference between the nominal and the actual loads is normally distributed, for both kinds of tankers. Now the following hypothesis is to be tested: The average difference between the nominal and actual loads is the same for tankers operated by oil firms as for those leased by the Navy. First, a value of 0.10 is chosen for α (meaning that we are willing to accept a 10-percent chance that if the hypothesis is true we will reject it). The permissible difference in means associated with β is fixed at 400 tons and a value of 0.05 is set for β (meaning that we are willing to accept a 5-percent chance that if the hypothesis is false we will accept it).

The choices of these error levels were based on several considerations. As is often the case in simulation development, the purpose of this test is to decide whether or not to include a particular variable in the model. We want to know whether it is necessary to tag each tanker as either commercial or Navy-lease in order to estimate more precisely the time required to unload its oil cargo. If the hypothesis of equal means is accepted, the attribute variable of "commercial" or "Navy-lease" will be left out of the model. In this situation, it is reasonable to use larger values of α than usual and smaller values of β than usual, because a type I error would result only in keeping the extra variable even though it were not needed, whereas a type II error would seriously harm the validity of the simulation by leading us to drop an important variable. The value of 400 tons for the permissible difference in means associated with β was selected because smaller differences in load make very little difference in the length of time required to unload the oil. In other words, this is the level of difference at which the unloading-time consequences of the difference become appreciable.

The next step is determination of the sample size needed in order to be certain that the test will meet these specified error characteristics. An estimate of the standard deviation of the differences between nominal and actual loads is required in order to determine the sample size. (Because the t test is used when the real standard deviation is unknown, estimates of this standard deviation may not be readily available. However, a rough estimate usually is adequate for planning purposes. In any case, it always is possible to repeat the procedure using larger and smaller estimates of the standard deviation to see how much an error in this estimate will affect the sample size.) In this case, the standard deviation of the differences is estimated to be about 500 tons. The necessary sample size is a function of α, β, and D, where D is calculated by

$$D = \frac{\text{difference associated with } \beta}{\text{estimated standard deviation}} = \frac{400}{500} = 0.80. \qquad (4.1)$$

Tables showing the necessary sample size as a function of α, β, and D are given by Johnson and Leone (1964, Vol. 1, pp. 479–482). Without such tables, the sample size must be estimated from tables of the noncentral t distribution, using a procedure discussed in the same book (p. 203). The procedure is fairly complex, and use of the tables is strongly recommended.

The tables indicate that a sample size of 35 is needed to reach the test objectives (that is, 35 observations for each class of ship of the difference between actual and nominal loads). However, the port being simulated is not very busy, and it will take several months to collect data on 35 ships of each class being unloaded at the port. Because we do not want to spend this much time on data collection, some compromise is needed between the desired error levels and the practical limitations of the study. One possible approach involves a sequential test (see Wald 1947). Data are accumulated as they are collected, and a decision is made after each addition of data: whether to conclude that the means are equal, to conclude that they are unequal, or to wait for more data. Such a test may lead to a conclusion in a shorter time. Alternatively, we might decide to accept a value of $\beta = 0.10$, or to retain $\beta = 0.05$ but allow a difference of 600 tons between the means. These modifications would result in sample sizes of 28 and 16 observations, respectively, for each class of ship. In most cases, we would examine several such alternatives and arrive at a decision after some further analysis of the problem.

In this case, we decide to retain the values of $\alpha = 0.10$ and $\beta = 0.05$, but we conclude that detecting a difference of 600 tons between the means for the two populations will be adequate for our purposes. We are able to obtain the necessary 16 observations of difference between actual and nominal loads for each of the two classes of ships (Table 4.3).

Now we are ready to make the actual statistical calculations for the t test. The statistic used in the t test is the following ratio:

$$t = \frac{(\bar{x}_1 - \bar{x}_2)}{\sqrt{n_1\,s_1^2 + n_2\,s_2^2}} \sqrt{\frac{n_1\,n_2\,(n_1 + n_2 - 2)}{n_1 + n_2}}, \tag{4.2}$$

where n_1 and n_2 are the sample sizes, $\bar{x}_1$ and $\bar{x}_2$ are the sample means, and s_1^2 and s_2^2 are the unbiased estimates of the population variances obtained from the sample (see Problem 4.2 at the end of the chapter for a more precise definition of s^2). If the means of the two samples are exactly equal, the t statistic has the value of zero. Suppose that there are two populations whose true means are exactly equal. If random samples are drawn from each of these populations, the t statistic observed for the samples usually will not be exactly zero. However, suppose that we repeat the experiment many times, each time drawing new random samples and calculating t. In this way, we could establish a density function indicating the probability of obtaining any certain value of t if the true means of the populations are exactly equal. This density function has a t distribution with degrees of freedom given by $df = n_1 + n_2 - 2$. Table A.2 (Appendix A) summarizes the functions for various values of df. For example, with $df = 1$, we see that an area of 0.5 is included under the t density curve from values of $t = -1.000$ to $t = +1.000$. In other words, there is a probability of 0.50 that the observed value of t will lie within this range if the true population means are equal and

TABLE 4.3 Observed Differences Between Actual and Nominal Oil Loads*

Owner of Tanker	Actual Minus Nominal Oil Load
Oil corporation	340, −460, −535, −210, −410, −240, 50, −80, −720, 140, −200, −280, −910, 205, −645, −310
Company operating under Navy lease	−615, −420, −100, −440, 220, −820, −375, 105, −290, −675, −480, −370, −60, −770, 105, −255

*Values given in this table are observed values for each of 16 ships of each owner class unloading at the port being studied. The nominal load for each ship is 12,000 tons of oil.

$df = 1$ for the samples. In our problem about the ship loads, $df = 16 + 16 - 2$ $= 30$. From the appropriate row of the table, we find a probability of 0.50 that the observed value of t will fall in the range $-0.683 \leq t \leq +0.683$, a probability of 0.80 that the observed value will fall in the range $-1.310 \leq t \leq +1.310$, and so on. Because we chose a value of $\alpha = 0.10$, we agreed to accept the hypothesis if there is a probability of 0.90 that t could have the observed value. From the table, we see that there is a probability of 0.90 that the observed value will fall in the range $-1.697 \leq t \leq +1.697$. Therefore, the *critical value* of t for this test is 1.697; if the observed value is smaller than 1.697, we will accept the hypothesis that the true means are equal. Note that we are using a two-tailed test, because we wish to reject the hypothesis if either mean is significantly larger than the other.

In our sample data on tanker loads, $\bar{x}_1 = -266.56$, $\bar{x}_2 = -327.50$, $n_1 = n_2$ $= 16$, $s_1^2 = 112,117.87$, $s_2^2 = 93,384.375$, and the calculated value of $t = 0.52$. Because this is less than the critical value, we accept the hypothesis. Within the error levels we have agreed to permit, the means of the two populations may be regarded as equal, and therefore the attribute variable of ship-ownership class will not be included in the port simulation.

4.5 The *F* Test

The *F* test is used to test hypotheses about differences between the dispersions of two normally distributed populations. In most cases, it is used to test the hypothesis that the variances of the two populations are equal. The test statistic is the ratio of the larger sample variance to the smaller one. If the hypothesis is true, the true ratio of population variances must be one. The test will involve establishing a critical value for the *F* ratio of the sample data, based upon permissible error levels. Johnson and Leone (1964, Vol. 1, p. 484) give a table that is useful in choosing appropriate sample sizes for given values of α, β, and the difference in the variances that we wish to be able to detect (expressed, of course, as a ratio).

Suppose, for example, we wished to determine whether the observed values of s_1^2 and s_2^2 obtained in the study of actual and nominal oil loads indicate a significant difference in the variances of the true populations. The test statistic (*F* ratio) is given by

$$F = \frac{larger\ variance}{smaller\ variance} \tag{4.3}$$

In this case, $F = 112,117.87/93,384.375 = 1.20$. Table A.4 (Appendix A) summarizes the distribution functions for the *F* ratio. From this table (using 15 degrees of freedom for the numerator and 15 for the denominator, and $\alpha = 0.10$), we find a critical value for *F* of 1.97. Because the observed value (1.20) is smaller than the critical value (1.97), we conclude that there is no significant difference between the true variances.

An *F* test frequently is used as a preliminary to tests on levels, because many parametric tests for differences in levels assume that there is no difference between the population variances. In our example, it would have been appropriate to make this *F* test first, to be sure that the *t* test (Section 4.4) can be applied with confidence in its validity.

4.6 Testing the Poisson Parameter

In simulating discrete stochastic systems, the Poisson distribution frequently is encountered. In the simulation models, a value for the Poisson parameter must be chosen to characterize this distribution. In this section we discuss the test of the hypothesis that the Poisson parameter is equal to a prescribed constant. This discussion serves both to present a useful test for this parameter and to illustrate the concept of a confidence interval.

In Section 3.6, the Poisson parameter was denoted by λt; here it will be more convenient to use the single Greek letter σ (sigma) to designate the parameter. Suppose that we wish to test the hypothesis that σ is equal to a prescribed constant *T*. An estimated value of σ can be calculated from a set of observations (sample); we will call this estimate $\hat{\sigma}$. (In the statistical literature, the symbol $\hat{x}$, read as "x cap," commonly is used to denote a sample estimate of x.) Denoting the permissible type I error again by α, we can determine two values σ_1 and σ_2 such that (given $\hat{\sigma}$) there is a probability of $\alpha/2$ that $\sigma < \sigma_1$ and a probability of $\alpha/2$ that $\sigma > \sigma_2$. Then, if the hypothesis is true, the probability that *T* falls within the range $\sigma_1 \leq T \leq \sigma_2$ is $(1 - \alpha)$. We would reject the hypothesis (that $\sigma = T$) if and only if *T* falls outside this range. This range is called the $100(1 - \alpha)$-percent *confidence interval*. For example, if $\alpha = 0.10$, this range is the 90-percent confidence interval.

The confidence interval can be used to indicate how well the sample serves to estimate the parameter. It is widely used where the objective of the statistical analysis is to estimate a parameter rather than to test an hypothesis. The confidence interval is stated along with the estimated value of the parameter. A confidence interval can be determined for any parameter estimated from any distribution.

Johnson and Leone (1964, Vol. 1, p. 478) give a table of values for σ_1 and σ_2 for $\alpha = 0.01$ and 0.05. We will use this table in an example drawn from the social security district office study, involving the occurrence of visitor reneges in the office operations. A renege occurs when a visitor to the office, who presumably wished to use the office facilities, leaves the office without making use of any facilities (for example, because he became tired of waiting for service). Earlier studies suggest that the occurrence of reneges follows a Poisson distribution. A field study of a particular district office yielded the following number of reneges for each day in a two-week period: 4, 5, 1, 5, 4, 2, 6, 7, 5, 3. Suppose we wish to test the hypothesis that $\sigma = 3.0$. In this case we choose $\alpha = 0.01$, because we expect to make several tests of this kind and do not wish to single out too many offices for having an unusual incidence of reneges. From the sample data, we find $\hat{\sigma} = 4.2$. From the table in Johnson and Leone's book, we find $\sigma_1 = 2.72$ and $\sigma_2 = 6.17$. Because our chosen value of $T = 3.0$ is inside this interval, we accept the hypothesis. We also can say that the 99-percent confidence level for the Poisson parameter of the renege distribution for this district office is given by $2.72 \leq \sigma \leq 6.17$.

4.7 The Kolmogorov-Smirnov Test

The Kolmogorov-Smirnov test is the first of the nonparametric techniques that we will discuss in this chapter. This test can be used to test the hypothesis that two populations have identical distributions, on the basis of samples drawn from each of the populations. The test is based on the difference between the two cumulative sample distributions. The difference between the cumulative sample distributions is computed for each interval for which the data are tabulated. The difference D with the greatest absolute value is used to carry out the test, according to the critical values given in Table A.5 (Appendix A).

Table 4.4 summarizes data obtained in a field study of class-A and class-D district offices, concerning the time required to interview claimants submitting a claim for old-age benefits. The table shows the cumulative distributions of interview times for each class of offices; the last column shows the differences between the cumulative distributions for each interval. Suppose we wish to test the hypothesis that the distributions of interview times are identical for the two classes of offices. From the table, we see that D (the largest difference between the cumulative distributions) is 0.0429 (for the fifth interval in the table). The sample sizes are $n_1 = 747$ and $n_2 = 140$. In Table A.5, we find that use of such large samples requires the calculation of the quantity $\sqrt{(n_1 + n_2)/n_1 n_2} = 0.0921$. As in the port study, we choose $\alpha = 0.10$ because we do not wish to rule out prematurely the possibility that class of office is a significant variable involved in the distribution of interview lengths. From Table A.5, we find that the critical value of D is given by $1.22 \times 0.0921 = 0.1124$. Because the observed value (0.0429) is smaller than the critical value (0.1124), we accept the hypothesis and do not include the class of the district office as a factor in determining the distribution of interview times for old-age benefit claimants.

For large sample sizes, the calculations involved in the Kolmogorov-Smirnov test may be excessive. Most computer program libraries include a program for this purpose. For example, the FORTRAN scientific subroutine package available with IBM System/360 and 370 computers includes a program (labeled KOLM2)

TABLE 4.4 Distributions of Interview Times for Old-Age
Benefit Claimants

Time Interval (*minutes*)	Class-A Offices		Class-D Offices		Difference Between Distributions
	Cumulative Frequency	Cumulative Distribution	Cumulative Frequency	Cumulative Distribution	
6 or less	9	0.0080	1	0.0071	0.0009
7–8	11	0.0147	3	0.0214	−0.0067
9–10	28	0.0375	8	0.0571	−0.0196
11–12	57	0.0763	15	0.1071	−0.0308
13–14	96	0.1285	24	0.1714	−0.0429
15–16	137	0.1834	26	0.1857	−0.0023
17–18	197	0.2637	36	0.2571	0.0066
19–20	247	0.3307	47	0.3357	−0.0050
21–22	303	0.4056	56	0.4000	0.0056
23–24	359	0.4806	62	0.4429	0.0377
25–26	393	0.5261	71	0.5071	0.0190
27–28	431	0.5770	78	0.5571	0.0199
29–30	466	0.6238	87	0.6214	0.0024
31–32	505	0.6760	91	0.6500	0.0260
33–34	534	0.7149	100	0.7143	0.0006
35–36	568	0.7604	103	0.7357	0.0247
37–38	586	0.7845	111	0.7929	−0.0084
39–40	606	0.8112	113	0.8071	0.0041
41–42	620	0.8300	117	0.8357	−0.0057
43–44	639	0.8554	118	0.8429	0.0125
45–46	651	0.8715	122	0.8714	0.0001
47–48	661	0.8849	126	0.9000	−0.0151
49–50	674	0.9023	127	0.9071	−0.0048
51–52	682	0.9130	127	0.9071	0.0059
53–54	688	0.9210	130	0.9286	−0.0076
55–56	693	0.9277	132	0.9429	−0.0152
57–58	704	0.9424	132	0.9429	−0.0005
59–60	712	0.9532	136	0.9714	−0.0182
61–62	719	0.9625	137	0.9786	−0.0161
63–64	721	0.9652	137	0.9786	−0.0134
65–66	723	0.9679	137	0.9786	−0.0107
67–68	726	0.9719	137	0.9786	−0.0067
69–70	731	0.9786	138	0.9857	−0.0071
71–72	732	0.9799	138	0.9857	−0.0058
73–74	735	0.9839	138	0.9857	−0.0018
75–76	737	0.9866	139	0.9929	−0.0063
77 or more	747	1.0000	140	1.0000	0.0000

for a Kolmogorov-Smirnov test. (The IBM manual on the FORTRAN scientific subroutine package is No. GH20–0205. A similar scientific subroutine package is available with PL/I; this manual is No. GH20–0586.)

The Kolmogorov-Smirnov test also can be used to test the hypothesis that a sample distribution is identical to a prescribed theoretical distribution. In this case, D is the maximal difference between the sample cumulative distribution and the theoretical cumulative distribution among the intervals for which the sample distribution is tabulated. Siegel (1956, pp. 47–52) discusses this test and gives (on p. 251) critical values for the test. The applicable program in the FORTRAN scientific subroutine package is labeled KOLM1.

4.8 The Runs Test

Data obtained from field studies or records usually are sequenced according to time of occurrence. For example, the record of interarrival times at a district office is sequenced according to time of day of the arrival, the times required to unload an oil cargo are sequenced by the day of the unloading operation, and the times required to check out a customer at a supermarket are sequenced according to the time of day of the checkout. In developing simulations of these activities, several important questions may arise about these sequences: (1) Are there busy periods and slow periods for the arrivals? (2) Is there a seasonal variation in the time required to unload an oil tanker? or (3) Do checkout times vary with the time of day?

The runs test provides one way to answer such questions on the basis of the sample data. A *run* is a sequence of identical results, preceded and followed by nonidentical results. For example, suppose that ten tosses of a coin produce the following results: HTHHH TTHHT. These results can be described as consisting of six runs: a run of one head, a run of one tail, a run of three heads, a run of two tails, a run of two heads, and a run of one tail. It is possible to calculate the probability of getting six or more runs in a series of ten throws that produces six heads and four tails. If this probability were very small, we could say that we observe an unusually large number of runs — in other words, the heads and tails are alternating more than would be expected with a typical unbiased coin. It is possible also to calculate the probability of getting six or fewer runs. If this probability were very small, we could say that we observe an unusual bunching of results — heads and tails are not alternating as often as would be expected.

The runs test and tables of significance are designed to deal with binomial data — that is, with a variable that has only two possible values (such as "head" or "tail") and that is binomially distributed. Results that have other discrete or continuous distributions must be reformulated before the runs test can be applied to them. In simulation applications, the data for a runs test usually is reformulated to reduce it to a sequence of pluses and minuses, with plus indicating values greater than the median and minus indicating values smaller than the median. (The *median* is that value of the random variable that is exceeded by 50 percent of the results. More precisely, if *m* denotes the median, then $F(m) = 0.50$.)

For example, Table 3.2 lists a sequence of interarrival times at a district office during a single day. The runs test can be used to find out whether there are busy and slow periods at the office during the day — in other words, whether there tend to be long runs of large interarrival times at some parts of the day and long runs of small interarrival times at other parts of the day. The median interarrival time can be computed. Each interarrival time greater than the median is replaced by a plus, and each interarrival time smaller than the median is replaced by a minus. If the number of runs is significantly smaller than expected, we will conclude that there are busy and slow periods during the day at this office.

Of the 122 interarrival-time observations, 60 are less than three minutes, 15 are three minutes, and 47 are greater than three minutes. Therefore, the median is the interval labeled "three minutes." In order to use Table A.6 (Appendix A), we must have equal numbers of pluses and minuses; therefore, we must assign pluses to 14 of the three-minute interarrival times and a minus to 1 of them. In order to avoid biasing the data, we will resort to a special randomization mechanism to assign the pluses and minus for the three-minute values. For example, we can use a table of random digits such as that in Table A.7. We might scan the table two digits at a time until we come to the first two-digit number less than or equal to 15 (call it *n*); we then could assign the minus sign to the *n*th three-minute interarrival time. Using this method with Table A.7, we proceed down the first column of two-digit numbers and encounter 07 in the seventh row as the first number within the required range. Therefore we convert the 7th value of 3 minutes to a minus, and we convert all other values of 3 to pluses. The sequence of interarrival times from Table 3.2 now can be reformulated as −−−++ ++++− +−+−− −−−+− −−−−− ++−−− −+−+− −+−+− +++−+ +−++− −−−−+ +−−++ +++−− +−++− +++−− +−−++ ++−++ ++++− +++−+ +−−+− −+−−+ −−−+− −−−+− −−+++ ++.

There are 56 runs in these data. Table A.6 indicates that we may expect a mean of 62 runs for many repetitions of such an experiment with random sequences. Is the observed value of 56 significantly smaller than this value? In the columns of critical values for too few runs, we see that we must have 52 runs or fewer to make this result statistically significant with $\alpha = 0.05$ (the largest value of α tabulated here). Therefore, we conclude that there are no significant busy and slow periods at this office during the day. (However, we shall return to this problem in Part Five.)

Although Table A.6 can be used only with sequences that include equal numbers of each alternative value for the variable, tables are available for use with small samples having unequal numbers of the two values. For example, such tables are given by Siegel (1956, pp. 252–253).

4.9 The Mann-Whitney U Test

The Mann-Whitney U Test is a relatively powerful nonparametric test that provides a useful alternative to the t test for testing differences in levels. Although the hypothesis tested is that the two *distributions* are identical, the Mann-Whitney U test is particularly sensitive to differences in levels. The test involves rank-ordering all the observations from the two samples. Suppose, for example, we apply this test to the data on tanker loads in Table 4.3. First we must order all 32 observations and assign ranks to them (Table 4.5). The test statistic U can be computed from the rank orders using the following formulae:

$$U_1 = n_1 \, n_2 + \frac{n_1 \, (n_1 + 1)}{2} - R_1 \quad \text{and} \quad U_2 = n_1 \, n_2 - U_1, \qquad (4.4)$$

where $n_1 \le n_2$ are the two sample sizes, and R_1 is the sum of the ranks associated with the smaller sample. The smaller of the two values U_1 or U_2 is used as the test statistic.

For the data in Table 4.5, $n_1 = n_2 = 16$, so U_1 may be computed from either sample. We arbitrarily choose to compute the sum of ranks for the observations

TABLE 4.5   Rank Ordering of Data on Oil Cargoes from Table 4.3

Rank	Observation	Owner	Rank	Observation	Owner
1	−910	Corp.	17	−290	Navy
2	−820	Navy	18	−280	Corp.
3	−770	Navy	19	−255	Navy
4	−720	Corp.	20	−240	Corp.
5	−675	Navy	21	−210	Corp.
6	−645	Corp.	22	−200	Corp.
7	−615	Navy	23	−100	Navy
8	−535	Corp.	24	−80	Corp.
9	−480	Navy	25	−60	Navy
10	−460	Corp.	26	50	Corp.
11	−440	Navy	27	105	Navy
12	−420	Navy	28	105	Navy
13	−410	Corp.	29	140	Corp.
14	−375	Navy	30	205	Corp.
15	−370	Navy	31	220	Navy
16	−310	Corp.	32	340	Corp.

associated with Navy ownership. We get $R_1 = 248$, $U_1 = 144$, $U_2 = 112$, and therefore the test statistic $U = 112$.

Tables of critical values for U (with n_1 and n_2 in the range from 3 to 20) are given by Siegel (1956, pp. 271–275). From these tables, we find a critical value of $U = 83$ for $\alpha = 0.10$. Because a value smaller than the critical value is needed for significance, we confirm our earlier decision to accept the hypothesis that there is no significant difference between the means of the two ownership classes.

If either n_1 or n_2 is greater than 20, the critical value of U can be approximated using the normal distribution. The test statistic $U = $ smaller (U_1, U_2) is computed as before. Another statistic Z, which approximates $N(Z;0,1)$ then is computed by

$$Z = \frac{U - (n_1\, n_2)/2}{\sqrt{n_1\, n_2\, (n_1 + n_2 + 1)/12}} \tag{4.5}$$

The value of this statistic Z then is tested as a normal distribution. Because of the way that Z is obtained, a one-tailed test is appropriate.

Tables of critical values for small values of n are not given in Appendix A because in most simulation applications of this test one of the samples will be larger than 20 and the normal approximation will be applicable.

If the samples are large, a computer program may be needed for the extensive calculations involved in this test. The appropriate program is labeled UTEST in the scientific subroutine package available with the IBM System/360 and 370 computers.

4.10 The *Chi* Square Test

The *chi* square (χ^2) test is used widely for testing the goodness of fit between observed data and a theoretical pattern. In this section we discuss the use of this test to check the goodness of fit between an empirical density function and a theoretical one. [The test also is used for other purposes, particularly for testing contingency tables (see Siegel 1956, pp. 104–111, 175–179). Here we note only that *contingency tables* result when data are classified into several mutually exclusive, exhaustive categories according to values of several (usually two) variables of classification. The result is a contingency table such as that in Table 4.6. In simulation development, tests of contingency tables do not arise very often because usually there are many variables that affect a result (requiring multi-dimensional contingency tables), and because the result itself usually can be measured on some scale rather than merely being counted as alternative outcomes. Consequently, regression techniques (Chapter 5) and the analysis of variance (Chapter 6) are much more commonly used in simulation development than is the testing of contingency tables.]

Using the hypothesis that a given theoretical density is the correct underlying probability density, a statistic can be computed that has the *chi* square distribution. More specifically, suppose the sample data are expressed as a frequency table with n intervals, and the observed frequencies are denoted by A_i for $i = 1, 2, \ldots, n$. Using the information in the hypothesis, we then calculate the expected, or theoretical, frequencies, denoted by T_i for $i = 1, 2, \ldots, n$. If necessary, intervals should be combined in order to make $T_i \geq 5$ for every i. (If it should become necessary to use the *chi* square test with small frequencies in some intervals, complex corrections should be applied. Program B.1 in Appendix B can be used to make the calculations with these corrections.) The test statistic is given by

$$\chi^2 = \sum_{i=1}^{n} \frac{(A_i - T_i)^2}{T_i}. \tag{4.6}$$

Table 4.7 summarizes data on the length of time required to complete an interview of claimants submitting a disability claim at a social security district office. In Section 4.7 we discussed similar data for claimants submitting old-age benefit claims. In that case we used the Kolmogorov-Smirnov test to find out whether interview times were the same for class-A and class-D offices. In this case, we will use the *chi* square test to find out whether interview times for disability claims can be assumed to be normally distributed. The calculation of the test statistic χ^2 is shown in Table 4.7.

Because of the large sample size (a total of 495 observations), a computer program (Program B.2 in Appendix B) was used in making the test calculations. Among other things, this program calculates the mean, standard deviation, skewness, and kurtosis of the sample data. These statistics are useful in gaining further insight into the empirical distribution.

The theoretical frequencies are calculated by using tables of the appropriate distribution to determine the proportion of observations that could be expected in each interval. Each proportion then is multiplied by the total number of observations to get the theoretical frequency for the interval.

For example, the first interval in Table 4.7 is for interview times of 13.5 minutes or less. Assuming that interview times were rounded to the nearest minute, we may consider this equivalent to a recorded interview time of 13

TABLE 4.6 An Example of a Contingency Table

Length of Job (*minutes*)	Number of Jobs in One Day That Were Programmed in		
	FORTRAN	PL/I	Other Languages
Less than 1	44	30	0
1–5	16	6	12
5–30	9	2	0
30–60	4	16	1
More than 60	2	1	1

minutes or less. (The interview times actually were calculated from punch-clock records of the beginning and end of each interview, in the same fashion as inter-arrival times were calculated—see Section 3.10. However, because the inter-view times are much longer than the interarrival times, and because there was some manual adjustment of these data, it is considered appropriate to treat these times as being rounded to the nearest minute.) According to the table, there were 19 interview times in the first interval. In order to determine the theoretical frequency for this interval, we must use the moments of the em-pirical distribution to calculate a theoretical normal distribution. The mean of the interview-times data is 45.5919 minutes, with a standard deviation of 20.1981 minutes. Using these values, the endpoint of the interval can be re-duced to standardized units (see Section 3.8): $z = (x - \mu)/\sigma = (13.5 - 45.5919)/20.1981 = -1.589$. From tables of the standardized normal distribution, we find that: $\int_{-\infty}^{-1.589} N(z;0,1)dz = 0.0562$. This is the proportion of observations ex-pected in this interval according to the normal distribution. Multiplying this by the total number of observations, we obtain $T_1 = 495 \times 0.0562 = 27.819$. From

TABLE 4.7 *Chi* Square Test of Hypothesis That Empirical Density of Interview Times Is Normally Distributed

Interview Time Interval (*minutes*)	Empirical Frequency (A)	Theoretical Frequency		$\frac{(A - T)^2}{T}$
		Relative Frequency	Absolute Frequency (T)	
13.5 or less	19	0.0562	27.819	2.796
13.5 to 17.5	19	0.0261	12.920	2.861
17.5 to 21.5	25	0.0343	16.978	3.790
21.5 to 25.5	20	0.0434	21.483	0.102
25.5 to 29.5	32	0.0530	26.235	1.267
29.5 to 33.5	39	0.0620	30.690	2.250
33.5 to 37.5	35	0.0696	34.452	0.009
37.5 to 41.5	26	0.0753	37.274	3.410
41.5 to 45.5	40	0.0785	38.858	0.034
45.5 to 49.5	38	0.0785	38.858	0.019
49.5 to 53.5	35	0.0756	37.422	0.157
53.5 to 57.5	36	0.0699	34.600	0.057
57.5 to 61.5	25	0.0623	30.838	1.105
61.5 to 65.5	20	0.0532	26.334	1.523
65.5 to 69.5	23	0.0439	21.730	0.074
69.5 to 73.5	20	0.0347	17.176	0.464
73.5 to 77.5	12	0.0264	13.068	0.087
77.5 to 81.5	10	0.0195	9.652	0.013
81.5 or more	21	0.0376	18.613	0.360
Totals	495	1.0000	495.000	$\chi^2 = 20.378$

the values $A_1 = 19$ and $T_1 = 27.819$, we can then calculate the contribution of this interval to the *chi* square statistic: $(A_1 - T_1)^2/T_1 = 2.796$.

Similarly, the endpoint of the second interval in standardized units is $(17.5 - 45.5919)/20.1981 = -1.390$. Because $\int_{-\infty}^{-1.390} N(z;0,1)dz = 0.0823$, then $\int_{-1.589}^{-1.390} N(z;0,1)dz = 0.0823 - 0.0562 = 0.0261$. Thus, $T_2 = 495 \times 0.0261 = 12.920$. We continue in this fashion, converting each of the interval endpoints to standardized units, determining areas under the standardized normal density function corresponding to each interval (using tables of this density function), and multiplying each area by the total number of observations to get the theoretical frequency for the interval. Finally, the contribution to the *chi* square statistic is calculated for each interval.

The value of χ^2 for all the intervals is 20.378. In general, the degrees of freedom in the *chi* square distribution is the number of intervals minus the number of parameters used in fitting the theoretical distribution. In this case, the mean and standard deviation were used to fit the theoretical curve to the empirical data, and there are twenty intervals, so $df = 20 - 2 = 18$. Again setting $\alpha = 0.10$, we obtain from Table A.3 (Appendix A) the critical value of 25.9894. Because the observed value of χ^2 is less than the critical value, the hypothesis that the underlying distribution is a normal one is accepted, and the normal distribution will be used to generate interview times for the simulation.

Problem 4.4 involves a *chi* square test on another empirical distribution of interview times. The distribution of interview times is discussed extensively in Part Five.

4.11 Supplementary Reading

The most comprehensive reference works on statistical tests are those by Johnson and Leone (1964) for parametric tests and by Siegel (1956) for nonparametric tests. An excellent, less mathematical discussion of parametric tests is given by Dixon and Massey (1969); their book may be a useful reference for those who have difficulty mastering Johnson and Leone's book. Massey also discusses the up-and-down, sequential procedure for estimating the central tendency of a distribution—a procedure that is ignored in many references. Walsh (1962, 1965, 1968) gives a monumental summary of virtually every nonparametric technique that is available; the usefulness of this reference work fully justifies the difficulty of mastering the succinct notation used in it.

Sarhan and Greenberg (1962) summarize that part of statistical methodology related to the use of order statistics. They summarize the more elementary statistical tests based on order statistics (Chapter 7), multiple tests and comparisons using order statistics (Chapter 9), and some techniques useful in dealing with censored samples—those drawn from a truncated distribution (Chapter 11).

Cohen (1969) provides probably the most comprehensive and readable reference on determination of the power of a parametric test, although some of the material is awkwardly organized and some of the notation is poor.

PROBLEMS

4.1   The t distribution can be applied to tests of the differences in levels between two samples that are paired. The test statistic used is $t = $ (*average paired difference*)/(*standard deviation of the paired differences*). This statistic has the t distribution with $n - 1$ degrees of freedom, where n is the paired number of samples. Table 4.8 summarizes the data obtained in making a series of runs of certain programs with standard data on each of two digital computers. Calculate the paired differences in running times and the average and standard deviation of these differences. Use the t test to test the hypothesis that the average paired difference is zero.

4.2   The *chi* square test can be applied to a test of the hypothesis that a sample variance differs from a prescribed constant, C. This test is applicable only if the sample is drawn randomly from a normally distributed population, so in this context the *chi* square test is a parametric test. The test statistic is $\chi^2 = (k - 1)s^2/C$, where k is the sample size and s^2 is the unbiased estimate of the population variance, given by

$$s^2 = \frac{k \sum_{i=1}^{k} x_i^2 - \left(\sum_{i=1}^{k} x_i \right)^2}{k(k - 1)}.$$

Test the hypothesis that the variance of the differences in running times summarized in Table 4.8 is equal to 6. Use $\alpha = 0.05$. Note that this is a two-tailed *chi* square test; therefore, Table A.3 is not complete enough for

TABLE 4.8   Running Times of Programs Using Standard Data on Two Computers

Program	Running Time of Program (*seconds*)	
	On Computer A	On Computer B
Sort	39	31
Matrix inversion	47	63
File merge	32	27
Test for normality	54	52
Correlation coefficient	29	34
Nonlinear least squares	31	37
KWIC index	51	40
File restructuring	24	19
Random number generation	12	19
Payroll processing	57	43

this test. The following additional critical values may be needed to complete the test:

df	P		
	0.01	0.025	0.05
9	2.0879	2.7004	3.3251
10	2.5582	3.2470	3.9403

4.3   Use the Kolmogorov-Smirnov test to test the hypothesis that the distribution of arrivals at one social security district office in all days of one week combined (see Problem 3.4 and Table 3.6) is identical to the distribution of arrivals at all class-B offices combined during this same weekly period (see Problem 3.5 and Table 3.7).

4.4   Use the *chi* square test to test the hypothesis that interview times for preparing old-age benefits claims are normally distributed. Use the data given in Table 4.9 (interview times for all offices combined) rather than the data in Table 4.4 (interview times for class-A and class-D offices only). The data in Table 4.9 include 1,490 observations, with a mean interview time of 28.5174 minutes and a standard deviation of 14.7900.

4.5   Use the Mann-Whitney U test to test the hypothesis that the running times for computer A and those for computer B (Table 4.8) are identically distributed.

TABLE 4.9   Empirical Distribution of Times Required to Conduct Interviews of Claimants for Old-Age Benefits

Time Interval (*minutes*)	Absolute Frequency	Time Interval (*minutes*)	Absolute Frequency
8.5 or less	27	36.5 to 38.5	39
8.5 to 10.5	41	38.5 to 40.5	40
10.5 to 12.5	62	40.5 to 42.5	31
12.5 to 14.5	79	42.5 to 44.5	32
14.5 to 16.5	78	44.5 to 46.5	26
16.5 to 18.5	107	46.5 to 48.5	22
18.5 to 20.5	100	48.5 to 50.5	23
20.5 to 22.5	109	50.5 to 52.5	18
22.5 to 24.5	108	52.5 to 54.5	12
24.5 to 26.5	86	54.5 to 56.5	12
26.5 to 28.5	76	56.5 to 58.5	15
28.5 to 30.5	82	58.5 to 60.5	13
30.5 to 32.5	68	60.5 to 62.5	11
32.5 to 34.5	65	62.5 to 64.5	5
34.5 to 36.5	65	64.5 or more	38

5

Regression

5.1 BACKGROUND   From one point of view, a model of a stochastic system is merely a mechanism for relating output variables to input variables. Among the inputs may be such things as arrival patterns, numbers and capabilities of system components, and exogenous factors such as the general economic level or the weather. Outputs include a wide variety of data on system performance. In some cases, it may be possible to state the relationship between outputs and inputs on the basis of a theoretical understanding of the system. At other times, it may be necessary to determine the relationship empirically. Data are obtained from observation of system outputs and the corresponding inputs. Functions are fitted to these data in order to obtain the required relationship. When this function-fitting process is placed in a statistical framework, it is called *regression*.

There are three major steps in the process of fitting a relationship between a dependent variable and a set of independent variables: (1) choosing the appropriate set of independent variables; (2) selecting an appropriate functional form; and (3) fitting the function. The first step is discussed both in Section 5.5 and in Chapter 6, and a very brief discussion of the second step is included in Section 5.6. The third step is the subject of most of this chapter.

The use of regression techniques in model building seldom is as straightforward as we have implied thus far. In many cases, the outputs cannot be related directly to inputs, and intermediate variables must be introduced to model these more complex relationships. For example, in a model of a social security district office, the output variables may include such measures of performance as the cost of operating the office, the rate at which work is done, and the number of errors made in getting the work done. In order to estimate the cost of operating the office, it is necessary to introduce intermediate variables associated with the numbers of various types of employees and the number of hours worked by each employee. In order to obtain data on errors, intermediate variables related to the reprocessing of claims must be introduced.

In the use of regression techniques in simulation, it almost always is necessary to combine the direct modeling approach with the function-fitting approach. A function that is first fitted empirically then is adjusted according to direct considerations of the nature of the system. Examples of this approach are given in this chapter and in Part Five.

5.2 The Framework

Scientists and other research investigators face the problem of how best to describe or summarize data that seem to follow a smooth pattern when plotted; the same problem is of importance in model building during simulation development. In many applications, it is enough merely to draw a smooth curve through the data points on a graph and to use the resulting graph to represent the function. However, computer simulation development often requires that the data be represented by an explicit mathematical function. *Least-squares techniques* can be used to determine which function of a prescribed form best fits a set of data; the least-squares criterion results in the choice of that function that minimizes the sums of the squares of the differences between the observed values and the fitted function (see Chapter 9 of the book by Cramer 1955 for a discussion of least squares). At times some other criterion for fitting a function may be more appropriate. For example, *Chebyshev's* criterion (also called the *minimax* criterion) has been applied to the problem of tabulating a relation that is known quite precisely; this criterion results in the choice of a function that minimizes the maximal difference between the fitted function and the observed values. A technique for fitting functions using Chebyshev's criterion is given by Ralston and Wilf (1968, Chapter 13). However, because there is a body of statistical methodology associated with the least-squares approach, this criterion is the most appropriate one for use in simulation development. In the remainder of this chapter, it is assumed that the least-squares criterion is to be used.

The general *model for a regression* is

$$y = f(x_1, x_2, \ldots, x_j; a_1, a_2, \ldots, a_k) + \epsilon. \tag{5.1}$$

The dependent variable y is assumed to be related to j independent variables $(x_1, x_2, \ldots, x_j)$ by means of the function f. This function has k parameters $(a_1, a_2, \ldots, a_k)$. Finally—because of the stochastic behavior of the system— the result is assumed to contain a certain amount of fluctuation or error, which is represented by the variable ϵ.

In later sections of this chapter, several specific examples of such models are given. However, in this section we discuss in more general terms the way that this model is used in fitting functions.

In using this approach, it generally is assumed that f is known and that $a_1, a_2, \ldots, a_k$ are to be estimated. Observations are made; that is, values of y and corresponding values of $x_1, x_2, \ldots, x_j$ are obtained. From these observations, the parameters must be estimated. In most regression models, the error ϵ is assumed to be normally distributed with a mean of zero and some fixed but unknown variance σ^2. In other words, $N(\epsilon; 0, \sigma^2)$. With these assumptions, it can be shown for a certain class of functions that the least-squares estimate is the best estimate of the parameters $a_1, a_2, \ldots, a_k$. According to the Gauss-Markov theorem, the least-squares estimate is best in the sense that it is unbiased and that it has minimal variance among all possible linear estimates (that is, among all estimates of the parameters that can be written as a linear combination of the observations). A proof of this theorem is given by Scheffe (1959, pp. 13–19).

The assumption that $N(\epsilon; 0, \sigma^2)$ makes it possible to do such things as to construct confidence intervals for values of y that are estimated from the regression and to test hypotheses about the parameters.

Note that the values of x are assumed to be known without error, and that the corresponding values of y are assumed to be subject to chance fluctuation. Although at first this may seem a dubious assumption, it does prove valid in simulation applications. For example, the presence of statistical fluctuation introduces an error into the prediction of the time of the next arrival at a district office. However, in a simulation of the office activities on a computer, the exact time of the next arrival must be specified without error. The pattern of arrival times is fixed so that the set of arrivals, taken as a whole, has the desired statistical distribution.

5.3 Fitting a Straight Line

Consider a regression model with just one independent variable x and with f assumed to be a straight line. The model becomes $y = a_1 x + a_2 + \epsilon$. Values of a_1 and a_2 are estimated by least-squares techniques from a series of n observations of y and the corresponding values of x. These pairs of observations may be denoted by (x_1, y_1) (x_2, y_2), . . . , (x_n, y_n), and the estimates of a_1 and a_2 may be denoted by $\hat{a}_1$ and $\hat{a}_2$. The least-squares estimates are calculated by

$$\hat{a}_1 = \frac{n \Sigma x_i y_i - \Sigma x_i \Sigma y_i}{n \Sigma x_i^2 - (\Sigma x_i)^2}, \tag{5.2}$$

and

$$\hat{a}_2 = \frac{\Sigma y_i - \hat{a}_1 \Sigma x_i}{n}, \tag{5.3}$$

where all sums Σ are from $i = 1$ to n. For each x_i, the estimate of y is given by $\hat{y}_i = \hat{a}_1 x_i + \hat{a}_2$. Because $\hat{a}_1$ and $\hat{a}_2$ are least-squares estimates, the quantity $\Sigma (y_i - \hat{y}_i)^2$ is a minimum. The differences $(y_i - \hat{y}_i)$ are called *residuals*.

Although linear regression is used widely in many areas of statistical application, this technique is not so widely used in simulation development. Most systems worth simulating are complex enough that several—not just one— independent variables are required to predict the behavior of a dependent variable. The multiple linear regression, discussed in the next section, is the natural extension of the linear approach to the situation with several independent variables. However, the straight line model is used occasionally, and a computer program useful in fitting straight lines to observed data is given in Appendix B (Program B.3). This program has several options that permit some analyses of the residuals to be made.

Before discussing multiple linear regression, we illustrate the basic concept of correlation and define several important terms. We also give a specific example to illustrate the concepts and formulae presented in this section.

From a given set of observations (x_i, y_i) for $i = 1$ to n, the fitted function, $\hat{y} = \hat{a}_1 x + \hat{a}_2$, is obtained by least-squares technique, resulting in a minimization of the *sum of the squares of the residuals*, $SSR = \Sigma (y_i - \hat{y}_i)^2$. If y were estimated without using the detailed knowledge of x, this estimate $\hat{y}$ could be based on its mean. That is (for all x) $\hat{y} = \bar{y} = (\Sigma y_i)/n$. The mean of the squared differences between the estimate and the observations is given by the variance of y; that is, by $\sigma_y^2 = [\Sigma (y_i - \bar{y})^2]/n$. Using the *total sum of squares*, $TSS = \Sigma (y_i - \bar{y})^2$, it is possible to calculate the sum of squares due to regression, or the *explained sum of squares*, $SSE = TSS - SSR$. Clearly, $TSS > SSR$ and $SSE > 0$. The *mean square about the regression* (that is, the *residual variance*) is given by $SSR/(n - 2)$. This residual variance also serves as an estimate of the variance of ϵ—in other words, as an estimate of σ^2 in $N(\epsilon; 0, \sigma^2)$. The square root of the residual variance is called the *standard error of the estimate*.

If the model is inappropriate—that is, if the relation between y and x is not a straight line—then the residual variance contains a component other than σ^2. In their very useful book, Draper and Smith (1966, Section 1.5) discuss this component, how it might be estimated, and how it might be used to determine a more appropriate model.

The *correlation coefficient* may be regarded as a measure of the degree of association of y and x. It is related to the amount of variation in y that is explained by the linear relation. Its sign is the same as the sign of $\hat{a}_1$. The sample correlation coefficient r is given by

$$r = \frac{n \sum x_i y_i - \sum x_i \sum y_i}{\sqrt{[n \sum x_i^2 - (\sum x_i)^2][n \sum y_i^2 - (\sum y_i)^2]}}, \tag{5.4}$$

where all sums are from $i = 1$ to n. If all observed data were colinear, r would have the value $+1$ or -1. If $\hat{a}_1 = 0$, so that $\bar{y}$ is the best estimate of y and $SSE = 0$, then $r = 0$.

A variety of hypotheses about this linear regression may be tested. For example, the hypothesis that $a_1 = 0$, or the hypothesis that $a_2 = $ (*some prescribed constant*), can be tested. Also, confidence intervals may be given for the estimate $\hat{y}$ for each value of x. Confidence intervals also may be given for the estimates of a_1, a_2, and σ^2. Finally, there are appropriate procedures and formulae that can be used for fitting straight lines to data in which only x is subject to error, or to data in which both x and y are subject to error; these procedures and formulae are different from, but analogous to, those given here. All of these topics and many more are discussed by Acton (1959) in his comprehensive book on the analysis of straight-line data.

We end this section with a numerical example of the fitting of a straight line to a series of observations, in order to illustrate the concepts and formulae discussed above. Suppose that we are attempting to simulate a horse race. We might proceed by first gathering data about all the horses that may run in the race. We then could analyze these data, trying to determine which factors affect the running time of the race for each horse. One factor that might affect the running time in a given race is the class of competition that the horse faces. For many races, the class of competition is best indicated by the claiming value of the race. (We shall refer to the simulation of a horse race again in this book. For a precise definition of claiming value, and for definitions and discussions of other terms that may be used in reference to this simulation, see the book by Ainslie 1968. All other things being equal, a larger claiming value indicates a better quality of horses in the race.) Table 5.1 summarizes the finish times and corresponding claiming values for a horse named Smooth Seas in twelve races, each run at a distance of 3/4 mile.

The first step to be taken in analyzing data is to plot them, if this is at all possible. Figure 5.1 shows the plot of the data summarized in Table 5.1. Using the least-squares technique, a line was fitted to these data with the following re-

TABLE 5.1   Claiming Values and Finishing Times for 3/4-Mile Races
of Smooth Seas

Claiming Value	Finishing Time (seconds)	Claiming Value	Finishing Time (seconds)
$5,000	73.03	$ 8,500	74.20
6,300	72.37	14,000	72.50
6,500	71.33	15,000	71.87
7,500	71.50	15,500	72.77
8,000	70.90	12,500	71.53
9,000	70.60	20,000	71.03

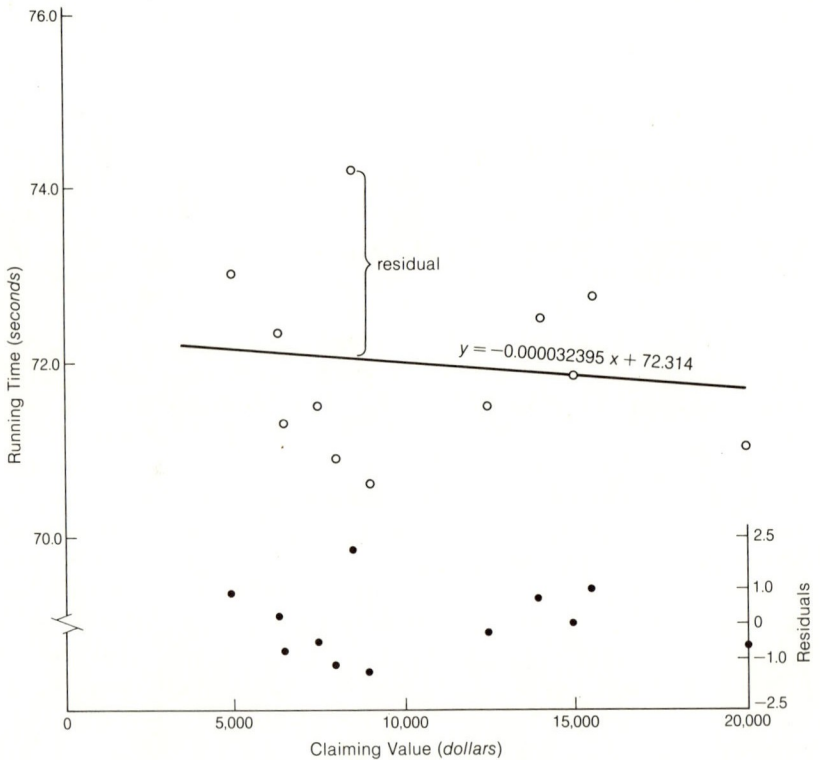

FIG. 5.1   Finish Time *vs.* Claiming Value for 3/4-Mile Races of Smooth Seas

sults: $\hat{a}_1 = -0.000032395$, $\hat{a}_2 = 72.314$, $\bar{y} = 71.8025$, $\bar{x} = 10.650$, $\sigma_y^2 = 0.99307$, $SSR = 11.6511$, $r = -0.1444$, $SSE = $ (mean square due to regression) $= 0.266$, and residual variance $= 1.165$. This line is plotted in Figure 5.1, and a typical residual is indicated. Table 5.2 shows all of the residuals. Clearly, very little of the variance of running times is accounted for by this linear relation, using claiming value as the independent variable. In other words, the fit is poor.

In general, residuals also should be plotted against the independent variable. This plot is a useful analytical tool. For example, it helps to determine whether a nonlinear relation could improve the fit. The plot of the residual is included in Figure 5.1.

As a second example, consider the data in Table 5.3, which summarizes the percentage of decisions in social security disability cases that were reversed at the hearings level each month. These data are plotted in Figure 5.2. A linear relation was fitted to these data, producing the line shown in the plot. Again the residuals were plotted, and in this case the residuals seem to follow a sinusoidal pattern, suggesting that a regular nonlinear relation might improve the fit to these data. We shall return to this example in the discussion of fitting nonlinear relations.

5.4 Multiple Linear Regression (MLR)

In a case with several independent variables, the simplest relation would be a weighted sum of the variables, with a constant added; such a relation is a *multiple linear regression* (MLR). More specifically, the MLR model is $y = a_1 x_1 + a_2 x_2 + \ldots + a_j x_j + a_0 + \epsilon$. The parameters to be fitted are $a_0, a_1, a_2, \ldots, a_j$.

If the number of parameters to be estimated, $j + 1$, is large, the calculations are extensive and the use of a computer is recommended. A computer program for this purpose (labeled MULTR) is included in the IBM System/360 and 370 scientific subroutine package. In addition, Hemmerle (1967, Chapter 3) discusses multiple regression calculations quite extensively.

TABLE 5.2   Residuals in Fitting Line by Least Squares
to Data in Table 5.1

x	y	$\hat{y}$	Residual $(y - \hat{y})$	x	y	$\hat{y}$	Residual $(y - \hat{y})$
5,000	73.03	72.15	0.88	8,500	74.20	72.04	2.16
6,300	72.37	72.11	0.26	14,000	72.50	71.86	0.64
6,500	71.33	72.10	−0.77	15,000	71.87	71.83	0.04
7,500	71.50	72.07	−0.57	15,500	72.77	71.81	0.96
8,000	70.90	72.05	−1.15	12,500	71.53	71.91	−0.38
9,000	70.60	72.02	−1.42	20,000	71.03	71.67	−0.64

TABLE 5.3 Reversal Rates in Hearings on Disability Cases

Month	Percentage of Reversals During					
	1965	1966	1967	1968	1969	1970
January	—	43.1	42.7	40.4	42.7	50.9
February	—	43.0	47.7	41.6	44.0	—
March	—	41.8	45.5	43.5	42.6	—
April	—	40.7	47.2	44.5	44.5	—
May	—	41.8	44.8	43.1	45.1	—
June	—	41.9	46.1	43.7	47.0	—
July	—	42.5	45.9	43.8	48.0	—
August	—	40.3	44.8	41.1	49.2	—
September	41.1	42.6	43.7	41.4	49.2	—
October	43.1	45.3	45.8	42.1	49.5	—
November	41.7	43.9	44.2	40.7	50.5	—
December	41.8	44.7	43.7	42.2	49.9	—

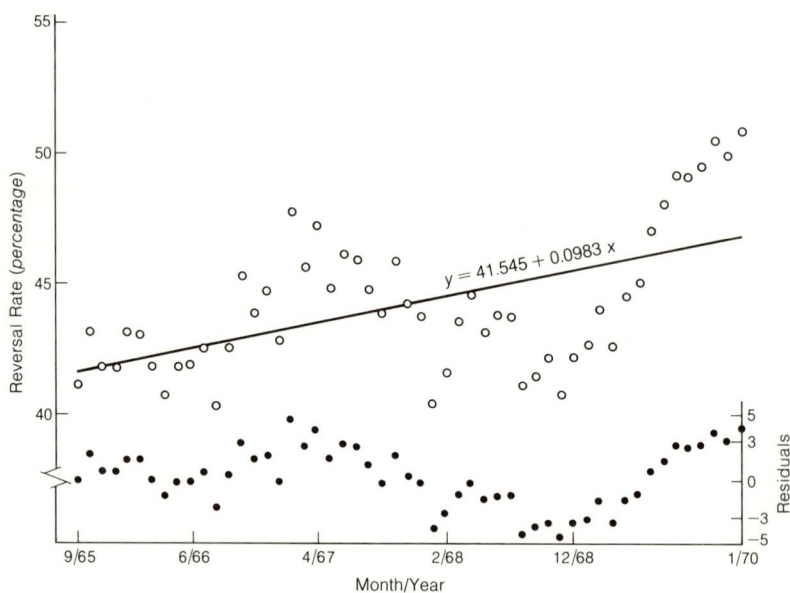

$$y = 41.545 + 0.0983\,x$$

FIG. 5.2 Reversal Rate vs. Month in Hearings on Disability Cases

The MLR is an important tool in the regression studies that are needed during simulation development. Simulations often require functional relations involving one dependent and several independent variables, and the MLR usually is the first model used in such a case. Its popularity is due partly to the simplicity of the model, the widespread availability of suitable computer programs, and the techniques that are available to determine which independent variables are relevant. These techniques are discussed in the next section, and an example of an MLR also is given there.

5.5 Selecting the Best MLR

Simulation development often involves the empirical fitting of relations involving many independent variables. One approach to this problem is the fitting of an MLR, using any one of several available techniques to decide which independent variables should be retained in the model. Here we briefly describe four of these techniques and give an example of the use of one of them in the simulation of a horse race. Many such techniques are discussed in detail by Draper and Smith (1966, Chapter 6).

Assume that we start with a set of n data points and j possible independent variables (n must be greater—preferably much greater—than $j + 1$). We are looking for the best subset of the independent variables to use in an MLR. The best subset ordinarily is defined in terms of a minimization of the SSR. However, addition of another variable cannot possibly increase the SSR. (Suppose we have k independent variables and a regression model of

$$y = \hat{a}_0 + \sum_{i=1}^{k} \hat{a}_i x_i.$$

If another variable, x_{k+1}, is added, then either $\hat{a}_{k+1} = 0$ or $\hat{a}_{k+1} \neq 0$. In the former case, the SSR is exactly the same as for the set of k variables; in the latter case, the SSR is smaller than that for the set of k variables.) Therefore, the criterion must specify not merely that addition of another variable causes a reduction in the SSR, but must specify that the reduction be meaningful according to some test. One approach is to add a variable only if it causes a statistically significant reduction in the SSR. In this approach, we would use an F test similar to the one discussed in Chapter 4. However, experience in simulation development indicates that too few variables are retained if the F test is used in this criterion. Another alternative is to continue to add variables as long as the standard error of the fit, $\sqrt{SSR/(n-2)}$, decreases. A reasonable compromise that works well in most cases is to plot the standard error of the fit against the number of variables used in the model. If the result resembles curve **A** in Figure 5.3, the decision is clearcut; in this case, four variables should be used. If the result resembles curve **B** in Figure 5.3, the decision may be difficult to make, but the validity of the

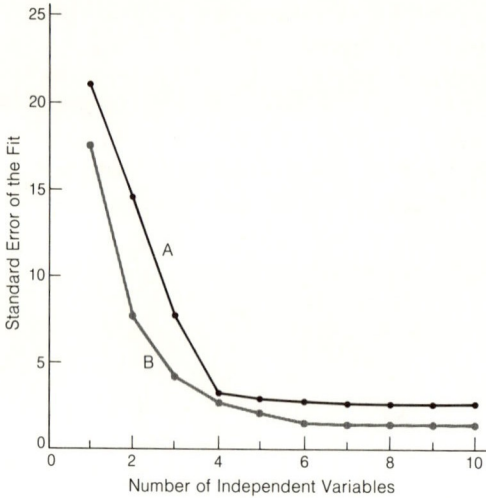

FIG. 5.3   Standard Error of the Fit *vs.* Number of Independent Variables

model will not be much affected by the particular decision made; in this case, three, four, five, or even six variables might be used.

The four techniques for variable selection that we discuss here are called: (1) all possible combinations; (2) backward elimination; (3) relaxed forward stepwise; and (4) fitting to the residuals. [Other names for these techniques also are used. For example, Draper and Smith (1966) call them: (1) all possible regressions; (2) backward elimination; (3) a variation of stepwise regression; and (4) stagewise regression.]

In the first approach (*all possible combinations*), every possible MLR using every subset of the j independent variables is fitted. The best fit with one variable, that with two variables, that with three variables, and so on are tabulated and plotted; a decision then is reached on the basis of this plot. Because there are 2^j such MLRs, this approach is both thorough and cumbersome. Suitable computer programs are available with some computers. However, this approach is not recommended for use in simulation development, because frequently there are too many independent variables. However, in those cases where j is only about 5 or less, this is a reasonable approach to use.

In the second approach (*backward elimination*), an MLR involving all j variables is fitted first. The SSR for each regression involving $j - 1$ variables then is calculated. If the largest of these SSRs (call it SSR_{j-1}) is less than some prescribed multiple of SSR, the set of j variables is retained and used. If SSR_{j-1} is greater than the prescribed multiple of SSR, the process is repeated to see whether SSR_{j-2} is less than the prescribed multiple of SSR_{j-1}. The process is repeated until some set of variables meets the criterion.

The third approach (*relaxed forward stepwise*) is a variation of the stepwise approach. In the stepwise approach, the SSR for each regression involving a single variable is calculated first, and that with the smallest SSR is chosen. Next the SSR for each regression with two variables is calculated; if the smallest of these SSRs does not decrease the SSR by a prescribed amount, the procedure is halted and the single-variable regression is used. The process is continued as long as addition of another variable continues to reduce the SSR by the prescribed amount. Computer programs for the stepwise approach are available in most computer libraries; that in the scientific subroutine package for the IBM System/360 and 370 is labeled STPRG. Ralston and Wilf (1960, pp. 191–203) present a description of Efroymson's stepwise procedure and a computer program for carrying it out.

In the usual stepwise approach, the decrease in the SSR required in order to add a new variable is prescribed in terms of the values of the F distribution. Experience with simulation development indicates that this requirement is too strict; a relaxed criterion should be used. We suggest that the criterion for continuing the computer program should be a reduction of any amount in the standard error of the fit. However, this criterion should be supplemented by examination of a plot such as that given in Figure 5.3. A numerical example of this approach is given below.

The fourth approach (*fitting to the residuals*) results in something other than a least-squares solution. The first step is to fit y to the single variable that gives the smallest SSR, as in the first step of the relaxed forward approach. The residuals in this fit then are regressed against each of the remaining $j-1$ variables. The best fit is retained. This process is continued until addition of another variable fails to produce a prescribed reduction in the SSR. Back substitution then gives the final function. The authors have not used this approach, but it is reported to be useful in development of some economic models, although it has not proven useful in developing industrial simulations (see Draper and Smith 1966, pp. 175–177).

Selection of the best MLR is particularly difficult if two or more of the independent variables are highly correlated. Inclusion of one of the correlated variables in the model usually precludes the addition of the others, because the additional variables do not significantly reduce the SSR. In such a case, it probably is wise first to determine which of the independent variables are highly correlated. Then, the decision of which of these variables to include in the regression should be made on the basis of appropriateness to the system description, rather than on the basis of reducing the SSR. The matter of appropriateness *versus* goodness of fit is discussed further in Section 5.8.

Another consequence of the presence of correlated variables is that, in moving from one stage of the fitting process to the next, the set of variables that give the best fit may have to be changed radically. Suppose for example, that the variables x_1 and x_8 (among the possible independent variables x_1, x_2, . . . , x_{12}) give the best fit among all possible fits using two independent variables. If one or both of these variables is correlated with some other independent variable, the best fit with three variables may prove *not* to include one or both of these variables, x_1 and x_8.

Calculation of all possible pairwise correlations can be very cumbersome. Fortunately, these correlations often can be obtained as optional byproducts of the regression calculations.

For a numerical example of the fitting of an MLR, let us return to the simulation of a horse race, this time dealing directly with the problem of predicting the outcome. One approach would involve first seeking the best relation between the time required to complete the first quarter-mile of the race and various independent variables. Next the time required to complete the first half-mile is related to another set of independent variables, including among them the quarter-mile time. Finally the finish time is related to a third set of independent variables, including the half-mile time. There are several reasons for using this approach rather than predicting finish time directly from a single MLR: (1) realistic charts of the race can be produced as byproducts of this approach; (2) the results of this approach are "smoother"—that is, the horses run a consistent race over the entire length of the race; (3) preliminary study of the system shows that different facts affect the early and later portions of the race; and (4) this approach permits appropriate adjustment of the results—for example, if several horses have nearly identical times for the first quarter-mile, adjustments can be made to simulate the blocking out and bumping of some of the horses that probably would occur in such a situation.

Separate regressions are used for each horse for each of the three distances. Table 5.4 summarizes data used as possible independent variables for predicting the quarter-mile times of a horse named Gordorigo; values of these variables and the corresponding quarter-mile times are given for each of several races. Using the stepwise approach for fitting the MLR, the *SSRs* shown in Table 5.5 were obtained with each added variable. After study of a plot of these values, it was decided to fit the MLR using the first five variables. This gave an MLR of: (*Quarter time*) = 0.41207 (*days of rest*) + 1.65884 (*track condition code*) + 2.42556 (*post position*) + 0.00492 (*dollar odds*) −0.18256 (*number of horses in race*). (Units of measurement for each variable are those indicated in Table 5.4.) The standard error of the estimate in using this regression is 15.08 thirtieths of a second, or about 1/2 second.

TABLE 5.4   Quarter-Mile Times and Values of Corresponding Independent Variables in 19 Races of Gordorigo

1/4-Mile Time (thirtieths of a second)	Number of Days of Rest	Track Condition*	Distance of Race (sixteenths of a mile)	Claiming Value (hundreds of dollars)	Post Position	Weight Carried (pounds)	Equivalent Dollar Odds (cents)	Number of Horses in Race
699	17	1	14	90	5	115	570	7
721	35	2	14	90	6	113	1760	12
698	7	1	14	100	3	121	410	8
734	14	1	14	150	11	119	550	12
699	7	1	14	150	1	117	900	6
710	21	1	17	150	3	115	1760	10
701	37	1	14	125	2	119	960	11
720	5	1	18	95	6	114	140	7
683	4	2	14	95	8	110	230	8
710	8	1	12	85	3	119	1390	11
680	7	1	16	75	9	116	150	9
710	7	1	16	125	7	117	920	12
731	26	1	14	100	14	119	1320	14
730	53	1	18	225	3	114	2310	9
690	6	2	16	180	3	118	1530	8
691	22	1	14	0	1	119	3590	11
710	13	3	16	250	6	113	630	7
730	0	3	12	0	6	117	4360	9
711	6	3	12	0	6	120	390	7

*Track condition code: 1 = fast; 2 = good; 3 = muddy; 4 = sloppy.

5.6 Analysis of the Residuals

Regression often is used in simulation development as a means of empirically establishing functional relationships between inputs and outputs. When using regression techniques in this way, it becomes particularly important to analyze thoroughly the residuals that are obtained. At least three objectives are kept in mind as this analysis is made: (1) to determine if the form of the function is suitable; (2) to determine if there are any values (called *outliers*) that are very unlikely to occur if the model for the relation is correct; and (3) to determine if additional independent variables will help to account for the residual fluctuations.

In order to reach the first two objectives, residuals are plotted against the independent variables. (We are speaking here of plots against a single independent variable. Although there are techniques for plotting against two or more independent variables, these more complicated plots usually will be supplemented or preceded by plots of the residuals against each independent variable separately.) If the plots indicate that there is a functional relation between the residuals and any independent variable, then the original functional form is inadequate to explain the behavior of the data. If the plot indicates that certain individual points lie well above or below the level of the other residuals, these values should be examined to determine if they are indeed outliers.

Figure 5.2 illustrates an example of a functional relation between the residuals and the independent variable. The example is somewhat unusual, because the solution in this case seems to be to accept the linear relationship as the long-term trend, and to use the sinusoidal relation to depict short-term fluctuations from this trend. The fitting of a sinusoidal function to the residuals is discussed in the next section. In many cases, a functional relation between the residuals and the independent variable can best be accommodated by modifying the form of the original function that was used. For example, a curvilinear relation be-

TABLE 5.5 *SSRs* for Each Additional Variable in Stepwise Approach to MLR Fitting

Total Number of Variables	Variables Added	*SSR*
1	Number of horses in race	4,107
2	Track condition	3,840
3	Days of rest	3,570
4	Post position	3,270
5	Dollar odds	2,957
6	Weight carried	2,812
7	Claiming value	2,602
8	Distance of race	2,601

tween the residuals and the independent variable will result if a straight line was used for data that are best fitted using a second or third degree polynomial.

When the parameters in a regression are estimated by least squares, extreme values may have a pronounced effect on the estimate of these parameters. Statistical tests may be used to answer the question, How unlikely is this observed outlier? Anscombe et al. (1960) give a comprehensive discussion of these techniques. However, the ultimate question to be answered is the following: Is this value erroneous, and should it be omitted from the analysis? Bross (1961) discusses outliers from this point of view. As might be expected, there is no clearcut strategy to adopt in dealing with outliers. The first step ordinarily is to seek an explanation for the extreme value; such an explanation should determine whether or not to omit the value. In the absence of an explanation, appropriate statistical tests are made, and a decision is reached on whether or not to omit the values and to take the associated risks.

Many systems are characterized by the infrequent occurrence of extreme values in certain variables. These values are unusual, but they are a real part of the system and they should be simulated. In most cases, two distributions will be used: one for the usual data and the other for the extreme data. For example, interview times in certain district offices might best be characterized by saying that 96 percent of the interview times are distributed as $N(20,7)$ and 4 percent of the times as $N(60,20)$.

The third objective of residual analysis — that of determining whether additional variables are required — is discussed in the context of the analysis of variance in Chapter 6. The article by Anscombe and Tukey (1963) is a good overall reference on the subject of the analysis of residuals.

5.7 Nonlinear Regression

The straight line and the MLR are two examples of the general linear model:

$$y = \sum_{i=1}^{k} a_i f_i (x_1, x_2, \ldots , x_j) + \epsilon. \tag{5.5}$$

In the case of the straight line, $f_1 \equiv x$ and $f_2 \equiv 1$. In the case of the MLR, $f_i \equiv x_i$ for $i = 1$ to j, and $f_{j+1} \equiv f_k \equiv 1$. A polynomial $(a_1 + a_2 x + a_3 x^2 + \ldots + a_k x^{k-1})$ is another example of the linear model, with $f_i = x^{i-1}$. The least-squares estimate of the parameters, $a_1, a_2, \ldots , a_k$, can be written in terms of the observations. The solution is directly obtainable, although the calculations may be lengthy.

There are many relations that do not fit the general linear model — for example: $y = a_1 e^{a_2 x}$. In this case, the variables may be transformed to give $\ln y = \ln a_1 + a_2 x$, which has a linear form. However, for many relations (such as $y = a_1 \sin a_2 x$, or $y = a_1 e^{a_2 x} + a_3 e^{a_4 x}$), it may be impossible to reduce the relation to linear terms through a transformation of the variables. If the variables are transformed, it is important to note that the solution of the regression minimizes the *SSR* in the transformed, not the original, variable. It generally is not the same solution that would be obtained by minimizing the *SSR* in the original variable.

There is a whole series of procedures for the solution of nonlinear forms, developed to take advantage of high-speed computers. Examples of these procedures are described by Hartley (1961), Spang (1962), and Draper and Smith (1966, Chapter 10). The basic problem involves finding the lowest point in a multi-dimensional surface. The difficulty is that there may be several separate valleys in this surface, and each of the techniques can do no better than to find the local minimum (rather than the lowest point of the entire surface). Experience with these techniques suggests that a straightforward searching procedure is probably the best to use. First, the form of the function to be fitted is prescribed and sets of values of the independent variables are chosen. Then the computer prints out the *SSR* corresponding to each combination of the independent variables. Several runs are made, until the user is satisfied that he has estimated the parameters with sufficient accuracy. A FORTRAN program for this purpose is included in Appendix B (Program B.4). Its use is illustrated in the following example.

Table 5.6 summarizes the residuals obtained in fitting a straight line to the reversal-rates data first summarized in Table 5.3. A sinusoidal relation between the residuals and the variable was indicated by the plot in Figure 5.2. The fitting of sine functions is discussed by Wolberg (1967, Chapter 7). We will use the nonlinear least-squares approach embodied in Program B.4.

Both the plot and the tabulated data indicate that the sinusoidal pattern is particularly pronounced in the period beginning with June 1966. We will fit the function using that point as the origin and omitting the data for the period from September 1965 through May 1966. The form of the function that will be fitted is $y = a_1 \sin a_2 x$. We need a first approximation to a_1 (the amplitude of the function) and a_2 (related to the period of the function). A superficial analysis of the plot in Figure 5.2 and the data in Table 5.6 indicates that the amplitude (a_1) is about 3 to 5 and that the period is about 28 to 34 months. Because $a_2 = 2\pi/(period)$, we estimate a_2 to be about 0.2. Using these estimates, the least-squares program was run with a_1 varying from 2.6 to 5.0 in increments of 0.2, and with a_2 varying from 0.15 to 0.40 in increments of 0.05. Figure 5.4 shows the output for this run. Note that the *SSR*s are recorded in floating point notation. Further runs then were made with smaller increments to search for the exact minima. Figure 5.5 shows part of the output for the fourth and final run, in which a_1 varied from 2.80 to 3.00 in increments of 0.01, and a_2 varied from 0.175 to 0.185 in increments of 0.001. No further runs were made because accuracies of 0.01 in a_1 and 0.001 in a_2 were sufficient for our purposes. Therefore, the final fitted function is: $y = 2.93 \sin (0.179 \, x)$.

5.8 Regression and Validity

Some caution is required in the use of regression techniques to establish relations in simulations. Sometimes the result just doesn't make sense. Every fitted function should be reviewed to make sure that it results in a reasonable relationship. An example will serve both to clarify and to illustrate this precautionary remark.

Consider again the use of an MLR to relate the time required by a horse to finish a race to several independent variables. In using this relation in a simulation, we could proceed by predicting the quarter-mile, half-mile, and finish times using each of three regressions for each horse. We then would generate a random number with the distribution N(0, *standard error of the estimate*) and add it to the finish time obtained from the MLR, in order to introduce the appropriate stochastic behavior. This is consistent with the general MLR model:

$$y = \sum_{i=1}^{k} a_i x_i + \epsilon.$$

The regression gives $\Sigma a_i x_i$, and the random number generator adds in ϵ.

TABLE 5.6   Residuals Obtained in Fitting a Straight Line to Relation Between Reversal Rates and Month* for Data in Table 5.3

Month (x)	Residual (y)	Month (x)	Residual (y)	Month (x)	Residual (y)
1	−0.543	19	2.087	37	−3.783
2	1.358	20	3.688	38	−3.182
3	−0.140	21	1.190	39	−4.680
4	−0.138	22	2.392	40	−3.278
5	1.063	23	2.093	41	−2.876
6	0.865	24	0.895	42	−1.675
7	−0.433	25	−0.303	43	−3.173
8	−1.632	26	1.698	44	−1.371
9	−0.630	27	0.000	45	−0.870
10	−0.628	28	−0.598	46	0.932
11	−0.127	29	−3.997	47	1.834
12	−2.425	30	−2.895	48	2.935
13	−0.223	31	−1.093	49	2.837
14	2.378	32	−0.192	50	3.039
15	0.880	33	−1.690	51	3.940
16	1.582	34	−1.188	52	3.242
17	−0.517	35	−1.187	53	4.144
18	4.385	36	−3.985		

*Month 1 is September 1965; Month 10 is June 1966; Month 53 is January 1970.

PARAM1	PARAM2	DIFSQ		PARAM1	PARAM2	DIFSQ	
2.6000	0.1500	0.208060D	03	3.8000	0.3000	0.710767D	03
2.6000	0.2000	0.134649D	03	3.8000	0.3500	0.442825D	03
2.6000	0.2500	0.484427D	03	3.8000	0.4000	0.659991D	03
2.6000	0.3000	0.505804D	03	4.0000	0.1500	0.292299D	03
2.6000	0.3500	0.318431D	03	4.0000	0.2000	0.190712D	03
2.6000	0.4000	0.468408D	03	4.0000	0.2500	0.720484D	03
2.8000	0.1500	0.215061D	03	4.0000	0.3000	0.750822D	03
2.8000	0.2000	0.137139D	03	4.0000	0.3500	0.469815D	03
2.8000	0.2500	0.512987D	03	4.0000	0.4000	0.698055D	03
2.8000	0.3000	0.535753D	03	4.2000	0.1500	0.311045D	03
2.8000	0.3500	0.334693D	03	4.2000	0.2000	0.206080D	03
2.8000	0.4000	0.495958D	03	4.2000	0.2500	0.761089D	03
3.0000	0.1500	0.223740D	03	4.2000	0.3000	0.792562D	03
3.0000	0.2000	0.141468D	03	4.2000	0.3500	0.498593D	03
3.0000	0.2500	0.543268D	03	4.2000	0.4000	0.737871D	03
3.0000	0.3000	0.567388D	03	4.4000	0.1500	0.331468D	03
3.0000	0.3500	0.352743D	03	4.4000	0.2000	0.223289D	03
3.0000	0.4000	0.525260D	03	4.4000	0.2500	0.803415D	03
3.2000	0.1500	0.234096D	03	4.4000	0.3000	0.835986D	03
3.2000	0.2000	0.147636D	03	4.4000	0.3500	0.529159D	03
3.2000	0.2500	0.575270D	03	4.4000	0.4000	0.779439D	03
3.2000	0.3000	0.600706D	03	4.6000	0.1500	0.353569D	03
3.2000	0.3500	0.372582D	03	4.6000	0.2000	0.242337D	03
3.2000	0.4000	0.556314D	03	4.6000	0.2500	0.847462D	03
3.4000	0.1500	0.246130D	03	4.6000	0.3000	0.881094D	03
3.4000	0.2000	0.155645D	03	4.6000	0.3500	0.561514D	03
3.4000	0.2500	0.608993D	03	4.6000	0.4000	0.822760D	03
3.4000	0.3000	0.635709D	03	4.8000	0.1500	0.377347D	03
3.4000	0.3500	0.394208D	03	4.8000	0.2000	0.263225D	03
3.4000	0.4000	0.589121D	03	4.8000	0.2500	0.893229D	03
3.6000	0.1500	0.259842D	03	4.8000	0.3000	0.927887D	03
3.6000	0.2000	0.165494D	03	4.8000	0.3500	0.595656D	03
3.6000	0.2500	0.644436D	03	4.8000	0.4000	0.867833D	03
3.6000	0.3000	0.672395D	03	5.0000	0.1500	0.402803D	03
3.6000	0.3500	0.417622D	03	5.0000	0.2000	0.285954D	03
3.6000	0.4000	0.623680D	03	5.0000	0.2500	0.940717D	03
3.8000	0.1500	0.275232D	03	5.0000	0.3000	0.976364D	03
3.8000	0.2000	0.177183D	03	5.0000	0.3500	0.631586D	03
3.8000	0.2500	0.681600D	03	5.0000	0.4000	0.914658D	03

FIG. 5.4 Output of First Run in Fitting Sine Function to Residuals by Nonlinear Least Squares

PARAM1	PARAM2	DIFSQ		PARAM1	PARAM2	DIFSQ
2.8900	0.1770	0.858001D 02		2.9400	0.1750	0.878533D 02
2.8900	0.1780	0.852139D 02		2.9400	0.1760	0.866436D 02
2.8900	0.1790	0.849307D 02		2.9400	0.1770	0.857518D 02
2.8900	0.1800	0.849453D 02		2.9400	0.1780	0.851733D 02
2.8900	0.1810	0.852524D 02		2.9400	0.1790	0.849030D 02
2.8900	0.1820	0.858463D 02		2.9400	0.1800	0.849358D 02
2.8900	0.1830	0.867213D 02		2.9400	0.1810	0.852660D 02
2.8900	0.1840	0.878713D 02		2.9400	0.1820	0.858878D 02
2.8900	0.1850	0.892904D 02		2.9400	0.1830	0.867951D 02
2.9000	0.1750	0.878821D 02		2.9400	0.1840	0.879817D 02
2.9000	0.1760	0.866754D 02		2.9400	0.1850	0.894413D 02
2.9000	0.1770	0.857819D 02		2.9500	0.1750	0.878566D 02
2.9000	0.1780	0.851972D 02		2.9500	0.1760	0.866463D 02
2.9000	0.1790	0.849165D 02		2.9500	0.1770	0.857549D 02
2.9000	0.1800	0.849347D 02		2.9500	0.1780	0.851780D 02
2.9000	0.1810	0.852464D 02		2.9500	0.1790	0.849104D 02
2.9000	0.1820	0.858459D 02		2.9500	0.1800	0.849469D 02
2.9000	0.1830	0.867272D 02		2.9500	0.1810	0.852818D 02
2.9000	0.1840	0.878846D 02		2.9500	0.1820	0.859093D 02
2.9000	0.1850	0.893117D 02		2.9500	0.1830	0.868231D 02
2.9100	0.1750	0.878685D 02		2.9500	0.1840	0.880171D 02
2.9100	0.1760	0.866611D 02		2.9500	0.1850	0.894849D 02
2.9100	0.1770	0.857680D 02		2.9600	0.1750	0.878642D 02
2.9100	0.1780	0.851848D 02		2.9600	0.1760	0.866532D 02
2.9100	0.1790	0.849067D 02		2.9600	0.1770	0.857623D 02
2.9100	0.1800	0.849285D 02		2.9600	0.1780	0.851870D 02
2.9100	0.1810	0.852448D 02		2.9600	0.1790	0.849222D 02
2.9100	0.1820	0.858498D 02		2.9600	0.1800	0.849624D 02
2.9100	0.1830	0.867376D 02		2.9600	0.1810	0.853020D 02
2.9100	0.1840	0.879022D 02		2.9600	0.1820	0.859351D 02
2.9100	0.1850	0.893374D 02		2.9600	0.1830	0.868555D 02
2.9200	0.1750	0.878592D 02		2.9600	0.1840	0.880569D 02
2.9200	0.1760	0.866511D 02		2.9600	0.1850	0.895329D 02
2.9200	0.1770	0.857584D 02		2.9700	0.1750	0.878759D 02
2.9200	0.1780	0.851767D 02		2.9700	0.1760	0.866643D 02
2.9200	0.1790	0.849012D 02		2.9700	0.1770	0.857740D 02
2.9200	0.1800	0.849266D 02		2.9700	0.1780	0.852003D 02
2.9200	0.1810	0.852475D 02		2.9700	0.1790	0.849382D 02
2.9200	0.1820	0.858581D 02		2.9700	0.1800	0.849822D 02
2.9200	0.1830	0.867523D 02		2.9700	0.1810	0.853265D 02
2.9200	0.1840	0.879243D 02		2.9700	0.1820	0.859653D 02
2.9200	0.1850	0.893676D 02		2.9700	0.1830	0.868923D 02
2.9300	0.1750	0.878541D 02		2.9700	0.1840	0.881011D 02
2.9300	0.1760	0.866452D 02		2.9700	0.1850	0.895853D 02
2.9300	0.1770	0.857530D 02		2.9800	0.1750	0.878919D 02
2.9300	0.1780	0.851728D 02		2.9800	0.1760	0.866797D 02
2.9300	0.1790	0.848999D 02		2.9800	0.1770	0.857899D 02
2.9300	0.1800	0.849291D 02		2.9800	0.1780	0.852179D 02
2.9300	0.1810	0.852546D 02		2.9800	0.1790	0.849585D 02
2.9300	0.1820	0.858707D 02		2.9800	0.1800	0.850063D 02
2.9300	0.1830	0.867715D 02		2.9800	0.1810	0.853554D 02
2.9300	0.1840	0.879508D 02		2.9800	0.1820	0.859999D 02
2.9300	0.1850	0.894022D 02		2.9800	0.1830	0.869335D 02

FIG. 5.5 Part of the Output of Final Run in Fitting Sine Function to Residuals by Nonlinear Least Squares

For one horse (Armed Warrior) the regression resulted in an enormous standard error. In other words, it was impossible to find a good fit to the empirical data, no matter how many variables were used. When this horse was run in simulations, he sometimes would win by 60 lengths, but at other times would lose by 40 lengths. This behavior was judged to be unrealistic. Temporarily, it was decided to retain the MLR but arbitrarily to reduce the standard error to about one-sixth of the calculated value for purposes of generating the random number. If this horse is to be retained in the simulation, further analysis should be made of the data in order to arrive at a more suitable prediction of his finish times. Nonlinear regressions may be needed.

5.9 Supplementary Reading

The most important references on the subject of regression have been mentioned in the text of this chapter, but a few comments may be added here. The book by Acton (1959) is the most comprehensive reference currently available on the subject of fitting straight lines. It tends to treat the most common case (y stochastic and x known without error) too briefly, but even this treatment is useful. The most important single reference on regression for those engaged in simulation development is that by Draper and Smith (1966); this book should be in your library. *Technometrics* is the most relevant periodical; it is relevant to problems of simulation development, even though it is intended for physical scientists who use statistical methodology. Two articles in this journal, by Box and Hunter (1962) and Cramer (1964), are of interest to those working on simulations; these articles deal with the use of statistical methods to develop models in the sciences. This journal should be available for easy access. Wolberg (1967) discusses the subject of fitting functions for purposes of prediction. This useful book includes discussions of the fitting of sine functions, polynomials, the exponential function, and the normal curve. Rosenfeld (1969) gives an interesting example of the application of regression techniques to the results of a set of simulation runs.

PROBLEMS

Problems 5.1 through 5.3 should be assigned if a computer is available. Problems 5.4 and 5.5 should be assigned if no computer is available.

5.1   Table 5.7 summarizes reversal rates in hearings of disability cases for the period immediately preceding that summarized in Table 5.3. (a) Plot the data from both tables. (b) Do you think that a single regression should be fitted to all of these data? (c) Fit an appropriate linear relation to the data in Table 5.7. Would you consider the point for August 1965 to be an outlier? (d) Adjust the data from Table 5.7 so that a single linear relation can be fitted to all the data from both tables, and fit such a relation. Be sure to obtain the residuals. **(e)** Plot the residuals obtained in d as a dependent variable, with month as an independent variable. **(f)** Would you be surprised to hear that new legislation relating to disability definitions was enacted early in 1965? Explain your answer.

5.2   Table 5.8 contains data on finish times, half-mile times, distance of race, weight carried, and days of rest for several races of a horse named Dig We Must. Fit a series of relations in which the dependent variable is finish time and the independent variables are: **(a)** distance alone; **(b)** distance and half-mile time; **(c)** distance, half-mile time, and weight carried; and finally **(d)** all four possible variables. Compute the SSR in each case. Which MLR would you be inclined to use?

5.3   Data' are given below on the proportion of breaking strengths retained by cotton duck fabric that was buried in soil for varying numbers of days. Using nonlinear least squares, fit to these data a function of the form

$$y = \frac{a_1 e^{-a_2 x} - a_2 e^{-a_1 x}}{a_1 - a_2},$$

where y is the proportion of breaking strength retained, x is the number of days of burial, and a_1 and a_2 are the parameters. Estimate a_1 and a_2 to the nearest hundredth. Try initial values of a_1 in the range 1 to 5, and initial values of a_2 in the range 0.1 to 0.9.

Days Buried:	0	1	2	3	4	5	6	7
Strength Retained:	1.00000	0.66623	0.44503	0.22906	0.08050	0.06872	0.05759	0.04123

TABLE 5.7   Monthly Reversal Rates in Hearings of Disability Cases

Month	Percentage of Reversals During		
	1963	1964	1965
January	—	33.3	30.4
February	—	35.2	33.3
March	—	34.7	31.8
April	—	36.8	34.6
May	—	35.0	33.7
June	—	30.9	33.9
July	24.0	32.3	32.9
August	28.3	33.3	46.5
September	32.0	29.4	—
October	28.8	32.8	—
November	31.7	31.3	—
December	29.9	33.5	—

5.4 Using the data in Table 5.8, make a plot using finish time as the dependent variable y and distance as the independent variable x. **(a)** Would you say that there is a linear relation between these variables? **(b)** Given that $\Sigma y = 46{,}339$, $\Sigma y^2 = 109{,}239{,}183$, $\Sigma x = 258$, $\Sigma x^2 = 3{,}378$, and $\Sigma xy = 607{,}403$, determine the least-squares line and the correlation coefficient r. **(c)** Calculate the residuals and, using these residuals as a new dependent variable z, plot them against half-mile time as the independent variable. From this plot, what are your conclusions about this relation? **(d)** Given the results of your analysis of the plot in c, describe the next steps you would take in the analysis of these data.

5.5 Table 5.9 shows the *SSR*s obtained in fitting each of the three usual regressions relating quarter-mile time, half-mile time, and finish time to a number of independent variables. The data used in the regressions were twenty races of the horse Smooth Seas. Plot the *SSR* *versus* the number of variables in each case. For each case, state which variables you would include in the model, and explain your answers.

TABLE 5.8 Finish Times and Values of Corresponding Independent Variables in 20 Races of Dig We Must

Finish Time (thirtieths of a second)	Distance (sixteenths of a mile)	1/2-Mile Time (thirtieths of a second)	Weight Carried (pounds)	Days of Rest
2,118	12	1,391	117	7
2,139	12	1,399	119	14
2,152	12	1,411	115	21
2,142	12	1,395	117	14
2,176	12	1,423	119	7
2,156	12	1,395	115	7
2,176	12	1,408	117	14
2,157	12	1,386	119	7
2,185	12	1,420	118	0
2,131	12	1,395	119	10
2,511	14	1,386	119	21
2,153	12	1,386	119	7
2,520	14	1,374	119	21
2,115	12	1,368	119	7
2,533	14	1,411	119	36
2,501	14	1,381	116	14
3,093	17	1,424	115	10
3,148	17	1,454	115	15
2,143	12	1,403	120	62
2,090	12	1,377	117	8

TABLE 5.9 New *SSR*s Resulting from Addition of Indicated
Independent Variable

Number of Variables in Regression	Independent Variable Added	New *SSR*
Dependent Variable = 1/4-Mile Time:		
1	Distance	3,407
2	Number of horses in race	3,248
3	Track condition	3,016
4	Dollar odds	2,977
5	Post position	2,968
6	Days of rest	2,951
7	Claiming value	2,949
Dependent Variable = 1/2-Mile Time:		
1	1/4-mile time	1,855
2	Dollar odds	1,531
3	Post position	1,342
4	Track condition	1,216
5	Claiming value	1,123
6	Days of rest	1,084
7	Number of horses in race	1,057
Dependent Variable = Finish Time:		
1	Distance	19,729
2	1/2-mile time	13,043
3	Days of rest	10,740
4	Track condition	7,934
5	Post position	7,382
6	1/4-mile time	6,623
7	Claiming value	5,834
8	Weight carried	5,741
9	Number of horses in race	5,711

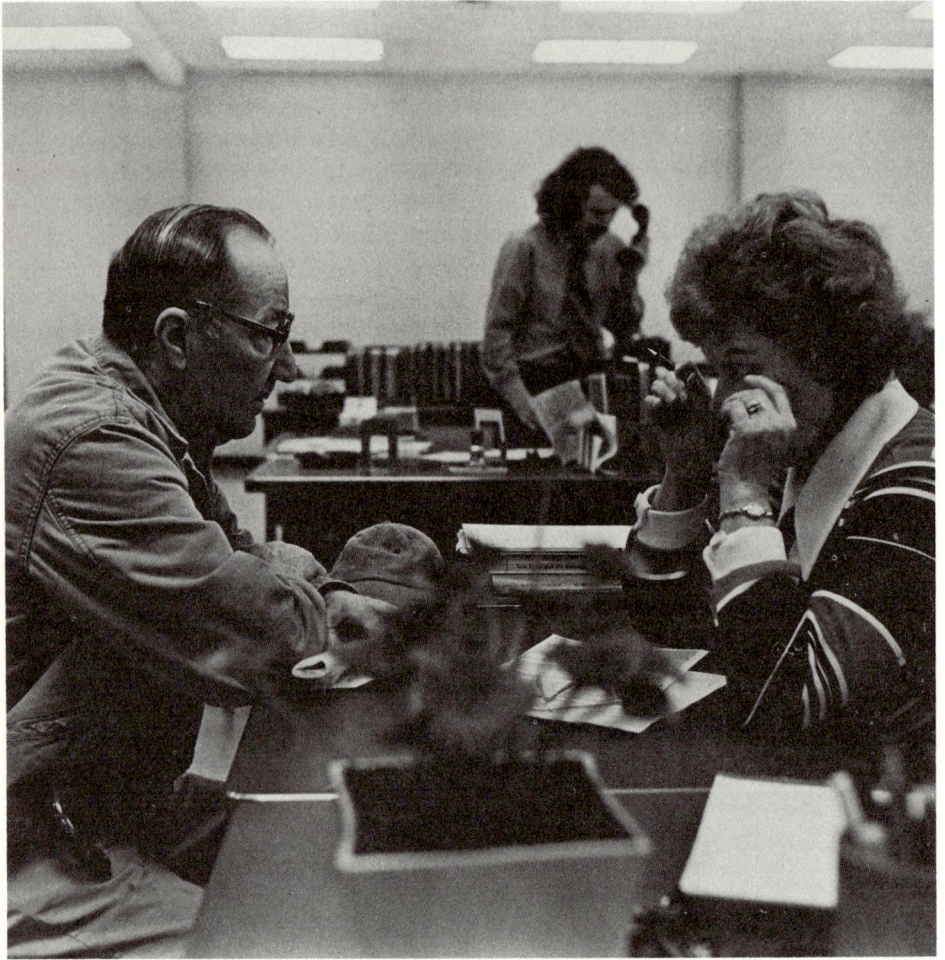

6

The Analysis of Variance

6.1 BACKGROUND   Many of the techniques that are useful in experimental design also are useful in simulation development and application. During development of a model for a stochastic system, the following question arises often: Which of many possible independent variables affect this dependent variable? In Chapter 5, regression techniques are used to help answer this question. However, regression techniques may be unwieldy if there are too many potential independent variables. This chapter deals with the application of 2^n designs in such situations, where they can be used to screen out unimportant variables before proceeding with a regression.

A simulation application is, in fact, a form of experiment. The simulation is used as a substitute for the real system. A series of carefully designed runs is made in order to experiment with this substitute system, much as a physicist, chemist, or biologist carries out experiments with laboratory systems. If the simulation is to be applied in a statistically valid fashion, the application must be made within this experimental-design framework. This chapter concentrates upon just one—the most important one—approach to experimental design: the use of the analysis of variance.

Entire books have been written on experimental design (for example, Cochran and Cox 1957) and on the analysis of variance (for example, Scheffe 1959). Our introductory discussion in this chapter is supplemented by references to these and other more extensive treatments of the topics.

6.2 The Framework

The *analysis of variance* is a technique used to test differences between means through the comparison of variances. For example, consider two sets of numbers. The variance of each set is computed separately; then the two sets are combined and the variance of the combined set is computed. The greater the difference between the means of the two sets of numbers, the greater will be the ratios of the variance of the combined set to the variances of the separate sets.

This relation may be illustrated with a simple numerical example. Consider the following three sets of numbers: set 1 is {23, 46, 15, 24, 29, 37, 17}; set 2 is {28, 29, 41, 18, 50, 22, 27}; and set 3 is {98, 114, 87, 112, 108, 120, 84, 107, 116}. The variance of set 1 is 104.8; the variance of set 2 is 105.6; and the variance of set 3 is 144.8. If sets 1 and 2 are combined, the variance of the combined set is 108.1. This value is not far different from the variances of the separate sets, and we may conclude that the means of the two sets are similar. However, if sets 1 and 3 are combined, the variance of the combined set is 1,617.8. This value is much greater than the variance of either separate set, and we may conclude that the means of the two sets are different. In fact, the mean of set 1 is 27.3; the mean of set 2 is 30.7; and the mean of set 3 is 105.1. The same relation can be used to compare the means of three or more sets, with a single variance being computed for the combined sets.

With certain assumptions about distributions, about the ways the means can differ, and about the consistency of the variance within each set, it is possible to make statistical tests of hypotheses about these means in the usual fashion (see Chapter 4). The values of the variances for separate sets are used to gauge the inherent variability. The variance of the combined set is split into two components: one related to the inherent variability of the separate sets, and the other measuring the variation between sets—in other words, the differences in means. With the appropriate assumptions, the F distribution then can be used to test the hypothesis that there is no difference in the means.

Section 6.3 lists and discusses some of the assumptions that are needed in order to make these tests and defines some terms used in connection with the tests. The other sections of this chapter discuss several useful tests in greater detail.

6.3 Underlying Assumptions and Factorial Designs

Experimental designs based on the analysis of variance often are called *factorial designs*. In a factorial design, factors that might influence the outcome are identified, and results are obtained at various prescribed *levels* of each factor. For example, the time required for a horse to race a given distance might depend on factors such as the position of the horse in the starting gate (the post position), the track condition, and the claiming value of the race. Levels of these factors might be: post positions 1, 2, 3, and so on; track conditions fast, good, slow, muddy, or sloppy; and claiming values in various dollar amounts. The design of a factorial experiment involves the choice of the factors and of the levels that are to be used. In the usual design, one or more observations is obtained for each possible combination of levels for all factors. A single combination is called a *cell*. Suppose that we are designing a study of the performance of a given horse. We choose to consider the three factors mentioned above, with the following levels: post positions 1, 2, 3, or 4; track conditions fast, slow, or sloppy; and claiming values of $3,000, $5,000, or $7,000. This experimental design has $4 \times 3 \times 3 = 24$ cells. The number of observations that are obtained for each cell is called the number of *replications* of the experiment.

In order to discuss the assumptions underlying the analysis of variance, we could present a general mathematical model for the technique and then precisely and succinctly discuss the assumptions associated with the model. However, the general model is very cumbersome, so we shall not present it here. Models for the one-way and two-way analysis of variance are given in Sections 6.4 and 6.5. In this section, we describe and discuss the general assumptions less formally.

The observed result is assumed to be a linear combination of a base mean and the contributions from each of the factors and each of their possible interactions. (The term *interaction* is defined more precisely in Section 6.5. Here we simply note that a special contribution to the result may come from the interacting consequences of a particular level of one factor with a particular level of another factor.) An error term also is added in, much as it was in the model for regression (Section 5.2). As in that case, the error is assumed to be $N(0,\sigma^2)$. Thus, the major assumptions underlying the analysis of variance are (1) that the effects of the factors are linear and additive; (2) that the error term is independently and normally distributed; and (3) that the variance of the error is independent of the cell — in other words, that the variance of the error is independent of the particular factor-level combination. The third assumption is called the assumption of *homoscedasticity*.

The assumption of homoscedasticity is the least crucial of the three assumptions, particularly if there are equal numbers of replications in each cell. Studies indicate that variances in one cell may be as much as three times greater than variances in another cell without substantially affecting the properties of the test (Box 1954). Other studies indicate that inferences about means are relatively insensitive to the effects of non-normal distributions for the error term (see Scheffe 1959, p. 337).

Scheffe (1959, pp. 360–362) rather generally characterizes the analysis of variance as a *robust* procedure; that is, its inferences are not seriously altered by small modifications in the assumptions underlying its use. This robustness is illustrated by the insensitivity of the procedure to relatively large deviations from homoscedasticity among the cells.

The analysis of variance permits tests to be made of hypotheses such as the following: (1) the observed values at different levels of a given factor are the same; in other words, the contribution of this factor to the observed result is zero; and (2) the contribution of certain interactions to the observed result is zero. The following sections of this chapter describe how such tests are made for several kinds of models.

6.4 The One-Way Classification

The *one-way analysis of variance* can be applied to the case where there is a single factor at each of several levels. In this case, the model is

$$y_{ij} = y + y_i + \epsilon_{ij}, \quad \text{with } i = 1, 2, \ldots, L,$$
$$\text{and } j = 1, 2, \ldots, n_i, \quad (6.1)$$

where y_{ij} is the jth observed value at the ith level; y is the overall mean of the observations; y_i is the contribution of the ith level of the factor; ϵ_{ij} is the error term; L is the number of levels; and n_i is the number of replications at the ith level. It is assumed that

$$\sum_{i=1}^{L} y_i = 0$$

and that ϵ_{ij} is $N(0, \sigma^2)$ independently of i and j. There are L cells in this case. If the number of replications in each cell is equal, then $n_i = n$ for all i, and the total number of observations $N = nL$. If the number of replications is not the same for each cell, then the total number of observations is

$$N = \sum_{i=1}^{L} n_i.$$

In most cases, the purpose of the analysis is to test the hypothesis that $y_1 = y_2 = \ldots = y_L$; in other words, that the factor has no effect on the observations.

A one-tailed F test is used. The numerator of the F statistic is a measure of variation between cells, and the denominator is a measure of the variation within cells. In other words, the numerator is a measure of the variance of y_i, and the denominator is a measure of σ^2.

The first step of the computational procedure is to compute the means within each cell ($\bar{y}_i$) and the overall mean ($\bar{y}$):

$$\bar{y}_i = \left(\sum_{j=1}^{n_i} y_{ij} \right)/n_i,$$

and

$$\bar{y} = \left(\sum_{i=1}^{L} \sum_{j=1}^{n_i} y_{ij} \right)/N.$$

Next calculate the between-cells mean square, BMS, and the within-group mean square, WMS:

$$BMS = \left[\sum_{i=1}^{L} n_i(\bar{y}_i - \bar{y})^2 \right]/(L-1),$$

and

$$WMS = \left[\sum_{i=1}^{L} \sum_{j=1}^{n_i} (y_{ij} - \bar{y}_i)^2 \right]/(N-L).$$

The test statistic F then is given by $F = BMS/WMS$, with $L-1$ and $N-L$ degrees of freedom.

These are not the most convenient formulae to implement on a desk calculator. However, calculations for a one-way classification are relatively simple, and the formulae given here serve to illustrate the meaning of "between" and "within" variations and to force the user to see the individual terms in these variances. It also is possible to test the hypothesis that y_i takes on different prescribed values for various values of i (however, Σy_i for $i = 1$ to L must equal zero). In this case, the noncentral F distribution is used to test the ratio with

$$noncentrality\ parameter = \left(\sum_{i=1}^{L} n_i y_i^2 \right)/\sigma^2.$$

This test is discussed by Cochran and Cox (1957, pp. 9–10).

As an example of the one-way analysis, consider a test of the hypothesis that post position does not affect the time required for a horse to complete a race. Table 6.1 contains data on the finish times of a horse called Armed Warrior for several races at each of several post positions. The levels of this factor have been grouped in order to get enough observations at each level to permit estimation of the within-group mean square. In this case, $L = 3$, $n_1 = n_3 = 4$, $n_2 = 5$, and $N = 13$. The computations give

$\bar{y}_1 = 8564/4 = 2141.0,$

$\bar{y}_2 = 10819/5 = 2163.8,$

$$\bar{y}_3 = 8628/4 = 2157.0,$$

$$\bar{y} = 28011/13 = 2154.7,$$

$$BMS = [4(-13.7)^2 + 5(9.1)^2 + 4(2.3)^2]/2 = 752.985,$$

$$WMS = [(-11)^2 + 25^2 + 5^2 + (-19)^2 + (8.2)^2 + (-6.8)^2 + (12.2)^2$$
$$+ (35.2)^2 + (-48.8)^2 + (-6)^2 + 20^2 + (-36)^2 + 22^2]/10 = 723.08,$$

and $F = (752.985)/(723.08) = 1.041.$

From a table of critical values for the F test (Table A.4, Appendix A), we find values of $F_{m,n,\alpha}$, where m is the degrees of freedom in the numerator, n is the degrees of freedom in the denominator, and α is the size of the acceptable type I error. In this case, $m = L - 1 = 2$, and $n = N - L = 10$. From the table, we see that $F_{2,10,0.05} = 4.10$, and $F_{2,10,0.10} = 2.92$. With either value of α, the observed value of F is smaller than the critical value. Therefore, the hypothesis that $y_1 = y_2 = y_3 = 0$ is not contradicted by these data, and we may conclude from this test that the finishing times of Armed Warrior are not affected by post position.

This example helps to illustrate why a one-way classification seldom is used in simulation development. We rarely wish to ask whether one factor (and one factor only) affects a dependent variable. As discussed in Chapter 5, post position is only one of several factors that might be included as independent variables in the simulation of a horse race. However, the one-way classification may be useful in answering questions about the effects of a single factor in a real system, through analysis of the results of simulation runs.

A nonparametric one-way analysis of variance, using the rank orders of the observations, is described by Siegel (1956, pp. 184–193).

6.5 The Two-Way Classification

The next most complex model for analysis of variance is the *two-way classification,* which is applicable to study of the effects of two factors on a dependent variable. The model for the two-way classification is

$$y_{ijk} = y + y_i + y_j' + y_{ij} + \epsilon_{ijk}, \quad \text{with } i = 1, 2, \ldots, L_1;$$

$$j = 1, 2, \ldots, L_2; \text{ and } k = 1, 2, \ldots, r. \quad (6.2)$$

TABLE 6.1   Finishing Times As a Function of Post
Position in 13 Races of Armed Warrior

Post Position	Finishing Times (*thirtieths of a second*)				
1, 2, or 3	2,130	2,166	2,146	2,122	
4, 5, or 6	2,172	2,157	2,176	2,199	2,115
7, 8, or 11	2,151	2,177	2,121	2,179	

This model assumes r replications for each cell. (Use of equal numbers of replications in each of the cells improves the robustness of the test, and also makes the computations much easier.) There are L_1 levels of the first factor and L_2 levels of the second factor. The total number of cells is $L_1 L_2$, and $N = L_1 L_2 r$. The term y_i accounts for the effect of the first factor; y_j' accounts for the second factor; and y_{ij} accounts for their interaction. In other words, we now assume that some special contribution to the result may come from the interacting consequences of the ith level of the first factor and the jth level of the second factor. For example, if we were predicting the finish times of a horse race, using the two factors of distance and post position, we might expect a greater effect of the post position for shorter race distances. This effect would be reflected in a set of non-zero values for y_{ij}.

In most cases, the hypotheses to be tested are

(1) that $y_1 = y_2 = \ldots = y_{L_1} = 0$,

(2) that $y_1' = y_2' = \ldots = y_{L_2}' = 0$,

and (3) that $y_{11} = y_{12} = \ldots = y_{1L_2} = y_{21} = y_{22} = \ldots = y_{2L_2}$
$$= \ldots = y_{L_1 L_2} = 0.$$

The computations are performed in the following sequence. (1) Compute the sum of the elements in each cell. That is, compute

$$y_{ij\cdot} = \sum_{k=1}^{r} y_{ijk} \qquad \text{for } i = 1, \ldots, L_1 \text{ and } j = 1, \ldots, L_2.$$

A dot in the subscript replaces a variable over which a sum is to be made. Also compute the sums of the cell totals by factor. That is, compute

$$y_{i\cdot\cdot} = \sum_{j=1}^{L_2} y_{ij\cdot} \qquad \text{for } i = 1, \ldots, L_1,$$

and compute

$$y_{\cdot j\cdot} = \sum_{i=1}^{L_1} y_{ij\cdot} \qquad \text{for } j = 1, \ldots, L_2.$$

(2) Compute the sum, $y_{\ldots}$, and the sum of the squares, SQ, of all the elements. That is, compute

$$y_{\ldots} = \sum_{i=1}^{L_1} y_{i\cdot\cdot} = \sum_{j=1}^{L_2} y_{\cdot j\cdot}.$$

and

$$SQ = \sum_{k=1}^{r} \sum_{j=1}^{L_2} \sum_{i=1}^{L_1} y_{ijk}^2$$

(3) Calculate a correction factor, $C = y_{\ldots}^2 / L_1 L_2 r$. (4) Calculate the sum of squares for the first factor, $SQ1$, and the sum of squares for the second factor, $SQ2$. That is, compute

$$SQ1 = \left(\sum_{i=1}^{L_1} y_{i..}^2 \right) / L_2 r - C,$$

and
$$SQ2 = \left(\sum_{j=1}^{L_2} y_{.j.}^2 \right) / L_1 r - C.$$

(5) Calculate the main effects. That is, compute the mean square effect for the first factor, $MSQ1 = SQ1/(L_1 - 1)$, and compute the mean square effect for the second factor, $MSQ2 = SQ2/(L_2 - 1)$. (6) Calculate the total sum of squares, $TSQ = SQ - C$, and calculate the subtotal sum of squares,

$$SSQ = \left(\sum_{j=1}^{L_2} \sum_{i=1}^{L_1} y_{ij.}^2 \right) / r - C.$$

(7) Calculate the estimate of error, also called the within-cells mean square,

$$MWSQ = (TSQ - SSQ)/L_1 L_2 (r - 1).$$

(8) Calculate the sum of squares of interaction, $ISQ = SSQ - SQ1 - SQ2$, and calculate the mean square for interaction, $MISQ = ISQ/[(L_1 - 1)(L_2 - 1)]$.

These calculations are summarized in the analysis-of-variance table of Table 6.2, and the results of the calculations should be summarized in a similar table. The three hypotheses are tested with the following F ratios: (1) to test for the first effect, $F = MSQ1/MWSQ$; (2) to test for the second effect, $F = MSQ2/MWSQ$; and (3) to test for interaction, $F = MISQ/MWSQ$. Each test statistic is F distributed with degrees of freedom as indicated for the numerator and denominator in Table 6.2. For example, the test statistic for interaction is F distributed with $(L_1 - 1)(L_2 - 1)$ degrees of freedom for the numerator and with $L_1 L_2 (r - 1)$ degrees of freedom for the denominator.

The following example illustrates these calculations. Table 6.3 summarizes data on the percentage of the daily total of visitors that entered a district office

TABLE 6.2   Analysis-of-Variance Table for Two-Way Classification

Factor	Sum of Squares	Degrees of Freedom	Mean Square
First main	$SQ1 = \left(\sum_{i=1}^{L_1} y_{i..}^2 \right)/L_2 r - C$	$L_1 - 1$	$MSQ1 = SQ1/(L_1 - 1)$
Second main	$SQ2 = \left(\sum_{j=1}^{L_2} y_{.j.}^2 \right)/L_1 r - C$	$L_2 - 1$	$MSQ2 = SQ2/(L_2 - 1)$
Interaction	$ISQ = SSQ - SQ1 - SQ2$	$(L_1 - 1)(L_2 - 1)$	$MISQ = ISQ/[(L_1 - 1)(L_2 - 1)]$
Subtotals	$SSQ = \left(\sum_{j=1}^{L_2} \sum_{i=1}^{L_1} y_{ij.}^2 \right)/r - C$	$L_1 L_2 - 1$	—
Within-cells	$WSQ = TSQ - SSQ$	$L_1 L_2 (r - 1)$	$MWSQ = WSQ/L_1 L_2 (r - 1)$
Total	$TSQ = SQ - C$	$L_1 L_2 r - 1$	—

during each of eight one-hour periods. These data are averages over a two-week period for each of eleven offices in each of three classes: B, C, and D. The objective of the analysis of variance is to determine whether (1) arrival patterns are affected by the time of day, (2) arrival patterns differ according to the class of office, and (3) there is an interaction effect between class of office and time of day. In most cases, percentage data (particularly those in the range from 0 to 25 percent) are non-normally distributed. However, a test of these data using Program B.2 (Appendix B) indicated that the assumption of normality is tenable.

TABLE 6.3   Percentage of Total Daily Arrivals by Hour of Day and Class of Office*

| Hour | Percentage of Total Daily Arrivals in Given Hour and Given Class of Office | | |
	Class B Offices	Class C Offices	Class D Offices
9 to 10 AM	12.3, 12.8, 9.8, 12.7 13.2, 12.7, 13.3, 14.3 12.9, 14.7, 10.1	12.2, 11.5, 11.4, 10.8 14.5, 13.5, 11.9, 9.7 14.7, 11.0, 8.7	7.0, 8.1, 14.2, 12.1 17.2, 10.3, 12.2, 12.8 15.6, 13.5, 12.7
10 to 11 AM	16.5, 12.1, 14.1, 15.0 13.0, 17.4, 17.8, 15.0 16.3, 15.3, 14.2	15.7, 16.9, 13.7, 16.0 19.6, 16.2, 13.3, 15.0 20.7, 17.2, 14.2	16.2, 13.7, 15.2, 20.0 18.3, 13.6, 15.8, 22.1 16.2, 14.3, 15.4
11 AM to noon	12.3, 14.5, 14.2, 14.5 13.5, 15.4, 14.9, 11.4 12.1, 13.9, 11.6	15.2, 13.9, 16.0, 16.8 12.4, 12.9, 14.0, 12.7 17.1, 13.7, 13.6	14.1, 9.9, 13.9, 11.8 13.7, 16.0, 13.6, 12.4 12.3, 15.2, 14.8
noon to 1 PM	12.3, 12.9, 10.6, 11.4 11.1, 10.7, 10.9, 12.7 9.6, 9.4, 9.9	8.3, 8.3, 8.1, 11.3 10.3, 10.1, 12.3, 11.2 8.1, 10.8, 11.2	10.3, 4.3, 7.0, 9.2 11.1, 11.4, 13.6, 12.1 8.6, 8.1, 11.4
1 to 2 PM	13.3, 13.9, 13.0, 14.2 12.8, 11.6, 11.5, 12.1 12.3, 12.0, 14.7	16.0, 14.6, 12.4, 12.7 15.8, 14.3, 14.4, 16.6 13.4, 12.4, 14.1	13.4, 13.0, 14.9, 13.3 17.1, 14.8, 16.3, 12.8 14.5, 8.1, 16.4
2 to 3 PM	12.2, 15.2, 14.1, 12.2 13.2, 11.8, 11.9, 11.8 12.1, 13.0, 11.1	16.6, 13.4, 15.1, 12.6 14.3, 13.1, 16.1, 15.3 11.2, 11.3, 14.3	14.6, 22.0, 14.8, 13.2 13.7, 13.2, 9.5, 10.9 16.9, 14.3, 11.6
3 to 4 PM	7.8, 12.7, 9.0, 9.4 10.0, 10.3, 9.3, 8.3 8.1, 13.8, 11.2	10.4, 9.8, 9.4, 8.9 6.9, 9.3, 9.8, 10.0 9.3, 8.1, 12.6	11.7, 12.1, 11.4, 11.5 10.4, 10.0, 9.5, 6.8 7.8, 13.4, 7.8
4 to 5 PM	9.0, 2.0, 5.1, 6.8 5.4, 8.0, 4.3, 4.6 7.4, 4.3, 5.7	5.4, 3.2, 6.9, 4.0 4.7, 6.2, 4.4, 6.1 2.1, 5.3, 6.3	6.2, 5.7, 3.0, 6.7 6.1, 3.2, 5.5, 2.5 5.5, 6.7, 3.8

*Data given are for 33 social security district offices (11 offices of each class) averaged over a two-week period during 1967.

In this case, $r = 11$, $L_1 = 8$, and $L_2 = 3$. Table 6.4 summarizes the results of the calculations of the sums y_{ij}. $y_{i..}$ $y_{.j}$ and $y...$ The results of other intermediate calculations are $SQ = (12.3)^2 + (12.8)^2 + (9.8)^2 + (12.7)^2 + \ldots + (2.5)^2 + (5.5)^2 + (6.7)^2 + (3.8)^2 = 40,443.29$, and $C = (3121.5)^2/264 = 36,908.19$. The sums of squares, degrees of freedom, and mean squares are summarized in Table 6.5. These values are calculated according to the formulae in Table 6.2. As an illustration, the sum of squares for class of office was calculated by $[(1027.8)^2 + (1045.8)^2 + (1047.9)^2]/88 - 36,908.19 = 2.66$. The F ratios are: F for time of day $= 94.8$; F for class of office < 1.0; and F for interaction $= 1.15$. From the critical values in Table A.4 (Appendix A), we see that the only significant effect is time of day.

TABLE 6.4   Sums for Each Cell and for Main Factors in Analysis of Variance of Data in Table 6.3

Time	Class of Office			Sums for Time Over Class
	B	C	D	
9–10	138.8	129.9	135.7	404.4
10–11	166.7	178.5	180.8	526.0
11–12	148.3	158.3	147.7	454.3
12–1	121.5	110.0	107.1	338.6
1–2	141.4	156.7	154.6	452.7
2–3	138.6	153.3	154.7	446.6
3–4	109.9	104.5	112.4	326.8
4–5	62.6	54.6	54.9	172.1
Sums for Class Over Time	1027.8	1045.8	1047.9	3121.5

TABLE 6.5   Summary of Results of Analysis-of-Variance Calculations on Data of Table 6.3

Factor	Sum of Squares	Degrees of Freedom	Mean Square
Time of day	2,548.15	7	364.02
Class of office	2.66	2	1.33
Interaction	62.12	14	4.44
Subtotal	2,612.93	23	—
Within-cells	922.17	240	3.84
Total	3,535.10	263	—

In Section 4.8, the effect of time of day on arrivals was tested in terms of runs in the interarrival times. From that test, we concluded that time of day does not affect the arrival pattern. The results of the analysis of variance rather firmly contradict the earlier conclusion. Although the two tests were conducted with different sets of data, in this case it does appear that the analysis of variance is more sensitive than the runs test to patterns in the arrivals. In Part Five, we do in fact simulate arrivals at a district office using different patterns at different times of the day.

6.6 2^n Designs

In computer simulation, the 2^n design is the most useful of the analysis-of-variance designs. This design permits a study of the effects of n factors at each of two different levels. There are 2^n cells in this design; if r replications are made for each cell, the total number of observations, $N = r2^n$. A little calculation will show that the required number of observations becomes quite large for values of n above a half-dozen or so. If there is no need to test for some of the interactions, larger values of n may be accommodated in a *fractional design,* one that does not require observations at all combinations of levels and factors. Such fractional designs are said to *confound* the effects of the interactions with the effects of the factors. The effects of the factors themselves are called the *main effects.* Cochran and Cox (1957, pp. 183–192) discuss confounded 2^n designs.

The levels of each factor usually are chosen so as to represent the maximal observed effect of that factor. For example, the two levels chosen for post position as a factor probably would be positions of 1, 2, or 3 for one level and 8, 9, or 10 for the other.

The 2^n design often is used for a *screening* test, which is a first step in the study of variables that might affect the result. The 2^n design is appropriate for screening purposes, because it is a minimum design that includes n factors. In simulation development, the 2^n-design screening test often is applied to a list of all the potential independent variables. Observations are obtained for each of two extreme levels of each variable. The results of the screening test help to determine which variables to retain for further data collection and function testing. If there are many potential independent variables, a fractional design is used. The next step in study of the variables selected by the screening test might be a regression or a more dense analysis-of-variance design, involving several levels of each factor.

In using a 2^n design to screen variables, the user primarily wishes to test the statistical significance of the main effects. However, the mean squares for the main effects also may be used as an estimate of the magnitude of these effects. The user may decide either to screen out those variables that do not give statistically significant F ratios or to screen out those variables that do not have a practically significant magnitude of mean square. The latter approach may be preferable in simulation development if it is possible to translate the application specifications for the simulation into a measure of the practical significance of an effect. This problem is discussed in a somewhat different context in Section 6.8.

The calculations involved in analysis of a 2^n design can become quite cumbersome, and the use of a computer is recommended. Ralston and Wilf (1960, pp. 221–230) describe a general analysis-of-variance computational algorithm. the FORTRAN scientific subroutine package for the IBM System/360 and 370 computers uses three programs (labeled AVDAT, AVCAL, and MEANQ) to carry out an analysis of variance.

6.7 The Analysis of Variance and Validity

Several methods of determining the validity of a simulation are discussed in Section 2.9. The analysis of variance often is a useful tool in implementing such checks on validity.

Consider, for example, the use of expert opinion. An expert may state that he would expect a particular factor to become significant at approximately certain levels. Two analysis-of-variance designs—one that incorporates levels within the range that the expert expects will be significant, and one that does not—can be used to provide estimates of the effects on the result. If the expert's estimates are verified, the developer gains confidence in the validity of his model. If the estimates are not verified, further study of the model will be needed. A sensitivity analysis (Section 6.8) might be used for this further study.

Analysis of variance also may be applied to the analysis of historical data in order to determine which factors have affected the result in the real system, thus helping to test the validity of the simulation. Of course, the data used in this test of validity should not be the same data that were used in developing the models, because the simulation-development procedures ensure that the simulation will mimic the behavior of these data. Only with new historical data can an analysis of variance give a meaningful test of the validity of the simulation.

6.8 Sensitivity Analysis

A *sensitivity analysis* is useful in screening variables, in establishing values for parameters, and in validating the simulation. In this analysis, the simulation is run with several different levels of a given factor, in order to determine how sensitive the result is to fluctuations in this factor. Clearly, this is a kind of analysis of variance. The user of a sensitivity analysis may be more interested in measures of the main effects and their magnitudes than in tests of the significance of these effects.

A 3^n design often is used for a sensitivity analysis. Three levels are used for each factor: an expected or middle level, a high level, and a low level. Cochran and Cox (1957, pp. 164–175, 193–203) discuss 3^2 and 3^3 designs.

A common problem in simulation development involves the decision of whether to represent a particular variable by a constant value or to use a random number generator to assign a value from a distribution of possible values; in other words, whether to represent the variable deterministically or stochastically. This problem is best solved with the help of a sensitivity analysis rather than a 2^n design. The middle level for the sensitivity analysis is the constant value that would be assigned for the variable if it is treated deterministically. Values from the upper and lower tails of the distribution are used as the other two levels of the factor. Commonly, the two values are chosen to encompass about 90 or 95 percent of the possible values for the stochastic variable. More precisely, if $F(x)$ is the distribution function and m is the middle value, then the upper and lower values are chosen as $m + a$ and $m - a$, where $F(m + a) - F(m - a)$ equals about 0.90 or 0.95. If a more sensitive test is desired, some additional levels may be added to the design.

In much the same way, a sensitivity analysis may be used to establish validity. In this case, the effects of high, low, and middle levels are somehow anticipated (from historical data, expert opinion, or direct observation of the system) and a set of simulation runs is tested to verify the expectations.

An example of a sensitivity analysis may help to illustrate its use. In the model of the operation of a social security district office, service times for conducting claims interviews were found to have a *gamma* distribution. The *gamma* density is not discussed in Chapter 3, but this distribution is used in Part Five. The density function is $f(x) = [\lambda/\Gamma(r)]/(\lambda x)^{r-1} e^{-\lambda x}$, where λ and r are parameters. Wadsworth and Bryan (1960, pp. 88–100) define and discuss this distribution. A sensitivity analysis was used to determine whether these service times should indeed be generated by sampling from a *gamma* distribution, or whether the use of a constant (mean) service time to conduct an interview would be adequate. Here we note only that a 3^n design was used in the analysis.

6.9 Error Reduction: Analysis of Covariance

If the error term ϵ is made to have smaller and smaller variance, the analysis of variance can detect smaller and smaller effects of a factor. The variance of the error term often is reduced by identifying additional factors. In simulation development, independent variables may be added to the model in order to permit more precise predictions of results. In Section 5.8 we mention the example of the horse Armed Warrior that was likely either to win by 40 lengths or to lose by 60 lengths because the variance of ϵ was very large.

We failed to identify additional variables for Armed Warrior, but such variables can be found in many systems. Of special interest is the identification of variables that can be related functionally to the result. This functional relation then can be included in the analysis-of-variance model. Exogenous variables often are handled in this fashion. The analysis of covariance is applied to adjust the results to a constant level of the covariant variables; the analysis of variance then is applied to the adjusted results, thereby minimizing the error term.

Another example may be drawn from the simulation of the horse race. When the finishing time of a horse was related to various independent variables, the distance of the race always turned out to be the most important independent variable. As a result, the fit could be improved only slightly by adding other independent variables to the MLR (see Table 5.9, for example). Data more sensitive to these other variables could be obtained by first using a covariant relation between finishing time and distance to correct all finishing times to a constant distance. These corrected finishing times then could be used as the dependent variable in studying the effects of the other independent variables. (This essentially is what was done in Problem 5.4. First a linear relation was fitted between finishing time and distance. Then the residuals of this linear relation were related to other independent variables. Because the residuals actually are equal to the corrected finish times minus a constant, the solution of Problem 5.4 actually involved an analysis of covariance.)

6.10 Concluding Remarks

This chapter serves more as a guide to the literature on experimental design and the analysis of variance than as a self-contained description of the techniques. Numerical examples in Part Five can serve to illustrate and enhance the discussion in this chapter. Our major purpose in this chapter is to point out that the techniques of the analysis of variance are relevant to simulation development. Although many relevant terms are defined and the simplest designs are described in this chapter, it is clear that a more extensive repertoire of designs will be needed, particularly if many factors are to be considered. The fractional factorial designs mentioned in Section 6.5 can be helpful. More sophisticated and complicated fractional designs can permit estimation and testing of the main effects confounded with interactions, using a minimum of observations. Among these designs discussed by Cochran and Cox (1957) are randomized blocks (pp. 106–117), latin squares (pp. 117–127), cross-over designs (pp. 127–142), incomplete blocks (pp. 376–395), lattice designs (pp. 396–438), balanced and partially balanced incomplete block designs (pp. 439–463), and incomplete latin squares (pp. 507–544).

Both the analysis of variance and regression techniques are used in studying the relation between a dependent variable ("the result") and a set of independent variables. Regression techniques are appropriate when explicit functional relations between the dependent and independent variables are required. If the only problem is to find out whether or not certain variables can be said to affect the result, the analysis of variance is more appropriate. Also, nominal variables (that is, variables of classification such as binomial variables) can be handled in a straightforward manner in the analysis of variance. In dealing with such variables in regressions, we must fit separate functions for each level of the variable and then must determine whether these functions really are distinct from one another. If they are distinct, then more than one regression must be used in the model; if they are not, then this nominal variable is ignored in refitting the regression.

6.11 Supplementary Reading

The book by Cochran and Cox (1957) probably is the best source for a variety of designs for use in developing, testing, and applying a simulation. Scheffe (1959) provides one of the most rigorous and mathematically sophisticated treatments available of the analysis of variance. Dixon and Massey (1969) give an unusually lucid discussion of the analysis of variance, describe computations for one-way and two-way classifications with examples, and give an example of the calculations in a two-way classification without replication.

A paper by Sakai and Nagao (1969) provides a very interesting example of a simulation and its application to traffic control problems. This simulation undoubtedly involved several structured sequences of runs similar to the analysis of variance, but the authors do not make explicit use of the analysis of variance. There is some indication either that too many runs were made or that the study could have been improved by making explicit use of the analysis of variance.

Howell (1969) gives a FORTRAN program to calculate the main effects and interactions in a factorial design. He also suggests ways to modify the algorithm to make it suitable for hand calculation.

A volume edited by Naylor (1969b) contains papers presented at a symposium (Duke University, October 1968) on the design of computer simulation experiments. It includes four papers on experimental design, five on methodology for data analysis, seven on applications, and eight on a variety of methodological problems ranging from validation and programming languages to a series of papers on Monte Carlo techniques. This book contains enough useful material to justify its purchase by anyone seriously interested in simulation.

PROBLEMS

6.1   Table 6.6 summarizes data on the times required to complete interviews for submission of disability claims in each of four different social security district offices. Test the hypothesis that there is no difference among these offices in the average length of their disability interviews.

6.2   Write a computer program—in any language that can be implemented on the computer to which you have access—to carry out a two-way analysis of variance with equal replication (see Section 6.5). Try to write a completely general program that will treat any number of levels of each factor and any number of replications. If you are successful, apply this program to the solution of Problems 6.3 through 6.7. If you are forced to simplify the program by restricting its generality, then write it so that it can deal with ten levels of one factor, five levels of the other, and either one or two replications. This simplified program can be used in solving Problems 6.5 through 6.7.

6.3   Table 6.7 summarizes estimated times required to perform each of seven operations on each of three different computers. Assuming that there is no interaction between computer and operation, carry out a two-way analysis of variance to test the hypothesis that there are no differences among these times due either to computer or to operation.

TABLE 6.6   Disability Claim Interview Times for Four District Offices*

Office Number	Interview Times (*minutes*)
218	25, 27, 43, 43, 49, 62, 67, 69, 70, 71
080	14, 25, 42, 45, 47
658	20, 36, 40, 41, 44, 48, 48, 76, 77, 107
285	19, 20, 31, 31, 32, 39, 49, 56, 56, 65, 72, 74, 101, 103

*Times required to complete interviews for disability claims at each of the four offices during a two-week period in 1967.

TABLE 6.7   Estimated Times Required for Various Operations on Three Computers

Operation	Estimated Time (*microseconds*) for Operation on		
	Computer A	Computer B	Computer C
Load/store	3.0	2.4	3.0
Fixed point add	3.1	2.4	3.0
Fixed point multiply	11.1	7.6	17.7
Fixed point divide	16.5	16.2	29.8
Floating point add	7.0	8.1	5.3
Floating point multiply	10.9	11.4	15.6
Floating point divide	14.7	17.1	24.7

6.4 Table 6.8 contains data on percentage of arrivals in district offices by hour of the day for eleven class-A social security district offices. Combine these data with those in Table 6.3 and recompute the analysis of variance for all the data. Tabulate the results of the calculations as in Table 6.5. Are the conclusions any different than those for the smaller set of data?

6.5 Table 6.9 summarizes the percentages of the total number of jobs submitted in each hour during each of five days at a university computer center by day of the week. Assuming that there is no interaction between day and time, carry out a two-way analysis of variation to test the factors of day of of the week and time of the day.

TABLE 6.8 Percentages of Total Daily Arrivals by Hour of Day at Class-A Offices*

Time of Day	Percentage of Daily Arrivals at Each Office During Time Interval
9 to 10 AM	13.9, 12.3, 12.9, 12.2, 14.3, 17.9, 13.9, 11.3, 12.7, 14.4, 12.8
10 to 11 AM	15.0, 17.5, 14.8, 15.9, 14.1, 15.8, 14.4, 18.8, 16.8, 15.5, 15.6
11 AM to noon	15.0, 13.1, 11.4, 14.2, 14.7, 13.3, 12.2, 15.1, 12.9, 13.6, 13.8
noon to 1 PM	9.3, 11.6, 10.4, 9.4, 12.4, 10.4, 11.0, 8.9, 10.9, 13.9, 10.9
1 to 2 PM	13.9, 15.8, 15.1, 13.7, 10.6, 14.9, 12.1, 12.7, 12.4, 12.8, 12.0
2 to 3 PM	12.6, 12.2, 10.9, 12.2, 10.9, 13.6, 10.2, 12.5, 11.2, 10.4, 11.6
3 to 4 PM	11.3, 12.1, 9.7, 10.3, 9.3, 7.8, 9.9, 10.0, 8.4, 9.0, 10.3
4 to 5 PM	3.6, 4.1, 5.6, 5.2, 6.7, 3.4, 4.0, 5.1, 4.7, 4.6, 3.7

*Data for eleven class-A social security district offices during a two-week period in 1967.

TABLE 6.9 Percentage of Total Daily Job Arrivals by Hour of Day and Day of Week*

Hour of Day	Percentage of Total Daily Job Arrivals Submitted in Given Hour on				
	Monday	Tuesday	Wednesday	Thursday	Friday
9–10 AM	4.1	8.6	6.2	7.3	2.0
10–11 AM	9.6	6.9	14.4	8.2	15.7
11 AM– noon	12.3	6.9	7.2	10.0	3.9
noon–1 PM	11.0	6.9	7.2	8.2	7.8
1–2 PM	21.9	17.2	20.6	14.5	19.6
2–3 PM	12.3	12.1	11.3	17.3	7.8
3–4 PM	4.1	19.0	11.3	14.5	11.8
4–5 PM	11.0	6.9	10.3	11.8	11.8
5–6 PM	8.2	12.1	6.2	8.2	11.8
6–7 PM	5.5	3.4	5.2	0.0	7.8

*At a university computer center during a week in April 1971.

6.6   Table 6.10 summarizes the numbers of jobs submitted to a university computer center by hour of the day and by day of the week. (The data of Table 6.9 were computed from these data.) (a) Assuming no interaction, carry out a two-way analysis of variance to test the factors of day of the week and hour of the day. (b) Compare this result with the result obtained in Problem 6.5 and give reasons for the differences.

6.7   Table 6.11 summarizes the numbers of jobs submitted at the same university computer center (see Problem 6.6) in a different week. (a) Assuming no interaction, carry out a two-way analysis of variance to test the factors of day of the week and hour of the day. (b) Combine the data from Tables 6.10 and 6.11 by adding together the numbers in corresponding cells. Again assuming no interaction, carry out a two-way analysis of the combined data to test the factors of day of the week and hour of the day. (c) Combine the data from Tables 6.10 and 6.11 by treating the two sets of data as two replications. Again assuming no interaction, carry out a two-way analysis of these combined data with two replications per cell. Compare and discuss the results of (b) and (c).

6.8   Either regression techniques or the analysis of variance techniques can be applied in dealing with a dependent and several independent variables. In the first case, each independent variable is treated as a variable in a functional relation, the function is fitted by least squares, and the regression analysis is carried out. In the second case, each independent variable

TABLE 6.10   Number of Job Arrivals by Hour of Day and Day of Week*

Hour of Day	Number of Jobs Submitted in Given Hour on				
	Monday	Tuesday	Wednesday	Thursday	Friday
9–10 AM	3	5	6	8	1
10–11 AM	7	4	14	9	8
11 AM– noon	9	4	7	11	2
noon–1 PM	8	4	7	9	4
1–2 PM	16	10	20	16	10
2–3 PM	9	7	11	19	4
3–4 PM	3	11	11	16	6
4–5 PM	8	4	10	13	6
5–6 PM	6	7	6	9	6
6–7 PM	4	2	5	0	4

*At the same university computer center as that in Table 6.9 during the same week in April 1971.

is treated as a factor, observations are obtained of the dependent variable at several levels of each factor, and the analysis of variance is carried out. In some cases, however, regression techniques cannot be applied because the independent variable is a variable of classification, not a measurement. For example, the presence or absence of blinders on a horse might affect its performance in a race, but this binomial variable cannot be treated as an independent variable in an MLR. In such cases, the analysis of variance is used first in order to determine if this factor has a statistically significant effect on the dependent variable. If it does, separate models must be developed for each level of the factor. (a) List as many independent variables as you can that might affect the performance of a horse in a race. Which of these can be included in a regression, and which cannot? (b) Design an analytical procedure using both the analysis of variance and regression (and perhaps the analysis of covariance) that will produce a model for the performance of a horse in a race. (c) Assume that you already have developed a simulation that can predict the performance of a horse in a race under given conditions (subject, of course, to stochastic fluctuation). Design a series of runs of this simulation that will help you to determine how to bet on a particular race.

6.9 Design a series of runs of the traffic simulator described by Sakai and Nagao (1969) that would help to answer the questions posed in that study.

TABLE 6.11 Number of Job Arrivals by Hour of Day and Day of Week During Another Week*

Hour of Day	Number of Jobs Submitted in Given Hour on				
	Monday	Tuesday	Wednesday	Thursday	Friday
9–10 AM	4	4	6	2	8
10–11 AM	0	6	7	3	7
11 AM–noon	3	5	9	6	8
noon–1 PM	8	4	9	3	6
1–2 PM	2	3	6	5	13
2–3 PM	17	12	10	7	16
3–4 PM	11	11	10	6	5
4–5 PM	9	15	10	6	8
5–6 PM	2	6	12	2	8
6–7 PM	2	3	3	0	1

*At the same university computer center as that in Table 6.10, but during a week in May 1971.

Part Three

RANDOM NUMBER GENERATION

Random numbers are used to introduce the necessary stochastic behavior in computer simulations. They also are used in other contexts to solve complicated numerical and statistical problems, to simulate games of chance on the computer, and to generate test data for checking algorithms. Because of their widespread use, they have been studied extensively by computer scientists. In this book, however, we discuss the generation and use of random numbers only insofar as it is relevant to simulation development and application.

Random numbers are used in simulations to introduce any one of a wide variety of stochastic patterns, ranging from standard distributions, such as the uniform and the normal, to empirical distributions defined only by a set of coordinates on the density or distribution function. In almost every case, uniformly distributed random numbers are generated first, and the distribution then is modified in an appropriate way. Accordingly, the first chapter of this section discusses the generation of uniformly distributed numbers, and the second chapter discusses the generation of other distributions. Appendix B.5 lists several computer programs that can be used to generate random numbers; it also discusses random numbers from a somewhat different point of view than that in these chapters. The reader with a special interest in this subject might well treat Appendix B.5 as if it were a third chapter in Part Three.

CHAPTER 7   Generating Uniformly
Distributed Numbers

CHAPTER 8   Generating Random Numbers
with Nonuniform Distributions

7

Generating Uniformly Distributed Numbers

7.1 INTRODUCTION   Almost every random number generator used for simulations utilizes a completely determined calculation, based on a set of unique and rigid rules, to generate a sequence of numbers. Given the same starting conditions, the generator always will produce the same sequence of numbers. The appropriate random behavior is ensured by designing the calculating procedure so that sets (very large sets) of numbers so generated will pass all appropriate tests for randomness. Obviously, it becomes very important to check the procedure used to generate random numbers before making use of these numbers in a simulation, in order to be sure that the numbers are validly random according to the criteria appropriate for the application. This is not a trivial point. It is

135

insufficient to assume that, because the particular random number generator is widely used, it must be a good one. Many random number generators in current use are not very good ones.

The sets of random numbers generated by a computer are called *pseudorandom numbers*, because they are obtained from strictly determined calculations but meet the appropriate tests for random properties. There are some procedures that generate true random numbers rather than pseudorandom numbers. For example, the low-order digits on a microsecond clock have been used to generate random numbers. Sequences of such numbers are not reproducible; this can be a disadvantage in simulation applications.

It is not easy to develop a procedure for generating pseudorandom numbers. Most procedures are iterative; that is, they generate the next number from the preceding one(s), and thus they will repeat the sequence of numbers after they return to an earlier value. The number of numbers that the process generates before restarting the sequence is called the *length*, or the *period*, of the generator. Obviously, it is desirable to make this period as great as possible. In order to save storage space and search time, it also is desirable to generate the numbers with a calculating procedure that relies on a few preceding values, rather than to read the numbers from a table previously calculated and stored in the computer.

The first random-number-generating procedure for a digital computer was proposed in 1946 by J. von Neumann. This *mid-square method* was found by Forsyth (1951) and others to be of limited usefulness. We briefly describe the method here, chiefly because of its historical interest.

The mid-square method uses as the next random number the middle digits of the square of the preceding random number. For example, suppose that we wish to generate four-digit numbers. (Usually, random numbers are generated within the range between 0 and 1; in this case, the random number itself is obtained by placing a decimal point in front of the first digit.) Suppose that the preceding number in the sequence (or the starting number) is 3,187. Computing $(3,187)^2 = 10,156,969$ and taking the middle four digits of this result, the next random number is found to be 1,569 (or 0.1569). Because $(1569)^2 = 2,461,761$, the next number in the sequence is 4,617 (or 0.4617). The shortcoming of this procedure is that most sequences generated by it tend to have a very short period. Of the sequences generated in this way that do have sufficiently long periods, many do not pass the statistical tests for randomness discussed in the next section. The congruential method, first proposed by Lehmer in 1948, has become the most widely used method for generating pseudorandom numbers (see Lehmer 1959). Before discussing this method, we discuss in the next section a few tests of the randomness of number sequences.

7.2 Testing Sequences of Random Numbers

A useful random number generator should be very fast, and it should generate a sequence of numbers that have a uniform distribution — in other words, each number should be equally likely to appear at any point in the sequence. The second criterion can be taken as a definition of *randomness*. It is relatively easy to construct fast generators. However, the second criterion cannot be met with sequences of pseudorandom numbers; because each number is strictly determined by the preceding numbers in the sequence, there certainly is not an equal probability that any possible number will appear at a given point in the sequence. However, the generator may be acceptable if the sets of numbers in the sequence that it generates can pass certain reasonable statistical tests, based upon the properties of sequences of truly random numbers.

In this section, we list a few of the tests that have been applied to sequences of numbers uniformly distributed over the range from 0 to 1. Similar tests can be developed for sequences with other distributions. Several tests are discussed with examples in Chapter 4; here we merely list these tests and indicate how they can be applied to testing sequences of random numbers.

The Kolmogorov-Smirnov goodness-of-fit test (Section 4.7) can be applied to the overall distribution of the sequence; this application is called the *frequency*, or *equidistribution, test*. This test compares the distribution of the set of numbers to a theoretical distribution — in this case, to the standard uniform distribution. The unit interval is divided into a number of subintervals, and the cumulative relative frequency of the sequence of pseudorandom numbers is calculated up to the endpoint of each subinterval. If the ith endpoint is denoted by x_i and the cumulative relative frequency to this endpoint is denoted by f_i, because $F(x) = x$, all that is required for this test is to find the maximal value of the difference $|f_i - x_i|$.

A second test (called the *serial test*) applies the *chi* square test (Section 4.10) to pairs of successive numbers. The computer must use a finite number of digits to represent the random number; thus, only a finite number of distinct numbers can be generated. For example, if the random number is represented by eight bits, then only $2^8 = 256$ distinct numbers can be represented. If d distinct numbers can be represented, then there are d^2 possible pairs of successive numbers. For a random sequence, the theoretical relative frequency of each possible pair in the sequence should be $1/d^2$. With this expected frequency, a *chi* square value can be calculated for each of the d^2 possible combinations, and these values then can be added to obtain the test statistic. This approach can be extended to sets of three, four, or more successive numbers. However, the number of possible combinations can become quite large, particularly if d is fairly large. In order to generate n independent pairs for the test data, $2n$ random numbers must be generated. (From the sequence, the first and second numbers are paired, then the third and fourth numbers, the fifth and sixth numbers, and so on.) For a valid *chi* square test, n must be at least $5d^2$, and even larger values of n are preferable.

In a more general test design, certain categories of combinations of r numbers are defined, the theoretical frequency is estimated for each category, and a *chi* square test is used to determine if the random number sequence conforms to the expectations. A popular test (called the *poker test*) based on this approach takes $r = 5$ and uses as categories the most likely kinds of poker hands.

Another test, called the *permutation test,* also is based on sets of r numbers. The entire sequence is divided into distinct sets, each with r elements. A frequency is obtained for each possible permutation of the r elements, and a *chi* square test is used to compare these frequencies to theoretical expectations.

The *runs test* (Section 4.8) can be applied directly to the sequence of random numbers. Experience with tests of random number sequences indicates that the runs test is probably the most discriminating of the tests listed here—that is, this test "fails" more sequences than do other tests. The poker test is probably the second most discriminating, and the serial and frequency tests are probably the least discriminating. Almost any carefully designed generation procedure will produce sequences that pass the serial and frequency tests.

The *spectral test* described by Knuth (1969, pp. 82–96) is characterized by him as the most discriminating test known; this test originally was introduced by Coveyou and MacPherson (1969). The spectral test measures the independence of adjacent sets of n numbers. Knuth's description of the test includes a description of an algorithm to implement it.

Two other tests—the D^2, or distance, test and the gap test—have proven particularly useful in testing sets of random numbers. Because these tests were not discussed in Chapter 4, we describe them in some detail here.

In the *distance* (D^2) test, successive pairs of random numbers are regarded as coordinates for points in the unit square. For example, consider the sequence of random numbers: r_1, r_2, r_3, and r_4. These may be regarded as coordinates for the two points (r_1, r_2) and (r_3, r_4) in the (x, y) plane. The square of the distance between these two points is given by $D^2 = (r_1 - r_3)^2 + (r_2 - r_4)^2$. If the points are distributed randomly in the unit square, then the probability that the observed value of D^2 is less than or equal to x is given by the following expression (see Wilson 1891, p. 390):

$$F(x) = \begin{cases} \pi x - \dfrac{8}{3}x^{3/2} + \dfrac{x^2}{2}, & \text{for } x \leq 1.0, \text{ and} \\[2em] \dfrac{1}{3} + (\pi - 2)x + 4(x - 1)^{1/2} + \dfrac{8}{3}(x - 1)^{3/2} - \dfrac{x^2}{2} \\[1.5em] \quad - 4x \operatorname{arcsec} \sqrt{x}, & \text{for } 1.0 \leq x \leq 2.0. \end{cases} \tag{7.1}$$

A few values of the probability corresponding to selected values of x are $F(0.0)$ = 0.0; $F(0.25) = 0.483$; $F(0.50) = 0.753$; $F(0.75) = 0.905$; $F(1.0) = 0.975$; $F(1.50)$ = 0.999; and $F(2.0) = 1.0$. Jaffray and Gruenberger (1965) give a more extensive discussion of the calculation of these probabilities; they also discuss the poker and gap tests. Using these probabilities, theoretical frequencies can be calculated for values of D^2 in prescribed intervals, and a *chi* square test then can be made.

The *gap test* is based upon the length of the "gap" (measured in number of occurrences of an event) between the occurrence of a particular outcome and the next occurrence of that same outcome. This approach may be applied to sequences of random numbers in either of two ways. In the first approach, a subinterval (α to β) of the unit interval is defined, with $0 < \alpha < \beta < 1$. The length of the gap is the number of numbers in the sequence between occurrences of numbers that lie within the subinterval. For example, suppose $\alpha = 0.25$ and $\beta = 0.41$, and the following sequence of random numbers is to be tested: 0.3187, 0.1569, 0.4617, 0.3166, 0.0235, 0.0552, 0.3047, 0.2842, 0.0769, 0.5913, 0.9635, 0.8332, 0.4222, 0.8252, 0.0955, 0.9120, 0.1744, 0.0415, 0.1722, 0.9652, 0.1611, 0.5953, 0.4382, 0.2019, 0.0763, 0.5821, 0.8840, 0.1456, 0.1199, 0.4376, 0.1493, 0.2290, 0.2441, 0.9584, 0.8530, 0.7609, 0.8968, 0.4250, 0.0625, 0.3906.

In this case, the first and fourth numbers fall within the subinterval, so the first gap is of length 2. The next gap also is of length 2 (from the fourth to the seventh number), the next of length 0, and the next of length 31. Because the probability that a number drawn from a standard uniform density lies between α and β is equal to $\beta - \alpha$, then the probability that a gap of length k occurs is given by $(\beta - \alpha)(1 - \beta + \alpha)^k$. Ordinarily, the numbers of gaps of length 0, 1, 2, . . . , n are counted, and all gaps of length greater than n are combined into a single category. The theoretical frequencies can be calculated from the stated probability, and a *chi* square test can be made to test these expectations.

In the second approach to the use of the gap test, the set of random numbers is treated as a sequence of digits. One digit is chosen as the test value, and the numbers of digits between recurrences of this test digit are counted (of course, ignoring the zeros placed before the decimal points in the list above). Suppose that 3 is chosen as the test digit for the sequence above. The gap lengths between recurrences of this digit are: 11, 5, 5, 14, 2, 2, 0, 40, 1, 9, 17, 5, 14, and 17. If 2 is chosen as the test digit, then the gap lengths are: 5, 4, 2, 15, 1, 0, 0, 1, 1, 6, 11, 0, 3, 11, 0, 9, 21, 0, 2, 20, and 4. In this case, the probability of a gap of length k is given by $0.1(0.9)^k$. The *chi* square test is used to compare the actual frequencies of gap lengths with those expected theoretically. Table 7.1 summarizes the results of *chi* square test calculations on the gap lengths using 2 as the test digit. Note that sets are grouped in order to assure a theoretical frequency of at least 5 for each cell. The observed value of χ^2 (4.904) is smaller than the critical value of 5.99 for $df = 2$ and $\alpha = 0.05$ (see Table A.3, Appendix A), and therefore we conclude that this sequence passes the gap test.

7.3 Congruential Methods

The congruential method is the method most widely used for generating uniformly distributed numbers. The goal is to generate numbers with the standard uniform distribution (compare Equation 3.12):

$$F(x) = \begin{cases} 0, & \text{for } x \le 0, \\ x, & \text{for } 0 < x \le 1, \text{ and} \\ 1, & \text{for } x > 1. \end{cases} \tag{7.2}$$

In Section 3.7, a transformation is given to convert numbers with a standard uniform distribution to numbers with any prescribed uniform distribution. Use of uniformly distributed numbers to generate numbers with other distributions is discussed in Chapter 8.

The first step in the congruential method is the choice of four nonnegative numbers: x_0 (the starting value, or *seed*, for the generator); a (the *multiplier*); c (the *increment*); and m (the *modulus*). The modulus, m, must be greater than both c and a. In this method, each number x_{n+1} is generated from the preceding one x_n by the following process: first calculate $N = ax_n + c$; then set x_{n+1} equal to the remainder obtained when N is divided by m. This process is represented symbolically as

$$x_{n+1} \equiv ax_n + c \pmod{m}. \tag{7.3}$$

Once again, the standard uniformly distributed number is obtained by placing a decimal point (or binary point if base 2 is used) to the left of the first digit. For example, suppose that the following initial values are chosen: $x_0 = 3$; $a = 7$; $c = 3$; and $m = 10$. The sequence generated is: 3, 4, 1, 0, 3, 4, 1, 0, 3, ... This generator has a period of only four numbers.

TABLE 7.1   Results of *Chi* Square Test Calculations on Gap Lengths (see text)

Length of Gap	Probability	Theoretical Frequency (T)	Actual Frequency (A)	$\dfrac{(A-T)^2}{T}$
0, 1, or 2	0.1 + 0.09 + 0.081	5.691	10	3.263
3, 4, 5, or 6	0.0729 + 0.06561 + 0.059049 + 0.0531441	5.265	5	0.013
Greater than 6	0.4783	10.044	6	1.628
Totals	1.0000	21.000	21	$\chi^2 = 4.904$

Generators using $c = 0$ are called *multiplicative congruential generators,* and those for which $c \neq 0$ are called *mixed congruential generators.* Lehmer's original congruential generator was multiplicative. Such generators are faster than mixed generators, but they tend to have shorter periods. Thomson (1958) first proposed the use of mixed congruential generators.

The best choice of values for x_0, a, c, and m is a problem of great interest. Because the period of the generator always is less than m, very large values of m are desirable. The value of m also should be chosen to permit rapid solution of the congruence relation — in other words, so that the remainder in dividing by m is easily found. One particularly convenient solution to this latter problem is to set m equal to the word size of the computer. The result of the multiplication and addition automatically will be reduced modulo w, if w is the word length of the computer. (The word length is the number of bits that are retained as a unit during processing activities. Some computers can have variable word lengths. The reasons for the automatic reduction modulo w are described by Knuth 1969, pp. 11–14.) However, a multiplicative method frequently results in a short period for the generator if $m = w$. If $m = w - 1$, this difficulty does not arise, and the multiplicative method can be used with its simpler calculations. Because of these considerations, values for m of $2^{32} - 1$ or $2^{36} - 1$ commonly are used with computers that have word lengths of 32 or 36 bits.

The choice of a value for the multiplier a is based almost entirely on considerations of increasing the period of the generator. The maximal period is of length m. The period of the generator will be exactly m if and only if (1) c is relatively prime to m (that is, 1 is the only common integer divisor of c and m); (2) $a - 1$ is a multiple of every prime dividing m; and (3) $a - 1$ is a multiple of 4, if m is a multiple of 4. [It always is possible to obtain a period of length m, although the resulting sequence may not be useful. For example, take $x_{n+1} = x_n + 1 \pmod m$ to produce the far-from-random sequence: x_0; $x_0 + 1$; $x_0 + 2$; . . . ; $m - 1$; 0; 1; 2; . . . ; $x_0 - 1$; x_0; . . . .] The considerations listed above result in the common use of multipliers $a = Z^k + 1$, where Z is the radix used in the computer, $m = Z^e$, and $2 \leq k < e$. Although these simple choices are recommended frequently in the literature, Knuth (1969, pp. 21–24) discusses reasons for using multipliers that are more complicated. For example, in the case $e = 35$, he suggests $a = 2^{23} + 2^{14} + 2^2 + 1$.

If the period of the generator is m, the choice of a starting value, or seed, is not particularly critical, because in such a case all possible alternatives will be generated. However, when using a congruential random number generator in simulations, it is important not to use the same seed in each run of the simulation, because this practice will tend to produce stereotyped behavior. A common alternative is to use the final number generated in the preceding run as the seed for the next run. On the other hand, the ability to use the same seed in successive runs is useful in debugging the programs. In this case, it is very helpful to be able to duplicate earlier results in order to uncover errors in the program.

Except for the requirement that c be relatively prime to m, the choice of the increment c usually is discussed only in terms of whether or not it should be zero; in other words, of whether the generator should be multiplicative or mixed. Greenberger (1961) placed bounds on the correlation of successive random numbers that depended on c as well as on values of a and m. This result does not seem very useful in selecting values for the increment, and it has not been used widely. In general, there seems to be a tendency to choose $c = 0$; in other words, to use multiplicative congruential generators. If the choice of values for m and a is made carefully, such generators are faster than mixed ones and probably are as good.

7.4   Additive Congruential Generators

A strictly additive congruential generator was introduced by Green et al. (1959). In Section 7.3 we mention some of the results of studies applying mathematical theorems to the behavior of multiplicative and mixed congruential generators. Some of these theorems are merely interesting, but others are both interesting and useful, particularly in helping to determine the multiplier. Experience shows, however, that these theorems can act only as guides; empirical tests of the generator still must be made. Knuth (1969, pp. 15–19) states some of the more important theorems and gives their proofs. There are very few mathematical theorems that can be applied to the study of the behavior of additive congruential generators. However, empirical tests have been made, and additive generators have been used in some simulation studies.

In this type of generator, the seed consists of a sequence of n numbers, $x_1, x_2, \ldots, x_n$, that are random numbers from a standard uniform distribution. The next number x_{n+1} is obtained by computing $x_1 + x_n$ and reducing this sum modulo m. In this case, because $0 \le x_1 < 1$ and $0 \le x_n < 1$, then $0 \le (x_1 + x_n) < 2$. If m is the word size of the computer, reduction modulo m is equivalent to retaining the fractional portion of the sum. Thus, the procedure followed by this generator can be summarized as (1) Compute $x'_j = x_{j-1} + x_{j-n}$; (2) Set x_j = (fractional part of x'_j). For binary computers, it has been demonstrated that the length of this generator is $k_n \times 2^{w-1}$. Values of k_n corresponding to $n = 2, 3, \ldots, 16$ are given by Green (1963). For example, if $n = 15$ and $w = 24$, the length of the generator is $32,767 \times 2^{23}$, or about 27,000,000,000,000. Statistical tests on this generator indicate that nonrandom patterns appear for $n < 6$, that the same nonrandom patterns appear for $6 \le n < 16$ but can be avoided by use of every other number that is generated, and that for $n = 16$ the numbers passed the statistical tests used (Green et al. 1959).

7.5 Other Generators of Pseudorandom Numbers

Many other methods for generating random numbers have been proposed. Many of these proposals consist of slight modifications to standard procedures, making them "more random." Others are based on random selection (in some sense) of some or all of the steps or constants used in the generating procedure. These attempts have not produced successful results.

Here we wish to discuss three promising procedures that differ from the multiplicative, additive, and mixed congruential procedures in some way — but not by introducing an "extra touch of randomness." The first method is a quadratic congruence method proposed by R. L. Coveyou, a method that is applicable when m is a power of 2. In this method, the product $x_n(x_n + 1)$ is reduced modulo m. The seed, x_0 may be any number congruent to 2 mod 4. This method proves to be almost equivalent to von Neumann's mid-square method using double-precision arithmetic (which involves the use of two words rather than one to carry out arithmetic calculations in the computer). However, Coveyou's method has a longer period than von Neumann's, and it appears to generate sequences that are better able to pass some of the statistical tests.

The second method is a more complex additive method mentioned by Knuth (1969, p. 27), which is applicable when m is a prime. For example, m might be chosen as the largest prime less than w. This prime modulo is denoted by p. The initial constants include k numbers as seeds $(x_1, x_2, \ldots, x_k)$ and k multipliers $(a_1, a_2, \ldots, a_k)$. The next number in the sequence is generated by the relation, $x_n \equiv (a_1 x_{n-1} + a_2 x_{n-2} + \ldots + a_k x_{n-k}) \bmod p$. The choice of appropriate multipliers is not trivial. Although the necessary properties for these multipliers can be derived from mathematical theory, it is a difficult matter to find a set of multipliers that have these properties. Knuth (1969, pp. 27–28) discusses an approach to selecting the multipliers. With a proper selection of multipliers, this generator has a period of $p^k - 1$.

The third method was proposed by Marsaglia and MacLaren (1965). Two independent sequences of random numbers first are generated by some other method; call these sequences $x_1, x_2, \ldots$ and $y_1, y_2, \ldots$. A table of length k (usually k is chosen to be about 100) is set up and the first k values of the x sequence are stored in it; the elements in the table may be denoted as $t_1, t_2, \ldots, t_k$. The first step in generating a new random number by this method is to generate the next numbers, x_n and y_n, in the x and y sequences. The number y_n then is transformed to produce a random number j within the range $1 \leq j \leq k$. Then t_j is taken from the table and used as the next random number for the generator output, while x_n replaces t_j in the table. This method has been recommended highly. It gives an exceptionally long period and requires little more time to implement than the time required to generate the two basic sequences used.

7.6 The GPSS Random Number Generator

Several versions of GPSS are available. In this section we describe the random number generator used in GPSS/360. Although it is a type of multiplicative congruential generator, it is not a straightforward generator of this type.

Three kinds of numbers are used in the generator. They are the base numbers, the multipliers, and the indices. Eight of each of these three kinds of numbers are stored in the generator at any one time. In effect, this multiplicity of constants is intended to permit the GPSS programmer to call on any one of eight random number generators. However, these eight generators are not truly independent of one another.

The eight base numbers differ from one another; each is a positive integer less than 2^{31} — in other words, each is a positive integer that can be represented by 31 bits. These eight base numbers do not change during use of the generator, and they cannot be changed by the programmer.

Each of the eight multipliers also is a positive integer that can be represented by 31 bits. However, these multipliers are changed during the process of generating random numbers, and they also can be changed by the programmer.

Each of the eight indices is a positive integer that can be represented by 3 bits. The indices also are changed as random numbers are generated.

The generation of random numbers follows the procedure diagrammed in Figure 7.1. The user specifies which of the eight random number generators he wishes to use; for example, he might ask for RN3. In that case, the third index, I_3, is selected. The generator multiplies the third multiplier, M_3, by the base that is in the position indexed by the third base, B_{I_3}, thus producing a new 62-bit number. The middle 32 bits of this number are used to generate the next random number; three of the sixteen higher-order (leftmost) bits replace I_3; and the lower-order (rightmost) 31 bits replace M_3. This splitting of the 62-bit product is diagrammed in Figure 7.2.

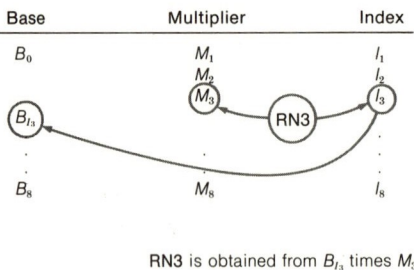

RN3 is obtained from B_{I_3} times M_3

FIG. 7.1   Procedure Used in Generating RN3 (*see text*)

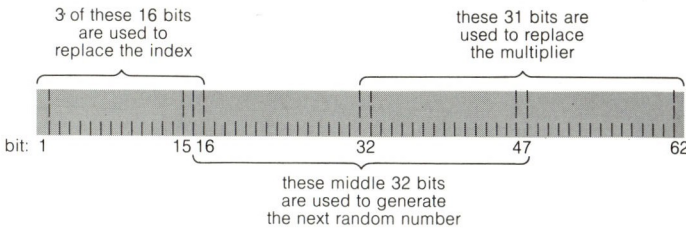

FIG. 7.2   Division of the 62-bit Product in the GPSS Random Number
Generator (*see text*)

The procedure by which the next random number is generated from the
middle 32 bits of the 62-bit product is fairly complex. Integers are represented
by a 32-bit code in the System/360; one bit is the sign and the other 31 bits are
the number. The GPSS compiler can produce three-decimal-digit random numbers that are either between 0 and 0.999 inclusive or between 0 and 999 inclusive. If numbers between 0 and 1 are required, the 31-bit result is divided
by 10^6. and the three digits to the right of the decimal in the result are used.
If numbers between 0 and 1,000 are required, the result is divided by 10^3, and
the three-digit remainder is used. It is not clear from the IBM users' manual
for GPSS (IBM Application Program Manual GH20–0326) how the three bits
that replace the index are selected from among the sixteen higher-order bits
in the 62-bit product.

The eight GPSS random number generators are not independent because
all of the indices are initialized at zero, and all of the multipliers are initialized
at one. Thus, the sequence of random numbers generated by each of the generators is the same. However, this identity of sequences can be modified by
the programmer, because he can specify his own set of initial values for the
multipliers.

7.7 Supplementary Reading

One of the most comprehensive references on random number generation is
Chapter 3 of the book by Knuth (1969). This book and other references giving
more complete discussions of procedures have been cited at appropriate places
in the text of the chapter. The following two references are appropriate both for
this chapter and for Chapter 8 (no section of supplementary reading suggestions
is included in Chapter 8).

The bibliography compiled by Naylor (1969a) includes 29 references on
random number generators. Reprints of these bibliographies can be purchased
from the Association for Computing Machinery. Naylor et al. (1966) give a good

introduction to random number generation in their Chapters 3 and 4; they discuss both the generation of uniformly distributed numbers and the generation of numbers with other distributions. They also describe FORTRAN subroutines for generating numbers with nonuniform distributions.

PROBLEMS

Problems 7.1 through 7.5 can be worked with a pencil and paper. Problems 7.6 through 7.8 require the use of a computer and presuppose an ability to write computer programs in a general purpose language.

7.1 Using the mid-square method, generate the next twenty numbers in the sequence of four-digit numbers begun in Section 7.1 and continued in Section 7.2. Does zero occur with greater than chance frequency in the first digit? If so, suggest an explanation.

7.2 (a) With $m = 10$, find values of a, c, and x_0 that will result in a mixed congruential generator that produces all the odd digits and no even digits (it will have a period of 5). (b) Again with $m = 10$, find values of a, c, and x_0 that will generate only the even digits (period 5). If the values of a and c from part (a) are retained, how can x_0 be modified to produce the even digits? (c) Once more with $m = 10$, find values of a and c (other than $a = c = 1$) that will give a period of 10. Generate these ten numbers and comment on their sequential behavior.

7.3 Find a set of values for a and c in the mixed congruential generator that will assure a period of 256 in a computer of word length $2^8 = 256$. Generate the first ten numbers in this sequence and comment on their behavior.

7.4 Generate 32 two-digit random numbers using the additive generator discussed in Section 7.4. Use $n = 16$ and get the seed of sixteen numbers from Table A.7 in Appendix A.

7.5 Suppose that j is selected from y_n in Marsaglia and MacLaren's procedure, by taking $y_n \equiv j \pmod{k}$, where $1 \leq j \leq k$ (so that, if y_n is a multiple of j, take $j = k$). Generate 15 two-digit numbers by taking $k = 10$ and by using the numbers in the first two and last two columns of Table A.7 for the x_n and y_n sequences, respectively.

7.6 (a) Write a computer program that implements the procedure developed in answer to Problem 7.3. (b) Calculate and print out the 256 numbers that would be generated with each of three seeds. (c) Apply a runs test to one of the three sets of 256 numbers. (d) Apply any other statistical test that is available in the program library of your computer center to the same sequence that was checked with the runs test. Discuss the results of the two tests.

7.7 (a) Write a computer program that will generate random numbers using the Marsaglia and MacLaren procedure. Use one of the three sets produced in answer to Problem 7.6 as the x sequence. Take $k = 50$. Use another set of values for a and c to generate the y sequence. (b) Calculate and print out 500 numbers produced by this program. (c) Apply a runs test to this set of 500 numbers. (d) Apply any other available statistical test to this set of 500 numbers. Discuss the results of the tests.

7.8 If a random number generator is available in your computer center, generate 500 numbers using this generator. Make the same statistical tests on these numbers that you made on the 500 numbers generated and studied in Problem 7.7. If a program to compute correlation coefficients is available in your program library, compute the correlation coefficient between the two sets of 500 numbers from Problems 7.7 and 7.8. (Pair the two sets of numbers according to the sequence in which they were generated.)

8

Generating Random Numbers
with Nonuniform Distributions

8.1 INTRODUCTION The stochastic behavior of many real-system entities cannot be characterized by the uniform distribution. In fact, other theoretical distributions—such as the normal, exponential, and *gamma* distributions—are encountered more frequently than is the uniform distribution. In many cases, no appropriate theoretical distribution can be found, and an empirical distribution is used. Thus, the introduction of appropriate stochastic characteristics in simulations requires the use of random number generators that produce numbers with distributions other than the uniform one.

Sections 8.2 through 8.4 describe general procedures for generating numbers with a prescribed density from numbers with a uniform density. Sections 8.5

149

through 8.9 discuss specific procedures that are used to obtain each of several important theoretical distributions and the empirical distributions.

8.2 The Inverse Transformation

Suppose we wish to generate random variables from a distribution $F(x)$. [Recall that $0 \le F(x) < 1$.] If we generate standard uniform numbers, say r, and if we knew $F^{-1}(x)$ — that is, if we knew how to get x from $F(x)$ — we could generate the numbers with distribution $F(x)$ by first generating r and then taking $x = F^{-1}(r)$. This procedure, called the *inverse transformation method*, is illustrated graphically in Figure 8.1. Note that $F(x)$ must be strictly increasing as x increases for all values of x if this procedure is to yield unique values of x. For example, if $F(x_1) = F(x_2) = r_1$, there cannot be a unique value of x corresponding to r_1. This ambiguity also is illustrated in Figure 8.1.

As an example, suppose that the random variables to be generated are to have the discrete distribution illustrated in Figure 8.2. Formally, $F(x)$ is a sequence of straight lines through the points $(x_0, a_0 = 0), \ldots, (x_i, a_i), \ldots, (x_n, a_n = 1)$. In this case, $F(x)$ is given by

$$F(x) = \begin{cases} \dfrac{a_1(x - x_1)}{x_1 - x_0} + a_1, & \text{for } x_0 \le x < x_1; \\[2mm] \vdots & \vdots \\[2mm] \dfrac{(a_{i+1} - a_i)(x - x_{i+1})}{x_{i+1} - x_i} + a_{i+1}, & \text{for } x_i \le x < x_{i+1}; \\[2mm] \vdots & \vdots \\[2mm] \dfrac{(1 - a_{n-1})(x - x_n)}{x_n - x_{n-1}} + 1, & \text{for } x_{n-1} \le x < x_n. \end{cases} \qquad (8.1)$$

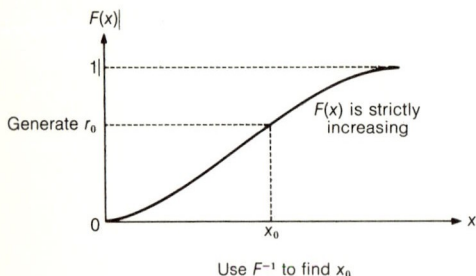

Use F^{-1} to find x_0

Unambiguous Inverse Transformation

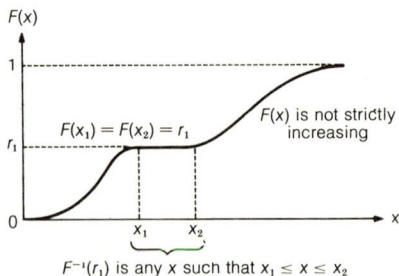

$F^{-1}(r_1)$ is any x such that $x_1 \le x \le x_2$

Ambiguous Inverse Transformation

FIG. 8.1   Use of the Inverse Transformation to Generate Random Numbers

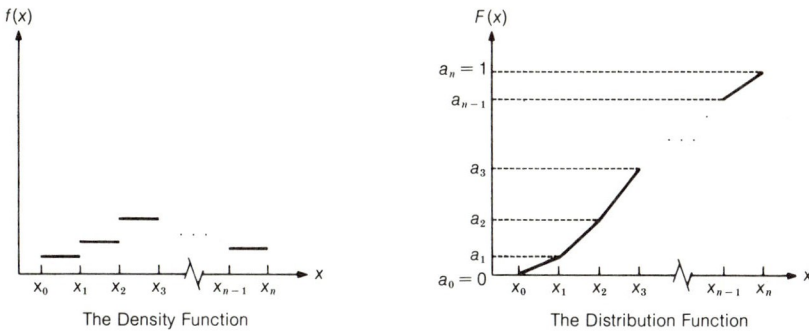

The Density Function   The Distribution Function

FIG. 8.2   Density and Distribution Functions for a Discrete Probability Distribution

Similarly, the inverse transformation for a is given by

$$F^{-1}(a) = \begin{cases} \dfrac{(a - a_1)(x_1 - x_0)}{a_1} + x_1, & \text{for } a_0 = 0 \leq a < a_1; \\ \vdots & \vdots \\ \dfrac{(a - a_{i+1})(x_{i+1} - x_i)}{a_{i+1} - a_i} + x_{i+1}, & \text{for } a_i \leq a < a_{i+1}; \\ \vdots & \vdots \\ \dfrac{(a - 1)(x_n - x_{n-1})}{1 - a_{n-1}} + x_n, & \text{for } a_{n-1} \leq a < a_n = 1. \end{cases} \quad (8.2)$$

To generate random numbers with the distribution indicated in Equation 8.1, it is necessary to take the numbers r with standard uniform distribution and to apply to them the inverse transformation of Equation 8.2. Thus, if $a_i \leq r < a_{i+1}$, the appropriate transformation (from the central line of Equation 8.2) is used to get the corresponding variable x.

As a numerical example, suppose that

$$f(x) = \begin{cases} 1, & \text{for } 0 \leq x < 1/4; \text{ and} \\ 3/7, & \text{for } 1/4 \leq x < 2. \end{cases} \quad (8.3)$$

The corresponding distribution function, $F(x)$, is represented by two line segments connecting the points (0,0), (1/4, 1/4), and (2, 1), Therefore,

$$F^{-1}(a) = \begin{cases} a, & \text{for } 0 \leq a < 1/4; \text{ and} \\ \dfrac{7(a - 1)}{3} + 2, & \text{for } 1/4 \leq a < 1. \end{cases} \quad (8.4)$$

If the standard uniform generator produces $r = 0.1034$, then the corresponding random number for the distribution $F(x)$ is $x = F^{-1}(r) = r = 0.1034$. If $r = 0.9021$, then $x = [7(r - 1)/3] + 2 = 1.7716$.

As another example, suppose that $f(x) = 2x$ and $F(x) = x^2$, for $0 \leq x < 1$. The inverse transformation is $F^{-1}(a) = \sqrt{a}$. Random numbers with this distribution may be produced by taking the square root of standard uniform random numbers. In this case, however, there is a better approach. It happens that, if x_1 has distribution $F_1(x)$ and x_2 has distribution $F_2(x)$, then $\max(x_1, x_2)$ has distribution $F_1(x) \times F_2(x)$. Therefore, random numbers with distribution $F(x) = x^2 = x \times x$ in the range 0 to 1 can be produced by drawing pairs of standard uniform random numbers and using the larger value of the pair as the random number with distribution x^2. Because this procedure (drawing two standard uniform numbers and choosing the larger value) almost always is faster than the procedure of taking a square root, the procedure of selecting from pairs is preferred.

8.3 The Rejection Method

Suppose that $f(x) \leq K$, for $a \leq x < b$. Then $k[f(x)] \leq 1$, where $k = 1/K$. If r_1 is a random number from the standard uniform density, then (from the definition of a uniform density) the probability that $r_1 \leq k[f(x)]$ is $k[f(x)]$. Suppose now that we choose x_1 at random from the interval $a \leq x < b$ by selecting a second random number, say r_2, and setting $x_1 = a + (b - a)r_2$. We use this number if and only if $r_1 \leq k[f(x_1)]$. This procedure is called the *rejection method* and is illustrated in Figure 8.3.

Suppose that $f(x) = 2x$, for $0 \leq x < 1$. Then $f(x) \leq 2$, and the scaled $f(x)$ is given by $k[f(x)] = (1/2)f(x) = f(x)/2 = x$. Also, $F(x) = x^2$. The rejection method

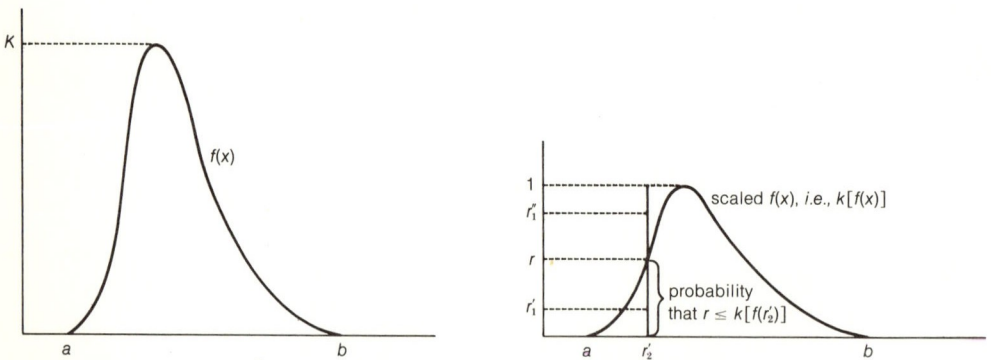

Choose r_1 and r_2. Compute $r_2' = a + (b - a)r_2$. Use r_2' if and only if $r_1 \leq k[f(r_2')]$. Thus, r_2' would be used if $r_1 = r_1'$ and would not be used if $r_1 = r_1''$.

FIG. 8.3   Illustration of the Rejection Method

then is equivalent to the use of the maximum of a pair of random standard uniform numbers. The linear transformation is $x = 0 + (1 - 0)r = r$. So we generate r_2 and set $x_1 = r_2$. We then use r_2 if and only if $r_1 \leq x_1 = r_2$. That is, we generate pairs of random numbers and use the greater of the pair.

8.4 The Composition, or Mixture, Method

Suppose that $F(x)$ can be expressed in the following form:

$$F(x) = \sum_{i=1}^{n-1} a_i F_i(x) + \left(1 - \sum_{i=1}^{n-1} a_i\right) F_n(x),$$

$$\text{with } a_1, a_2, \ldots, a_{n-1} > 0 \quad \text{and with } \sum_{i=1}^{n-1} a_i < 1.$$

A random number r_1 is drawn from the standard uniform distribution. Because of the restrictions on a_i, if

$$s_j = \sum_{i=1}^{j} a_i \qquad \text{for } j = 1, 2, \ldots, n,$$

then there is a value m of j such that $s_{m-1} < r_1 < s_m$. The random number to be used then is generated using a procedure that generates numbers with distribution F_m. For example, suppose that $n = 2$. Then, $F(x) = pF_1(x) + (1 - p)F_2(x)$. In this case, if $r < p$, then x is chosen from $F_1(x)$, and if $r \geq p$, then x is chosen from $F_2(x)$.

Knuth (1969) states that this procedure—a *composite*, or *mixed*, method—can be extremely useful if one of the values of a_i is near 1 and if F_i is an easily accommodated distribution. The mixed procedure discussed in Section 8.5 is a mix of 145 distributions.

8.5 Generating Normally Distributed Numbers

Normally distributed variables are encountered frequently in the simulation of stochastic systems. If standardized normal numbers can be generated—that is, random numbers with the distribution $N(0,1)$—then numbers with any normal distribution can be generated by a simple linear transformation. If y is $N(0,1)$ and $Y = \mu + \sigma y$, then Y is $N(\mu, \sigma^2)$. Therefore, in this section we discuss only the generation of normally distributed numbers with a mean of zero and a standard deviation of one.

One easy method suggested by Box and Muller (1958) involves generation of a pair of standardized normal numbers, x_1 and x_2, from two standard uniform numbers, r_1 and r_2, by letting $x_1 = \sqrt{-2 \ln r_1} \cos(2\pi r_2)$; and $x_2 = \sqrt{-2 \ln r_1} \sin(2\pi r_2)$.

Knuth (1969, p. 104) gives a procedure for generation of these numbers.

Because it is short and interesting, we present it here. First the two uniformly distributed numbers, r_1 and r_2, are generated. Then V_1 is set equal to $2r_1 - 1$ and V_2 is set equal to $2r_2 - 1$. Next compute $S = V_1^2 + V_2^2$. If $S \geq 1$, two new uniformly distributed numbers are generated and the procedure begins again. If $S < 1$, then $x_1 = V_1 \sqrt{(-2 \ln S)/S}$ and $x_2 = V_2 \sqrt{(-2 \ln S)/S}$. The numbers x_1 and x_2 have the desired normal distribution. Note that the calculation of $2r_1 - 1$ and $2r_2 - 1$ and the squares of these values, and the drawing of excess pairs of r_1 and r_2 (when $S \geq 1$), makes it possible to avoid having to calculate sines and cosines. However, square roots and natural logarithms still must be calculated. It is estimated that about 127 pairs of r_1 and r_2 will be needed in order to generate 100 pairs of x_1 and x_2.

A second direct method for generation of normally distributed numbers is due to Teichroew; this method and several others are discussed by Muller (1959). This procedure begins with the drawing of twelve uniformly distributed numbers, $r_1, r_2, \ldots, r_{12}$. Then compute

$$R = \left(\sum_{i=1}^{12} r_i - 6 \right)/4.$$

Finally set

$$x = \left(\{ [(C_1 R^2 + C_2) R^2 + C_3] R^2 + C_4 \} R^2 + C_5 \right) R,$$

where $C_1 = 0.029899776$, $C_2 = 0.008355968$, $C_3 = 0.076542912$, $C_4 = 0.252408784$, and $C_5 = 3.949846138$. The number x has the desired normal distribution.

The third and fastest of the procedures discussed here is due to Marsaglia, MacLaren, and Bray. This procedure requires three tables; initial entries for these tables are suggested by Marsaglia et al. (1964a) for both binary and decimal computers. This procedure is very fast if the tables are stored in a clever way. (Many random number generators use tables somewhere in the procedure. The speed and efficiency of such generators often can be enhanced by clever storage techniques for the tables.) The procedure is described in detail by Knuth (1969, pp. 105–112). It is a mixed generator that uses a sum of 145 densities. Of these, 48 are uniform in a small range – in other words, they are small rectangles.

8.6 Generating Exponentially Distributed Numbers

The standard exponential distribution is $F(x) = 1 - e^{-x}$, which has a mean of 1. Any exponential distribution with mean μ can be produced by the simple transformation of replacing x by μx. Therefore, again, we discuss only the generation of the standard distribution.

The inverse method can be applied, because $F^{-1}(a) = -\ln(1 - a)$. However, if a is uniformly distributed, $(1 - a)$ also is uniformly distributed, and the exponentially distributed numbers can be obtained directly from standard uniformly distributed numbers r merely by taking $x = -\ln r$.

As might be expected, this procedure is easy to program, but not very efficient to run because of the need to calculate natural logarithms. Knuth (1969, p. 114) describes a method (developed by Marsaglia) that produces exponentially distributed numbers from a table of numbers of the form: $P_j = 1 - 1/e^j$ and $Q_j = [1/(e-1)] [(1/1!) + (1/2!) + \ldots + (1/j!)]$. Knuth says that this method is reasonably fast, but it is not clear whether it is much faster than the direct calculation of the logarithm of the uniformly distributed number.

Marsaglia et al. (1964b) describe and discuss a very fast mixed method for generation of exponentially distributed numbers.

8.7 Generating Binomially and Geometrically Distributed Numbers

In this and in the next section, we discuss the generation of random numbers from three important discrete distributions: the binomial, the geometric, and the Poisson.

The simplest method for generating random binomial numbers is to use the rejection method. Given p (the probability of success) and n (the number of trials), the binomial number x (the number of successes in n trials) can be obtained by first generating n standard uniform numbers. The number of these n numbers that are less than or equal to p then is determined, and x is set equal to this value.

Also note that for large n the binomial distribution can be approximated by the normal distribution. That is, the binomial distribution approximates $N[np, np(1-p)]$. Thus, for large n, binomial numbers can be generated by a transformation of the output of a normal number generator.

The *geometric distribution* is closely related to the binomial distribution. In the geometric distribution, the variable is the number of trials preceding the first success in a sequence of independent binomial trials with probability of success p. In this case, $f(x) = p(1-p)^{x-1}$ for $x = 1, 2, \ldots$, and $f(x) = 0$ otherwise. This distribution has been used in some econometric models and in studies of quality control. It is discussed by Naylor et al. (1966, pp. 102–104). The mean of the distribution is $1/p$ and the variance is $(1-p)/p^2$.

The geometrically distributed variable can be generated directly from a standard uniformly distributed number r, by taking x equal to the greatest integer that is less than or equal to $[\ln r/\ln (1-p)]$.

8.8 Generating Poisson Distributed Numbers

The Poisson distribution is of some importance in simulations, and the need to generate Poisson distributed numbers is likely to arise. Poisson distributed numbers with parameter λ are generated by counting the number of standard uniformly distributed numbers that must be generated before the product of these numbers is less than $e^{-\lambda}$. Specific procedures for generating this distribution are given by Knuth (1969, p. 117) and by Naylor et al. (1966, p. 114). A more elaborate procedure, using specially designed tables for generating the numbers, has been developed by Kribs and is described by Knuth (1969, p. 118); it can be faster than the basic method.

8.9 Generating Numbers with Empirical Distributions

In many simulations, an empirical distribution is used to characterize the stochastic behavior of certain entities. No theoretical analog is available, and no theoretical distribution has been found to approximate the behavior of the empirical one. Therefore, a way must be found to generate random numbers with this empirical distribution.

In most cases, the empirical density is defined as a frequency distribution. Thus, the distribution function is given by a sequence of straight lines. In such a case, the inverse transformation method can be used as demonstrated in Section 8.2. In most cases, the distribution is defined by a set of ten or more points; the calculations then are more tedious than those for the simple three-point example of Section 8.2, but the formulae developed there still are applicable.

Butler (1970) describes in the FORTRAN programming language an algorithm that is a general purpose random number generator. In this algorithm, the given density (theoretical or empirical) is approximated by a sequence of straight lines, and random numbers then are generated with a density given by the sequence of lines. This algorithm can be applied to generation of random numbers with any empirical distribution.

Random numbers can be generated in GPSS with any prescribed empirical distribution, using a tabulation of the coordinates of the set of points defining the distribution. Theoretical distributions are prescribed in much the same way in GPSS, resulting in an approximation to the distribution by a sequence of straight lines. Although adequate approximations can be obtained by using enough points, this method does make it awkward to precribe theoretical densities in GPSS. The generation of random numbers with an empirical distribution in GPSS is discussed more fully in Part Four.

PROBLEMS

Problems 8.1 through 8.4 should be worked by those who do not have access to an electronic digital computer. Problems 8.5 through 8.9 should be worked by those who can write computer programs and also have access to an electronic digital computer.

8.1   A distribution is given by the sequence of straight lines through the following points: $(-4, 0)$, $(-2, 0.0228)$, $(-1, 0.1611)$, $(-0.5, 0.3085)$, $(0, 0.5)$, $(0.5, 0.6915)$, $(1, 0.8438)$, $(2, 0.9772)$, $(4, 1)$. **(a)** Plot this distribution. **(b)** Regarding this as an empirically defined distribution, describe in detail the procedure to be used in obtaining numbers with this distribution from numbers with a standard uniform density. **(c)** What theoretical distribution might be approximated by this empirical distribution?

8.2   **(a)** Using Table A.7 (Appendix A) to "generate" uniformly distributed two-digit numbers, write a procedure (using the rejection method) that will generate numbers with density $f(x) = 2x$. **(b)** Use this procedure to generate 50 numbers with density $f(x) = 2x$. **(c)** Write a procedure (using the inverse method) that will generate numbers with density $f(x) = 2x$. **(d)** Generate 50 numbers with $f(x) = 2x$, using the procedure written in c. **(e)** Pair the 50 numbers generated in b with the 50 numbers generated in d, pairing the first with the first, second with second, and so on. Plot these pairs with values of the b set as the abscissa and corresponding values of the d set as the ordinate. Discuss these results.

8.3   **(a)** Using Table A.7 to "generate" four-digit standard uniformly distributed numbers, generate ten normally distributed numbers by using the Box-Muller method. **(b)** Using Table A.7 to generate two-digit standard uniformly distributed numbers, generate five normally distributed numbers using the Teichroew method.

8.4   The *gamma* distribution with positive integer parameter r also is called the Erlang distribution. Numbers with this distribution can be generated by taking a sum of r numbers, each with an exponential distribution with parameter $\sigma = 1/\lambda$. (The *gamma* density is defined in Section 6.8.) Given r standard uniformly distributed numbers, write a procedure that would generate numbers from a *gamma* distribution with parameters (r, λ).

8.5   Write a computer program that will accept as input the standard uniformly distributed numbers generated in either Problem 7.7 or Problem 7.8, and that will produce as output numbers with the distribution defined in Problem 8.1.

8.6 Write a computer program that will use as input the numbers generated in either Problem 7.7 or Problem 7.8, and that will produce as output numbers with density $f(x) = 2x$.

8.7 Write a computer program that will use as input the numbers generated in either Problem 7.7 or Problem 7.8, and that will produce as output standard normally distributed numbers. Use either the Box-Muller method or the Teichroew method. Compare the running times of programs developed by the students in your class, and try to determine the reasons for any differences in running times.

8.8 Write a computer program that will use as input the numbers generated in either Problem 7.7 or Problem 7.8 and the parameters r and λ, and that will produce as output numbers with the corresponding Erlang distribution (see Problem 8.4).

8.9 Write a computer program that will use as input the numbers generated in either Problem 7.7 or Problem 7.8 and the parameter λ, and that will produce as output numbers with the corresponding Poisson distribution.

Part Four

THE COMPUTER AND SIMULATION

A simulation is implemented only in the form of a series of computer programs. No matter how carefully the objectives are stated, or how effectively the field study is conducted, or how comprehensively the statistical analyses are made — when all is said and done, the computer program must do the job.

The first chapter in this part describes the algorithmic process that is followed in carrying out a simulation of a discrete system on a computer, and it provides an overview of the programming languages used in simulations, with special emphasis on FORTRAN, PL/I, SIMSCRIPT, and GPSS. The implementation of a single example in each of these four languages is illustrated with actual programs.

The next chapter (Chapter 10) introduces GPSS and describes the basic facilities of the language. This chapter can be read without first reading Chapter 9 — in fact, if both chapters are to be read, Sections 9.14 through 9.16 can be skipped, because this material is treated in greater detail in Chapter 10. Chapter 11 discusses the more advanced features of the GPSS

language, including many features that are ignored in most existing texts but are required in most simulation applications. The problems in Chapter 11 include suggestions for term projects; such projects, however, should be started before beginning Part Four, in order to allow time for their completion. Even the extensive discussion of GPSS in these two long chapters cannot cover all features of the language; see Section 10.16 for more comprehensive references.

Chapter 12 concludes this part with a discussion of a computer simulation of computer systems. The chapter describes why, when, and how computer systems are simulated, provides references to the literature on the simulation of computers, and presents examples of the techniques that have been developed. In addition, this chapter serves to illustrate the programming and other techniques described in earlier chapters. The case study in Part Five provides a full example of the application of these techniques — we believe that it is an essential part of the book.

CHAPTER 9   Simulation Programming and Languages

CHAPTER 10   GPSS: An Introduction

CHAPTER 11   Additional GPSS Features

CHAPTER 12   Simulation of Computer Systems

9

Simulation Programming and Languages

9.1 INTRODUCTION   This chapter provides a general description of some techniques and languages used in the computer simulation of discrete systems. A simple example is introduced first, and the typical requirements for programming this simulation on a computer are discussed. The remainder of the chapter shows how some of these requirements may be implemented with the general purpose languages FORTRAN and PL/I and with the simulation languages SIMSCRIPT and GPSS. It also describes the kinds of information processing activities common to simulation runs and compares the capabilities of the languages.

The reader probably will wish to develop a more detailed understanding of at least one of these languages. Chapters 10 and 11 discuss GPSS in detail.

References to more detailed descriptions of FORTRAN, PL/I, SIMSCRIPT, and other simulation languages are given in Section 9.18.

The four languages described here were chosen because they are widely available and commonly are used in simulations. At a general session of a simulation conference held in 1967, a show of hands indicated that more than two-thirds of those attending who had written programs for simulation applications had written them in FORTRAN. GPSS was the next most widely used language — about one in five of those who had written simulation programs had used GPSS. SIMSCRIPT was the third most widely used language; about one in ten had used SIMSCRIPT. When the chairman asked about other languages such as COBOL, SIMULA, and GASP, only one or two hands were raised in each case. PL/I was not widely used at the time, and the chairman did not ask about it. Although some shifts in the use of languages have occurred since that conference, FORTRAN probably is still the most widely used language for simulation programming, with GPSS as the second most widely used language.

FORTRAN and PL/I are described fairly briefly in this chapter, because it is assumed that the reader already knows something about them — if not, he can easily find many good books on these languages. SIMSCRIPT is described in the greatest detail because it is an example of the special purpose simulation languages that the reader may not have encountered before, and because it is a difficult language to describe briefly. GPSS also is an important simulation language, but it is discussed relatively briefly here, because the following two chapters are devoted to an extensive discussion of GPSS.

9.2 The Example

The use of a telephone booth serves as an example of a simple system that shares many properties with systems likely to be simulated. During any given time interval, customers may arrive at the booth and wish to make telephone calls. If the booth is occupied at the time of arrival, the prospective caller must join the waiting line. When the phone is available, the first person in line will enter the booth and use the phone for a certain amount of time. He then leaves, making the booth available for the next user. Figure 9.1 presents an abstracted description of this system, and this diagram is a fairly typical representation of the use of an equipment item. This system (with slight variations) is used as an example throughout this chapter.

9.3 Review of Simulation Terminology

Several terms and concepts introduced and defined in Part One are used in this discussion. It will be useful to review briefly some terminology and concepts. *Entities*, you will recall, are the components of the system — the objects that are interacting over time; in this case, the callers and the telephone booth are entities.

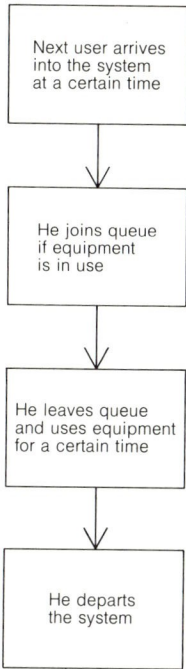

FIG. 9.1   Use of One Equipment Entity

The characteristics, or qualifying properties, of the entities are called *attributes*. The *state of the system* at any given time is specified by the attributes of the system entities and the relations among the entities at that time. In the usual computer simulation, the progress of the system is followed by analyzing changes of state; this approach is called the *critical-event approach* (see Section 1.9). Any process that causes a change of system state is called an *activity*; in other words, the entities engage in activities. For example, the arrival or departure of a telephone caller is an activity. An *event* is the occurrence of an activity at a particular instant of time. For example, an event occurs at the instant of time at which the telephone booth becomes empty. The simulation process must keep track of activities and of the entities affected, and it must schedule events within the system so that activities will occur in the correct time sequence.

9.4 Time

If the simulation is to proceed properly, the passage of simulated time must be controlled. This control may be accomplished through a user-designed algorithm; it is done automatically in most of the special purpose simulation languages. The mechanism called the *simulation clock* is connected intimately with the occurrence and scheduling of events within the system. The time units accumulated by this clock must be chosen appropriately. For example, in a simulation of the telephone booth system, the basic unit of time might be a minute; arrivals into the system and phone usage could be scaled to integral numbers of minutes. In a simulation of the activities of a computer, the simulation time unit might be a nanosecond, with instruction timing and job arrivals given in integral numbers of nanoseconds.

The simulation clock is independent of actual computer running time for the simulation programs. For example, either the simulation of 600 simulation-clock minutes for the phone booth system or the simulation of 5,000 nanoseconds of computer activity actually might require one-half second of computer running time. In the one case, 10 hours of real-world activities are simulated in one-half second on the computer; in the other case, 5 microseconds of real-world activity are simulated in one-half second. The simulation clock ordinarily is controlled by event scheduling. Scheduled activities are ordered chronologically by the scheduled time of their occurrence, and the simulation clock is updated to the time of the next event. With this critical-event approach, the simulation clock increments by discrete jumps, which generally are not evenly spaced.

Table 9.1 shows the phone booth simulation for the first five arrivals and departures. Ten events are scheduled: five arrivals and five departures. The program to simulate the system must order the events according to increasing event time; it then must update the simulation clock to each new event time and must perform the activities associated with that event, before updating the clock to the time of the next scheduled event.

9.5 Arrivals

In the telephone booth example, all state changes are forced by arrivals into the system. As soon as a caller enters the system, the event of his departure can be scheduled, using only information about the present state of the system and about the distribution of the duration of phone calls. For example, note the information associated with caller number 1 in the first line of Table 9.1. His arrival is scheduled at simulation time 0, and he is assigned to make a call of length 3 minutes. The booth is empty when he arrives, so he does not have to wait. Because there is no waiting time, his total time in the system will be the length of his call, 3 minutes. His call can be placed as soon as he arrives (at time 0) and therefore he will depart at time 3. The waiting line was empty at his arrival. Caller number 2 is scheduled to arrive at simulation time 2 and to make a call of length 4 minutes. Because caller no. 1 does not depart until time 3, the booth is occupied when no. 2 arrives, and he must wait for 1 minute. His total time in the system is 5 minutes — the 1 minute of waiting and the 4 minutes of his call. His call can be placed when he enters the booth at the departure of no. 1, which occurs at time 3. His time of departure is 4 minutes (the length of his call) later, at time 7. There was 1 person in the waiting line after he joined it (in other words, only himself). In similar fashion, all information can be generated for each caller, given only his time of arrival and the length of his call. The only events in this system are the arrivals and departures of callers; joining or leaving the waiting line and placing of calls can be regarded as parts of the events associated with arrivals and departures. Therefore, a complete schedule of events can be set forth from the times listed in the second and seventh columns of the top part of the table.

In general, there must be some rule that governs the arrival times of the callers. For example, an empirical distribution might be used as a source for arrival times. In many cases, a well-known distribution, such as the uniform or normal distribution (either of which easily can be programmed into the computer simulation), provides a valid pattern for arrival times. When the arrival pattern is known, it is possible to begin scheduling arrival events. Two methods are in

TABLE 9.1   System State Changes and Event Schedule for
First Five Callers

Caller Number	Arrival Time	Length of Call	Waiting Time	Time in System	Time Call Is Placed	Time of Departure	Number Waiting
1	0	3	0	3	0	3	0
2	2	4	1	5	3	7	1
3	6	1	1	2	7	8	1
4	10	2	0	2	10	12	0
5	11	1	1	2	12	13	1

System State Changes

Event Number	Event Time	Activity Scheduled
1	0	Arrival of caller no. 1
2	2	Arrival of caller no. 2
3	3	Departure of caller no. 1
4	6	Arrival of caller no. 3
5	7	Departure of caller no. 2
6	8	Departure of caller no. 3
7	10	Arrival of caller no. 4
8	11	Arrival of caller no. 5
9	12	Departure of caller no. 4
10	13	Departure of caller no. 5

Event Schedule

general use. The simplest method is to record (in a table, for example) all arrival times before the simulation begins. These arrivals can be ordered by increasing event times, and each arrival then is allowed to occur as the simulation clock is updated to the appropriate time. The other method, which is more prevalent and which conserves computer storage space, is to schedule the next arrival each time that an arrival event occurs. In this method, only the events scheduled for the immediate future are stored in the computer at any moment.

9.6 FORTRAN

In the United States, FORTRAN is the most commonly used general purpose programming language. It also is one of the most commonly used languages for computer simulation. Figure 9.3 is a listing of a FORTRAN program for the simulation of the telephone booth system; Figure 9.2 is the flowchart for this program.

The general outline of the program is clear from the flowchart. All arrivals are scheduled before the simulation clock starts to run. The system is to be simulated for 1,000 arrivals. The program listing shows that the arrival events are recorded in a two-dimensional array named ARVLS; for each arrival J between 1 and 1,000, the time of arrival is stored in ARVLS(J,1), and the time that the user will use the equipment (that is, the length of his call) is stored in ARVLS(J,2). This array is computed by the two DO loops contained in FORTRAN statements 9 through 15. Because arrival and usage times generally are not deterministic, the function IRND is used to insert a degree of random behavior into the model. It is assumed that the interarrival time is given by the uniform distribution on the interval [NFROM, NTO] and that usage times are uniformly distributed on [IFROM, ITO]. The function IRND (listed in Figure 9.4) is a variation of the standard uniform random number generator common on 32-bit-per-word computers such as the IBM 360/370 series. Of course, other distributions could be used if they are more appropriate; it is the responsibility of the analyst to select the most appropriate distribution.

After the arrival event records are created, the simulation algorithm can begin. Because the first arrival will be allowed immediate access to the phone (the booth is assumed to be empty initially), the simulation clock TIME is set to his departure time. The DO loop at statement 19 then takes control to schedule the remaining events. The algorithm proceeds by calculating for each arrival the event time at which he will cease to wait in line and will be able to place his call, and also the event time of his departure. As each event occurs and the system state changes, statistics are accumulated to measure waiting time, CUMQ, and transit time, XTME. The algorithm may be followed quite easily, using the arrival times and call lengths in Table 9.1. The problem of gathering statistics is discussed in the following sections.

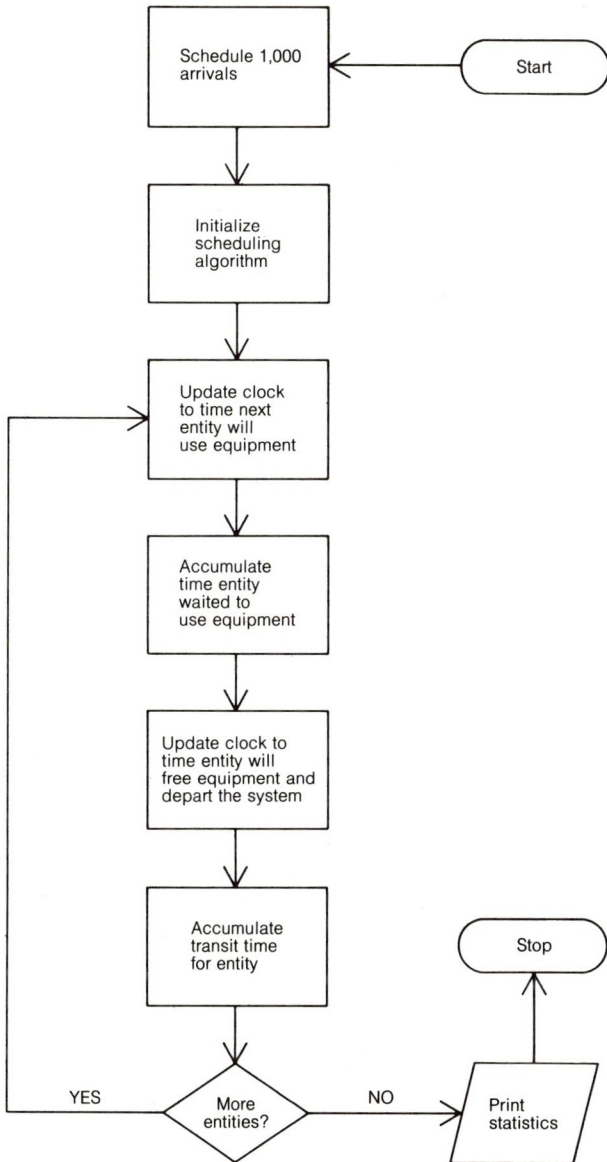

FIG. 9.2   Flowchart for FORTRAN Simulation of Telephone Booth System

```
            C
            C FORTRAN
            C -------
            C      SIMULATION OF USE OF ONE ITEM OF EQUIPMENT
            C
            C      FOLLOWING INFORMATION IS REQUIRED BY PROGRAM
            C          NFROM,NTO:RANGE OF INTER ARRIVAL RATES FOR EQUIPMENT USERS.
            C          IFROM,ITO: RANGE OF TIME EQUIPMENT WILL BE USED
            C
            C PROGRAM GATHERS STATS ON UTILIZATION AND DELAY
            C
            C
            C          THE ARRAY 'ARVLS' CONTAINS FOR EACH USER:
            C                USER ARRIVAL TIME
            C                TOTAL TIME EQPMNT WILL BE NEEDED
            C
0001               DIMENSION ARVLS(1000,2)
0002               COMMON IX
            C
            C
            C IX,NFROM,NTO,IFROM,ITO ARE SUPPLIED AS DATA
            C IX IS A RANDOM NUMBER SEED
            C
            C
0003        8132 READ (5,999,END=8133) IX,NFROM,NTO,IFROM,ITO
0004        999  FORMAT(5I5)
0005             WRITE (6,998) NFROM,NTO,IFROM,ITO
0006        998  FORMAT('1','NFROM=',I6,'    NTO=',I6,'        IFROM=',I6,
                .     '      ITO=',I6)
            C
0007               CTEL=0.0
0008               ACC=0.0
            C
            C CREATE THE   ARRAY OF ACTION TIMES
            C
0009               DO 1 J=1,1000
0010               ARVLS(J,1)=ACC
0011               ACC=ACC+IRND(NFROM,NTO)
0012        1      CONTINUE
0013               DO 11 J=1,1000
0014               ARVLS(J,2)=IRND(IFROM,ITO)
0015        11     CTEL=CTEL+ARVLS(J,2)
            C
            C
            C  MAIN BODY OF SIMULATION ALGORITHM
            C
            C
0016               TIME=ARVLS(1,2)
0017               XTME=TIME
0018               CUMQ=0.0
            C
0019               DO 1000 NOW=2,1000
0020               TIME=AMAX1(TIME,ARVLS(NOW,1))
0021               CUMQ=CUMQ+TIME-ARVLS(NOW,1)
0022               TIME=TIME+ARVLS(NOW,2)
0023        1000 XTME=XTME+TIME-ARVLS(NOW,1)
            C
            C CALCULATE STATS AND PRINT
            C
0024               XTME=XTME/1000.
0025               CTEL=CTEL/TIME
0026               AVGTT=CUMQ/1000.
0027               WRITE (6,333)  TIME,CTEL,AVGTT,XTME
0028        333  FORMAT ('0TIME=',F15.0/
                .          ' EQP UTLZTN=',      F15.6/
                .          ' AVG WAIT TME=',     F15.6/
                .          ' TRANSIT TME AVG=',F15.6)
0029             GO TO 8132
0030        8133 STOP
0031             END
```

FIG. 9.3   FORTRAN Program for Simulation of Telephone Booth System

```
        C
        C        IRND IS A FUNCTION RETURNING UNIF DSTRBTD INTGR BETWEEN
        C        LIMITS DEFINED BY ARGUMENTS
        C
0001             FUNCTION IRND   (LOW,LHI)
0002             COMMON IX
0003             IY=IX* 65539
0004             IF  ( IY )  1,  2,  2
0005     1       IY=IY+2147483647+1
0006     2       IX=IY
0007             YFL=IY
0008             YFL=YFL*.4656613E-9
0009             IRND=(LHI+1-LOW)*YFL+LOW
0010             RETURN
0011             END
```

FIG. 9.4   Listing of FORTRAN Function IRND Used in Program of Figure 9.3

9.7 Queues

When entities use the same resources, a certain amount of contention may arise. For example, Table 9.1 shows that three of the first five arrivals into the system had to wait while previous arrivals finished their calls. If shorter interarrival times or longer call lengths were used, rather long waiting lines might result. The study of waiting lines, or *queues*, and their causes is one of the more important objectives of simulation.

Queues are characterized by the manner in which entities pass through them. This characterization is called the *queuing discipline*. Some common types of queues are: (1) FIFO (first in, first out) — entities are serviced in the order in which they arrived; (2) LIFO (last in, first out) — the last entity to arrive is serviced first; (3) RANDOM — each entity in the queue has an equal chance of being serviced next, regardless of the time of its arrival into the queue; and (4) RANKED — entities are ordered for service according to the value of an attribute associated with each of them. The most common queuing discipline is FIFO. In the phone booth example, the line waiting to use the phone is treated as a FIFO queue. Cars arriving at a toll station are treated in a FIFO manner. LIFO queuing disciplines occur in stockrooms in which materials are stacked in a vertical pile, or on a ferryboat with a single loading/unloading ramp, so that the last car loaded must be the first unloaded. RANDOM disciplines characterize the drawing of ticket stubs at raffles; the order in which stubs are drawn presumably is independent of the order in which they were deposited. Most of us have experienced the RANKED discipline when ordered alphabetically by name for various functions such as dental examinations in grade school, graduation exercises, registration, and so on. A common example of a RANKED discipline is queuing by priority. In such situations, the value of a priority attribute associated with each entity is used to determine which members of the queue are to be serviced first. Diplomatic protocol is an example of a RANKED discipline in which priority is the controlling factor. In most cases, if two entities have equal priority, the discipline reverts to FIFO.

9.8 Queues and List Processing

The representation of entities such as queues in computer programs involves the representation of sets and set membership relations. Such representations commonly are implemented by the use of list-processing techniques. A *linked list*, or *chain*, is a set of data items with associated locators or pointers connecting the items, as diagrammed in Figure 9.5. Each FOLL is a pointer to the next item in the chain, and each PREC points to the preceding member. Note that a single item of data may contain pointers to several other items in the set. Two special pointers generally are reserved to locate the first and last members in the chain. FIRST is called the *head pointer*, and LAST is called the *tail pointer*.

If a FIFO queue is being represented, the arriving entities might be stored in a manner like that of chain I in Figure 9.5. The last entity to arrive will join the queue at the bottom (tail), and thus it will be the last to be serviced. The procedure of joining the queue is shown in Figure 9.6. Note that the pointers are recalculated, so that LAST points to the new arrival, who is now the tail of the queue. The symbol $\varnothing$ is used in the FOLL pointer to indicate that the entity is at the end of the queue, with no following entity. A similar procedure is followed when the first entity is allowed to leave the queue. In this case, the pointer FIRST is recalculated to point to the next data item in the chain. Note that this procedure of recalculating pointers equally well can be used to insert or delete entities in the middle of the queue. Thus, chaining methods can be used to simulate any of the queuing disciplines described above. For example, events might be ordered in a queue according to increasing event times. When a new event is to be queued, a search must be made in the queue to find the relative position at which the new event is to be inserted. Such a scheduling algorithm ensures that the event located by the pointer FIRST always is the next in time to be serviced.

Multilinked lists simplify the simulation of more complicated queuing disciplines and other relationships, but at the price of the additional memory space required for the pointers. In multilinked lists, many pointers may be associated with each element, thus establishing linkages that may become very intricate. Chain II in Figure 9.5 represents a doubly linked list; each element has a pointer PREC to the preceding element of the list as well as the pointer FOLL to the following element. This list may be processed in either a LIFO or a FIFO manner. In many situations, doubly linked lists are used to simulate RANDOM or RANKED queuing disciplines, because any element can be reached from any other element of the list.

Pointers also can be used to link those elements within a queue that have similar attributes. For example, each element in a linked list might have an additional pointer COL, which links this element to another element in the list with the same color; this element in turn is linked by a COL pointer to another element of the same color; and so on. Hence, all green elements in the queue can

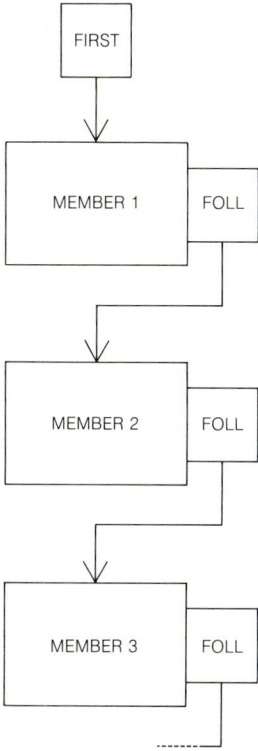

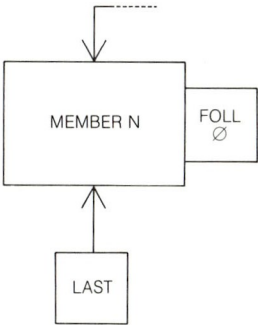

I. Singly Linked

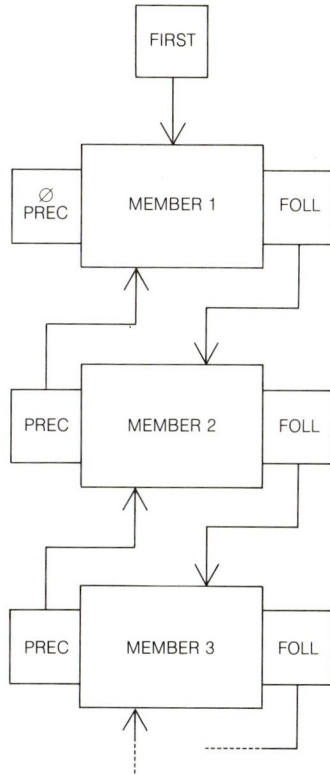

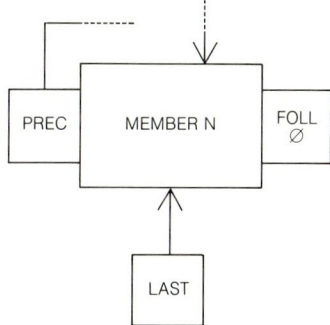

II. Doubly Linked

FIG. 9.5 Examples of Chains

QUEUE

FIRST

Arrival Time
10
Usage Time
5
FOLL

NEW ARRIVAL

Arrival Time
12
Usage Time
4

Arrival Time
11
Usage Time
6
FOLL
∅

LAST

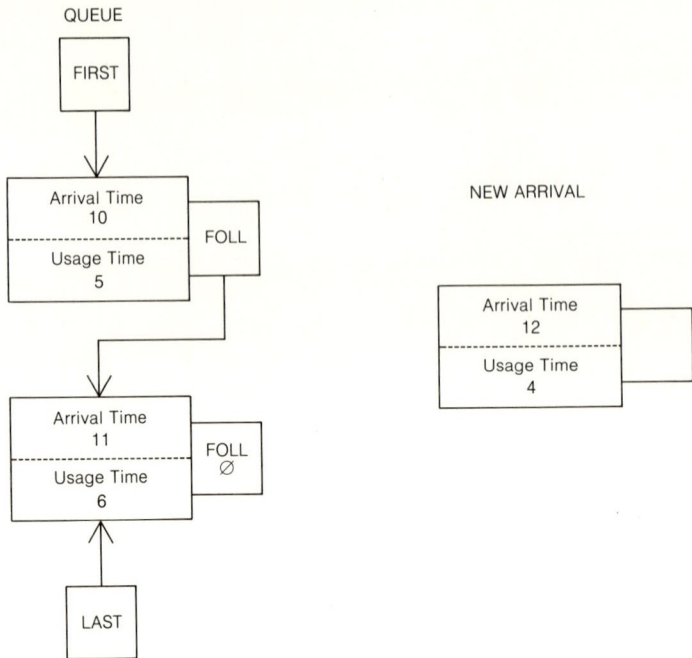

UPDATED QUEUE

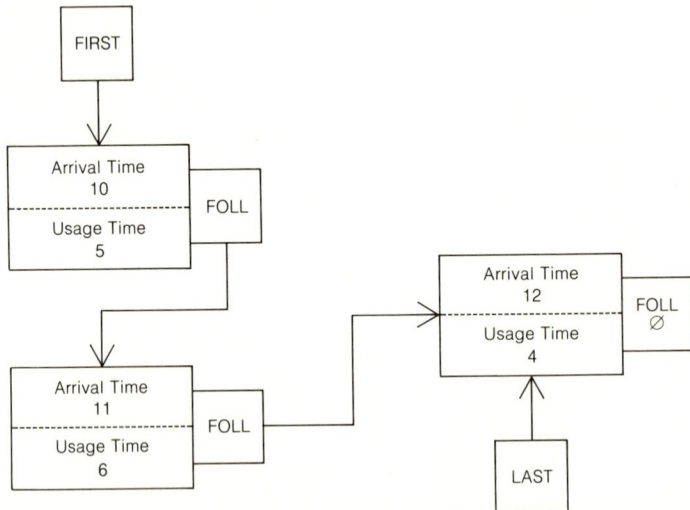

FIRST

Arrival Time
10
Usage Time
5
FOLL

Arrival Time
12
Usage Time
4
FOLL
∅

Arrival Time
11
Usage Time
6
FOLL

LAST

FIG. 9.6 Entity Joining a FIFO Chain Representing a Queue with Two Elements

be serviced easily by finding the first green element. Just as the pointer FIRST was used to locate the beginning of the list, a pointer GREEN could be used to locate the first green element.

An element can be a member of many different queues with differing disciplines if enough pointers are associated with the element. For example, there could be a set of N head and tail pointers (FIRST1, LAST1, FIRST2, LAST2, . . . , FIRSTN, LASTN) and N pairs of pointers (PREC1, FOLL1), . . . , (PRECN, FOLLN) associated with each element. With this arrangement, N different queues can be simulated, and any element may belong to any queue. For example, the values of PREC3 and FOLL3 would connect the element with the preceding and following elements in queue number 3, while the values of PREC8 and FOLL8 would connect the element into queue number 8. Values of $\emptyset$ for both members of any pair (PRECN and FOLLN, for example) would indicate that the element is not a member of queue N.

There are storage problems associated with list processing. As indicated in Figure 9.6, the process of creating or extending a list requires that a certain amount of storage be acquired for each additional element and that the associated pointers be adjusted to reflect properly the queuing discipline. The removal of list elements is carried out similarly. For example, if MEMBER 2 of Chain I (Figure 9.5) has been serviced and is to be removed from the queue, the pointer FOLL in MEMBER 1 would be modified to point to MEMBER 3. The list then effectively bypasses MEMBER 2, because MEMBER 2 no longer can be found by following pointers in the chain. Care must be taken to make available the storage that had been used for discarded MEMBER 2, so that it can be reused for future additions to the queue. In most applications, this need to keep track of discarded storage elements becomes a critical problem, because new elements frequently are added and existing elements frequently are deleted from the chains. The process of keeping track of and reusing storage space is called *garbage collection* and is an important consideration in list processing. Fortunately, languages such as GPSS, PL/I, and SIMSCRIPT alleviate many of the problems associated with the details of garbage collection. In most other languages — for example, in assembly languages — garbage collection is a difficult and time consuming problem.

Maisel (1969, pp. 105–110) discusses list processing at an elementary level; Knuth (1968) gives a more advanced discussion. For a discussion of list processing and garbage collection using PL/I, see IBM Report F20–0015 (1969).

9.9 PL/I

As more manufacturers implement PL/I compilers, this general purpose language is gaining fairly widespread use. PL/I not only encompasses all the capabilities of FORTRAN, but it also has additional, powerful dynamic storage allocation and list-processing features that are very helpful in the simulation of such system entities as queues. Figure 9.9 shows the listing of a PL/I program for simulation of the phone booth system. The essential logic of the program is diagrammed in Figure 9.7; a more complete flowchart of the program is shown in Figure 9.8.

The timing algorithm (clocking routine) updates the clock to the next scheduled event and determines whether that event is an arrival or a departure. If it is an arrival, the PL/I procedure named ARRIVE is executed; if it is a departure, DEPART is executed. The routine ARRIVE performs operations associated with the arrival of caller entities and then schedules the next arrival event, which is inserted into the event queue that feeds the clocking routine. Similarly, DEPART performs the necessary operations involved in caller departure and then schedules the next departure event. The event queue thus holds only two events at a time: the next arrival event, which is held in TNXT_ARV; and the next departure event, which is held in TNXT_DPRT. The clocking routine is contained in statements 21 through 29 of the program (Figure 9.9).

A caller arriving into the system is represented by the structured data item named USER. Execution of the ALLOCATE USER; statement in the program causes a sufficient amount of computer core to be reserved for this data item and assigns the location of this core to the pointer P—in other words, this statement creates a new arrival. USER has two attributes: ARVL_TIME to store the time of his arrival and USE_TIME to store the amount of time that the caller will require on the equipment. USER also contains a pointer named FOLL, which is used to locate the next caller to arrive into the system. Thus, the data item USER is structured similarly to those items forming the queue in Figure 9.6.

When the clock is updated to an arrival event, the routine ARRIVE is called. This routine consists of statements 33 through 57 (Figure 9.9). Statement 34 creates the new arrival; statements 35 and 36 create its attributes—arrival time and duration of call. Note that stochastic behavior has been introduced through

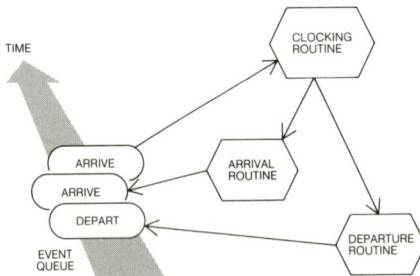

FIG. 9.7 Gross Flow of Logic for PL/I Simulation of the Phone Booth System

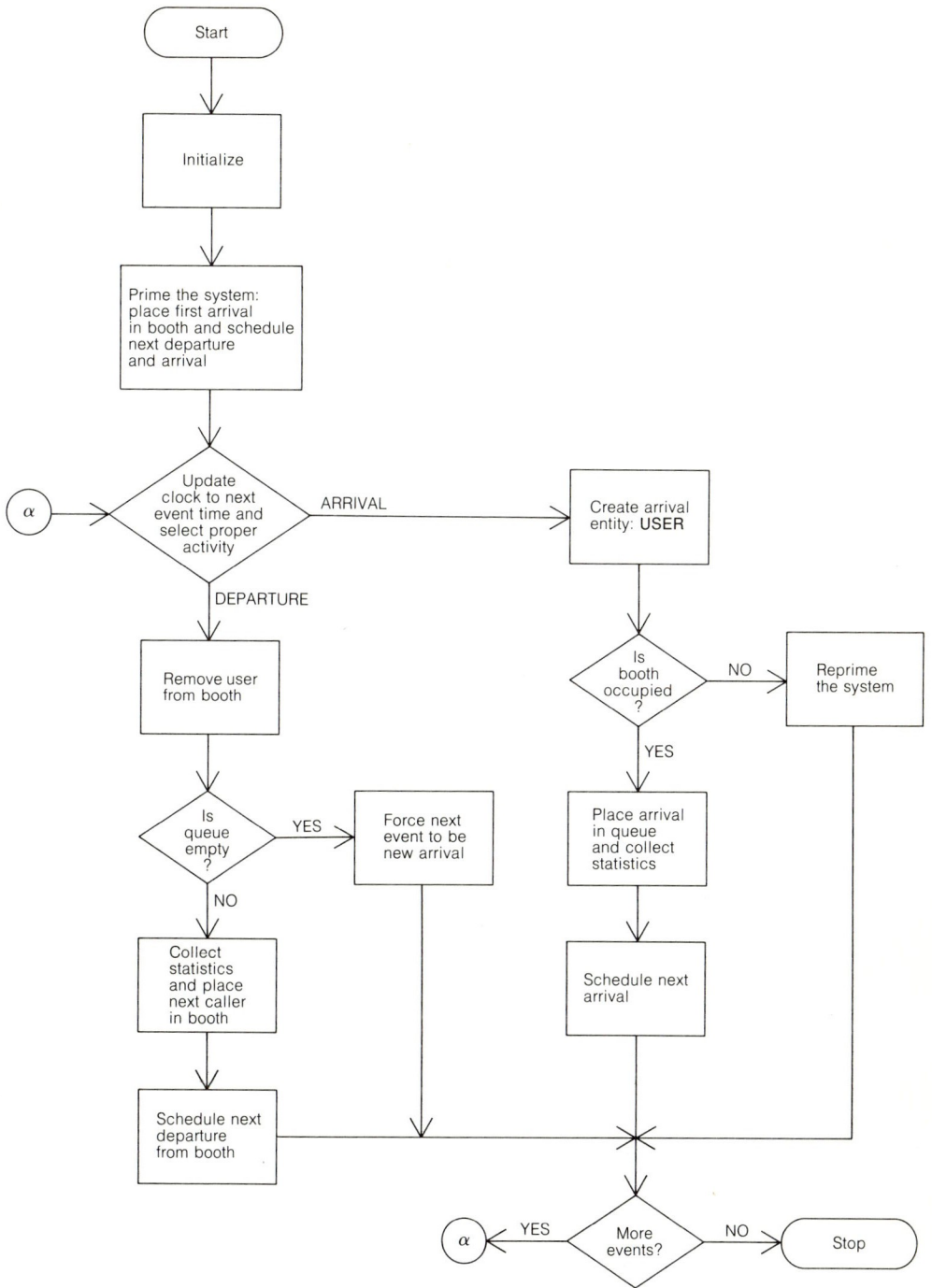

FIG. 9.8   Flowchart of PL/I Simulation of Phone Booth System

```
            SIM: PROCEDURE OPTIONS (MAIN);


STMT LEVEL NEST
   1                        SIM: PROCEDURE OPTIONS (MAIN);
   2     1                    DCL 1 USER BASED (P),
                                2 ARVL_TIME,
                                2 USE_TIME,
                                2 FOLL POINTER,
                                (LAST,FIRST,TEL) POINTER;
   3     1                    DCL (USE_FROM,USE_TO,RATE_FROM,RATE_TO) FIXED BIN;
   4     1                    ON ENDFILE (SYSIN ) STOP;

   6     1             STARTIT:    GET LIST (RATE_FROM,RATE_TO,USE_FROM,USE_TO);
   7     1                    PUT PAGE DATA(RATE_FROM,RATE_TO,USE_FROM,USE_TO);
   8     1                    CTEL,CLOCK,CUMQ,CUMT=0;
   9     1                    STATE=1;
  10     1                    NUSE=1;
  11     1                    NQUE=0;
  12     1                    NMAX=0;
                            /* PRIME THE SYSTEM */
  13     1                    ALLOCATE USER;
  14     1                    TEL=P;
  15     1                    USE_TIME=IRND(USE_FROM,USE_TO);
  16     1                    ARVL_TIME=CLOCK;
  17     1                    TNXT_ARV=CLOCK+IRND(RATE_FROM,RATE_TO);
  18     1                    TNXT_DPRT=CLOCK+USE_TIME;
  19     1                    TLAST=TNXT_ARV;

  20     1                    DO WHILE(NUSE<1000);
                            /* CLOCKING ROUTINE */
  21     1    1                 IF TNXT_ARV > TNXT_DPRT THEN DO;
  23     1    2                    CLOCK=TNXT_DPRT;
  24     1    2                    CALL DEPART;
  25     1    2                    END;
  26     1    1                 ELSE DO;
  27     1    2                    CLOCK=TNXT_ARV;
  28     1    2                    CALL ARRIVE;
  29     1    2                    END;
  30     1    1                 END;

  31     1                    PUT PAGE EDIT( 'TIME=',CLOCK,
                                 'CUM TME INTGRL=',CUMQ,
                                 'CUM DLY TMES=',CUMT,
                                 'EQPMNT UTLZTN=',CTEL/CLOCK,
                                 'MAX IN QUE=',NMAX,
                                 'AVG DELAY =',CUMT/1000.0,
                                 'AVG CONTENTS=',CUMQ/CLOCK)
                                 (SKIP,A,F(15,6));
  32     1                    GO TO STARTIT;

                            /* ARRIVAL ROUTINES */
  33     1             ARRIVE:     PROCEDURE;
  34     2                STRT: ALLOCATE USER;
  35     2                    ARVL_TIME=CLOCK;
  36     2                    USE_TIME=IRND(USE_FROM,USE_TO);
```

FIG. 9.9   Listing of PL/I Program for Simulation of Phone Booth System

use of a random number generator similar to that for the FORTRAN example (Figure 9.4). Statements 37 through 46 are executed only if the system needs repriming—that is, if the telephone booth is not in use (as indicated by a value of zero for the telephone booth attribute STATE). In such a case, the system has been empty since the previous departure time, and the new arrival goes directly

```
37      2              IF STATE=0 THEN DO;
                         /* REPRIME THE SYSTEM */
39      2     1          TEL=P;
40      2     1          TNXT_DPRT=CLOCK+USE_TIME;
41      2     1          STATE=1;
42      2     1          NUSE=NUSE+1;
43      2     1          TNXT_ARV=CLOCK+IRND(RATE_FROM,RATE_TO);
44      2     1          TLAST=TNXT_ARV;
45      2     1          RETURN;
46      2     1          END;
                       /* PLACE ENTITY IN WAITING LINE */
47      2              IF NQUE=0 THEN FIRST=P;
49      2                   ELSE LAST->FOLL=P;
50      2              CUMQ=CUMQ+NQUE*(CLOCK-TLAST);
51      2              TLAST=CLOCK;
52      2              NQUE=NQUE+1;
53      2              NMAX=MAX(NMAX,NQUE);
54      2              LAST=P;
55      2              TNXT_ARV=CLOCK+IRND(RATE_FROM,RATE_TO);
56      2              RETURN;
57      2              END;

                       /* DEPARTURE ROUTINE */
58      1      DEPART:     PROCEDURE;
                         /* FREE BOOTH */
59      2              CTEL=CTEL+TEL->USE_TIME;
60      2              STATE=0;
61      2              FREE TEL->USER;
62      2              IF NQUE=0 THEN DO;
                         /* SYSTEM IS EMPTY. FORCE NEXT */
                         /* EVENT TO BE ARRIVAL.        */
64      2     1          TNXT_DPRT=1E50;
65      2     1          RETURN;
66      2     1          END;
67      2              CUMQ=CUMQ+NQUE*(CLOCK-TLAST);
68      2              TLAST=CLOCK;
69      2              CUMT=CUMT+     (CLOCK-FIRST->ARVL_TIME);
                       /* PLACE FIRST WAITING CALLER IN BOOTH */
70      2              TEL=FIRST;
71      2              FIRST=TEL->FOLL;
72      2              NQUE=NQUE-1;
73      2              NUSE=NUSE+1;
74      2              STATE=1;
75      2              TNXT_DPRT=CLOCK+TEL->USE_TIME;
76      2              RETURN;
77      2              END;

                       /* RANDOM NUMBER GENERATOR */
78      1      IRND:      PROCEDURE(FROM,TO);
79      2              DCL (FROM,TO) FIXED BIN;
80      2              DCL (IX,IY) STATIC FIXED BIN(31) INIT(1);
81      2                  CALL RANDU(IX,IY,YFL);
82      2                  IX=IY;
83      2              M=FROM+YFL*(TO+1-FROM);
84      2              RETURN(M);
85      2              END;
86      1      END SIM;
```

FIG. 9.9—Continued

to use the phone. The system is primed in the same way (statements 13 through 19) when the first arrival occurs. If the telephone booth is in use (as indicated by a value of one for STATE), the entity USER will not go directly to the phone, but will join the queue instead. The code to enter an element onto the queue consists of the following statements from the program:

47	2	IF NQUE=0 THEN FIRST=P;
49	2	ELSE LAST->FOLL=P;
52	2	NQUE=NQUE+1;
54	2	LAST=P;

First, the value of the queue attribute NQUE (which counts the number of elements presently in the queue) is checked. If it is zero, then the queue is reconstructed to contain one new element. This is done by setting the pointer FIRST equal to the pointer P (which already points to the last allocation of USER; in other words, to the new arrival). The pointer LAST also is set to P, and NQUE is incremented by one. Thus, the queue contains only the new arrival, and the head and tail pointers both point to this same element. If the queue is not empty (NQUE≠0), then FIRST points to the location of the first caller in the queue, and LAST points to the last caller. Addition of the new caller to the queue requires execution of the process diagrammed in Figure 9.6. In this case, the pointer FIRST is not affected, but continues to point to the head of the queue. However, the pointer FOLL in the last entity of the queue is given the value P, thus adding the new arrival onto the end of the queue (statement 49). Finally, LAST is updated to the value P (thus pointing to the new tail of the queue), and the size of the queue (NQUE) is incremented by one. The remaining statements of the ARRIVE routine schedule the next arrival event and RETURN to the clocking routine.

The routine DEPART handles departures and, if the queue is not empty, handles the entry into the phone booth (freed by the departure) of the first entity in the queue. Execution of the DEPART routine begins whenever a departure event is scheduled to occur. Immediately upon entry to the routine, the booth is freed by the code

60	2	STATE=0;
61	2	FREE TEL->USER;

First the STATE of the equipment is set to zero, indicating that it is not in use. Next the USER presently in the booth is eliminated from the system. The pointer TEL is used to identify this USER, and statement 61 releases the space occupied by this USER.

Because the booth now is free, the queue is checked to see if there is another USER waiting. If no USER is waiting (NQUE=0), then the system is empty, and the next event is forced to be an arrival. This is accomplished (in statements 62 through 66) by the simple mechanism of making the next departure time so high that the clocking routine always will choose the next arrival as the most imminent event.

If the queue is not empty, statistics are updated and the next USER in line is placed into the booth by the code

70	2	TEL=FIRST;
71	2	FIRST=TEL->FOLL;
72	2	NQUE=NQUE−1;
73	2	NUSE=NUSE+1;
74	2	STATE=1;

Because FIRST points to the USER first in line, statement 70 sets the pointer TEL to locate the first USER waiting. After this is done, the head pointer FIRST is recalculated to point to the entity that FOLLowed the entity just removed from the queue. The size of the queue (NQUE) then is decreased by one, and the STATE of the phone booth is set to busy (1). Finally, the routine schedules the next departure event and RETURNs to the clocking routine.

The queuing discipline established by this program is FIFO. Entities are added to the tail of the chain and are removed from the head of the chain. Other queuing disciplines could be simulated in similar ways. For example, a RANDOM discipline could be simulated by the code listed in Figure 9.10, which removes a USER selected RANDOMly from the queue and places him into the booth. Of course, this code must replace correctly the equivalent statements (70 through 74) in the DEPART routine. The RANDOM discipline routine is quite simple. A random number is chosen between 1 and the present length of the queue. This number, contained in CHOICE, indicates which entity of the

```
/* CHOICE IS RANDOM INTG BETWEEN 1 AND NQUE INCLUSIVELY.
   REMOVE IS POINTER LOCATING THE RANDOMLY SELECTED USER.
   LINK POINTS TO HIS PREDECESSOR AND IS USED TO CLOSE THE
      GAP IN THE CHAIN WHEN THE USER IS REMOVED. */

   CHOICE=IRND(ONE,NQUE); /* SELECT ENTITY ON QUE.*/
   IF CHOICE=1 THEN DO;
      /* FIRST ELEMENT ON QUE WAS CHOSEN */
      REMOVE=FIRST;          /* POINT TO ENTITY REMOVED */
      FIRST=TEL->FOLL;       /* SECOND ENTITY BECOMES FIRST */
      END;
   ELSE DO;   /* ENTITY CHOSEN WAS NOT THE FIRST ENTITY ON QUE */
      LINK=FIRST;            /* ROUTINE TO FIND   */
      DO J=1 TO CHOICE-2;    /* POINTER TO ENTITY */
      LINK=LINK->FOLL;       /* TO BE REMOVED */
      END;                   /* FROM THE QUEUE. */
      REMOVE=LINK->FOLL;
      IF REMOVE=LAST THEN LAST=LINK;    /* CLOSE THE */
         ELSE LINK->FOLL=REMOVE->FOLL;  /* CHAIN.    */

   /* PLACE THE CHOSEN USER IN BOOTH */
   TEL=REMOVE;
   NQUE=NQUE-1;
   STATE=1;
```

FIG. 9.10 Listing of PL/I Code to Implement RANDOM Queuing Discipline in Phone Booth System

queue will be allowed to use the phone next. The pointer REMOVE then is cal-culated to locate the selected USER. Because a gap will develop when the USER is removed, the routine also relinks the chain to eliminate the gap.

9.10 Statistics

This section discusses some of the statistics commonly gathered during simula-tion runs and the general manner in which they are collected.

The simplest type of statistical information is a count—for example, the amount of elapsed clock time, the number of entities in a queue, the total num-ber of arrivals, and so forth. Some, such as clock time, are cumulative; others, such as queue length, are used to specify certain measures of the system state. For measures of the latter kind, it often is of interest to record such things as the maximal and minimal values assumed by the counter during the entire run. For example, in the PL/I simulation program, the maximal length of the queue waiting for the telephone is calculated by the statement,

```
53      2              NMAX=MAX(NMAX,NQUE);
```

MAX is a function in the PL/I language; it extracts the maximal value from its argument list. Because this statement is executed each time the length of the queue is increased, the final value of NMAX will be the maximal length of the queue during the run.

The calculation of the mean and standard deviation of some of the statistics also may be of interest. These quantities are obtained during a simulation run through the use of two cumulative counters for each statistic—one counter to accumulate the sum of the observations, and the other to accumulate the sum of the squares of the observations. In the PL/I program, the mean length of the queue and the standard deviation of the length could be calculated by inserting the following three statements into the program:

```
SUM=SUM+NQUE;                 /*  SUM,SUM_SQRS,NCHNGES  ARE  ASSUMED */
SUM_SQRS=SUM_SQRS+NQUE**2; /*  INITIALLY  TO  BE  ZERO             */
NCHNGES=NCHNGES+1;            /*  NCHANGES  COUNTS  NUMBER  OF       */
                              /*  OBSERVED  QUEUE  LENGTH  CHANGES.  */
```

at the points where NQUE changes value (immediately following statements 52 and 72 in Figure 9.9). At the end of the run, the mean and standard deviation of the length of the queue can be calculated as follows:

```
QML=SUM/NCHNGES;
QLSS=SQRT((SUM_SQRS**2−NCHNGES*QML**2)/(NCHNGES−1));
```

The mean as defined above is not always a satisfactory measure of central tendency for entities that change size as simulation time passes. It is more informative to know the proportion of the time that a queue was a given length, rather than simply how many times it reached that length. The former type of queue length may be measured by weighting queue length by its duration when calculating statistics of interest. The time-weighted measure of central tendency is termed the "average contents" of the queue. This measure is discussed further below.

Statistics must be gathered at certain specified points in the model — at the event times where the system changes states in such a way as to affect the statistics of interest. For example, NQUE is affected each time that a caller enters or departs the queue. However, the event of entering the queue does not affect any statistic concerned with direct measurement of telephone use. Thus, in the PL/I program, the counter NUSE is incremented only when the telephone booth is entered — not when the queue is entered. Care is needed to gather statistics at all of the appropriate event times. This event-time dependency becomes even more explicit in measuring time-dependent status-change statistics such as utilization of entities, average queue contents, and so forth.

Two other statistics are of special interest: the average utilization of an entity that provides service, and the average contents of certain sets. Each statistic is based on a counter known as the *cumulative time integral*, C, which is defined as

$$C = \Sigma \phi_i \Delta t_i = \Sigma \phi_i (t_{i+1} - t_i), \qquad (9.1)$$

where ϕ_i is the level of utilization of contents during the time interval Δt_i, which is the time between t_i (the time of the preceding change in utilization of contents) and t_{i+1} (the time of the next change in utilization of contents). The sum is accumulated over all times. (Cumulative time statistics are illustrated in Figure 10.19.)

The *average contents* (AC) of a set is defined as

$$AC = C/T, \qquad (9.2)$$

where T is the total elapsed simulation time. This statistic is important in dealing with queues. It measures the average number of entities waiting in the queue during a simulation run. *Average utilization* can be calculated for sets of entities that have the attribute of capacity, or maximal size. Average utilization, AU, is defined as

$$AU = AC/N, \qquad (9.3)$$

where N is the capacity. For example, if the model has six booths whose usage was simulated for one hour, average utilization would be calculated as

$$AU = [(\Sigma \phi_i \Delta t_i)/60]/6 = (\Sigma \phi_i \Delta t_i)/360,$$

where ϕ_i is the number of booths in use during the time interval Δt_i. Note that, when the use of only one booth is being simulated, average utilization and average contents are calculated from the same expression (because $N = 1$):

$$AC = AU = \Sigma \Delta t_i' / T,$$

where $\Delta t_i'$ represents only the time intervals during which the entity was in use. Because ϕ_i is 0 when the entity is not in use and is 1 when the entity is in use, the time intervals when the entity is not in use can be ignored in the case of a single booth. In the example, the phone booth utilization is calculated as CTEL/CLOCK, where CTEL is the total amount of time the booth was in use. In the PL/I program, the statement

CUMQ=CUMQ+NQUE*(CLOCK−TLAST);

(used as statements 50 and 67) computes the cumulative time integral for the queue. In the output section (statement 31), the average contents of the waiting line is calculated as CUMQ/CLOCK.

The transit time through the system and the interarrival time at specified points in the system are two other statistics commonly calculated during simulation runs. In the FORTRAN program, for example, the *transit time* is calculated as the difference between the arrival and departure times. These differences are accumulated into the counter XTME, which finally is used to calculate the average transit time. The *interarrival time* (time between successive arrivals) could be accumulated by a counter and then used to compute average interarrival time. However, often it is more useful to record the exact distribution of interarrival times, thus giving the analyst a more detailed and meaningful view of the nature of the flow through the system.

Distributions commonly are recorded by means of a frequency table. For example, suppose that FR has been declared to be an array containing 51 elements; this array is to be used to record the distributions of queue lengths in the PL/I program. The frequency classes to be recorded are

Class 1	$0 \leq$ NQUE < 2
Class 2	$2 \leq$ NQUE < 4
Class 3	$4 \leq$ NQUE < 6
.	.
.	.
.	.
Class 50	$98 \leq$ NQUE < 100
Class 51	NQUE ≥ 100

The recording can be done by inserting the following code after each point at which the queue length (NQUE) changes:

```
IF  NQUE>100  THEN FR(51)=FR(51)+1;
              ELSE FR(NQUE/2+1)=FR(NQUE/2+1)+1;
```

Here FR(51) is the overflow class, which counts the number of times that the queue size exceeded 99. If NQUE does not exceed 100, then the correct frequency class is incremented. For example, if NQUE=5, then (NQUE/2+1) = 5/2 + 1 = 3.5, which is truncated to the integer 3. Thus, FR(3) is incremented by 1; as can be seen above, NQUE=5 does fall within frequency class 3.

9.11 SIMSCRIPT: Basic Concepts

SIMSCRIPT is a discrete simulation language with its origins in FORTRAN. There are several versions of this language; the examples here are given in SIMSCRIPT 1.5, which is more widely available.

The basic concepts of SIMSCRIPT are much the same as those discussed in the preceding sections. There are entities, which can be assigned various attributes. Sets may be defined to simulate various membership relationships such as queues. Activities that interact with sets and entities can be defined by subroutines called *event routines*.

All of these concepts can be handled by using general purpose languages such as FORTRAN or PL/I. However, SIMSCRIPT offers some advantages for simulation programming: not only does it have most of the capabilities of FORTRAN, but it also contains terminology and tools specifically designed for simulation of discrete systems. For example, the clocking mechanism for event scheduling is handled automatically. Also, complicated queuing disciplines can be simulated easily, without the programming overhead required in PL/I list processing. In SIMSCRIPT, pointers are adjusted automatically whenever set membership changes.

A SIMSCRIPT simulation has five major parts: (1) definition section; (2) event routines list; (3) event routines; (4) initialization section; and (5) exogenous event list. In the following paragraphs, these parts and their interactions are described in general terms.

In the *definition section*, entities, attributes, and other system variables are defined. Figure 9.11 shows an example of the coding for a definition section. SIMSCRIPT provides for two types of entities: temporary and permanent.

Temporary entities are used to represent items that are created and destroyed at various times during the simulation. For example, the code T in column 2 of the form marks MAN as a temporary entity. This entity can be used to represent a telephone caller who enters the system to place a call at the booth and is removed from the system when he is finished. Associated with MAN are several attributes: TIBTH, TTOQ, SQUE, STEL, and so on. These attributes can be used to carry such information as the total time the entity will use the telephone (TIBTH). MAN and its attributes can be used in much the same way that the PL/I structure named USER was used to represent dynamic entities in the telephone booth system.

Permanent system variables are used to define entities, variables, pointers, arrays, and so forth — items that are permanent characteristics of the entire model, and that can be referenced throughout the entire simulation. They cannot be

FIG. 9.11 SIMSCRIPT Definition Form

```
Column 7

  │
  ↓
  EVENTS
  1 EXOGENOUS
        CRNKUP (1)
  2 ENDOGENOUS
        ARVE
        LEAV
  END
```

FIG. 9.12   Example of a SIMSCRIPT Events List

created or destroyed at will. Such variables can be used to communicate information between different parts of the model, to gather information concerning the entire system, or to define attributes of the entire system. For example, the permanent variable FNUSE could be used to count the number of MAN entities that entered the phone booth.

Queues and their queuing disciplines also are defined in the definition section. For example, QUE and TEL are defined to be FIFO queues (by the code F in column 57). Temporary entities that may belong to the sets must have as attributes pointers that will be used to chain them onto the set. MAN uses SQUE and STEL to point to the successor entity on the sets. The sets also must have head and tail pointers defined for them. The head pointer FQUE and the tail pointer LQUE are defined as permanent variables; FTEL and LTEL perform the same function for the set TEL.

The *event routine list* is used to name each of the routines that will perform system activities; these routines are called event routines. SIMSCRIPT allows two types of event routines: endogenous and exogenous.

As the names suggest, *endogenous routines* can be scheduled only from event routines within the simulation, whereas *exogenous routines* are scheduled externally by input from the exogenous event list. Figure 9.12 is an example of an event routine list. On this list, one exogenous routine (named CRNKUP) is listed along with two endogenous routines (named ARVE and LEAV). The number 1 to the right of CRNKUP links this exogenous event routine with a correspondingly numbered entry in the exogenous event list. Note that the number of routines of each type must be specified before naming the type—for example, 2 before ENDOGENOUS.

After the event routine list come the event routines. Each of these event routines consists of a series of FORTRANlike statements which describe activities affecting the state of the model. The general form of a routine is

$$\left\{ \begin{array}{l} \text{ENDOGENOUS} \\ \text{EXOGENOUS} \end{array} \right\} \text{EVENT name of routine}$$

. . . . statements . . . .
RETURN
END

where the brackets indicate a choice. The statements that comprise event routines are discussed in Section 9.12.

In SIMSCRIPT, permanent system variables must be initialized before simulation. The *initialization section* supplies the appropriate values for this initialization. Figure 9.13 is an example of an initialization section, initializing the permanent system variables defined in Figure 9.11. Two options have been used here. The first option is to set groups of variables to zero initially; this is done by specifying the number range of the variables to be set to zero and then placing a Z in column 12. For example, the first line sets variables 1 through 4 to zero initially, and the last line sets variables 9 through 14 to zero initially. Variables 5 through 8 (corresponding to LOWT, HIT, LOWC, and HIC) are initialized individually by using the other option. This option is signaled by an R in column 12, indicating that the value specified in the initial value field (columns 50–66) is to be used to initialize the variable. For example, LOWT will be set to a value of 5 at the beginning of the simulation.

The final section is the *exogenous event list*, which consists of records that each have an ID number corresponding to an exogenous event routine. The record also contains a time, which will be the event time at which the corresponding exogenous event routine will be executed. Many such records may appear for each of the exogenous event routines defined in the model. In a SIMSCRIPT I.5 simulation, at least one exogenous event routine with at least one exogenous event notice must be used to start the simulation.

Finally, we wish to discuss the clocking mechanism in SIMSCRIPT. The algorithm follows essentially the same logic as that diagrammed for the PL/I program in Figure 9.7. Statements are available in SIMSCRIPT to create endogenous event notices at various times during the simulation. Each such notice has an event time attribute, which indicates the time at which the associated event routine is to be executed. After they are created, the endogenous event notices are inserted into the event queue, which also contains all exogenous event notices. All of the notices in the event queue are kept sorted into chronological order throughout the simulation. The control algorithm then proceeds as follows: The next scheduled event notice in the event queue is examined. The clock is updated to the specified event time, and the associated event routine is initiated. When the event routine has been completed, the process of examining the next event notice from the queue is repeated. Note that new endogenous event notices may be issued during any event routine. The event queue must be continuously updated as new event notices are added and old ones are removed from the head of the queue; this updating is done automatically by the control programs.

FIG. 9.13 SIMSCRIPT Initialization Form

Row	ARRAY NUMBER FROM	TO	NO. OF SUBSCRIPTS	READ-IN VALUES	SET TO ZERO	INITIAL VALUE OR DESCRIPTION
1	1	4			N	
2	5		O	R		5
3	6		O	R		15
4	7		O	R		8
5	8		O	R		16
6	9	14	O		N	
7						
8						
9						
10						
11						
12						
13						
14						
15						
16						

9.12 SIMSCRIPT: Language Elements

SIMSCRIPT is similar to FORTRAN in many ways. This similarity is particularly evident in the form of the statements and coding formats used to define event routines. These statements are discussed in this section, with some general comments about their use in SIMSCRIPT simulations. Table 9.2 lists the more common simulation-oriented statements of this language. A complete description of the syntax used in SIMSCRIPT I.5 is given in the *SIMSCRIPT I.5 Univac 1106/1107/ 1108 User Manual* (available from Univac Federal Systems Division).

SIMSCRIPT statements are coded on cards in exactly the same way as are FORTRAN statements. The body of the statement is contained in columns 7 through 72. Column 6 is reserved for card continuation. Columns 2 through 5 are reserved for statement labels, and columns 73 through 80 are ignored by the compiler. As in FORTRAN, a letter C appearing in column 1 indicates a comment card.

The statements comprising the language generally can be divided into seven major classifications (Table 9.2). In the class of entity operations appear the CREATE and DESTROY statements. The CREATE statement is used to allocate space for a temporary entity; it is used similarly to the ALLOCATE statement that creates the entity USER in the PL/I program. For example, the statement

> CREATE MAN

would cause storage space to be reserved for the temporary entity named MAN, which was defined in Figure 9.11. Without some systematic method of freeing storage space after a temporary entity has left the system, a SIMSCRIPT simulation soon would run out of computer memory. The statement DESTROY is available to free the space that has been allocated to any temporary entity; for example, the statement

> DESTROY MAN

would release the storage space created by the statement just above.

When it is necessary to create two MAN entities that will exist simultaneously within the system, local variables may be used to differentiate between them. A *local variable* is one that is known only within the extent of the event routine where it is defined. For example, the statements

> CREATE MAN CALLED JERRY
> CREATE MAN CALLED LARRY

define the local variables JERRY and LARRY and make it possible to distinguish between attributes of these two MAN entities coexisting within the system. For example, TIBTH(JERRY) would be a reference to the length of the call made by JERRY, whereas TIBTH(LARRY) would define the length of LARRY's call.

TABLE 9.2   SIMSCRIPT I.5 Statements

Entity Operations

      CREATE temporary entity [CALLED local variable]

      DESTROY temporary entity [CALLED local variable]

      CAUSE event notice [CALLED local variable] [AT expression]

      CANCEL event notice [CALLED local variable]

      FILE pointer variable IN set

      REMOVE pointer variable FROM ranked set

      REMOVE FIRST pointer variable FROM set

Arithmetic Statements

      LET variable = expression [,control phrase] . . . [,control phrase]

Control Phrases and Modifiers

      FOR variable = (expression) (expression) [(expression)]

      FOR EACH entity

      FOR EACH variable IN set

      WITH (expression) comparison code (expression)

      OR (expression) comparison code (expression)

      AND (expression) comparison code (expression)

Iteration Statements

      DO [TO statement label], control phrase [,control phrase] . . . [,control phrase]

Decision Statements

      IF (expression) comparison code (expression), any statement

      IF set $\left\{ \begin{matrix} \text{IS} \\ \text{IS NOT} \end{matrix} \right\}$ EMPTY, any statement

      FIND variable = $\left\{ \begin{matrix} \text{MAX} \\ \text{MIN} \end{matrix} \right\}$ OF expression, control phrases [WHERE pointer variable] [, IF NONE statement]

Computational Statements

      ACCUMULATE variable list = variable list SINCE time list [, $\left\{ \begin{matrix} \text{POST} \\ \text{ADD} \end{matrix} \right\}$ phrases]

      COMPUTE variables = statistics list OF expression [, control phrases]

Input-Output Statements

      SAVE [optional test]

      READ FROM [TAPE] expression, variable list [, control phrases]

      WRITE ON [TAPE] expression, variable list [, control phrases]

In this case, the DESTROY statement must specify which MAN entity is to be DESTROYed. For example, the statement

DESTROY MAN CALLED JERRY

would free the space that had been allocated to the MAN entity named JERRY.

Event routines often contain a sequence of operations that create and schedule an endogenous event. Because an endogenous event notice is a type of temporary entity, the creation of an event notice is accomplished with a CREATE statement. For example, the statement

CREATE ARVE

creates an event notice named ARVE. The name used for the event notice must also be the name of one of the endogenous event routines defined in the event routines section. This event notice will trigger the execution of the endogenous event routine ARVE when the control program detects it as the next event on the event queue. The CAUSE statement is used to insert the event notice into its proper place in the event queue; for example,

CAUSE ARVE AT TIME + 12.5

Because TIME is an automatically defined system variable, which gives the value of the present clock time, the event notice will be inserted into the event queue with an event time 12.5 units in the future. The event routine named ARVE will be executed at that time.

Arrival notices that have been entered into the event queue may be removed from the queue by use of a CANCEL statement. For example, the routine named ARVE may have been scheduled already, when a check on the size of the line at the booth indicates the wisdom of not creating new arrivals for a time. In such a case, the statement

CANCEL ARVE

would remove the event notice from the queue. Such statements often are useful in the simulation of reneges.

Either the execution of the endogenous event routine or the CANCEL statement will remove the event notice from the event queue. However, neither one frees the space that had been allocated to the event notice; this must be done with the DESTROY statement. Because event notices are temporary entities and can have attributes, they often are used to transmit information from the event routine that scheduled them to the event routine that they trigger.

Several statements are available to permit simulation of set operations such as queuing. The FILE statement can be used to place a temporary entity into a set. For example, the statements

CREATE MAN CALLED LARRY
FILE LARRY IN QUE

would create a temporary entity and place it into a set named QUE. If QUE has been defined as a ranked set, then a specific entity can be removed according to its local variable identifier by means of the statement

REMOVE LARRY FROM QUE

This specific type of removal from ranked sets is allowed because ranked sets are doubly linked chains in SIMSCRIPT. For LIFO and FIFO sets, which are singly linked, a simpler type of removal is required, using statements such as

CREATE MAN

    .

    .

    .

FILE MAN IN QUE

    .

    .

    .

REMOVE FIRST MAN FROM QUE

If QUE was defined as FIFO, MAN will be placed by the FILE statement at the tail of QUE; if QUE was defined as LIFO, MAN will be placed at the head of QUE. The REMOVE FIRST statement always will remove the entity at the head of the set.

The set IF statement is of particular interest in dealing with decisions involving sets. This statement allows the analyst to test whether or not a set is empty. For example, the series of statements

  6 IF QUE IS EMPTY, GO TO 7
     REMOVE FIRST MAN FROM QUE
     GO TO 1000
  7 . . .

will cause the REMOVE statement to be bypassed if the set QUE is empty. If QUE is not empty, the first entity of the set will be removed.

Arithmetic and computational statements are provided to extend the capabilities of FORTRAN. The LET statement is the SIMSCRIPT equivalent of the assignment statement. For example, in execution of the statement

LET IX(3)=Y+1.5*Z

the expression to the right of the equal sign is evaluated, and this value is placed into location IX(3), with a conversion from floating point to integer mode if necessary.

The ACCUMULATE and COMPUTE statements are two purely computational statements that are extremely useful in gathering statistics. The ACCUMULATE statement generally is used to accumulate totals over time. For example, the cumulative time integral for a set named QUE could be calculated through execution of the statement

ACCUMULATE FNQUE INTO CUMQ SINCE TLAST

before each change of QUE size. Here TLAST is the time of the last status change in QUE size and FNQUE is the number of elements on the QUE. The statement causes execution of the assignments CUMQ=CUMQ+FNQUE*(TIME−TLAST) and TLAST=TIME, which define the cumulative time integral for the QUE and update the time of the last status change.

The COMPUTE statement will cause the automatic calculation of any number of options from the set of statistics in Table 9.3. For example, to calculate the mean XMEAN and standard deviation XSTD of the first K elements of the array X, the following statement can be used:

COMPUTE XMEAN,XSTD=MEAN,STD-DEV OF X(I) FOR I=(1)(K)

The preceding statement also provides an example of the use of a control phrase. Control phrases are the main reason why SIMSCRIPT can be considered a more powerful general purpose language than FORTRAN. The control phrase FOR and its modifiers (AND, OR, and WITH) extend the scope and power of many of the statements. As an example, the single SIMSCRIPT statement

LET X(I)=Z(I)*Y(I) FOR I=(1)(K*J)WITH(Z(I))LT(6.3)

is equivalent to the three FORTRAN statements:

```
      M=K*J
      DO 1 I=1,M
    1 IF (Z(I).LT.6.3), X(I)=Z(I)*Y(I)
```

It is not difficult to see that one SIMSCRIPT compound statement involving many control phrases and modifier phrases may be the equivalent of dozens of FORTRAN statements. The FOR phrase also allows repetitive operations involving sets. For example, the statement

LET TOTME=TOTME+TIME−TTOQ(JOE),FOR EACH JOE IN QUE

will accumulate the sum of delay times for the entities of the set QUE.

Iterative operations requiring more than one statement can be implemented by a DO LOOP similar to FORTRAN DO LOOPs. The typical form of a SIMSCRIPT DO LOOP can be seen in the following example:

```
        DO TO 13, FOR I=(1)(20)
        CREATE MAN CALLED NEXT
        FILE NEXT IN QUE
   13   LOOP
```

In this example, twenty MAN entities are created and filed into the set named QUE.

One decision statement already has been discussed: the set IF statement used to test set occupancy. IF statements similar to FORTRAN IV IF statements also are available. In addition, SIMSCRIPT implements the GO TO and the computed GO TO available in FORTRAN. A true extension of FORTRAN is seen in the FIND statements. For example, the statement

FIND GR8TST=MAX OF X(I), FOR I=(1)(20)

will set GR8TST to the maximal value in the first 20 elements of the array X.

SIMSCRIPT has most of the input-output capabilities of FORTRAN, with several minor modifications and with several extensions. For example, the READ/WRITE statements allow for freer formats in the variables list, but they require that the associated FORMAT statements follow immediately. A true extension of FORTRAN capabilities is the SIMSCRIPT option of defining a routine known as the *report generator*, which simplifies such output as the tabular output very often encountered in simulation problems. Details of this option are described in the *User Manual* mentioned at the beginning of this section.

SIMSCRIPT also has many of the usual automatically defined functions available in FORTRAN, such as SQRT for square root, ABS for absolute value, and so on. In addition, system-wide variables and functions are available to aid in simulation applications. For example, TIME already has been mentioned as a system-wide variable specifying current simulation time in decimal units (days). Random number generating functions are available for use in introducing stochastic behavior. For example, the function RANDI(I,J) produces an integer

TABLE 9.3   Statistics Available with SIMSCRIPT I.5
COMPUTE Statement

Mnemonic	Description
NUMBER	Number of cases satisfying specified conditions
SUM	Sum of elements satisfying specified conditions
MEAN	Mean of elements = SUM/NUMBER.
SUM-SQUARE	Sum of squares of elements satisfying specified conditions
MEAN-SQUARE	(SUM-SQUARE)/NUMBER
VARIANCE	(MEAN-SQUARE)$-$(MEAN$**$2)
STD-DEV	VARIANCE$**$0.5

random variable uniformly distributed between the integer values I to J, and RANDM produces a floating point random variable uniformly distributed between 0.0 and 1.0. These generators can be used in SIMSCRIPT programs to generate a variety of different distributions.

9.13 SIMSCRIPT: An Example

This section discusses the use of SIMSCRIPT for a simulation of the telephone booth system (Section 9.2). Figure 9.14 is the flowchart of the SIMSCRIPT program listed in Figure 9.15. The program contains three event routines: the exogenous event routine CRNKUP, and the two endogenous event routines ARVE and LEAV.

In SIMSCRIPT I.5, at least one exogenous event notice is required to initiate the scheduling algorithm, because no endogenous event notices can be placed into the event queue until some event routine is in execution. In the example, CRNKUP is used both for this purpose and for initializing the model. As soon as the corresponding exogenous event notice forces CRNKUP into execution, the temporary entity MAN is created and its attributes are assigned. TTOQ, which later will be used to calculate the total time in minutes that MAN remained in the waiting line, is initialized to the present time by the statement

LET TTOQ(MAN)=TIME

In this case, the present time is exactly the time coded onto the exogenous event card associated with CRNKUP. The attribute TIBTH is used to store the amount of time that it will take the MAN to make his call. This time is calculated as a random integer uniformly distributed on the interval (LOWT,HIT) by use of the random number generator RANDI. Because time is carried in days by the SIMSCRIPT clock, whereas LOWT and HIT are expressed in minutes, the value of the random number variable is divided by 1,440 (the number of minutes in a day) before it is assigned to TIBTH. Because this MAN is the first entity in the system, it will have immediate access to the telephone booth. Therefore, its departure can be scheduled to occur exactly TIBTH(MAN) days in the future, by use of the statements

CREATE LEAV
CAUSE LEAV AT TIME+TIBTH(MAN)

MAN then is placed into the set TEL, which represents the telephone booth. This set will contain only one entity at a time, and the permanent system variable FNUSE will count the number of entities that have used it. As soon as MAN is placed into TEL, the endogenous event notice ARVE is scheduled to create the next arrival. This notice will be the first notice on the event queue after

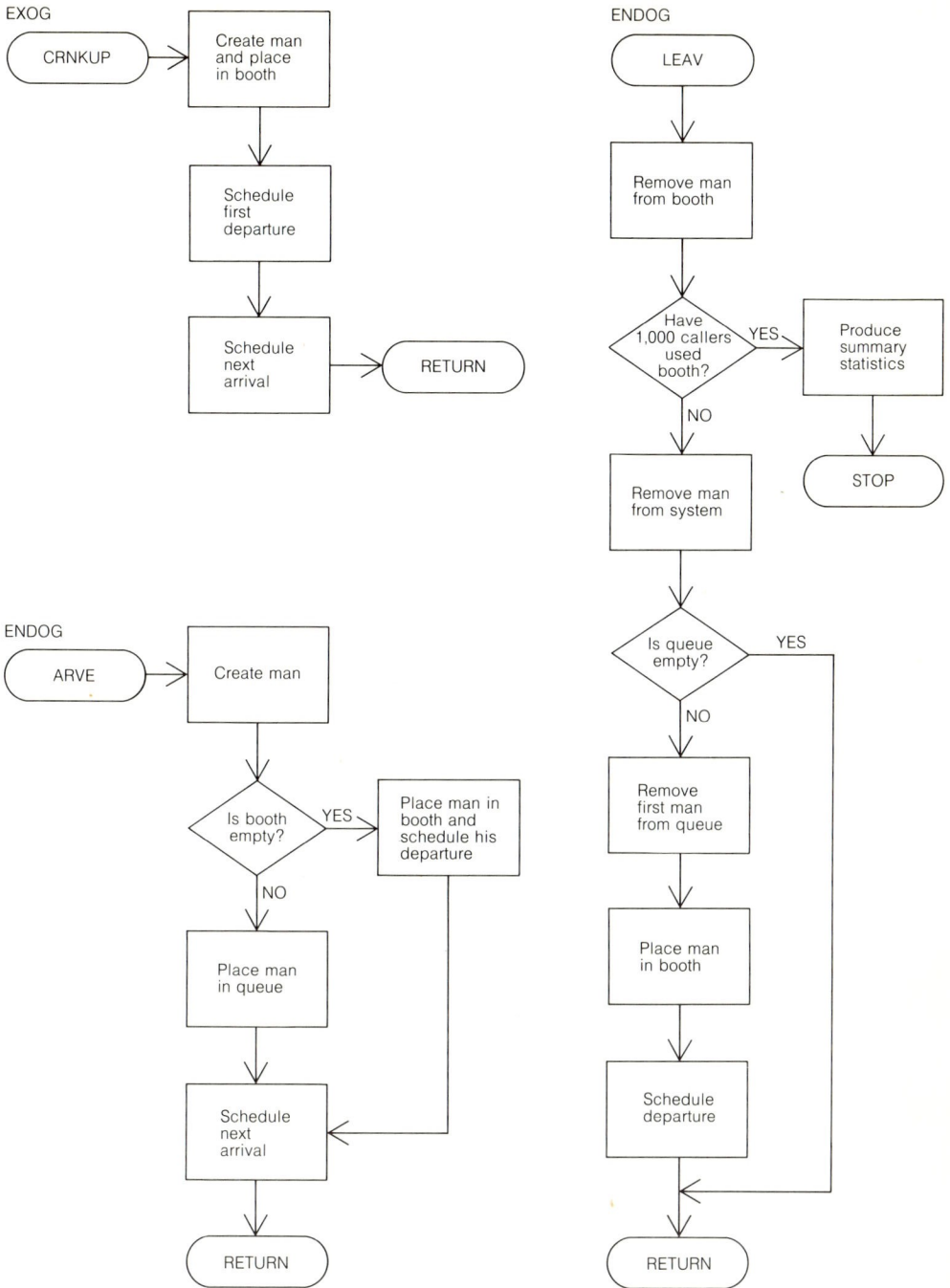

FIG. 9.14 Flowchart for SIMSCRIPT I.5 Simulation of Telephone Booth System

```
C       EXOGENOUS EVENT CRNKUP
C
C
C       THE EXOGENOUS EVENT ROUTINE 'CRNKUP' IS USED TO
C       PRIME THE SYSTEM WITH ONE USER. THE ROUTINE SCHEDULES THE
C       FIRST ARRIVAL AND IS NOT USED PASSED THE INITIALIZATION
C       STAGE
C
        LET FNUSE=1.0
        CREATE MAN
        LET TT=RANDI(LOWT,HIT)
        LET TIBTH(MAN)=TT/1440.
        LET TTOQ(MAN)=TIME
        CREATE  LEAV
        CAUSE   LEAV AT TIME+TIBTH(MAN)
        FILE MAN IN TEL
        CREATE  ARVE
        CAUSE ARVE AT TIME
        RETURN
        END


        ENDOGENOUS EVENT ARVE
C
C
C
C THE ENDOGENOUS EVENT ROUTINE 'ARVE' SCHEDULES ARRIVALS INTO
C    THE MODEL. THE ROUTINE WILL QUE AN ARRIVAL INTO THE WAITING
C    LINE UNLESS THE EQUIPMENT IS FREE FOR USE.
C
        DESTROY ARVE
        CREATE MAN
        LET TT=RANDI(LOWT,HIT)
        LET TIBTH(MAN)=TT/1440.
        LET TTOQ(MAN)=TIME
        IF TEL IS NOT EMPTY, GO TO 333
        CREATE LEAV
        CAUSE LEAV AT TIME+TIBTH(MAN)
        FILE MAN IN TEL
        GO TO 334
  333   ACCUMULATE FNQUE INTO CUMQ SINCE TLAST
        LET FNQUE=FNQUE+1.0
        FILE MAN IN QUE
  334   LET TT=RANDI(LOWC,HIC)
        LET TT=TT/1440.
        CREATE ARVE
        CAUSE ARVE AT TIME+TT
        RETURN
        END


        ENDOGENOUS EVENT LEAV
C
C
C
C   THE ENDOGENOUS ROUTINE 'LEAV' HANDLES STATISTICS AND SCHEDULES
C    USER DEPARTURE TIME. THE ROUTINE ALSO TERMINATES THE PROGRAM
C    AND CAUSES SUMMARY STATS TO BE ISSUED.
C
        DESTROY LEAV
        REMOVE FIRST MAN FROM TEL
        LET CTEL=CTEL+TIBTH(MAN)
        IF FNUSE LS 1000.,GO TO 200
C
        LET UE=CTEL/TIME
        LET AE=CUMQ/TIME
        LET BE=CINT/FNUSE
        WRITE ON TAPE 6
        FORMAT(* NO.          TEL UTLZTN      AVG IN QUE          AVG TME IN
      . QUE *)
        WRITE ON TAPE 6,FNUSE,UE,AE,BE
        FORMAT(D5.0,S4,D2.7,S5,D2.7,S10,D7.4)
        WRITE ON TAPE 6,TIME
        FORMAT(* TIME IS   *,M3.2.2)
        STOP
C
  200   DESTROY MAN
  250   IF QUE IS EMPTY, GO TO 300
        REMOVE FIRST MAN    FROM QUE
        LET CINT=CINT+TIME-TTOQ(MAN)
        ACCUMULATE FNQUE INTO CUMQ SINCE TLAST
        LET FNQUE=FNQUE-1.0
        LET FNUSE=FNUSE+1.0
        CREATE  LEAV
        CAUSE LEAV AT TIME+TIBTH(MAN)
        FILE MAN IN TEL
  300   RETURN
        END
```

FIG. 9.15 SIMSCRIPT I.5 Program for Simulation of Telephone Booth System

control is returned to the SIMSCRIPT control program by execution of the RE-TURN statement. The event routine CRNKUP never will be executed again in the run, because no other exogenous event notices have been supplied to this model.

Each time that a RETURN statement is executed, the SIMSCRIPT 1.5 scheduling algorithm finds the most imminent event notice—that is, the event notice at the head of the event queue, whose members are ordered according to increasing event times. If the notice is an ARVE notice, the scheduling algorithm updates the clock time to the time of that notice and then turns control over to the endogenous routine ARVE. The ARVE routine has four purposes: (1) to destroy the event notice ARVE, which is used only to schedule execution of the event routine ARVE; (2) to reinitialize the system if the telephone booth is empty; (3) to create the next arrival and place it into the waiting line; and (4) to perpetuate itself. The creation of MAN is performed exactly as in the exogenous routine CRNKUP. If the booth is empty, then the system is reinitialized by immediately placing MAN into the booth, scheduling his departure, and then scheduling the next arrival. If the booth is occupied, MAN is placed into the set QUE, a FIFO set representing the waiting line, and system statistics are updated. The updating of the system statistics is accomplished by execution of the statements

```
ACCUMULATE FNQUE INTO CUMQ SINCE TLAST
LET FNQUE=FNQUE+1.0
```

The first statement accumulates the cumulative time integral associated with the set QUE into the system variable CUMQ. TLAST automatically is updated to present time and is used to indicate the time of the last QUE status change. FNQUE indicates the size of the QUE. Because MAN is being placed into QUE, FNQUE is incremented by 1. The final purpose of this routine is to schedule the next arrival, thus perpetuating its own execution. The event time of the next arrival is assigned by choosing an interarrival time from the uniform distribution on the interval (LOWC, HIC).

If the SIMSCRIPT scheduling algorithm finds that the most imminent event notice is a LEAV notice, it updates the clock time to the time of that notice and then turns control over to the endogenous routine LEAV. The LEAV routine has five purposes: (1) to destroy the event notice LEAV, which is no longer needed; (2) to handle the departure of the MAN using the telephone; (3) to place the next MAN in QUE into the booth; (4) to terminate the simulation and produce summary statistics if 1,000 MAN entities have used the booth; and (5) to perpetuate itself. The first operation performed by this routine is to destroy the event notice that caused its execution. MAN then is removed from TEL, and the cumulative time integral for TEL usage is updated. A choice then is made: whether to go to the statement labeled 200, which eliminates MAN from the system, or to terminate the simulation and produce summary statistics. The simulation will be terminated after 1,000 entities have used the booth. If FNUSE is less than 1,000 or if TEL is empty, control will go to the statement labeled 250. At this point, the set TEL will be empty and an attempt will be made to remove the next MAN entity from the QUE and to place it into TEL. (If QUE is empty, control RETURNs to the SIMSCRIPT control program—in this case, the next LEAV event will be scheduled by the reinitialization procedure in the next ARVE routine execution.) Because removal of an entity from the QUE involves a change in the size of QUE, statistics for that set are calculated. Because the amount of time that the entity MAN will remain in TEL is contained in the attribute TIBTH, the routine creates the next LEAV endogenous event notice and schedules it at time TIME+TIBTH(MAN), thus perpetuating itself. MAN then is placed into TEL and RETURN is made to the control program.

This program produces three pertinent summary statistics at the end of the simulation run: (1) the utilization of TEL (CTEL/TIME); (2) the average size of QUE (CUMQ/TIME); and (3) the average time MAN remained in QUE (CINT/FNUSE).

9.14 GPSS: Basic Concepts

The General Purpose Simulation System, or GPSS, is one of the oldest and most widely used discrete simulation languages. As with SIMSCRIPT, many different versions of GPSS have been produced since its original development. In this book, we discuss GPSS/360; more recent versions of GPSS do not differ markedly from GPSS/360.

The design of GPSS departs radically from that of statement-oriented languages. Its design is based upon the fundamental assumption that most systems can be simulated adequately through use of just a few types of entities: dynamic entities, equipment entities, statistical entities, and operational entities.

Dynamic entities in GPSS are called *transactions*. Transactions are created and destroyed as required during a simulation, much like temporary entities in SIMSCRIPT. For example, the telephone users in the phone booth example would be simulated by transactions in GPSS. Activities are caused by the interaction of transactions with other entities, as transactions flow through the system. Transaction attributes are defined by assigning values to sets of *parameters* associated with each transaction. These parameters also may be used for complex and versatile references to other system attributes.

Equipment entities are available to simulate items of equipment that are used by transactions. *Facilities*, for example, are used to simulate equipment that processes one transaction at a time—a telephone booth, for example. Equipment entities that can service more than one transaction at a time are called *storages* — thus, a bank of twelve telephone booths could be simulated as a single unit by using a storage entity. GPSS automatically maintains statistics on utilization, average contents, and so forth of such equipment entities. The final values of these statistics automatically are output at the end of the simulation. Such statistical information is treated as an entity attribute, and therefore reference can be made at any time within the run to the values accumulated up to that time.

Several statistical entities are available to analyze the simulation. *Queue entities* and *chain entities* are used to simulate and measure the contention arising from competition among transactions for the use of equipment entities. Chain entities also may be used to simulate the more complex types of queuing disciplines. *Tables* are used to collect the different frequency distributions that arise naturally during the modeling process.

The operational entities of GPSS are called *blocks*; blocks are the GPSS equivalents of statements. In GPSS, the blocks determine the logic of the system by controlling the flow and interaction of transactions. For example, some blocks control the ways in which transactions can use equipment entities; other blocks affect transaction parameters; some control output; some control the direction of transaction flow; and two types of blocks control transaction creation and destruction. About forty different types of blocks are available in GPSS. The essence of GPSS simulation lies in the actions caused as blocks interact with transactions.

GPSS automatically controls the flow of transactions from block to block. The control programs keep track of which block each transaction is to enter next, how long it will remain there, and so forth. A system-wide clock is maintained in order to schedule these operations correctly, and event times are scheduled in terms of this clock. Transactions generally are moved on a first-come, first-served basis. The control program updates the clock to the time that the next transaction is scheduled to move and then begins to move the transaction, performing the specified operations as it is moved along the sequence of blocks. Whenever an operation cannot be performed — for example, because a facility is not available for use — transaction movement will cease; the control program places the transaction into a temporarily inactive state. A search then is made to find the transaction with the most imminent block departure time. The clock is updated to this time, and that transaction is moved in the same fashion. The simulation usually ends after a specified number of transactions have moved through the model.

GPSS also defines many system-wide attributes and entities. Function entities can be used to define many complex empirical distributions as well as standard theoretical distributions. Computational variables can be used to evaluate algebraic formulae involving other attributes. Eight random number generators are available as system attributes (see Section 7.6).

9.15 GPSS: Language Elements

Some of the basic elements of the GPSS language are illustrated in this section. Appendix C contains a complete list of the blocks, definition cards, and control cards used in GPSS. Chapters 10 and 11 contain more detailed discussions of GPSS.

The GPSS block is laid out in an 80-column format. Columns 8–18 contain the key word or words that define the function of the block. Beginning in column 19, there are a series of operands, separated by commas, that specify the functions of the block. Columns 2–7 are used for reference labels. Comments may be inserted at the end of each block after the last operand; one or more blank columns must separate the last operand from the comment.

The birth and death of transactions are controlled, respectively, by the GENERATE and TERMINATE blocks. The function of the TERMINATE block is to destroy any transaction that enters the block, along with all of the parameters of that transaction. This block also is used to control termination of the run, by halting the run after a preset number of transactions have been terminated. For example, the block

        TERMINATE   1

will immediately remove from the system any transactions that enter this block. Each time a transaction is terminated, the operand 1 is subtracted from a counter that was set initially to a value prescribed by the programmer. When this counter is reduced to zero, the simulation run is terminated. The GENERATE block creates transactions. Among its operands are two that specify an interarrival time density. For example, the block

        GENERATE   22,12

will create transactions with interarrival times uniformly distributed in the interval [10,34] — that is, with mean 22 and spread 12. More complex distributions could be used to define the interarrival times, through use of computational system-wide attributes such as functions.

Simulation of the usage of an equipment entity usually requires three blocks. Two blocks are used to identify the entity that is to be used or to be freed; the third block is used to indicate how long the entity is to be used. This third block, which is used to indicate the service or delay time, is the ADVANCE block. For example, the block

        ADVANCE   15,5

would force any entering transaction to be delayed in this block for a time interval selected from the uniform distribution with mean 15 and spread 5 — that is, for anywhere from 10 to 20 time units. If no ADVANCE blocks are included anywhere in the system, each transaction will flow through all blocks in zero time. The two other blocks used to simulate equipment usage vary with the type of equipment. The SEIZE and RELEASE blocks are used for facilities. Thus, usage of a facility named PHONE for 10 to 20 minutes could be simulated by the blocks

```
SEIZE          PHONE
ADVANCE        15,5
RELEASE        PHONE
```

When a transaction enters the SEIZE block, the facility PHONE is recorded as being in use. The PHONE remains in use as long as the transaction is in the ADVANCE block. After the specified delay time, the transaction enters the RELEASE block and the facility is freed from use. For storages, the ENTER and LEAVE blocks are used in a similar manner. Because a storage can be used by many transactions simultaneously, more than one transaction may be allowed to ENTER a storage and the associated ADVANCE block. The number of transactions allowed to ENTER the storage is limited by the storage attribute known as its capacity. The movement of a transaction will be halted if it reaches a SEIZE block for a facility that is in use or an ENTER block for a storage that is filled to capacity. Movement of the transaction will be resumed as soon as the facility is RELEASEd or another transaction LEAVEs the storage. Statistics on the usage of a facility or storage are accumulated automatically by the blocks that control that usage.

A certain amount of congestion results when transactions are halted because a facility is in use or because a storage is full. Because measurement of such congestion often is a major objective of the simulation, several blocks are available to simulate queues. The QUEUE and DEPART blocks are used to simulate a FIFO discipline and to measure congestion. These two blocks act to force transactions into and out of a queue. In general, these blocks immediately surround the block(s) that cause congestion:

```
QUEUE          LINE
SEIZE          PHONE
DEPART         LINE
```

In this example, transactions that find the PHONE in use will remain in a waiting LINE until the PHONE is RELEASEd. At that time, the transaction at the head of the LINE is allowed to enter the SEIZE block and immediately passes through the DEPART block to leave the LINE. GPSS automatically accumulates many useful statistics on queues—for example, average queue contents, number of elements in the queue, average time per transaction in the queue, and so forth. These statistics form part of the standard output at the completion of the simulation run. They also may be tested by decision blocks to alter the logic of the program.

Among the more useful blocks in GPSS is the TEST block, which controls movement of transactions entering it. The TEST block allows the analyst to test the state of the system and to alter the destination of transactions according to the test results. For example, Q$LINE is an attribute for the queue LINE, whose value is the present size of the queue. The blocks

```
TEST L        Q$LINE,10,AWAY
QUEUE         LINE
```

will allow a transaction to enter the queue LINE only if the length of the queue is less than 10. Otherwise, the transaction will be transferred to another block with the symbolic name AWAY.

The TRANSFER block also is used to control the flow of traffic through the system. For example, the block

```
TRANSFER      6,BLCK1,BLCK2
```

will use the uniform distribution to send 40 percent of all entering transactions to the block named BLCK1 and 60 percent of them to BLCK2.

A simulation run is only as good as the valid statistical data that it generates. Much of this data is tabulated, and GPSS has a special block that facilitates the generation of tables. Whenever transactions enter a TABULATE block, values are accumulated into tables. Thus, the block

```
TABULATE      XTME
```

will cause an entry to be made into the table named XTME whenever a transaction enters the block. The exact definition of each table is made in a definition card.

GPSS uses special cards called *definition cards* to define many of the entities that are used in the simulation. For example, the table XTME for transit time could be defined by the table definition card,

```
XTME    TABLE          M1,0,20,50
```

This definition card calls for the transit time (code M1) to be accumulated in a table with lower limit 0, interval size 20, and 50 intervals. Storage capacity is defined similarly in a storage definition card. Definition cards also are used to define algebraic variables and computational entities such as functions.

In addition to the block and definition cards, GPSS uses *control cards* as an external control on the extent and length of computer time for the simulation. For example, the START card is used in conjunction with the TERMINATE block to limit the length of the run, by setting the initial value of the counter that is decremented as transactions are TERMINATEd. The card

```
START          2500
```

will cause the simulation to end after 2,500 transactions have entered TERMI-

NATE blocks that have a 1 in column 19. The CLEAR and RESET control cards may be used to restart the system, so that several runs can be made in a single batch with only minor modifications in the model. This capability facilitates such studies as sensitivity analyses. For example, the sequence

```
           GENERATE      15,5
              .
              .
              .
BLCK1      ADVANCE       10,5
              .
              .
              .
           TERMINATE     1
           START         1000
           CLEAR
BLCK1      ADVANCE       15,5
           START         1000
```

causes the model to be run twice, each time for 1,000 transaction terminations. The first run has an ADVANCE block service time mean of 10 with spread of 5; the second run redefines the ADVANCE block and increases the mean time to 15.

The SIMULATE control card actually initiates running of the program. If this card is not present, the GPSS compiler merely checks the syntax of the statements but will not attempt to execute them. Other important control cards include the END card, which must be the last card in a simulation program, and the JOB card, which allows many different models to be batched in an input deck.

9.16 GPSS: An Example

Figure 9.16 contains the flowchart and an equivalent GPSS block diagram of the GPSS source program (Figure 9.17) for simulation of the telephone booth simulation.

Transactions representing telephone callers arrive into the system at the GENERATE block, with interarrival times distributed according to the negative exponential density with a mean of 15 minutes. This distribution is specified in the function NEXPN that is defined at the beginning of the program. A transaction entering the system immediately is placed into the queue LINE, where it will remain until the facility PHONE is RELEASEd for its use and it is allowed to enter the SEIZE block. Because PHONE is a facility, only one transaction at a time is allowed through the SEIZE or DEPART blocks or into the ADVANCE block. The transaction reaching the ADVANCE block will remain there between 5 and 15 minutes, the exact time being a uniformly distributed integer within that range. After the PHONE has been used, the SEIZEing transaction will enter

```
┌─────────────┐                              ┌───────────────┐
│ Callers arrive │                            │   GENERATE    │
│ according to │                              │  15,FN$NEXPN  │
│ neg. exp.    │                              └───────────────┘
│ distribution │                                      │
└─────────────┘                                       ▼
       │                                      ┌───────────────┐
       ▼                                      │    QUEUE      │
┌─────────────┐                               │               │
│    Join      │                              │    LINE       │
│  waiting     │                              └───────────────┘
│    line      │                                      │
└─────────────┘                                       ▼
       │                                      ┌───────────────┐
       ▼                                      │    SEIZE      │
┌─────────────┐                               │               │
│   Enter      │                              │    PHONE      │
│  phone       │                              └───────────────┘
│  booth       │                                      │
└─────────────┘                                       ▼
       │                                      ┌───────────────┐
       ▼                                      │   DEPART      │
┌─────────────┐                               │               │
│   Stop       │                              │    LINE       │
│  waiting     │                              └───────────────┘
└─────────────┘                       TIME            │
       │                                              ▼
       ▼                                      ┌───────────────┐
┌─────────────┐                               │   ADVANCE     │
│   Place      │                              │               │
│   call       │                              │    10,5       │
└─────────────┘                               └───────────────┘
       │                                              │
       ▼                                              ▼
┌─────────────┐                               ┌───────────────┐
│   Free       │                              │   RELEASE     │
│   phone      │                              │               │
└─────────────┘                               │    PHONE      │
       │                                      └───────────────┘
       ▼                                              │
┌─────────────┐                                       ▼
│ Check watch  │                              ┌───────────────┐
│ for length   │                              │   TABULATE    │
│ of call      │                              │               │
└─────────────┘                               │    XTME       │
       │                                      └───────────────┘
       ▼                                              │
┌─────────────┐                                       ▼
│   Leave      │                              ┌───────────────┐
│   system     │                              │  TERMINATE    │
└─────────────┘                               │      1        │
                                              └───────────────┘
```

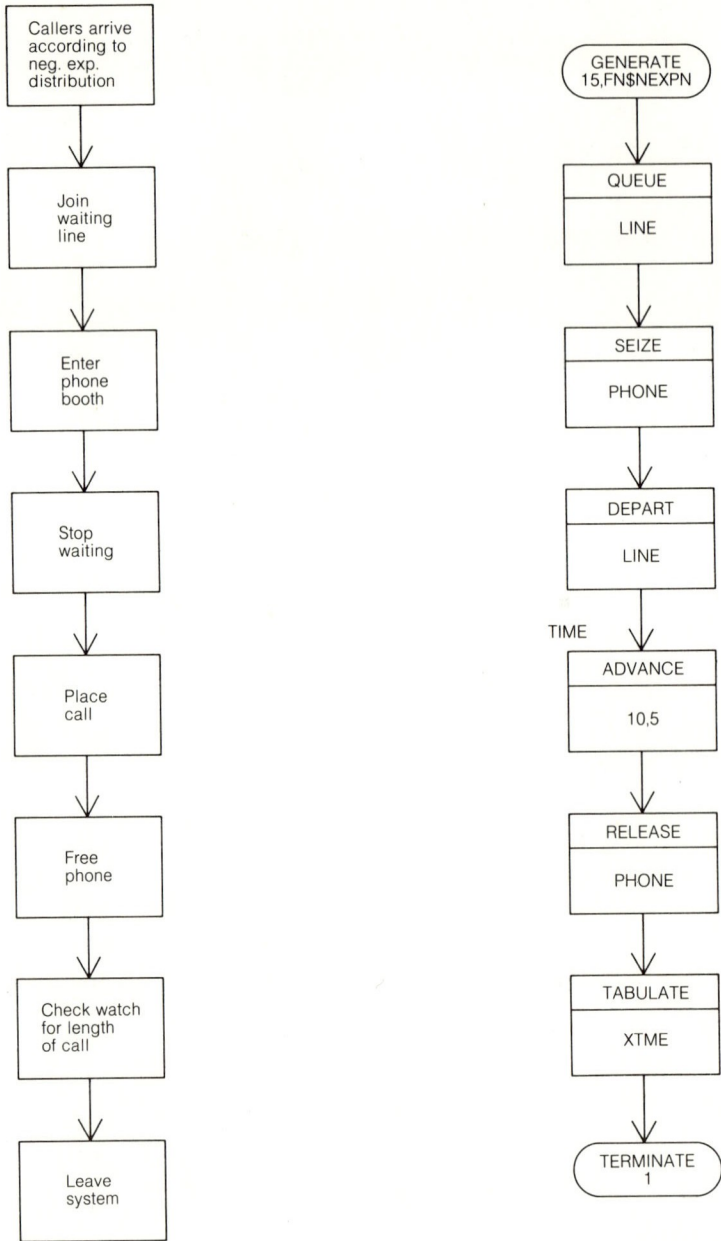

FIG. 9.16 Flowchart and GPSS Block Diagram for Telephone Booth Simulation

```
BLOCK
NUMBER  *LOC    OPERATION  A,B,C,D,E,F,G                COMMENTS
        *
        *       SIMULATION OF THE USE OF A TELEPHONE BOOTH
        *
        *       SIMULATE
        *
        NEXPN FUNCTION    RN2,C24
        0,0/.1,.104/.2,.222/.3,.355/.4,.509/.5,.69
        .6,.915/.7,1.2/.75,1.38/.8,1.6/.84,1.83/.88,2.12
        .9,2.3/.92,2.52/.94,2.81/.95,2.99/.96,3.2/.97,3.5
        .98,3.9/.99,4.6/.995,5.3/.998,6.2/.999,7.0/.9997,8.0
        *
1               GENERATE   15,FN$NEXPN       ARRIVALS ACCRDNG TO NEG EXP DSTR
2               QUEUE      LINE              JOIN WAITING LINE
3               SEIZE      PHONE             ENTER THE BOOTH AND
4               DEPART     LINE                        STOP WAITING IN LINE.
5       TIME    ADVANCE    10,5              USE PHONE
6               RELEASE    PHONE             FREE PHONE FOR NXT USER.
        *
7               TABULATE   XTME              TABULATE TRANSIT TIMES.
        *
8               TERMINATE  1                 LEAVE THE SYSTEM
        *
        XTME    TABLE      M1,0,10,20        TRANSIT TIME TABLE
        *
                START      1000              RUN FOR 1000 TERMINATIONS
        *
                CLEAR
5       TIME    ADVANCE    8,2               CHANGE PHONE USAGE TIME
MULTIPLE DEFINITION OF SYMBOL IN ABOVE CARD
                START      1000              START THE SECOND RUN
        *
                END
```

FIG. 9.17   Program Listing for GPSS Simulation of Telephone Booth System

the RELEASE block and free the facility for the next transaction waiting in LINE. The RELEASEing transaction will proceed through the TABULATE block to be destroyed at the TERMINATE block. As it passes through the TABULATE block, an entry is made into the table XTME to record the time taken by the transaction to pass through the system.

The control cards at the end of the program specify that the model is to be run twice, each run being terminated after 1,000 transactions have passed through the system. The first run is made with call lengths varying in the interval [5,15]. The system then is CLEARed and the calling time interval is set at [6,10] by redefining the block named TIME. Using the results of these runs, the two forms of the system can be compared to see how the change in AD-VANCE block delay time affects the model. Figure 9.18 shows queue statistics accumulated during these two runs.

9.17 General Remarks on Simulation Languages

Two additional discrete simulation languages, SIMULA and GASP, are mentioned and briefly discussed in this section. The major part of the section compares the SIMSCRIPT and GPSS languages.

QUEUE	MAXIMUM CONTENTS	AVERAGE CONTENTS	TOTAL ENTRIES	ZERO ENTRIES	PERCENT ZEROS	AVERAGE TIME/TRANS	$AVERAGE TIME/TRANS	TABLE NUMBER	CURRENT CONTENTS
LINE	8	.969	1003	310	30.9	14.581	21.103		3
$AVERAGE TIME/TRANS = AVERAGE TIME/TRANS EXCLUDING ZERO ENTRIES									

QUEUE	MAXIMUM CONTENTS	AVERAGE CONTENTS	TOTAL ENTRIES	ZERO ENTRIES	PERCENT ZEROS	AVERAGE TIME/TRANS	$AVERAGE TIME/TRANS	TABLE NUMBER	CURRENT CONTENTS
LINE	5	.379	1001	448	44.7	5.447	9.860		1
$AVERAGE TIME/TRANS = AVERAGE TIME/TRANS EXCLUDING ZERO ENTRIES									

FIG. 9.18   Queue Statistics for Two Runs of GPSS Telephone Booth Simulation

SIMULA is a discrete simulation language that is used more widely in Europe than in the United States. Like SIMSCRIPT, it was conceived as an extension of a general purpose language; whereas SIMSCRIPT is an extension of FORTRAN, SIMULA is an extension of ALGOL. In SIMULA, the system is viewed as sets of processes, and simulation is accomplished by program blocks that effect these processes. We feel that this language, particularly in its implementation as SIMULA 67, is an elegant and powerful discrete simulation language. However, because there is little interest in or availability of ALGOL and ALGOL-based languages in the United States, the use of SIMULA almost certainly will continue to be inhibited.

GASP II is another language that uses a design philosophy basically the same as that for SIMSCRIPT. GASP II consists of a series of FORTRAN subroutines that perform the special tasks required in a simulation. Therefore, this language is particularly useful in small to medium-sized computer facilities that have a FORTRAN compiler. However, because most simulations use a great deal of storage, it may be impossible to carry out sophisticated simulations on these smaller facilities.

Other languages have capabilities for discrete simulation, but the use of these other languages in the United States is relatively limited. Because GPSS and SIMSCRIPT are the simulation languages most widely used in the United States, we will direct most of our remarks in this section to a comparison of these two languages.

GPSS is easy to learn after the beginner clears the hurdle of dealing with a language that is not statement-oriented. Those who already have cleared this hurdle or those who never have programmed before will find it easier to simulate elementary models with GPSS than with SIMSCRIPT because (1) the block orientation of GPSS is easier to understand; (2) statistics are gathered automatically by GPSS; (3) all output is produced automatically by GPSS; and (4) there are no definition or initialization sections in GPSS as there are in SIMSCRIPT. (The definition and initialization sections have been eliminated in the newer versions of SIMSCRIPT, but this newer compiler is not yet widely available.) On the other hand, persons who are well versed in FORTRAN probably will find SIMSCRIPT easier to learn than GPSS.

The more complex the problems and models being studied, the more difficult it is to work with GPSS. SIMSCRIPT is more flexible in complex situations, because of its ability to handle very complex data structures. However, an experienced programmer in GPSS can handle problems just as complex as those handled by SIMSCRIPT programmers. In fact, the problem of programming large, complex models proves far less serious than the problem of finding computer resources for running the program.

An added disadvantage of most versions of GPSS is that values are kept as integral numbers, causing scaling problems and loss of precision in arithmetic computations such as division. For example, even though most operations being simulated can be measured in hours, it often is necessary to carry time in seconds rather than in hours, thus requiring rescaling of most values by a factor of 3,600. Languages such as SIMSCRIPT use scientific or floating point notation more freely and therefore avoid this difficulty.

SIMSCRIPT is a compiler language; the language statements comprising the program are translated into a machine-code equivalent that is efficient with respect to computer storage and running speed. GPSS, on the other hand, uses subroutines to interpret and execute the operations associated with each block. Therefore, GPSS models tend to be relatively time consuming to run and, for small simulations, to use more core storage space than other languages. However, it must be noted that most versions of the SIMSCRIPT compiler require a large amount of storage themselves, even though the compiled program is relatively small. For this reason, GPSS generally will run on machines with smaller core sizes than can accommodate SIMSCRIPT. For example, not long ago the latest version of GPSS required a 128K IBM 360/40, whereas the latest version of SIMSCRIPT required a 256K 360/40.

A compiler language, such as SIMSCRIPT, should produce reasonably good diagnostics to aid the user in correcting syntactic errors and in debugging his programs. This does not seem to be the case with SIMSCRIPT, and a SIMSCRIPT user may find it very difficult to debug his programs. Programs written in GPSS are easier to debug, although the diagnostics provided with GPSS also could be improved.

In one form or another, GPSS is the simulation language that has been implemented on the most machines. The most obvious reason for this extensive use is the fact that GPSS has been freely available on IBM computers since the 7040/44. SIMSCRIPT has not had the same massive support in its development, and the availability and usage of SIMSCRIPT have suffered accordingly. Recently CACI has acquired rights to the various versions of SIMSCRIPT, and it appears that this language is beginning to reach a larger audience. It is important to remember, however, that FORTRAN is and probably will continue to be the most widely used language in simulations.

To summarize: SIMSCRIPT is more versatile and is faster; GPSS is easier to learn, is more widely available, and is more widely used.

9.18 Supplementary Reading

We have not been able to find a reference dealing specifically with the use of FORTRAN in simulation, but a wide variety of good general references on this language is available. Gordon (1969) discusses several discrete and continuous simulation languages and also discusses the use of FORTRAN for simulation; his book is excellent as a survey of the more important simulation languages.

Fischer (1970) discusses a preprocessor extension of PL/I (called PL/I:SL) in conjunction with on-line simulations.

Kiviat et al. (1969) provide an excellent text on SIMSCRIPT II, going to great lengths to present the language's power and versatility, which often approach that of ALGOL and PL/I. Unfortunately, only about the last third of the book is devoted to discussion of the simulation aspects of the language. Wyman (1970) gives an introduction to discrete simulation and to SIMSCRIPT I.5; his book is clearly written, well presented, and useful, but some previous experience with FORTRAN is needed to follow the discussion. Weinert (1967) compares SIM-SCRIPT and FORTRAN programs in a case study.

Pritsker and Kiviat (1969) provide the only available text on GASP II, discussing many valuable techniques and problems. A firm grasp of FORTRAN is a prerequisite for reading their book, however.

Krasnow (1969) discusses GPSS, SIMSCRIPT, CSL, SIMULA, and SIMULATE. Dahl and Nygaard (1967) provide the basic manual for SIMULA. A study of simulation languages by Teichroew and Lubin (1966) is interesting and well written; they compare SIMSCRIPT, CLP, CSL, GASP, GPSS, and SOL. The most comprehensive and best written comparison known to the authors is given by Dahl (1968).

Further references dealing with GPSS are listed in Section 10.16.

10

GPSS: An Introduction

10.1 INTRODUCTION Several programming languages are discussed in Chapter 9 in relation to the simulation of discrete systems. In this chapter and the next, special attention is given to one of these languages: the General Purpose Simulation System (GPSS).

GPSS exists in several dialects. We discuss the language GPSS/360 as it is implemented on the IBM 360 and 370 computers, because of the widespread availability of these systems. Anyone mastering this version of GPSS should find it easy to adjust to other dialects of the language.

This chapter provides a general introduction to GPSS. Here we define block diagrams, equipment entities, control cards, and block types, and we illustrate each in several examples. Chapter 11 extends many of these concepts and introduces new ones; it defines more block types and discusses more advanced techniques, computational features, storage capabilities, and special output options.

Not all of the options and capabilities of the GPSS language can be discussed here. For a complete description of the language, see the *GPSS/360 User's Manual* (IBM Systems Reference Library Form H20–0326).

10.2 GPSS: Review of Basic Concepts

GPSS is a process-oriented language. It is particularly suited to the translation from a flowchart representation of a system into a computer program. GPSS has a large number of block entities, called *block types*, which function to simulate those activities that are most universally characteristic of discrete systems. The universality of these blocks is illustrated in Figure 10.1, which demonstrates

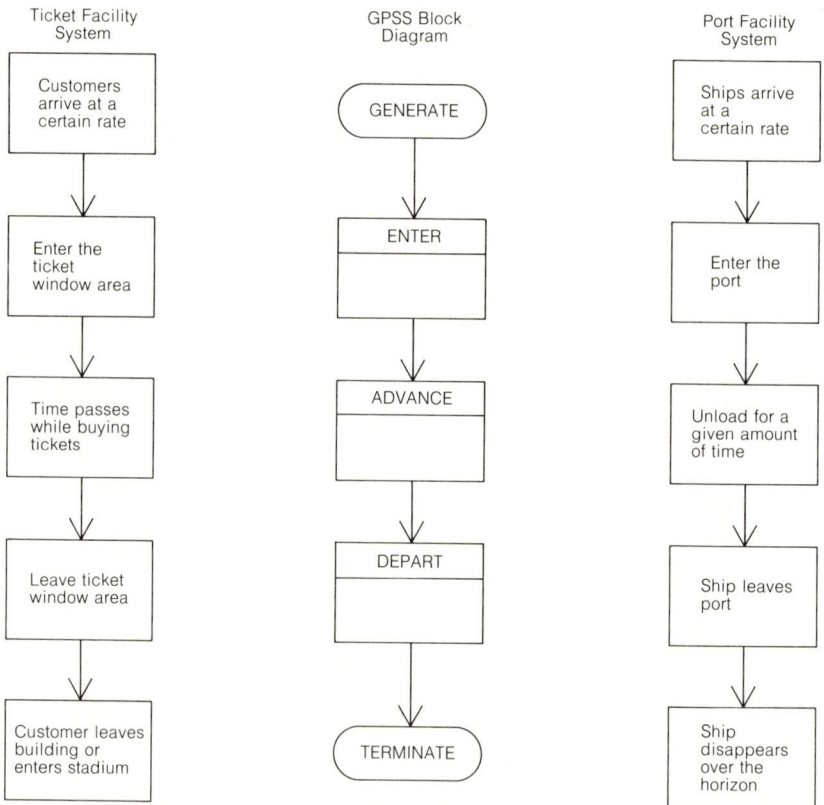

FIG. 10.1   Two Different Systems Depicted by a Single GPSS Block Diagram

how two apparently different systems can be represented by the same GPSS flowchart, or *block diagram*. Each system activity is equivalent to the adjacent GPSS block symbol.

The block types control and react with the elements of traffic flowing through the system. These traffic elements are called *transactions*; they are used to simulate such things as jobs being processed by a computer, cars being serviced at a gasoline station, ships unloading at a port, or claimants presenting a claim at a social security office. Because such transactions usually are serviced in some fashion within the system, GPSS also allows for *equipment entities*, which interact with the transactions. Equipment entities can be used to simulate such devices as computer processors, gasoline pumps and piers, or a pumping system that unloads oil cargoes at a port. They also can be used to simulate services such as those supplied by factory workers or secretarial pools.

A simulation language should be able both to introduce the necessary stochastic behavior and to accumulate and display the concomitant statistical information; GPSS provides both of these features. Eight random number generators are included as part of the language, and the user can construct his own special random number generators with the aid of computational functions. Special options enable the user freely to record information and to produce — either under his control or automatically — a great variety of statistical information, from simple frequency counts to complete distribution tables.

To summarize, the basic elements of the GPSS language are called entities and may be divided into six major classes according to their uses: (1) basic entities, such as block types and transactions; (2) equipment entities; (3) computational entities; (4) statistical entities; (5) reference entities; and (6) chain, or set, entities. All of these classes of entities are discussed in this chapter and the next.

10.3 A GPSS Program

A simple GPSS program will serve both to illustrate some of the entities mentioned in Section 10.2 and to provide an overall view of the layout of a GPSS program. The discussion of this section is general; details are provided in following sections.

The system to be simulated is the traffic flow through a branch office of an hypothetical bank; the simulation model will be a gross representation of this flow (Figure 10.2). The interarrival time is 3 ± 2 time units (in this case, the units can be assumed to be minutes). The symbolism $x \pm y$ generally is used to indicate a uniform distribution in the range $[x - y, x + y]$, with only integer values allowed. Thus, only the integer values $x - y, x - y + 1, x - y + 2, \ldots, x + y - 1, x + y$ are possible, and any particular interarrival time is equally likely to have any one of these values. After the customer arrives, he makes a decision either to use the available preparation facilities (table, pen, withdrawal

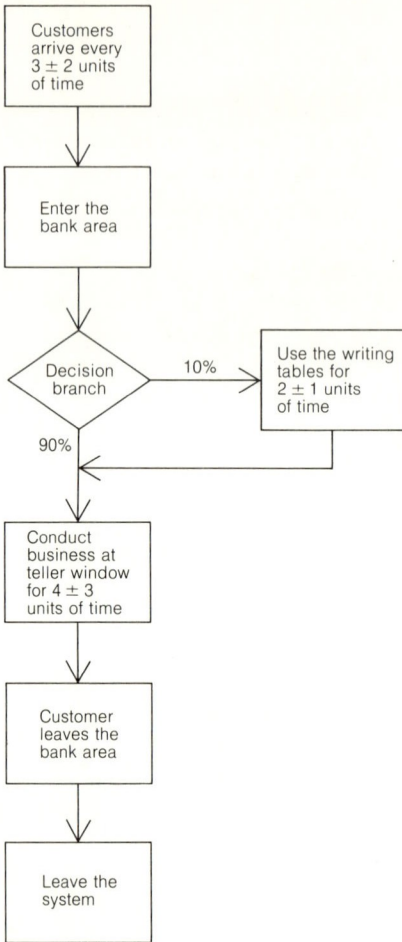

FIG. 10.2   Gross Flowchart of Customer Traffic Through Hypothetical Bank Branch

forms, and so forth) or to proceed directly to the teller windows. The flowchart indicates that there is a 10-percent chance that the customer will proceed to the writing tables. Thus, the probability that he will proceed directly to the teller is 0.9. The length of time spent at the writing table is 2 ± 1 time units; that spent at the teller window is 4 ± 3 units. After the customer completes his business at the teller window, he leaves the bank. In this case, the customers may be represented as transactions, and the object of the simulation is to describe their flow through the system. The flowchart indicates that seven processes are to be simulated, from arrival through departure.

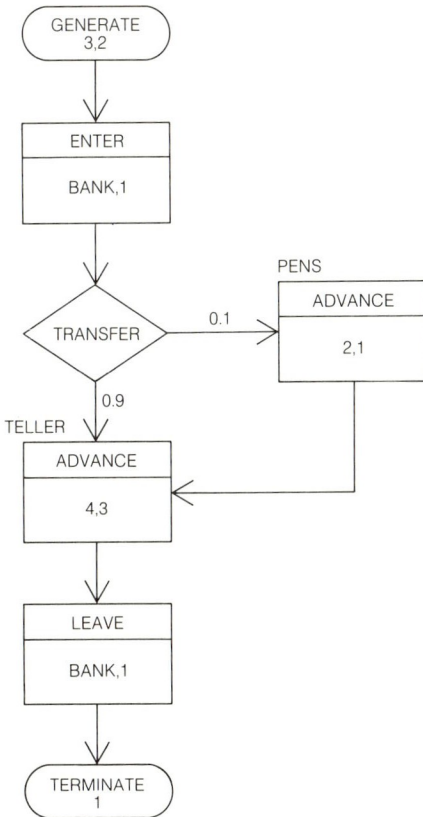

FIG. 10.3   GPSS Block Diagram Corresponding to Flowchart in Figure 10.2

The flowchart readily can be translated into a GPSS block diagram (Figure 10.3); each block type in the diagram corresponds to the associated process in the flowchart. Transactions are created at the GENERATE block with an inter-arrival distribution of 3 ± 2 units. They then ENTER the bank. They subsequently are TRANSFERred either to an ADVANCE block named PENS or to an ADVANCE block named TELLR, with probabilities of 0.100 and 0.900 respectively. The time spent at these ADVANCE blocks will be 2 ± 1 units for PENS and 4 ± 3 units for TELLR. The transactions then LEAVE the bank and, finally, leave the system at the TERMINATE block.

In order to make the actual simulation run on the computer, the block diagram first must be coded onto a computer-readable medium, such as punched cards. This coding was done for the bank-branch example, and Figure 10.4 is a listing of the resulting program.

```
BLOCK
NUMBER   *LOC    OPERATION   A,B,C,D,E,F,G              COMMENTS                              CARD
         *                                                                                   NUMBER
         * MODEL I                                                                           1
         *                                                                                   2
                 SIMULATE                                                                    3
         *                                                                                   4
1        INPUT  GENERATE     3,2                INTER-ARRIVAL RATE                            5
2               ENTER        BANK,1             CUSTOMER ENTERS BANK.                         6
3        WHICH  TRANSFER     .900,PENS,TELLR    DECISION BLOCK.                               7
4        PENS   ADVANCE      2,1                USE WRITING TABLE                             8
5        TELLR  ADVANCE      4,3                USE TELLER.                                   9
6               LEAVE        BANK,1             LEAVE BANK.                                   10
7               TERMINATE    1                  LEAVE SYSTEM.                                 11
         *                                                                                   12
         BANK   STORAGE      50                 UP TO 50 CUSTOMERS AT A TIME                  13
         *                                                                                   14
                START        1000               RUN MODEL FOR 1000 TRANSACTIONS.             15
         *                                                                                   16
                END                                                                          17
                                                                                             18
```

FIG. 10.4   Listing of GPSS Program Corresponding to Block Diagram in Figure 10.3

In Figure 10.4, each of the lines that are numbered on the right from 1 through 18 represents a card submitted for the computer run. These cards comprise the GPSS *source program* for the simulation—or, simply, the program. Cards 6 through 12 are the coded equivalents of the seven blocks in the block diagram. On each card, a key block type name (such as GENERATE or TRANSFER) is used to identify the process or operation to be performed. The remaining cards either are nonfunctional or are cards that aid the GPSS control program in further definition of the scope of the program. Each nonfunctional card begins with an asterisk (*); these cards are used for comments. The SIMULATE card (card 4) and the START card (card 16) are examples of *control cards*. The SIMULATE card indicates that a computer run is to occur; the START card limits the length of the run. In this case, the simulation is to continue until 1,000 customers have been serviced by the bank—that is, until 1,000 transactions have arrived at the TERMINATE block. Another control card, the END card, is used to indicate that there are no more cards following in this GPSS simulation; the END card always is the last card in the source program. The only other functional card is number 14, the STORAGE card, which is used to define the capacity of the bank as 50 customers at any one time.

Figure 10.5 is a listing of the output obtained from a run of this GPSS program. The actual output spans several pages, but the essential parts of the output have been compressed here into a single figure. The first page of the output contains *symbol tables*, which cross-reference and number the symbols used in the program. For example, INPUT is identified with block number 1; in other words, a reference to the block labeled INPUT is the same as a reference to block number 1. Similarly, storage number 1 can be referenced by the symbol BANK. The GPSS control program uses these numbers to replace all symbolic references by numeric references. The result of this translation is called the as-

```
BLOCK NUMBER    SYMBOL    REFERENCES BY CARD NUMBER

    1           INPUT
    4           PENS              8
    5           TELLR             8
    3           WHICH


STORAGE SYMBOLS AND CORRESPONDING NUMBERS

    1           BANK


*
* MODEL I
*
    1    GENERATE     3     2
    2    ENTER        1     1
    3    TRANSFER   .900    4     5
    4    ADVANCE      2     1
    5    ADVANCE      4     3
    6    LEAVE        1     1
    7    TERMINATE    1     1
*
    1    STORAGE     50
*
         START     1000


RELATIVE CLOCK          3051    ABSOLUTE CLOCK
BLOCK COUNTS
BLOCK CURRENT    TOTAL          BLOCK CURRENT    TOTAL
  1      0       1002
  2      0       1002
  3      0       1002
  4      0        100
  5      2       1002
  6      0       1000
  7      0       1000
```

STORAGE	CAPACITY	AVERAGE CONTENTS	AVERAGE UTILIZATION	ENTRIES	AVERAGE TIME/TRAN	CURRENT CONTENTS	MAXIMUM CONTENTS
BANK	50	1.414	.028	1002	4.308	2	5

FIG. 10.5 Condensed Output of a Run of the GPSS Program Listed in Figure 10.4

sembled form of the program; its listing immediately follows the symbol tables. Any entity can be referenced either by number or by symbolic reference in the original program—for example, the statements ENTER   BANK,1 and ENTER   1,1 can be used interchangeably in the cards of Figure 10.4. Clearly, however, use of symbolic references can make the program more legible and much simpler to revise. Therefore, symbolic rather than numeric references should be used in writing the program.

The actual statistical output is produced automatically, following the assembly listing. In this case, the output begins with *clock times*. The system ran for 3,051 units of simulation time before the simulation was finished—in other words, it took 3,051 time units (minutes) for the simulated bank branch to process 1,000 customers. Immediately following the clock time, *block counts* are listed. These statistics indicate how many transactions entered each block during the simulation run. Block number 4 processed only 100 transactions during the run. The symbol tables show that block number 4 is the ADVANCE block named PENS; in other words, only about 1 of every 10 transactions used the writing facilities, just as was intended in the model design. From the block counts, it can be seen that two customers were being serviced at the teller windows when the thousandth customer left the bank, terminating the simulation. The final part of the output is a table that contains statistical information about utilization of the bank as a whole. This table indicates that the average utilization of the bank facilities during the simulation was only 0.028 (an average of 1.414 customers in the bank at any given time, divided by a capacity of 50 customers) and that the average time spent in the system by each transaction was 4.308 units. During this simulation run, there never were more than 5 customers in the bank at any given time. Obviously, the information produced in such output tables is very helpful in the analysis of the system being simulated.

10.4 Movement, Events, and the Passage of Time

Simulation time passes in discrete intervals during a GPSS simulation; only an integral number of time units either can be made to elapse or can be recorded. The supervisory functions of the GPSS control programs include the ability to update automatically and to control a system-wide simulation clock, whose unit of time is chosen by the user. This time unit is chosen implicitly when the user specifies action and delay times in terms of his understood unit of time; the program itself deals only with time units that have no explicitly specified value. A time unit may represent a century, a nanosecond (billionth of a second), or any other unit of time. However, because only an integral number of time units can elapse between events in the simulation, the unit chosen must be a lowest common denominator of the times to be encountered during the simulation. For example, if the program must simulate some actions that are measured in integral numbers of minutes and other actions that are measured in seconds, the time unit must be chosen as one or a few seconds. It may even be necessary to express units of time in tenths of a second, in order to get sufficient detail for valid stochastic information. GPSS automatically keeps track of the number of time units that have passed since the simulation began in what is called the *relative clock*. The programmer can refer to the current value of this clock by using the symbol C1.

The GENERATE and ADVANCE blocks are used to define the time frame and to control simulation time. One function of the GENERATE block is to establish interarrival rates for transactions, by specifying the amount of time that is to pass between successive creations of transactions. Time passage also is forced when a transaction enters an ADVANCE block. In such a case, a number is calculated to determine how many units of time the transaction must be delayed at this block. In fact, this is the only function of the ADVANCE block, but it is a very important function because it is the only way in GPSS to simulate service or delay times. Therefore, this function is connected intimately with the pattern of flow of transactions through the system.

The flow of transactions in GPSS is controlled by two very important rules: (1) Only one transaction is moved at a given real time during the execution of the program (although another transaction may be moved before the relative clock is advanced); and (2) Each transaction is moved as far as possible in zero simulation time.

For example, as soon as a transaction issues from a GENERATE block, it is moved continuously through the system until some obstruction interrupts its flow. Until it encounters this obstruction, its rate of flow relative to the system is infinite — that is, no simulation time passes as the transaction moves from block to block. As soon as the transaction is stopped (for example, by the forced delay at an ADVANCE block), the GPSS control programs examine the system to see when the next scheduled event is to occur. If another transaction is scheduled to move at the current simulation time, it now will be moved as far through the system as possible. It is very important to note that, although the movements of these two transactions occur "simultaneously" in simulation time, they actually are carried out sequentially. Only after all transactions scheduled to be moved at the current simulation time have been moved as far as possible in zero simulation time — only then will the simulation (relative) clock be updated to the time of the next scheduled transaction movement. For example, if the next scheduled event is creation of a new transaction at a GENERATE block, the simulation clock will be updated according to the calculated interarrival time.

10.5 Block Type Symbols and Formats

Forty-three different block types are avilable in GPSS/360. Each block type has an associated keyword or descriptor called the *block name*. The block name not only identifies the block type, but also describes its function. For example, the

GENERATE block causes transactions to be created, or GENERATEd.

Two different conventions currently are used for the symbols representing block types in block diagrams. The convention adopted in this book uses the five shapes shown in Figure 10.6. We have chosen this convention because it is explicit (the block name appears in most cases) and because it is simple (only five shapes are used). The other convention requires 43 unique shapes, making it confusing to everyone except the expert—and tedious to use, even for the expert. The second convention is described in Appendix 6 of the *GPSS/360 Introductory User's Manual* (IBM Systems Reference Library Form GH20–0304).

After a block diagram has been constructed, it must be transformed into the allowed GPSS format for computer input. This transformation consists of a translation of the block diagram into lines of code that are suitable for keypunching onto cards. For block types, these lines of code are called *block definition cards*. The remainder of this section describes the format of these cards. The 43 possible block definition cards are described in Table C.1 (Appendix C); many of these cards will be discussed at length in the following pages.

Each block definition card has three functional fields and one nonfunctional field. The three functional fields are the LOC, OPERATION, and OPERANDS fields; the nonfunctional field is called the COMMENTS field. Figure 10.7 sum-

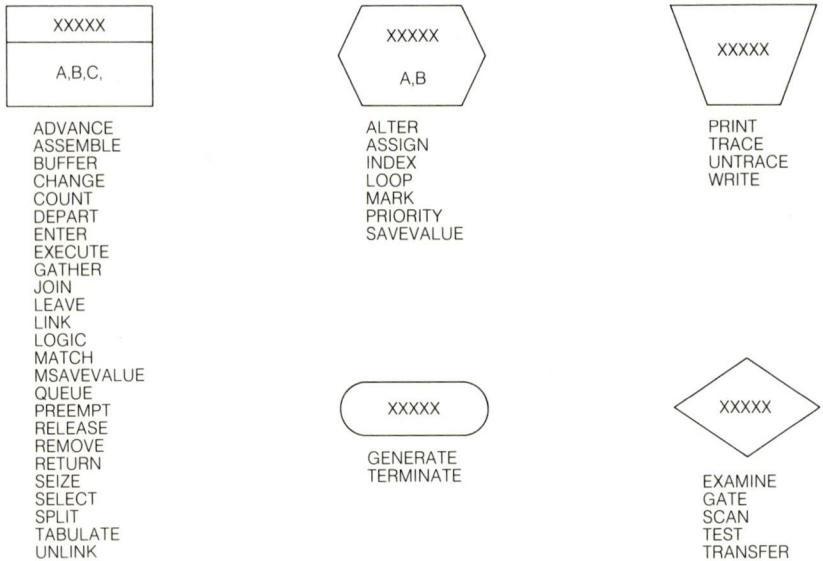

XXXXX		
A,B,C,		

ADVANCE
ASSEMBLE
BUFFER
CHANGE
COUNT
DEPART
ENTER
EXECUTE
GATHER
JOIN
LEAVE
LINK
LOGIC
MATCH
MSAVEVALUE
QUEUE
PREEMPT
RELEASE
REMOVE
RETURN
SEIZE
SELECT
SPLIT
TABULATE
UNLINK

XXXXX
A,B

ALTER
ASSIGN
INDEX
LOOP
MARK
PRIORITY
SAVEVALUE

XXXXX

PRINT
TRACE
UNTRACE
WRITE

XXXXX

GENERATE
TERMINATE

XXXXX

EXAMINE
GATE
SCAN
TEST
TRANSFER

XXXXX is to be replaced by the proper block name when the symbol is used.

FIG. 10.6   The Five Basic GPSS Block Diagram Shapes

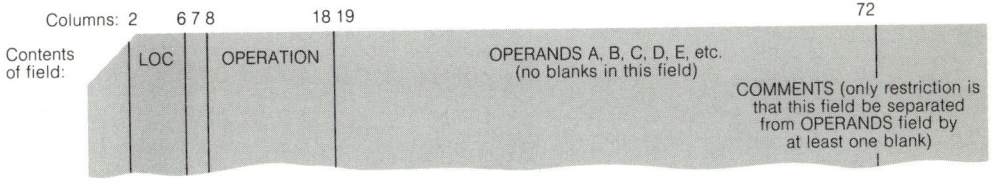

FIG. 10.7 Format of GPSS Block Definition Card

marizes the location and format of these fields. Figure 10.8 is an example of a coding sheet that may be used to program in accordance with this format.

The OPERATION field contains the block type name. For example, Figure 10.8 includes the block type names: GENERATE, MARK, TRANSFER, ADVANCE, SEIZE, and QUEUE. Each name represents a different process; each block type will affect a transaction in a different way. Any of the 43 possible block type names may appear in this field.

```
*LOC    OPERATION  A,B,C,D,E,F        COMMENTS
*
* MODEL I
*
        SIMULATE
*
 INPUT  GENERATE   3,2                INTER-ARRIVAL RATE
        ENTER      BANK,1             CUSTOMER ENTERS BANK.
 WHICH  TRANSFER   .9ØØ,PENS,TELLR    DECISION BLOCK.
 PENS   ADVANCE    2,1                USE WRITING TABLE
 TELLR  ADVANCE    4,3                USE TELLER.
        LEAVE      BANK,1             LEAVE BANK.
        TERMINATE  1                  LEAVE SYSTEM.
*
 BANK   STORAGE    5Ø                 UP TO 5Ø CUSTOMERS AT A TIME
*
        START      1ØØØ               RUN MODEL FOR 1ØØØ TRANSACTIONS.
*
        END
```

FIG. 10.8 Coding Sheet Containing a Simple GPSS Simulation Program

The last functional field in the definition card, the OPERANDS field, usually contains a list of operands that are defined positionally and are separated by commas. The first operand is called the A operand, the second the B operand, and so forth. An operand may be omitted, but this must be indicated explicitly by writing an additional comma. In the TRANSFER block named JUMP in Figure 10.9, the first operand was omitted, but its place is marked by the leading comma. In general, operands are used to control and to qualify the operation. For example, the first two operands of the GENERATE block are used to define the interarrival rate of transactions into the block. The block called CRE8 in Figure 10.9 creates transactions with a uniform distribution in the range [138,162].

The LOC, or location, field is used for referencing blocks. It may be left blank (in which case the block will be identified only by the numeric reference assigned to it in the assembly program), or it may contain a symbolic name. This symbolic name then may be used to refer to this block within the definitions of other blocks. *Symbolic names* may be any sequence of 3 to 5 alphameric characters, but they must begin with at least 3 alphabetic characters. The first example in Figure 10.9 has two ADVANCE blocks with symbolic names BLCKA and BLCKB. The TRANSFER block illustrates the use of these symbolic names to reference the ADVANCE blocks.

The COMMENTS field is nonfunctional. If any comments are placed in this field, they must be separated from the OPERANDS field by at least one blank column; accordingly, no blank columns may appear within the OPERANDS field. The COMMENTS field is used to annotate the program. Comments also may occupy an entire card (see Figure 10.4). Any card beginning with an asterisk (*) in column 1 will be ignored in the execution of the program, but it will appear in the program listing.

```
  2       8          19
 *LOC    OPERATION   A,B,C,D,E,F,G                    COMMENTS
  *
  *      EXAMPLE I
  *
         TRANSFER    .800,BLCKA,BLCKB
 BLCKA   ADVANCE     6,5                 THIS IS A COMMENT
 BLCKB   ADVANCE     7,3
  *
  *      EXAMPLE II
  *
 CRE8    GENERATE    150,12              THIS BLOCK CREATES XACTIONS
         MARK
 JUMP    TRANSFER    ,OUT                COMMAS INDICATE  MISSING PARAMETERS
 WAIT    QUEUE       TOOL
         SEIZE       DRILL
 TIME    ADVANCE     12,2
 OUT     TERMINATE   1                   REMOVE XACTIONS
```

FIG. 10.9 Examples of Block Definition Cards

10.6 The GENERATE, ADVANCE, TRANSFER, and TERMINATE Blocks

Each of the four important block types discussed in this section can perform one of the following four functions: (1) creation of transactions (the GENERATE block); (2) deletion of transactions (the TERMINATE block); (3) time delay (the ADVANCE block); and (4) flow modification (the TRANSFER block).

The main function of the GENERATE block is to initiate and to maintain the flow of transactions into the system. The block has several other functions that enable it to affect the type and the number of the transactions that are created. These functions are specified and controlled by the values of up to seven operands that may appear in the OPERANDS field of the block definition card. Here we discuss only a few of the more important operands; other options are discussed in later sections of this chapter.

In its simplest form, the GENERATE block has the operands A and B specified to represent what are called a mean time and a spread time. The block named RATE2 in Figure 10.10 has a mean time of 6 units and a spread time of 3 units. The interarrival times are calculated using these operands. The time interval is obtained from a uniformly distributed number in the range (mean time − spread time) to (mean time + spread time); in other words, the distribution of interarrival times can be represented as (mean time) ± (spread time) or, in terms of the operands, as A ± B. After a transaction issues from the GENERATE block named RATE2, from 3 to 9 time units will pass before the next transaction issues from this block. If the spread time is zero or is omitted (as in the blocks named RATE1 and RATE4 in Figure 10.10), the interarrival time is a constant given by the mean. The mean time must be greater than or equal to the spread time, because negative interarrival times are not allowed. Operand C may be used to specify an *offset time*; the value of this operand will determine the number of time units that are to pass before the first transaction is to be created. For example, the blocks named RATE3, RATE4, and RATE5 will not create any transactions during the first 24 time units of the simulation; thereafter, each will create transactions with the interarrival time distribution indicated by its operands A and B. Offset

```
  2       8         19
 *LOC   OPERATION  A,B,C,D,E,F,G                    COMMENTS
 *
 * EACH OF THE FOLLOWING CARDS IS A SEPARATE EXAMPLE OF A POSSIBLE
 * GENERATE BLOCK WHICH MAY APPEAR IN A GPSS SIMULATION.
 *
  RATE1 GENERATE   6            NEW XACTN EVERY 6 TIME UNITS
  RATE2 GENERATE   6,3          EVERY 6+-3 UNITS OF TIME
  RATE3 GENERATE   6,3,24       EVERY 6+-3 UNITS OF TIME STARTING AT TIME 24
  RATE4 GENERATE   6,,24        EVERY 6 UNITS STARTING AT TIME 24
  RATE5 GENERATE   6,3,24,15    GENERATE ONLY UP TO 15 XACTNS
```

FIG. 10.10   Examples of GENERATE Block Definition Cards

times are useful when more than one GENERATE block is used to create transactions, with the requirement that the load of transaction flow in the system be staggered at different times. Operand D is a *limit count* of the number of transactions to be created. For example, the block named RATE5 will create only 15 transactions. The functions of the operands E, F, and G are discussed in later sections.

No transaction may enter a GENERATE block from another block. Any attempt to program such a transaction movement will result in an error report.

The TERMINATE block complements the function of the GENERATE block by removing transactions from the system. The TERMINATE block is used to eliminate transactions no longer needed by the system (thus freeing storage space for new transactions) and to simulate transaction departure from the system. Any transaction entering this block is eliminated immediately. The only operand allowed in the TERMINATE block definition card is operand A, which contributes—if it appears at all—to the total *termination count*. When a transaction enters a TERMINATE block, the value of operand A is subtracted from the termination count value. The simulation is ended when the termination count value is reduced to zero. Because this is the only way that the simulation will end without external intervention by a computer operator, there must be at least one TERMINATE block with a nonzero operand A. (Specification of the initial value for the termination count is discussed in Section 10.10.) Figure 10.11 includes examples of TERMINATE block definition cards.

The ADVANCE block is used to simulate passage of time. In its simplest form, the ADVANCE block calculates delay times with a distribution indicated by the mean time and spread time specified by operands A and B. For example, transactions entering the ADVANCE block named PASS (Figure 10.11) will be delayed in the block for 2 ± 1 time units. Note that ADVANCE blocks often are used to simulate congestion in a system. For example, if a new transaction is being GENERATEd every 6 time units, but every transaction must pass through

```
   2      8          19
  *LOC   OPERATION   A,B,C,D,E,F,G                    COMMENTS
  *
  * EXAMPLES
  *
   BEGIN GENERATE    4,2          CREATE XACTN EVERY 4+-2 TIME UNITS
         TRANSFER    ,PASS        SEND XACTN TO BLOCK NAMED PASS
         GENERATE    2,1,3600,250    250 XACTNS WILL BE CREATED STARTING
  *                                  3600 TIME UNITS AFTER THE FIRST XACTN
  *                                  IS CREATED AT THE BLOCK NAMED BEGIN
   PASS  ADVANCE     2,1          XACTNS ENTERING HERE ARE DELAYED 2+-1 TIME UNITS
         TRANSFER    .900,DELAY,TERM2    STATISTICAL TRANSFER
   DELAY ADVANCE     1            DELAY EXACTLY 1 TIME UNIT
  *
         TERMINATE                REMOVE XACTN
   TERM2 TERMINATE   1            REMOVE XACTN AND ADJUST TERMINATION COUNT
```

FIG. 10.11　More Examples of Block Definition Cards

an ADVANCE block with mean time of 27 units and spread time of 2 units, then at least four new transactions will have been GENERATEd to compete for service at the ADVANCE block while a single transaction is being held in the ADVANCE block. The ADVANCE block is used most naturally to simulate time passage required to perform some operation such as parking a car, preparing a deposit slip, conducting an interview, and so on. Two examples of ADVANCE block definition cards are included in Figure 10.11.

The TRANSFER block is used to alter the flow of transactions through a system. This block works in many modes — we will discuss only two of them here: the unconditional transfer and the statistical transfer. In the *unconditional transfer*, operand A of the TRANSFER block definition card is omitted; in this case, the transaction will proceed immediately to the block specified by operand B. Thus, the first TRANSFER block in Figure 10.11 transfers all transactions unconditionally to the ADVANCE block named PASS. This transfer interrupts the natural sequential flow of transactions from one block to the next one defined in the program; in this case, the unconditional transfer is used to avoid the error that would be caused by allowing transactions to enter a GENERATE block. In the *statistical transfer*, a number between zero and one is specified as the A operand, and blocks are specified as operands B and C. The value in operand A specifies the probability that the transaction will be sent to the block specified by C; the probability that the transaction will be sent to the block specified by B is equal to $1 - A$. The second TRANSFER block definition card specifies a statistical transfer, with a probability of 0.900 that the transaction will be sent to TERMZ and a probability of 0.100 that it will be sent to DELAY.

10.7 Facilities and Facility-Oriented Blocks

In order to simulate processes that involve use of equipment or that require service, GPSS allows for several types of equipment entities. The most common equipment entity is the facility. The *facility entity* is used to simulate equipment that can service (or can be used by) only one transaction at a time. For example, in the simulation of an assembly line with transactions representing the parts being assembled, an electric hand drill can be used only on one part at a time. Similarly, the drill can be used by only one workman at a time. In this case, both the drill and the workman would be represented as system facilities.

Facility entities are defined by the appearance of a symbolic name or a number as operand A of a SEIZE or a PREEMPT block. For example, PREEMPT DRILL defines a facility with the symbolic name DRILL, and SEIZE 8 defines a facility that is identified by the number 8. Because GPSS automatically associates a number with each symbolic name (see Section 10.3), the symbolic name DRILL and the number 8 could actually represent the same facility. To avoid confusion, we shall use symbolic names whenever possible.

Two pairs of block types are used in GPSS to simulate the use of facilities: these are the SEIZE and RELEASE blocks and the PREEMPT and RETURN blocks. When a transaction is allowed entry into a SEIZE block, two things happen: (1) the facility specified by operand A of the SEIZE block is recorded as being in use; and (2) other transactions are refused entry into any SEIZE blocks that reference in operand A the facility that is now in use. This facility cannot be SEIZEd·by any other transaction until the transaction that has already SEIZEd it enters a RELEASE block that references this facility in its operand A. Thus, the function of the RELEASE block is to negate the effect of the SEIZE block. When a transaction enters the RELEASE block, the facility referenced in operand A of that block is recorded as no longer being in use, and other transactions are allowed to SEIZE the facility. The first example in Figure 10.12 simulates a sales pitch. In this case, the transactions represent customers, and the facility with symbolic name MAN represents a salesman.

The PREEMPT and RETURN blocks also control the usage of facilities; these blocks are used for high-priority transactions. For example, consider the simulation of an emergency ward, in which a facility represents a doctor and transactions represent patients. Patients will be treated according to the gravity of their condition and according to the order in which they arrive. However, a patient in extremely critical condition may arrive while the doctor is busy with a less serious case. In such a situation, the doctor will interrupt his treatment of the first case in order to treat the new arrival. The PREEMPT block is used in GPSS to simulate such processes. In its simplest form, the PREEMPT block is similar to the SEIZE block. Operand A of the PREEMPT block specifies the facility that is to be PREEMPTed. Any transaction entering a PREEMPT block will take over control of the facility specified in operand A from any transaction that may already have SEIZEd that facility. In the emergency ward simulation, normal incoming cases would SEIZE the doctor facility, whereas arriving critical cases would PREEMPT the facility. If the facility already has been

```
     2      8          19
    *LOC   OPERATION   A,B,C,D,E,F,G                COMMENTS
    *
    *    SEIZING AND PREEMPTING FACILITIES
    *
    *    EXAMPLE I:  SEIZE AND RELEASE BLOCKS
            SEIZE      MAN    SALESMAN BEGINS ATTEMPT TO SELL
            ADVANCE    15,5   PITCH TAKES 10 TO 20 MINUTES
            RELEASE    MAN    SALE COMPLETED
    *
    *    EXAMPLE II:  PREEMPT  AND RETURN BLOCKS
            PREEMPT    MAN    SALESMAN DRAWN AWAY BY SPECIAL CUSTOMER
            ADVANCE    30,10  SPECIAL ATTENTION GIVEN TO CUSTOMER
            RETURN     MAN    SALESMAN RETURNS TO ORIGINAL CUSTOMER
```

FIG. 10.12   Examples of Facility-Oriented Blocks

PREEMPTed, a new transaction attempting to PREEMPT the same facility will have to wait its turn.

The RETURN block functions in a manner similar to the RELEASE block. A facility remains in the PREEMPTed state until the transaction that PREEMPTed it enters a RETURN block that specifies the same facility in its operand A. When this happens, the facility is returned to its previous state — that is, either to the SEIZEd or to the available state, whichever was its condition at the time it was PREEMPTed. The second example in Figure 10.12 illustrates the use of PRE-EMPT and RETURN blocks in the sales-pitch example.

In both of the examples in Figure 10.12, an ADVANCE block is used to simulate use of the facility for a specified length of time. If no ADVANCE block is included, there will be zero simulation time between the SEIZEure or PRE-EMPTion of a facility and its RELEASE or RETURN. The ADVANCE block is the only block available in GPSS that can directly control the amount of time for which equipment entities are to be used.

10.8 Storages and Storage-Oriented Blocks

Another type of equipment entity available in GPSS is the *storage entity*, which is used most commonly to simulate a bank of facilities. For example, a facility could be used to simulate a single secretary, but a storage could be used to simulate a secretarial pool. Similarly, a parking space could be simulated as a facility, but a parking lot would be simulated as a storage. A facility can service or be used by only one transaction at a time; a storage can service a number of transactions simultaneously.

Each storage defined in a simulation has a specified *capacity*, which represents the maximal number of transactions that can be serviced simultaneously. The capacity of a storage can be specified in the *storage definition card* (see Figure 10.4). This card has the symbolic name or number of the storage in the LOC field and the capacity number as operand A. Thus, in Figure 10.4, the capacity of the BANK was specified as 50 transactions (customers). Similarly, in the first example of Figure 10.13, a capacity of one million is specified for the computer memory storage named CORE. The second way of specifying storage capacity is by default; if the capacity is not specified in operand A of the storage definition card, the maximal occupancy of a storage (defined by the implementation) will be used as the capacity of the storage. (On the System/360, this maximal capacity is 2,147,483,647.) The capacity will be defined by default if the storage definition card is omitted from the source program.

The ENTER and LEAVE blocks are available to simulate the usage of storages. In each of these blocks, operand A specifies the symbolic name or number of the storage referenced. Operand B specifies the number of storage units that are to be used (for the ENTER block) or released (for the LEAVE block) by each

```
   2      8        19
  *LOC   OPERATION  A,B,C,D,E,F,G                 COMMENTS
  *
  *    USING AND DEFINING STORAGES
  *
  *    EXAMPLEI:  DATA TRANSMISSION IN A COMPUTER
         ENTER      CORE,1000  1000 UNITS OF COMPUTER STORAGE NEEDED
         SEIZE      CHAN1      CHANNEL ONE SEIZED FOR THE TRANSMISSION
         ADVANCE    5000       TIME FOR TRANSMISSION
         RELEASE    CHAN1      CHANNEL NO LONGER NEEDED
         ADVANCE    1000000    PROCESSING TIME
         LEAVE      CORE,1000  COMPUTER STORAGE NO LONGER NEEDED
  *      DEFINE THE SIZE OF THE COMPUTER
   CORE  STORAGE    1000000    LARGE COMPUTER
  *
  *    EXAMPLE II: A SMALL STORAGE
         ENTER      1,2        OCCUPY TWO UNITS OF STORAGE
         ADVANCE    10         WAIT TEN UNITS OF TIME
         LEAVE      1,2        FREE THE CORE UNITS
  *      DEFINE THE STORAGE SIZE
   1     STORAGE    5          STORAGE SIZE IS 5
```

FIG. 10.13   Examples of Storages and Storage-Oriented Blocks

transaction. Each transaction ENTERing a storage uses the indicated number of units of the storage capacity. As long as enough units of the capacity still are available, additional transactions are allowed to ENTER the storage. However, any transaction that attempts to use more storage capacity than is currently available will be stopped from entering the ENTER block until sufficient capacity becomes available as other transactions return capacity at corresponding LEAVE blocks. In the second example of Figure 10.13, only two transactions at a time are permitted to use storage 1, because each incoming transaction uses two units of storage and the total capacity is only five. The first example shows how transactions may make use of both storages and facilities in the simulation of complex activities. In this case, both 1,000 units of core memory (defined as the storage named CORE) and a channel (defined as the facility named CHAN1) are needed for message transmission within the simulated computer.

10.9 Queues and Queue-Oriented Blocks

When a facility is in use or a storage is filled to capacity, some transactions may be forced to wait for their turns to use the equipment entities. In many cases, the study of such waiting lines, or queues, is a major purpose of the simulation. To permit the user to measure the behavior of waiting lines, GPSS allows for a statistical entity called a queue. The QUEUE and DEPART blocks are used in conjunction with this entity.

The queue entity and its associated blocks function very much like a storage entity and its blocks. There are three major differences between queues and storages: (1) the GPSS control programs automatically accumulate certain special statistics for the usage of queues; (2) the capacity of a queue is unlimited — a transaction never is prevented from waiting in line; and (3) the delay time in a queue is determined by the availability of the associated equipment entity rather than by a characteristic of the queue itself. As with the ENTER and LEAVE blocks, only operands A and B are allowed in the block definition cards for QUEUE and DEPART blocks. Operand A specifies the symbolic name or the number of the queue entity to be joined or departed. Operand B indicates how many units are to be added or subtracted from the current queue contents. (If operand B is omitted, a value of 1 is assigned automatically.)

Example I in Figure 10.14 is a typical three-block combination simulating the use of a facility named PHONE. If the interarrival time for transactions arriving at the SEIZE block is smaller than the delay time indicated by the ADVANCE block, then the SEIZE block will cause a certain amount of congestion. The second example shows how that congestion can be measured, using a queue entity named LINE. In this case, each transaction that arrives at the QUEUE block immediately joins the queue named LINE. Whenever the PHONE becomes available for use, it is SEIZEd by the first transaction in the LINE. This transaction immediately passes through the SEIZE and DEPART blocks (thus gaining control of the facility and leaving the queue) and into the ADVANCE block. This arrangement of the blocks ensures that only the time actually spent waiting for the facility will be recorded in the queue usage statistics kept by the system. If the DEPART block were placed before the SEIZE block, every transaction would leave the queue immediately after joining it; if the DEPART block were placed after the ADVANCE block, the statistics for the queue would include both waiting times and the times used in making phone calls (the delay times in the ADVANCE block). The handling of queues is discussed more extensively in Sections 9.8 and 9.15.

```
      2      8          19
     *LOC   OPERATION   A,B,C,D,E,F,G                    COMMENTS
     *
     *    QUEUE AND DEPART BLOCKS
     *
     *    EXAMPLE I:   PHONE CALL WITHOUT A LINE
            SEIZE        PHONE       GET THE PHONE WHEN FREE
            ADVANCE      5,3         MAKE THE CALL
            RELEASE      PHONE       FREE THE PHONE

     *
     *    EXAMPLE II:  FORMING A LINE
            QUEUE        LINE        WAIT FOR THE PHONE
            SEIZE        PHONE       GET THE PHONE WHEN FREE
            DEPART       LINE        NO LONGER WAITING IN LINE
            ADVANCE      5,3         MAKE THE CALL
            RELEASE      PHONE       FREE THE PHONE
```

FIG. 10.14   Examples of Queues and Queue-Oriented Blocks

10.10 GPSS Control Cards

An example of the use of GPSS control cards is mentioned in Section 10.3. Here we discuss several of the more important control cards and show how they affect an actual computer run. Figure 10.15 shows examples of these control cards; a full explanation of the cards and their operands is given in Table C.2 (Appendix C).

The SIMULATE control card, which may appear anywhere in the source deck, indicates that an actual run is to be made. If this card is omitted from the deck, the GPSS compiler will do nothing but scan the source program for coding errors.

The END control card must be physically the last card in the source deck. Its function is to delimit the set of cards that represents the program.

The START control card is as important as it is versatile. Its principal functions are to signal the start of a simulation and to limit the length of the run. The run is initiated when the GPSS control programs sense the appearance of a START card. Thus, all of the block definition cards that represent the logic of the model must appear before the START control card in the source deck. The length of the run is limited through the value of operand A of the START card. This operand specifies the initial value of the termination count. Each time that a transaction enters a TERMINATE block, the termination count is decreased

```
  2       8            19
*LOC    OPERATION    A,B,C,D,E,F,G                      COMMENTS
*
*       EXAMPLES OF CONTROL CARDS
*
*        1.          SIMULATE CONTROL CARD
        SIMULATE
*
*        2.          THE START CONTROL CARD
        START        1000         THE MODEL WILL BE RUN FOR 1000 TERMINATIONS
*                                 STANDARD STATISTICS WILL THEN BE PRINTED.
*
        START        300,NP       RUN FOR 300 TERMINATIONS BUT SUPPRESS
*                                 THE PRINTOUT OF STATISTICS.
*
        START        500,,100     RUN FOR 500 TERMINATIONS PRINTING
*                                 ACCUMULATED STATISTICS EVERY
*                                 100 TERMINATIONS.
*
*        3.          THE CLEAR CONTROL CARD
        CLEAR                     WIPES OUT MOST ACCUMUMULATED STATISTICS
*                                 AND REMOVES ANY REMAINING TRANSACTIONS.
*
*        4.          THE RESET CONTROL CARD
        RESET                     WIPES OUT MOST ACCUMULATED STATISTICS.
*                                 HOWEVER SYSTEM REMAINS PRIMED WITH
*                                 TRANSACTIONS.
*
*        5.          THE JOB CONTROL CARD
        JOB                       INDICATES A NEW JOB IS TO BE RUN.
*
*        6.          THE END CONTROL CARD
        END                       THAT'S IT FOLKS.
```

FIG. 10.15   Examples of GPSS Control Cards

by the amount specified in the A operand of the TERMINATE block. When the count is reduced to zero, the simulation of that particular model is ended. At this time, the GPSS control programs resume their scan for further cards immediately following the START card that initiated the run just completed. Thus, the same model can be redefined slightly and run again. If the JOB control card appears next, an entirely different model can be defined and run next. The control programs continue to search for additional run instructions until an END card is sensed.

The START control card also affects the automatic printing of statistics in GPSS. This card can be used to suppress printing of statistics by entering NP as operand B (this is the only permissible value for operand B). Operand C can be used to increase the number of statistical printouts; accumulated statistics will be printed after every C terminations (where C is the value of operand C). Examples of the use of operands B and C are included in Figure 10.15.

Two other control cards, the RESET and CLEAR cards, can be used in conjunction with the START card to control the actual computer run. The RESET card can be used to initialize the model, so that it achieves its steady state— that is, so that the statistical fluctuations produced during initial loading of the model with transactions will level off before statistics are gathered. The first START card in Figure 10.16 will cause transactions to be GENERATEd until 50 transactions have been TERMINATEd. At this time, the RESET control card is sensed and all accumulated statistics are set back to zero; the relative clock is set back to zero; but all transactions currently in the system are preserved and the states of all entities are left unchanged. The flow is reinitiated when the next START card is sensed. Allowances must be made in the final statistics, however, to account for the fact that the system was initialized.

The effect of the CLEAR control card essentially is to return the system to its original state—that is, to eliminate all transactions, to set all accumulated statistics and the relative clock back to zero, and to restore all entities to their

```
   2        8          19
  *LOC     OPERATION   A,B,C,D,E,F,G                    COMMENTS
  *
  *        RESET CARD
  *
           GENERATE    10,5    ARRIVALS AT AN OFFICE
  CHOSE    TRANSFER    .5,GIRLA,GIRLB   CHOOSE A CLERK
  GIRLA    ADVANCE     5,4     TIME AT CLERK A
           TERMINATE   1
  GIRLB    ADVANCE     6,3     TIME AT CLERK B
           TERMINATE   1
           START       50      RUN FOR 50 TERMINATIONS. INITIALIZES THE SYSTEM
  *                                    WITH TRANSACTIONS.
           RESET               WIPE OUT STATS
           START       500     RUN AT STEADY STATE FOR 500 TERMINATIONS.
```

FIG. 10.16   Examples of RESET Control Cards

initial states. This card can be used to compare the effects of different parameterizations of the same system — that is, to conduct a sensitivity analysis — by redefining block or entity defintion cards after the CLEAR card and before the next START card. Each new block must have the same symbolic name as the block that it is to replace; the new block will appear in exactly the same position as the old one did in the original program. Every block in the original program that is to be replaced should be given a symbolic name, in order to be certain that redefinitions will be applied to the correct blocks. In Figure 10.17, both the TRANSFER block named CHOSE and the ADVANCE block named GIRLB have been redefined immediately following the CLEAR card and before the system is to be run again for an additional 1,000 terminations. In this way, it is possible to compare the effects on the system of hiring a beautiful blonde as GIRLB *versus* hiring two girls of equal attractiveness as GIRLA and GIRLB. (Note that the redefinition of the TRANSFER block seems to imply that most of the customers in this system are male.)

10.11 GPSS Input Deck Format

Three of the four types of cards required for a GPSS simulation have been discussed in preceding sections. These are the block definition cards, the entity definition cards, and the control cards. In addition, most installations require that the user supply job control cards, which supply the computer with information such as accounting codes and the fact that the source deck is to be handled by the GPSS compiler. Because each installation has its own particular rules concerning the form of the job control cards to be used, here we only indicate that such cards will be needed.

```
     2        8          19
   *LOC    OPERATION   A,B,C,D,E,F,G              COMMENTS
   *
   *        THE CLEAR CARD
   *
            GENERATE    10,5
   CHOSE    TRANSFER    .500,GIRLA,GIRLB
   GIRLA    ADVANCE     5,4
            TERMINATE   1
   GIRLB    ADVANCE     6,3
            TERMINATE   1
            START       1000
            CLEAR                ALL STATS AND TRANSACTIONS WIPED OUT
   CHOSE    TRANSFER    .600,GIRLA,GIRLB  GIRL B IS A STATUESQUE BLOND
   GIRLB    ADVANCE     8,5    CUSTOMER TENDS TO STAY LONGER
            START       1000         SECOND RUN
            END
```

FIG. 10.17   An Example of the Use of the CLEAR Control Card

A typical input deck is diagrammed in Figure 10.18. Two START control cards are used, in order to run this program with two sets of parameters. The particular configuration of cards shown in this figure is not the only possible one; however, this is the usual configuration and it is recommended for ease of handling.

10.12 Utilization Statistics: The Cumulative Time Integral

Before discussing some of the statistics that are produced automatically by GPSS, we examine a few concepts that will aid in understanding these statistics. Our chief concern here is with those statistics that measure usage.

Two points should be noted concerning usage statistics. The first is that usage statistics—like all other statistics gathered in GPSS—are based on integral counters. The second is that the more important usage statistics are based on the unit of simulation time. In calculating the statistics, GPSS uses the simula-

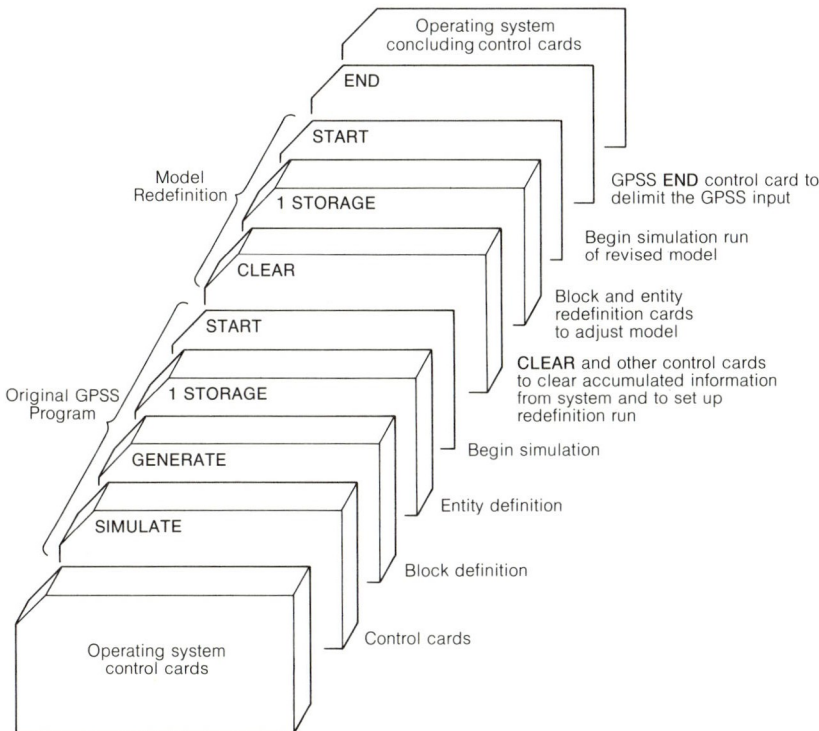

FIG. 10.18   Input Deck Format for a GPSS Computer Run

tion time recorded automatically in the relative clock, C1. This clock counts the number of time units that have passed since the beginning of a simulation job — or since the appearance of the last RESET, CLEAR, or JOB control card.

The *average utilization* of an equipment entity is an important statistic that measures the relative amount of time that the entity was in use during the simulation run. The GPSS control program automatically calculates a statistic called the *cumulative time integral*, which is used in the computation of statistics such as the average utilization. The cumulative time integral is computed in slightly different ways for entities that act as facilities and for entities such as queues and storages, which have capacities associated with them. In the latter case, calculation of the statistic involves consideration of the portion of the capacity that is being used as well as the time of use.

Each time that a facility is recorded as being put into use (that is, each time that a transaction enters an associated SEIZE or PREEMPT block), the relative clock time t_u is recorded. When the facility is freed (RELEASEd or RETURNed), the relative clock time t_f is recorded, and the difference $(t_f - t_u)$ is added to a running total. This total is defined as the *facility cumulative time integral C_F*, and it may be written as

$$C_F = \Sigma(t_f - t_u), \tag{10.1}$$

where the summation extends over all status changes during the run. In Figure 10.19, C_F is represented by the total of the shaded areas in the top part of the figure.

If the entity can service more than one transaction, the amount of time used must be weighted by the number of units used. Let t_i be the relative clock time for the *i*th status change, and let n_i be the number of units being used

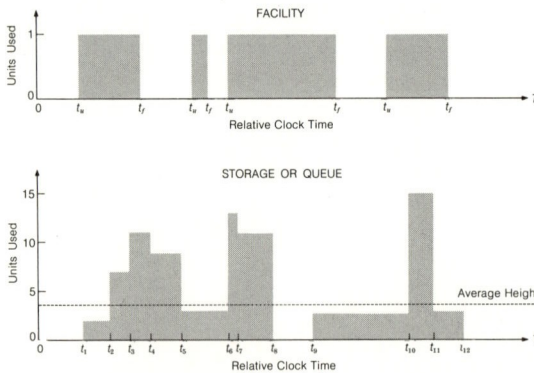

FIG. 10.19 Cumulative Time Integral (*total shaded area*) for Facilities (*top*) and for Storages or Queues (*bottom*)

after the status change. (For a storage, a status change will occur whenever a transaction enters an associated ENTER or LEAVE block; for a queue, it occurs whenever a transaction enters an associated QUEUE or DEPART block.) At the instant t_{i+1}, when the $(i + 1)$st status change is about to occur, the quantity $n_i(t_{i+1} - t_i)$ is added to a running total. This total is the *queue* or *storage cumulative time integral*, C_Q or C_S, and is written as

$$C = \Sigma n_i (t_{i+1} - t_i), \tag{10.2}$$

where the summation extends over all the status changes during the run. Whenever C1 is reset to zero, the values of C_F, C_Q, and C_S also are reset to zero.

10.13 Storage, Facility, and Queue Statistics

Each time that the termination count is reduced to zero, GPSS automatically produces summary statistics for queues, facilities, and storages, in the form of tables that list pertinent statistics for all entities of each type (Figure 10.20). These tables ordinarily appear on separate pages in the computer output, but they have been condensed in Figure 10.20. For consistency, the symbolisms used in GPSS as abbreviations for some of the more common statistics have been noted on the printout. As will be seen, similar abbreviations can be used in the program to access the current value of the statistic.

The first table in Figure 10.20 summarizes statistics produced for three facilities: FACA, FACB, and FACC. The *average utilization* of a facility is defined by

$$FR = C_F/T = [\Sigma(t_f - t_u)]/T, \tag{10.3}$$

where T is the simulation relative clock time at the end of the run — that is, the value of the relative clock C1 when the termination count is reduced to zero. It appears from the table that FACC was the most highly utilized facility; it was utilized 48 percent of the time during the run. The *number of entries*, FC, indicates how many transactions SEIZEd or PREEMPTed the facility during the run. The *average time per transaction*, FT, indicates the average amount of time that each transaction used the facility. For example, on the average, each transaction used FACA for 4.5 time units. The value of FT is calculated as

$$FT = C_F/FC. \tag{10.4}$$

The final two columns record the identification number of the transaction that might have been SEIZEing or PREEMPTing each facility at the moment that the termination count was reduced to zero. These numbers are assigned by the GPSS control programs for internal control purposes.

Storage summary statistics are more extensive. Figure 10.20 includes summary statistics for three storages, numbered 1, 2, and 3. The first column merely

FACILITY	FR AVERAGE UTILIZATION	FC NUMBER ENTRIES	FT AVERAGE TIME/TRAN	SEIZING TRANS. NO.	PREEMPTING TRANS. NO.
FACA	.069	2	4.500		
FACB	.317	4	10.250		
FACC	.480	5	12.399	3	

STORAGE	CAPACITY	SA AVERAGE CONTENTS	SR AVERAGE UTILIZATION	SC ENTRIES	ST AVERAGE TIME/TRAN	S CURRENT CONTENTS	SM MAXIMUM CONTENTS
1	20	.279	.013	8	4.500		4
2	40	1.069	.026	12	11.500		6
3	60	3.410	.056	25	17.599	5	10

QUEUE	QM MAXIMUM CONTENTS	QA AVERAGE CONTENTS	QC TOTAL ENTRIES	QZ ZERO ENTRIES	PERCENT ZEROS	QT AVERAGE TIME/TRANS	QX $AVERAGE TIME/TRANS	TABLE NUMBER	Q CURRENT CONTENTS
ONE	1	.003	36	34	94.4	.194	3.500		
TWO	1	.008	33	30	90.9	.545	6.000		
THREE	2	.050	31	21	67.7	3.451	10.699		

$AVERAGE TIME/TRANS = AVERAGE TIME/TRANS EXCLUDING ZERO ENTRIES

FIG. 10.20 Condensed Output of Standard Summary Statistics for Entities

lists the capacities that were assigned to each storage by the user. In this case, the capacities had been defined by the three storage definition cards as 20, 40, and 60, respectively. This value is included in the table because an important statistic is based on it.

The *average contents of a storage*, SA, is defined by

$$SA = C_S/T = [\Sigma n_i(t_{i+1} - t_i)]/T, \tag{10.5}$$

where T is the relative clock time at the end of the run, and C_S is the storage cumulative time integral. SA can be interpreted as the average height of the profile in Figure 10.19.

The *average utilization* of a storage, SR, is defined in terms of the capacity and the average contents:

$$SR = SA/(\text{storage capacity}). \tag{10.6}$$

For example, storage 2 has $SR = 1.069/40 = 0.026$.

The next statistic, *entries* (SC), indicates the number of transactions that used the storage during the run. The *average time per transaction*, ST, is calculated as

$$ST = C_S/SC. \tag{10.7}$$

The next two statistics indicate how many storage units were being used when the run terminated (*current contents*, S) and the maximal number of storage units being used at any one time during the run (*maximum contents*, SM).

In a practical situation, statistics about waiting lines, or queues, usually are among the most important outputs of the simulation run. It is important to know the average time that all transactions passing through the system spent waiting for various facilities and storages. It is equally important to know such things as the proportion of the transactions that were able to use the equipment entity without any wait time, and the average wait time for those transactions that were forced to wait. For example, in a simulation of a bank branch, suppose that one simulation run yields an average wait time of 2 minutes for all transactions using the teller windows, and an average wait time of 3 minutes for those transactions that are forced to wait at all. Another run with different parameters yields an average wait time of only 1 minute for all transactions, but an average wait time of 10 minutes for those transactions that did have to wait. It appears that a very small proportion of the transactions had to wait in the second run, but that there was a very long wait for those who did have to join a queue. If the simulation were being used to plan the design of the branch office, one might conclude that the first parameters were better than the second, even though the average wait time for all customers was reduced with the second set of parameters. In this case, the small reduction in wait time for most customers might be of little value, while the long wait times for a few customers might be completely unacceptable.

In order to accommodate such considerations, GPSS statistics record both overall statistics for all transactions passing through a queue, and statistics for just those transactions that are forced to wait in the queue. In the table of queue statistics in Figure 10.20, the column headed *zero entries*, QZ, records the absolute number of transactions that passed through the queue without being forced to wait. The next column, *percent zeros*, converts the preceding statistic to a percentage of the total number of transactions passing through the queue. The *average time per transaction*, QT, is calculated for all transactions passing through the queue. In the next column, the *$average time per transaction*, QX, is calculated for only those transactions that did have to wait in the queue. In these examples, note that the values of QX are much larger than the corresponding values of QT. For example, the queue named TWO has QT = 0.545 and QX = 6.000. In other words, although the average wait time for all transactions in this queue was little more than half a time unit, the average wait for those transactions that were delayed in the queue was 6 units. Looking back at the percent zeros column, we note that only about 9 percent of the transactions were delayed in the queue. Therefore, about 91 percent of the transactions using the equipment entity associated with this queue were able to use the equipment without any wait, but about 9 percent of the transactions were forced to wait for an average of 6 units each. This may mean that the equipment occasionally is tied up for long periods of time, or that the queue occasionally becomes very long because of a sudden cluster of arrivals. A glance at the first column, *maximum contents*, shows that the queue named TWO never contained more than one transaction, so we can eliminate the second possible explanation.

Table 10.1 summarizes the various statistics and their definitions.

10.14 A Second Example

Using the concepts discussed in preceding sections of this chapter, we now present a second example that extends the bank branch simulation (Section 10.3). Again, this example is hypothetical; it is designed chiefly to illustrate the use of the GPSS features discussed thus far.

Figure 10.21 is the block diagram of the system as it is to be simulated initially. The salient features are the following: (1) customers arrive at the bank with interarrival times distributed uniformly in the range from 20 to 120 seconds; (2) about 40 percent of the customers go directly to one of the two tellers; the remaining 60 percent go to the writing table; (3) the amount of time that a customer spends using the writing facilities is distributed uniformly in the range from 30 to 150 seconds; (4) customers choose either of the two tellers with equal probabilities; (5) the first teller can handle a customer in about 120 ± 90 seconds; and (6) the second teller requires about 120 ± 60 seconds per customer.

In this section we examine the GPSS program for this block diagram (see Figure 10.22). We also compare this model to several slightly altered versions in order to analyze the effects of such changes as increasing the efficiency of a teller or supplying more writing tables. In practical situations, such analyses might affect decisions about personnel changes or modernization of the bank.

In this example the time unit has been chosen as one second, rather than one minute as in the example of Section 10.3. The smaller time unit makes it possible to give action times more exactly and leads to the production of more precise statistics. In some situations, it might be necessary to refine the time unit even further.

The logic of the model is straightforward. The arrival pattern is set by the GENERATE block named INPUT. The TRANSFER block named CHSE simulates the second feature listed above; it sends 60 percent of the transactions (customers) to the block QPEN and 40 percent to SLCT. QPEN is the first of five blocks that simulate the use of the writing table (represented by the storage named PENS). The queue named PENQ measures waiting times for use of that storage. The ADVANCE block (card number 12) simulates the average time that the writing

TABLE 10.1   Summary of GPSS Equipment Statistics

Statistic	Symbol	Definition
Facility		
Average utilization	FR	$\Sigma (t_f - t_u)/T$
Number of entries	FC	———
Average time per transaction	FT	$\Sigma (t_f - t_u)/FC$
Storage		
Average contents	SA	$\Sigma n_i (t_{i+1} - t_i)/T$
Average utilization	SR	SA/(storage capacity)
Number of entries	SC	———
Average time per transaction	ST	$\Sigma n_i (t_{i+1} - t_i)/SC$
Current contents	S	———
Maximum contents	SM	———
Queue		
Average contents	QA	$\Sigma n_i (t_{i+1} - t_i)/T$
Number of entries	QC	———
Average time per transaction	QT	$\Sigma n_i (t_{i+1} - t_i)/QC$
Zero entries	QZ	———
Percent zeros	–	100 QZ/QC
$Average time per transaction	QX	$\Sigma n_i (t_{i+1} - t_i)/(QC - QZ)$

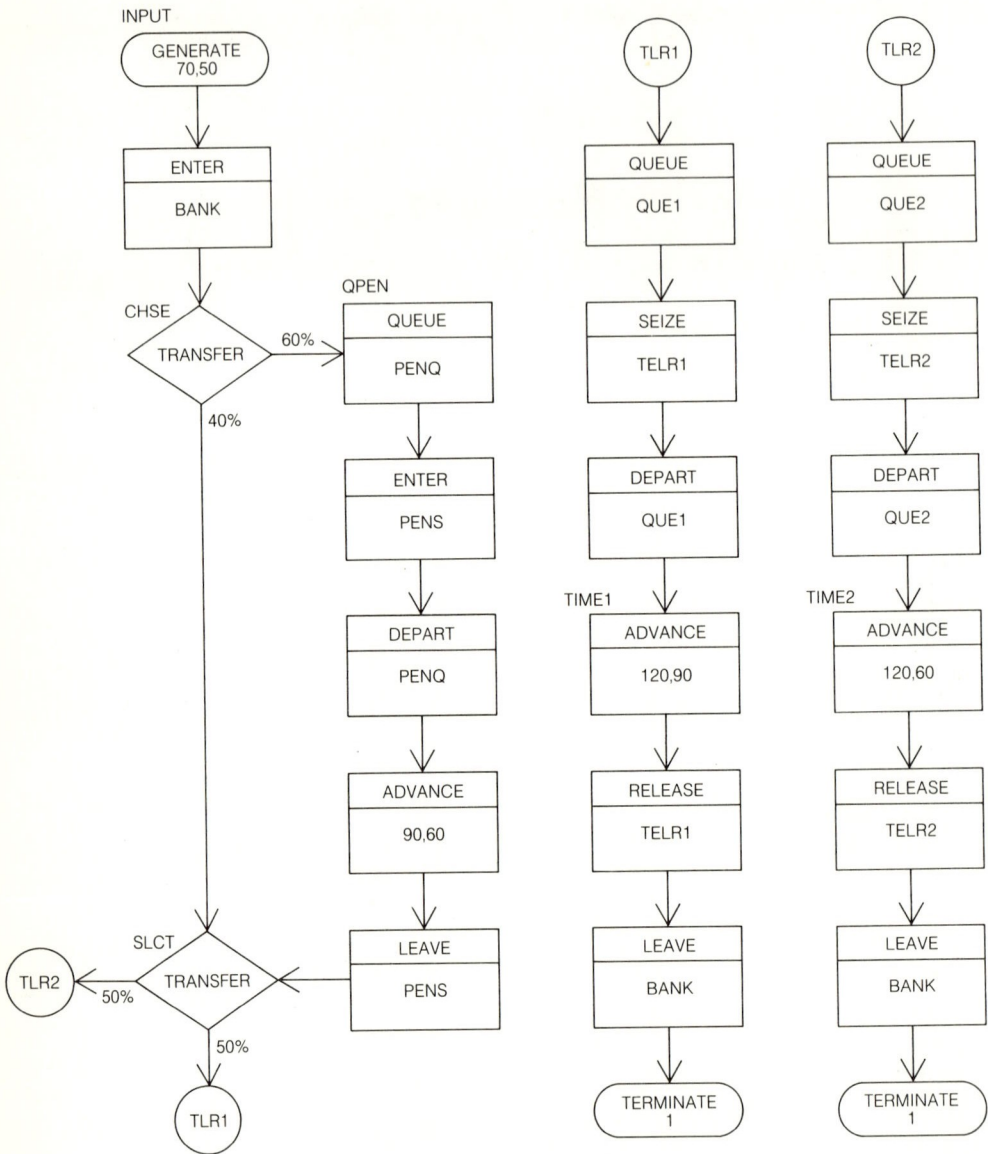

FIG. 10.21 Block Diagram of Revised Model of Bank Branch System

```
BLOCK
NUMBER  *LOC     OPERATION   A,B,C,D,E,F,G              COMMENTS                    CARD
        *                                                                          NUMBER
        *      BANK BRANCH SIMULATION II                                             1
        *                                                                            2
        *            SIMULATE                                                        3
        *                                                                            4
  1     INPUT    GENERATE    70,50       INTR ARRVL RTE 20 SECS TO 2 MINS            5
  2              ENTER       BANK        ENTER THE BANK.                             6
  3     CHSE     TRANSFER    .400,QPEN,SLCT   60% GO USE PENS                        7
  4     QPEN     QUEUE       PENQ        GET INTO LINE TO USE PENS.                  8
  5              ENTER       PENS        START USING PEN.                            9
  6              DEPART      PENQ        LEAVE THE LINE WAITING FOR PENS.           10
  7     PNTME    ADVANCE     90,60       USE 30 SECS TO 2 1/2 MINS                  11
  8              LEAVE       PENS        NO LONGER USING PENS.                      12
  9     SLCT     TRANSFER    .500,TLR1,TLR2  1/2 TO TELR 1, 1/2 TO TELR2.          13
 10     TLR1     QUEUE       QUE1        GET IN LINE AT WINDOW 1.                   14
 11              SEIZE       TELR1       REACH THE TELLER WINDOW.                   15
 12              DEPART      QUE1        NO LONGER WAITING.                         16
 13     TIME1    ADVANCE     120,90      30 SEC TO 3  1/2 MIN                       17
 14              RELEASE     TELR1       FINISHED BUSINESS.                         18
 15              LEAVE       BANK        LEAVE THE BANK                             19
 16              TERMINATE   1                                                      20
 17     TLR2     QUEUE       QUE2        JOIN LINE WAITING AT SECOND WINDOW.        21
 18              SEIZE       TELR2       REACH THE WINDOW.                          22
 19              DEPART      QUE2        NO LONGER WAITING.                         23
 20     TIME2    ADVANCE     120,60      1 MIN TO 3 M                               24
 21              RELEASE     TELR2       BUSINESS FINISHED.                         25
 22              LEAVE       BANK        LEAVE THE BANK.                            26
 23              TERMINATE   1                                                      27
        *                                                                          28
        PENS     STORAGE     1           ONLY ONE PEN AND WRITING STATION.          29
        *                                                                          30
                 START       5000                                                  31
        *                                                                          32
        *    INCREASE THE AVAILABLE WRITING AREAS                                  33
        *                                                                          34
                 CLEAR                                                             35
        PENS     STORAGE     2       INCREASE WRITING AREAS                        36
                 START       5000                                                  37
        *                                                                          38
        *    INCREASE EFFICIENCY OF THE TWO TELLERS                               39
        *                                                                          40
                 CLEAR                                                             41
 13     TIME1    ADVANCE     90,60        30 SECS TO 2 1/2 MINS                    42
MULTIPLE DEFINITION OF SYMBOL IN ABOVE CARD                                        43
 20     TIME2    ADVANCE     90,30        1 TO 2 MINS                              
MULTIPLE DEFINITION OF SYMBOL IN ABOVE CARD                                        44
                 START       5000                                                 
                 END                                                               45
                                                                                  46
```

FIG. 10.22   Source Cards for Program Corresponding to Model in Figure 10.21

table is used. The TRANSFER block named SLCT reflects the equal probability of choice between the two tellers. Queues are defined to measure the waiting lines: QUE1 for the first teller and QUE2 for the second teller. The ADVANCE blocks named TIME1 and TIME2 represent the times required for the two tellers to service their customers. The storage named BANK is used to measure transit time through the entire system; transactions ENTER this storage as soon as they leave the GENERATE block and LEAVE the storage only when they are about to be TERMINATEd. Thus, the average time per transaction produced for the storage BANK will coincide with the average transit time through the system. (A more satisfactory way of recording transit times through use of table entities is described in Chapter 11.)

Figure 10.23 shows the statistics produced by running the model for 5,000 terminations. A glance at the block counts confirms that the logic of the program corresponds to that of the model. For example, the count at block 4 (QPEN)

```
RELATIVE CLOCK      351931    ABSOLUTE CLOCK      351931
BLOCK COUNTS
BLOCK CURRENT  TOTAL     BLOCK CURRENT  TOTAL     BLOCK CURRENT  TOTAL
  1     0      5005       11     0      2611       21     0      2389
  2     0      5005       12     0      2611       22     0      2389
  3     0      5005       13     0      2611       23     0      2389
  4     0      2991       14     0      2611
  5     0      2991       15     0      2611
  6     0      2991       16     4      2611
  7     0      2991       17     4      2394
  8     0      2991       18     0      2390
  9     0      5005       19     0      2390
 10     0      2611       20     1      2390
```

FACILITY	AVERAGE UTILIZATION	NUMBER ENTRIES	AVERAGE TIME/TRAN	SEIZING TRANS. NO.	PREEMPTING TRANS. NO.
TELR1	.886	2611	119.432		
TELR2	.818	2390	120.525	19	

STORAGE	CAPACITY	AVERAGE CONTENTS	AVERAGE UTILIZATION	ENTRIES	AVERAGE TIME/TRAN	CURRENT CONTENTS	MAXIMUM CONTENTS
BANK	2147483647	7.584	.000	5005	533.311	5	27
PENS	1	.762	.762	2991	89.776		1

QUEUE	MAXIMUM CONTENTS	AVERAGE CONTENTS	TOTAL ENTRIES	ZERO ENTRIES	PERCENT ZEROS	AVERAGE TIME/TRANS	$AVERAGE TIME/TRANS	TABLE NUMBER	CURRENT CONTENTS
PENQ	9	.694	2991	978	32.6	81.742	121.457		
QUE1	23	3.267	2611	400	15.3	440.363	520.031		
QUE2	9	1.155	2394	567	23.6	169.811	222.511		4

$AVERAGE TIME/TRANS = AVERAGE TIME/TRANS EXCLUDING ZERO ENTRIES

FIG. 10.23 Condensed Output of Statistics for First Run of Bank Branch Simulation

shows that about 60 percent of all transactions did indeed use the writing table. The storage statistics for BANK indicate that the average time that a transaction remained in the system — the average transit time — is about 9 minutes. The queue statistics indicate that considerable bottlenecks developed at times, both at the writing table and at the teller windows. For example, waiting time at the first window averaged well over 7 minutes (440.363 seconds). The true nuisance value of the waiting line is measured better by the entry $average time/trans in the same table. Here we see that those transactions that did have to wait at the first window had an average waiting time of about 9 minutes.

The model is run again when cards 36 through 38 are sensed by the GPSS control programs. For this second run, all accumulated statistics and transactions are CLEARed from the system, and the model is reSTARTed for a run of 5,000 terminations with the capacity of storage PENS increased. This redefinition of the storage is caused by card 37, which sets the capacity of the storage to 2. This modification of the system represents the installation of a second writing table. The statistics output from this second run (Figure 10.24) show that transactions still require an average of about 8 minutes to get through the system. Although the delay at the writing table has been almost eliminated (an average wait of 2.2 seconds in run II, compared to an average wait of 81.742 seconds in run I), the bottlenecks at the teller windows have not changed significantly.

In the third run, ADVANCE blocks TIME1 and TIME2 are redefined by cards 43 and 44 to simulate more efficient tellers. In this run, the storage PENS retains its redefined (larger) capacity. (Redefinition is cumulative. In order to revert to the original capacity of PENS, it would be necessary to insert another redefinition card.) The statistics output for this run (Figure 10.25) shows a dramatic decrease in the average time that a transaction remains in the BANK — from a transit time of about 530 seconds in run I and 467 seconds in run II to a transit time of about 196 seconds in run III. In addition, the queues are generally shorter, and the waiting times have decreased to about one or two minutes.

10.15 Debugging

In order to ease the burden on the analyst, GPSS produces diagnostic messages whenever it detects an error or a possible error in the source program. For example, such a diagnostic appears near the end of the program listing in Figure 10.22. The message warns that two different definition cards have been included for blocks with the same symbolic name. In this case, the redefinition was intentional, but such messages would help the programmer catch his error if he had erroneously redefined the same facility.

Table C.4 (Appendix C) lists error messages by identifying number. The messages fall into four general categories, according to the type of error made. These error types correspond to the assembly, input, execution, and output

```
**   INCREASE THE AVAILABLE WRITING AREAS
**
2    CLEAR
     STORAGE    2
     START      5000


RELATIVE CLOCK  347106   ABSOLUTE CLOCK   347106
BLOCK COUNTS
BLOCK CURRENT  TOTAL    BLOCK CURRENT  TOTAL    BLOCK CURRENT  TOTAL
  1      0     5006      11     0       2576      21     0      2425
  2      0     5006      12     0       2576      22     0      2425
  3      0     5006      13     1       2576      23     0      2425
  4      0     3037      14     0       2575
  5      0     3037      15     0       2575
  6      0     3037      16     0       2575
  7      0     3037      17     3       2428
  8      0     3037      18     0       2425
  9      0     5006      19     0       2425
 10      2     2578      20     0       2425


FACILITY    AVERAGE        NUMBER     AVERAGE      SEIZING       PREEMPTING
            UTILIZATION    ENTRIES    TIME/TRAN    TRANS. NO.    TRANS. NO.
TELR1       .897           2576       120.873
TELR2       .846           2425       121.098      16


STORAGE   CAPACITY     AVERAGE    AVERAGE       ENTRIES   AVERAGE     CURRENT    MAXIMUM
                       CONTENTS   UTILIZATION             TIME/TRAN   CONTENTS   CONTENTS
BANK      2147483647   6.736      .000          5006      467.062     6          19
PENS      2            .792       .396          3037      90.629                 2


QUEUE   MAXIMUM   AVERAGE    TOTAL     ZERO      PERCENT   AVERAGE     $AVERAGE     TABLE    CURRENT
        CONTENTS  CONTENTS   ENTRIES   ENTRIES   ZEROS     TIME/TRANS  TIME/TRANS   NUMBER   CONTENTS
PENQ    3         .019       3037      2795      92.0      2.200       27.615
QUE1    15        2.448      2578      355       13.7      329.733     382.389               2
QUE2    12        1.731      2428      454       18.6      247.572     304.511               3
$AVERAGE TIME/TRANS = AVERAGE TIME/TRANS EXCLUDING ZERO ENTRIES
```

FIG. 10.24 Condensed Output of Statistics for Run II of Bank Branch Simulation

```
*    INCREASE EFFICIENCY OF THE TWO TELLERS
*
*
        CLEAR
13      ADVANCE    90    60
20      ADVANCE    90    30
        START      5000
```

RELATIVE CLOCK 348798   ABSOLUTE CLOCK   348798

BLOCK COUNTS

BLOCK	CURRENT	TOTAL	BLOCK	CURRENT	TOTAL	BLOCK	CURRENT	TOTAL
1	0	5003	11	0	2519	21	0	2481
2	0	5003	12	0	2519	22	0	2481
3	0	5003	13	0	2519	23	0	2481
4	0	2969	14	0	2519			
5	0	2969	15	0	2519			
6	0	2969	16	0	2519			
7	2	2969	17	0	2481			
8	0	2967	18	0	2481			
9	0	5001	19	0	2481			
10	1	2520	20	0	2481			

FACILITY	AVERAGE UTILIZATION	NUMBER ENTRIES	AVERAGE TIME/TRAN	SEIZING TRANS. NO.	PREEMPTING TRANS. NO.
TELR1	.656	2519	90.959		
TELR2	.638	2481	89.831		

STORAGE	CAPACITY	AVERAGE CONTENTS	AVERAGE UTILIZATION	ENTRIES	AVERAGE TIME/TRAN	CURRENT CONTENTS	MAXIMUM CONTENTS
BANK	2147483647	2.817	.000	5003	196.433	3	8
PENS	2	.764	.382	2969	89.827	2	2

QUEUE	MAXIMUM CONTENTS	AVERAGE CONTENTS	TOTAL ENTRIES	ZERO ENTRIES	PERCENT ZEROS	AVERAGE TIME/TRANS	$AVERAGE TIME/TRANS	TABLE NUMBER	CURRENT CONTENTS
PENQ	2	.015	2969	2759	92.9	1.769	25.023		
QUE1	6	.396	2520	1089	43.2	54.852	96.595		
QUE2	5	.345	2481	1089	43.8	48.601	86.623	1	

$AVERAGE TIME/TRANS = AVERAGE TIME/TRANS EXCLUDING ZERO ENTRIES

FIG. 10.25 Condensed Output of Statistics for Run III of Bank Branch Simulation

phases of the GPSS control programs. In each of these cases, the control programs report the error by its identifying number; the user may refer to Table C.4 for the appropriate explanation.

If an error occurs during the actual running of the model, information is printed about the status of the system at the time of the error. This information is immediately preceded by a message of the form

ERROR NO ___
TRANS ___ FROM ___ TO ___ CLOCK ___ TERMINATIONS TO GO ___

This message defines the error number, the transaction being moved at the time of the error, the block numbers FROM and TO which the transaction was being moved, the clock time at which the error occurred, and the number of terminations remaining in the run. For example, TRANSFER of a transaction to a GENERATE block will cause a message similar to this one:

ERROR 413
TRANS 1 FROM 16 TO 12 CLOCK 63 TERMINATIONS TO GO 873

Table C.4 indicates that error 413 is caused by an illegal entry to a GENERATE block. The diagnostic message indicates that the model and definition cards for blocks 12 and 16 should be checked first in a search for the cause of this error. As in this case, the error printout often makes it possible to locate the error immediately. In many cases, however, a deeper analysis is required to trace the causes of the error.

Further aids in *debugging* — as the process of program correction is called — are output-producing features of GPSS such as the PRINT and TRACE blocks. The PRINT block is discussed in Section 11.15. The TRACE and UNTRACE blocks are available to test the logic of a block diagram by tracing the flow of each transaction through a selected sequence of blocks. When a transaction enters a TRACE block, a record is printed of its progress through each successive block until it enters an UNTRACE block. Figure 10.26 is an example of output caused by the TRACE block. The first line of output produced for each block consists of the same information as that in an error diagnostic:

TRANS ___ FROM ___ TO ___ CLOCK ___ TERMINATIONS TO GO ___

The following lines contain information about the transaction being traced. Some of this information — specifically the entries under TRANS, BLOCK, and NBA — are merely repetitions of the information given by TRANS, FROM, and TO in the first line. MARK-TIME usually indicates when the transaction was GENERATEd. The columns marked P1, P2, P3, and P4 contain the values of the parameters that a transaction can have (see Chapter 11). Explanations of the remaining entries are given in the *GPSS/360 User's Manual* (see Section 10.16).

The TRACE and UNTRACE blocks must be used with discretion if you do not wish to wade through stacks of paper output many inches thick. However, these blocks do enable the programmer to follow a transaction step-by-step through the system. They not only can help to pinpoint the cause of an error, but they can be useful in validating the system.

10.16 Supplementary Reading

The basic reference for information about GPSS is the *GPSS/360 User's Manual* (IBM Systems Reference Library Form H20–0326). *The GPSS/360 Introductory User's Manual* (IBM Systems Reference Library Form H20–0304) also may be useful.

Problems

Prepare GPSS programs to simulate the activities described in each of the problems in this section. A complete solution will include a correct block diagram and a computer run. Be sure that all necessary output is produced by the program and that any additional questions posed in the problems are answered.

10.1 Simulate the port facility system discussed in Section 10.2. Assume that the port may service 5 ships at a time and that it takes about 20 ± 5 hours to unload a given ship. Assume that ship interarrival time at the port is given by 6 ± 1 hours. Run the system for 1,000 terminations. What changes must be made in the program in order to simulate a ticket-window facility with 5 windows, each of which can handle customers at the rate of one every 20 ± 5 seconds, with a customer interarrival time of 6 ± 1 seconds?

10.2 Consider the GPSS program discussed in Section 10.3 — the simulation of a small bank branch. Modify the original program in each of the following ways: **(a)** Represent all action times in seconds — for example, interarrival time given by (180,120), time at writing table given by (120,60), and time at teller given by (240, 180); **(b)** Represent all action times in hundredths of an hour. In a series of runs, compare these modifications with each other and with the original form of the program.

10.3 People arrive at an office at the rate of one every 10 ± 3 minutes and form a line at a receptionist's desk. The receptionist is able to handle the business of 10 percent of these people, with an average rate of 3 ± 1 minutes per person. The other 90 percent of the people are transferred immediately (after they reach the head of the line to speak to the receptionist) with equal probability to either clerk A or clerk B. Clerk A processes inquiries at a rate of one every 10 ± 3 minutes; clerk B works at a rate of one every 10 ± 6 minutes. Clerk A refers 5 percent of all inquiries reaching him to the manager; clerk B refers 8 percent of his inquiries to the manager. These references of inquiries to the manager are made

```
TRANS                                                                                          SI TI DI CI MC PC PF
TRANS  1  1 FROM  2 TO   3 CLOCK  SET  1 TERMINATIONS TO GO         2000                                    2
          BDT   BLOCK  PR SF NBA      MARK-TIME              P1  P2      P3      P4
          1     2              3          1            0           0 0     0 0     0 0     0 0 0
                                                                  0

TRANS                                                                                          SI TI DI CI MC PC PF
TRANS  1  1 FROM  3 TO   4 CLOCK  SET  1 TERMINATIONS TO GO         2000                                    2
          BDT   BLOCK  PR SF NBA      MARK-TIME              P1  P2      P3      P4
          1     3              4          1            1           0 0     0 0     0 0     0 0 0
                                                                  0

TRANS                                                                                          SI TI DI CI MC PC PF
TRANS  1  1 FROM  4 TO   5 CLOCK  SET  1 TERMINATIONS TO GO         2000                                    2
          BDT   BLOCK  PR SF NBA      MARK-TIME              P1  P2      P3      P4
          1     4              5          1            1           0 0     0 0     0 0     0 0 0
                                                                  0

TRANS                                                                                          SI TI DI CI MC PC PF
TRANS  1  1 FROM  5 TO   6 CLOCK  SET  1 TERMINATIONS TO GO         2000                                    2
          BDT   BLOCK  PR SF NBA      MARK-TIME              P1  P2      P3      P4
          1     5              6          1            1           0 0     0 0     0 0     0 0 0
                                                                  0

TRANS                                                                                          SI TI DI CI MC PC PF
TRANS  1  1 FROM  6 TO   7 CLOCK  SET  1 TERMINATIONS TO GO         2000                                    2
          BDT   BLOCK  PR SF NBA      MARK-TIME              P1  P2      P3      P4
          1     6              7          1            1           0 0     0 0     0 0     0 0 0
                                                                  0

TRANS                                                                                          SI TI DI CI MC PC PF
TRANS  2  2 FROM  2 TO   3 CLOCK  SET 11 TERMINATIONS TO GO         2000                                    2
          BDT   BLOCK  PR SF NBA      MARK-TIME              P1  P2      P3      P4
          11    2              3         11            0           0 0     0 0     0 0     0 0 0
                                                                  0

TRANS                                                                                          SI TI DI CI MC PC PF
TRANS  2  2 FROM  3 TO   4 CLOCK  SET 11 TERMINATIONS TO GO         2000                                    2
          BDT   BLOCK  PR SF NBA      MARK-TIME              P1  P2      P3      P4
          11    3              4         11            2           0 0     0 0     0 0     0 0 0
                                                                  0

TRANS                                                                                          SI TI DI CI MC PC PF
TRANS  2  2 FROM  4 TO   5 CLOCK  SET 11 TERMINATIONS TO GO         2000                                    2
          BDT   BLOCK  PR SF NBA      MARK-TIME              P1  P2      P3      P4
          11    4              5         11            2           0 0     0 0     0 0     0 0 0
                                                                  0
```

```
TRANS 2    2 FROM   5 TO    6 CLOCK            11 TERMINATIONS TO GO
TRANS 2         BDT 11  BLOCK 5   PR  SF  NBA 6   SET 2   MARK-TIME         P1 2   2000 P2      P3      P4      SI TI DI CI MC PC PF
                                                                              0        0        0        0                  2
                                                                              0        0        0        0

TRANS 2    2 FROM   6 TO    7 CLOCK            11 TERMINATIONS TO GO
TRANS 2         BDT 11  BLOCK 6   PR  SF  NBA 7   SET 2   MARK-TIME         P1 2   2000 P2      P3      P4      SI TI DI CI MC PC PF
                                                                              0        0        0        0                  2
                                                                              0        0        0        0

TRANS 1    1 FROM   7 TO    8 CLOCK            15 TERMINATIONS TO GO
TRANS 1         BDT 15  BLOCK 7   PR  SF  NBA 8   SET 1   MARK-TIME         P1 1   2000 P2      P3      P4      SI TI DI CI MC PC PF
                                                                              0        0        0        0                  2
                                                                              0        0        0        0

TRANS 1    1 FROM   8 TO    9 CLOCK            15 TERMINATIONS TO GO
TRANS 1         BDT 15  BLOCK 8   PR  SF  NBA 9   SET 1   MARK-TIME         P1 1   2000 P2      P3      P4      SI TI DI CI MC PC PF
                                                                              0        0        0        0                  2
                                                                              0        0        0        0

TRANS 1    1 FROM   9 TO   10 CLOCK            15 TERMINATIONS TO GO
TRANS 1         BDT 15  BLOCK 9   PR  SF  NBA 10  SET 1   MARK-TIME         P1 1   2000 P2      P3      P4      SI TI DI CI MC PC PF
                                                                              0        0        0        0                  2
                                                                              0        0        0        0

TRANS 1    1 FROM  10 TO   11 CLOCK            15 TERMINATIONS TO GO
TRANS 1         BDT 15  BLOCK 10  PR  SF  NBA 11  SET 1   MARK-TIME         P1 1   2000 P2      P3      P4      SI TI DI CI MC PC PF
                                                                              0        0        0        0                  2
                                                                              0        0        0        0

TRANS 3    3 FROM   2 TO    3 CLOCK            18 TERMINATIONS TO GO
TRANS 3         BDT 18  BLOCK 2   PR  SF  NBA 3   SET 3   MARK-TIME         P1 0   1999 P2      P3      P4      SI TI DI CI MC PC PF
                                                                              0        0        0        0                  2
                                                                              0        0        0        0

TRANS 3    3 FROM   3 TO    4 CLOCK            18 TERMINATIONS TO GO
TRANS 3         BDT 18  BLOCK 3   PR  SF  NBA 4   SET 3   MARK-TIME         P1 3   1999 P2      P3      P4      SI TI DI CI MC PC PF
                                                                              0        0        0        0                  2
                                                                              0        0        0        0
```

FIG. 10.26   Example of Output Resulting from Use of TRACE and UNTRACE Blocks

only after the clerk has spent the usual amount of time processing the inquiry. The manager handles inquiries at the rate of one every 15 ± 5 minutes. Simulate this system for 1,000 terminations and measure waiting lines at each point of congestion.

10.4   Augment the program written in answer to Problem 10.3, using START cards and additional block definition cards, to obtain results for each of the model revisions listed below. Retain all preceding revisions in each new model — in other words, make the revisions cumulative. Compare the outputs of statistics and discuss the reasons for any differences. (a) The receptionist requires 8 ± 7 minutes for the 10 percent of the customers that she is able to service, and requires 3 ± 1 minutes to make the transfer of the other 90 percent to a clerk. (b) The customers arrive at a rate of one every 5 ± 2 minutes. (c) A third clerk is added to the system. This clerk C processes one inquiry every 9 ± 3 minutes and refers 4 percent of his inquiries to the manager. Assume that customers are sent to the three clerks with equal probabilities. The manager now services inquiries at the rate of one every 12 ± 5 minutes.

10.5   Rewrite the GPSS program given in answer to Problem 10.3, so that clerks A and B are represented as a storage with a service-time distribution of 10 ± 4 minutes. Six percent of the inquiries processed by this storage are then forwarded to the manager. Compare the results of this program with those obtained in running the program written for Problem 10.3.

10.6   Revise the GPSS program written in answer to Problem 10.5, so that a third clerk is added to the storage. Do not change any of the other characteristics of the model. Compare the results of this program both with those obtained in answer to Problem 10.5 and with those obtained in answer to part c of Problem 10.4.

10.7   Cars arrive at a service station every 3 ± 2 minutes, with 60 percent of the cars requiring regular gas and 40 percent requiring premium gas. Each car requires an attendant for service. There are three attendants. There are two premium pumps, each of which can service a car in 4 ± 2 minutes. There are three regular pumps, each of which can service a car in 8 ± 3 minutes. Measure the utilization and the waiting lines formed for attendants and for pumps. Run the model until 500 cars have been serviced.

10.8 A gizmo factory produces gizmos at the rate of one every 5 ± 2 minutes. As they are produced, an inspector examines each gizmo for 2.5 ± 1 minutes. He immediately discards 10 percent of all the gizmos that he inspects. Of the remaining gizmos, 70 percent are accepted and 30 percent are sent to a touch-up line. Touch-up requires 2.5 ± 1 minutes per gizmo. Each gizmo leaving the touch-up line is reinspected under the same conditions as the original inspection and by the same inspector. Run this model until 1,000 gizmos have passed inspection. Use queues to measure utilization of the inspector.

10.9 Modify Problem 10.7 so that one of the regular pumps is converted to a self-service pump. At this pump, it takes the customer 6 ± 2 minutes to service his own car, after which an attendant is required for 2 ± 1 minutes to collect the money. Twenty-five percent of the customers requiring regular service will use the self-service pump. Run this model for 500 terminations and compare it with the results of Problem 10.7.

10.10 A bank branch has one writing table and ten teller windows. Twenty-five percent of the customers use the writing table and the other 75 percent go directly to a teller window. There are equal probabilities that the customer may choose any of the windows. The time spent at the writing table is 3 ± 2 minutes. Ninety percent of the customers spend 3 ± 2 minutes at the teller windows, while the remaining 10 percent spend 10 ± 5 minutes. Customers arrive at the bank with interarrival times of 2 ± 1 minutes. Run the model until 1,000 customers have been serviced. Then modify the model so that all customers wishing to use a teller window join a common waiting line. The person at the head of the line goes to the first available teller. Run the modified model for 1,000 customers and compare results for the two runs.

11

Additional GPSS Features

11.1 INTRODUCTION   This second chapter on GPSS describes and illustrates several useful and more advanced features of the language, including standard numerical attributes; the ASSIGN block; indirect addressing; savevalues; tabular output; random numbers and their use in GPSS to represent prescribed distributions; chains; and special output features such as the use of the PRINT block and the construction of graphical output.

The reader who masters the features discussed in this chapter will be able to program complex simulations. In particular, he will understand the GPSS programs that appear in the examples and case studies of the following chapters.

11.2 Standard Numerical Attributes

The GPSS programmer has easy access to certain numerical quantities that represent the status of the system and its entities. These quantities are called *standard numerical attributes*, or simply *SNAs*. For example, the present length of a queue entity named LINE is indicated by the current value of the SNA called Q$LINE. Because SNAs can be used as operands in almost any block, the current value of Q$LINE could be used to control transaction flow so as to prevent heavy congestion in the queue LINE.

Each SNA is identified by a name made up of one or two letter codes, followed by either a number or a symbolic name. For example, N17 has a value equal to the total number of transactions that so far have entered block 17. If block 17 has a symbolic name, say BLCK, then N17 and N$BLCK will be the same. The dollar sign ($) always must separate the SNA code from the symbolic name. This separation is necessary to avoid possible confusion between names such as S$PORT (which is the SNA equal to the current contents of the storage PORT) and SPORT (which is a symbolic name that might have nothing to do with storages or with SNAs).

Table 11.1 lists some of the SNAs available in GPSS. Many more will be introduced and discussed in this chapter; complete descriptions of all SNAs will be found in the *GPSS/360 User's Manual* (see Section 10.16).

TABLE 11.1   Major Standard Numerical Attributes (SNAs)

Associated Entity	Mnemonic	Description
Block	N	Entry count; that is, the total number of transactions that so far have entered the specified block.
Storage	S	Current contents of the storage; for example, S$BANK gives the current contents of the storage BANK.
	SR	Storage utilization in parts per thousand; for example, if utilization of storage ROAD is 0.980, then SR$ROAD has the value 980.
Facility	F	Present status of the facility; for example, if the facility DRILL is in use, then F$DRILL is 1; if it is not in use, then F$DRILL is 0.
	FR	Facility utilization in parts per thousand.
Queue	Q	Current length of specified queue.
	QA	Average contents of specified queue (truncated to an integer).
System-wide	C1	Relative clock time (set to zero at beginning of job or at a START control card).
	K	Integer constant; for example, K19634 for the integer 19634.

Many of the SNAs, such as QA, are truncated to integers. Others, such as SR and FR, whose values always range from 0 to 1, are given as three-digit numbers in parts per thousand. Some of the mnemonics used for SNAs are similar to the abbreviations introduced in Sections 10.12 and 10.13 for storage, queue, and facility statistics. In fact, they represent the same statistics. Notice, however, that reference to such an SNA always gives the value at the time of reference, whereas the statistical output gives the cumulative or final value of the SNA at the end of the run.

Two SNAs of particular interest are the *relative clock time* and the *integer constants*. Each of these is called a system-wide SNA, because it is unaffected by the GPSS program. The clock, for example, is maintained automatically by the GPSS control programs. The programmer may reference it by using the SNA symbolic code C1. Constant integers of up to six digits may use the SNA mnemonic K for identification; for example, K125 has the value of the integer 125. However, the K generally is omitted, and it is mentioned here chiefly for consistency with other references.

11.3 Transaction Parameters

Transaction parameters are probably the most versatile and important SNAs available in GPSS. These parameters can perform such functions as identifying transactions, accumulating computational results, holding and transmitting values between different portions of the model, and making traffic flow modification conditional on the state of the system. Parameters also are used in a technique called indirect addressing, which can enhance the sophistication of a GPSS model.

Each transaction can carry from 0 to 100 numerical parameters. Each parameter value is stored as a signed integer, occupying either a halfword or a fullword of core storage. (On an IBM/360 or 370, a fullword consists of 32 bits, or 4 bytes, of core storage; it allows integers to range from -2^{31} to $(2^{31} - 1)$. A halfword occupies 16 bits, or 2 bytes, and allows integers to range from -2^{15} to $(2^{15} - 1)$. It may be necessary to use halfwords when computer storage is limited.) The number and the size of parameters attached to a transaction are specified by operands F and G of the GENERATE block. The number of parameters is specified by operand F; if this operand is omitted, then 12 parameters will be created. The size of parameters is specified by operand G; the symbol F in operand G specifies that the parameters will occupy full words of storage; if operand G is omitted, parameter size will be halfword. The values of all parameters for newly created transactions are zero. The mnemonic code reference for a parameter is P; for example, P6 is a reference to the sixth parameter of the transaction.

The ASSIGN block provides the principal means of modifying the numerical values of transaction parameters. The ASSIGN block definition card has the following form: (1) the LOC field may contain a symbolic name for the block; (2) the OPERATION field contains the block name ASSIGN; and (3) the OPERANDS field contains as operand A an SNA that specifies the number of the parameter whose value is to be changed, and as operand B an SNA whose value replaces, is added to, or is subtracted from the current value of the parameter specified by operand A.

The ASSIGN block will operate in one of the three modes: replacement, addition, or subtraction. Without special instructions, the block operates in the replacement mode—that is, the value of the SNA specified as operand B replaces the value of the parameter specified as operand A. In Figure 11.1, the ASSIGN block named RPLCE will operate in the replacement mode. For example, if the contents of the queue LINE (given by the value of the SNA Q$LINE) are 68 at the time a transaction enters the block RPLCE, then the current value of the parameter P3 for that transaction will be replaced by the value 68. If a plus sign (+) immediately follows operand A in the ASSIGN block definition card, then the block will operate in the addition mode—that is, the value of the SNA specified as operand B will be added to the current value of the parameter specified by operand A, and this sum then will replace the current value of the specified parameter. The ASSIGN block named ADDIT (Figure 11.1) will operate in the addition mode. For example, if a transaction enters ADDIT with a current value of −200 for its parameter P2, then its parameter P2 will have the value 616 when the transaction leaves the block. If a minus sign (−) immediately follows operand A in the ASSIGN block definition card, then the block will operate in the subtraction mode—that is, the value of the SNA specified as operand B will be subtracted from the current value of the parameter specified by operand A, and the result then will replace the current value of the specified parameter.

```
   2      8           19
  *LOC   OPERATION   A,B,C,D,E,F,G                    COMMENTS
  *
  *   TRANSACTION PARAMETER EXAMPLES
  *
  *   I:GENERATE BLOCK EXAMPLE
         GENERATE    5,2,,,,6,F EACH XACT CARRIES 6 FULLWORD PARAMETERS
         GENERATE    8,6,,,,100 100 HALFWORD PARAMETERS
         GENERATE    10,2       STANDARD DEFAULT OF 12 HALFWORDS
  *
  * II:ASSIGN BLOCK EXAMPLE
   RPLCE ASSIGN      3,Q$LINE   REPLACE VALUE OF P3 BY LENGTH
  *                             OF QUEUE NAMED LINE
   ADDIT ASSIGN      2+,816     ADD 816 TO VALUE OF P2
   SUBTR ASSIGN      5-,N$RPLCE SUBTRACT THE ENTRY COUNT OF
  *                             BLOCK RPLCE FROM P5
```

FIG. 11.1 Transaction Parameters and ASSIGN Blocks

11.4 Indirect Addressing and Indirect Specification

An SNA ordinarily is designated by writing an integer immediately after the mnemonic code. For example, SR3 is the current value for the utilization of storage 3. It also is possible to use parameters to designate a particular SNA. This technique is called *indirect addressing*, and its use is signalled by the appearance of an asterisk (∗) immediately following the SNA mnemonic code. Thus, SR∗3 is the utilization of the storage whose number is the current value of P3 (parameter 3). For example, if the current value of P3 is 8, then SR∗3 is the same as SR8, and its value is equal to the current value for the utilization of storage 8.

Consider the following two block definition cards:

```
BLCK1    ASSIGN        1,Q2
BLCK2    ASSIGN        1,Q∗2
```

When a transaction enters block BLCK1, its parameter 1 is given a new value equal to the current length of queue number 2. For example, if queue 2 contains 14 transactions at this time, the value of P1 for the entering transaction will be replaced by the value 14. When a transaction enters BLCK2, the action is quite different because the queue number is found by indirect addressing. In this case, P1 will be ASSIGNed a value equal to the current length of the queue whose number is equal to the current value of P2. For example, if the current value of P2 for this transaction is 6, then BLCK2 will function as if it had been defined by:

```
BLCK2    ASSIGN        1,Q6
```

and the value of parameter 1 of the entering transaction will be replaced by a value equal to the current length of queue 6.

Example I in Figure 11.2 shows how parameters and indirect addressing may be used to modify and to keep track of transactions flowing through the program. Parameter 2 of a transaction reaching the block OUT will be ASSIGNed the value of the current utilization for the facility that the transaction SEIZEd at block BLK2. The facility number, which can be either 1 or 2, is computed in the first three blocks of the coding fragment and is carried in P1. Depending upon the value of P1, the value of either FR1 or of FR2 will be ASSIGNed to P2 at OUT. In this way, the programmer can assign a transaction to either of two facilities and can keep track of which facility it was assigned to, by using one of the parameters to store this information.

Indirect addressing may be used with any SNA except the clock (C1) and two others—transit time (M1) and random numbers (RNj), which are discussed in later sections. There also are certain blocks for which the use of indirect addressing is limited in certain operands. See Appendix C.1 for this information.

The concept of *indirect specification* has been implicit in most of the pre-

258   The Computer and Simulation

```
  2      8           19
*LOC    OPERATION   A,B,C,D,E,F,G                COMMENTS
*
*    EXAMPLES OF INDIRECT ADDRESSING
*
*    EXAMPLE I
 INTO   ASSIGN      1,1         1 PLACED INTO P1
        TRANSFER    .5,BLK1,BLK2  CONTROLS CHOICE OF FACILITY
 BLK1   ASSIGN      1+,1        ADD 1 TO P1; P1 NOW CONTAINS 2
 BLK2   SEIZE       P1          SEIZE FAC 1 OR 2 ACCORDING AS TO TRANSFER
        ADVANCE     6,2.
        RELEASE     P1
 OUT    ASSIGN      2,FR*1      P2 CONTAINS THE CURRENT LEVEL OF
*                               UTILIZATION OF FAC SEIZED BY XACTN
*
*    EXAMPLE II
        SEIZE       Q*6         SEIZE FAC WHOSE NUMBER IS GIVEN BY
*                               THE LENGTH OF QUEUE WHOSE NUMBER
*                               IS IN P6
        ASSIGN      P4+,F*1     ADD 1 TO CONTENTS OF P4 IF THE FAC
*                               WHOSE NUMBER IS IN P1 IS IN USE
*                               OTHERWISE LEAVE P4 AS IS
```

FIG. 11.2   Examples of Indirect Addressing

vious discussion. An operand is said to be indirectly specified whenever its value is specified by an SNA other than an integer constant. For example, ASSIGN P4,126 will cause the value 126 to be ASSIGNed to the parameter whose number is indirectly specified by the contents of parameter 4. In contrast, the block ASSIGN 4,126 will set the value of parameter 4 to 126. The block ASSIGN P4,126 will have this effect only if P4 contains the integer 4.

Indirect specification can reduce significantly the number of blocks required in a GPSS program. For example, the blocks

```
SEIZE       P1
ADVANCE     P2
RELEASE     P1
```

can be used to simulate the use of any number of facilities, simply by preASSIGN-ing the proper facility number to parameter 1 and the corresponding service time to parameter 2. If there were eight facilities, 24 blocks would be required to treat the facilities individually.

11.5 Savevalues

Parameters enable the programmer to record and to carry information along with transactions as they move through the system. However, it is not possible for one transaction directly to affect or to examine the information carried in the parameters of some other transaction. The need to preserve values for future reference in this dynamic environment can be satisfied by using savevalues and matrix savevalues.

Two SNAs are associated with *savevalues*: (1) X*j* is the current value of savevalue *j* (which occupies a fullword of core storage); and (2) XH*j* is the current value of halfword savevalue *j* (which occupies a halfword of core storage). The SAVEVALUE block is used to adjust the contents of savevalues. The form of the SAVEVALUE block definition card is the following: (1) the LOC field may contain a symbolic block name; (2) the OPERATION field contains the block name SAVEVALUE; and (3) the OPERANDS field contains operand A (an SNA specifying the name or number of the savevalue whose contents will be altered), operand B (an SNA whose value replaces, is added to, or is subtracted from the value of the parameter specified by operand A), and operand C (with the value H if the savevalue is a halfword; if the savevalue is a fullword, this operand is omitted).

Like the ASSIGN block, the SAVEVALUE block will operate in one of the three modes: replacement, addition, or subtraction. The mode of operation for the block is specified on the block definition card in exactly the same way as it is for the ASSIGN block. Remember that the letter H must appear as operand C of the SAVEVALUE block if the savevalue is a halfword. When operand C is omitted, the savevalue referenced will be a fullword. (Recall that parameters are created with halfword size if operand G of the GENERATE block is omitted. Thus, the default specification for the length of transaction parameters is a halfword, but the default specification for the length of savevalues is a fullword.)

Example I of Figure 11.3 shows how savevalues can be used to communicate information between transactions. The GENERATE block will create one transaction every 55 time units and will stop after GENERATEing two transactions. When the first transaction enters BLCK1 at time 55, 4 is added to the contents of

```
   2       8          19
  *LOC    OPERATION   A,B,C,D,E,F,G                COMMENTS
  *
  *    SAVEVALUES
  *
  *    EXAMPLE I
         GENERATE    55,,,2       2 XACTNS EVERY 55 UNITS
  BLCK1  SAVEVALUE   11+,K4       ADD 4 TO X11
         TRANSFER    ,X11         TRANSFER TO BLOCK NUMBER IN X11
         ADVANCE     10           10 UNIT DELAY
  BLCK2  SAVEVALUE   11,1         PLACE 1 INTO X11
         TERMINATE   1
  *
  *    EXAMPLE II : INDIRECT ADDRESSING
         SAVEVALUE   P2,S*8       PLACE CURRENT CONTENTS OF STORAGE WHOSE
  *                               NUMBER IS IN P8 INTO SAVEVALUE WHOSE
  *                               NUMBER IS IN P2
  *    EXAMPLE III: THREE MODES
         SAVEVALUE   10,K300,H    REPLACE CONTENTS OF HALFWORD SAVEVALUE
  *                               NUMBER 10 BY 300
         SAVEVALUE   5+,X10       ADD VALUE OF X10 TO X5
         SAVEVALUE   6-,X5        SUBTRACT X5 FROM X6
```

FIG. 11.3   Examples of the SAVEVALUE Block

X11. Because all savevalues originally are set to the value zero, the value of X11 now will be 4. Next the first transaction enters the TRANSFER block and is TRANSFERed to the block whose number is the current value of X11. In other words, the transaction will be TRANSFERed to block 4, which is the ADVANCE block immediately following. (Recall that the GPSS compiler automatically assigns reference numbers to each block in the sequence that their definition cards appear in the source program.) The first transaction will be delayed in the ADVANCE block for 10 time units, but the second transaction will not leave the GENERATE block until 55 time units after the generation of the first transaction. Therefore, the next event to be executed by the control programs (at C1 = 65 units) is the movement of the first transaction out of the ADVANCE block and into BLCK2, which sets the value of X11 to 1. The first transaction then is TERMINATEd. When the second transaction enters BLCK1 at time 110, the current value of X11 is 1. Therefore, addition of 4 to the current value causes the value of X11 to be reset to 5. When the second transaction enters the TRANS-FER block, therefore, it will be TRANSFERed to block 5, bypassing the AD-VANCE block. In this example, a previous transaction has altered the logic of the system for succeeding transactions. Techniques of this type can be used in GPSS to help in the implementation of complex models.

GPSS allows the programmer to group savevalues into reference entities called *matrix savevalues,* which are rectangular arrays of individual savevalue elements, each of which is identifiable uniquely by its row and column location. Once again, the elements of matrix savevalues may be stored either as fullword or as halfword signed integers. The two SNAs associated with matrix savevalues are: (1) MX$j(m,n)$, which is the current value saved in the mth row and nth column of fullword matrix savevalue j; and (2) MH$j(m,n)$, which is the current value saved in the mth row and nth column of halfword matrix savevalue j. Indirect addressing is implemented by specifying these SNAs as MX$*j(m,n)$ or MH$*j(m,n)$. For example, MX$*3(7,2)$ is a reference to the current value of the element in the 7th row and 2nd column of the fullword matrix savevalue whose number is equal to the current value of P3 for the transaction in question.

In order to use matrix savevalues in GPSS, a *matrix definition card* must be included. This card specifies the dimensions of the matrix (that is, the number of columns and rows) and the word size. This card must precede the START card and must have the following form: (1) the LOC field (columns 2–6) must contain the matrix savevalue number or a symbolic name; (2) the word MATRIX must appear in columns 8–13; and (3) the OPERANDS field (columns 19–72) must contain operand A (with value X for fullword or H for halfword), operand B (the number of rows), and operand C (the number of columns). Examples of matrix definition cards are included in Figure 11.4.

The MSAVEVALUE block is used to adjust values of matrix savevalues. Like the SAVEVALUE block, the MSAVEVALUE block will operate in the addition

```
  2        8          19
 *LOC    OPERATION   A,B,C,D,E,F,G                  COMMENTS
 *
 *       MSAVEVALUES
 *
 *       MATRIX DEFINITION
 TOP      MATRIX      H,4,4           4X4 SQUARE MATRIX OF HALFWORDS NAMED TOP
 *                                    AND REFERENCED BY THE NUMBER 1
  2       MATRIX      X,7,8           7X8 RECTANGULAR MATRIX OF FULLWORDS
 *                                    REFERENCED BY THE NUMBER 2
 *
 *       I:EXAMPLES OF MSAVEVALUE BLOCK AND SNA'S
 *
         ASSIGN      2,MX$TOP(2,3) REPLACE P2 BY ELEMENT (2,3) OF TOP
         QUEUE       MH1(4,4)   JOIN QUEUE WHOSE NUMBER IS IN MH1(4,4)
 *
 *       II:EXAMPLE OF USAGE HISTORY
         ENTER       P2
         SEIZE       P4
         MSAVEVALUE  1+,P2,P4,K1     CROSSTABULATION OF SIMULTANEOUS
 *                                   STORAGE AND FACILITY USAGE
 *
 *  III:MODES
         MSAVEVALUE P3,2,4,Q$LINE REPLACE ELEMENT(2,4)  OF MATRIX
 *                                   SAVEVALUE WHOSE NUMBER IS IN P3
 *                                   BY THE LENGTH OF QUEUE NAMED LINE
         MSAVEVALUE 6+,1,1,K20,H  ADD 20 TO ELEMENT (1,1) OF
 *                                   HALFWORD MATRIX SAVEVALUE 6
         MSAVEVALUE P2-,Q*4,MX2(6,5),S*9
```

FIG. 11.4   Examples of Matrix Savevalues and the MSAVEVALUE Block

mode if a plus sign (+) immediately follows operand A on the block definition card, in the subtraction mode if a minus sign (−) immediately follows operand A, and in the replacement mode otherwise. Because the element savevalue being referenced must be located by its row and column position, additional operands are needed for this block. The operands of the MSAVEVALUE block are (A) the matrix savevalue number; (B) the row number; (C) the column number; (D) the SNA whose value is to replace, to be added to, or to be subtracted from the value of the element referenced by the first three operands; and (E) the value H for halfword. Operand E is omitted for a fullword — in other words, the default specification for word length of matrix savevalues is a fullword.

Figure 11.4 includes examples of matrix savevalues and MSAVEVALUE blocks. Note how Example II uses a matrix savevalue to collect information about the simultaneous usage of facilities and storages. For example, if P2 = 1 and P4 = 3, then the contents of MX1(1,3) are incremented by 1. This savevalue element records the number of times that the same transaction both entered storage 1 and seized facility 3.

Matrix savevalues can be used also to record information that is time-dependent. For example, they can be used to record information about the way that the length of a particular queue varies over time. This information can be recorded in a matrix savevalue with 2 rows; a clock time and the queue length at that clock time will be recorded in corresponding columns. For example, consider the following code:

```
SAVEVALUE      1+.1
MSAVEVALUE     HIST,1,X1,C1
MSAVEVALUE     HIST,2,X1,Q1
```

The first block increments savevalue 1 by 1. The second block places the current clock time into M$HIST(1,X1), and the last block places the current length of queue 1 into M$HIST(2,X1). Column X1 of HIST now contains the clock time in row 1 and the queue length in row 2. By forcing a transaction to pass through these blocks at certain times, the programmer can record the size changes in queue 1 as simulation time passes. Use of this technique requires special care — both in order to avoid invoking these blocks so frequently that the number of columns in the matrix savevalue becomes excessive, and also in order to be able to anticipate how many columns will be needed in the matrix definition.

11.6 Initializing and Redefining Savevalues

Every savevalue and matrix savevalue initially is set to zero and subsequently is reset to zero whenever a CLEAR control card is processed. On the other hand, no savevalue or matrix savevalue is changed when a RESET control card is processed. The INITIAL control card can be used to assign initial values other than zero. The INITIAL control card has the following format: (1) the OPERATION field contains the word INITIAL; and (2) the OPERANDS field contains operand A (the SNA that specifies the savevalue or element of a savevalue matrix that is to be given an initial value), and operand B (the signed integer, up to 10 digits, that is to be placed in the indicated savevalue or savevalue matrix).

Example I of Figure 11.5 shows examples of this basic format. To save time and space, options are provided that permit the use of one INITIAL control card to assign initial values to many different savevalues. Example II shows how the slash (/) can be used to combine several different initializations on the same card. Example III initializes a range of savevalues to the common value −1. As in this example, the savevalues must be numbered consecutively in ascending order, and all must be of the same word length. The final example illustrates the INITIALization of matrices. For example, in the matrix savevalue MH2, the elements in the first and second columns of the second and third rows are given initial values of 30; the other elements of this matrix retain their initial values of zero. Matrix savevalues must be defined in a matrix definition card before they can be INITIALized.

Matrix savevalues and nonzero savevalues form part of the standard output produced when the START card termination count has been reduced to zero

```
  2     8          19
*LOC   OPERATION   A,B,C,D,E,F,G                 COMMENTS
*
*     EXAMPLES OF THE INITIAL CARD
*
*     EXAMPLE I
        INITIAL     X1,-200      SET X1 TO -200
        INITIAL     XH2,23       XH2 SET TO 23
        INITIAL     MX1(1,1),-6     MX1(1,1) SET TO -6
*
*     EXAMPLE II: SAME EFFECT AS ALL CARDS IN EXAMPLE I
        INITIAL     X1,-200/XH2,23/MX1(1,1),-6
*
*     EXAMPLE III:INITIALIZING A RANGE OF SAVEVALUES
        INITIAL     X1-X5,-1   SET X1,X2,X3,X4,X5 TO -1
        INITIAL     X1-X5,-1/XH12-XH14,22 SET X1 THROUGH X5 TO -5 AND
*                                    XH12,XH13,XH14 TO 22
*     EXAMPLE IV: INITIALIZING MATRICES
  1     MATRIX      X,3,3        DEFINE MX1 AS 3X3 FULLWORD MATRIX
  2     MATRIX      H,4,4        DEFINE MH2 AS 4X4 HALFWORD MATRIX
        INITIAL     MX1(1-3,1-3),1  EACH ELEMENT OF MX1 SET TO 1
        INITIAL     MH2(1-2,2-3),30 PART OF MH2 SET TO 30
```

FIG. 11.5   INITIALizing Savevalues and Matrix Savevalues

(Figure 11.6). In the first example, note the omission of savevalues 4 through 9, which have zero values.

11.7 Frequency Distribution Tables

The frequency distribution of any SNA can be tabulated at specified times during the execution of a program. This tabulation is stored in a GPSS statistical entity called a table. A *table entity* consists of a set of counters associated with a set

```
CONTENTS OF FULLWORD SAVEVALUES (NON-ZERO)
SAVEVALUE  NR,        VALUE      NR,        VALUE    NR,       VALUE    NR,      VALUE
           1           1         2          -46      3          85      10        460

CONTENTS OF HALFWORD SAVEVALUES (NON-ZERO)
SAVEVALUE  NR, VALUE     NR, VALUE     NR, VALUE     NR, VALUE     NR, VALUE
           4   800

MATRIX FULLWORD SAVEVALUE    1

           COLUMN   1           2           3

  ROW  1            88         -60         440
       2            -1           0          12

MATRIX HALFWORD SAVEVALUE    2

        COL. 1    2    3    4

  ROW  1     8    5   14   16
       2    13    2    7    0
       3     9    2    1    5
```

FIG. 11.6   Standard Statistics Output for Savevalues and Matrix Savevalues

of contiguous intervals, or *frequency classes*. The table entity records the number of times that the value of the SNA falls within each of these intervals at a moment when a tabulation is called for—that is, whenever a transaction enters a TABU-LATE block referencing that table.

The *table definition card* completely defines a table entity by specifying the SNA to be tabulated and the frequency classes to be used. This card has the following form: (1) the LOC field contains the number or symbolic name for the table; (2) the OPERATION field contains the word TABLE; and (3) the OPERANDS field contains operand A (the SNA to be tabulated), operand B (the upper limit of the lowest interval), operand C (the interval width), and operand D (the number of intervals). The frequency classes are shown in Table 11.2, with the values of operands B, C, and D represented by k_B, k_C, and k_D, respectively. The first and last classes always define the *spill classes*—that is, they encompass all values that fall below the lower limit or beyond the upper limit.

As an example, consider the SNA given by M1, which is called the transaction *transit time*. The current value of this SNA is the amount of clock time that has passed since the transaction was GENERATEd. M1 can be used to determine the distribution of time required for transactions to flow through the system. A table to record the distribution of such transit times could be defined by

XTIME   TABLE   M1,10,10,5

In this example, five frequency classes are defined: (1) transit times of 10 or less units of time; (2) transit times from 11 to 20 units of time; (3) transit times from 21 to 30 units of time; (4) transit times from 31 to 40 units of time; and (5) transit times greater than or equal to 41 units of time. When a transaction

TABLE 11.2   Table Frequency Classes*

Frequency Class	Extent (x = value of SNA being tabulated)	Width
First	$-2^{31} < x \le k_B$	$2^{31} + k_B$
Second	$k_B < x \le (k_B + k_C)$	k_C
Third	$(k_B + k_C) < x \le (k_B + 2k_C)$	k_C
.	.	.
.	.	.
	.	
$(k_D - 1)$th	$[k_B + (k_D - 3)k_C] < x \le [k_B + (k_D - 2)k_C]$	k_C
(k_D)th	$[k_B + (k_D - 2)k_C] < x \le (2^{31} - 1)$	$2^{31} - 1 - [k_B + (k_D - 2)k_C]$

*The symbols k_B, k_C, and k_D represent, respectively, the values of the B, C, and D operands on the table definition card.

enters a TABULATE block specifying this table, the current value of M1 for that transaction will be examined and the counter for the appropriate frequency class in the table will be incremented by 1. For example, if the transaction has a transit time of 23 units at the moment that it enters the TABULATE block, the counter for the third class of this table will be incremented by 1. Figure 11.7 shows other examples.

The points of tabulation are determined by the location of TABULATE blocks in the program. When a transaction enters a TABULATE block, the table specified in operand A of the block is adjusted according to the present value of the SNA associated with that table. For example, the block definition card

TABULATE   XTIME

will cause the transit time of any entering transaction to be tabulated in the table XTIME.

Figure 11.7 includes several examples of table entities and TABULATE blocks. The TABULATE block named TABQ records the distribution of queue lengths for the queue named WAIT in the table named QLONG. Note that the SNA recorded in QLONG is Q$WAIT, which gives the current length of the queue WAIT. The transit time of transactions is recorded into the table TRANS whenever the transactions pass through block TIME.

The table named IARRV, which is TABULATEd at the block TARRV, records the interarrival rate of transactions at IARRV. This function is signaled by the special code IA in operand A of IARRV. When a transaction enters the TABULATE block TARRV, the time elapsed since the previous transaction

```
  2      8         19
 *LOC   OPERATION  A,B,C,D,E,F,G                COMMENTS
 *
 *      EXAMPLES OF TABLE ENTITIES
 *
        GENERATE   25,7
        QUEUE      WAIT         JOIN WATING LINE
        SEIZE      FAC1         SEIZE FACILITY
 TABQ   TABULATE   QLONG        ENTRY ADDED TO TABLE NAMED QLONG
        DEPART     WAIT         LEAVE QUEUE
        ADVANCE    25,15
        RELEASE    FAC1         FREE FACILITY
 TARRV  TABULATE   IARRV        ENTRY ADDED TO TABLE IARRV
 TIME   TABULATE   TRANS        ENTRY MADE ON TABLE TRANS
        TERMINATE  1
 *
 QLONG  TABLE      Q$WAIT,2,2,5    TABULATES THE LENGTH OF THE
 *                                 QUEUE NAMED WAIT
 IARRV  TABLE      IA,5,5,7     TABULATES INTERARRIVAL RATE TO THE
 *                              TERMINATE BLOCK
 TRANS  TABLE      M1,5,5,7     TABULATES TRANSIT TIME THROUGH SYSTEM
 QTABS  QTABLE     WAIT,2,2,5 TABULATES QUEUE DELAY TIMES AUTOMATICALLY
 *                            WITHOUT A TABULATE BLOCK
```

FIG. 11.7   Examples of Tables and the TABULATE Block

entered TARRV is TABULATEd into the table IARRV. The reader is cautioned that, unlike M1, the code IA does not represent an SNA that can be referenced elsewhere in the GPSS program. IA is simply a code that indicates the table is to collect an interarrival distribution.

QTABS is a special entity called a queue table entity. *Queue table entities* are used to record the distribution of waiting times in the queues. On the definition card for a queue table entity, the name or number of a queue must appear in operand A, and the word QTABLE must appear in the OPERATIONS field. The GPSS control program automatically adjusts queue tables whenever transactions leave the specified queue, so TABULATE blocks are not used in conjunction with queue tables.

11.8 Standard Table Output

Figure 11.8 shows a typical example of the standard statistical printout produced for a table. The following notations are used in this section to explain the entries in the output: k_B = upper limit of first frequency class; k_C = width of frequency classes; k_D = number of frequency classes; x_i = the value of the ith SNA or argument tabulated; n_j = the number of arguments falling into the jth frequency class; and TC = the total number of entries into the table. The value of TC appears as the first entry in the first line of output for tables; it is given by

$$TC = \sum_{j=1}^{k_D} n_j. \tag{11.1}$$

The final entry (sum of arguments) in the first line is computed as

$$SUM = \sum_{i=1}^{TC} x_i. \tag{11.2}$$

TABLE 3						
ENTRIES IN TABLE	MEAN ARGUMENT		STANDARD DEVIATION	SUM OF ARGUMENTS		
500	53.301		21.062	26651.000		NON-WEIGHTED

UPPER LIMIT	OBSERVED FREQUENCY	PER CENT OF TOTAL	CUMULATIVE PERCENTAGE	CUMULATIVE REMAINDER	MULTIPLE OF MEAN	DEVIATION FROM MEAN
10	16	3.19	3.1	96.7	.187	-2.055
20	13	2.59	5.7	94.1	.375	-1.581
30	27	5.39	11.1	88.7	.562	-1.106
40	97	19.39	30.5	69.4	.750	-.631
50	87	17.39	47.9	52.0	.938	-.156
60	61	12.19	60.1	39.8	1.125	.318
70	77	15.39	75.5	24.4	1.313	.792
80	79	15.79	91.3	8.6	1.500	1.267
90	25	4.99	96.3	3.6	1.688	1.742
100	18	3.59	100.0	.0	1.876	2.217
REMAINING FREQUENCIES ARE ALL ZERO						

FIG. 11.8   Standard Statistical Output Produced for a Table Entity

The mean argument is defined as

$$TB = SUM/TC. \qquad (11.3)$$

Finally, the standard deviation is defined as

$$TD = \sqrt{\frac{\sum x_i^2 - (SUM^2/N)}{TC - 1}}. \qquad (11.4)$$

The balance of the output is concerned with the frequency distribution tabulated from the argument entries. The first column lists the frequency classes defined for the table, in increasing order according to the upper limit of each class. The second column gives the corresponding observed frequencies for each class. The third column gives the percentage of argument values that fell within each of the corresponding frequency classes. The next two columns are self-explanatory: the cumulative percentage and the cumulative remainder. Column six can be used to assist in comparison of the distribution to the exponential (Erlang) family of distributions. Column seven facilitates comparisons with the normal distribution. The multiple of the mean for the jth frequency class (column six) is defined as

$$MM_j = \frac{k_B + (j-1)k_C}{TB}, \qquad (11.5)$$

and the deviation from the mean for the jth frequency class (column seven) is defined as

$$D_j = \frac{k_B + (j-1)k_C - TB}{TD}. \qquad (11.6)$$

11.9 Random Numbers

GPSS has eight pseudorandom number generators, whose results are accessible through the eight system-wide SNAs: RN1, RN2, . . . , RN8. Each of the eight generators will produce the exact same sequence of numbers (except, as explained below, when the RMULT control card is used), using a variation of the congruential method (see Section 7.6).

Reference to RNj for any $j=1, 2, \ldots, 8$ normally will produce a uniformly distributed three-digit integer from 0 to 999 inclusively (an exception will be discussed in the next section). Figure 11.9 is a listing of the first few random integers produced by RN1. RN1 always is used automatically in any cases where the use of a random number generator is implied. For example, TRANSFER   .600,BLCKA,BLCKB requires invocation of RN1 to produce a random integer. This integer is compared with 600, and the transfer is made to BLCKB if the integer is < 600 and to BLCKA if it is ≥ 600. RN1 also is used to produce the (*mean,spread*) distribution specified for ADVANCE and GENERATE

1	573	30	777
2	675	31	795
3	337	32	820
4	177	33	407
5	871	34	384
6	160	35	277
7	719	36	784
8	667	37	943
9	340	38	16
10	420	39	140
11	431	40	859
12	36	41	954
13	449	42	239
14	202	43	958
15	693	44	743
16	580	45	250
17	218	46	705
18	428	47	90
19	125	48	404
20	96	49	399
21	340	50	515
22	318	51	491
23	343	52	818
24	961	53	715
25	610	54	843
26	512	55	372
27	339	56	754
28	485	57	755
29	507	58	637

FIG. 11.9 Pseudorandom Number Sequence Produced by the RN1 Generator (Sequence numbers are shown in the left columns)

blocks. In this case, the standard transformation is performed to produce an integer uniformly distributed on the interval [*mean − spread, mean + spread*].

The analyst has the option of making some or all of the generators produce unique sequences, through use of the RMULT control card. This card has the word RMULT in its OPERATION field, and it can contain any of up to eight operands, A through H. These operands can be used to redefine the initial values for the multipliers (these values ordinarily are 1) for each of the eight generators. Redefinition is done positionally; that is, operand A redefines the multiplier for RN1, operand B for RN2, and so on.

Certain rules should be followed when using the RMULT control card. **(1)** A redefined multiplier must be an odd integer less than 100,000. For example, RMULT   667,,9,,71 can be used to redefine the multipliers for RN1, RN3, and RN5. However, RMULT   72,101201,1,3 contains two errors that will prevent simulation: the first number is even, and the second number is too large. **(2)** At the beginning of the run, the RMULT card should be the very first card in the deck.

If multiple STARTs are used, the RMULT cards should immediately precede the CLEAR cards. Unexpected results and errors will be caused if this rule is not followed. **(3)** The CLEAR card does not reset the random number generators. Therefore, in the case of multiple starts, an RMULT card is required if a certain sequence of numbers is to be repeated in the next run. To repeat the standard sequence, the multiplier should be reset to 1.

11.10 Representing Densities and Distributions

In the simulation of a discrete stochastic system, the analyst often must represent prescribed density functions. In GPSS, the *function entity* is used to approximate densities. A *function* is a rule that assigns a value of the dependent variable y for each possible value of the independent variable x. For example, the arrival pattern for customers at a bank might vary with the time of day. The rule that gives the interarrival rate y in terms of the time of day x is a function.

Figure 11.10 includes examples of the two types of GPSS functions to be considered here: the continuous function and the discrete function. Discrete densities and continuous densities are defined and discussed in Chapter 3. The discrete function is used in GPSS to represent discrete densities, and the continuous function is used to represent continuous densities. In GPSS, a continuous function always is defined by a series of connected line segments; thus, the GPSS continuous function only can approximate a continuous density. A function is completely defined by specifying its type (discrete or continuous) and by specifying a sufficient number of points x and y (in order of ascending value of x) to determine its form. For example, the points x,y given by 0,1.5/1,2.5/2,1/3,2 are sufficient to determine the discrete function of Example I. Similarly, the four points -2,2/2,-2/6,2/8,-2 determine the continuous function of Example II. This information is specified in the function definition card and in function follower cards. Functions in GPSS need not necessarily be distributions or densities. It is obvious that this is the case for these two examples.

The *function definition card* specifies the function type, the number of points determining the function, and the SNA to be used as the independent variable x. The card has the following form: (1) the LOC field contains the symbolic name or the number of the function; (2) the OPERATION field contains the word FUNCTION; and (3) the OPERANDS field contains operand A (the SNA to be used as independent variable x) and operand B (with value either Cn or Dn, where C is the code for a continuous function, D is the code for a discrete function, and n is the number of points defining the function).

The list of points defining the form of the function appears on *function follower cards,* which must immediately follow the function definition card. The points x, y are listed starting in column 1 of the function follower cards in

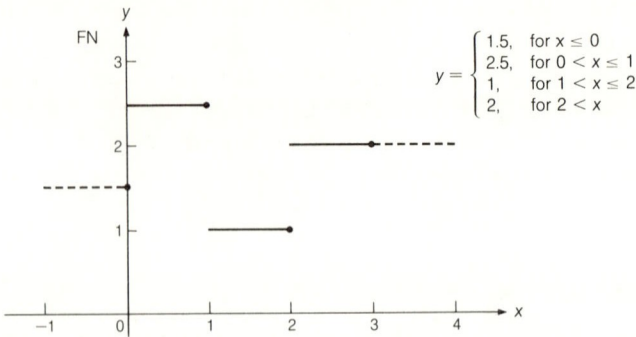

$$y = \begin{cases} 1.5, & \text{for } x \le 0 \\ 2.5, & \text{for } 0 < x \le 1 \\ 1, & \text{for } 1 < x \le 2 \\ 2, & \text{for } 2 < x \end{cases}$$

EXAMPLE I: Discrete Function

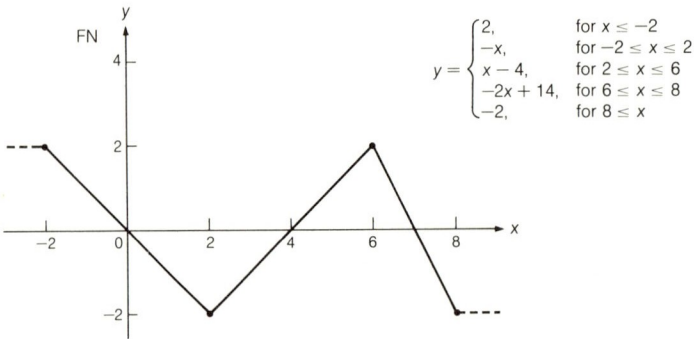

$$y = \begin{cases} 2, & \text{for } x \le -2 \\ -x, & \text{for } -2 \le x \le 2 \\ x - 4, & \text{for } 2 \le x \le 6 \\ -2x + 14, & \text{for } 6 \le x \le 8 \\ -2, & \text{for } 8 \le x \end{cases}$$

EXAMPLE II: Continuous Function

FIG. 11.10   Examples of Functions

ascending value of x. Contiguous pairs must be separated by a slash (/). The SNA code used to reference a function is FN.

Figure 11.11 includes several examples of discrete and continuous functions. For example, DISC is a discrete function defined by two points. If the value of the SNA argument Q1 is not greater than 100, then a reference to the SNA FN$DISC will produce the value 1. On the other hand, if the length of queue number 1 is greater than 100, the value of FN$DISC will be zero. The function named LINE is an example of a continuous function. For all practical purposes, this function is a straight line throught the point 0,0 at an angle of 45 degrees — in other words, the identity function. Thus, for −999999 S1 ≤ 999999, the value of FN$LINE will be exactly equal to the present value of S1. EXMP1 and EXMP2 are the functions graphed in Figure 11.10.

Functions often are used in conjunction with the random number gen-

```
   2       8            19
 *LOC    OPERATION    A.B.C.D.E.F.G                      COMMENTS
 *
 *    EXAMPLES OF FUNCTIONS
 *
 *    DISCRETE FUNCTIONS
 *
  DISC   FUNCTION     Q1,D2
 100,1/200,0
 *
  EXMP1 FUNCTION      X1,D4
 0,1.5/1,2.5/2,1
 3,2
 *
 *    CONTINUOUS FUNCTIONS
 *
  EXMP2 FUNCTION      RN1,C4
 -2,2/2,-2/6,2/8,-2
 *
  LINE   FUNCTION     S1,C2
 -999999,-999999/999999,999999
```

FIG. 11.11   Examples of Function Definition Cards and Function Follower Cards

erators to produce nonuniformly distributed numbers. (Chapter 8 includes a general discussion of the generation of nonuniform pseudorandom numbers.) When an RNj is used as the independent variable for a function, its value will have six significant digits and will be uniformly distributed in the range from 0.000000 to 0.999999. (This production of a six-digit rather than a three-digit random number is the exception mentioned in Section 11.9.)

The inverse transformation method is the method most commonly used in GPSS to develop distributions different from the uniform distribution. An approximation is made to the inverse of the cumulative distribution function. This inverse function, with an RNj as independent variable, then will produce random numbers with the required distribution. Because smooth functions only can be approximated by straight-line segments in GPSS, a satisfactory approximation sometimes is impossible. In general, the approximation becomes better as more points are used to approximate the smooth function.

As an example, suppose that a choice is to be made among three facilities, with the following empirical probability density function: facility 1 is to be chosen with a probability of 0.3; facility 2 is to be chosen with a probability of 0.4; and facility 3 is to be chosen with a probability of 0.3. Example I of Figure 11.12 shows the cumulative distribution function and the inverse of this function. The inverse function could be defined by

```
ABC        FUNCTION       RN1,D3
0.3,1/0.7,2/1.0,3
```

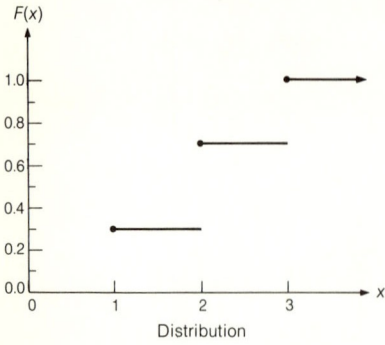

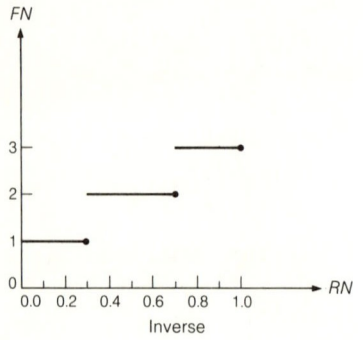

EXAMPLE I: A Discrete Distribution and Its Inverse Function

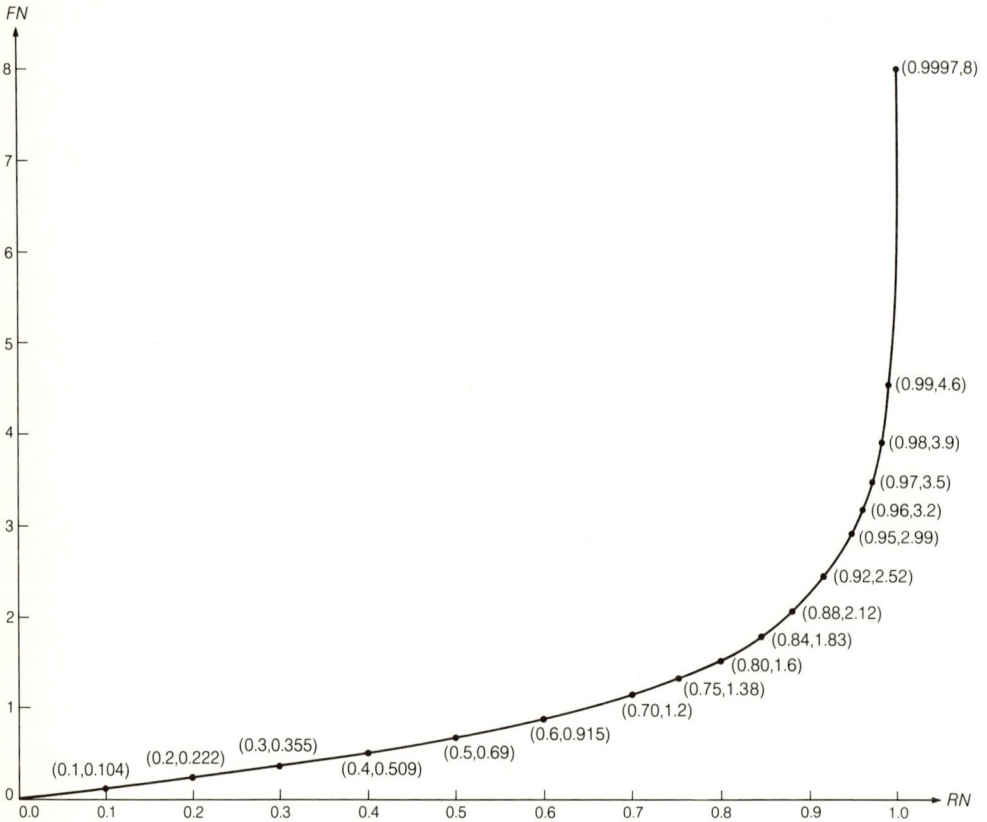

EXAMPLE II: Inverse of Negative Exponential Function

FIG. 11.12 Examples of Discrete and Continuous Inverse Functions

Thus, facility 1 would be used if $0 \leq$ RN1 ≤ 0.3, facility 2 if $0.3 <$ RN1 ≤ 0.7, and facility 3 if $0.7 <$ RN1 ≤ 1.

Example II of Figure 11.12 approximates the inverse cumulative of the negative exponential function. The function is determined by the following twenty-four points:

0,0/0.1,0.104/0.2,0.222/0.3,0.355/0.4,0.509/0.5,0.69/
0.6,0.915/0.7,1.2/0.75,1.38/0.8,1.6/0.84,1.83/0.88,2.12/
0.9,2.3/0.92,2.52/0.94,2.81/0.95,2.99/0.96,3.2/0.97,3.5/
0.98,3.9/0.99,4.6/0.995,5.3/0.998,6.2/0.999,7/0.9997,8.

This approximation gives results that are accurate within 0.1 percent when the mean of the exponential function is about 250; the accuracy decreases to 1 percent when the mean is about 45.

In most cases, reference to the function SNA yields an integer—that is, the function value FNj immediately is truncated to an integer. Two important exceptions occur when a function SNA appears as operand B in an ADVANCE or a GENERATE block. In these cases, the untruncated value returned by the function SNA is multiplied by the present value of the SNA in operand A. This product *then* is truncated to an integer and becomes the ADVANCE block delay time or the GENERATE block interarrival time. Thus, the analyst can represent delay and interarrival times according to distributions other than the uniform. For example, using the function ABC defined above as operand B in the block

GENERATE   10,FN$ABC

produces an interarrival rate computed as 10 if $0 \leq$ RN1 ≤ 0.3, as 20 if $0.3 <$ RN1 ≤ 0.7, and as 30 if $0.7 <$ RN1 ≤ 1.

11.11 Variables

At times, it becomes desirable to use SNAs as operands in performing calculations that involve standard arithmetic operations such as addition, division, and so forth. GPSS permits such operations to be performed by defining SNAs known as *variables* and *floating point variables*. Reference to such SNAs will produce a value computed from algebraic expressions defined in corresponding *variable* or *floating point variable definition cards*. For example, variable number 6 defined by the definition card

6   VARIABLE   Q7+Q8

will be assigned a value equal to the sum of the current lengths of queues 7 and 8. The variables and the floating point variables differ in the method used to evaluate the corresponding expression. For a variable, the value of each SNA involved in the expression is truncated to an integer *before* the expression is evaluated; for a floating point variable, the truncation occurs *after* all computations are completed. For example, the expression 2*(5/2) would be evaluated as 4 for a variable (5/2 is truncated to 2 before the multiplication) and as 5 for a floating point variable.

Care must be taken, however, in the use of floating point variables, because they can produce erroneous results. Fractional digits sometimes must be approximated in the computer. For example, 1/5 is represented as 0.1999 instead of 0.2000 in the IBM/360/370 computer series, because these computers represent floating point numbers in hexadecimal notation. Thus, the expression 100*(1/5) would yield 19.99, which is truncated to 19 when referencing the associated floating point variable.

Scaling and rounding may be needed to increase the precision of computed results. For example, consider the calculation of the number of entries per minute into block XXX in a model whose unit of time is one second. The expression required is (N$XXX*60)/C1. If 100 transactions have entered XXX after 1 hour, this expression will yield the value 1 because of truncation, in either the variable or the floating point variable case. The correct answer is (100 × 60)/3600, or about 1.6667. To increase precision, the computation could be scaled through multiplying by 100, thus giving the expression (N$XXX*6000)/C1. This expression yields a value of 166 when referencing the associated variable or floating point variable. If the expression is used in a floating point variable, rounding may be used. For example, the expression (N$XXX*6000)/C1+(1/2) yields a value of 167. Of course, if scaling is used, the resulting value must be properly interpreted. In this case, the label for the output should read "hundredths of entries per minute."

The variable or floating point variable definition cards have the following form: (1) The LOC field contains the number or symbolic name for the variable; (2) the OPERATION field contains the word VARIABLE for a variable or FVARIABLE for a floating point variable; and (3) the OPERANDS field contains the expression to be evaluated. The operations allowed in these expressions are: addition (+), subtraction (−), multiplication (*), division (/), and modulo division (@). The last operation gives as an answer the remainder in a division. For example, 6@4 has the value 2.

Any number of combinations of the operations may be used to form expressions, such as

| VAR1 | VARIABLE | FN3+K12 |
| 8 | FVARIABLE | Q7*S1/V6+K5*(FN4*FN2) |

In such cases, evaluation proceeds from left to right, with *, /, and @ taking precedence over + and −, unless the order is altered by the use of parentheses. Expressions within parentheses are evaluated first, using the same procedure. Care must be taken to differentiate between expressions such as S1*Q7*K5 (which involves the symbol $*$ as multiplication) and S$*$1 (which is an indirect reference). The value assigned to a variable can be recalled by using the SNA code V. For example, if FN3 has the value 33, then the use of V$VAR1 (defined above) would return the value 45.

Any SNA may be used in a variable expression — with the obvious limitation that, if an SNA referring to a variable is used, that variable must have been defined previously.

11.12 An Example

To illustrate several of the concepts discussed in the preceding sections, consider a simple model that simulates the flow of traffic at a ticket counter. Figure 11.13 shows the flowchart and block diagram for the model; the program listing is shown in Figure 11.14.

Transactions representing customers arrive at the GENERATE block according to the negative exponential distribution with mean of 1.25 minutes (the unit of time is 0.01 minute). The SNA FN$EXPON produces a negative exponentially distributed random number in the range $0 \leq$ FN$EXPON < 1 (see Section 11.10); this value then is multiplied by operand A (125) to calculate the interarrival rate.

Some customers need many tickets. Some will need change. To indicate whether these conditions apply to any particular transaction, parameters 2 and 3 are used as follows: P2 may have the values 1 (if the customer needs only one ticket) or 2 (if the customer needs more than one ticket); and P3 may have the values 1 (if the customer has exact change) or 2 (if the customer needs change). The discrete function TWO is used to ASSIGN these values to parameters 2 and 3. By definition, FN$TWO takes on the value 1 with a probability of 0.333 or the value 2 with the probability of 0.667. Therefore, approximately 2/3 of all customers will need more than one ticket, and approximately 2/3 will need change. Each of these conditions will affect the service time required from the facility CLERK.

This service time is computed at the ADVANCE block according to the uniform distribution with mean V$MEAN and spread 25. Because MEAN is defined by the formula $50*(P2+P3-1)$, the value of V$MEAN depends on P2 and P3 in the following manner: if P2=1 and P3=1, then V$MEAN $= 50$; if P2 $= 1$ and P3 $= 2$, then V$MEAN $= 100$; if P2 $= 2$ and P3 $= 1$, then V$MEAN $= 100$; and if P2 $= 2$ and P3 $= 2$, then V$MEAN $= 150$. Hence, the mean service time increases by 0.5 minutes, from a minimum of 0.5 minutes to a maximum of 1.5 minutes, for each additional service that the CLERK must perform.

Statistics concerning the simulation run are shown in Figure 11.15 and 11.16. The facility statistics show that the CLERK has been kept well-occupied,

FLOW CHART

```
┌─────────────────┐
│ Customers       │
│ arrive according│
│ to exponential  │
│ distribution    │
│ with mean of    │
│ 1.25 minutes    │
└─────────────────┘
        │
        ▼
┌─────────────────┐
│ Decides on      │
│ number of       │
│ tickets         │
│ needed          │
└─────────────────┘
        │
        ▼
┌─────────────────┐
│ Checks to see   │
│ if change       │
│ is needed       │
└─────────────────┘
        │
        ▼
┌─────────────────┐
│ Joins waiting   │
│ line at         │
│ ticket counter  │
└─────────────────┘
        │
        ▼
┌─────────────────┐
│ Arrives at      │
│ head of line    │
└─────────────────┘
        │
        ▼
┌─────────────────┐
│ Leaves line     │
│ to begin        │
│ transaction     │
│ with clerk      │
└─────────────────┘
        │
        ▼
┌─────────────────┐
│ Buys tickets;   │
│ time depends on │
│ number of tickets│
│ and on change   │
│ required        │
└─────────────────┘
        │
        ▼
┌─────────────────┐
│ Clerk records   │
│ type of         │
│ transaction     │
└─────────────────┘
        │
        ▼
┌─────────────────┐
│ Clerk free      │
│ for next        │
│ customer        │
└─────────────────┘
        │
        ▼
┌─────────────────┐
│ Note            │
│ interarrival    │
│ rate for        │
│ last customer   │
└─────────────────┘
        │
        ▼
┌─────────────────┐
│ Leave system    │
└─────────────────┘
```

BLOCK DIAGRAM

```
   GENERATE
   125,FN$EXPON
        │
        ▼
   ASSIGN
   2,FN$TWO
        │
        ▼
   ASSIGN
   3,FN$TWO
        │
        ▼
   QUEUE
   LINE
        │
        ▼
   SEIZE
   CLERK
        │
        ▼
   DEPART
   LINE
        │
        ▼
   ADVANCE
   V$MEAN,25
        │
        ▼
   MSAVEVALUE
   XTAB+,P2,P3,1,H
        │
        ▼
   RELEASE
   CLERK
        │
        ▼
   TABULATE
   IARRV
        │
        ▼
   TERMINATE
   1
```

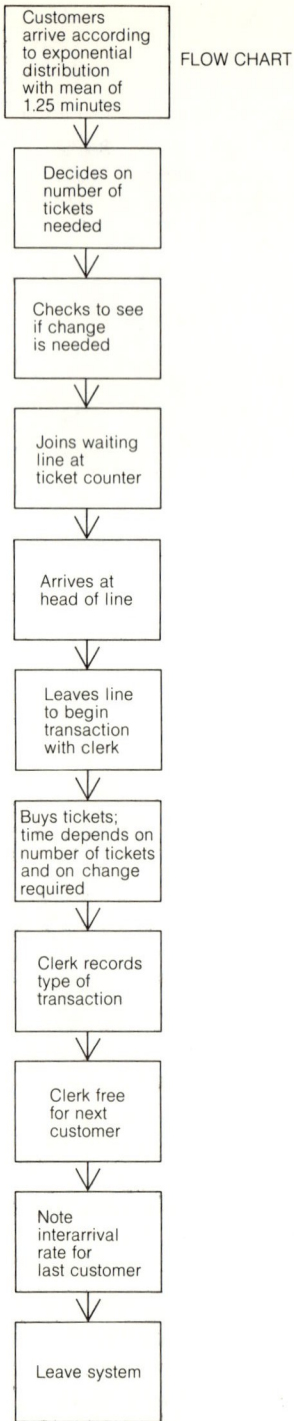

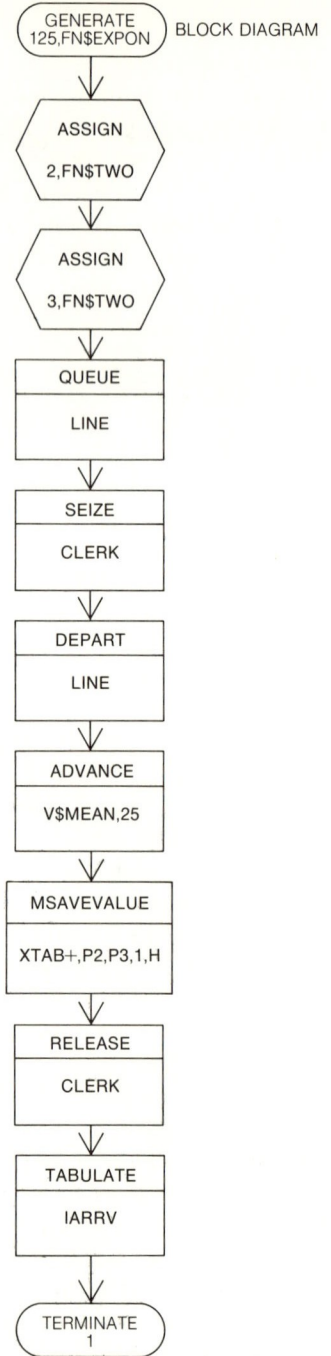

FIG. 11.13 Flowchart and Block Diagram of Ticket Counter Simulation

```
BLOCK                                                                   CARD
NUMBER  *LOC    OPERATION  A,B,C,D,E,F,G            COMMENTS            NUMBER
        *                                                                 1
        * DEFINITION OF THE EXPONENTIAL DISTRIBUTION                      2
         EXPON FUNCTION   RN8,C24                                         3
        0,0/.1,.104/.2,.222/.3,.355/.4,.509/.5,.69                        4
        .6,.915/.7,1.2/.75,1.38/.8,1.6/.84,1.83/.88,2.12                  5
        .9,2.3/.92,2.52/.94,2.81/.95,2.99/.96,3.2/.97,3.5                 6
        .98,3.9/.99,4.6/.995,5.3/.998,6.2/.999,7.0/.9997,8.0             7
        *                                                                 8
        * DISCRETE FUNCTION                                               9
         TWO    FUNCTION   RN2,D2                                        10
        0.333,1/1.0,2                                                    11
        *                                                                12
        * VARIABLE DEFINITION CARD                                       13
         MEAN   VARIABLE   50*(P2+P3-1)                                  14
        *                                                                15
        * MATRIX DEFINITION CARD                                         16
         XTAB   MATRIX     H,2,2                                         17
        *                                                                18
        *        SIMULATION OF A TICKET COUNTER QUEUE                    19
        *                                                                20
        *                                                                21
                 SIMULATE                                               22
        *                                                                23
   1             GENERATE   125,FN$EXPON   TIME IS CALCULATED IN HUNDRETHS  24
        *                              OF A MINUTE.                      25
   2             ASSIGN     2,FN$TWO   CUSTOMER MAY NEED MORE THAN ONE TICKET 26
   3             ASSIGN     3,FN$TWO   CUSTOMER MAY NEED CHANGE          27
   4             QUEUE      LINE       GET INTO LINE FOR TICKETS         28
   5             SEIZE      CLERK      REACH HEAD OF LINE                29
   6             DEPART     LINE       READY TO BE SERVED                30
   7             ADVANCE    V$MEAN,25  SERVICE TIME DEPENDS ON WHETHER CHANGE 31
        *                              IS NEEDED AND IF MORE THAN ONE TICKET 32
        *                              IS NEEDED.                        33
   8             MSAVEVALUE XTAB+,P2,P3,1,H    CROSSTABULATE TYPE OF SERVICE. 34
   9             RELEASE    CLERK      FINISHED                          35
  10             TABULATE   IARRV      TABULATE INTER ARRIVAL RATE TO END 36
  11             TERMINATE  1          LEAVE THE SYSTEM......            37
        *                                                                38
        * TABLE DEFINITION CARD                                          39
         IARRV  TABLE      IA,20,20,50                                   40
        *                                                                41
                 START      2500                                        42
                 END                                                    43
```

FIG. 11.14 Program for Simulation of Ticket Counter Model in Figure 11.13

with an average utilization of 0.921, processing customers at an average rate of one every 1.17 minutes. The queue statistics show that the length of the waiting line exceeded twenty people at least once. However, the average length of the line was only 4.5 people, and the average wait was only about 6 minutes—values that probably would be tolerable in most situations. Two additional statistics of interest have been collected in this simulation.

Statistics concerning the types of service rendered by the clerk are gathered at the MSAVEVALUE block. This block causes element (P2,P3) of the 2×2 halfword matrix savevalue XTAB to be incremented by 1 each time that a transaction enters the block. Thus, XTAB accumulates the frequency of each type of service performed by the CLERK. The types of service represented by the four elements are as follows: MH$XTAB(1,1) represents basic service (only one ticket purchased and no change required); MH$XTAB(2,1) represents sale of multiple tickets but no change required; MH$XTAB(1,2) represents sale of a single ticket with change required; and MH$XTAB(2,2) represents sale of multiple tickets with change required. The statistical output (Figure 11.15) shows that 260 customers needed only basic service; 1,090 needed both change

FACILITY   AVERAGE   NUMBER   AVERAGE   SEIZING   PREEMPTING

```
FACILITY        AVERAGE        NUMBER       AVERAGE         SEIZING      PREEMPTING
                UTILIZATION    ENTRIES      TIME/TRAN       TRANS. NO.   TRANS. NO.
CLERK           .921           2500         117.231


QUEUE    MAXIMUM    AVERAGE     TOTAL      ZERO       PERCENT    AVERAGE        $AVERAGE       TABLE      CURRENT
         CONTENTS   CONTENTS    ENTRIES    ENTRIES    ZEROS      TIME/TRANS     TIME/TRANS     NUMBER     CONTENTS
LINE     22         4.535       2507       195        7.7        575.122        623.630                   7
$AVERAGE TIME/TRANS = AVERAGE TIME/TRANS EXCLUDING ZERO ENTRIES


MATRIX HALFWORD SAVEVALUE XTAB

          COL. 1      2

ROW   1    260    562
      2    588   1090
```

FIG. 11.15   Facility, Queue, and Matrix Savevalue Output for Ticket Counter Simulation

TABLE TARRV
ENTRIES IN TABLE 2499
MEAN ARGUMENT 127.188
STANDARD DEVIATION 62.812
SUM OF ARGUMENTS 317845.000
NON-WEIGHTED

UPPER LIMIT	OBSERVED FREQUENCY	PER CENT OF TOTAL	CUMULATIVE PERCENTAGE	CUMULATIVE REMAINDER	MULTIPLE OF MEAN	DEVIATION FROM MEAN
20	0	.00	.0	100.0	.157	-1.706
40	72	2.88	2.8	97.1	.314	-1.388
60	115	4.60	7.4	92.5	.471	-1.069
80	186	7.44	14.9	85.0	.628	-.751
100	411	16.44	31.3	68.6	.786	-.432
120	436	17.44	48.8	51.1	.943	-.114
140	416	16.64	65.4	34.5	1.100	.203
160	411	16.44	81.9	18.0	1.257	.522
180	306	12.24	94.1	5.8	1.415	.840
200	18	.72	94.8	5.1	1.572	1.159
220	26	1.04	95.9	4.0	1.729	1.477
240	18	.72	96.6	3.3	1.886	1.795
260	12	.48	97.1	2.8	2.044	2.114
280	15	.60	97.7	2.2	2.201	2.432
300	7	.28	97.9	2.0	2.358	2.751
320	6	.24	98.2	1.7	2.515	3.069
340	7	.28	98.5	1.4	2.673	3.388
360	7	.28	98.7	1.2	2.830	3.706
380	2	.08	98.8	1.1	2.987	4.024
400	4	.16	99.0	.9	3.144	4.343
420	4	.16	99.1	.8	3.302	4.661
440	1	.04	99.2	.7	3.459	4.980
460	4	.16	99.3	.6	3.616	5.298
480	3	.12	99.5	.4	3.773	5.616
500	1	.04	99.5	.4	3.931	5.935
520	3	.12	99.6	.3	4.088	6.253
540	0	.00	99.6	.3	4.245	6.572
560	1	.04	99.7	.2	4.402	6.890
580	1	.04	99.7	.2	4.560	7.208
600	1	.04	99.8	.1	4.717	7.527
620	1	.04	99.8	.1	4.874	7.845
640	1	.04	99.8	.1	5.031	8.164
660	0	.00	99.8	.1	5.189	8.482
680	1	.04	99.9	.1	5.346	8.800
700	1	.04	99.9	.0	5.503	9.119
720	0	.00	99.9	.0	5.660	9.437
740	0	.00	99.9	.0	5.818	9.756
760	1	.04	99.9	.0	5.975	10.074
780	0	.00	99.9	.0	6.132	10.393
800	0	.00	99.9	.0	6.289	10.711
820	0	.00	99.9	.0	6.447	11.029
840	0	.00	99.9	.0	6.604	11.348
860	0	.00	99.9	.0	6.761	11.666
880	0	.00	99.9	.0	6.918	11.985
900	0	.00	99.9	.0	7.076	12.303
920	1	.04	100.0	.0	7.233	12.621

REMAINING FREQUENCIES ARE ALL ZERO

FIG. 11.16 Interarrival Table Output from Ticket Counter Simulation

and multiple tickets; 588 needed multiple tickets but no change; and 562 needed change but bought only one ticket.

The interarrival time at the TERMINATE block is TABULATEd in block 10. The distribution recorded in the output (Figure 11.16) might be used later to generate arrivals for followup simulations. In this case, the interarrival times at the TERMINATE block of the ticket counter model might be used to determine interarrival times for the GENERATE block of a simulation of the traffic in a movie theater lobby, where customers go after buying tickets.

11.13 The TEST Block

The TEST block makes it possible to alter the flow in a block diagram, contingent upon the present values of any two SNAs. The block defines conditions that must be met before transactions are allowed to enter it. The specified conditions need not directly involve the entering transaction, but can involve any SNA in the system.

The condition to be met is specified as an algebraic comparison between the operand A and operand B SNAs. The comparison to be made is specified as a part of the OPERATION field. Any one of the following six comparisons may be made: less than (L), less than or equal (LE), equal (E), not equal (NE), greater than (G), and greater than or equal (GE). For example, if LE is specified, the condition is met only if operand A does not exceed operand B. The TEST block definition card has the following form: (1) the LOC field may contain a symbolic name; (2) the OPERATION field contains the word TEST starting in column 8 and the comparison code starting in column 13; and (3) the OPER-ANDS field contains operand A (the first argument in the comparison), operand B (the second argument in the comparison), and operand C (the name or number of the block to which the transaction is to be transferred if the condition is not met).

If operand C is omitted, the TEST block operates in the refusal mode. In this mode, a transaction will not be allowed to enter the TEST block until the condition is met. For example, no transaction is allowed to enter the TEST block NOGO (Figure 11.17) until C1 is greater than 500—in other words, until 500 units of simulation time have passed since the beginning of the simulation.

If a block name or number is specified in operand C, the TEST block will operate in the transfer mode. In this mode, the transaction will be allowed to enter the TEST block, whether or not the condition is met. If the condition is met, the attempt will be made to move the transaction to the next sequential block. If the condition is not met, the attempt will be made to transfer the transaction to the block specified by operand C. The TEST block MAYBE (Figure 11.17) works in the transfer mode. When a transaction enters this block, V1 is evaluated and is compared with zero. If V1 is not zero (in other words, if P1 is not even),

```
    2        8           19
  *LOC    OPERATION   A,B,C,D,E,F,G              COMMENTS
   *
   *   TEST BLOCK EXAMPLES
   *
   *   TRANSFER MODE
   *
   1      VARIABLE    P1ә2
  MAYBE TEST NE       V1,K0,EVEN      IF CONTENTS OF P1 ARE EVEN THEN
   *                                  GO TO BLOCK NAMED EVEN.
   *
   *   REFUSAL MODE
   *
   NOGO   TEST GT     C1,500          BLOCKS ALL TRANSACTIONS UNTIL
   *                                  CLOCK TIME REACHES 500
   *
   EVEN   TERMINATE   1
   *
```

FIG. 11.17 Examples of the TEST Block

then the condition NE is met, and the transaction will attempt to enter the next sequential block, NOGO. If P1 is even, then V1 equals zero, and the condition NE will not be met. In this case, the transaction will be transferred to the TERMINATE block named EVEN.

11.14 User Chains

The movement of transactions during the simulation is handled automatically by the GPSS control program. However, entities called *user chains* enable the analyst to override the control program and to place transactions into an inactive state. User chains chiefly are used to model queuing disciplines such as the LIFO and the RANKED disciplines (see Section 9.6), which cannot be simulated using the standard FIFO queue discipline available in GPSS. In addition, chains sometimes are used in conjunction with queue entities to decrease running time, because user chains place the burden of controlling the queues on the analyst instead of on the control program and may permit him to develop algorithms that run faster.

Two blocks are used to define and to control user chains: the LINK and UNLINK blocks. The LINK block is used to remove transactions from the control of the control programs and to place them on a user chain in an inactive state. The LINK block definition card has the following form: (1) the LOC field may contain a symbolic block name; (2) the OPERATION field contains the word LINK; and (3) the OPERANDS field contains operand A (an SNA specifying the name or number of the user chain on which the entering transaction is to be placed), operand B (a symbol specifying the type of queuing disciplines to be used on the user chain), and operand C (the name or number of a block to which the entering transaction will be transferred if the link indicator is off). The code used to specify queuing discipline in operand B may be FIFO (which will place the transaction at the tail of the user chain), LIFO (which will place the transaction at the head of the user chain), or Pj (which will put the transaction into the chain in RANKED order according to ascending value of parameter j—in other words, the transaction with the smallest value of Pj will be at the head of the chain, and the transaction with the largest value will be at the tail of the chain).

If operand C is omitted, then the entering transaction is forced to join the specified user chain, and the associated *user chain link indicator* is turned on. This indicator is used by the LINK and UNLINK blocks to test the state of the user chain; it is explained in an example below. If operand C is supplied, it represents the number or name of the block to which the entering transaction is transferred if the link indicator is off. The indicator will be turned back on when the transaction is transferred. If the link indicator is on, then the entering transaction is placed on the user chain and the indicator is left on.

Example I of Figure 11.18 shows the two forms of the LINK block. Transactions entering LONE are forced unconditionally to join the chain named LINE, whereas transactions entering LTWO join chain 6 only if the indicator is on. Note that the transactions in chain 6 will be ordered according to increasing values of parameter 2.

```
 2      8          19
*LOC    OPERATION  A,B,C,D,E,F,G                    COMMENTS
*
*   USER CHAINS
*
*   EXAMPLE I: LINK BLOCKS
*
 LONE   LINK       LINE,FIFO       JOIN FIFO CHAIN NAMED LINE AND
*                                  TURN LINK INDICATOR ON.
 LTWO   LINK       6,P2,LOOSE      IF INDICATOR IS ON, JOIN CHAIN 6.
*                                  IF OFF, TURN ON AND GO TO LOOSE.
*
*   EXAMPLE II: UNLINK BLOCKS
*
 UONE   UNLINK     LINE,KILL,X1    SAVEVALUE 1 CONTAINS THE NUMBER
*                                  OF XACTS TO BE REMOVED FROM
*                                  LINE AND SENT TO KILL.
 UTWO   UNLINK     6,BEGIN,ALL     EMPTY CHAIN 6 THROUGH BLOCK BEGIN.
*
*   EXAMPLE III: A LIFO QUEUE FOR FACILITY USAGE.
*
        QUEUE      STACK           PLACE ON STACK IN A
        LINK       WAIT,LIFO,TAKE       LAST-IN-FIRST-OUT MANNER.
 TAKE   SEIZE      DRILL           TAKE ASSEMBLY PART OFF TOP OF
        DEPART     STACK                STACK TO DRILL HOLE.
        ADVANCE    25,9            DRILL HOLE.
        RELEASE    DRILL           RELEASE DRILL AND READY TOP
        UNLINK     WAIT,TAKE,1          PART ON STACK FOR DRILLING.
```

FIG. 11.18 Examples of User Chains and of the LINK and UNLINK Blocks

The UNLINK block is used to remove transactions from a user chain and place them back under the direction of the control program. The more common form of the UNLINK block definition card is the following: (1) the LOC field may contain a symbolic name; (2) the OPERATION field contains the word UNLINK; and (3) the OPERANDS field contains operand A (an SNA specifying the name or the number of the user chain from which transactions will be removed), operand B (the number or name of the block to which the UNLINKed transaction will be sent), and operand C (the number of transactions to be UNLINKed, or the word ALL if all transactions in the chain are to be UNLINKed).

When a transaction enters an UNLINK block of the above form, the following sequence of operations occurs: (1) the user chain number is determined from the SNA specified by operand A; (2) if the user chain is empty, the indicator is set to off; (3) if the user chain is not empty, as many transactions as possible to satisfy operand C are removed, starting at the head of the chain; (4) these transactions are returned to the active state and will be transferred by the control programs to the block specified by operand B; and (5) the transaction that entered the UNLINK block immediately proceeds to the next sequential block.

When a transaction enters the UNLINK block UONE (Example II, Figure 11.18), fullword savevalue 1 is evaluated and that number of transactions is scheduled to leave the chain LINE and to enter the block KILL. If the number of transactions is less than or equal to the value of X1, then the chain will be emptied just as if ALL had been specified as operand C. The block UTWO uses the latter method to remove all transactions from user chain 6.

The SNAs associated with user chains are: CA_j, the average contents of user chain j (truncated to an integer); CH_j, the number of transactions currently on chain j; CM_j, the maximal number of transactions on chain j; CC_j, the total number of entries on chain j; and CT_j, the average time per transaction on chain j. The statistics CA_j and CT_j are computed exactly as are the average contents and average time per transaction for queues (see Section 10.13).

Example III (Figure 11.18) shows how a user chain may be used in the simulation of a LIFO queuing discipline. This example also will serve to explain how the link indicator works and how the use of user chains can enhance program efficiency. The link indicator initially is off. Therefore, when the first transaction enters the LINK block, it is transferred to the block named by operand C. In other words, the first transaction does not join the chain, but immediately transfers to the block TAKE and SEIZEs the idle facility. At the same time, the link indicator is turned on. As long as the SEIZEing transaction is in the AD-VANCE block, any other transactions arriving at the LINK block will find the link indicator on; therefore they will immediately join the chain WAIT in LIFO order. When the transaction using the facility leaves the ADVANCE block and RELEASEs the facility, it then enters the UNLINK block. This causes the transaction at the head of the WAIT chain to be placed in the active mode and scheduled to enter the block named in operand B of the UNLINK block—in other words, the first available transaction on WAIT is scheduled to enter TAKE and to SEIZE the facility. In this case, the indicator remains on. However, if the user chain is empty when the RELEASEing transaction enters the UNLINK block, then the indicator is turned off so that the next transaction to enter the LINK block will transfer immediately to SEIZE the now-idle facility. In this manner, only one transaction is allowed to attempt to SEIZE the facility at any given time. Without the use of a user chain, many transactions would attempt to SEIZE the facility, and the control programs are forced to search through the entire set of contending transactions to decide which one will be allowed to SEIZE the facility next. Because user chains avoid this search procedure, they can lead to significant reductions in running time.

11.15 The PRINT Block

GPSS produces standard statistical output each time that the transaction termination count is reduced to zero. The PRINT block enables the analyst to print selected portions of the standard printout before the termination count is reduced to zero. This permits him to obtain intermediate results and is particularly useful in debugging the program.

The form of the PRINT block definition card is the following: (1) the LOC field may contain a symbolic name; (2) the OPERATION field contains the word PRINT; and (3) the OPERANDS field contains operand A (the smallest value of the entity identification number for which results are to be printed), operand B (the largest value of the entity identification number), operand C (the entity mnemonic code), and operand D (the paging control).

TABLE 11.3   Mnemonic Codes for Operand C
of the PRINT Block

Code	Output
C	Relative and absolute clock times
N	Block count
S	Storage statistics
Q	Queue statistics
F	Facility statistics
X	Fullword savevalue contents
XH	Halfword savevalues
MX	Fullword matrix savevalues
MH	Halfword matrix savevalues

For example,

PRINT   3,6,F

will cause output of the standard statistics associated with facilities 3, 4, 5, and 6. The values that are printed out are those that have been accumulated up to the instant that a transaction enters this block. In this example, operand D is omitted. In such a case, the printer will position itself to the beginning of a new page each time that a transaction enters the PRINT block. Because this may lead to a very voluminous output, omission of operand D is not recommended. Specification of any nonblank character for operand D will result in a more compact spacing of printed output.

Table 11.3 lists some of the mnemonic codes that may be used in operand C to specify the output required. (A complete description of all codes is given in the *GPSS/360 User's Manual* — see Section 10.16.)

Operands A and B determine the range of the statistics to be printed. If these operands are omitted, the full range of statistics is printed. For example,

PRINT   ,,F,X

will cause the printout of statistics for all facilities active in the system. (Note the use of the character X in operand D to suppress page skipping.) If only one entity is of interest, the values of operands A and B should be the same. Thus,

PRINT   3,3,S

will cause the printer to skip to a new page and to print statistics only for storage number 3.

In some cases, operands A and B are meaningless and should be omitted. For example, in printing clock time,

PRINT   ,,C,X

should be used because the clock does not have a range of identification numbers.

11.16 Special Output

The GPSS/360 output editing features allow the analyst to replace the standard statistical output with output of his own design. A series of output editing request cards are used to select the desired statistics, format these statistics, and annotate the output.

The first card in the set of editing request cards, which we will call the *editing packet*, must be a *report request card*. The general deck format for a GPSS simulation including an editing packet is shown in Figure 11.19. Once an editing packet has been defined, it cannot be redefined. The packet will

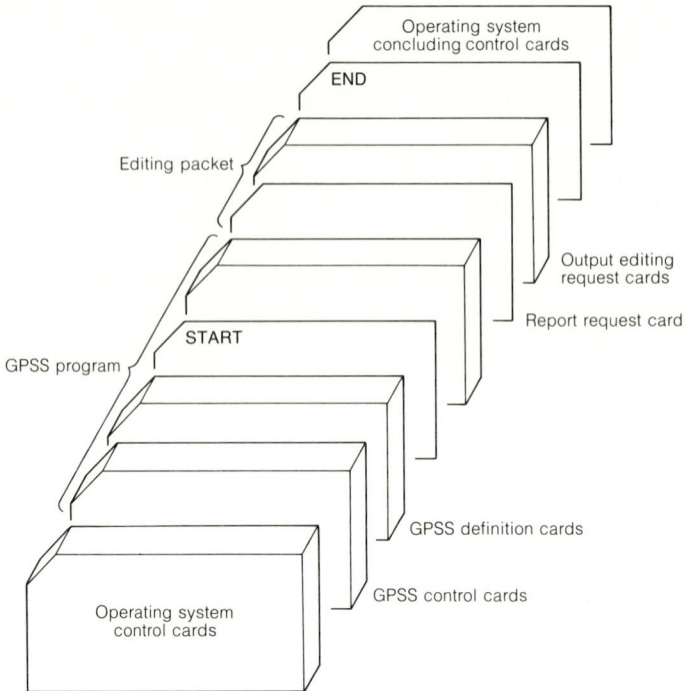

FIG. 11.19   Input Deck Format for GPSS Computer Run Including Editing Packet

apply to every run made in the batch. Each run in the batch will have identically formatted output.

In this section we discuss the request cards that control tabular output. Request cards dealing with graphic output are discussed in the next section. A complete discussion of all request cards is given in the *GPSS/360 User's Manual* (see Section 10.16).

The report request card serves to indicate the beginning of the editing packet. It contains only the word REPORT in the OPERATION field.

The *title request card* will cause the printing of standard statistical output for specified entities and will precede this output with a heading or title line that is specified by the user. The LOC field of this card contains a mnemonic code representing the particular entity type whose statistics are to be printed and titled. Some of these entity codes are listed in Table 11.4. The OPERATION field of the card contains the word TITLE. Operand B of the card is used to specify the title or heading for the statistical output. This title may extend to column 71 of the card, and it may be continued up to a total of 124 characters (including blanks) by placing any nonblank character in column 72 and con-

TABLE 11.4   Entity-Type Codes for Title and
Include Request Cards

Code	Entity Type
BLO	Block counts
SAV	Fullword savevalues
HSAV	Halfword savevalues
MSAV	Fullword matrix savevalues
MHSA	Halfword matrix savevalues
FAC	Facility statistics
STO	Storage statistics
QUE	Queue statistics
TAB	Table statistics
CLO	Clock statistics
CHA	User chain statistics

tinuing the title in column 1 of the next card. Operand A of the card is used to
specify the number or symbolic name of the specific entity whose statistics are
to be printed. For example,

    MSAV   TITLE   6,   TRANSIT MATRIX

will print and title only the output for matrix savevalue number 6 (Figure 11.20).
Note that blanks can appear as part of operand B on this card, including blanks
preceding the first word of the title. If operand A is omitted, as in

    MSAV   TITLE   ,   MATRICES FOLLOW

the entire range of matrix savevalues defined in the model will be produced. In
each case, the title given in operand B will be printed on the line just preceding
the first line of the usual statistical output.

```
        TRANSIT MATRIX

    MATRIX FULLWORD SAVEVALUE      6

                    COLUMN    1          2          3

        ROW   1              48          0          0
              2               0          0         63
```

FIG. 11.20   Output Obtained with Example Title Request Card

The *include request card* is used to extract certain statistics of interest from the standard set of statistical output produced for each entity. The OPERATION field of this card contains the word INCLUDE. The LOC field contains the entity-type code in the same fashion as that of the title request card (Table 11.4). There are two different forms for the OPERAND field of the include request card. The first form applies to all entities for which the standard output is given in columnar form—facilities, storages, queues, and tables—whereas the second form applies to noncolumnar forms of output produced for entities such as savevalues and matrix savevalues. In the first form (for columnar output), operand A specifies the range of entity identification numbers for which statistics are to be produced. This is done by giving an entity code and the upper and lower limits of the range of identification numbers. The code consists of a single letter: F for facilities, S for storages, Q for queues, and T for tables. Thus, if only storages 3 through 5 are of interest, the range is written as S3-S5. If statistics are wanted for queues 1 through 6, the range is written as Q1-Q6. Immediately following the range (without an intervening comma) is a slash (/) followed by a list of integers that specify the statistics to be produced. These numbers and their meanings are given in Table 11.5. Thus, the card

     FAC   INCLUDE   F2-F5/1,3,4

would cause the printing of facility numbers, numbers of entries, and average times per transaction for facilities 2 through 5. Similarly, the card

     STO   INCLUDE   S2-S3/1,3,4

would cause the printing of storage numbers, average contents, and average utilizations for storages 2 and 3 (Figure 11.21).

The second form of the include request card omits operand A and specifies the range of savevalues or matrix savevalues in operand B. The codes used in operand B are: X for fullword savevalues, XH for halfword savevalues, MX for fullword matrix savevalues, and MH for halfword matrix savevalues. The ranges

STORAGE	AVERAGE CONTENTS	AVERAGE UTILIZATION
2	.361	.120
3	.337	.067

FIG. 11.21   Output Obtained with Example Include Request Card

TABLE 11.5   Selected Codes for Include and Format Request Cards

Entity and Statistic	Include Code	Format Code
Facility (F)		
1. Name or number	1	F1
2. Average utilization	2	F2
3. Number of entries	3	F3
4. Average time per transaction	4	F4
Storage (S)		
1. Name or number	1	S1
2. Capacity	2	—
3. Average contents	3	S3
4. Average utilization	4	S4
5. Number of entries	5	S5
6. Average time per transaction	6	S6
Queue (Q)		
1. Queue name or number	1	Q1
2. Maximum contents	2	Q2
3. Average contents	3	Q3
4. Total entries	4	Q4
5. Zero entries	5	Q5
6. Percent of zero entries	6	Q6
7. Average time per transaction	7	Q7
8. Average time per transaction of nonzero entries	8	Q8
Savevalues (X or XH)		
1. Savevalue name or number	—	X1
2. Contents of savevalue	—	X2
3. Halfword savevalue name or number	—	XH1
4. Halfword savevalue contents	—	XH2
Tables (T)		
1. Name or number	1	T1
2. Entries in table	2	T2
3. Mean argument	3	T3
4. Standard deviation	4	T4
5. Sum of arguments	5	—

are specified as in the first form. Example cards for each of the four kinds of entities are

SAV	INCLUDE	,X7-X8
MSAV	INCLUDE	,MX1-MX2
HSAV	INCLUDE	,XH2-XH3
MHSA	INCLUDE	,MH4-MH5

The title and include request cards may be paired. In this case, the statistics to be produced are specified on the include card; the title card specifies only the heading that is to appear on the line before the statistics. To function as a pair, both cards must have the same entity-type code in the LOC field, they must appear in succession, and operand A of the title card must be omitted. For example,

QUE	TITLE	, QUEUE 1 AND 2 STATS
QUE	INCLUDE	Q1-Q2/1,3

This combination would cause the printing of the title QUEUE 1 AND 2 STATS, followed by the queue numbers and average contents of queues 1 and 2 (Figure 11.22).

Statistic selection also can be made by use of the *format request card*. Unlike the include card, which produces output for only one entity type, the format card allows mixed types. The LOC field of this card is not used; the OPERATION field contains the word FORMAT. The OPERANDS field specifies a range of identification numbers, followed by a slash and a list of codes for the statistics to be output. These codes are listed and explained in Table 11.5. For example, suppose that facilities 2 through 4 represent phone booths, and that queues 2 through 4 measure the waiting lines at these booths. The card

FORMAT   2-4/F1,F3,Q2

will produce the output shown in the first part of Figure 11.23. The first column contains the values of F1 (facility numbers) for facilities 2 through 4. The second column contains the values of F3 (numbers of entries) for facilities 2 through 4.

```
QUEUE 1 AND 2 STATS
QUEUE       AVERAGE
            CONTENTS
   1          .219
   2          .194
```

FIG. 11.22   Output Obtained with Example Title and Include Request Cards

```
              2             169             4
              3             171             4
              4             148             3
         PART I:  Output of format request card alone


         FACILITY      NUMBER OF       MAX IN
         NUMBER        ENTRIES         QUEUE
         PART II:  Output of comment request cards alone


         FACILITY      NUMBER OF       MAX IN
         NUMBER        ENTRIES         QUEUE
              2             169             4
              3             171             4
              4             148             3

     PART III:  Output of combined comment and format request cards
```

FIG. 11.23   Output Obtained with Example Format and Comment Request Cards

The third column contains the values of Q2 (maximum contents) for queues 2 through 4. In general, a column of output is produced for each item appearing in the output statistics list, but no titles or headings are printed.

The *comment request card* is similar to the standard GPSS/360 comment card. An asterisk appears in column 1. The contents of the remaining columns of the card will be printed out just as they appear on the card. For example, the cards

```
*  FACILITY      NUMBER OF       MAX IN
*  NUMBER        ENTRIES         QUEUE
```

would produce the output shown in the second part of Figure 11.23. By placing these comment cards immediately before the format card described above, the comment cards can be used to produce a heading for the output of the format card, as in the third part of Figure 11.23.

Two request cards are used exclusively for spacing. The *eject request card* causes the printer to proceed to the top of the next page before any more output requests are processed. This card contains only the word EJECT in the OPER-ATION field. The *space request card* causes n lines to be skipped before the next request is processed, where $n = 1$, 2, or 3. The card contains the word SPACE in the OPERATION field and the desired value of n as operand A.

The *output request card* enables the user to obtain all of the standard GPSS/360 output in addition to the other requests in the output editing packet. If this card is not present in the packet, the standard output will be suppressed and will be replaced by the output specified in the packet. This card consists simply of the word OUTPUT in the OPERATION field.

11.17 Graphic Output

Among the GPSS/360 output editing features is the capability of producing graphic output in the form of histograms. When used in conjunction with table entities, this option becomes particularly useful in displaying the shape of distributions. For example, Figure 11.26 graphs a distribution of transit times. Each graph is scaled within the 60-line by 132-column matrix of different print positions in a standard page of output. All of the information needed to define the histogram within this matrix is supplied within the editing packet by a set of request cards called a *graphing packet*. One such packet must be supplied for each graph requested. The graphing packet may contain six types of request cards, which must be ordered in the sequence in which they are discussed below.

The *graph request card* must appear first in the graphing packet; it specifies the SNA values to be plotted. There are two forms for this card. Form A is the following: (1) the LOC field is left blank; (2) the OPERATION field contains the word GRAPH; and (3) the OPERANDS field contains operand A (a permissible SNA code representing the SNA to be graphed), operand B (the lower limit of the range of entities to be graphed), operand C (the upper limit of the range of entities), and operand D (the character to be used for graph lines; if this operand is omitted, an asterisk is used). Table 11.6 lists some of the SNAs that may be plotted. For example, the graph card

GRAPH   X,6,8

would be used to graph the values of savevalues 6, 7, and 8. The card

GRAPH   SR,1,8,.

would be used to graph the utilizations of the first eight storages. Note that the second graph would be plotted with a period (.) as the plotting symbol, whereas the first graph would be plotted with an asterisk (because operand D is omitted). Symbolic names can be used in operands B and C. For example, if storages 1 and 8 in the example above were named STOR1 and STOR8, then the graph request card could equally well be written as

GRAPH   SR,STOR1,STOR8,.

However, note that the range of SNAs to be plotted is determined by the numbers assigned to these symbolic names. For example, if STOR8 happens to be the symbolic name of storage number 4, the card above will produce a graph only for the first four storages.

To plot a distribution associated with a table entity, form B (the distribution form) of the graph request card is used. Only the operands of this form differ from form A. The operands for form B are: operand A (a permissible SNA code representing the distribution to be graphed), operand B (the table name or number), operand C (omitted), and operand D (the plotting character; an asterisk will be used if operand D is omitted). For example, the card

GRAPH   TF,XTME,,+

would be used to graph the frequencies accumulated in the table named XTME, with a plus sign used to plot the histogram.

The *origin request card* appears second in the graphing packet; it is used to locate the origin of the graph axes — that is, the point of intersection for the x and y axes. The LOC field of this card is left blank; the OPERATION field contains the word ORIGIN. Operand A locates the line (among the 60 lines of the page) along which the x axis is to be drawn. Operand B locates the column (among the 132 columns of the page) along which the y axis is to be drawn. For example, the card

ORIGIN   55,10

will cause the x axis to be drawn on the 55th line from the top of the page, and the y axis to be drawn along the 10th column from the left of the page.

The *X request card* appears third in the graphing packet; it is used to scale the values of the abscissa and to label the x axis. This card has either form A or form B, corresponding to the forms of the graph request card. In both forms,

TABLE 11.6   Selected SNA Codes for Graph Request Card

SNA Code	Statistic to Be Graphed
Form A	
FR	Facility utilization
FT	Facility average time per transaction
SR	Storage utilization
SA	Storage average contents
ST	Storage average time per transaction
QA	Queue average contents
QT	Queue average time per transaction
QX	Queue average time per nonzero transaction
X	Fullword savevalues
XH	Halfword savevalues
TB	Table mean
TS	Table standard deviation
Form B	
TF	Table observed frequencies
TP	Percent of total

the LOC field is left blank, and the OPERATION field contains the letter X. For form A, the operands are operand A (the code SYM causes entity symbolic names to be listed along the x axis; if this operand is omitted, entity numbers will appear); operand B (width, in columns and including endpoints, of the histogram rectangles to be plotted; 3 will be assumed if this operand is omitted); operand C (spacing, in columns, between rectangles; 1 will be assumed if this operand is omitted); operands D, E, F (omitted); operand G (if NO is specified, all x axis labeling will be suppressed). For example, the card

                    X   ,,3

will cause the x axis to be labeled with entity numbers, the histogram rectangles to be 3 columns wide, and 3 spaces to appear between adjacent rectangles. Figure 11.25(a) was graphed using this card. The card

                    X   SYM,4,3

was used in graphing Figure 11.25(b); in this case, symbolic names label the rectangles and each rectangle is four columns wide.

```
            GRAPH        SR,1,8,.
            ORIGIN       55,10
            X            ,,3
            Y            .000,.003,53,1
     23     STATEMENT    58,20,STORAGE UTILIZATION
            ENDGRAPH


            GRAPH        SR,1,8,.
            ORIGIN       55,10
            X            SYM,4,3
            Y            .036,.003,42,1
            ENDGRAPH


            GRAPH        TF,XTME,,+
            ORIGIN       55,10
            X            ,1,1,125,1,42,NO
            Y            0,1,32,1
     25     STATEMENT    25,30,TRANSIT TIME DISTRIBUTION
     25     STATEMENT    26,30,FOR EXPERIMENTAL MODEL
            ENDGRAPH


            GRAPH        TF,XTME
            ORIGIN       55,10
            X            ,2,1,130,2,21,NO
            Y            0,2,32,1
            ENDGRAPH
```

FIG. 11.24 Graphing Packets Used to Define Figures 11.25 and 11.26

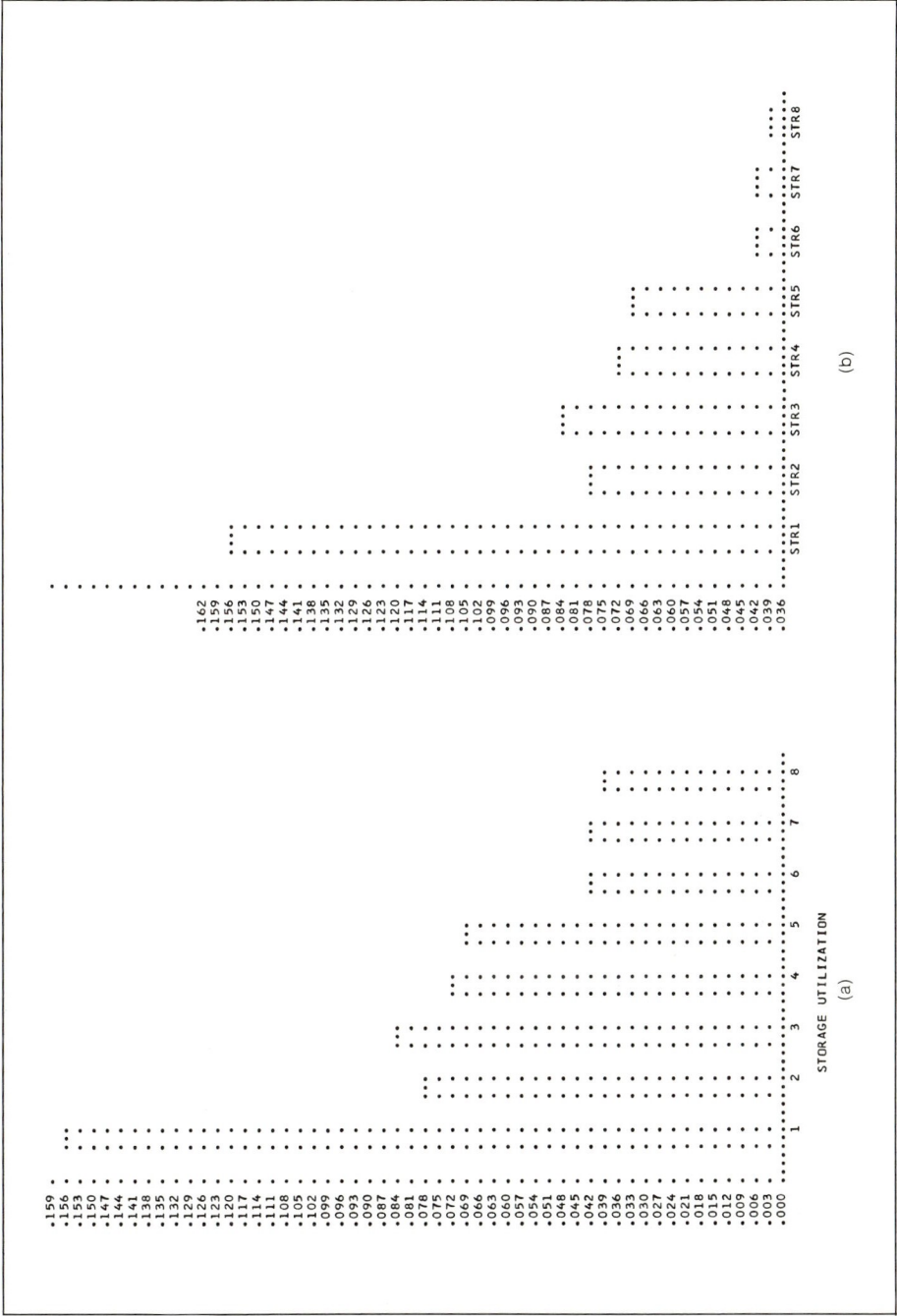

FIG. 11.25 Storage Utilization for Eight Storages

Form B of the X request card is used for plotting distributions associated with table entities. The operands used with this form are operand A (omitted); operand B (width, in columns and including endpoints, of histogram rectangles); operand C (spacing between rectangles); operand D (upper limit of lowest frequency class to be plotted); operand E (number of frequency classes to be included per x axis increment; 1 is assumed if this operand is omitted); operand F (number of increments to be plotted); and operand G (if NO appears here, then no numeric values will appear on the x axis). As an example, consider the table entity defined by the definition card,

XTME   TABLE   M1,125,5,42

This table records transaction transit times into 42 frequency classes, each of length 5 time units. The first frequency class has an upper limit of 125. The request card

X   ,1,1,125,1,42,NO

was used in producing the output of Figure 11.26(a). The rectangles are simply lines (width 1 column) with 1 space separating them. The upper limit of the lowest frequency class is 125, and exactly 1 frequency class is plotted for each of the 42 increments to be plotted; in other words, each line represents one frequency class from the table. Notice that judicious use of operands D, E, and F permit the analyst to condense or to select table frequency classes. For example, the same table was condensed to produce Figure 11.26(b) by using the card

X   ,2,1,130,2,21,NO

in which pairs of adjacent frequency classes are combined into single classes of the histogram.

The Y *request card* is used to scale and label the y axis; this card appears fourth in the graphing packet. The y axis automatically is labeled according to the information specified on this card. The LOC field of the card is left blank; the letter Y appears in the OPERATION field. The operands are operand A (lower limit for y axis label); operand B (the increment size for y axis label); operand C (the number of increments to be included on y axis); and operand D (the number of page lines or rows per increment). The following Y request cards, for example, were used in producing the histograms of Figures 11.25 and 11.26:

Y   .000,.003,53,1
Y   .036,.003,42,1
Y   0,1,32,1
Y   0,2,32,1

The *statement request card* is used to annotate graphic output. Many statement cards may appear in a graphing packet. They must follow the Y request card and precede the endgraph request card, and they must be arranged in order of increasing value of operand A. The OPERATION field of the card contains the word STATEMENT. The statement that is to be printed appears as operand C. Operand A specifies the page line or row on which the statement is to be printed; operand B specifies the number of characters (including blanks) in the statement; and the LOC field contains a number specifying the column in which printing of the statement is to begin. For example, the card

    23   STATEMENT   58,19,STORAGE   UTILIZATION

was used to annotate Figure 11.25(a).

The *endgraph request card* must appear as the last card in each graphing packet. It contains only the word ENDGRAPH in the OPERATION field.

The complete graphing packets used to produce the graphs of Figures 11.25 and 11.26 are listed in Figure 11.24.

It is difficult to produce time plots in GPSS. Information for such plots may be recorded either by storing the necessary coordinate information in matrix savevalues (see Section 11.5), or by using the PRINT block to output the information as it is produced. Either of these outputs then can be used to make plots by hand after the run.

11.18 The Bank Branch Simulation

In this section, we use the features described in this chapter to extend the bank branch simulation discussed in Section 10.14. The flowchart for the extended model is shown in Figure 11.27, the block diagram in Figure 11.28, and the GPSS program in Figure 11.29.

The flowchart shows that the model is much the same as in the earlier version, with two additional services available and with the option for customers to renege. The additional services consist of a managerial staff and a receptionist to screen demands for the services of that staff.

Interarrival times into the model are defined at the GENERATE block named INPUT, by the negative exponential distribution with mean 60. The mean is defined by XH6, which was initialized to 60, and the distribution is defined by the function named EXPON.

Blocks 2 through 4 are used to simulate reneges when the BANK is too full. If the contents of the BANK, given by S$BANK, are more than or equal to XH7, which was INITIALized to 30, transactions are routed to the TRANSFER block. From here, 60 percent of them are TRANSFERed to the TERMINATE block named RENG. Thus, the probability that a customer will ENTER the BANK when thirty or more other customers already are there is 0.40.

After a transaction arrives at the block INTO and ENTERs the BANK, parameter 1 is ASSIGNed the value 1. This parameter will be used in the system to help record the type of services rendered to the transaction, as described

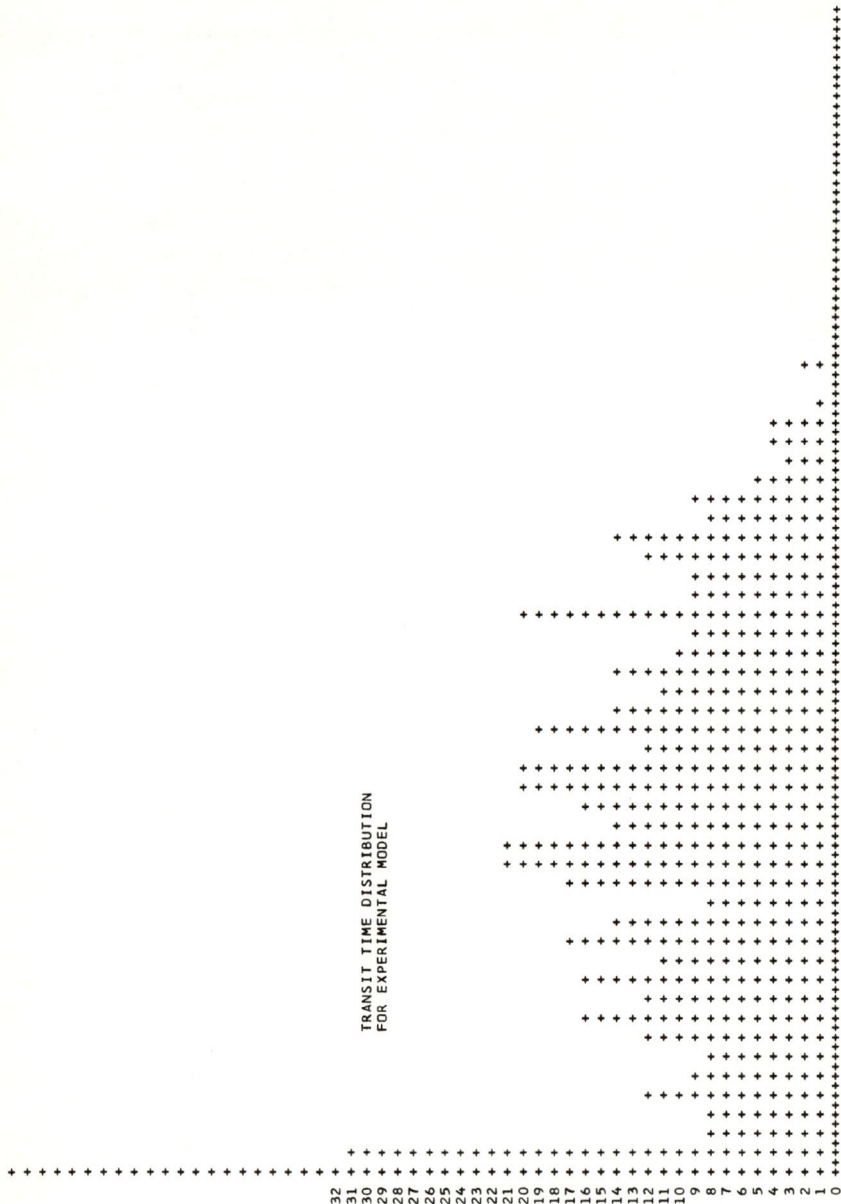

TRANSIT TIME DISTRIBUTION
FOR EXPERIMENTAL MODEL

(a)

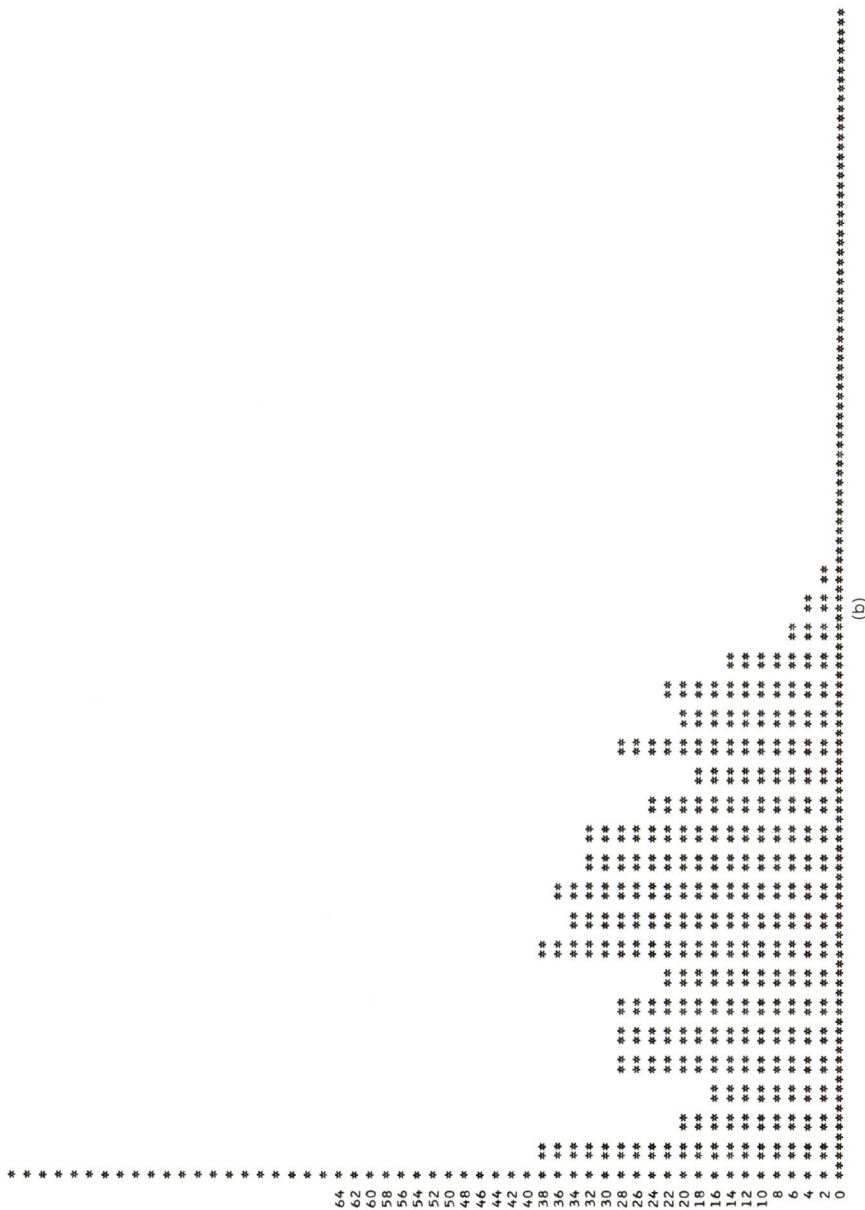

FIG. 11.26 Distribution of Transit Times

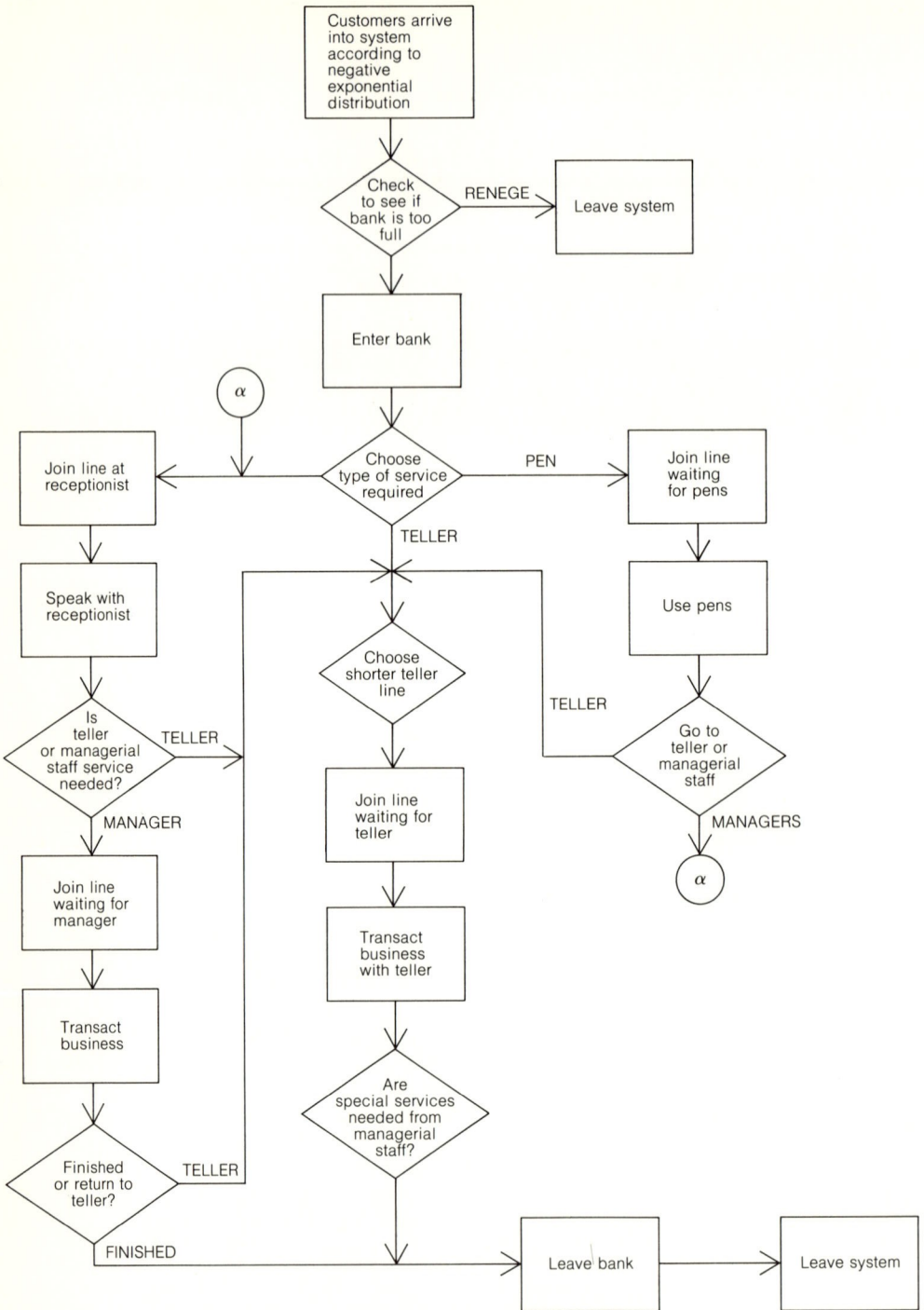

FIG. 11.27 Flowchart of Extended Bank Branch Simulation

below. Blocks 7 and 8 are TRANSFER blocks, which control the initial choice of service needed by the transaction. Of the transactions entering block 7, 10 percent are TRANSFERed to the block named MNGT1 for special services that only the managerial staff can provide; the remaining 90 percent of the transactions immediately pass on to the next block named CHSE1, which also is a TRANSFER block. Here the choice is between using the writing facilities (45 percent) or going directly to the teller lines at CHSE2 (55 percent).

Blocks 9 through 15 simulate the use of the writing facilities. The storage PENS contains six writing stations. A user chain, CHN1, is used in conjunction with the queue PENQ. Here, as in other occurrences of user chains in this model, the chain is FIFO and is used only for the purpose of decreasing computer running time. Of the customers who have used the writing facilities, 7 percent will TRANSFER at block number 16 to seek special services; the remaining 93 percent will proceed to the teller lines.

As in the earlier model (Chapter 10), there are two tellers available to service customers. These two tellers are represented by facilities 4 and 5; the lines at the tellers are represented by queues 4 and 5; and user chains 4 and 5 are used in conjunction with these queues. In blocks 20 through 27, the choice of the teller to be used is specified indirectly by parameter—for example, a transaction will enter the queue whose number is in P3, SEIZE the facility whose number is in P3, and so forth. This indirect specification makes it possible to simulate both tellers with a single set of blocks (compared to the two parallel sets of blocks used in the earlier model). The particular teller to be used depends upon the lengths of the teller lines, the choice being made at blocks 17 through 19. When a transaction arrives at CHSE2, the value 4 is ASSIGNed to P3. The TEST block then checks to see whether facility 5 has a line of length less than or equal to that of facility 4. If it does, P3 is increased to 5 at block 19. If it does not, the transaction goes to TPARM with P3 unchanged at a value of 4. Through indirect addressing, the value of P3 also determines the spread time ($XH*3$) at the ADVANCE block. After passing through the teller lines, most of the transactions proceed to the termination routine, but 5 percent of those transactions who have not already sought special services now will seek them.

All customers who need special services must enter the receptionist queue, RCPTQ, at block 34. Block 41 indicates that the receptionist will intercept 25 percent of the demands and redirect these customers back to the teller lines. The remaining customers will be allowed to use the managerial pool of three managers, after which 30 percent will return to the tellers for unfinished business, and 70 percent will proceed to the termination routine, which will remove them from the BANK.

Blocks 51 through 55 are used to gather some final statistics and to remove the transaction from the system. Note that a termination count has not been specified either here or at the block RENG that TERMINATEs reneges. Instead, termination of the simulation has been placed under the control of a separate

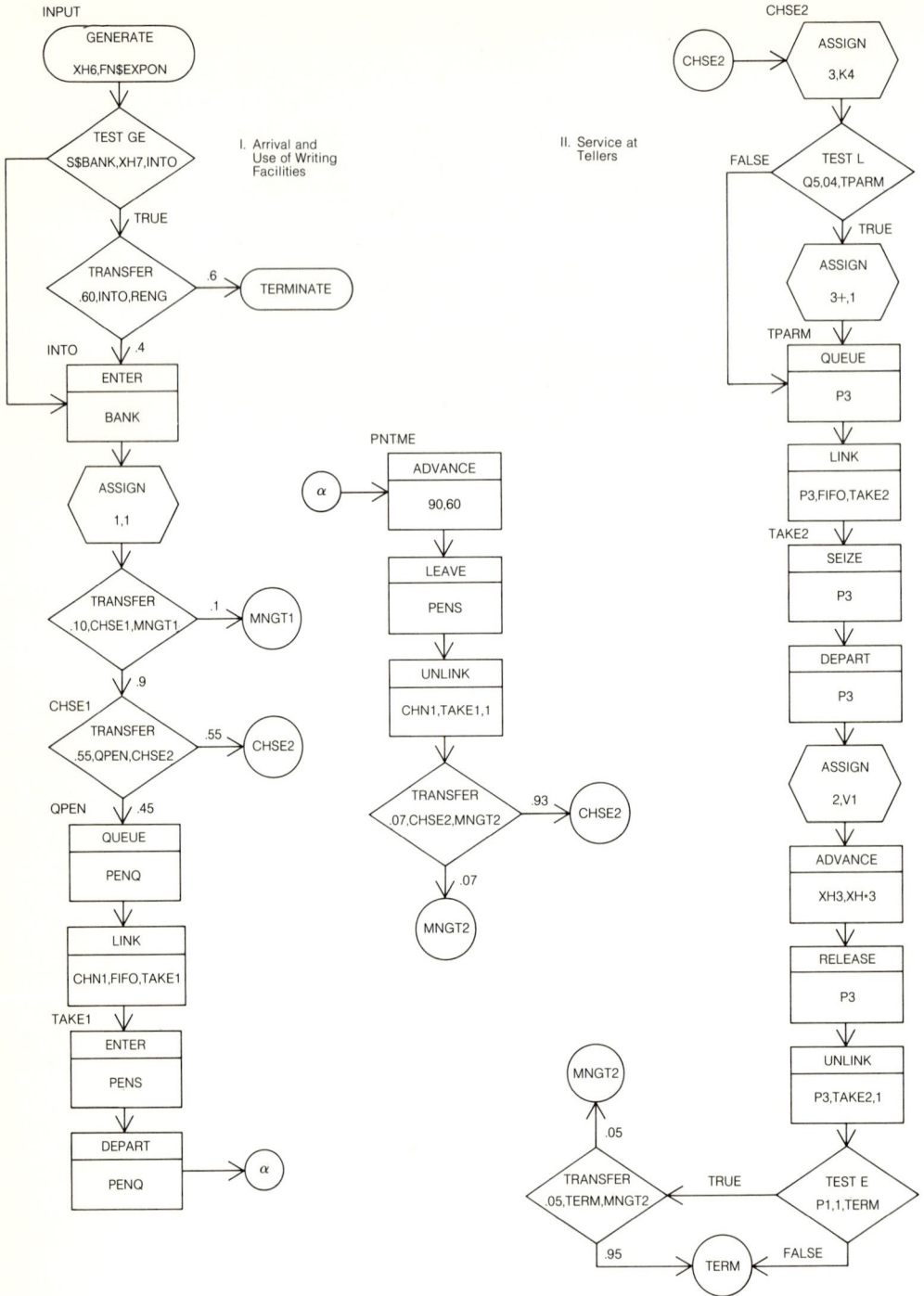

FIG. 11.28 Block Diagram of Extended Bank Branch Simulation

III. Service by the Receptionist

IV. Service by the Managerial Staff

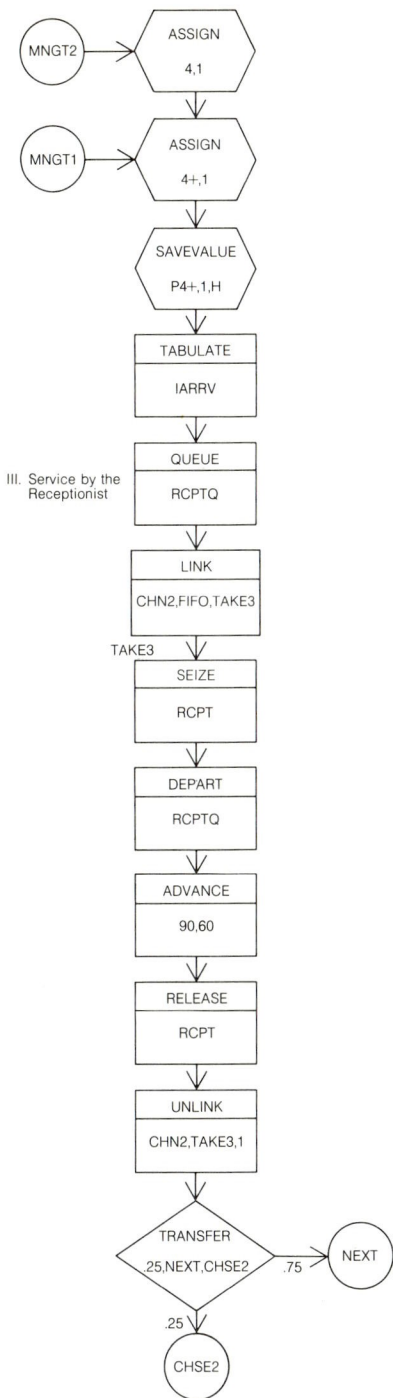

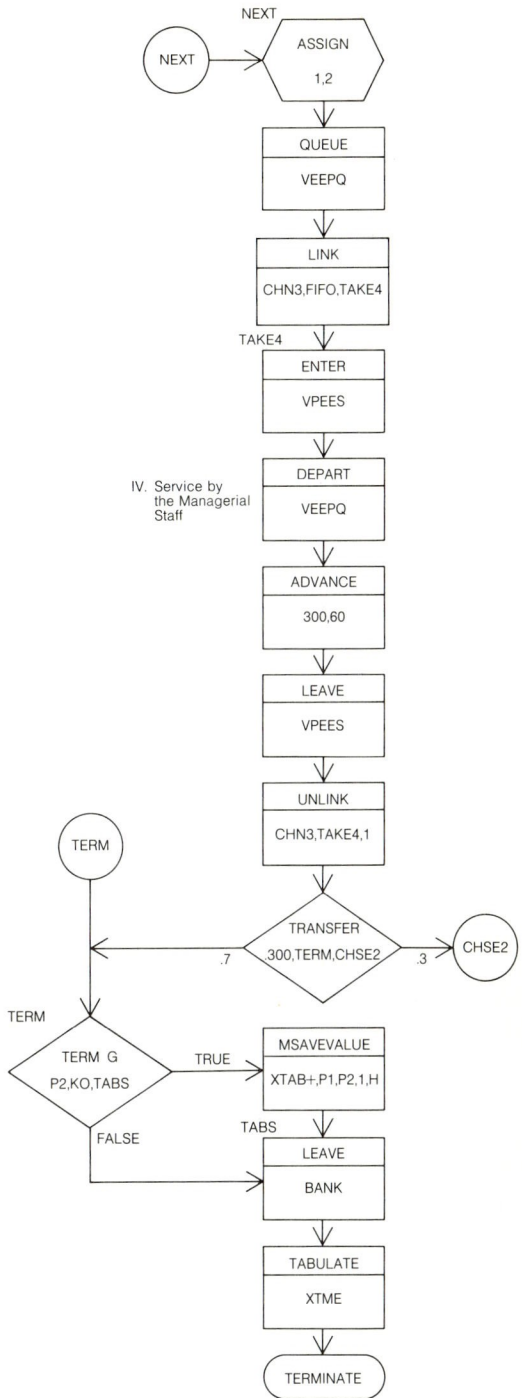

FIG. 11.28—Continued

```
BLOCK                                                                            CARD
NUMBER  *LOC   OPERATION  A,B,C,D,E,F,G            COMMENTS                      NUMBER
        *                                                                          1
        *      BANK BRANCH SIMULATION III                                          2
        *                                                                          3
        *      MSAVEVALUE TO CROSS TABULATE SERVICE ACTIVITIES                     4
        XTAB   MATRIX     H,2,2                                                     5
        *                                                                          6
        *      INITIALIZATION OF SAVEVALUES                                        7
               INITIAL    XH3,120            TELLER MEAN SERVICE TIME              8
               INITIAL    XH4,90             SPREAD TIME FOR TELLER 1              9
               INITIAL    XH5,60             SPREAD TIME FOR TELLER 2             10
               INITIAL    XH6,60             INTR ARVL MEAN TME                  11
               INITIAL    XH7,30             TOLERANCE LEVEL FOR RENEGS          12
        *                                                                         13
        * FUNCTION USED TO DEFINE NEGATIVE EXPONENTIAL DISTRIBUTION.              14
        EXPON  FUNCTION  RN8,C24                                                  15
        0,0/.1,.104/.2,.222/.3,.355/.4,.509/.5,.69                                16
        .6,.915/.7,1.2/.75,1.38/.8,1.6/.84,1.83/.88,2.12                          17
        .9,2.3/.92,2.52/.94,2.81/.95,2.99/.96,3.2/.97,3.5                         18
        .98,3.9/.99,4.6/.995,5.3/.998,6.2/.999,7.0/.9997,8.0                      19
        *                                                                         20
        *      VARIABLE USED TO COMPUTE FREQUENCY TABLE ASSIGNMENT                21
        1      VARIABLE   P3-3                                                    22
        *                                                                         23
               SIMULATE                                                           24
        *                                                                         25
        *                                                                         26
1       INPUT  GENERATE   XH6,FN$EXPON  INTR ARVL TIME IS EXP DSTRBTD             27
2              TEST GE    S$BANK,XH7,INTO    WHEN BANK TOO FULL.                  28
3              TRANSFER   .60,INTO,RENG     A CERTAIN % WILL RENEG.               29
4       RENG   TERMINATE                    RENEG BEFOR ENTERING.                 30
5       INTO   ENTER      BANK              CUSTOMER ENTERS THE BANK              31
6              ASSIGN     1,1               INITIALIZE PARAMETER FOR LATER        32
        *                                    USE IN CROSS TABULATIONS.            33
7              TRANSFER   .10,CHSE1,MNGT1        10% OF ARRVALS GO TO SEE BANK    34
        *                                    MANAGEMENT FOR SPECIAL SERVICES.     35
8       CHSE1  TRANSFER   .55,QPEN,CHSE2     CERTAIN % GO TO PENS                 36
        *                                                                         37
        *      USE OF WRITING AREAS.                                              38
        *                                                                         39
9       QPEN   QUEUE      PENQ                                                    40
10             LINK       CHN1,FIFO,TAKE1                                         41
11      TAKE1  ENTER      PENS                                                    42
12             DEPART     PENQ                                                    43
13      PNTME  ADVANCE    90,60                                                   44
14             LEAVE      PENS                                                    45
15             UNLINK     CHN1,TAKE1,1                                            46
16             TRANSFER   .07,CHSE2,MNGT2        7% OF PEN USERS GO TO MNGMT      47
        *                                                                         48
        *                                                                         49
        *      TELLER LINES                                                       50
        *                                                                         51
17      CHSE2  ASSIGN     3,K4               REINITIALIZE P3                      52
18             TEST LE    Q5,Q4,TPARM        CHOOSE TELLER WITH SHORTER QUEUE     53
19             ASSIGN     3+,1               P3 WILL CONTAIN TELLER NUMBER        54
20      TPARM  QUEUE      P3                                                      55
21             LINK       P3,FIFO,TAKE2                                           56
22      TAKE2  SEIZE      P3                                                      57
23             DEPART     P3                                                      58
24             ASSIGN     2,V1               P2 RECORDS WHICH TELLER WAS USED     59
25             ADVANCE    XH3,XH*3           XH3 CONTAINS MEAN TIME--SPREAD TIME  60
        *                                    DEPENDS ON WHICH TELLER WAS CHOSEN.  61
26             RELEASE    P3                                                      62
27             UNLINK     P3,TAKE2,1                                             63
28             TEST E     P1,1,TERM          CUSTMRS WHO ARE FINISHED GO TO TERM. 64
29             TRANSFER   .05,TERM,MNGT2     TELLERS SEND 5% TO SEE              65
        *                                    MANAGERIAL STAFF.                    66
        *                                                                         67
        *      SPECIAL SERVICES REQUIRED....                                      68
        *                                                                         69
30      MNGT2  ASSIGN     4,1               RECORD WHETHER THE CUSTOMER HAS       70
31      MNGT1  ASSIGN     4+,1              PREVIOUSLY USED ANY SERVICES.         71
32             SAVEVALUE  P4+,1,H           RECORD IN XH1 OR XH2.                 72
33             TABULATE   IARRV                                                   73
        *      RECEPTIONIST                                                       74
34             QUEUE      RCPTQ             GET IN LINE FOR RECEPTIONIST          75
35             LINK       CHN2,FIFO,TAKE3                                         76
36      TAKE3  SEIZE      RCPT                                                    77
37             DEPART     RCPTQ                                                   78
38             ADVANCE    90,60             TALK WITH RECEPTIONIST                79
39             RELEASE    RCPT                                                    80
40             UNLINK     CHN2,TAKE3,1                                            81
41             TRANSFER   .25,NEXT,CHSE2         25% HANDLED BY RECEPTIONIST      82
```

FIG. 11.29 GPSS Program for Extended Bank Branch Simulation

```
         *        MANAGERIAL STAFF                                              83
42    NEXT  ASSIGN     1,2              RECORD USAGE FOR XTAB                    84
43          QUEUE      VEEPQ            WAIT FOR MANAGERIAL STAFF               85
44          LINK       CHN3,FIFO,TAKE4                                          86
45    TAKE4 ENTER      VPEES                                                    87
46          DEPART     VEEPQ                                                    88
47          ADVANCE    300,60                                                   89
48          LEAVE      VPEES                                                    90
49          UNLINK     CHN3,TAKE4,1                                             91
50          TRANSFER   .300,TERM,CHSE2   30% RETURN TO TELLERS.                 92
      *                                                                         93
      *                                                                         94
      *    TERMINATION ROUTINE TO REMOVE CUSTOMERS FROM BANK AND SYSTEM         95
      *                                                                         96
51    TERM  TEST G     P2,K0,TABS    IF P2 NOT 0 THEN CRSTBLTE                  97
52          MSAVEVALUE XTAB+,P1,P2,1,H       CROSSTABULATE TYPES OF SERVICE     98
53    TABS  LEAVE      BANK             CUSTOMER LEAVES THE BANK.               99
54          TABULATE   XTME                                                    100
55          TERMINATE                                                          101
      *                                                                        102
      *                                                                        103
      *    STORAGE DEFINITIONS                                                 104
      VPEES STORAGE   3                 POOL OF MANAGERS                       105
      PENS  STORAGE   6                 WRITING STATIONS                       106
      *                                                                        107
      *    TABLES                                                             108
      XTME  TABLE     M1,80,80,50       TRANSIT TIME THRU BANK                 109
      IARRV TABLE     IA,30,30,50                                             110
      *                                                                        111
      *                                                                        112
      *                                                                        113
      *    ROUTINE TO CONTROL TOTAL TIME OF SIMULATION.                       114
      *    EACH TERMINATION REPRESENTS ONE HOUR OF SIMULATION.                115
      *                                                                        116
56          GENERATE   3600                                                    117
57          TERMINATE  1                                                       118
      *                                                                        119
      *                                                                        120
      *                                                                        121
            START      30,NP            REACH STEADY STATE.                    122
            RESET                       START THE STATISTICAL RUN              123
            INITIAL    XH1-XH2,0/MH1(1-2,1-2),0    REINIT SAVEVALUES          124
            START      8                RUN FOR EIGHT HOURS.                   125
      *                                                                        126
            REPORT                                                             127
            EJECT                                                              128
      *                                                                        129
      **********   OUTPUT FOR BANK SIMULATION III    **********               130
      *                                                                        131
            SPACE      3                                                       132
      STO   TITLE      ,    STORAGE STATS FOR BANK, PENS AND VPEES.           133
      STO   INCLUDE    S1-S3/1,3,4,6                                          134
            SPACE      3                                                       135
      FAC   TITLE      ,    STATS FOR RECEPTIONIST AND TWO TELLERS.           136
      FAC   INCLUDE    F1-F5/1,2,4                                            137
            SPACE      3                                                       138
      HSAV  TITLE      ,    HALFWORD SAVEVALUES                               139
      HSAV  INCLUDE    ,XH1-XH2                                               140
            SPACE      3                                                       141
      QUE   TITLE      ,    QUEUE STATS: LAST TWO LINES FOR TELLERS           142
      QUE   INCLUDE    Q1-Q5/1,2,3,6,7,8                                      143
            SPACE      3                                                       144
      *     CROSS TABULATION OF USAGE OF TELLERS AND SPECIAL SERVICES         145
      *                                                                        146
      *     COL 1: ENTRIES FOR FIRST TELLER                                   147
      *     COL 2: ENTRIES FOR SECOND TELLER                                  148
      *     ROW 1: ENTRIES FOR NON USAGE OF SPECIAL SERVICES                  149
      *     ROW 2: ENTRIES FOR SPECIAL SERVICE USAGE                          150
      *                                                                        151
      MHSA  INCLUDE    ,MH$XTAB                                               152
            EJECT                                                             153
            GRAPH      TF,XTME                                                154
            ORIGIN     55,10                                                  155
            X          ,2,1,80,1,50,NO                                        156
            Y          0,2,25,2                                               157
56          STATEMENT  15,35,TRANSIT TIME THRU BANK                           158
            ENDGRAPH                                                          159
            EJECT                                                             160
            GRAPH      TF,IARRV                                               161
            ORIGIN     55,10                                                  162
            X          ,2,1,30,1,50,NO                                        163
            Y          0,1,15,3                                               164
56          STATEMENT  15,45,INTERARRIVAL RATE FOR SPECIAL SERVICES           165
            ENDGRAPH                                                          166
            END                                                              167
```

FIG. 11.29—Continued

clocking routine: the GENERATE and TERMINATE blocks numbered 56 and 57. One transaction is GENERATEd every 3,600 clock units and immediately is TERMINATEd, reducing the termination count by 1. Because the time unit represents seconds, each termination at this block marks the completion of an hour of simulation time. Thus, use of a START card specifying a termination count of 8 would cause the model to run for exactly 8 simulation hours. Of course, throughout this time, INPUT is GENERATEing the transactions that move through the main part of the model, and these transactions are being terminated after they leave the BANK. In this program (Figure 11.29), the model was initialized to a steady state, then RESET and run for 8 simulation hours.

Note the heavy use of savevalues throughout the simulation, thus making it rather easy to reparametrize the model. For example, the spread times for the service times of the two tellers are contained in halfword savevalues XH5 and XH6, respectively. These values easily can be INITIALized to new values before a rerun of the simulation model, thus exploring the effects of changes in the efficiencies of the two tellers. In the earlier model (Section 10.14), this same effect was produced by redefining the ADVANCE blocks that represent teller service times. Such redefinition is not possible in the extended model of this section, because a single ADVANCE block represents time for both tellers through indirect addressing. The major advantage of the use of savevalues in this model is the ability to reparametrize the model extensively through the use of one or two INITIAL control cards.

Savevalues also can be used to affect parts of the model while simulation is being performed. For example, the mean interarrival time at a bank is likely to decrease during the lunch hour, because many people then are free to run errands such as going to the bank. This lunch-hour rush easily can be simulated in this model by inserting the following cards to replace the START card numbered 125:

START	3	9 TO 12 O'CLOCK.
INITIAL	XH6,30	CUSTOMERS ARRIVE AT
START	1	FASTER RATE
*		UNTIL 1 O'CLOCK.
INITIAL	XH6,60	RETURN TO NORMAL RATE
START	4	FOR REMAINING TIME.

The interarrival mean time is 60 for the first three hours; it decreases to 30 for the lunch hour; and then it returns to the normal rate for the afternoon. Because no RESET or CLEAR cards are included in this sequence, the model is not affected in any other way by the temporary pauses to reINITIALize parameters.

Halfword savevalues XH1 and XH2 and matrix halfword savevalue XTAB are used to collect frequency statistics concerning the types of services required by transactions. XH1 contains the number of transactions that sought special services immediately upon entry into the BANK. XH2 records the number of customers who sought managerial assistance after first using some other facility, such as a writing station or a teller. These statistics are gathered by blocks 30 through 32. Customers previously using some other facility arrive at MNGT2. By the time they reach block 32, P4 will be increased to 2 and the SAVEVALUE block will add one to the contents of XH2. Customers who go directly to the receptionist queue on entry into the BANK arrive at MNGT1 with P4 having a value of 1, thus causing XH1 to be incremented by 1. The halfword matrix savevalue XTAB tabulates the type of services rendered to customers. This information is gathered at the MSAVEVALUE block TERM just before the customer leaves the system. At this block, the element XTAB(P1,P2) is incremented by 1. The four elements of this matrix savevalue represent the numbers of customers who fell into each of the following four classes of services: XTAB(1,1) = number of customers who used the first teller and required no special services; XTAB(1,2) = number of customers who used the second teller and required no special services; XTAB(2,1) = number of customers who used the first teller and did require special services; and XTAB(2,2) = number of customers who used the second teller and did require special services.

Further statistics are gathered by the tables XTME and IARRV. XTME is TABULATEd by block 54 and defines the distribution of transit times through the model. IARRV describes the distribution of interarrival times at the receptionist's desk; it is TABULATEd at block 33.

Figures 11.30 through 11.32 show output obtained for a run of eight simulation hours. GPSS editing features have been used (see Figure 11.29) to alter and select from the standard statistical output those items of most interest. Note how the TITLE and INCLUDE cards have been paired to label and select the output displayed in Figure 11.30. The tables XTME and IARRV are represented by the graphs in Figures 11.31 and 11.32.

```
*********     OUTPUT FOR BANK SIMULATION III     *********

   STORAGE STATS FOR BANK, PENS AND VPEES.
   STORAGE     AVERAGE       AVERAGE        AVERAGE
               CONTENTS    UTILIZATION     TIME/TRAN
     BANK       11.500        .000          648.183
     PENS         .706        .117           87.386
     VPEES        .648        .216          291.921

   STATS FOR RECEPTIONIST AND TWO TELLERS.
   FACILITY      AVERAGE        AVERAGE
              UTILIZATION      TIME/TRAN
     RCPT         .263          90.285

        4         .957         119.320
        5         .998         118.345

HALFWORD SAVEVALUES

CONTENTS OF HALFWORD SAVEVALUES (NON-ZERO)
SAVEVALUE  NR, VALUE   NR, VALUE   NR, VALUE   NR, VALUE   NR, VALUE   NR, VALUE   NR, VALUE   NR, VALUE
    1   46     2   37


QUEUE STATS: LAST TWO LINES FOR TELLERS
          MAXIMUM    AVERAGE    PERCENT      AVERAGE      $AVERAGE
QUEUE     CONTENTS   CONTENTS    ZEROS      TIME/TRANS    TIME/TRANS
  PENQ        8       .958        28.8       118.978       167.290
  RCPTQ       2       .019        81.9         6.662        36.866
  VEEPQ       3       .340        37.5       153.437       245.500
  4          10      3.074         6.0       379.974       404.264
  5          10      3.533          .8       415.359       418.777


CROSS TABULATION OF USAGE OF TELLERS AND SPECIAL SERVICES

COL 1: ENTRIES FOR FIRST TELLER
COL 2: ENTRIES FOR SECOND TELLER
ROW 1: ENTRIES FOR NON USAGE OF SPECIAL SERVICES
ROW 2: ENTRIES FOR SPECIAL SERVICE USAGE


MATRIX HALFWORD SAVEVALUE XTAB

        COL. 1      2

  ROW 1   210    228
      2    15      9
```

FIG. 11.30   Selected Output from Extended Bank Branch Simulation

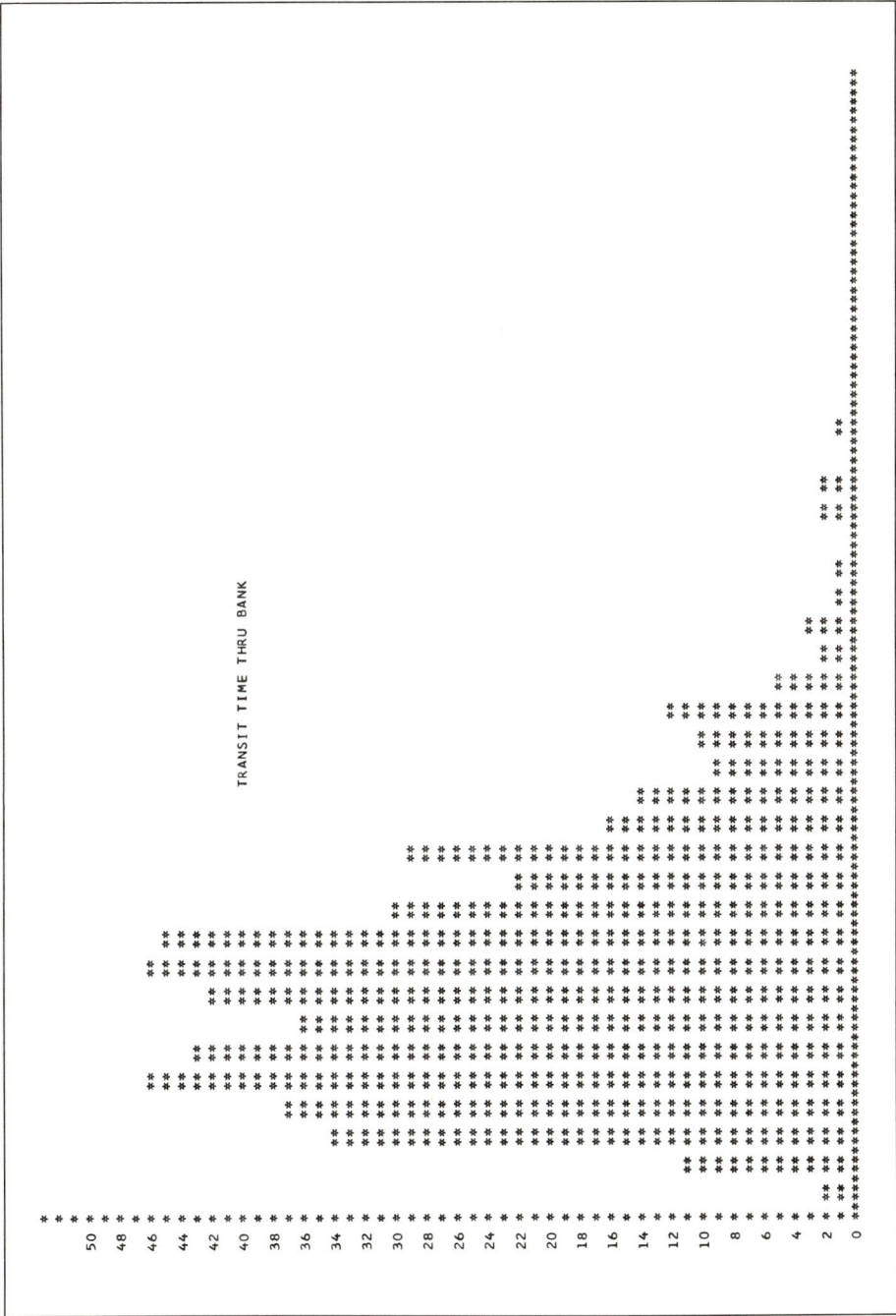

FIG. 11.31   Distribution of Transaction Transit Times

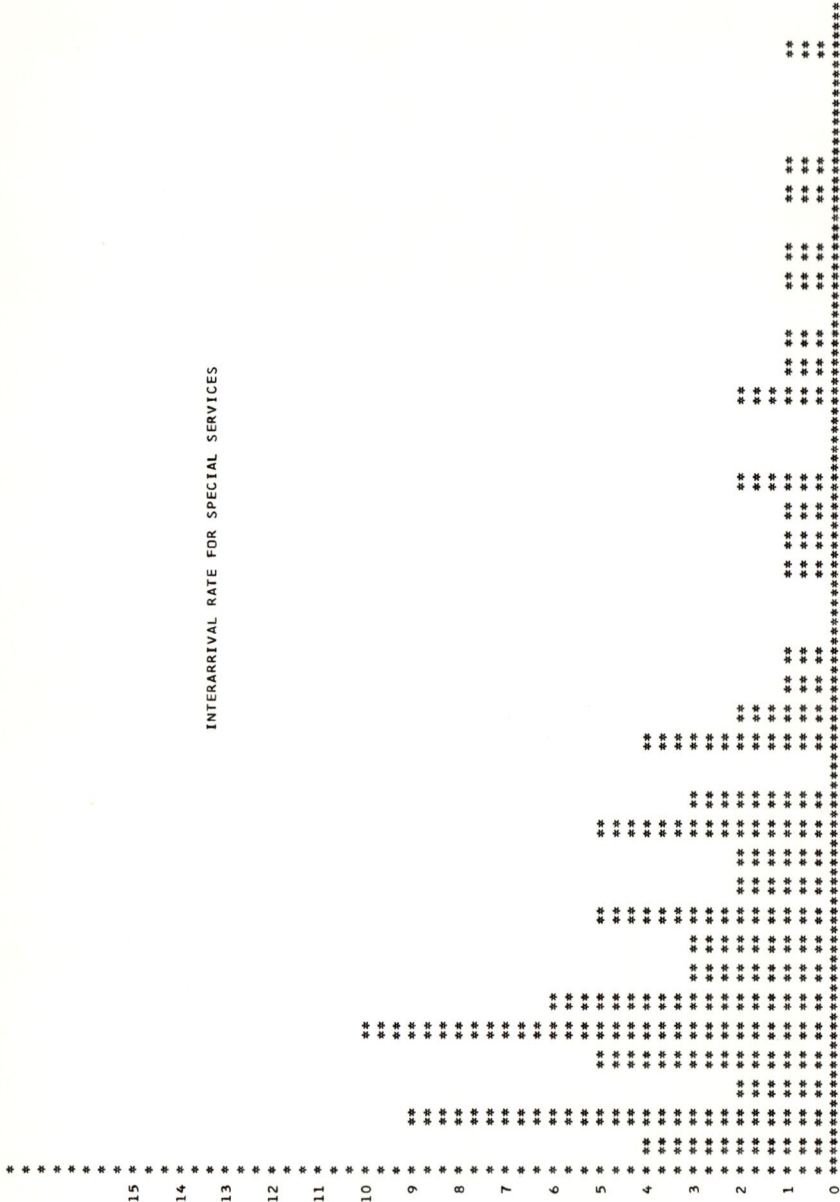

FIG. 11.32 Distribution of Transaction Interarrival Times for Special Services

PROBLEMS

11.1   Adjust your model of the service station (developed in answer to Problem 10.7) so that (1) cars will renege if ten cars already are present in the service station; (2) cars always will join the shortest of the lines for the type of gas required; and (3) the attendants always will be used in order of increasing utilization. Write a program incorporating all three changes and compare the results obtained in running this program with those obtained for the solution of Problem 10.7.

11.2   Adjust the model of the gizmo factory (Problem 10.8) to reflect the different queuing disciplines required if gizmos are stacked one on another at the inspection station and touchup line, with the top gizmo on the pile always being removed for further processing. Compare the results obtained from running this adjusted model to the results obtained in running your solution to Problem 10.8.

11.3   Use indirect specification to reduce the amount of code needed in the program developed for Problem 10.3 (carry the specification of a choice of clerk in the transaction parameters). Base the choice of which clerk will be used on the length of the waiting lines. Again, compare the results obtained in running the original and the modified programs.

11.4   (a) If your installation is capable of producing running times for you, run the bank branch simulation of Section 11.18 once with and once without the LINK/UNLINK blocks, and compare the running times for the two runs. (b) Note that the bank branch simulation is run for eight simulation hours *after* it reaches steady state. Examine the startup effects by replacing the clocking mechanism used in the problem, and by producing statistics each time that 100 transactions have passed through the bank. This modified system should be run until 5,000 customers have used the bank.

11.5   (a) One approach to producing normally distributed random numbers with mean of zero and standard deviation of one is given by

$$y = \sum_{i=1}^{12} x_i - 6.0,$$

where the x_i are random numbers uniformly distributed in $[0,1]$. The transformation $z = y\sigma + \mu$ then will approximate normally distributed random numbers z with mean of μ and standard deviation of σ. Taking into account the fact that GPSS produces random integers uniformly distributed in the range $0 \leq x < 1,000$, code GPSS blocks that will enable transactions to produce a normally distributed random integer. The required mean will be carried in P2 and the required standard deviation in P3. The resultant random number should be placed in P4 of the transaction. (b) Define a continuous function entity to approximate the normal distribution. It should use RN8 as an independent variable to produce normally distributed random numbers with the same mean and standard deviation as in part (a). **(c)** Compare the two methods for implementing the normal distribution by tabulating 1,000 random integers produced by each of the two methods.

11.6   A small computer installation runs a batch operation. The jobs that are run fall into four major groups by language used: 60 percent of the runs are in FORTRAN; 30 percent are in PL/I; 7 percent are in COBOL; and 3 percent are in other languages. Table 11.7 shows five classes associated with each group according to expected run times (in minutes). Jobs arrive at the dispatcher at the rate of one every 13 ± 5 minutes and are placed in the job queue. CPU time is calculated with the mean given by the times in Table 11.7, and with a spread time equal to 20 percent of the mean time. **(a)** Simulate the installation for one week of its operation. Two distributions should be recorded for each of the four groups: the distribution of queue waiting times, and the distribution of turnaround times (in other words, transit times). Also record the distribution of turnaround times for each of the five time frequency classes. **(b)** Alter the above system so that jobs are run according to their class, with class 1 given highest priority and class 5 given lowest priority. Gather the same statistics as in part a and compare the two systems.

TERM PROJECTS

The following problems are term projects that have been assigned to students in the second semester of a two-semester course taught by one of the authors. Each project requires a great deal of effort and can best be undertaken by a three- or four-student team. The most time-consuming effort is the gathering and analyzing of relevant data. The project should be assigned at the beginning of the semester, with a target date for checking the first results of the data analysis about one-third of the way through the semester. This check almost always will reveal a need to gather more data and to do more analyses.

Because most students in the course already know a general purpose language such as FORTRAN or PL/I, it is instructive to require the students to

TABLE 11.7   Expected Run Times for Jobs at Computer Installation (Problem 11.6)

Frequency Class	Expected Run Time (T)	Cumulative Percentages of Runs Falling in Intervals			
		FORTRAN	PL/I	COBOL	Other Languages
1	$0 < T \le 5$	94	88	90	93
2	$5 < T \le 15$	96	90	95	95
3	$15 < T \le 30$	98	98	97	99
4	$30 < T \le 60$	99	99	99	100
5	$60 < T \le 120$	100	100	100	100

program all or part of their simulations both in GPSS and in one of these general purpose languages.

Project 1: A Horserace Simulation. Simulate the running of a horserace. The book by Ainslie (1968) should be available as a basic reference. The project may be defined with either of the following objectives: **(a)** Simulate the running of a specific race that actually will be run near the end of the semester. This race should be for a substantial purse and at a well-known track. It should be for horses at least 3 years old, and preferably older, so that adequate data on past performances will be available. The simulation should be written in such a way that all data on performance of horses in the race, up to and including the day of the race, can be incorporated into it. **(b)** Simulate the running of a hypothetical race, involving any subset of a dozen or so real horses that are in the same class and for which extensive performance data are available.

In either case, Ainslie's book will be needed to help specify the variables that may relate to a horse's performance and for ideas on how to simulate a race. Recall from the discussion in Chapter 5 that it probably will be wise to attack the race piecemeal—that is, to simulate the early, middle, and late portions of the race in distinct segments of the program.

A precisely defined objective or measure of performance should be chosen. For example, one might plan the simulation to predict the order of finish, or to predict the time of finish for each horse (which gives both the order of finish and the degree of separation among the horses). A most ambitious measure would involve maximization of profits in placing bets upon the outcome of the race. In order to deal with this objective, the simulation would have to be able to predict mutual prices, relate these prices to the predicted order of finish, and arrive at both the expected payoffs from various betting strategies and the greatest loss or profit that is reasonably likely to occur with each betting strategy.

Project 2: A Stock Market Simulation. Previous experience with student simulations of common stocks indicates that (1) only stocks listed on the New York Exchange should be included; (2) the simulation should be restricted to stocks of companies in a single industry; and (3) the measure of performance incorporated into the simulation should be the cost consequences of various strategies for the purchase and sale of stock.

If a wide variety of stocks is to be studied, separate simulations should be developed for various industries. The cost consequences in any case should include both expected gains or losses and reasonably likely extreme gains or losses.

A precisely defined time unit should be established from the start. For example, one might attempt to predict the behavior of the price of a stock in week n, using all data available through week $n - 1$. It would be more ambitious to make predictions for month n or year n from all data available through month $n - 1$ or year $n - 1$. These different time scales probably would result in very different approaches to the simulation.

The simulation should be able to deal with a variety of sophisticated strategies for buying and selling stocks. Buying on margin and the use of puts and calls should be included in the simulation. No additional remarks on the development of such a simulation are offered here. Most of the students who choose this project probably will be economics majors and will have their own favorite references and approaches.

Project 3: A Bank Branch Simulation. The simulation of a bank branch is discussed extensively in this book, and this project probably is the least innovative of those listed here. The value of this project will lie in the attempt to simulate an actual bank branch office. The team should visit a branch of a local bank, explain their purpose to the manager, and obtain his permission to proceed with a study of the branch. They then should obtain data on arrival patterns, service times, work flow, and so forth. If possible, these data should be gathered for all days and hours that the branch is in operation; if such a complete study is impossible, be sure that all data are gathered at a specific day-hour combination. In either case, the bank must be studied and data obtained in each of several weeks. If a specific day-hour combination is to be simulated, initial conditions (queue lengths, number of servers, and so forth) must be recorded. Be sure to enlist the cooperation of all bank personnel. You will be relying on them in obtaining data, and you should seek their expert opinions on how representative your data really are of typical conditions in the bank. Remember that your activities are likely to be an annoyance to them, unless you take great care to win their support.

Simulate the bank's activities with a view toward testing such standard modifications as changes in the number of tellers, modifications in the customer flow patterns, changes in the numbers of nonteller personnel, and the impact of increased or decreased workload. Be sure to solicit the manager's views on the kinds of modifications that the simulation should be able to handle; his cooperation may be more enthusiastic if you can provide some useful information for him in return.

Project 4: A Basketball Game Simulation. Use a simulation to predict the final score of a basketball game between your school and an opposing school. Do not attempt to simulate the play-by-play action of the game, but rather try to predict the number of points that each player on the team will score. Determine—from past performances of the players—those factors that affect the number of points scored by each player. Simulate each player's performance in the game for which you are predicting the score by making defensive assignments and by determining the values that each of the relevant factors takes on in this game. Be sure to allow for modifications resulting from injuries, last-minute decisions by the coaches, and similar effects. This simulation might be extended to make possible the prediction of outcomes for any game between two schools in the league. A far more ambitious objective would be the prediction of the final league standings on the basis of the games played up to a certain point in the season and the schedule of games remaining to be played.

Project 5: A Computer Center Simulation.   Simulate the activities of the computer center at your university. Treat the computer itself as a single entity, with well-defined service characteristics. Enlist the cooperation of the center director and his staff. Study the center operations in the same fashion as that described for the study of the bank branch (Project 3) in order to obtain data on workload, service characteristics, queue disciplines, priorities, and so forth. If possible, simulate the workflow from the keypunch operation right through to the delivery of output to the user.

If the center provides timesharing services, simulate only those activities related to batch processing; then degrade the computer performance appropriately to take account of the workload generated at the terminals.

Do a preliminary study to determine whether time of day and day of week are relevant factors for this simulation. It is very likely that the conditions of the system will vary over the course of a semester, so be sure to get workload data both near the beginning of a semester (probably a slower period) and near the end of a semester (probably a busy period).

If you feel confident, ask the computer center director or the operations manager to participate in the simulation development, with a view toward using the result as a management tool.

Project 6: Simulation of a Presidential Election.   Simulate the next presidential election by predicting the outcome of the popular vote in each of the fifty states and then determining the electoral vote totals. Use socio-economic variables and data from past elections to predict results within each state. Write the simulation in such a way that any one of at least three candidates from each major party could be the actual nominee of that party. Try to predict the result both with and without a conservative third-party candidate from the South in the race, and both with and without a fourth-party candidate (taking a position to the Left of the Democratic Party) in the race.

Simulation of Computer Systems

12.1 THE OBJECTIVES Simulations of computer systems usually are undertaken in order to evaluate systems performance more effectively. In a comprehensive article on systems evaluation, Lucas (1971) notes that simulation is "the most potentially powerful and flexible of the evalution techniques" and is "the most adequate technique for all purposes of evaluation," but that "the greatest drawback of simulation is its relatively high cost." Simulation has been used widely for systems evaluation, particularly for evaluation of new systems. Examples of the application of simulation techniques to performance evaluation are given by Katz (1966, 1967) and by Nielsen (1967). An introduction to computer-systems simulation from a somewhat different point of view from that in this chapter and an extensive bibliography on this subject are given by MacDougall (1970).

In a typical case, a simulation of a computer system is developed to answer questions such as the following: (1) If the present workload of the facility were put on a new computer, would the unused capacity of the new computer be sufficient for servicing the projected increase in facility workload? (2) For this new facility without increased workload, what would be the quality of service, measured in turn-around time as a function of priority level? What would be the quality of service with the projected increase in workload? (3) What system of priority levels for the different kinds of jobs to be processed could yield the best quality of service? (4) What would be the impact on unused capacity and on quality of service if timesharing services were added to the facility? (5) What job-scheduling algorithms would be most appropriate for the new facility?

12.2 Level of Detail

In simulation of a computer facility, a critical issue is the level of detail at which the simulation is to operate. We can distinguish two extreme levels of detail; in practice, of course, there exists between the two extremes a whole spectrum of levels. We will call the extremely fine level of detail the *micro level* and the extremely aggregated level the *macro level*.

At the micro level, the effects of each individual machine-language instruction are simulated. The transactions are machine-language instructions and, perhaps, input-data sets. The state of the system includes the contents of core storage, auxilliary storage, and other output-data sets. The processor and the channels are treated as servicing entities. At this level of detail, simulation of a unit of real time may be expected to require ten or more units of simulation time. For example, micro models of the System/360 operating system required five to fifty units of simulation time for each unit of real time (Seaman and Soucy 1969). The exact ratio varied with the processor used and depended strongly on whether or not timesharing capabilities were simulated. Thus, micro-level simulations are expensive both in terms of programming time and in terms of running time. Furthermore, simulation at the micro level requires an extremely detailed understanding of the functions of the operating system, because these details must be incorporated into the logic of the models.

Micro-level simulations are useful for study of computer-design problems. They can give the designer insight into the consequences of modifying the instruction set or the hardware and software capabilities. However, in a simulation intended to determine how to process a user's workload, this level of detail seems to be unnecessary and probably undesirable.

At the macro level, the effects of processing complete jobs are simulated, with each transaction representing a total job. The state of core storage is described, not in terms of its contents, but rather in terms of the number of storage locations that are busy or idle. This is the level most often used in simulation of computer systems for purposes of answering questions like those listed in Section 12.1. The simulations discussed in the following sections of this chapter are all at this macro level.

12.3 The Job Generator

In a simulation of a computer system, a critical component is the program that generates jobs. If the simulation program is written in GPSS, then this is the component that generates transactions. At least three questions must be considered in the design of a job generator: (1) What parameters should be used to characterize a job? (2) What values should be assigned to these parameters in order to duplicate effectively the workload that is anticipated for the facility being studied? and (3) What is the distribution of interarrival times for jobs at this facility?

The choice of parameters depends on the objectives of the simulation and on the nature of the workload being processed. However, certain characteristics of jobs almost always are included in this set of parameters: (1) identification of the job; (2) time and place that the job was submitted to the system; (3) its priority; and (4) the resource demands of the job—including such things as (a) auxiliary and main storage space requirements: (b) required input/output facilities and set-up, which may include such detailed information as the number of times that I/O channels are utilized; and (c) time demands on each facility that is used.

The generation of a representative job stream involves three considerations. First, these parameters must be assigned values that will reflect the characteristics of individual jobs that are processed by the computer that is being simulated. Second, a set of such individual jobs must be selected to represent the total workload of the computer. This problem often is approached through the use of artificial jobs whose characteristics can be carefully controlled and manipulated. In other words, the jobs can be "tuned up" until they match the real workload (see Section 12.4).

The third consideration involves generation of jobs with a pattern of interarrival times that matches the actual workload on the computer system. Empirical distributions should be used. Poisson and exponential distributions have been used in some simulations. However, almost every computer center has busy and slow periods during the day and busy and slow seasons during the year. Empirical densities are required to match such patterns. Although the time scale may be somewhat different, the problem here is not unlike that of characterizing the interarrival times at a social security district office. The discussions of those interarrival times in earlier chapters and in Section 14.2 should be helpful references in dealing with this problem.

12.4 Synthetic Job Streams

In evaluating computer performance, some systems analysts use representative synthetic workloads. They obtain benchmark measures of the processing time for this workload on different computer systems. The programs that make up this synthetic workload are written in such a way that the demands they place upon the computer resources can be modified easily by varying either input parameters or some of the instructions. Thus it is easy to "tune up" the synthetic workload, giving it characteristics that match those of the real or projected job stream on the computer system currently in use. Because synthetic job streams are easier to assemble, operate, and maintain than are the real workloads, the synthetic job streams may be preferred for use in benchmark measurements.

An example of a synthetic job stream is discussed here, both because this technique should be of interest to systems analysts, and because it relates directly to the specification of job attributes in the generator. The example discussed here is one developed by Wood and Forman (1971). It was developed in order to measure performance improvement resulting from the use of HASP and to measure the improvement in performance that might result from the replacement of an IBM 360/50I (512K bytes of core) with an IBM 360/65I (512K bytes of core) or an IBM 360/65J (1,024K bytes of core). (In this chapter, it is assumed that the reader is familiar with the technical jargon in common use in the computer industry, especially those terms used with IBM computers.)

The synthetic job stream was developed to match the characteristics of a corresponding real job stream, with respect to region, CPU time, I/O time (measured by the number of EXCPs, or executions of a channel program), tape and disk use, and printer output. A PL/I program was used to generate the synthetic jobs (Figure 12.1). Parameters in the PL/I program were modified in order to obtain twenty-three distinct representative jobs from this one program. On an IBM 360/50, the compute-kernel portion of the program was estimated to require 30 milliseconds of processor time for execution. The five input parameters are (1) NMASTER, the number of master records to be created; (2) R, the number of records to be processed from the master file (R ≤ NMASTER) — this parameter, in conjunction with the JCL (job control language) commands that are used, determines the number of EXCPs; (3) N, the number of times that the compute kernel is executed; (4) L, the total number of lines to be printed; and (5) LPR, the number of lines printed per record.

Two difficulties were encountered when this program was tuned to match the characteristics of a real job stream on the 360/50 under HASP. First, N proved not to be as directly related to the processor time as had been expected. Even with N held fixed, the processing times varied; the relation between processing time and N was subject to statistical fluctuation. In order to arrive at a useful

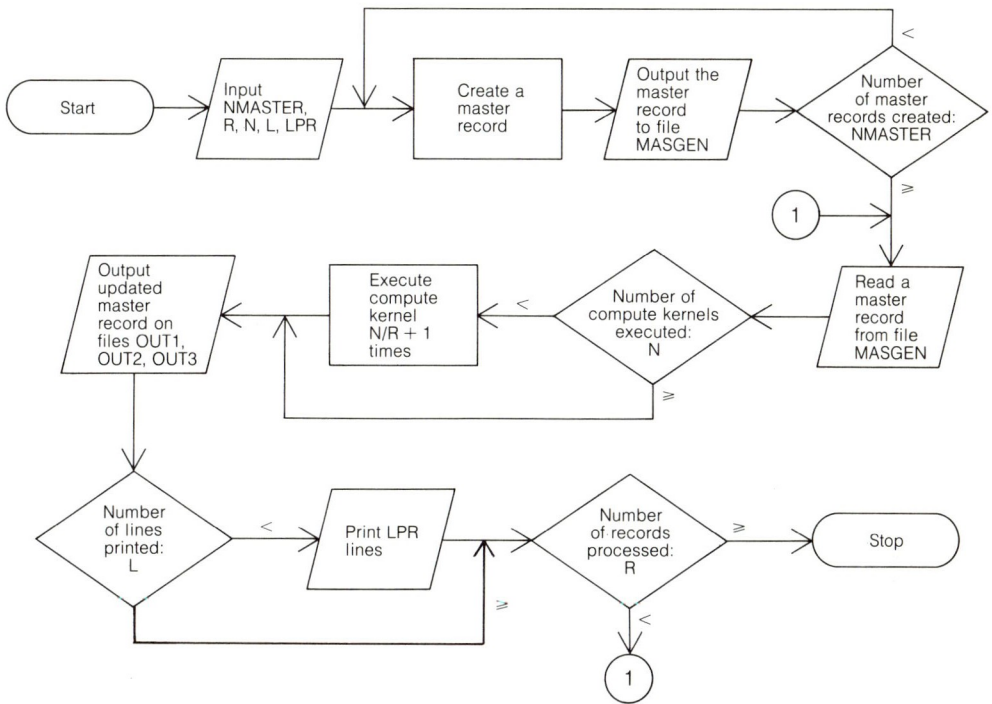

FIG. 12.1   Flowchart for PL/I Program Used to Generate Synthetic Job Streams

relation between N and processor demand, a special statistical analysis was made of a series of runs with varying N. This relation then was used to help tune up the synthetic stream. The second difficulty involved I/O times. These times were substantially shorter in runs of the synthetic job streams than those in runs of the real job stream, even though the number of EXCPs executed in both streams was the same. Apparently, this discrepancy occurred because the record lengths in the synthetic stream were shorter than those in the real stream. Blocking factors were adjusted accordingly.

The results of this study have important implications for the simulation of computer systems. First, the following job attributes almost certainly should be included in a simulation: the expected processing time, the I/O time, the number of lines of printing, the demands placed on disk and tape facilities, and the main-storage requirements. Second, I/O time might be estimated by multiplying the number of channel executions by the average record length. Third, I/O time and processing time should be treated stochastically.

12.5 The Processor and Main Storage

Simulation of the processor and main-storage components of the computer is particularly sensitive to the choice of level of detail. For simulation of the processor, the crucial decisions are the choices of the smallest time interval and the shortest job step. For main storage, the critical decision is the choice of the number of bits of storage that will be the smallest unit of storage to be simulated. For example, in a simulation of a timesharing system with virtual memory capabilities (Nielsen 1967), 100 microseconds was chosen as a unit of time and a page was chosen as the unit of storage space. The shortest job step simulated was a task (there are several tasks in a job). In this simulation, combinations of artificial, representative tasks were used to construct job streams. The page was chosen as a unit for main storage in order to simplify simulation of virtual memory systems; in other contexts, this would be an unlikely choice.

Another important consideration in simulation of the processor and main storage is the logic of the operating system that is used. This is best described in a flowchart that outlines the sequence of processing steps required by the operating system for running different types of jobs. Thus, for example, a compilation-execution job in OS/360 can be expected to require several more processor-storage steps for completion than would the execution of a program already stored in a program library. The simulation must be able to deal with each of these situations.

In some applications, it may be feasible to aggregate all processor-storage activities, representing them by a single GPSS facility or storage block with appropriate ADVANCE statistics that are a function of the job parameters. This is especially easy to do when an artificial job stream is used. The parameters of the ADVANCE block can be determined, with appropriate provision for stochastic behavior, from such parameters as the number of compute kernels. Not only can the processor-storage activities be aggregated in this way, but it also may be feasible to aggregate into this single set of blocks all exchanges with auxiliary storage that are made during the running of the job. This is particularly true for systems that spool input and output. Simulation of job processing in such a system might best be made in three major steps: input spooling, execution, and output spooling. The example discussed in Section 12.8 illustrates how this might be done.

The preceding discussion has concentrated on the simulation of the sequence of activities of the processor-storage unit. Simulation of these facilities also requires information on the storage and timing requirements associated with the processing of the job stream. The literature does not contain extensive data on this subject. In development of a simulation of an existing computer system, it may be easy to obtain the necessary data through monitoring the activities of the facility. In simulation of new systems, these data must be extrapolated from a knowledge of the design characteristics of the system. We can offer no standard procedure for attacking this problem. Bonner (1969) gives a rather general description of the use of equipment monitoring to gather statistics. In highly aggregated simulations, accounting statistics may prove sufficient.

12.6 Simulation of Input/Output

For purposes of simulation, it is useful to divide input/output (I/O) activities into two categories: those associated with relatively slow devices, and those associated with relatively fast devices. The major units in the slow category are the card reader, card punch, and printer. In some systems, a paper-tape reader and/or remote facilities would have to be added to this list. The major units in the fast category are the magnetic-tape, disk, and drum auxiliary-storage units and, in some systems, an interface to remote units.

As already noted, I/O exchanges with fast devices often may best be simulated by aggregating these activities into the simulation of the processor. However, some applications may require that these devices be simulated specifically. For example, the application might involve evaluation of alternative configurations, or of the effects of adding a multiplexor to the current system. In such cases, the first question to be considered is, How are the high-speed devices connected to the main storage? The second question would be, What is the logic used in implementing these connections? For example, in the System/360 it would be necessary to consider channels, EXCPs, and the channel-buffering and priority logic. In quantifying performance for simulation, the manufacturer's specifications for equipment performance should be accepted with caution. For example, access time to disk units may be more than one cycle (rather than a half cycle) on the average, if the processor activities between disk seeks are timed inappropriately. (This phenomenon is discussed by Patrick 1966). Also, time wasted in recovering from a tape error may be inordinately long if the software is not well designed (Domnauer 1969). The simulation must represent the system as it actually functions—not as it is supposed to function.

For simulation of slower devices currently in use, the computer center usually has data readily available on the time actually required to read or punch cards or to print a page of output. Again, however, care is needed to see that actual rather than nominal statistics are used.

In most simulations, I/O activities can be simulated adequately by treating each slow unit as a separate facility with its own queue, and either aggregating fast-unit I/O into other simulation steps or simulating the activity of the fast units in some detail. Aggregation probably will be adequate for simulation of fast units in all cases where the application is concerned merely with the speed at which these units process information, rather than with the way that the fast I/O units function. In those cases where the way that the fast I/O units function is of interest, a detailed simulation of their activities will be needed in order to deal with alternative functional arrangements.

12.7 Simulation of a Batch System: An Example

This section discusses the simulation of a hypothetical system similar to an IBM 360-series computer, operating under a simple batching operating system (OS/PCP). Under this operating system, only one job is processed at a time, and the unit of core storage is of no significance to the simulation (because a job either fits or does not fit, and we will assume that applications involving jobs that do not fit in core are of no interest). We also will assume that the time unit of one second will be adequate, because micro-level statistics are not required for this application. A simulation of this kind would be appropriate in an attempt to answer questions such as the following: (1) What would be the consequences to this facility of an increase in the workload from 150 to 200 jobs per day? (2) What would be the consequences of a shift in the workload to a greater proportion of student jobs, or to a greater proportion of research jobs? and (3) What would be the impact on the computer center of a substantial expansion of the psychology department?

Simulation of a center such as this requires the gathering of statistics on the current workload, on the projected workload under the new arrangements, and on the time required to process representative jobs from these workloads. In this case, the distributions of the simulated workloads were based on experience with a university facility operating under OS/PCP.

Neither this simulation nor the one described in Section 12.8 were developed through use of the elaborate, systematic approach described in Chapter 2. Thus they should be viewed not as case studies, but merely as examples of the techniques and concepts discussed in this chapter. It is unlikely that a simulation would be developed in most cases to answer the kinds of questions that these simulations can help to answer. Such questions usually can be answered by statistical analyses of the data that must be gathered before developing a simulation. However, simulations of computer systems are useful tools in performance evaluation, and—as noted in Section 12.1—more elaborate and more widely applicable simulations of computer systems frequently are developed.

Four priority categories are assumed for the jobs processed by this computer: the highest priority category includes jobs that require 0 to 300 seconds; those that require 300 to 1,800 seconds fall in the next category; those that require 1,800 to 3,600 seconds fall in the third category; and those requiring more than 3,600 seconds fall in the lowest priority category. It also is assumed that 82 percent of the jobs fall in the highest priority category, 10 percent in the second category, 6 percent in the third category, and 2 percent in the lowest category. It is assumed that the center opens at 7 A.M. and stops accepting jobs at 9 P.M., but the computer continues to function until all of the day's workload is processed. Several jobs are submitted to the center between 9 P.M. and 7 A.M., using some kind of night depository system, for processing the next morning. Table

12.1 summarizes the processing-time distribution for jobs in each priority category.

The GPSS program that was written to simulate this system is listed in Figure 12.2. We will discuss several features of this program. First, note that both the number of jobs waiting at 7 A.M. and the expected total number of jobs per day are assigned through INITIALization of halfwords XH1 and XH2, respectively. Thus, these values can be changed merely by substitution of new INITIAL statements. Second, note that a somewhat complicated mechanism is used to implement the distribution for the duration of the jobs (Table 12.1). Standard uniformly distributed numbers are generated; the inverse distributions, appropriately scaled, then are used to modify these numbers in order to get a correct duration for each job. These steps are carried out by the series of statements headed "job timings." Third, block number 9 (the second GENERATE block) is somewhat more complicated than might seem necessary. We tried to use V6 and V7 directly in this GENERATE block, but the compiler would not permit it. As a result of this apparent compiler error, we were forced to create savevalues

TABLE 12.1   Distribution of Processing Times by Priority Category

Priority Category	Processing Time (*seconds*)	Proportion of Jobs in Category Requiring That Time or Less
1	60	0.20
	120	0.65
	180	0.85
	240	0.95
	360	1.00
2	600	0.35
	900	0.61
	1,200	0.79
	1,500	0.93
	1,800	1.00
3	2,160	0.35
	2,520	0.61
	2,880	0.79
	3,240	0.93
	3,600	1.00
4	5,040	0.35
	6,480	0.61
	7,920	0.79
	9,360	0.93
	10,800	1.00

```
BLOCK                                                                        CARD
NUMBER  *LOC    OPERATION  A,B,C,D,E,F,G          COMMENTS                   NUMBER
        *                                                                       1
        *       SIMULATE BATCH                                                  2
        *                                                                       3
        * INITIALIZE ...  # JOBS IN BACKLOG (ONE LESS THAN )                    4
        * INITIALIZE ...  # JOBS GENERATED DURING WRKNG HRS                     5
        *                                                                       6
                INITIAL    XH1,6                                                7
                INITIAL    XH2,150                                              8
                INITIAL    X1,1                                                 9
                INITIAL    X3,360000                                           10
                INITIAL    X4,3600000                                          11
        *                                                                      12
        * JOB TIMINGS                                                          13
        *                                                                      14
         PRI1   FUNCTION   RN3,C6   CLASS 1                                    15
        0,0/.2,20/.65,40/.85,60/.95,80/1,100                                  16
        *                                                                      17
         PRALL  FUNCTION   RN3,C6   CLASSES 2,3,4                              18
        0,0/.35,20/.61,40/.79,60/.80,93/1,100                                 19
        *                                                                      20
         1      VARIABLE   FN$PRI1*3                                           21
         2      VARIABLE   (FN$PRALL*15)+300                                   22
         3      VARIABLE   (FN$PRALL*18)+1800                                  23
         4      VARIABLE   (FN$PRALL*12)+3600                                  24
        *                                                                      25
        *                                                                      26
        * PRIORITY                                                             27
        *                                                                      28
         PRIOR  FUNCTION   RN2,D4                                              29
        .82,1/.92,2/.98,3/1,4                                                  30
        *                                                                      31
        *                                                                      32
        * MEAN AND SPREAD TIMES FOR JOB GENERATION                            33
        *                                                                      34
         MESP   FUNCTION   C1,D14                                             35
        3600,25/7200,47/10800,67/14400,94/18000,84/21600,65/25200,70         36
        28800,83/32400,103/36000,102/39600,80/43200,75/46800,58/50400,47     37
        *                                                                      38
         5      VARIABLE   FN$MESP*XH2                                         39
         6      VARIABLE   X4/V5                                               40
         7      VARIABLE   X3/V5                                               41
        *                                                                      42
        *                                                                      43
        * MONEY CHARGES                                                        44
        *                                                                      45
         8      VARIABLE   25*P3                                               46
        *                                                                      47
        *                                                                      48
        *                                                                      49
         9      VARIABLE   CH1+W$WAIT                                          50
        *                                                                      51
        * MATRIX STATS                                                         52
        *                                                                      53
         1      MATRIX     X,4,5                                               54
        *                                                                      55
        *                                                                      56
        *                                                                      57
   1            GENERATE   1,,,1,,3    CREATES BACKLOG.                        58
   2            SAVEVALUE  3+,XH1,H    COMPUTES TOTAL # OF JOBS.               59
   3            SAVEVALUE  3+,1,H                                              60
   4            SAVEVALUE  3+,XH2,H                                            61
   5            SAVEVALUE  1,V6                                                62
   6            SAVEVALUE  2,V7                                                63
   7            SPLIT      XH1,START   CREATE COPIES                           64
   8            TRANSFER   ,START                                             65
        *                                                                      66
        *                                                                      67
        * JOB ARRIVAL                                                          68
        *                                                                      69
   9            GENERATE   X1,X2,,XH2,,3                                       70
  10            SAVEVALUE  6,C1   LAST GENERATION TIME                         71
  11            SAVEVALUE  1,V6                                                72
  12            SAVEVALUE  2,V7                                                73
```

FIG. 12.2 GPSS Program for Simulation of Computer Operating Under a Batch System

```
              *                                                                    74
              * ACCEPT NO JOBS AFTER CLOSING BUT RUN OUT THE JOBQ                   75
              *                                                                    76
13                    TEST G      C1,50400,START                                    77
14                    SAVEVALUE   4+,1,H      COUNT JOBS.                            78
15                    SAVEVALUE   5+,1        COUNT #DISCARDED                       79
16      TSTQ  TEST G  V9,0,STOP                                                      80
17            TEST L  XH4,XH3,STOP                                                   81
18            TERMINATE                                                             82
              *                                                                    83
              *                                                                    84
19      START ASSIGN  1,FN$PRIOR PICK UP PRIORITY CLASS.                            85
20            ASSIGN  3,V*1 TOTAL CPU TIME.                                         86
              *                                                                    87
21            SAVEVALUE   7,C1  LAST ARRIVAL TIME                                   88
22            SAVEVALUE   9,Q$JOBQ  BACKLOG AT CLOSING TIME                         89
23            QUEUE       JOBQ  JOIN QUEUE BY PRIORITY.                             90
24            LINK        JOBQ,P1,CPUIN                                             91
25      CPUIN SEIZE       CPU                                                       92
26            DEPART      JOBQ                                                      93
27      WAIT  ADVANCE     P3                                                        94
28            RELEASE     CPU                                                       95
29            UNLINK      JOBQ,CPUIN,1                                              96
              *                                                                    97
              *                                                                    98
              * ACCUMULATE STATS                                                    99
              *                                                                   100
30            MSAVEVALUE  1+,P1,1,1        #JOBS/CLASS                             101
31            MSAVEVALUE  1+,P1,2,P3       CPU TIME/CLASS                          102
32            MSAVEVALUE  1+,P1,3,V8       CHARGES/CLASS*1000                      103
33            MSAVEVALUE  1+,P1,4,M1       TOT TME/CLASS                           104
              *                                                                   105
34            TABULATE    TMES                                                    106
35            TABULATE    XTME                                                    107
              *                                                                   108
36            SAVEVALUE   4+,1,H     COUNT JOBS.                                   109
37            SAVEVALUE   8,C1  LAST DEPARTURE TIME                               110
38            TEST L      XH4,XH3,TSTQ                                            111
39            TERMINATE                                                           112
40      STOP  TERMINATE   1                                                       113
              *                                                                   114
              *                                                                   115
        XTME  TABLE       M1,100,360,100                                          116
        TMES  TABLE       V*1,30,30,160  DSTRBTN OF CPU USAGE                     117
              *                                                                   118
              *                                                                   119
              START       1                                                       120
              INITIAL     X1,1                                                    121
              INITIAL     XH1,9                                                   122
              INITIAL     XH2,200                                                 123
              CLEAR       XH1-XH2,X1,X3-X4                                        124
              START       1                                                       125
              *                                                                   126
              * STUDENT LOAD                                                      127
              *                                                                   128
              INITIAL     X1,1                                                    129
              INITIAL     XH1,6                                                   130
              INITIAL     XH2,150                                                 131
        PRIOR FUNCTION    RN2,D4                                                  132
        .88,1/.96,2/.99,3/1,4                                                    133
              CLEAR       XH1-XH2,X1,X3-X4                                        134
              START       1                                                       135
              *                                                                   136
              * RESEARCH LOAD                                                     137
              *                                                                   138
              INITIAL     X1,1                                                    139
              INITIAL     XH1,6                                                   140
              INITIAL     XH2,150                                                 141
        PRIOR FUNCTION    RN2,D4                                                  142
        .78,1/.87,2/.96,3/1,4                                                    143
              CLEAR       XH1-XH2,X1,X3-X4                                        144
              START       1                                                       145
              END                                                                 146
```

FIG. 12.2—Continued

X1 and X2 for this purpose. Unfortunately, such difficulties are not uncommon in the use of special-purpose languages; the programmer must learn to circumvent them. Finally, a JOBQ chain is used in blocks 23 to 29. The elements of the chain are ordered according to the priority given in P1; this value was assigned to the parameter in block 19.

Four runs of this simulation were made; their results are summarized in Table 12.2. These runs might be appropriate to help answer questions similar to those posed at the beginning of this section. As the table shows, use of this simulation makes it relatively easy to obtain insight into the effects of changes in the workload. Note that the final column of the table is actually the turn-around time.

The results summarized in Table 12.2 indicate that (1) the normal workload (run 1) can be accommodated in about 20 hours, with average turn-around times ranging from about 17 minutes for highest-priority jobs to more than 9 hours for the lowest-priority category; (2) an increase in the workload that might be expected to result from development of new applications (run 2) will not saturate the facility (there are 86,400 seconds in a day), but it will increase the turn-around times for jobs in the three lower-priority categories; (3) a shift in the workload from research toward student use (run 3) will leave the center substantially underutilized, and will decrease the turn-around time for jobs in the three lower-priority categories; and (4) a shift in the workload from student toward research use (run 4) will result in more work than the center can handle, but will cause substantial increases in turnaround times only for the lowest-priority category.

12.8 Simulation of a Multiprogrammed System

This section discusses the simulation of a hypothetical computer and operating system, functioning in a multiprogrammed mode with spooling capabilities. Although the reader may recognize similarities between existing systems and the one simulated here, we did not attempt to simulate any particular system.

The objectives for undertaking a simulation of this type of computer system would be similar to those listed at the beginning of Section 12.7. In this case, the workloads would be expected to be substantially greater than those for a batch system. The user also probably would be interested in questions relating to the effects of inefficient dispatching, of improvements in auxiliary storage capacity, and of changes in main storage capacity.

For this system, we are not attempting to simulate total turn-around. Spooling activities are simulated only insofar as they require CPU and channel capabilities. With this simulation, it is impossible to determine the time required to complete the printing activities associated with the workload.

TABLE 12.2 Summary of Results of Four Runs of the Batch Simulation

Run No.	No. of Jobs Submitted		Actual Number of Jobs in Run	Processing Time for Workload (seconds)	Priority Category	Jobs in This Category		Avg. Time per Job (seconds)	
	During Night	During Day				Proportion	Actual Number	Processing Time	Transit Time
1	7	150	156	70,360	1	0.82	123	113.5	1,025.8
					2	0.10	21	1,004.4	3,409.1
					3	0.06	9	2,490.0	17,157.7
					4	0.02	3	4,300.0	32,473.3
2	10	200	208	74,228	1	0.82	171	110.6	887.6
					2	0.10	25	844.8	3,954.2
					3	0.06	11	2,505.3	25,388.2
					4	0.02	1	3,912.0	50,338.0
3	7	150	155	53,482	1	0.88	136	104.4	908.9
					2	0.08	11	988.6	2,591.9
					3	0.03	7	2,175.7	6,368.9
					4	0.01	1	4,272.0	17,666.0
4	7	150	156	97,322	1	0.78	114	116.3	991.4
					2	0.09	19	745.3	2,184.7
					3	0.09	16	2,390.0	20,442.0
					4	0.04	7	3,888.0	49,797.9

The job stream used in this simulation is made of combinations of seven basic jobs, each of which was chosen to be representative of real jobs submitted to an academic computation center. These seven jobs are best described by indicating the sequence and frequency of I/O and processing activities associated with each algorithm (Table 12.3). The notation used to describe the sequence of operations is straightforward. Each description should be read from left to right. Integer numbers are premultipliers; the notation is like that used in FORTRAN formats—for example, 30(input, 3 compute) indicates that 30 repetitions are to be carried out of the pair of activities consisting of one input and three units of computation. A unit of input is the reading of a card record; a unit of output is the writing of a line. (In each case, the I/O is to or from disk, because these activities are spooled. However, note that job 4 uses tape I/O and job 6 uses disk I/O; these I/O activities are not spooled.) A unit of computing is 10 microseconds of CPU time. Sets consisting of an input or output and a brief compute activity—for example, 30(input, 3 compute) or 11(output, 3 compute)—represent the processing in sequence of several input or output records. The brief CPU activity is required to carry out these I/O operations.

The computer system being simulated functions in the following way: input from the card reader and output to a printer are spooled onto or from a disk; exchanges among auxiliary storage, main storage, and the CPU are made

TABLE 12.3   Jobs Used in the Simulation of a Multiprogrammed Computer System

Job Number	Description of Job	Sequence of Operations
1	Student: statistical computation	input; 25(input, 300 compute); 3,000 compute; 2(output, 3 compute).
2	Research: short compute bound	30(input, 3 compute); 3,000,000 compute; 11(output, 3 compute).
3	Research: longer compute bound	30(input, 3 compute); 18,000,000 compute; 11(output, 3 compute).
4	Research: I/O bound	3(input, 3 compute, output, 3 compute); 10 compute; 1,000(input tape, 5 compute, output tape, 3 compute).
5	Student: simple computation	4(input, 3 compute); 17(30 compute, 1 output).
6	Research: statistical tabulation	8,400 compute; output; 5(input, 200 compute); 10(output, 100 compute, output, 5 compute, output, 100 compute); 250 compute; 1,000(input, 100 compute, output disk, 3 compute); 100 (input disk, 100 compute); 150(100 compute, output).
7	Student: record manipulation	input; 3 compute; output; 3 compute; 20(input, 20 compute, output, 3 compute); 10 compute; output.

through the use of either of two fast channels. It is assumed that a separate dedicated auxiliary-storage device and fast channel are available for exchanges with the operating system. In addition, another slow channel is used for exchanges between the CPU and the printer and card reader. This fourth (slow) channel sometimes is called a multiplexor channel. The channel and device dedicated to the operating system are not simulated specifically; their effects are aggregated into increased time requirements that are characterized as operating-system overhead. This approach is used with the assumption that no questions are to be answered about the effects of changes in hardware or software on this overhead.

The first major problem encountered in this simulation design is that of an appropriate time unit. Even with some aggregation of operations, CPU activities in executing jobs can be measured in units of 10 microseconds (μs). With similar degrees of aggregation, channel activities would be measured in units of 30 milliseconds (ms). If the system is simulated using the smaller time unit (10 μs), the running time needed for simulation of several hours of activity may become excessive. With simulation of shorter periods of activity, it may be difficult to obtain realistic statistics on queue lengths, throughput, and other quantities of interest. On the other hand, if 30 ms is used as the basic time unit, it will be necessary to aggregate the effects of CPU activities. Because one of the purposes of the simulation is to provide insight into these activities, we cannot assume that we know enough to aggregate them correctly. This dilemma could be resolved by first simulating activities for short periods with the 10-μs unit, and then analyzing these results to obtain sufficient insight for aggregating them in a representative manner. With such an approach, it would be necessary to develop two simulations: one with 10 μs as the unit of time and a second with about 1/30 second as the unit of time. This was the approach we had in mind when we began developing this simulation. However, as you will see, the results of the first simulation indicated that the second simulation was unnecessary.

Table 12.4 presents a general description of the GPSS program used in the simulation with a 10 μs time unit. Figure 12.3 is a block diagram for the processing of one type of job (job number 5); the corresponding portion of the GPSS program is listed in Figure 12.4. Two of the blocks used in this segment of the program have not been described previously: the PRIORITY and LOOP blocks. The PRIORITY block sets priorities for transactions from the value given by its operand. The LOOP block makes it possible to use repeatedly certain segments of the program; its use and effect are described in greater detail in Figure 12.3 in connection with block 243.

The entire GPSS program contains about 400 blocks. In addition, about 50 cards are used to define matrices and storages and to initialize savevalues. Of the 400 blocks, approximately 280 are used either to generate jobs or to assign attributes to these jobs. Some of these attribute assignments are made at the time the job is generated; others are made during the course of executing the job. Both forms of assignment are illustrated in Figures 12.3 and 12.4. Several other routines are required to complete the processing of any job, including procedures to perform input operations, perform output operations, use the CPU in connection with a compute segment, carry out input spooling, carry out output spooling, and terminate running of the simulation (based on elapsed-time). These routines are shown in Figures 12.5 and 12.6. In these program segments, we use an extension of the PREEMPT block that has not been discussed previously (see, for example, block 103 in Figure 12.5). This usage permits a transaction to preempt a facility if its priority is higher than that of the transaction currently using the facility.

This simulation program was run in order to illustrate its use in helping to answer two questions: (1) What would be the effect on processing time of inefficient dispatching? and (2) How much time would be required to process a representative job stream? In order to obtain some insight into the answer to

TABLE 12.4   General Description of GPSS Program for Simulation of Multiprogrammed Computer at the Microsecond Level

Block Numbers	Usage
1–96	Job generation section. Each of the six different jobs is generated at each of four specified times. The jobs are transferred to each of the six different execution sections according to job type.
97–110	INP1/INP: subroutine for simulation of the input operation. Jobs are transferred to this section to simulate input, with parameter P4 for the extent of channel usage and P5 for the extent of CPU usage.
111–124	OUTP1/OUTP: subroutine for simulation of output operation. Timing is controlled by P6 and P7.
125–130	COMP: subroutine for simulation of compute operation. Timing in P8.
131–160	Scheduling and execution of job-type 1. Transaction then is transferred to SUMUP (block 394) for termination.
161–188	Scheduling and execution of job-type 2.
189–227	Scheduling and execution of job-type 3.
228–252	Scheduling and execution of job-type 4.
253–326	Scheduling and execution of job-type 5.
327–363	Scheduling and execution of job-type 6.
364–378	SPOOLIN: this routine simulates a spooling operation from card reader to disk.
379–393	SPOOLOUT: this routine simulates a spooling operation from disk to printer.
394–397	SUMUP: this routine terminates transactions that have been processed. A count is kept of the number processed, and the simulation is terminated if a specified limit is reached.
398–400	TIMER: this routine will terminate the simulation after a specified time is reached.

BLOCK NUMBER	BLOCK	FUNCTION OF BLOCK

49 — GENERATE 1,,,1,,,F — Generate job at time 1.

50 — ASSIGN 2,MH4(1,1) — Record execution priority from halfword matrix savevalue 4 into P2.

51 — PRIORITY MH4(1,2) — Pick up scheduling priority.

52 — TRANSFER DRT0 — Transfer to the execution section for this job type.

DRT0

228 — ASSIGN 3,PR — Record scheduling priority in P3.

229 — QUEUE JOBQ — Join job queue according to scheduling priority.

230 — SEIZE P2 — Enter CPU area P2 to begin execution.

231 — DEPART JOBQ — No longer in JOBQ.

232 — PRIORITY P2 — Set execution priority.

α

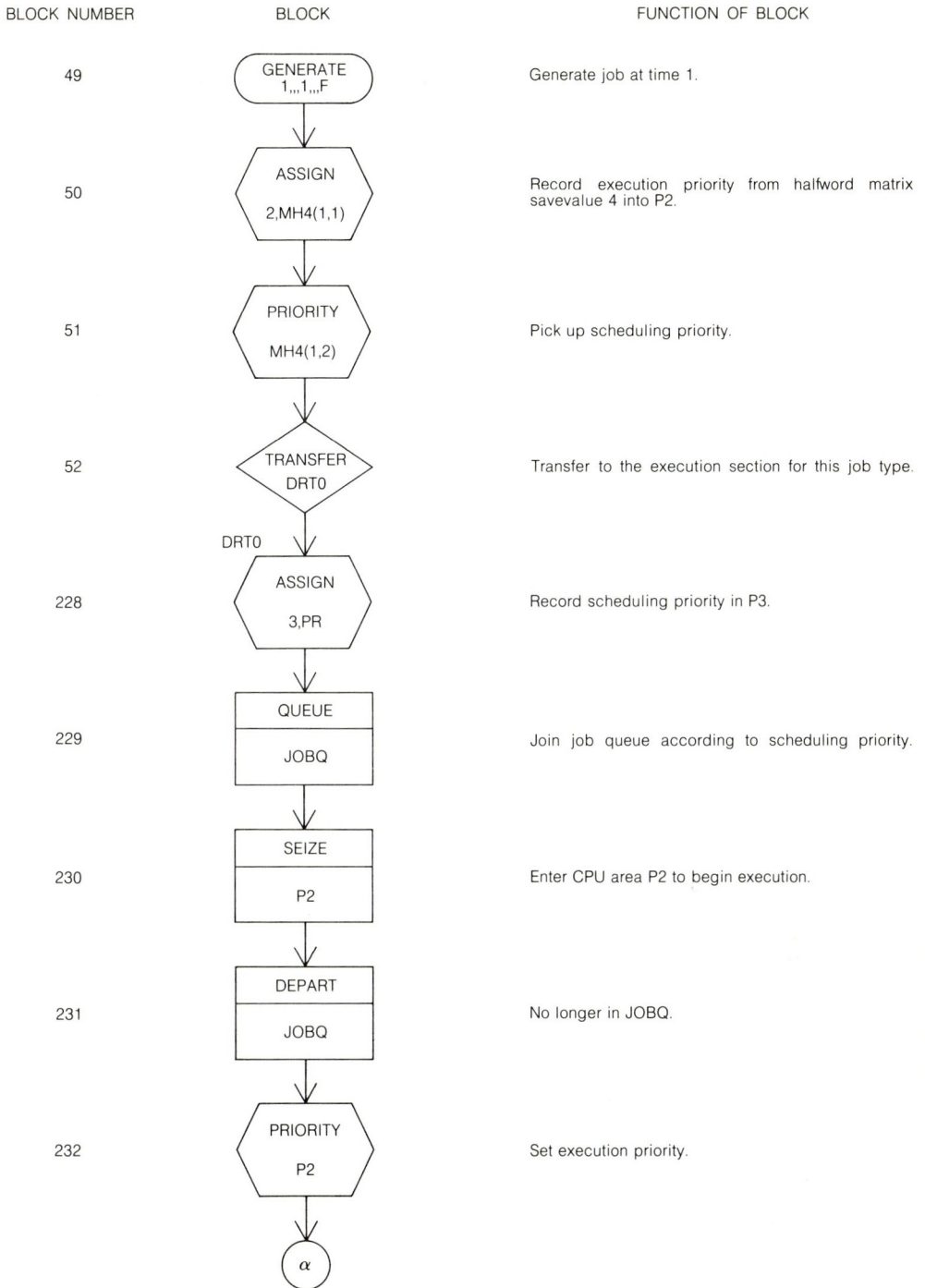

FIG. 12.3   Block Diagram for GPSS Program Segments That Process Job-Type 5

BLOCK NUMBER	BLOCK	FUNCTION OF BLOCK

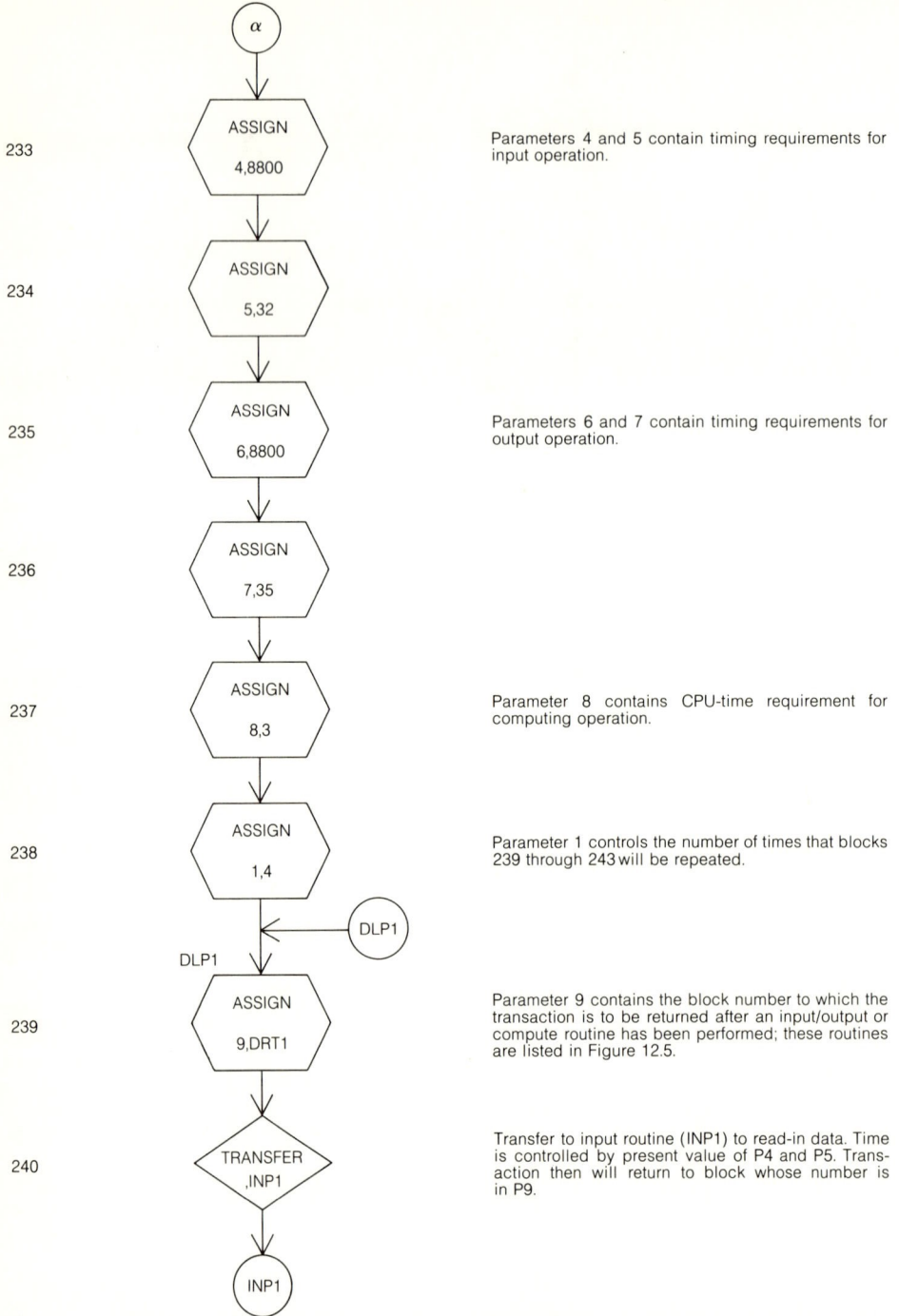

α

| 233 | ASSIGN 4,8800 | Parameters 4 and 5 contain timing requirements for input operation. |

| 234 | ASSIGN 5,32 | |

| 235 | ASSIGN 6,8800 | Parameters 6 and 7 contain timing requirements for output operation. |

| 236 | ASSIGN 7,35 | |

| 237 | ASSIGN 8,3 | Parameter 8 contains CPU-time requirement for computing operation. |

| 238 | ASSIGN 1,4 | Parameter 1 controls the number of times that blocks 239 through 243 will be repeated. |

DLP1

DLP1

| 239 | ASSIGN 9,DRT1 | Parameter 9 contains the block number to which the transaction is to be returned after an input/output or compute routine has been performed; these routines are listed in Figure 12.5. |

| 240 | TRANSFER ,INP1 | Transfer to input routine (INP1) to read-in data. Time is controlled by present value of P4 and P5. Transaction then will return to block whose number is in P9. |

INP1

FIG. 12.3—Continued

BLOCK NUMBER	BLOCK	FUNCTION OF BLOCK

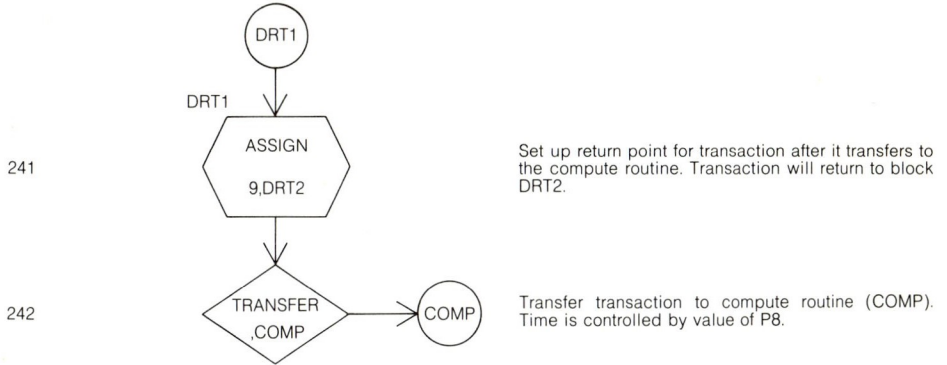

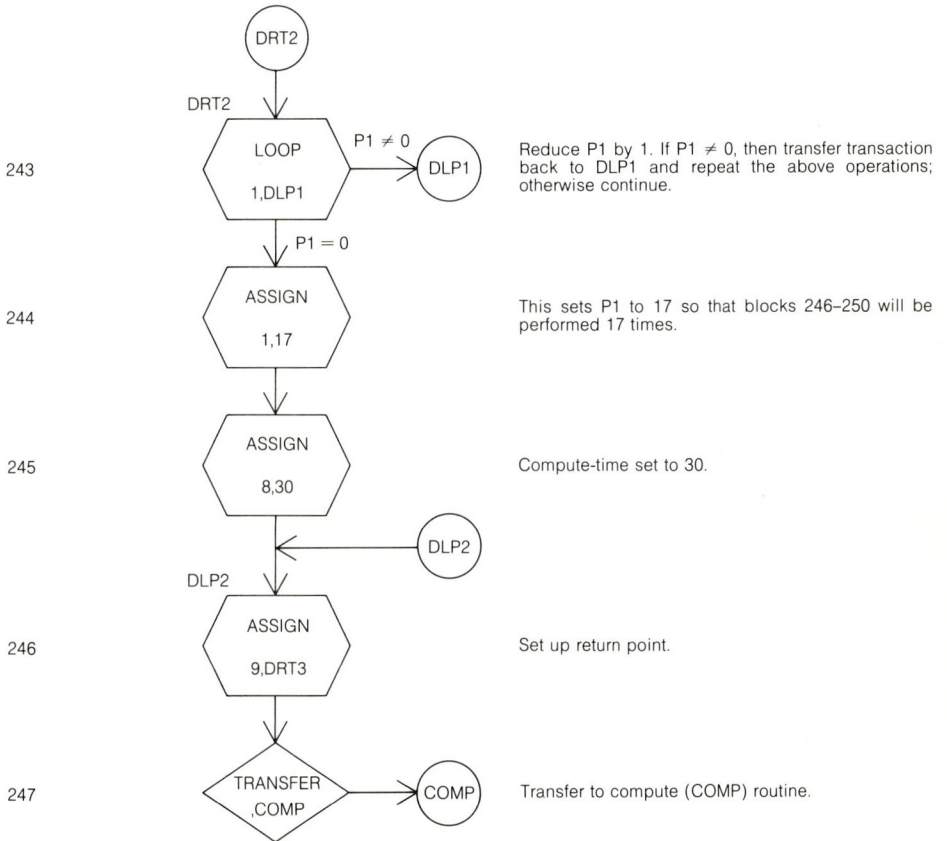

241 — Set up return point for transaction after it transfers to the compute routine. Transaction will return to block DRT2.

(DRT1)

DRT1

ASSIGN
9,DRT2

242 — TRANSFER ,COMP → (COMP)

Transfer transaction to compute routine (COMP). Time is controlled by value of P8.

(DRT2)

DRT2

243 — LOOP 1,DLP1 — P1 ≠ 0 → (DLP1)

Reduce P1 by 1. If $P1 \neq 0$, then transfer transaction back to DLP1 and repeat the above operations; otherwise continue.

P1 = 0

244 — ASSIGN 1,17

This sets P1 to 17 so that blocks 246–250 will be performed 17 times.

245 — ASSIGN 8,30

Compute-time set to 30.

(DLP2)

DLP2

246 — ASSIGN 9,DRT3

Set up return point.

247 — TRANSFER ,COMP → (COMP)

Transfer to compute (COMP) routine.

FIG. 12.3—Continued

BLOCK NUMBER	BLOCK	FUNCTION OF BLOCK

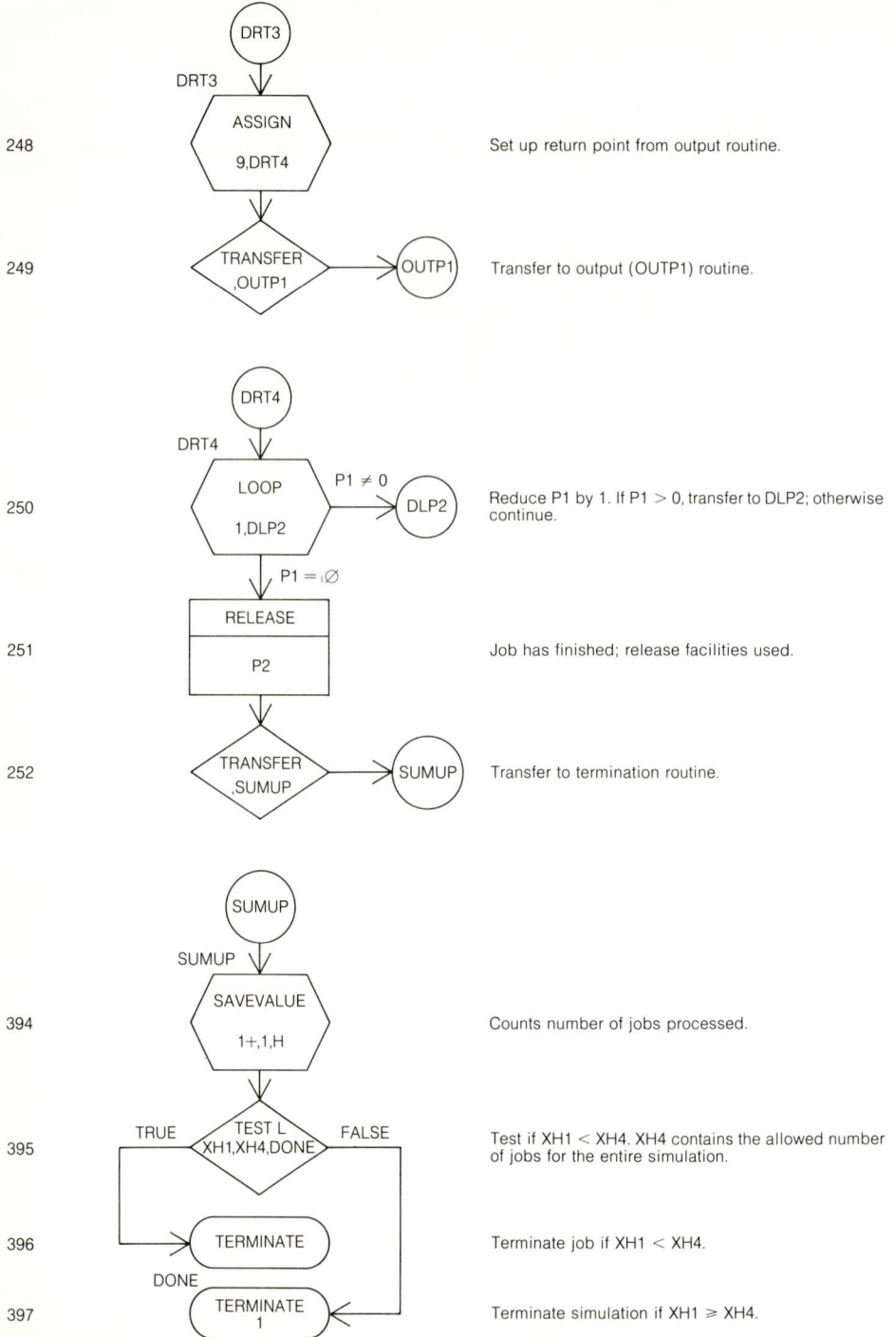

DRT3

DRT3

248
ASSIGN
9,DRT4

Set up return point from output routine.

249
TRANSFER
,OUTP1 → OUTP1

Transfer to output (OUTP1) routine.

DRT4

DRT4

250
LOOP
1,DLP2   P1 ≠ 0 → DLP2

Reduce P1 by 1. If P1 > 0, transfer to DLP2; otherwise continue.

P1 = ,∅

251
RELEASE
P2

Job has finished; release facilities used.

252
TRANSFER
,SUMUP → SUMUP

Transfer to termination routine.

SUMUP

SUMUP

394
SAVEVALUE
1+,1,H

Counts number of jobs processed.

395
TRUE   TEST L
XH1,XH4,DONE   FALSE

Test if XH1 < XH4. XH4 contains the allowed number of jobs for the entire simulation.

396
TERMINATE

Terminate job if XH1 < XH4.

DONE

397
TERMINATE
1

Terminate simulation if XH1 ≥ XH4.

FIG. 12-3—Continued

```
            *
            *
49              GENERATE    1,,,1,,,F
50              ASSIGN      2,MH4(1,1)
51              PRIORITY    MH4(1,2)
52              TRANSFER    ,DRTO
            *
            *
            * STD JOB 2    4(I,3),17(30,0)
            *
228     DRTO  ASSIGN      3,PR
229           QUEUE       JOBQ
230           SEIZE       P2
231           DEPART      JOBQ
232           PRIORITY    P2
            *
            * EXECUTION
            *
233           ASSIGN      4,8800
234           ASSIGN      5,32
235           ASSIGN      6,8800
236           ASSIGN      7,35
237           ASSIGN      8,3
238           ASSIGN      1,4
239     DLP1  ASSIGN      9,DRT1
240           TRANSFER    ,INP1
241     DRT1  ASSIGN      9,DRT2
242           TRANSFER    ,COMP
243     DRT2  LOOP        1,DLP1
        **
244           ASSIGN      1,17
245           ASSIGN      8,30
246     DLP2  ASSIGN      9,DRT3
247           TRANSFER    ,COMP
248     DRT3  ASSIGN      9,DRT4
249           TRANSFER    ,OUTP1
250     DRT4  LOOP        1,DLP2
            *
251           RELEASE     P2
252           TRANSFER    ,SUMUP
            *
            *
394     SUMUP SAVEVALUE   1+,1,H      # JOBS PROCESSED
            *
395           TEST L      XH1,XH4,DONE
396           TERMINATE
397     DONE  TERMINATE   1
            *
```

FIG. 12.4   Listing of GPSS Program Segments That Process Job-Type 5

the first question, two runs were made. In each run, each job type except job-type 3 was processed four times. In the first run, I/O-bound jobs were assigned higher execution priority; in the second run, compute-bound jobs were assigned higher execution priority. In each run, the jobs were loaded so as to assure competition between I/O-bound and compute-bound jobs for the use of the computer. In this way, we hoped to estimate the extreme effects of poor dispatching. In the first run, about 9.5 minutes of simulation time elapsed before execution of the last job was completed. (Recall that time needed for printing is not included in this simulation.) In the second run, about 11.5 minutes of

```
              *
              * SPOOLIN:   X2 # CARDS, XH1 # JOBS
              *
    364                 GENERATE     1,,,1,100,,F
    365                 ASSIGN       6,8800        DSKOUT
    366                 ASSIGN       7,35
    367                 ASSIGN       8,186
    368       SPLOP     TEST G       X2,0
    369                 ASSIGN       9,SRT1
    370                 ENTER        CHANX
    371                 ADVANCE      6000
    372                 TRANSFER     ,COMP
    373       SRT1      ASSIGN       9,SRT2
    374                 TRANSFER     ,OUTP
    375       SRT2      SAVEVALUE    2+,1
    376                 LEAVE        CHANX
    377                 TEST E       XH1,XH4,SPLOP
    378                 TERMINATE    1
              *
              * SPOOL OUT: X3 # PRNT : XH1 # JOBS
              *
    379                 GENERATE     1,,,1,100,,F
    380                 ASSIGN       4,8800        DSKIN
    381                 ASSIGN       5,38
    382                 ASSIGN       8,68
    383       SPOUT     TEST G       X2,0
    384                 ASSIGN       9,SPRT1
    385                 TRANSFER     ,INP
    386       SPRT1     ENTER        CHANX
    387                 ASSIGN       9,SPRT2
    388                 TRANSFER     ,COMP
    389       SPRT2     ADVANCE      5450
    390                 LEAVE        CHANX
    391                 SAVEVALUE    3-,1
    392                 TEST E       XH1,XH4,SPOUT
    393                 TERMINATE    1
              *
              *
              *
              * TIMER
              *
    398                 GENERATE     1,,,1
    399                 ADVANCE      X4
    400                 TERMINATE    1
                        START        1
              *
              *
              *
```

FIG. 12.5   GPSS Program Segments for Spooling Operations and for Termination of Execution Based on Elapsed Time

simulation time elapsed before execution of the last job was completed. Each of these runs required about 20 minutes of real time on an IBM 360/40 computer. This means that—even at the μs level and on a medium-speed computer—the ratio of computer time required to carry out the simulation to the amount of simulation time that elapsed is only about 2 to 1.

If our objective actually had been to obtain better insight into the effects of poor dispatching, we would have made several more runs. Because our objective was merely to illustrate how a computer system could be simulated, we did not make any other runs in connection with this question.

```
            *
            *
            *  INPUT OPERATIONS: P4 ; P5 CPU
            *
 97    INP1    SAVEVALUE    2,1,H         SPOOL COUNT
 98    INP     QUEUE        CHNQ1
 99            ENTER        CHAN
100            DEPART       CHNQ1
101            ADVANCE      P4            TYPE OPR
102            QUEUE        CPUQ1
103            PREEMPT      CPU,PR
104            DEPART       CPUQ1
105            ADVANCE      P5
106            RETURN       CPU
107            SAVEVALUE    2-,XH2
108            SAVEVALUE    2,0,H
109            LEAVE        CHAN
110            TRANSFER     ,P9           P9 HAS RET POINT
            *
            *
            *  OUTPUT :   P6 CHAN     P7  CPU
111    OUTP1   SAVEVALUE    3,1,H
112    OUTP    QUEUE        CHNQ2
113            ENTER        CHAN
114            DEPART       CHNQ2
115            QUEUE        CPUQ2
116            PREEMPT      CPU,PR
117            DEPART       CPUQ2
118            ADVANCE      P7
119            RETURN       CPU
120            ADVANCE      P6
121            LEAVE        CHAN
122            SAVEVALUE    3+,XH3
123            SAVEVALUE    3,0,H
124            TRANSFER     ,P9
            *
            *
            *  CPU OPERATION: P8 CPU
            *
125    COMP    QUEUE        CPUQ3
126            PREEMPT      CPU,PR
127            DEPART       CPUQ3
128            ADVANCE      P8
129            RETURN       CPU
130            TRANSFER     ,P9           RETURN
            *
```

FIG. 12.6   GPSS Program Segments for Input, Output, and Compute Operations

Because the ratio of computer running time to simulation time was so low, we decided to attempt the simulation of a realistic job mix without aggregating the model. To illustrate how this might be done, we made one run for this purpose. We chose a realistic job mix, which is outlined with associated execution priorities (the greater the number, the higher the priority) in Table 12.5. These jobs were loaded as outlined in Table 12.6.

About 16.5 minutes of simulation time elapsed before execution of the last job was completed. The simulation run required about 30 minutes of real time on the 360/40. Statistics were obtained on facility utilization and on queue lengths. One interesting result was that the proportion of time that the CPU was utilized nearly doubled in this run, as compared with either of the runs made to check on the efficiency of the dispatcher.

The most annoying problem encountered in writing this GPSS program was the need to specify each of the attributes used to characterize jobs explicitly by an ASSIGN block. It would have been much easier to write this program if it were possible to read-in the appropriate attributes from cards at the time that the program was run.

We already have noted that several more runs would have been made if this simulation were being used to answer questions about the efficiency of

TABLE 12.5   Job Mix Used for Simulation Run

Job Type	Number of Jobs of This Type in Mix	Execution Priority
1	20	1
3	2	1
4	4	2
5	8	1
6	7	2
7	10	2

dispatching. The same is true, of course, for estimation of the time required to process a realistic job stream. In addition, if this simulation were intended to solve these and other real problems, then (1) data would have to obtained on the performance characteristics of the computer being simulated; (2) the simulation should be modified in order to include the time required to complete printing operations; and (3) it might be necessary to give detailed consideration to job steps related to exchanges within the operating system.

This simulation of a multiprogrammed system at the microsecond level does not contain any stochastic elements; it is a completely deterministic simulation. It is not unreasonable to expect that a simulation of computer functions at this detailed level should be deterministic, whereas one at a more aggregated level (such as the one described in Section 12.7) should be stochastic. The stochastic behavior that might be expected in the results of applications of this simulation could be introduced by generation of realistic job streams with the aid of a stochastic mechanism. Stochastic behavior in the results also could be obtained merely by applying the simulation to each of several different prescribed job streams.

TABLE 12.6   Loading of Jobs for Simulation Run

Time ($10 \,\mu s$ *units*)	Input at This Time
1	5 of job-type 1; 1 of job-type 3; and 2 each of job-types 4 through 7
6,000,000	5 of job-type 1; 1 of job-type 3; and 2 each of job-types 4 through 7
18,000,000	5 of job-type 1; and 2 each of job-types 5 through 7
30,000,000	5 of job-type 1; 2 of job-type 5; 1 of job-type 6; and 4 of job-type 7

Part Five

A CASE STUDY

This final part of the book describes a case study, which illustrates many of the concepts and techniques discussed in the preceding parts. The case study is a simulation of the district office network of the United States Social Security Administration (see Section 1.5). Data on arrival patterns at district offices are discussed in Sections 3.3, 3.9, 3.10, 4.7, and 6.6, and in Problems 3.4, 3.5, 4.3, and 6.3. Data on interview lengths are discussed in Sections 4.7 and 4.10 and in Problems 4.4 and 6.1. All of this information should be reviewed as an introduction to this case study; it is assumed here that the reader already is familiar with the general working of a district office, the sizes of the offices, and the arrival and interview time distributions for them.

A complete documentation of the district office simulation would fill several volumes. Here we provide both a sketchy overall view of the whole simulation and a detailed view of just a few components of the developmental effort and of the simulation. The components treated in detail were chosen to illustrate most effectively the concepts and techniques discussed in earlier chapters.

Development of the district office simulation followed the procedure described in Chapter 2. This general procedure involved (1) the establishment of the need for a computer simulation; (2) the specification of the characteristics of the simulation, with the aid of management's questions; (3) the collection and analysis of data; (4) the construction of models; (5) the computer programming; and (6) validation. Chapter 13 discusses some of the effort that went into the first three steps of this process. Chapter 14 discusses the modeling of arrival and service characteristics and of other components of district office activities. Chapter 15 gives a sketchy description of the whole simulation, along with an additional detailed view of one part of the computer program, a discussion of validity, and an example of the application of this simulation.

CHAPTER 13   Planning, Design,
          and the Field Study

CHAPTER 14   Model Development

CHAPTER 15   The District Office
          Network Simulation

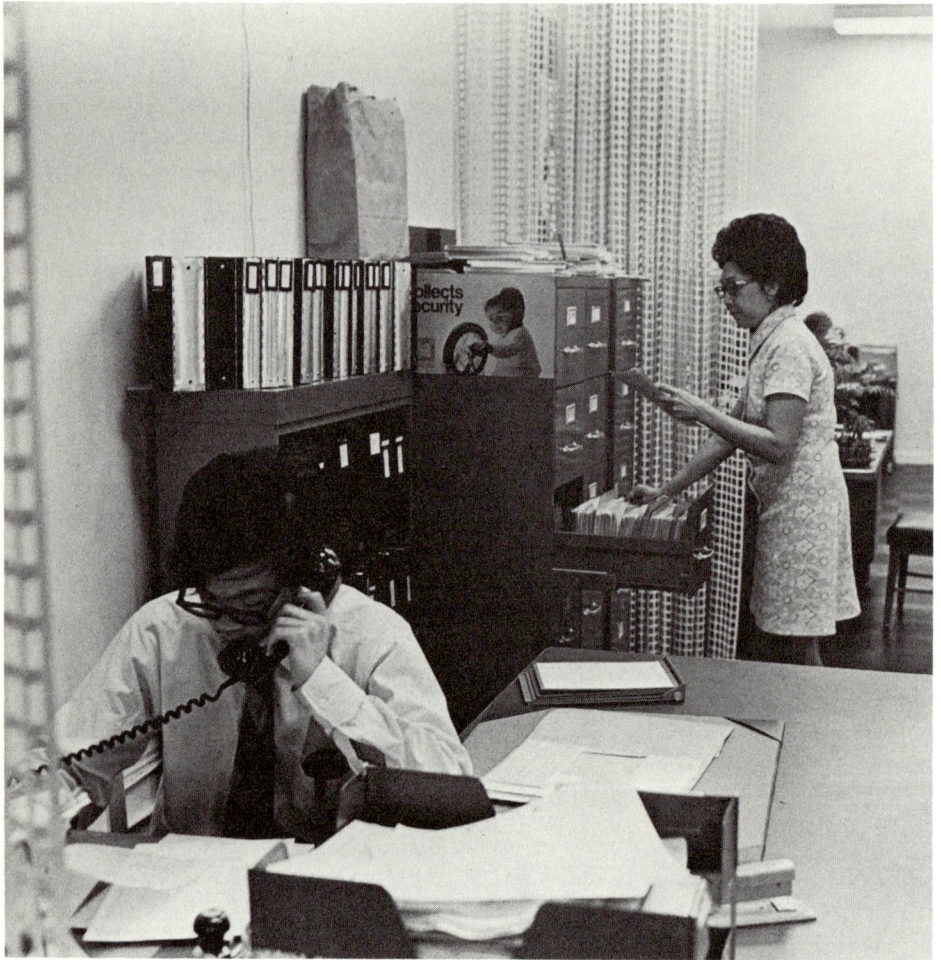

13

Planning, Design, and the Field Study

13.1 THE NEED FOR A SIMULATION   Responsibility for the overall supervision of the social security district offices rests with the Bureau of District Office Operations in the Headquarters of the Social Security Administration, near Baltimore, Maryland. Regional offices, in each of eleven regions, exercise line supervision over district office operations. During 1966 and 1967, staff of both the bureau headquarters and some of the regional offices discussed the need for a simulation with the staff of the Operations Research Office in the administration headquarters. After a study of the kinds of applications that were desired and of the nature of district office operations, the operations research staff concluded that a simulation would be justified. Estimates of the resources required and a schedule for the development of a simulation were completed early in 1967. Work began in mid-1967, with the establishment of specifications for the simulation by means of a series of questions posed by personnel in the regions, the bureau, and the Office of Administration (which assists headquarters and field staffs in their efforts to provide more effective and efficient service to the public; the Operations Research Staff is a part of this office).

13.2 Management's Questions

Table 13.1 lists a few of the questions originally formulated by management personnel in response to the following queries: What questions could this simulation help to answer if it were available now? What questions could it help answer for you if it is available two or three years from now? seven or eight years from now? The table also shows the reformulated versions of these questions, as they finally were worded after further discussion and analysis.

It soon became clear that most of the questions posed by management were related to functioning of the whole district office network, rather than to the

TABLE 13.1   Examples of Questions Posed by Management

Original Question	Reformulated Question
What expansion in facilities and staff should be realized over the next ten years in order to maintain the current level of service?	Assuming that there are no changes either in the operational procedure or in the guidelines for the size and location of district offices, what are the projected facility and staff requirements for the district office network over the next ten-year period? Make these estimates in two-year increments, using population projections supplied by the Office of the Actuary.
What is the most efficient makeup of the reception unit in offices with a sizeable walk-in traffic?	For those offices with a relatively small ratio of claims initiated to customers serviced, and for a specified set of revised operational and staffing arrangements for the reception unit, determine the distributions of waiting times and operating costs.
What would be the impact on staffing of a possible overall staff rollback such as we now face or might face in the future?	For the whole district office network and for a specified set of revised operational and staffing patterns, determine the distributions of waiting times, the extent of overtime required, and the operating costs that would result if staffing were reduced by 5 percent. What would be the effects of a 10-percent reduction in staff?
What would be the effect of decentralizing large offices in urban areas?	For a specified set of revised district office sizes and locations in certain urban areas and for a specified family of staffing patterns and operational procedures for these offices, compare with the existing setup the new distributions of waiting times, the costs of operation, and the ease of accessibility for these new office arrangements.

functioning of any single office. This observation resulted in a change of the scope of the planned simulation. The original plan had called for a simulation that would be able to model a district office of virtually any size and shape and with a broad range of actual and hypothetical operating and staffing policies. The decision now was made to extend the scope of the simulation in order to simulate a variety of structures and combinations of such offices and to examine the functioning of the network as a whole with various changes in the offices and their interrelations. The problem became much more complex.

At the same time, it was becoming clear to management that the simulation would not be able to determine what should be done. The differences between the original questions and the reformulated questions in Table 13.1 reflect this realization. The simulation will provide estimates of the consequences of certain prescribed changes in policies, procedures, and conditions. It cannot make policy decisions. It is an analytical tool, not a magic wand.

13.3 Review of the Literature

Isolated studies of district offices had been made prior to 1967. Some mathematical models had been proposed for the relations among district office staffing, service characteristics, and operating costs. Flowcharts had been developed for the way that an individual district office functions. Regular reports to management of detailed office activities were available. A thorough review of all this material was necessary, in order to determine to what extent these reports could be used in developing the simulation.

The detailed literature review was completed at about the same time that management's questions had been reformulated and absorbed. The literature review made it clear that the existing literature could not provide a detailed, quantitative description of the functioning of a district office. It also indicated that the weekly reports from district offices would provide the most useful source for quantitative information about the system. However, even these reports could not provide data on arrival patterns, service times, employee activities, or on such exogenous factors as the availability of transportation and parking and the socio-economic measures of the population served by each district office. Table 13.2 summarizes the data that were contained in the weekly office reports.

After completion of the literature review, discussions were held with subject-matter experts in the Bureau of District Office Operations, the regions, and some district offices. In these discussions, it was agreed that a field study would be necessary and that the weekly reports could provide control data for such a study.

At this point in the development of the simulation, all of the personnel that conducted the literature review, planned the development, and discussed the objectives of the simulation with operating personnel were on the operations research staff—with the exception of one computer programmer from the Bureau of Data Processing. This effort involved a senior operations analyst, two junior operations analysts, a consultant, and the director of the operations research staff. The senior operations analyst worked fulltime on this project throughout its development. The consultant also worked throughout the development of the project, but he devoted only about one day per week to it. This consultant and the senior operations analyst served as the control group for this project. The junior operations research analysts and the director of the operations research staff worked on this project intermittently. In these early stages of its development, they each devoted about one day per week to it.

13.4 Designing the Field Study

The next task was to design the field study. District offices to be studied were chosen, times for conducting the study were selected, the data to be recorded were decided upon, and the necessary resources for the study were marshaled.

The principal factor in the study design was the class of district office. It was decided to observe an equal number of offices in each of four classes: A, B, C,

TABLE 13.2   Summary of Information Reported in District Office Weekly Reports (DOWR)*

Kind of Information	Description of Information Reported
Claims processed	Three numbers are reported for each type of claim processed in the district office; they are the numbers of claims of this type that are (a) pending at the beginning of the 1-week period; (b) received or initiated in the office during this period; and (c) completed or cleared in the office during this period.
Development actions processed	This information includes data about such work as assisting other offices in development of their claims or taking special action on cases after payments have been made. The latter category of postentitlement actions includes such things as checking on the earnings and number of dependents of beneficiaries, and activities relating to the processing of health benefits (Medicare) through insurance carriers or other intermediates in arranging payment.
Miscellaneous items	This includes: (a) the numbers of certain forms processed (which may relate to workload also reported elsewhere), such as change of address notices and death benefit notices; (b) counts of activities not reported elsewhere, such as preparation of annual reports, issuance of new account numbers, and responses to requests for information that do not result in initiation of any action; and (c) special information for regional offices on the workload that has been pending in the district office for 20 days or more.
Employee hours worked	Gross number of hours worked; number of hours of annual leave; number of hours of sick leave; number of hours of overtime.

*The DOWR covers a one-week period from the start of business on Thursday to the close of business on the following Wednesday. The report is divided into four major sections as shown.

and D. Class-E offices were not studied because they clearly were "relics of the past." The next problem was to determine how many offices to sample from each class. Because of possible regional differences—and because each regional manager was interested in obtaining data on offices within his own region—it was decided to make region a second factor in the study design. This resulted in the selection of 44 district offices: one office of each class in each of eleven regions. Replication within a region and class was not considered possible because of the great cost associated with the study of additional offices. Furthermore, it was expected that the regions would tend to cluster into not more than two or three categories, with regions in the same category yielding similar results. The study design could then be regarded as providing replication within these categories.

Sites were chosen at random. A few changes in this random site list were made later because of special considerations—chiefly because of requests from management for data on certain offices of particular interest to them. Finally, it was decided to make a pilot study at some district offices, in order to iron out any kinks in the procedures and forms to be used for the full field study.

The field study occupied a special place in the development of the district office simulation (it accounted for about one-third of the total cost of the simulation development). Furthermore, field studies often are important in the simulation of complex systems. Therefore, a number of sections of this chapter are devoted to a more detailed description of the design, conduct, and analysis of this study.

13.5 Preliminary Design of the Simulation

The variables to be included in the simulation were listed even before the field study was made. Furthermore, management's questions made it clear that the major application of the simulation would be the estimation of effects of policy and procedural changes on the whole district office network. The effort required to elicit these questions indicated that it would be necessary to set up a special procedure for definition of the precise applications of the simulation. This procedure should permit management and operational personnel to state desired applications in their own terms. The procedure then would elicit from them—probably through a combination of interviews and questionnaires—a more and more precise statement of the application, suitable for use in preparing inputs to the simulation program. Finally, the questions initially posed by management made it clear that output from the simulation would have to be specially tailored to each application. For all these reasons, preliminary simulation design could proceed even while the field study was being planned and conducted.

The scope of the simulation as indicated by the list of variables, the need for answering questions relating to the whole network, and the need to tailor-make the output—all of these factors led to the decision to partition the simulation into three major divisions: a preprocessor, a district office simulation, and a postprocessor. The preprocessor would (1) help in translating the user's statement of the application into specific inputs; (2) define the sequence of runs of specific district office types that would be needed to satisfy the needs of the user—in effect, providing a kind of automated experimental design; (3) set up the runs by creating the input required for the district office simulation; and (4) select the outputs to be generated, thus creating the inputs for the postprocessor. The district office simulation would be used to generate data on what could happen under certain conditions in various district offices, and would pass these data on to the postprocessor. The postprocessor would analyze the data from the simulation and would set up and generate output tables and reports according to instructions from the preprocessor.

This preliminary design was in fact the overall design of the simulation that finally was developed (see Chapter 15).

13.6 Further Study Design

After the district offices to be studied were chosen (Section 13.4), it was necessary to choose dates for the study and to specify the data to be collected, in order to complete the design of the field study.

The study was conducted from June 1967 through January 1968. It included a "horizontal" phase, during which operational data was collected during a one-week period at each of the 44 offices. This phase was followed by a "longitudinal" phase, during which every case generated during the one-week study was monitored until it left the district office. Because one purpose of the field study was to provide data on district office operations for managerial personnel, reports on the horizontal phase were made to district office managers and other personnel early in 1968. Reports on the longitudinal phase were made in May 1968 (Operations Research Staff 1968) and July 1969 (Ozarowski et al. 1969).

The data collected were grouped into three general categories: visitors, employees, and cases. Each visitor to an office was given a form that was time-stamped as he entered and left the office, and on which entries were made as he proceeded through the office. Each employee was given a form on which he listed his activities for the day. In addition, employees completed forms that gave detailed information on incoming telephone calls and interviews. Finally, several forms were kept with each case in order to gather sufficient data for the longitudinal phase. Figure 13.1 shows a completed visitor form; Figure 13.2 shows a completed employee activity form; and Figure 13.3 shows a completed case form. Some of the identifying entries in the forms have been blocked out in order to protect the privacy of the persons involved.

SSA FIELD FACILITY NETWORK*(Interview)*								

PART I – INTERVIEW RECORD

A. SEQUENCE NO. **72735**	B. DISTRICT OFFICE CODE *387*	C. JULIAN DATE *272*	D. 1 ☐ ACCOUNT NUMBER	2 ☐ REFERRAL	3 ☐ RENEGE	4 ☐ VOID

E. ARRIVAL TIME IN OFFICE **SEP 29 9 25 AM '67**	F. START TIME-BEGINNING OF INTERVIEW **SEP 29 9 29 AM '67**	G. EXIT TIME FROM OFFICE **SEP 29 9 34 AM '67**

H. WAGE EARNER'S NAME	J. WAGE EARNER'S ACCOUNT NUMBER	K. NAME OF CALLER *(Other than Item H)*

L. PURPOSE OF VISIT *(For DO use only)*

EVIDENCE CODE

1. Wage Record
2. Proof of Age
3. Proof of Death
4. Relationship
5. Earnings Development
6. Student
7. Medical Evidence
8. Rep. Payee
9. Payment Burial Exp.
10. Deductions and Retirement Test
11. Other

PART II – TYPE OF INTERVIEW

A. CATEGORY OF INTERVIEW *(Check appropriate box)*

1 ☐ RSI   2 ☐ DIB   3 ☒ HIB   4 ☐ _____

B. PURPOSE OF INTERVIEW

1 ☐ FILING OF CLAIM(S) *(Claims received during interview)*

OA-C _____
OA-C _____
OTHER _____

1a ☐ EVIDENCE CODES

REQUESTED DURING INT.	RECEIVED DURING INT.

2 ☐ CLAIMS DEVELOPMENT
3 ☐ POST-ADJUDICATION OR NON-CLAIMS ACTIONS INITIAL
4 ☐ POST-ADJUDICATION OR NON-CLAIMS DEVELOPMENT
5 ☐ HEARINGS REQUEST *(HA-501)*
6 ☐ INQUIRY
7 ☒ BENEFICIARY NOTICES AND REPORTS
8 ☐ SMI PAYMENT CLAIMS
9 ☐ OTHER

C. REMARKS: *(For DO use only)*

☒ CLAIMANT PARTICIPATION

MONITOR ID NUMBER

INTERVIEWER ID NUMBER *309*

FORM **SSA-9426** (8-67)

FIG. 13.1   A Completed Visitor Form Used in the Field Study

13.7 Preparation for the Study

Preparations for the field study — in addition to the design of the study — included (1) the design and printing of appropriate forms; (2) the conduct of pilot studies; (3) the training of study personnel (which included the preparation of manuals and other training materials); (4) the purchase and issuance of other study materials (such as special time stamps, binders, and so forth); (5) the design of punchcard formats to be used in recording the data after they were collected; and (6) the development of computer programs to process the data that were collected.

Figures 13.1, 13.2, and 13.3 are examples of some of the forms that were designed for and used in the field study. Pilot studies were made in district

SSA FIELD FACILITY NETWORK *(Activity Record)*								A. DO CODE 821		B. JULIAN DATE 277

C. TIME		DOCUMENTATION OF EVIDENCE		D. ACTIVITY *(Record number of cases or one check as appropriate)*						
BEGINNING 1	ENDING 2	CLAIMS 1	NON CLAIMS 2	ADJUDICATION 3	RECOMM. & DETER. 4	ADDITIONAL WORKLOAD 5	CLERICAL SUPPORT 6	CONSUL-TATION 7	TRAINING 8	PERSONAL TIME 9	OTHER 10
7:45	8:25								✓		
8:51	9:10	2									
9:40	9:55									✓	
9:56	10:00	1									
10:01	10:08	1									
10:09	10:15							✓			
10:16	10:31	c									
10:40	11:28	2									
11:29	1:45	2									
12:40	1:25									✓	
1:26	2:15								✓		

FORM SSA-9426B (8-67)

EMPLOYEE ID NUMBER 218

FIG. 13.2   The First of Two Pages of a Completed Employee Activity Form

offices in Pittsburgh, Pennsylvania, and in Towson, Maryland. As a result of these pilot studies, procedures and forms were revised.

Thirty-two members of the headquarters and regional offices staffs helped to conduct the study. A series of training sessions were held in the headquarters office to instruct these people in the purposes of the study and in the procedures to be followed in completing it. A 46-page manual was prepared for use both as a text during the training sessions and as a reference during the actual study. In addition, instructions for study representatives were prepared for use as a reference during the conduct of the study and during the reporting of the study results (Operations Research Staff 1967).

13.8 Conduct of the Study

The horizontal phase of the study involved observation of operations at each of the 44 offices during a one-week (Thursday through Wednesday) period. Two

SSA FIELD FACILITY NETWORK *(Report of Claims Flow)*

A. DO CODE	B. JULIAN DATE	C. WAGE EARNER'S NAME	D. WAGE EARNER'S NUMBER	E. TYPE OF CLAIM
285	275			C 1

F. EMPLOYEE ID NUMBER	G. JULIAN DATE	H. TIME BEGINNING 1	H. TIME ENDING 2	J. ACTION CODE	K. REQUEST FOL.UP 1	K. REQUEST INITIAL 2	K. RECEIPT SUFF. 3	K. RECEIPT NOT SUFF. 4	L. IN OFFICE INTERVIEW 1	L. TEL. 2	L. MAIL 3	L. FIELD CONTACT 4	L. ARS 5
210	275	Interview		A									
440	276	1015	1020	C									
500	276	9:32	936	C	I								I
408	299	3:00	3:03	C			I					I	
500	310 / 308	12:53	12:58	B									
210	316	255	300	B									

K. DOCUMENTATION OF EVIDENCE (REQUEST / RECEIPT)
L. SOURCE OF EVIDENCE

ACTION CODE
A. Documentation of Evidence
B. Final Adjudication
C. Clerical Support
D. Consultation
E. Other

EVIDENCE CODE
1. Wage Record
2. Proof of Age
3. Proof of Death
4. Relationship
5. Earnings Development
6. Student
7. Medical Evidence
8. Rep. Payee
9. Payment Burial Exp.
10. Deductions and Retirement Test
11. Other

35
1 3 12
11

M. APPLICATION FORWARDED TO: 1 ☐ PC 2 ☐ BDI 3 ☐ SA 4 ☐ DO	N. JULIAN DATE FORWARDED 310	O. EMPLOYEE ID NUMBER 210

FORM SSA-9426C (8-67)

FIG. 13.3 A Completed Form Showing the Sequence of Action Required in Processing a Claim

study representatives normally were sent to each office, arriving on Monday to brief office personnel on the objectives of the study and on the procedures that would be followed. On Tuesday, they gave special instructions in the preparation of the half-dozen or so forms to be completed by district office personnel. The two time clocks used in the study also were set up on Tuesday, one ordinarily being placed at the entrance to the office and the other at a location near the receptionist's desk (near the spot at which a claimant is introduced to an interviewer by the receptionist). On Wednesday, pilot runs were made during each of several short time periods. The results of these runs were reviewed jointly by district office and study personnel, in order to be sure that the correct data were being recorded.

On Thursday morning, one of the two study representatives would station himself at the entrance to the office, in order to distribute and time-stamp the visitors' forms and to explain to visitors that a study was underway and that their cooperation would be required. The other study representative wandered about the office, answering questions and checking to be sure that procedures were being followed. During later days of the study, the study representative not working at the entrance would review and correct forms collected during previous days of the study.

On the Friday following the last day of the study, both study representatives would review, correct, and box the forms for shipment to the Division of Statistical Services in the administration headquarters. The case forms were retained in the case folders for use in the longitudinal study. Just before each case was sent out of the district office for further processing elsewhere, a district office employee would remove the forms from the folder and mail them to the Division of Statistical Services.

13.9 Analysis of Results

As forms were received from the district offices, the Division of Statistical Services reviewed them and prepared punchcards using the previously designed card format. Figure 13.4 shows a typical card format; this particular format was used to record the data on the visitor's form shown in Figure 13.1. The division also obtained and analyzed the distributions of various statistics, including arrival times by day of week, interview times by type of employee and type of claim, telephone service times, types of evidence accumulated, and many others. The statistical analysis of the data collected in both phases of the field study continued into 1971. Several special reports to management were made on the results of these analyses (for example, see Haskins 1969b, 1969c). Other analyses were required for the development of the simulation—for example, the characterization of the arrival and service patterns, and the determination of the factors that are significant in characterizing a district office. This characterization of an office was needed in order to enable the preprocessor automatically to select a set of offices and a set of runs for those offices that would satisfy the needs of a particular application. Examples of these analyses are given in Chapter 14.

With respect to the resources required to conduct this field study, it already has been noted that about one-third of the total cost of developing the simulation was spent on this field study, and that the services of 42 persons from several units at the headquarters and regional levels were required in the on-site observation of district offices. In addition, as noted above, the resources of the Division of Statistical Services were required in analyzing the study results. Also, the services of a senior programmer in the Bureau of Data Processing were required to write computer programs used in the analysis of study results. From this point on in the development of the simulation, at least one and sometimes two or three programmers from the Bureau of Data Processing worked on this project. One of these programmers was assigned to this project nearly fulltime. In addition, a programmer-consultant was added to the project in the concluding stages of its development in 1971. The operations research staff also supplied

Part	Item	No. of Card Columns	Name of Item
I Interview Record			
	A	–	Sequence Number – Don't punch
	B	3	District Office Code
	C	3	Julian Date
	D	1	Account Number, Referral, Renege, or Void
	E	4	Arrival Time in Office
	F1	4	Beginning of First Interview or Claimant Participation
	G1	4	Exit Time from Office
	F2	4	Beginning of Second Interview
	G2	4	Exit Time from First Interview or Claimant Participation
	H	6	Wage Earner's Name – Punch first six alphabetic letters of last name
	I	9	Wage Earner's Account Number
	K	–	Name of Caller – Don't punch
	L	–	Purpose of Visit – Don't punch
II Type of Interview			
	A	1	Category of Visit
	B1	12	Filing of Claim(s) – The claims application area will contain a variable number of lined entries. In punching this section, allow for four application numbers, containing three columns each.
	B1a	5	Evidence Requested During Interview – Punch evidence codes as shown. However, punch evidence codes "10" as "0" (numeric zero) and "11" as "X" (zone).
	B1a	5	Evidence Received During Interview – Punch data as described for evidence requested during interview.
	B2 – 9	1	*Other Purpose of Interview – Punch codes as annotated.
	C	–	Remarks – Don't punch
	–	1	Claimant Participation
	–	3	Monitor ID Number
	–	3	First Interview ID Number
	–	3	Second Interview ID Number
	–	2	Card Identification – Punch code "12"
Total Card Column		78	

FIG. 13.4 Punchcard Format Used for Recording Data from Visitor Form

additional resources to help conduct the field study and analyze its results. About 2 man-years of effort by members of the operations research staff were devoted to the analysis of the study results. In addition, a junior operations analyst was assigned fulltime to the development of the simulation in its concluding stages in 1971.

13.10 Effects on Modeling Activities

As might be expected, the results of the field study were used in all parts of the simulation. Chapter 14 discusses some examples of the use of these results in the preprocessor and in the characterization of arrival and interview times. In this section, we discuss the effect of the field study on the basic description of the way that a district office functions (as might be contained, for example, in a flowchart of the district office activities).

A detailed flowchart of district office activities, for use in this simulation, first was prepared after the consultations with subject-matter specialists that led to the decision that a simulation was needed. This flowchart was revised on the basis of further discussions before the field study began. However, it was only after the completion of the field study that a detailed knowledge was obtained of the wide variety of operating policies and procedures that actually are implemented at the district offices. Flowcharts were revised extensively to permit each of these alternatives to be implemented in any particular run of the simulation.

Study representatives and members of the simulation team jointly prepared flowcharts of each office's activities. These charts were reviewed systematically by the operations analyst developing the district office model. She was able to develop a single overall chart that provided for the alternative policies and procedures by means of gates, which restrict or channel the workflow in appropriate ways.

For example, the study results showed that various procedures are used in different offices to verify that all necessary evidence has been collected to establish a claim. In every office, the claims representative reviews the results of the interview and lists for a clerical assistant the nature of the additional evidence required. The clerical assistant then attempts to collect all of the required information. Each item is reviewed as it is received. However, three different procedures are followed in different offices after all of the additional evidence has been collected: (1) in some offices, the clerical assistant—on her own initiative—always passes the folder to another unit for clearance of the case from the office; (2) in other offices, the clerical employee always passes the folder to the claims representative, who verifies that it indeed is complete before he passes it to the clearance unit; and (3) in a third type of office, the clerical employee sometimes passes the folder to a claims representative for review and sometimes passes it directly to the clearance unit. The relative frequency of the two choices in the third type of office is related to the length of experience of the clerical employee. New employees tend to pass the folder to the claims representative, whereas more experienced clerical employees are more certain of their judgment that a case is completed and they tend to pass the folder directly to the clearance unit.

The district office model handles these alternatives by setting up a gate that each claims transaction must pass through before leaving the claims representative files and proceeding to the clearance unit. The characteristics of this gate may be adjusted to model any of the three procedures: it may be set to provide automatic branching to the clearance unit, to provide automatic routing through the claims representative, or to branch through a program segment that sets up a probability (related to the experience of the clerical employee handling the transaction) for routing through the claims representative. Stored in the preprocessor is the appropriate structure of this gate for each office.

13.11 Supplementary Reading

Haskins (1969a) summarizes many of the results of the district office simulation that are of general interest. More specialized reports and documents related to this simulation are referenced within the earlier sections of this chapter. General references on concepts and techniques are given in earlier chapters of this book.

Readers who may be interested in obtaining further reports on this project should write to the Operations Research Staff, Social Security Administration, Woodlawn, Maryland.

Those who wish to learn more about the simulation of other kinds of activities will find the following books useful in the listed fields of application: business, Bonini (1963); economics, Naylor et al. (1966); geology, Harbaugh and Bonham-Carter (1970); behavioral sciences, Borko (1962) and Tompkins and Messick (1963); politics and international relations, Guetzkow et al. (1963), Coplin (1968), and de Sola Pool et al. (1960); and socioeconomics, Orcutt et al. (1961).

14

Model Development

14.1 INTRODUCTION Development of the models used in the district office network simulation required about 6 man-years of effort, spread over three calendar years. (This figure does not include the effort required in planning, field studies, or computer programming.) Obviously, this development effort cannot be described in detail in a single chapter. Several volumes have already been filled, and documentation of the models still is underway. In this chapter we provide a glimpse of each of several different aspects of model development. The analyses made to characterize arrival and service times are discussed in some detail. The development of the preprocessor is described in more general terms. Finally, a model of one small part of district office operations (the assignment of work to claims representatives) will be discussed in moderate detail.

As pointed out in Section 2.8, model development does not proceed in a simple linear way. There is a great deal of back-tracking. Analyses of field data and interviews with experts lead to first models and computer programs. Re-working of these leads to newer, improved results. Eventually, the first version is produced that is considered worthy of being marked as suitable for use. Further modification and improvement of the models normally will continue throughout the application. The descriptions in this chapter and the next deal mainly with the effort and results associated with the first marked version of the district office simulation, which became available for use late in 1971. Little will be said about the back-tracking efforts required in earlier developmental stages in order to arrive at this functioning model.

14.2 Simulating Arrivals

In earlier chapters of this book, a great deal of data concerning interarrival times and arrival patterns is presented. However, the data are presented and analyzed in the context of illustrating various statistical concepts and techniques, and little is said there about the process of determining how to represent arrivals in the simulation.

The determination of how best to treat arrivals was based on two statistical analyses. The first sought to characterize the volume—that is, the number—of arrivals at various offices on different days; the other sought to characterize the pattern—that is, the distribution—of the arrivals within a day.

Table 14.1 summarizes the data for the first analysis. The appropriate statistical model for these data is a three-way analysis of variance without replication. The factors are office class, day of the week, and region. Table 14.2 summarizes the results of the analysis of variance. Although nearly all of the effects are statistically significant when compared with the residue mean square, it is clear that the office class is the major factor in determining the number of arrivals at a district office. This analysis also led to the conclusion that the effect of the day of the week is great enough to warrant including this variable as a factor in determining the number of arrivals.

Further analysis revealed that office class really is too crude an indicator of office size, or volume of arrivals. This is reflected in the large interaction values. It is illustrated, for example, by the fact that the class-A office in region 1 has substantially fewer arrivals than the class-B office in region 2. Similarly, the class-B office in region 8 has fewer arrivals than the class-C office in region 6. As a result of this analysis, the simulation was designed to determine the mean number of arrivals on a given day from a knowledge of the history of the particular office and from the day of the week. The number of arrivals was assumed to be normally distributed around this mean. It also was decided to vary the variance of this distribution somewhat in proportion to the mean. A random number generator was used to generate the exact number of arrivals for each office on each day.

The second analysis was designed to determine the pattern of arrivals within a day. The preliminary stages of this analysis showed that there are indeed busy and slow periods during the day, and that a single exponential function cannot be used to characterize the interarrival times (see Section 4.8). The characteristic shape of the density function proved to be two-peaked, or bimodal, as shown by the typical empirical function in Figure 14.1.

The next approach used was to attempt to fit a function of the form $f(x) = a_1 \sin x + a_2 \sin 2x + a_3 \sin 3x$ to each of the 44 densities. The function is linear in its parameters, and a standard library program was used to fit it to the observed data. Wolberg (1967, Chapter 7) discusses this and related functional forms. The intention of this analysis was to determine if the parameters could be related systematically to such things as office class, region, and day of the week. No statistically significant relationships were found. Therefore, it was concluded that the distribution of arrivals could best be treated empirically, using a single density function of the form shown in Figure 14.1 for all offices on all days of the week.

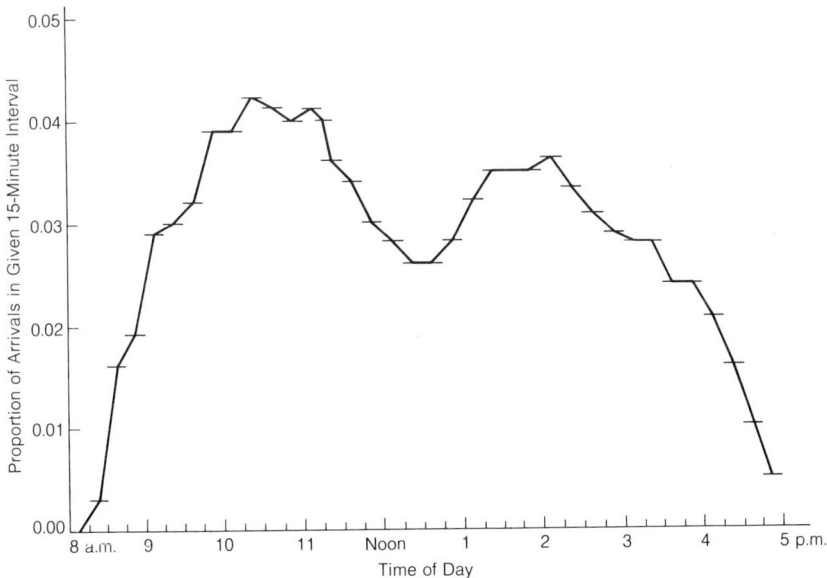

FIG. 14.1 Empirical Density Function for Arrivals at District Office

TABLE 14.1   Data on Volume of Arrivals at 44 District Offices by Day of Week

Class	Region	Number of Arrivals on Given Day					Total Arrivals for Week
		Thursday	Friday	Monday	Tuesday	Wednesday	
A	1	137	104	198	201	176	816
	2	210	148	238	249	236	1,081
	3	144	180	255	228	306	1,113
	4	153	136	289	310	355	1,243
	5	270	233	337	344	335	1,519
	6	214	188	270	306	308	1,286
	7	213	167	295	232	297	1,204
	8	188	130	258	237	243	1,056
	9	161	145	281	260	323	1,170
	10	233	174	378	296	278	1,359
	11	220	168	275	290	314	1,267
B	1	225	141	204	151	127	848
	2	313	195	285	223	196	1,212
	3	137	141	178	144	116	716
	4	103	91	138	105	138	575
	5	202	98	175	151	121	747
	6	204	132	159	120	116	731
	7	194	159	305	214	158	1,030
	8	129	81	156	85	81	532
	9	100	140	176	139	121	676
	10	175	157	235	176	165	908
	11	196	182	215	159	167	919
C	1	110	69	108	96	65	448
	2	100	92	177	96	73	538
	3	51	69	96	78	49	343
	4	88	81	182	126	105	582
	5	126	132	147	125	110	640
	6	189	123	144	110	101	667
	7	106	88	113	81	87	475
	8	46	82	75	73	74	350
	9	42	43	75	43	52	255
	10	63	67	111	85	60	386
	11	94	109	147	128	123	601
D	1	105	89	134	91	78	497
	2	47	40	53	38	43	221
	3	74	76	134	89	86	459
	4	59	53	70	56	29	267
	5	41	26	64	51	22	204
	6	81	100	125	100	97	503
	7	63	77	95	62	62	359
	8	45	46	66	46	53	256
	9	63	52	89	64	57	325
	10	52	73	101	75	83	384
	11	71	78	98	79	98	424

TABLE 14.1—*Continued*

Class	Region	Number of Arrivals on Given Day					Total Arrivals for Week
		Thursday	Friday	Monday	Tuesday	Wednesday	
TOTALS:							
A	—	2,143	1,773	3,074	2,953	3,171	13,114
B	—	1,978	1,517	2,226	1,667	1,506	8,894
C	—	1,015	955	1,375	1,041	899	5,285
D	—	701	710	1,029	751	708	3,899
—	1	577	403	644	539	446	2,609
—	2	670	475	753	606	548	3,052
—	3	406	466	663	539	557	2,631
—	4	403	361	679	597	627	2,667
—	5	639	489	723	671	588	3,110
—	6	688	543	698	636	622	3,187
—	7	576	491	808	589	604	3,068
—	8	408	339	555	441	451	2,194
—	9	366	380	621	506	553	2,426
—	10	523	471	825	632	586	3,037
—	11	581	537	735	656	702	3,211
All Offices		5,837	4,955	7,704	6,412	6,284	31,192

TABLE 14.2 Results of Analysis of Variance on Arrival Volumes at District Offices

Factor	Degrees of Freedom	Mean Square	Ratio to Residue
Day of week	4	26,560.10	102.8
Class of office	3	289,424.28	1,120.0
Region	10	5,170.12	20.0
Interactions:			
Day-Class	12	8,418.07	32.6
Day-Region	40	394.14	1.53
Region-Class	30	4,579.05	17.7
Residue	120	258.41	—

As a result of these two analyses, the generation of arrivals at district offices in the simulation was planned according to the following model. First, given the office and the day of the week, the total number of arrivals for that day is determined by using a normally distributed random number generator, with mean and variance related to the office and day. Second, the average proportion of arrivals within each 15-minute period during the day is given by the density shown in Figure 14.1. The program generates random fluctuations about this density, by assuming that these proportions are normally distributed with mean equal to the given proportion and variance approximately equal to one-fifth of the proportion. The factor one-fifth was estimated from the data obtained in the field study. Each proportion generated is rounded to the nearest thousandth. In other words, each proportion is of the form 0.xxx. The program generates proportions in this fashion only until 2:30 P.M. After that time, the proportions are determined in a different way that is designed to both to preserve the shape of the density and to ensure that the sum of all proportions over the whole day will equal 1.000.

The combination of the two steps described above (which yield the total number of arrivals for the day and the proportion of arrivals within each 15-minute period) determines the number of arrivals within each 15-minute period. Because some applications would require it, the preprocessor also permits the specification of the number and distribution of arrivals directly as inputs for a simulation run. The arrivals within each 15-minute period are assumed to be uniformly distributed over the period, an assumption that results in an adequate approximation to the empirical distribution. From another point of view, any bunching of the approximately one to twelve arrivals that occur within a 15-minute interval would not seriously affect queue lengths or office operations, and so is relatively unimportant to the simulation.

14.3 Simulating Interview Lengths: The *Gamma* Distribution

In the statistical analyses that were made to characterize the length of interviews, the sole concern was the distribution of this statistic. It was evident immediately that the distributions are different for different types of interviews. However, a single distribution type with modified parameters proved to be useful for the characterization of these distributions.

At this point, we digress briefly to define and discuss the *gamma* distribution, both because it proved applicable to the characterization of the interview times, and because it is of some importance in simulating discrete stochastic systems. A more detailed discussion of this distribution is given by Wadsworth and Bryan (1960, pp. 88–101).

The *gamma* density is given by

$$f(x) = \frac{x^{\alpha} e^{-x/\beta}}{\beta^{\alpha+1} \Gamma(\alpha+1)}, \qquad \text{for } 0 \le x < \beta, \tag{14.1}$$

where $\Gamma(\alpha + 1) = \alpha\Gamma(\alpha)$. If α is an integer, then $\Gamma(\alpha + 1) = \alpha!$ and $f(x)$ is integrable. If α is not an integer, then $\Gamma(\alpha + 1) = \int_0^\infty x^\alpha e^{-x} dx$. The parameters α and β take on values $\alpha > -1$ and $\beta > 0$. If $\alpha = 0$, then $f(x)$ is the exponential distribution. Furthermore, the *gamma* distribution with integer values for α can be related to the Poisson distribution. Finally, we note that the sum of independent variables that have a *gamma* distribution with parameters (α_1, β), (α_2, β), . . . , (α_k, β) has a *gamma* distribution with parameters $(\alpha_1 + \alpha_2 + . . . + \alpha_k + k - 1, \beta)$.

In particular, if $\alpha_1 = \alpha_2 = . . . = \alpha_k = 0$, then the sum of exponentially distributed variates has a *gamma* distribution. This is one reason for the widespread applicability of the *gamma* distribution in simulations.

With negative values of α, the density function has a shape sloping steeply downward to the right and then leveling off — what is sometimes called a "reverse-J" shape. As α changes from negative to positive, the shape of the density changes to a skewed unimodal density — that is, it has a central peak, with values sloping down steeply to the left and less steeply to the right. The degree of skewness decreases as α increases. β acts as a scale factor. Tables of the *gamma* function — that is, of $\Gamma(\alpha + 1)$ — and of the *gamma* density (called the incomplete *gamma*) are given by the National Bureau of Standards (1964).

Returning to the interview times, we note that the interview-times data obtained in the field study were analyzed to determine if a *gamma* density could be used to characterize these data. The *gamma* density was fitted by least squares (using the nonlinear least squares program given in Appendix B) to several sets of data on interview times, with the results summarized in Table 14.3. The procedure used to convert the observed frequency distributions to points on the density to be used in the least squares fitting calculations is described in the next section. Verification that we do indeed have points on a density is a more complicated task than it might appear to be.

The fits obtained by least squares were quite good, and a Kolmogorov-Smirnov test verified that there were no statistically significant differences between the empirical and the fitted functions. Therefore, the *gamma* density was used to characterize interview times. The parameters were estimated by least

TABLE 14.3 Results of Least Squares Fittings of *Gamma* Density to Interview Times

Claim Type	Sample Size	Least Squares Estimates of		Sum of Squares of Residuals
		α	β	
Retirement	1,490	3.21	6.37	0.713×10^{-5}
Death Benefit	960	2.76	4.41	0.174×10^{-4}
Disability	495	3.14	11.90	0.308×10^{-4}

squares for those interview types studied in the field study. For some interview types, the data were inadequate to fit a density. For these types and for new interview types, it was decided to set $\alpha = 3$ and $\beta = (average\ interview\ length)/(\alpha + 1)$, because the least squares estimates of α gave values of approximately 3 for most interview types and because, in general, $\beta = mean/(\alpha + 1)$. Estimates of average interview length were obtained either from small sets of data or from expert opinion.

This approach (in dealing with interview times for which sufficient data were not available) was checked by means of a sensitivity analysis. In this case, the simulation was run with interview times determined both from the least squares estimates of the parameters and from the estimates that would have been obtained if the $\alpha = 3$, $\beta = average/(\alpha + 1)$ procedure had been used. Runs were made with all of the parameters for interview times estimated by least squares, with none estimated by least squares, and with various alternatives involving some estimated by least squares and some by the short-cut procedure. The results indicated that within these limits for parameter values, the outputs were not sensitive to the way that the *gamma* parameters are estimated.

14.4 Converting Frequencies to Densities

In order to fit the *gamma* density to observed data by least squares, it was necessary to obtain points on the empirical density to be used in the least squares calculations. It turned out that this procedure was a little more complicated than anticipated. Because theoretical densities frequently must be fitted to observed data in developing simulations, the procedure is described in some detail here.

First, the observed frequency table was converted to an empirical distribution. Next, the empirical distribution was numerically differentiated at those values of the variate that were to be used to characterize the density. The result was a table of abscissas (the variate) and ordinates (the corresponding density). These results were then smoothed (a smoothing of the graph of the data by eye proved adequate). Next, the area under the smoothed density was calculated, using Simpson's rule. Finally, the density was adjusted in order to make the area under it equal to one. These adjusted pairs of variables were used in the least squares fitting procedure. Table 14.4 illustrates the calculations for a fit to data on disability interviews.

14.5 Development of the Preprocessor

The functions of the preprocessor are: to translate users' specifications to program inputs, to determine how many runs of which office types are required to satisfy the application, and to create inputs for both the district office simulation and the postprocessor. The input-creating facilities of the preprocessor are discussed in Chapter 15. Here we wish to concentrate on the developmental effort required to satisfy the first two objectives of the preprocessor.

The procedure to accomplish the first objective—translation of a user's specification of a problem into computer inputs—was established by a team that included an operations research analyst, a subject-matter specialist, and a human-factors specialist. The subject-matter specialist headed the team and worked fulltime on this problem over a period of about six months. He also called in other subject-matter specialists from time to time. The other two team members worked parttime on the problem, as their services were requested by the subject-matter specialist.

The approach used was (1) to master the input specifications for the simulation; (2) to construct several hypothetical applications and to arrive at precise input formats for them from a knowledge of the input specifications; (3) to have one team member explain one of the problems to a subject-matter specialist and to ask the subject-matter specialist then to describe the problem to another

TABLE 14.4 Calculations to Produce Empirical Density
Corresponding to Observed Frequencies

Interview Length (L) (minutes)	Number of Interviews Shorter than L	Cumulative Distribution, Proportion of Interviews Shorter than L	Estimated Density*	Smoothed Density	Scaled Density†
0	0	0.00000	——	——	——
7	4	0.00808	0.00303	0.00300	0.00294
12	15	0.03030	0.00687	0.00680	0.00666
17	38	0.07677	0.01051	0.01010	0.00989
22	67	0.13535	0.01232	0.01290	0.01263
27	99	0.20000	0.01475	0.01500	0.01468
32	140	0.28283	0.01818	0.01690	0.01654
37	189	0.38182	0.01778	0.01800	0.01762
42	228	0.46061	0.01677	0.01850	0.01811
47	272	0.54949	0.01939	0.01900	0.01860
52	324	0.65455	0.01859	0.01830	0.01791
57	364	0.73535	0.01434	0.01540	0.01507
62	395	0.79798	0.01131	0.01190	0.01165
67	420	0.84848	0.01030	0.01000	0.00979
72	446	0.90101	0.00889	0.00780	0.00763
77	464	0.93737	0.00586	0.00550	0.00538
82	475	0.95960	0.00323	0.00350	0.00343
87	480	0.96970	——	——	——

*Estimated density was obtained for each point by taking the cumulative distribution at the next point minus the cumulative distribution at the preceding point, divided by the difference in abscissas at these two points. This is a crude but adequate estimate of the slope of the tangent at a point, obtained by using the slope of the chord that connects the preceding and succeeding points.

†The estimate of the area under the smoothed points, obtained using Simpson's rule, was 0.99617. If the area under the density over the whole range is to be 1.000, the area under the density to $x=87$ should be about 0.975. A factor of 0.975/0.99617 or 0.97875 therefore was used to adjust the smoothed data.

team member, eventually determining from several of these exchanges the kinds of questions that would be required in order to elicit the appropriate responses; and (4) to prepare carefully formatted questionnaires with the aid of the human-factors specialist.

A pilot test of the preprocessor was made in the first real application of the simulation. This test led to revisions, and further revisions probably will be made from time to time. The ultimate objective is to permit the simulation to be used without the need for a staff of experts to make sure that the inputs are properly defined. At present, however, expert review still is required.

The problem-definition procedures used in the preprocessor are as much a part of the simulation as is the computer program. This simulation, therefore, is more than just a set of computer programs.

The determination of the particular runs needed to satisfy an application is based upon relations discovered through factor analysis (Harman 1967). The data used in the analysis were the results of the district office field study and the responses to a questionnaire sent to the 44 district offices in the study. This questionnaire was designed to obtain information about a wide variety of ex-ogenous variables. It included questions related to such things as parking, public transportation, population characteristics, and socio-economic characteristics of the area served by the district office. It also included questions about the educational level and experience of district office employees and about the poli-cies and procedures followed in the office. Figure 14.2 shows one page from the 16-page questionnaire.

Haskins (1968) describes the factor analysis in greater detail. The approach involved obtaining and relating two different sets of variables. First, those varia-bles that best measure the performance of the office network as a whole were listed. Then, all variables that are associated with outputs from a single run of a district office simulation and that might contribute to these overall network results were listed. A factor analysis was used to obtain a series of multiple linear relations between these two sets of variables. That is, the entire second set was partitioned into subsets, and each subset was viewed as accounting for one aspect of the network's performance. Finally, the usual regression techniques were used to relate each of the subsets in the second set to inputs.

This method of developing the preprocessor makes it possible to use the description of the application in order to design the set of runs. The descrip-tion is transformed into a set of inputs and also is reduced to a set of significant factor areas. The definition of the factor areas determines which offices are to be used in the run. These offices then are used to represent the performance of the whole district office network.

This part of the questionnaire is designed to provide a description of the environmental conditions of your office. Be precise, if possible, but if exact figures are unavailable, please give your best estimate. Demographic considerations: Indicate the sources used in answering questions 1-6 and the years the sources were published.

		Answer	Source	Year
1.	Service Area population			
	a. Population under age 19	_____	_____	_____
	b. Population 19-62	_____	_____	_____
	c. Population over age 62	_____	_____	_____
	d. Population within 20-mile radius of district office.	_____	_____	_____
2.	Total square miles of service area.	_____	_____	_____
3.	Percent of population that is literate.	_____	_____	_____
4.	Income per capita of service area.	_____	_____	_____
5.	Total number of self-employed farmers.	_____	_____	_____
6.	Total number of large employers (employing over 200 people) in service area.	_____	_____	_____
7.	Number of contact stations in service area.	_____		
8.	Description of Service Area. Check the 3 categories which best describe your DO's service area:			
	a. residential	_____		
	b. commercial	_____		
	c. light industry	_____		
	d. heavy industry	_____		
	e. agricultural	_____		

FIG. 14.2 Page from Questionnaire Sent to District Offices

14.6 Assigning Work to Claims Representatives

In order to simulate the operations of any facility, it is necessary to describe each aspect of those operations in a complete, unambiguous, and detailed way. Such an algorithmic description of an operation often results in a complicated and lengthy description of something that seemed at first to be a simple process. As an example, we present here the results of a study of the way in which work is assigned to a claims representative (CR) in a district office. Using the terminology of GPSS, we may say that a series of priorities applies if a transaction attempts to SEIZE a CR who is present for work in the office. For example, if the transaction attempting to SEIZE the CR is a claimant seeking an interview, the CR might interrupt either a telephone call or work on claim development in order to conduct the interview. In other offices, the CR might interrupt an interview in order to take a phone call—that is, the priorities of interviews and phone calls might be reversed. In general, the following series of priorities applies: (1) lunch; (2) interview; (3) telephone call; (4) development work. In some offices, the second and third priorities are reversed. This priority schedule applies only to a CR who is present for work in the office. Arrangements also must be made to assign to someone else the work that ordinarily would be given to a CR who is absent.

The treatment of the lunch period itself proved to be a complex matter. In the first place, a CR who is scheduled to begin his lunch period at 11:30 ordinarily is not available to be SEIZEd by a transaction at 11:25. This phenomenon was modeled by extending the lunch period to include the 5 minutes preceding its actual beginning. For another thing, the CR normally does not interrupt or terminate an interview because it is time for his lunch period. Instead, he completes the interview and then takes his lunch period, extending the period to make up for the time lost in the interview at the beginning of the period. This phenomenon was modeled by an appropriate change in the priority routine. Finally, in some offices, the claimant may be assigned to a specific CR. If this CR is out to lunch or taking a coffee break, the claimant is required to wait until he returns, although the claimant will be assigned to another CR if his own CR is not available for work in the office that day. These offices are called "wait-for-CR" offices and are modeled by an appropriately modified procedure for assigning the claimant to the CR.

The procedure used to assign a particular case to a particular CR varies from office to office. In some offices, the assignment is made from consideration of the last digit or two in the account number. In other offices, the first initial of the claimant's last name is used. In still other offices, work is assigned on a "first-available-CR" basis. Also, in some offices, CRs are grouped into clusters. Each cluster handles a particular set of account numbers or last initials, but within the cluster work is assigned on a first-available-CR basis.

It also must be noted that some visitors to the office require an interview that is not related to a claim. For example, they may be seeking information more extensive than that the receptionist can provide. Such interviews are assigned to service representatives (SR) with similar sets of priorities and special modeling procedures.

Let us return to the problem of assigning an interview when the CR who normally would handle the claimant is not available. The flowchart of Figure 14.3 outlines the procedure to be followed. Figure 14.4 shows the portion of the GPSS program that implements the part of the procedure related to handling

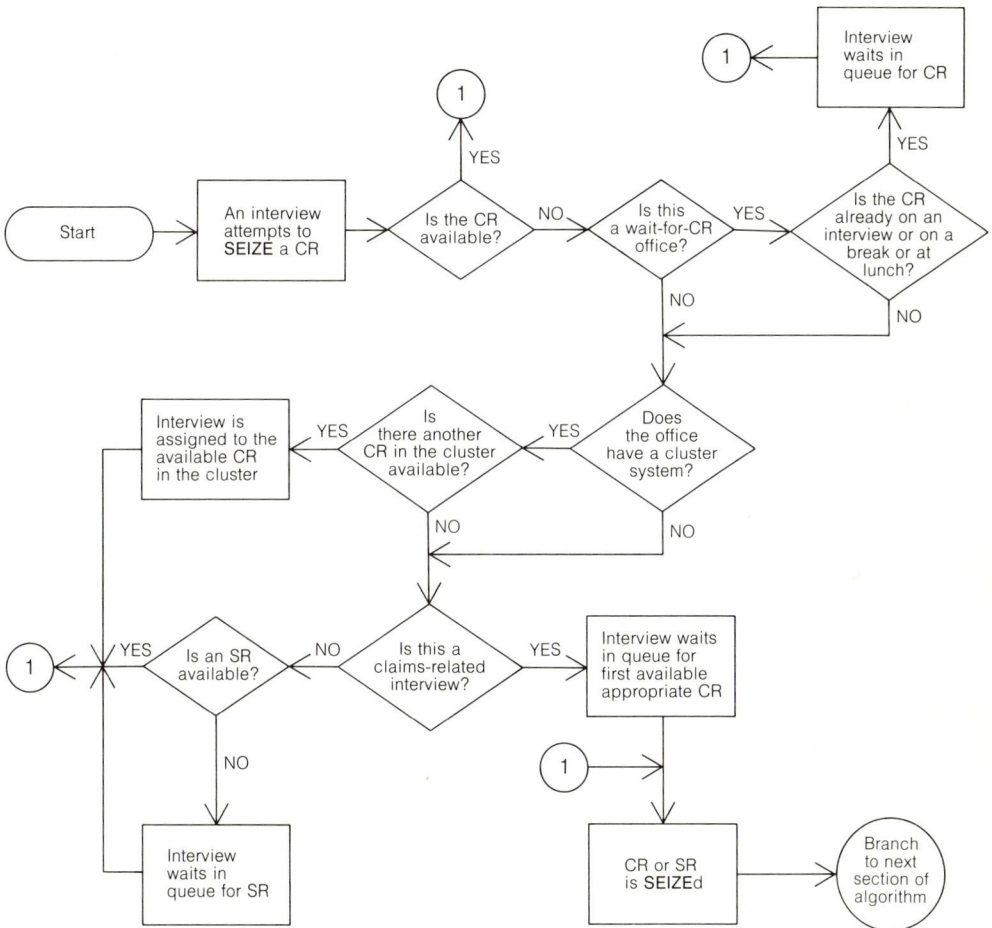

FIG. 14.3   Flowchart of Interview-Assignment Procedure in a District Office

```
*LOC    OPERATION A,B,C,D,E,F,G  COMMENTS
*                            * ROTATION WITHIN CLUSTER SYSTEM
 CLSTR TEST L    P10,17,NONCL   IF THIS IS A CLAIM, ANY CR WILL TAKE,
       ASSIGN    3,V31          BEGINNING WITH 1ST CR IN UNIT
       TRANSFER  ,CKNXT         USING REGULER ROTATION ROUTINE
 NONCL TEST L    P10,30,SRCAS IF THIS IS CR NON-CLAIM
       ASSIGN    5,XH13         ASSIGN NO OF CRS FOR LOOP
       ASSIGN    3,V31          ASSIGN FIRST UNIT CR NUMBER
 CRROT TRANSFER  SBR,NOTIN,7    CHECK FOR FREE CLUSTER CR
       GATE N1   P3,*+2         IF A CLUSTER CR IS FREE
       GATE LS   P3,INTVW       UTILIZE
       TEST E    P5,0,CRROT     IF NO CLUSTER CR IS FREE,
       TEST NE   XH14,0,ANYCR   IS THERE A CLUSTER SR
       ASSIGN    2,4
       ASSIGN    5,XH14         ASSIGN NO OF SRS FOR LOOP
       ASSIGN    3,V30          ASSIGN 1ST UNIT SR NUMBER
 SRROT TRANSFER  SBR,NOTIN,7    CHECK FOR FREE CLUSTER SR
       GATE NI   P3,*+2         IF A CLUSTER SR IS FREE,
       GATE LS   P3,INTVW       UTILIZE
       TEST E    P5,0,SRROT     IF NO CLUSTER SR IS FREE
       GATE SNF  5,CWAIT        IF NO CR FREE,WAIT - ELSE
 ANYCR ASSIGN    2,5            GIVE INTERVIEW
       ASSIGN    5,XH10         TO ANY
       ASSIGN    3,V13          FREE CR
       TRANSFER  ,CKNXT
 SRCAS TEST NE   XH14,0,NOSRS   IF UNIT HAS ANY SR
       ASSIGN    5,XH14         ASSIGN NUMBER OF SRS FOR LOOP
       ASSIGN    3,V30          ASSIGN 1ST SR IN CLUSTER
 SRCHK TRANSFER  SBR,NOTIN,7    CHECK FOR FREE SR
       GATE NI   P3,*+2         IF CLUSTER SR IS FREE,
       GATE LS   P3,INTVW       UTILIZE
       TEST E    P5,0,SRCHK     IF NO SR AVAILABLE IN UNIT,
 NOSRS ASSIGN    2,5            CHECK FOR FREE CLUSTER CR
       ASSIGN    5,XH13
       ASSIGN    3,V31
 CRCHK TRANSFER  SBR,NOTIN,7
       GATE NI   P3,*+2
       GATE LS   P3,INTVW
       TEST E    P5,0,CRCHK     IF NO ONE IN CLUSTER AVAILABLE,
       GATE SNF  4,SWAIT        IF NO SR FREE, WAIT - ELSE
       ASSIGN    2,4            GIVE INTERVIEW TO ANY FREE SR
       ASSIGN    5,XH8
       ASSIGN    3,V12
       TRANSFER  ,CKNXT
```

FIG. 14.4 GPSS Code Relating to Handling of Clusters in Assigning Interview to CRs and SRs

CR clusters. This small example may make it clear why the entire GPSS program to simulate the activity of a district office requires more than 1,300 GPSS blocks.

In addition to the tediously complex code that must be developed to mimic these various procedures, it also is necessary to associate a long list of descriptions with each district office, in order to provide information needed within the code. Differences among offices in details of priorities, procedures, and policies must be available to the program during a run in order to make appropriate choices within the model. These differences are recorded in parameters associated with each office in a master file of offices. This master file is used both by the preprocessor and by the district office simulation. It may be that a sensitivity analysis would reveal that some of these details are insignificant and could be eliminated from the model without seriously changing the results of runs. However, many of management's questions are related to these different district office policies. Therefore, this level of detail in the model is necessary to make it possible to satisfy applications related to such questions.

15

The District Office Network Simulation

15.1 INTRODUCTION   This chapter provides an overview of the simulation of the social security district office network and provides some glimpses of details of its structure and use. The following sections give an outline of the simulation, describe the use of the simulation, describe the three parts of the simulation (the preprocessor, the district office simulation, and the postprocessor), and give some examples of the simulation GPSS code (both to illustrate GPSS programming and to provide a second detailed view of this component of the simulation). The chapter ends with a discussion of the debugging of the simulation, a discussion of a few of the validity checks that were made, and a discussion of an application of the simulation.

15.2 Overall Structure

The district office network simulation consists of the following major subelements: (1) a set of questionnaires (this is the only part of the simulation that is neither a program nor a set of data stored in computer-compatible form); (2) extensive demographic data; (3) extensive data on the structure of a variety of district offices; (4) a COBOL program (the preprocessor) that accepts as input data from the questionnaires and demographic and district office data, and that produces output to be used in the GPSS program and postprocessor; (5) the GPSS program that simulates district office operations, accepts the preprocessor output as its input, and produces output for the postprocessor; and (6) a COBOL program (the postprocessor) that accepts the output of the GPSS and preprocessor programs as its input, and produces output both on tape and on the printer.

The questionnaires are discussed briefly in Section 14.5, and little more will be said about them here. They are intended to elicit from the user a description of his intended application—a description that can be translated into an appropriate set of runs for the simulation. There are several different sections to the questionnaire. The first section introduces the user to the questionnaire (Figure 15.1). The second section contains a flowchart that helps to guide the user through the task of filling out the questionnaire (Figure 15.2 shows the first page of this flowchart). Then follows a table of contents for the questionnaires and the questionnaires themselves. One page from the first questionnaire, relating to work experience of the DO staff, is shown in Figure 15.3. Each questionnaire contains several pages. It is expected that new questionnaires will need to be developed and old ones will need to be modified substantially as the simulation is used.

Some of the demographic data stored in the simulation are related directly to the district offices; for example, there are various data concerning the socioeconomic characteristics of the population served by each office. The information on the structure of each office also is filed by district office. All of this information is stored in a 480-character (six 80-character card images) data record that is maintained for each district office. The structure of this record is described in Figure 15.4. Note that the first two cards of the record relate to district office policies; the third card relates to demographic characteristics; and the final three cards relate to district office staffing characteristics.

Arrangements also have been made to obtain demographic information from the Bureau of the Census and from the Office of the Actuary of the Social Security Administration, and to incorporate these data into the simulation. The demographic data appearing in the third card of the district office record were obtained from reports made by the district office itself. These data periodically must be supplemented and updated.

The remaining parts of the simulation are discussed in the following sections.

Introduction

The D/O network simulator is comprised of many variables, any of which could be the subject of simulation. However, to a user of the simulator, some variables will be undoubtedly more important than others, in fact, some may be of no importance whatsoever. The variables selected in any simulation will, of necessity, be a function of the area or areas of D/O operations in which the user is interested. For this reason, rather than include all variables in a single questionnaire; variables have been grouped by category into eleven questionnaires.

The enclosed package consists of a flow chart, a table of contents of each questionnaire and, of course, the questionnaires themselves. To locate the questionnaire or questionnaires that contain the variables to be simulated, we suggest that you first study the flow chart. If the questionnaire or questionnaires containing the relevant variables can be identified, go directly to them and complete the items. If identification of the questionnaire or questionnaires cannot be accomplished from the flow chart, study the table of contents of D/O network simulator questionnaires. This is more detailed than the flow chart and should enable you to find the desired variables.

FIG. 15.1 Introduction to the Questionnaire Used in the Preprocessor

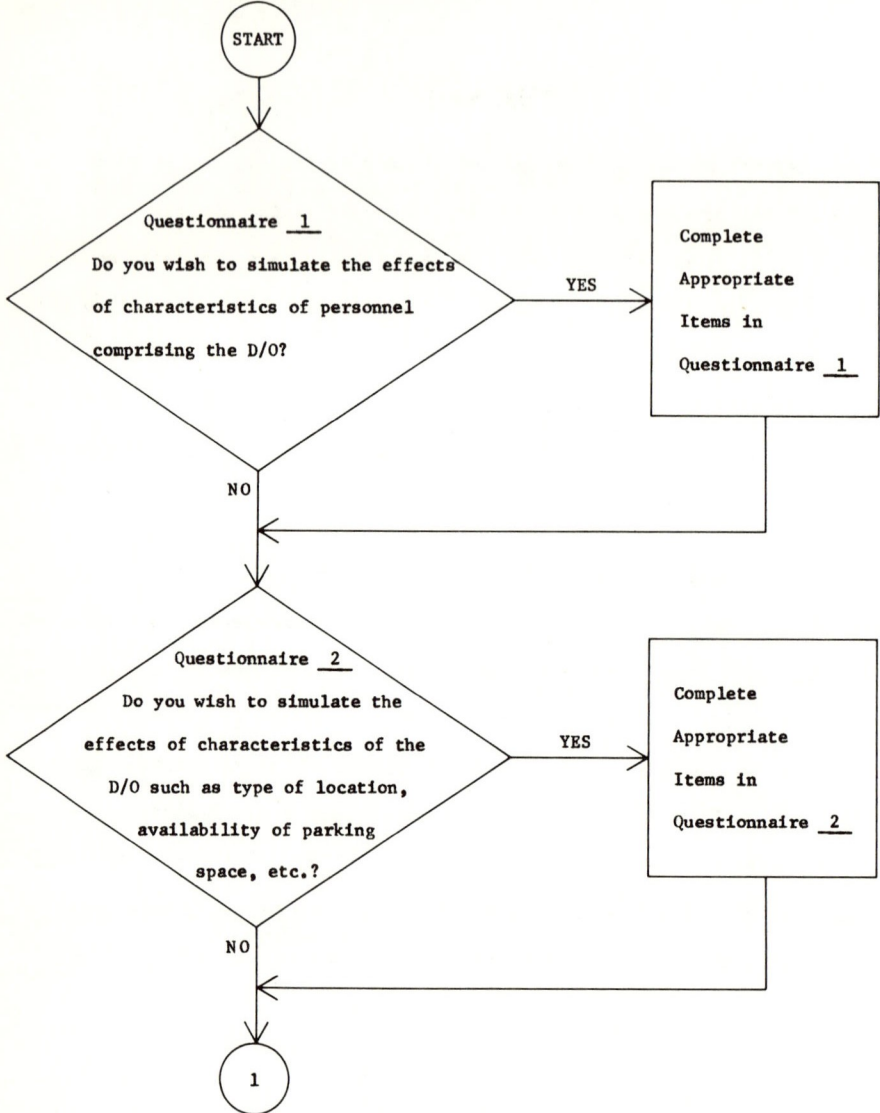

FLOW CHART OF D/O NETWORK SIMULATOR QUESTIONNAIRES

START

Questionnaire 1
Do you wish to simulate the effects of characteristics of personnel comprising the D/O?

YES

Complete Appropriate Items in Questionnaire 1

NO

Questionnaire 2
Do you wish to simulate the effects of characteristics of the D/O such as type of location, availability of parking space, etc.?

YES

Complete Appropriate Items in Questionnaire 2

NO

1

FIG. 15.2 First Page of the Flowchart in the Preprocessor Questionnaire

District office personnel characteristics. This refers to the average length of service in district offices for each personnel type listed. Include all DO experience but no other SSA or Federal service. To compute the average length of service, divide the number of assigned employees for a position into their total number of years of DO experience. For example, if an office has three FR's with a total of 25 years DO experience, the average length of service for this position would be 8.3 years.

1. Average length of DO service of employees in years:

    a. Manager   _____

    b. Assistant Manager   _____

    c. Staff Assistant   _____

    d. Operations Supervisors   _____

    e. Field Representative   _____

    f. Claims Representative   _____

    g. Service Representatives _____

    h. Claims Development Clericals _____

    i. Data Review Technicians _____

    j. Receptionists   _____

    k. Account Number Clerk and other clericals _____

    l. Administrative Clerk   _____

FIG. 15.3 First Page of Questionnaire 1 of the Preprocessor

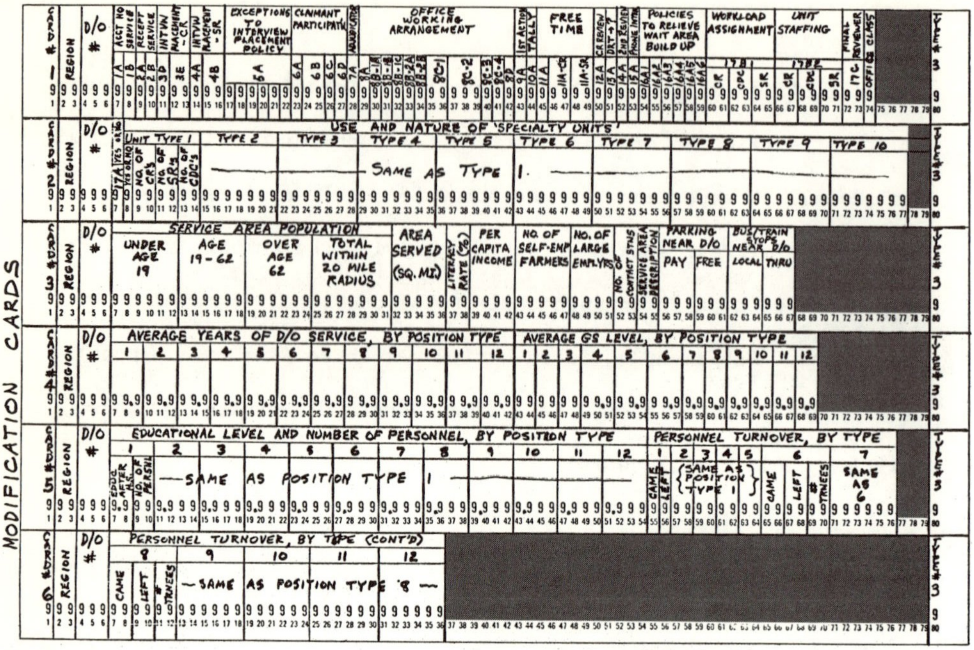

380   A Case Study

FIG. 15.4   Layout of the Data Record Associated with Each District Office

15.3 How the Simulation is Used

Figure 15.5 is a schematic description of the way that the simulation is carried out. The user first completes a series of questionnaires and other forms, which lead him—step by step—to a detailed specification of the objectives of his particular request for use of the simulation. These forms result in a complete specification of the input parameters for this run. In the early stages of development of the simulation, these forms are reviewed by persons familiar with the simulation, in order to be sure that the specifications are complete and consistent. The forms will be modified and improved on the basis of experience. As more people become familiar with their use, it will be possible to pass them more directly to an input device with a minimum of review.

The runs of the simulation are not very different from any other computer run requiring the use of auxiliary storage facilities.

The preprocessor uses input from the demographic tape and from the input deck. The major functions of the preprocessor are (1) to transmit information from the input deck that determines how many runs of which kinds of district offices are required; (2) to transform input data into the format and values needed

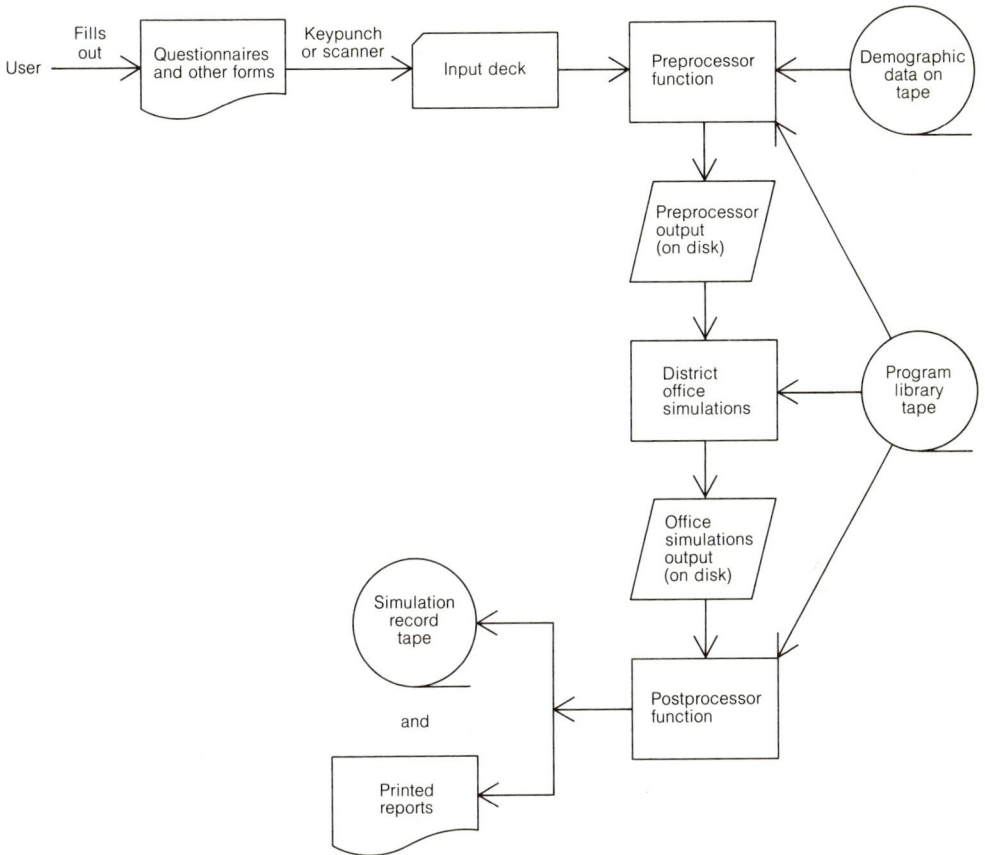

FIG. 15.5   Schematic Description of the Use of the District Office Network Simulation

in the GPSS program; (3) to determine the kinds of output needed; and (4) to prepare records containing the definition of the problem and its input characteristics (these records are incorporated into the printed report generated by the postprocessor).

District office simulations then are carried out as required by repeatedly calling up a series of GPSS programs that were modified in accordance with blocks produced by the preprocessor and producing output to be passed to the postprocessor.

The office simulations file serves as input to the postprocessor program. The postprocessor produces the bulk of the printed report, appropriately organized and formatted. In addition, it writes a complete history of the purposes and results of this run onto the simulation-record tape, which is made in order to have a comprehensive record of all runs. It serves both as backup in case some data for previous runs are lost or destroyed, and as a basis for periodic validity checks. These validity checks are discussed in Section 15.8.

15.4 The Preprocessor

The preprocessor is the biggest component of the simulation; it contains 1,450 COBOL statements. Its size is related to the enormous number of housekeeping activities that must be initiated and developed in order to carry out the simulation successfully. In addition to accepting specifications for the simulation run (from the questionnaires), the preprocessor also (1) formats and prints descriptive information on the objectives of the run and the input specifications, information that will become a part of the final report; (2) notes the appropriate representative district offices specified in the input deck and determines which features these offices should have; (3) modifies input parameters so that they can be used in the GPSS run; (4) inserts GPSS blocks into the GPSS program as necessary (in most cases, this involves changing parameters by replacing blocks; modification of the logic of the GPSS program rarely is necessary); and (5) controls the modification of a succession of GPSS runs.

Figure 15.6 is a general flowchart of the preprocessor functions. In this section we provide a detailed description of parts of the aspect of the preprocessor that carries out function 3 above: the modification of the parameters.

The detailed aspect of the preprocessor that we consider here is the calculation of the claims workload. This calculation is done in several steps (each of which is described in detail in a later paragraph): (1) the total workload for one week is calculated, using a linear combination of demographic and office characteristics; (2a) the proportions of claims of different types are obtained from the district office characteristics file if the office is not to be modified in this respect; or (2b) if the office is to be modified in this respect, the proportions are estimated from a linear combination of demographic data; (3) the weekly totals are reduced to daily totals; (4) the daily totals are further subdivided into 15-minute subtotals for the whole day; and (5) this information is converted into a GPSS function, is stored, and is passed to the GPSS program.

The weekly total is calculated by the expression,

$$Weekly\text{-}Claims = 81 + 0.0158(Population\text{-}1) + 0.0239(Population\text{-}2)$$
$$+ 0.0739(Population\text{-}3) - 0.903(Literacy\text{-}Rate)$$
$$- 0.0014(Farmowners) + 0.7114(Local\text{-}Drpoff).$$

To this result then is added a normally distributed random number, with mean of zero and standard deviation of 20.76. The variables used in the function are defined as follows: *Population-1* = number of people in service area under age 19; *Population-2* = number of people in service area between ages 19 and 62;

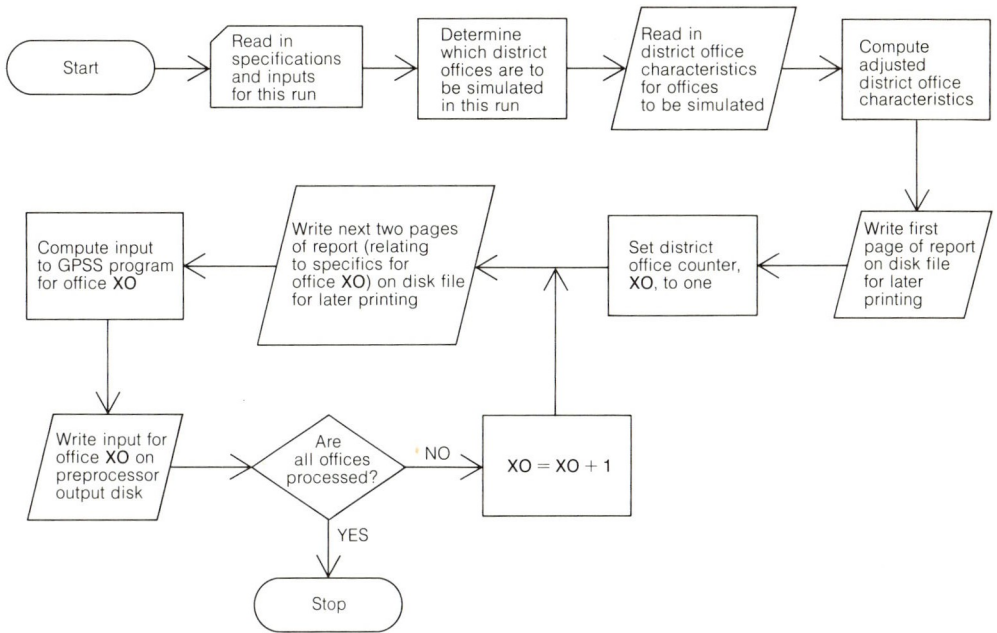

FIG. 15.6　General Flowchart of the Preprocessor Function

Population-3 = number of people in service area over age 62; *Literacy-Rate* = literacy rate (as a percentage) in service area; *Farmowners* = number of self-employed farmers in the service area; and *Local-Drpoff* = number of local bus or train stops near the district office.

The proportions of claims of each type then are obtained, either directly from a table for the particular district office, or by using functions similar to the one above (for those offices whose workload is being modified as part of the application). For example, the number of C1-type claims in a week can be calculated from

$$\textit{Weekly-C1} = 5.1 + 0.0073(\textit{Population-1}) + 0.0061(\textit{Population-2})$$
$$- 0.0007(\textit{Farmowners}) + 0.1007(\textit{Large-Emplrs}).$$

In this case, a normally distributed number with mean of zero and standard deviation of 12.96 is added to the result. The variable *Large-Emplrs* is defined as the number of large employers in the service area; a large employer is one that has 200 or more employees in his enterprise. These estimates for each type are totaled and the proportion of each type then is calculated.

Finally, the pattern of arrivals within a week and the pattern within a day are used to reduce these totals to the number of arrivals in each 15-minute interval. These patterns are described in Chapter 13. This breakdown into intervals is passed to the GPSS program in the form of a GPSS function.

15.5 The GPSS District Office Simulation

The GPSS program that simulates district office operations contains about 1,350 blocks. More than 100 of these blocks are function definitions, and more than 500 others are definitions of variables, savevalues, and matrix savevalues. The program also has a long series of SAVEVALUE, MSAVEVALUE, and ASSIGN blocks near the end. These blocks serve to accumulate and process crucial data. In addition, comments cards have been used very freely to provide headings for various subsections of the program, and to give brief English-language definitions of the parameters and variables that are used.

The earliest operational parts of the program deal with the processing of telephone calls and the non-claims workload. The claims workload is handled in different ways for different offices (see Section 14.6). The GPSS statements in Figure 14.4 are used to implement the choice of a CR or SR in an office that uses a cluster system. Several other segments of the GPSS program are used to assign claims in offices that use other systems. However, every office in the simulation uses the same sequence of instructions to obtain work for an employee after completion of an interview or of any other activity. This segment of the GPSS program is listed in Figure 15.7. In a sense, this segment represents the other side of the coin. The problem discussed in Section 14.6 was how to find a CR to handle a claimant that needs servicing — in other words, how to decide what a claimant is to do next. The problem handled by the program segment of Figure 15.7 is to decide what an office staff member should do next after completing a particular task.

The GETWK subroutine checks the queue of work waiting for the employee whose identification number is given in P3, in order to determine what this employee is to do next. The work-waiting queue is stored in a chain and includes all of the work that is waiting for employee P3. Included in this queue is a special transaction, tagged with an 8888 in P5, which is used to indicate that a break is due to the employee. This transaction is linked, on a LIFO basis, to the chain at the appropriate time for the break. In other words, once the time for the break arrives, the employee will take the break as soon as he finishes the task at hand. Blocks 249 and 250 check to determine if a break is due next and, if it is, transfer is made to GOTWK and out of the subroutine. Block 251 checks on whether P3 is less than 6. If P3 is less than 6, the employee is an account number clerk and work is assigned in block 252. If $P3 \geq 6$, there is a branch to block 254, which is used to check on whether the employee is a receptionist. Receptionists are numbered 6 to 10, inclusively. By means of this series of TEST, UNLINK, and TRANSFER blocks, the type of employee is identified,

```
BLK.
NO.  *LOC    OPERATION A,B,C,D,E,F,G COMMENTS
     *                              *SUBROUTINE TO OBTAIN WORK AFTER
     *                               INTERVIEW BY CR OR SR
     *                               OR ON COMPLETION OF ANY ACTIVITY
249  GETWK   UNLINK    P3,GOOUT,1,5,8888,*+2 CHECK IF LUNCH OR BREAK TIME
250          TRANSFER  ,GOTWK
251          TEST L    P3,6,*+3       IF A/N CLERK SEEKING WORK,
252          UNLINK    3,ANSVC,1      GIVE HER SOME
253          TRANSFER  ,GOTWK
254          TEST L    P3,11,*+3      IF RECEPTIONIST SEEKING WORK,
255          UNLINK    10,GREET,1     GIVE HER SOME
256          TRANSFER  ,GOTWK
257          TEST G    P3,20,CKTEL    IF DRT, WILL RETURN CALL
258          TEST L    P3,91,CKTEL    CDC WILL RETURN PHONE CALL
259          TEST L    P3,41,GETCR    DETERMINE IF SR NEEDING WORK
260          UNLINK    40,INTVW,1,3,,*+2  ANY INTERVIEW FOR THIS CR
261          TRANSFER  ,GOTWK
262          TEST NE   XH23,1,CKTEL   IF OK TO TAKE ANY SR INTERVIEW
263          SAVEVALUE 43,P3,H        STORE THIS SERVERS NUMBER AND
264          UNLINK    40,TKANY,1,,,CKTEL      GET NEXT IN LINE
265          TRANSFER  ,GOTWK
266  GETCR   UNLINK    90,INTVW,1,3,,*+2  ANY INTERVIEW FOR THIS CR
267          TRANSFER  ,GOTWK
268          TEST NE   XH23,1,CKTEL   IF OK TO TAKE ANY INTERVIEW
269          SAVEVALUE 43,P3,H        STORE THIS SERVERS NUMBER AND
270          UNLINK    90,TKANY,1,,,*+2   GET NEXT CR INTERVIEW
271          TRANSFER  ,GOTWK
272          UNLINK    40,TKANY,1,,,CKTEL   IF NO CR INTVW , TAKE SR INTVW
273          TRANSFER  ,GOTWK
274  CKTEL   UNLINK    P3,ANSWR,1,5,7777,*+2 CHECK FOR DEFERRED PHONE CALL
275          TRANSFER  ,GOTWK
276          TEST L    P3,21,*+3      IF DRT SEEKING WORK,
277          UNLINK    20,DRT,1       GIVE HER SOME
278          TRANSFER  ,GOTWK
279          GATE NU   P3,GOTWK
280          UNLINK    P3,DEVEL,1,,,GOTWK
281  GOTWK   TRANSFER  P,7,1          RETURN TO PARENT ROUTINE
282  TKANY   ASSIGN    3,XH43         ASSIGN FREE SERVER NUMBER
283          TRANSFER  ,INTVW         GO TO HAVE INTERVIEW
```

FIG. 15.7 GPSS Program Segment That Finds New Work for Employee after
Completion of a Task

and appropriate work is assigned. Most of the remainder of the subroutine is
devoted to the details of this function.

The middle of the GPSS program is devoted to processing the office workload and to the housekeeping associated with this processing. Figures 14.4
and 15.7 are examples of this middle aspect of the program. The concluding
portions of the program are devoted to (1) accumulating results (through the
long series of SAVEVALUE and ASSIGN blocks that have already been mentioned); (2) dealing with exceptional situations, such as the assignment of annual-
leave status, the processing of work from other offices, and the assignment of
employees to training activities; and (3) printing output via the PRINT block.
Figure 15.8 is a listing of a portion of the segment of the GPSS program that is
used to allow for training time. Note the extensive use of the TEST block, first
to determine if it is a work period and then to determine if training is permitted
and what the duration of the training should be.

```
BLK.
NO.    *LOC    OPERATION  A,B,C,D,E,F,G COMMENTS
       *                         *ROUTINE TO ALLOW TRAINING TIME
846    TRNG    TEST L     V18,6,OCUPY IF WEEKEND,PREMPT TWO DAYS
847            TEST NE    V17,XH71,ENDRT IS IT CLOSING TIME
848            TEST GE    V18,XH33,TERM TEST IF TRAINING PERMITTED TODAY
849            TEST NE    P2,4,SRTNG    ASSIGN LENGTH OF TRAINING SESSIONS
850            TEST NE    P2,5,CRTNG
851            ASSIGN     4,79
852            TRANSFER   ,TRAIN
853    SRTNG   ASSIGN     4,80
854            TRANSFER   ,TRAIN
855    CRTNG   ASSIGN     4,81
856    TRAIN   ASSIGN     5,XH*4
```

FIG. 15.8   GPSS Program Segment That Assigns Training Time for Employees

15.6 The Postprocessor

The postprocessor is the smallest of the three major parts of the simulation; it contains about 500 COBOL statements. Its main function is to structure and to fill in printed reports and to prepare the simulation record tape. The printed reports contain two major sections: (1) detailed statistics on the performance of each office that is simulated; and (2) network-wide summaries.

The office statistics always contain the following information: (1) workload (number of people walking in, number of telephone calls, and number of transactions entering the office by mail or from field activities); (2) processing time (for each claim type or for non-claims items, the average processing time in days); (3) queue lengths (for each queue, the average queue length as calculated by GPSS); (4) waiting times (average time elapsed, for claimants who are interviewed, between the time they enter the office and the time the interview begins); (5) reneges (total number of arrivals that left the office before being served); (6) initial load statistics (the total number of claims and non-claims items that are in the office at the beginning of the simulation—in other words, the startup workload); and (7) processed statistics (the number of claims that were completed during the simulation—with two subtotals, one representing the number of claims completed that were part of the startup workload, and the other representing the number of claims completed that entered the office during the simulation).

More detailed information, such as frequency tables, is produced for those statistics that are of special importance to the particular application. The input from the preprocessor includes the specifications for these special outputs.

Figure 15.9 is a general flowchart of the functions of the postprocessor. Offices are processed one at a time. This sequential processing is used, even though some activities—such as the selection of variables and the specification of the level of detail to be included in the office reports—are the same from one office to the next. If it also is necessary to combine results into network or sub-

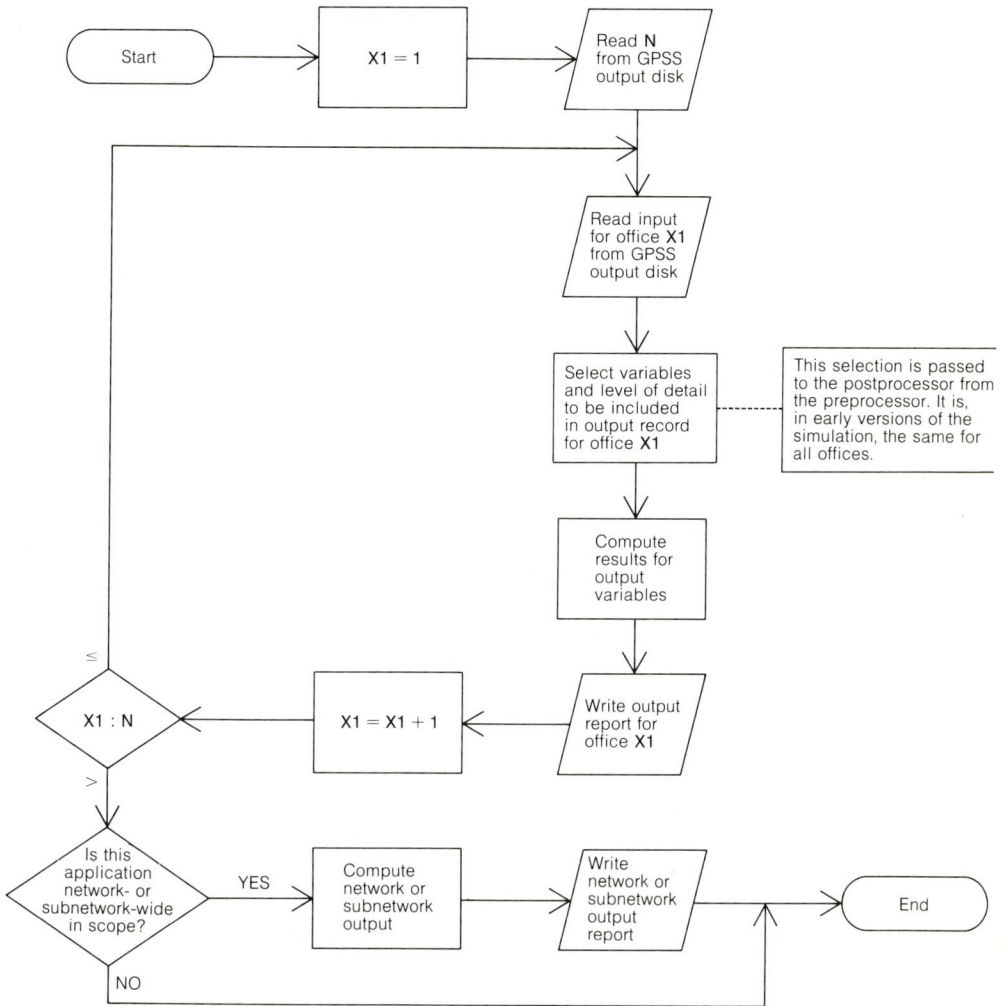

FIG. 15.9 General Flowchart of Postprocessor Functions

network summaries, then a whole new series of calculations is made. Nearly all of the network- or subnetwork-wide statistics are obtained from linear combinations of results in individual offices. The coefficients for these linear relations were determined in the preprocessor run and were passed to the postprocessor.

15.7 Debugging the Simulation

Each of the three subelements of the simulation was debugged separately. When these had been debugged successfully, the whole simulation was put together and checked as a unit.

Debugging was accomplished by constructing sets of test inputs and running them through the subelement. In debugging the questionnaires, operational personnel were asked to fill out the forms and then were closely monitored in their formulation and entering of responses to the questions. In debugging the computer programs, test inputs were fed directly into the program, and intermediate and final outputs from these test runs were monitored. In some cases, exact values for the output were known; in other cases, it was necessary to conclude that the programs were correctly programmed if the data made sense. As is usually the case in debugging, a great deal of additional output was obtained in these runs to check various details and options of the model. Except for the debugging of the questionnaires, the test data used were entirely hypothetical. The test data were chosen in order to be sure that each branch of the program was executed, that erroneous data could be screened out of the models, and that representative data would be processed correctly.

Debugging is not a check on the validity of the model. It merely checks on whether the programs correctly implement the model. It does not evaluate the extent to which the programs satisfy the design objectives.

15.8 Validity

Evaluation of the extent to which the programs satisfy the design objectives is made in the checks of the validity of the simulation. Section 2.9 discusses the methods of checking validity. All three of the channels diagrammed in Figure 2.3 were applied to the district office simulation.

The field study was a major source of performance data against which the district office simulation was checked. In order to help ensure validity of the field study results, some of the data obtained in the field study were compared with corresponding data from the district office weekly reports. For example, the weekly reports include data on incoming workloads and numbers of items processed. These data, as well as a great number of other and more detailed data, were obtained in the field study. A series of analyses of variance was made on each of the incoming-workload and processing statistics. The factors in the analysis were (1) week, and (2) whether or not the office was included in the study.

With respect to the second factor, each of the 44 offices in the study was matched with a similar office that was not included in the study. Data were obtained for both offices, so that there were two levels for this second factor.

There were five levels for the first factor: the two weeks preceding the study, the study week, and the two weeks following the study. Table 15.1 describes this two-way layout.

The first results of the analyses indicated that week was a significant factor. After some review, it was discovered that some of the 5-week periods included holidays and others did not. After correcting the data for the presence of holidays, another analysis was made and no significant effects of week were found. The first analysis also revealed significant differences in the definitions of claims workloads between the weekly report and the reports of the study team and headquarters personnel. After redefining these statistics and correcting for the effects of holidays, there were no further significant effects due to this factor. In many analyses, there was a significant difference between the study office and the corresponding control office. In each case, this difference proved to be consistent and to reflect true differences between conditions at the two offices. This approach to building validity combines the first and second channels of Figure 2.3, because historical data were used to validate field-study results before these results were incorporated into the program.

A second check to ensure validity involved expert review of results obtained in subelement debugging, before the subelements were assembled into the complete simulation. In a sense, this check combines the first and third channels. The subject-matter experts were given the input for the debugging runs and were asked to predict the outputs that could be expected. The control group then resolved any differences between the predictions and the actual results, deciding either (1) that the programs needed further debugging, (2) that the model was invalid, or (3) that the subject-matter experts could not predict results efficiently. Some — but only a very few — modifications in the subelements were made as a result of this review. A similar check was made by asking subject-matter experts to predict results for and to review results of the first few applications of the simulation.

TABLE 15.1   Data Sources for Analyses of Variance Comparing Data from Weekly Reports to Data from the Field Study

| Week | Data Source (WR = Weekly Report; FS = Field Study) | |
	Study Office	Control Office
−2	WR	WR
−1	WR	WR
Study	FS	WR
+1	WR	WR
+2	WR	WR

The simulation record tape is one of the principal devices that is used to ensure validity. This is done in many different ways; the major one is periodically to analyze results obtained for what might be called "the standard district office network." In most applications with network- or subnetwork-wide objectives, a series of runs is made of the present system, in order to compare these results with the modified or hypothetical system. Because the district office network is reasonably stable, runs with the current system made at different times can be expected to give similar results, or can be expected to vary in a prescribed way that can be predicted from a knowledge of the ways that the system is supposed to have changed since the last application of the simulation. After each application of the simulation, a calibration analysis is made to determine if there has been any significant drift in the standard district office network. This analysis uses regression techniques, in which the independent variable is time in most cases. Clearly, the calibration improves as additional reference data are added— in other words, as more simulations are made. These data for the standard network also are systematically analyzed after each few runs, using either regression techniques with several independent variables to detect spurious relationships, or analyses of variance to deal with factors that are not quantitative.

The district office weekly reports also are compared with results for the standard network, in order to see if the real system has drifted in directions not anticipated by the group responsible for maintaining the validity of the simulation.

The description above implies the existence of a permanent facility with responsibility for validity, and this indeed is the case. This facility includes a statistician with very nearly fulltime responsibility for establishing and maintaining validity of the simulation. He is assisted by subject-matter specialists and by computer programmers, who are on call as the need arises. These people make up the post-implementation control group.

15.9 An Application

One of the first applications of the district-office-network simulation was used to assist in the selection of branch-office locations in the states of Georgia and Virginia. This application was made in the fall and winter of 1971. The objective was to determine the consequences of opening new branch offices at proposed sites in each of these two states. Management personnel selected the sites, and simulations were run involving various combinations of these sites, in order to help determine where the branches might best be located.

It was assumed that no existing district offices would be replaced, and that personnel would be transferred to the new branches from existing offices. It also was assumed that all localities in these states that now obtain services from offices in neighboring states will continue to do so. (For example, the northwestern counties of Georgia use the office in Chattanooga, Tennessee, and the counties on the eastern shore of the Chesapeake Bay in Virginia use the office in Salisbury, Maryland.) Subsets of district offices were defined for each state so as to include all existing offices plus proposed branches. Subsets of service areas were selected so as to omit counties serviced by out-of-state offices.

The effect of additional branch offices was measured by using all the standard statistics on workloads, processing times, queue lengths, and so forth. However, in this instance it was decided to develop a special measure of effectiveness to give a quantitative index of the service to the public that results from a particular geographical distribution of offices. Because the development of this index may well prove one of the major benefits to the administration from this particular application, the index is defined here. (It is not unusual for the mere use of a simulation to reveal the need for improved measurements of system performance. Use of these improved measurements often helps to enhance future performance.)

The measure was defined in the following way. For the ith county in the state, let (x_i, y_i) be the coordinates of the geographical center of the county (measured in any convenient and consistent coordinate system), and let p_i be the population of this county. In this particular application, each state contains about 100 counties, so that i takes on integer values from 1 to about 100. For the jth district office in the state, let (u_j, v_j) be the coordinates of its geographical location. In this application, the number of offices varied with the number of branches included in the simulation; in general, the maximal value of j was about 25 for Georgia and about 20 for Virginia. For each i, let

$$D_i = \min_j \sqrt{(x_i - u_j)^2 + (y_i - v_j)^2},$$

so that D_i is the shortest distance from the center of the ith county to a district office. The service measure, S, is given by

$$S = (\sum_i D_i p_i) / \sum_i p_i.$$

One difficulty with this measure is that some district offices maintain contact stations in post offices and other locations that are closer to the public. For such offices, calculations were made both with and without contact stations included in the office structure. If the proportion of the time that the contact station is open is represented by q, the results for the associated office with the station were weighted by q, and the results without the station were weighted by $(1 - q)$.

A second difficulty arose in the application of this measure in large cities, such as Atlanta. Several offices are located in such cities; county-wide population and location statistics are not detailed enough to permit calculation of meaningful values for S. The decision was made to ignore offices in these large cities when calculating S, because the addition of a branch to a city-wide complex of offices usually is made either to reduce congestion in existing offices or to enhance accessibility by locating the branch near public transportation or parking facilities. Distance, in itself, usually is not the critical factor in such cases.

Except for these two difficulties, the measure of service readily was implemented because population statistics were available in computer-compatible form and it was easy to obtain the geographical coordinates and carry out the calculations on a computer.

Two further problems were encountered in the implementation of this application. First, most branch offices—because they are so small—have a structure somewhat different than that of other district offices. For example, a claims representative may act as a receptionist. Because application of the simulation to the study of branch offices had not been anticipated during the design stage, it was necessary to modify some of the models and programs. This modification was relatively easy; had it proven difficult, this study of branch offices would not have been chosen as one of the first applications for the simulation.

The second problem arose in the estimation of workloads. Very few of the offices involved in this study had been surveyed in the field study. Therefore, the workloads of most of the offices had to be estimated indirectly. Two approaches were tried. In the first approach, multiple linear functions were fitted to the survey data as the estimating tool. In the second, data from yearly workload reports were used. Using estimates from each approach, runs were made to gather statistics about the system under its current workload. These statistics then were compared with actual statistics reported by the real offices. The estimates based on the data in the workload reports produced simulation results far more consistent with the real system than did the estimates based on the regression. Therefore, the estimates based on workload reports were used in the application.

To illustrate the results of the application, we will discuss some of the findings about the Georgia network. Three branches were planned for Georgia: one at Milledgeville, a second at Statesboro, and a third on Cascade Avenue in Atlanta. (These branch offices are represented by the abbreviations MIB, STB, and ACB.) Runs also were made to simulate two of the three existing offices that would be split to form branches and four other offices that would be unaffected by establishment of the branches: the Atlanta Downtown office (ADN without branch, ADY with branch), the Macon office (MAN without branch, MAY with branch), the Atlanta Southeast office (ASE), the Eastpoint office (EPT), the Marietta office (MAR), and the Augusta office (AUG).

Table 15.2 summarizes the sequence of runs used in the study of the Georgia network. Each run except for the last involves simulation of six offices; each office was simulated three times altogether. In each case, a total of 42 days of office activities was simulated. Of these 42 days, 14 were used for initialization of the system, and operational statistics were accumulated over the last 28 days. The multipliers in the GPSS random number generator were modified at the beginning of each run, in order to be sure that a new sequence would be generated in each case.

For the existing network, the value of S was calculated as 4.227. Addition of MIB reduced the value of S to 4.199, and addition of STB reduced it to 4.160. (Recall that offices within Atlanta are ignored in the calculation of S.)

Table 15.3 gives a subset of the results of the runs. As can be seen from the results, the opening of branch offices in Georgia can be expected to produce a substantial reduction of waiting time to see the receptionist, which in turn reduces the time spent in the office prior to an interview. The use of smaller offices slightly increases the ratio of receptionists to total office personnel. However,

TABLE 15.2   Summary of Runs Made in Study of Georgia District-Office Network

Run	Offices Simulated (in the Order in Which They Were Simulated)
1	ADN, ASE, EPT, MAN, MAR, AUG
2	ADY, MAY, MIB, STB, ACB, ADN
3	ASE, EPT, MAN, MAR, AUG, ADY
4	MAY, MIB, STB, ACB, ADN, ASE
5	EPT, MAN, MAR, AUG, ADY, MAY
6	MIB, STB, ACB

TABLE 15.3   Some Results of the Simulation of Georgia District Offices

Office	Time in Office Before Seeing				Time per Transaction for			
	Receptionist		A CR or SR		Receptionists		Claim Representatives	
	Avg.	Stand. Dev.	Avg.	Stand. Dev.	Avg.	Stand. Dev.	Avg.	Stand. Dev.
ADN	29.2	1.74	33.6	1.51	3.5	0.01	12.6	0.16
ADY	14.7	0.22	19.1	0.11	3.6	0.01	12.9	0.05
ASE	4.2	0.17	8.9	1.11	3.5	0.01	15.3	0.31
EPT	7.1	1.50	11.9	1.86	3.6	0.01	13.5	0.30
MAN	13.1	0.64	17.7	0.72	3.6	0.06	13.4	0.07
MAY	11.3	0.70	15.9	0.55	3.6	0.06	42.7	0.11
MAR	5.3	0.52	10.7	0.56	3.7	0.02	41.5	0.21
AUG	11.3	0.06	15.9	0.15	3.7	0.05	44.8	0.15
MIB	2.6	2.49	8.3	0.73	3.7	0.01	43.4	0.75
STB	2.0	0.70	8.6	1.19	3.8	0.02	43.0	0.46
ACB	2.8	0.44	8.3	1.08	3.5	0.02	41.4	0.46

because this ratio is small, a slight increase in it causes a substantial improvement in receptionist services with little degradation in the services provided by other personnel. These results suggest that it might be appropriate to consider increasing the ratio of receptionists to other office personnel in any large office.

The columns headed "Stand. Dev." are the standard deviations of the three averages obtained for the separate runs for each office. The small standard deviations of the average time per transaction for receptionists caused us some concern; we were afraid that the simulation was yielding unrealistic, stereotyped behavior. However, an analysis of the results showed that they are not unreasonable. The fairly limited range of values for the duration of receptionists' transactions results in averages over 28 days of operations that have very small standard deviations.

Although results from this application were put on the history tape, they are not expected to provide a yardstick for the behavior of the present network, because this application dealt only with a small portion of the whole network.

Appendix A

Miscellaneous Statistical Tables

TABLE A.1   The Standard Normal Density and Distribution
TABLE A.2   Critical Values of the *t* Distribution
TABLE A.3   Critical Values of the *Chi* Square Distribution
TABLE A.4   Critical Values of the *F* Distribution
TABLE A.5   Critical Values for the Kolmogorov-Smirnov Test
TABLE A.6   Critical Values for the Runs Test
TABLE A.7   500 Five-Digit Random Numbers
TABLE A.8   The Exponential and Negative Exponential Functions

TABLE A.1   The Standard Normal Density and Distribution

x	f(x)*	F(x)†	x	f(x)*	F(x)†
0.0	0.39894	0.50000	1.6	0.11092	0.94520
0.1	0.39695	0.53983	1.7	0.09405	0.95543
0.2	0.39104	0.57926	1.8	0.07895	0.96407
0.3	0.38139	0.61791	1.9	0.06562	0.97128
0.4	0.36827	0.65542	2.0	0.05399	0.97725
0.5	0.35207	0.69146	2.1	0.04398	0.98214
0.6	0.33322	0.72575	2.2	0.03547	0.98610
0.7	0.31225	0.75803	2.3	0.02833	0.98928
0.8	0.28969	0.78814	2.4	0.02239	0.99180
0.9	0.26609	0.81594	2.5	0.01753	0.99379
1.0	0.24197	0.84134	2.6	0.01358	0.99534
1.1	0.21785	0.86433	2.7	0.01042	0.99653
1.2	0.19419	0.88493	2.8	0.00792	0.99744
1.3	0.17137	0.90320	2.9	0.00595	0.99813
1.4	0.14973	0.91924	3.0	0.00443	0.99865
1.5	0.12952	0.93319	3.5	0.00087	0.99977

* $f(x) = \dfrac{1}{\sqrt{2\pi}}\, e^{-x^2/2}$ and $f(-x) = f(x)$.

† $F(x) = \int_{-\infty}^{x} f(t)\,dt$ and $F(-x) = 1 - F(x)$.

TABLE A.2 Critical Values of the *t* Distribution*

df	P						
	0.5	0.8	0.9	0.95	0.98	0.99	0.999
1	1.000	3.078	6.314	12.706	31.821	63.657	636.619
2	0.816	1.886	2.920	4.303	6.965	9.925	31.598
3	0.765	1.638	2.353	3.182	4.541	5.841	12.924
4	0.741	1.533	2.132	2.776	3.747	4.604	8.610
5	0.727	1.476	2.015	2.571	3.365	4.032	6.869
6	0.718	1.440	1.943	2.447	3.143	3.707	5.959
7	0.711	1.415	1.895	2.365	2.998	3.499	5.408
8	0.706	1.397	1.860	2.306	2.896	3.355	5.041
9	0.703	1.383	1.833	2.262	2.821	3.250	4.781
10	0.700	1.372	1.812	2.228	2.764	3.169	4.587
11	0.697	1.363	1.796	2.201	2.718	3.106	4.437
12	0.695	1.356	1.782	2.179	2.681	3.055	4.318
13	0.694	1.350	1.771	2.160	2.650	3.012	4.221
14	0.692	1.345	1.761	2.145	2.624	2.977	4.140
15	0.691	1.341	1.753	2.131	2.602	2.947	4.073
16	0.690	1.337	1.746	2.120	2.583	2.921	4.015
17	0.689	1.333	1.740	2.110	2.567	2.898	3.965
18	0.688	1.330	1.734	2.101	2.552	2.878	3.922
19	0.688	1.328	1.729	2.093	2.539	2.861	3.883
20	0.687	1.325	1.725	2.086	2.528	2.845	3.850
21	0.686	1.323	1.721	2.080	2.518	2.831	3.819
22	0.686	1.321	1.717	2.074	2.508	2.819	3.792
23	0.685	1.319	1.714	2.069	2.500	2.807	3.768
24	0.685	1.318	1.711	2.064	2.492	2.797	3.745
25	0.684	1.316	1.708	2.060	2.485	2.787	3.725
30	0.683	1.310	1.697	2.042	2.457	2.750	3.646
40	0.681	1.303	1.684	2.021	2.423	2.704	3.551
60	0.679	1.296	1.671	2.000	2.390	2.660	3.460
∞	0.674	1.282	1.645	1.960	2.326	2.576	3.291

*The values of P (column headings) are areas under the *t* density from minus the tabulated value of *t* to plus the tabulated value of *t*. The values of *df* (row headings) are the number of degrees of freedom, or values of the parameter associated with the *t* distribution. The table can be used directly to determine critical values of *t* for two-tailed tests. For such tests, if the type I error is α, the critical value of *t* is found in the row with the appropriate *df* and the column with $P = 1 - \alpha$. For one-tailed tests, critical values corresponding to a type I error of α are found by taking $P = 1 - 2\alpha$.

TABLE A.3   Critical Values of the *Chi* Square Distribution*

df	P					
	0.50	0.75	0.90	0.95	0.99	0.999
1	0.45494	1.32330	2.70554	3.84146	6.63490	10.828
2	1.38629	2.77259	4.60517	5.99147	9.21034	13.816
3	2.36597	4.10835	6.25139	7.81473	11.3449	16.266
4	3.35670	5.38527	7.77944	9.48773	13.2767	18.467
5	4.35146	6.62568	9.23635	11.0705	15.0863	20.515
6	5.34812	7.84080	10.6446	12.5916	16.8119	22.458
7	6.34581	9.03715	12.0170	14.0671	18.4753	24.322
8	7.34412	10.2188	13.3616	15.5073	20.0902	26.125
9	8.34283	11.3887	14.6837	16.9190	21.6660	27.877
10	9.34182	12.5489	15.9871	18.3070	23.2093	29.588
11	10.3410	13.7007	17.2750	19.6751	24.7250	31.264
12	11.3403	14.8454	18.5494	21.0261	26.2170	32.909
13	12.3398	15.9839	19.8119	22.3621	27.6883	34.528
14	13.3393	17.1170	21.0642	23.6848	29.1413	36.123
15	14.3389	18.2451	22.3072	24.9958	30.5779	37.697
16	15.3385	19.3688	23.5418	26.2962	31.9999	39.252
17	16.3381	20.4887	24.7690	27.5871	33.4087	40.790
18	17.3379	21.6049	25.9894	28.8693	34.8053	42.312
19	18.3376	22.7178	27.2036	30.1435	36.1908	43.820
20	19.3374	23.8277	28.4120	31.4104	37.5662	45.315
21	20.3372	24.9348	29.6151	32.6705	38.9321	46.797
22	21.3370	26.0393	30.8133	33.9244	40.2894	48.268
23	22.3369	27.1413	32.0069	35.1725	41.6384	49.728
24	23.3367	28.2412	33.1963	36.4151	42.9798	51.179
25	24.3366	29.3389	34.3816	37.6525	44.3141	52.620
30	29.3360	34.7998	40.2560	43.7729	50.8922	59.703
40	39.3354	45.6160	51.8050	55.7585	63.6907	73.402
50	49.3349	56.3336	63.1671	67.5048	76.1539	86.661
100	99.3341	109.141	118.498	124.342	135.807	149.449

*The values of P (column headings) are values of the *chi* square distribution corresponding to the tabulated value of χ^2. The values of df (row headings) are the degrees of freedom, or values of the parameter associated with the *chi* square distribution. For a one-tailed test for significantly large values, critical values corresponding to a type I error of α are found by taking $P = 1 - \alpha$.

TABLE A.4   Critical Values of the F Distribution*

PART I: $\alpha = 0.1$

n	\multicolumn{13}{c}{m (degrees of freedom in the numerator)}
	1	2	3	4	5	6	8	12	15	20	30	60	∞
1	39.86	49.50	53.59	55.83	57.24	58.20	59.44	60.71	61.22	61.74	62.26	62.79	63.33
2	8.53	9.00	9.16	9.24	9.29	9.33	9.37	9.41	9.42	9.44	9.46	9.47	9.49
3	5.54	5.46	5.39	5.34	5.31	5.28	5.25	5.22	5.20	5.18	5.17	5.15	5.13
4	4.54	4.32	4.19	4.11	4.05	4.01	3.95	3.90	3.87	3.84	3.82	3.79	3.76
5	4.06	3.78	3.62	3.52	3.45	3.40	3.34	3.27	3.24	3.21	3.17	3.14	3.10
6	3.78	3.46	3.29	3.18	3.11	3.05	2.98	2.90	2.87	2.84	2.80	2.76	2.72
7	3.59	3.26	3.07	2.96	2.88	2.83	2.75	2.67	2.63	2.59	2.56	2.51	2.47
8	3.46	3.11	2.92	2.81	2.73	2.67	2.59	2.50	2.46	2.42	2.38	2.34	2.29
9	3.36	3.01	2.81	2.69	2.61	2.55	2.47	2.38	2.34	2.30	2.25	2.21	2.16
10	3.29	2.92	2.73	2.61	2.52	2.46	2.38	2.28	2.24	2.20	2.16	2.11	2.06
11	3.23	2.86	2.66	2.54	2.45	2.39	2.30	2.21	2.17	2.12	2.08	2.03	1.97
12	3.18	2.81	2.61	2.48	2.39	2.33	2.24	2.15	2.10	2.06	2.01	1.96	1.90
13	3.14	2.76	2.56	2.43	2.35	2.28	2.20	2.10	2.05	2.01	1.96	1.90	1.85
14	3.10	2.73	2.52	2.39	2.31	2.24	2.15	2.05	2.01	1.96	1.91	1.86	1.80
15	3.07	2.70	2.49	2.36	2.27	2.21	2.12	2.02	1.97	1.92	1.87	1.82	1.76
16	3.05	2.67	2.46	2.33	2.24	2.18	2.09	1.99	1.94	1.89	1.84	1.78	1.72
17	3.03	2.64	2.44	2.31	2.22	2.15	2.06	1.96	1.91	1.86	1.81	1.75	1.69
18	3.01	2.62	2.42	2.29	2.20	2.13	2.04	1.93	1.89	1.84	1.78	1.72	1.66
19	2.99	2.61	2.40	2.27	2.18	2.11	2.02	1.91	1.86	1.81	1.76	1.70	1.63
20	2.97	2.59	2.38	2.25	2.16	2.09	2.00	1.89	1.84	1.79	1.74	1.68	1.61
21	2.96	2.57	2.36	2.23	2.14	2.08	1.98	1.87	1.83	1.78	1.72	1.66	1.59
22	2.95	2.56	2.35	2.22	2.13	2.06	1.97	1.86	1.81	1.76	1.70	1.64	1.57
23	2.94	2.55	2.34	2.21	2.11	2.05	1.95	1.84	1.80	1.74	1.69	1.62	1.55
24	2.93	2.54	2.33	2.19	2.10	2.04	1.94	1.83	1.78	1.73	1.67	1.61	1.53
25	2.92	2.53	2.32	2.18	2.09	2.02	1.93	1.82	1.77	1.72	1.66	1.59	1.52
26	2.91	2.52	2.31	2.17	2.08	2.01	1.92	1.81	1.76	1.71	1.65	1.58	1.50
27	2.90	2.51	2.30	2.17	2.07	2.00	1.91	1.80	1.75	1.70	1.64	1.57	1.49
28	2.89	2.50	2.29	2.16	2.06	2.00	1.90	1.79	1.74	1.69	1.63	1.56	1.48
29	2.89	2.50	2.28	2.15	2.06	1.99	1.89	1.78	1.73	1.68	1.62	1.55	1.47
30	2.88	2.49	2.28	2.14	2.05	1.98	1.88	1.77	1.72	1.67	1.61	1.54	1.46
40	2.84	2.44	2.23	2.09	2.00	1.93	1.83	1.71	1.66	1.61	1.54	1.47	1.38
60	2.79	2.39	2.18	2.04	1.95	1.87	1.77	1.66	1.60	1.54	1.48	1.40	1.29
120	2.75	2.35	2.13	1.99	1.90	1.82	1.72	1.60	1.55	1.48	1.41	1.32	1.19
∞	2.71	2.30	2.08	1.94	1.85	1.77	1.67	1.55	1.49	1.42	1.34	1.24	1.00

TABLE A.4—Continued

PART II: $\alpha = 0.05$

m (degrees of freedom in the numerator)

n	1	2	3	4	5	6	8	12	15	20	30	60	∞
1	161.4	199.5	215.7	224.6	230.2	234.0	238.9	243.9	245.9	248.0	250.1	252.2	254.3
2	18.51	19.00	19.16	19.25	19.30	19.33	19.37	19.41	19.43	19.45	19.46	19.48	19.50
3	10.13	9.55	9.28	9.12	9.01	8.94	8.85	8.74	8.70	8.66	8.62	8.57	8.53
4	7.71	6.94	6.59	6.39	6.26	6.16	6.04	5.91	5.86	5.80	5.75	5.69	5.63
5	6.61	5.79	5.41	5.19	5.05	4.95	4.82	4.68	4.62	4.56	4.50	4.43	4.36
6	5.99	5.14	4.76	4.53	4.39	4.28	4.15	4.00	3.94	3.87	3.81	3.74	3.67
7	5.59	4.74	4.35	4.12	3.97	3.87	3.73	3.57	3.51	3.44	3.38	3.30	3.23
8	5.32	4.46	4.07	3.84	3.69	3.58	3.44	3.28	3.22	3.15	3.08	3.01	2.93
9	5.12	4.26	3.86	3.63	3.48	3.37	3.23	3.07	3.01	2.94	2.86	2.79	2.71
10	4.96	4.10	3.71	3.48	3.33	3.22	3.07	2.91	2.85	2.77	2.70	2.62	2.54
11	4.84	3.98	3.59	3.36	3.20	3.09	2.95	2.79	2.72	2.65	2.57	2.49	2.40
12	4.75	3.89	3.49	3.26	3.11	3.00	2.85	2.69	2.62	2.54	2.47	2.38	2.30
13	4.67	3.81	3.41	3.18	3.03	2.92	2.77	2.60	2.55	2.46	2.38	2.30	2.21
14	4.60	3.74	3.34	3.11	2.96	2.85	2.70	2.53	2.46	2.39	2.31	2.22	2.13
15	4.54	3.68	3.29	3.06	2.90	2.79	2.64	2.48	2.40	2.33	2.25	2.16	2.07
16	4.49	3.63	3.24	3.01	2.85	2.74	2.59	2.42	2.35	2.28	2.19	2.11	2.01
17	4.45	3.59	3.20	2.96	2.81	2.70	2.55	2.38	2.31	2.23	2.15	2.06	1.96
18	4.41	3.55	3.16	2.93	2.77	2.66	2.51	2.34	2.27	2.19	2.11	2.02	1.92
19	4.38	3.52	3.13	2.90	2.74	2.63	2.48	2.31	2.23	2.16	2.07	1.98	1.88
20	4.35	3.49	3.10	2.87	2.71	2.60	2.45	2.28	2.20	2.12	2.04	1.95	1.85
21	4.32	3.47	3.07	2.84	2.68	2.57	2.42	2.25	2.18	2.10	2.01	1.92	1.82
22	4.30	3.44	3.05	2.82	2.66	2.55	2.40	2.23	2.15	2.07	1.98	1.89	1.79
23	4.28	3.42	3.03	2.80	2.64	2.53	2.37	2.20	2.13	2.05	1.96	1.86	1.76
24	4.26	3.40	3.01	2.78	2.62	2.51	2.36	2.18	2.11	2.03	1.94	1.84	1.73
25	4.24	3.39	2.99	2.76	2.60	2.49	2.34	2.16	2.09	2.01	1.92	1.82	1.71
26	4.23	3.37	2.98	2.74	2.59	2.47	2.32	2.15	2.07	1.99	1.90	1.80	1.69
27	4.21	3.35	2.96	2.73	2.57	2.46	2.31	2.13	2.06	1.97	1.88	1.79	1.67
28	4.20	3.34	2.95	2.71	2.56	2.45	2.29	2.12	2.04	1.96	1.87	1.77	1.65
29	4.18	3.33	2.93	2.70	2.55	2.43	2.28	2.10	2.03	1.94	1.85	1.75	1.64
30	4.17	3.32	2.92	2.69	2.53	2.42	2.27	2.09	2.01	1.93	1.84	1.74	1.62
40	4.08	3.23	2.84	2.61	2.45	2.34	2.18	2.00	1.92	1.84	1.74	1.64	1.51
60	4.00	3.15	2.76	2.53	2.37	2.25	2.10	1.92	1.84	1.75	1.65	1.53	1.39
120	3.92	3.07	2.68	2.45	2.29	2.17	2.02	1.83	1.75	1.66	1.55	1.43	1.25
∞	3.84	3.00	2.60	2.37	2.21	2.10	1.94	1.75	1.67	1.57	1.46	1.32	1.00

TABLE A.4—Continued

PART III: $\alpha = 0.025$

n	\multicolumn{13}{c}{m (degrees of freedom in the numerator)}
	1	2	3	4	5	6	8	12	15	20	30	60	∞
1	647.8	799.5	864.2	899.6	921.8	937.1	956.7	976.7	984.9	993.1	1001	1010	1018
2	38.51	39.00	39.17	39.25	39.30	39.33	39.37	39.41	39.43	39.45	39.46	39.48	39.50
3	17.44	16.04	15.44	15.10	14.88	14.73	14.54	14.34	14.25	14.17	14.08	13.99	13.90
4	12.22	10.65	9.98	9.60	9.36	9.20	8.98	8.75	8.66	8.56	8.46	8.36	8.26
5	10.01	8.43	7.76	7.39	7.15	6.98	6.76	6.52	6.43	6.33	6.23	6.12	6.02
6	8.81	7.26	6.60	6.23	5.99	5.82	5.60	5.37	5.27	5.17	5.07	4.96	4.85
7	8.07	6.54	5.89	5.52	5.29	5.12	4.90	4.67	4.57	4.47	4.36	4.25	4.14
8	7.57	6.06	5.42	5.05	4.82	4.65	4.43	4.20	4.10	4.00	3.89	3.78	3.67
9	7.21	5.71	5.08	4.72	4.48	4.32	4.10	3.87	3.77	3.67	3.56	3.45	3.33
10	6.94	5.46	4.83	4.47	4.24	4.07	3.85	3.62	3.52	3.42	3.31	3.20	3.08
11	6.72	5.26	4.63	4.28	4.04	3.88	3.66	3.43	3.33	3.23	3.12	3.00	2.88
12	6.55	5.10	4.47	4.12	3.89	3.73	3.51	3.28	3.18	3.07	2.96	2.85	2.72
13	6.41	4.97	4.35	4.00	3.77	3.60	3.39	3.15	3.05	2.95	2.84	2.72	2.60
14	6.30	4.86	4.24	3.89	3.66	3.50	3.29	3.05	2.95	2.84	2.73	2.61	2.49
15	6.20	4.77	4.15	3.80	3.58	3.41	3.20	2.96	2.86	2.76	2.64	2.52	2.40
16	6.12	4.69	4.08	3.73	3.50	3.34	3.12	2.89	2.79	2.68	2.57	2.45	2.32
17	6.04	4.62	4.01	3.66	3.44	3.28	3.06	2.82	2.72	2.62	2.50	2.38	2.25
18	5.98	4.56	3.95	3.61	3.38	3.22	3.01	2.77	2.67	2.56	2.44	2.32	2.17
19	5.92	4.51	3.90	3.56	3.33	3.17	2.96	2.72	2.62	2.51	2.39	2.27	2.13
20	5.87	4.46	3.86	3.51	3.29	3.13	2.91	2.68	2.57	2.46	2.35	2.22	2.09
21	5.83	4.42	3.82	3.48	3.25	3.09	2.87	2.64	2.53	2.42	2.31	2.18	2.04
22	5.79	4.38	3.78	3.44	3.22	3.05	2.84	2.60	2.50	2.39	2.27	2.14	2.00
23	5.75	4.35	3.75	3.41	3.18	3.02	2.81	2.57	2.47	2.36	2.24	2.11	1.97
24	5.72	4.32	3.72	3.38	3.15	2.99	2.78	2.54	2.44	2.33	2.21	2.08	1.94
25	5.69	4.29	3.69	3.35	3.13	2.97	2.75	2.51	2.41	2.30	2.18	2.05	1.91
26	5.66	4.27	3.67	3.33	3.10	2.94	2.73	2.49	2.39	2.28	2.16	2.03	1.88
27	5.63	4.24	3.65	3.31	3.08	2.92	2.71	2.47	2.36	2.25	2.13	2.00	1.85
28	5.61	4.22	3.63	3.29	3.06	2.90	2.69	2.45	2.34	2.23	2.11	1.98	1.83
29	5.59	4.20	3.61	3.27	3.04	2.88	2.67	2.43	2.32	2.21	2.09	1.96	1.81
30	5.57	4.18	3.59	3.25	3.03	2.87	2.65	2.41	2.31	2.20	2.07	1.94	1.79
40	5.42	4.05	3.46	3.13	2.90	2.74	2.53	2.29	2.18	2.07	1.94	1.80	1.64
60	5.29	3.93	3.34	3.01	2.79	2.63	2.41	2.17	2.06	1.94	1.82	1.67	1.48
120	5.15	3.80	3.23	2.89	2.67	2.52	2.30	2.05	1.94	1.82	1.69	1.53	1.31
∞	5.02	3.69	3.12	2.79	2.57	2.41	2.19	1.94	1.83	1.71	1.57	1.39	1.00

TABLE A.4—Continued

PART IV: $\alpha = 0.001$

n	\multicolumn{13}{c}{m (degrees of freedom in the numerator)}
	1	2	3	4	5	6	8	12	15	20	30	60	∞
1	4052	4999.5	5403	5625	5764	5859	5982	6106	6157	6209	6261	6313	6366
2	98.50	99.00	99.17	99.25	99.30	99.33	99.37	99.42	99.43	99.45	99.47	99.48	99.50
3	34.12	30.82	29.46	28.71	28.24	27.91	27.49	27.05	26.87	26.69	26.50	26.32	26.13
4	21.20	18.00	16.69	15.98	15.52	15.21	14.80	14.37	14.20	14.02	13.84	13.65	13.46
5	16.26	13.27	12.06	11.39	10.97	10.67	10.29	9.89	9.72	9.55	9.38	9.20	9.02
6	13.75	10.92	9.78	9.15	8.75	8.47	8.10	7.72	7.56	7.40	7.23	7.06	6.88
7	12.25	9.55	8.45	7.85	7.46	7.19	6.84	6.47	6.31	6.16	5.99	5.82	5.65
8	11.26	8.65	7.59	7.01	6.63	6.37	6.03	5.67	5.52	5.36	5.20	5.03	4.86
9	10.56	8.02	6.99	6.42	6.06	5.80	5.47	5.11	4.96	4.81	4.65	4.48	4.31
10	10.04	7.56	6.55	5.99	5.64	5.39	5.06	4.71	4.56	4.41	4.25	4.09	3.91
11	9.65	7.21	6.22	5.67	5.32	5.07	4.74	4.40	4.25	4.10	3.94	3.78	3.60
12	9.33	6.93	5.95	5.41	5.06	4.82	4.50	4.16	4.01	3.86	3.70	3.54	3.36
13	9.07	6.70	5.74	5.21	4.86	4.62	4.30	3.96	3.82	3.66	3.51	3.34	3.17
14	8.86	6.51	5.56	5.04	4.69	4.46	4.14	3.80	3.66	3.51	3.35	3.18	3.00
15	8.68	6.36	5.42	4.89	4.56	4.32	4.00	3.67	3.52	3.37	3.21	3.05	2.87
16	8.53	6.23	5.29	4.77	4.44	4.20	3.89	3.55	3.41	3.26	3.10	2.93	2.75
17	8.40	6.11	5.18	4.67	4.34	4.10	3.79	3.46	3.31	3.16	3.00	2.83	2.65
18	8.29	6.01	5.09	4.58	4.25	4.01	3.71	3.37	3.23	3.08	2.92	2.75	2.57
19	8.18	5.93	5.01	4.50	4.17	3.94	3.63	3.30	3.15	3.00	2.84	2.67	2.49
20	8.10	5.85	4.94	4.43	4.10	3.87	3.56	3.23	3.09	2.94	2.78	2.61	2.42
21	8.02	5.78	4.87	4.37	4.04	3.81	3.51	3.17	3.03	2.88	2.72	2.55	2.36
22	7.95	5.72	4.82	4.31	3.99	3.76	3.45	3.12	2.98	2.83	2.67	2.50	2.31
23	7.88	5.66	4.76	4.26	3.94	3.71	3.41	3.07	2.93	2.78	2.62	2.45	2.26
24	7.82	5.61	4.72	4.22	3.90	3.67	3.36	3.03	2.89	2.74	2.58	2.40	2.21
25	7.77	5.57	4.68	4.18	3.85	3.63	3.32	2.99	2.85	2.70	2.54	2.36	2.17
26	7.72	5.53	4.64	4.14	3.82	3.59	3.29	2.96	2.81	2.66	2.50	2.33	2.13
27	7.68	5.49	4.60	4.11	3.78	3.56	3.26	2.93	2.78	2.63	2.47	2.29	2.10
28	7.64	5.45	4.57	4.07	3.75	3.53	3.23	2.90	2.75	2.60	2.44	2.26	2.06
29	7.60	5.42	4.54	4.04	3.73	3.50	3.20	2.87	2.73	2.57	2.41	2.23	2.03
30	7.56	5.39	4.51	4.02	3.70	3.47	3.17	2.84	2.70	2.55	2.39	2.21	2.01
40	7.31	5.18	4.31	3.83	3.51	3.29	2.99	2.66	2.52	2.37	2.20	2.02	1.80
60	7.08	4.98	4.13	3.65	3.34	3.12	2.82	2.50	2.35	2.20	2.03	1.84	1.60
120	6.85	4.79	3.95	3.48	3.17	2.96	2.66	2.34	2.19	2.03	1.86	1.66	1.38
∞	6.63	4.61	3.78	3.32	3.02	2.80	2.51	2.18	2.04	1.88	1.70	1.47	1.00

*Column headings (m) are the number of degrees of freedom in the numerator; row headings (n) are the number of degrees of freedom in the denominator. Four separate tables are given, for $\alpha = 0.1$, $\alpha = 0.05$, $\alpha = 0.025$, and $\alpha = 0.01$.

TABLE A.5   Critical Values for the Kolmogorov-Smirnov Test

PART I* $n_1 = n_2 = N \leq 40$

N	Critical Value $\alpha=0.05$	$\alpha=0.01$	N	Critical Value $\alpha=0.05$	$\alpha=0.01$	N	Critical Value $\alpha=0.05$	$\alpha=0.01$
5	4	5	16	7	9	26	9	11
6	5	6	17	8	9	27	9	12
7	5	6	18	8	10	28	10	12
8	5	6	19	8	10	29	10	12
9	6	7	20	8	10	30	10	12
10	6	7						
			21	8	10	35	11	13
11	6	8	22	9	11			
12	6	8	23	9	11	40	11	12
13	7	8	24	9	11			
14	7	8	25	9	11			
15	7	9						

PART II† $n_1 > 40$ and $n_2 > 40$

	α					
	0.10	0.05	0.025	0.01	0.005	0.001
Multiplier	1.22	1.36	1.48	1.63	1.73	1.95

*With small and equal sample sizes, the maximal difference in the cumulative frequencies (that is, in the numerator of D) has the critical values tabulated in Part I, for $\alpha = 0.01$ and $\alpha = 0.05$ in two-tailed tests. If the numerator is greater than or equal to the tabulated value, the hypothesis is rejected.

†With large sample sizes (and n_1 not necessarily equal to n_2), the critical value for a two-tailed test is obtained by multiplying the values in Part II by the expression $\sqrt{(n_1 + n_2)/n_1 n_2}$.

TABLE A.6   Critical Values for the Runs Test*

N	Crit. Vals. for Too Few Runs			Crit. Vals. for Too Many Runs			Mean	S.D.
	α=0.01	α=0.025	α=0.05	α=0.01	α=0.025	α=0.05		
11	6	7	7	17	16	16	12	2.3
12	7	7	8	18	18	17	13	2.4
13	7	8	9	20	19	18	14	2.5
14	8	9	10	21	20	19	15	2.6
15	9	10	11	22	21	20	16	2.7
16	10	11	11	23	22	22	17	2.8
17	10	11	12	25	24	23	18	2.9
18	11	12	13	26	25	24	19	3.0
19	12	13	14	27	26	25	20	3.0
20	13	14	15	28	27	26	21	3.1
25	17	18	19	34	33	32	26	3.5
30	21	22	24	40	39	37	31	3.8
35	25	27	28	46	44	43	36	4.1
40	30	31	33	51	50	48	41	4.4
45	34	36	37	57	55	54	46	4.7
50	38	40	42	63	61	59	51	5.0
55	43	45	46	68	66	65	56	5.2
60	47	49	51	74	72	70	61	5.5
65	52	54	56	79	77	75	66	5.7
70	56	58	60	85	83	81	71	5.9
75	61	63	65	90	88	86	76	6.1
80	65	68	70	96	93	91	81	6.3
85	70	72	74	101	99	97	86	6.5
90	74	77	79	107	104	102	91	6.7
95	79	82	84	112	109	107	96	6.9
100	84	86	88	117	115	113	101	7.1

*This table can be used to test the hypothesis that the number of runs is equal to the expected value, either against the alternative that too few runs occur, or against the alternative that too many runs occur. It is applicable only to data from two equal samples of size N each. In addition to the critical values, the mean and standard deviation of the expected number of runs is given for each N. The levels of α given are appropriate for one-tailed tests. Significance is indicated by an observed number of runs less than or equal to the tabulated value if the alternative is that too few runs occur. If the alternative is that too many runs occur, significance is indicated by an observed value greater than or equal to the tabulated value.

TABLE A.7   500 Five-Digit Random Numbers

55034	81217	90564	81943	11241	84512	12288	89862	00760	76159
25521	99536	43233	48786	49221	06960	31564	21458	88199	06312
85421	72744	97242	66383	00132	05661	96442	37388	57671	27916
61219	48390	47344	30413	39392	91365	56203	79204	05330	31196
20230	03147	58854	11650	28415	12821	58931	30508	65989	26675
95776	83206	56144	55953	89787	64426	08448	45707	80364	60262
07603	17344	01148	83300	96955	65027	31713	89013	79557	49755
00645	17459	78742	39005	36027	98807	72666	54484	68262	38827
62950	83162	61504	31557	80590	47893	72360	72720	08396	33674
79350	10276	81933	26347	08068	67816	06659	87917	74166	85519
48339	69834	59047	82175	92016	58446	69591	56205	95700	86211
05842	08439	79836	50957	32059	32910	15842	13918	41365	80115
25855	02209	07307	59942	71389	76159	11263	38787	61541	22606
25272	16152	82323	70718	98081	38631	91956	49909	76253	33970
73003	29058	17605	49298	47675	90445	68919	05676	23823	84892
81310	94430	22663	06584	38142	00146	17496	51115	61458	65790
10024	44713	59832	80721	63711	67882	25100	45345	55743	67618
84671	52806	89124	37691	20897	82339	22627	06142	05773	05547
29296	58162	21858	33732	94056	88806	54603	00384	66340	69232
51771	94074	70630	41286	90583	87680	13961	55627	23670	35109
42166	56251	60770	51672	36031	77273	85218	14812	90758	23677
78355	67041	22492	51522	31164	30450	27600	44428	96380	26772
09552	51347	33864	89018	73418	81538	77399	30448	97740	18158
15771	63127	34847	05660	06156	48970	55699	61818	91763	20821
13231	99058	93754	36730	44286	44326	15729	37500	47269	13333
50583	03570	38472	73236	67613	72780	78174	18718	99092	64114
99485	57330	10634	74905	90671	19643	69903	60950	17968	37217
54676	39524	73785	48864	69835	62798	65205	69187	05572	74741
99343	71549	10248	76036	31702	76868	88909	69574	27642	00336
35492	40231	34868	55356	12847	68093	52643	32732	67016	46784
98170	25384	03841	23920	47954	10359	70114	11177	63298	99903
02670	86155	56860	02592	01646	42200	79950	37764	82341	71952
36934	42879	81637	79952	07066	41625	96804	92388	88860	68580
56851	12778	24309	73660	84264	24668	16686	02239	66022	64133
05464	28892	14271	23778	88599	17081	33884	88783	39015	57118
15025	20237	63386	71122	06620	07415	94982	32324	79427	70387
95610	08030	81469	91066	88857	56583	01224	28097	19726	71454
09026	40378	05731	55128	74298	49196	31669	42605	30368	96424
81431	99955	52462	67667	97322	69808	21240	65921	12629	92896
21431	59335	58627	94822	65484	09641	41018	85100	16110	32077

TABLE A.7 – *Continued*

95832	76145	11636	80284	17787	97934	12822	73890	66009	27521
99813	44631	43746	99790	86823	12114	31706	05024	28156	04202
77210	31148	50543	11603	50934	02498	09184	95875	85840	71954
13268	02609	79833	66058	80277	08533	28676	37532	70535	82356
44285	71735	26620	54691	14909	52132	81110	74548	78853	31996
70526	45953	79637	57374	05053	31965	33376	13232	85666	86615
88386	11222	25080	71462	09818	46001	19065	68981	18310	74178
83161	73994	17209	79441	64091	49790	11936	44864	86978	34538
50214	71721	33851	45144	05696	29935	12823	01594	08453	52825
97689	29341	67747	80643	13620	23943	49396	83686	37302	95350

TABLE A.8   The Exponential and Negative Exponential Functions

x	e^x	e^{-x}	x	e^x	e^{-x}	x	e^x	e^{-x}
0.0	1.00000	1.00000	2.6	13.4637	0.074274	5.2	181.272	0.0055166
0.1	1.10517	0.90484	2.7	14.8797	0.067206	5.4	221.406	0.0045166
0.2	1.22140	0.81873	2.8	16.4446	0.060810	5.6	270.426	0.0036979
0.3	1.34986	0.74082	2.9	18.1741	0.055023	5.8	330.300	0.0030276
0.4	1.49182	0.67032	3.0	20.0855	0.049787	6.0	403.429	0.0024788
0.5	1.64872	0.60653						
0.6	1.82212	0.54881	3.1	22.1980	0.045049	6.2	492.749	0.0020294
0.7	2.01375	0.49659	3.2	24.5325	0.040762	6.4	601.845	0.0016616
0.8	2.22554	0.44933	3.3	27.1126	0.036883	6.6	735.095	0.0013604
0.9	2.45960	0.40657	3.4	29.9641	0.033373	6.8	897.847	0.0011138
1.0	2.71828	0.36788	3.5	33.1155	0.030197	7.0	1096.63	0.00091188
1.1	3.00417	0.33287	3.6	36.5982	0.027324	7.2	1339.43	0.00074659
1.2	3.32012	0.30119	3.7	40.4473	0.024724	7.4	1635.98	0.00061125
1.3	3.66930	0.27253	3.8	44.7012	0.022371	7.6	1998.20	0.00050045
1.4	4.05520	0.24660	3.9	49.4024	0.020242	7.8	2440.60	0.00040973
1.5	4.48169	0.22313	4.0	54.5982	0.018316	8.0	2980.96	0.00033546
1.6	4.95303	0.20190	4.1	60.3403	0.016573	8.2	3640.95	0.00027465
1.7	5.47395	0.18268	4.2	66.6863	0.014996	8.4	4447.07	0.00022487
1.8	6.04965	0.16530	4.3	73.6998	0.013569	8.6	5431.66	0.00018411
1.9	6.68589	0.14957	4.4	81.4509	0.012277	8.8	6634.24	0.00015073
2.0	7.38906	0.13534	4.5	90.0171	0.011109	9.0	8103.08	0.00012341
2.1	8.16617	0.12246	4.6	99.4843	0.010052	9.2	9897.13	0.00010104
2.2	9.02501	0.11080	4.7	109.947	0.0090953	9.4	12088.4	0.000082724
2.3	9.97418	0.10026	4.8	121.510	0.0082297	9.6	14764.8	0.000067729
2.4	11.0232	0.090718	4.9	134.290	0.0074466	9.8	18033.7	0.000055452
2.5	12.1824	0.082085	5.0	148.413	0.0067379	10.0	22026.5	0.000045400

Appendix B

Computer Programs

PROGRAM B.1   The Exact Mean and Variance of *Chi* Square
When Expectations Are Small
PROGRAM B.2   Test for Normality with Provision for
Standardization of Variables
PROGRAM B.3   Linear Regression in Two Variables
PROGRAM B.4   Nonlinear Least Squares
PROGRAM B.5   Generation of Random Numbers

NOTE   Programs B.1 through B.4 were developed by the authors and their associates at the Georgetown University Computation Center. The material in Program B.5 was prepared by Professor Nunamaker of Purdue University and is used here with his permission.

PROGRAM B.1 The Exact Mean and Variance of *Chi* Square When Expectations Are Small

This program carries out the computations for a statistical analysis devised by Haldane (1939). The data to be analyzed are arranged in a matrix, such as that shown in Figure B.1, with r rows and c columns.

Here, each x_{ij} may represent a number of individuals observed;

$$s_i = \sum_{j=1}^{r} x_{ij}; \qquad t_j = \sum_{i=1}^{c} x_{ij};$$

and

$$N = \sum_{i=1}^{c} s_i = \sum_{j=1}^{r} t_j.$$

The table may represent r samples of $s_1, s_2, \ldots, s_r$ individuals, each sample falling into c classes, with $t_1, t_2, \ldots, t_c$ being the grand total in each class. Or it may represent c samples of $t_1, t_2, \ldots, t_c$ individuals, each falling into r classes, the class totals being $s_1, s_2, \ldots, s_r$.

Given this matrix, the program computes *chi* square, the standard deviation S of *chi* square, and the numbers T and E, which are defined below.

Haldane's procedure has a particular advantage, in that it does not assume that the number of samples is large.

Given a matrix, the program first computes s_i, for all i from 1 to r, and then computes t_j, for all j from 1 to c. It then computes N.

Chi square is computed next. The value of *chi* square is given by

$$\chi^2 = \sum_{i=1}^{c} \sum_{j=1}^{r} \frac{x_{ij} - \dfrac{s_i t_j^2}{N}}{\dfrac{s_i t_j}{NN}} = N \sum_{i=1}^{c} \sum_{j=1}^{r} \frac{x_{ij}^2}{s_i t_j} - N.$$

x_{11}	x_{12}	x_{13}	. . . .	x_{1c}	s_1
x_{21}	x_{22}	x_{23}	. . . .	x_{2c}	s_2
x_{31}	x_{32}	x_{33}	. . . .	x_{3c}	s_3
. . . .	. . . .	. . . .	. . . .	. .	.
. . . .	. . . .	. . . .	. . . .	.	.
. . . .	. . . .	. . . .	. . . .		.
x_{r1}	x_{r2}	x_{r3}	. . . .	x_{rc}	s_r
t_1	t_2	t_3	. . . .	t_c	N

FIG. B.1 Matrix of Data for Analysis by Program B.1

The final expression is the one actually used by the program to calculate *chi* square. The value of *chi* square is given in the output.

The number E is defined by

$$E = \frac{(c-1)(r-1)N}{N-1}.$$

The value of E is computed and given as output.

The numbers s and t are defined by

$$s = \sum_{i=1}^{c} \frac{1}{s_i} \quad \text{and} \quad t = \sum_{j=1}^{r} \frac{1}{t_j}.$$

These numbers are used in the following sequence of calculations, leading to the computation of the variance, V:

$$P_1 = N/[(N-1)(N-2)(N-3)].$$
$$P_2 = 2(r-1)(c-1)N^3.$$
$$P_3 = (r^2 c^2 + 2r + 2c - 4)N^2.$$
$$P_4 = rc(r-1)(c-1).$$
$$P_5 = (r+c)(r+c-2).$$
$$P_6 = rc(r-2)(c-2).$$
$$P_7 = (r^2 + 2r - 2)t.$$
$$P_8 = (c^2 + 2c - 2)s.$$
$$P_9 = r(r-2)t.$$
$$P_{10} = c(c-2)s.$$
$$P_{11} = stN^2(N-1).$$
$$Q_1 = [P_2 + P_3 - 2N(P_4 + P_5) - P_6]/(N-1).$$
$$Q_2 = -N^2(P_7 + P_8) + N(P_9 + P_{10}) + P_{11}.$$
$$V = P_1(Q_1 + Q_2).$$

The standard deviation S is defined as

$$S = \sqrt{V}.$$

The value of S is computed and given as output.

The value of T is defined as

$$T = (\chi^2 - E)/S.$$

The value of T is computed and given as output.

From one to ninety matrices may be input at one time. The maximal size of the matrices is 40 by 40. The matrix elements may be positive or negative decimal numbers with up to eight digits. Any rows or columns whose elements add up to zero should be deleted before inputting the matrix. N, the sum of all the elements in the matrix, must not be 1, 2, or 3.

The *input format* is as follows: On the very first card, punch the number of matrices to be analyzed on this particular run. This number is to be punched in the first two columns, right adjusted. (For example, if 6 matrices are to be analyzed, punch "6" in the second column. If 23 matrices are to be analyzed, punch "2" in the first column and "3" in the second.) Leave the rest of this card blank.

Next, punch the data for the first matrix to be analyzed. Let R be the number of rows in this matrix, and C the number of columns. In the first two columns of the card, punch R, right adjusted in the field. In the next two columns, punch C, right adjusted. Leave the rest of this card blank.

On the next card, begin to punch the numbers in the first matrix. Punch eight numbers on each card. (The last card for the matrix may contain fewer than eight numbers.) The first number is punched anywhere in the first ten columns of the card, the second number anywhere in the second ten columns, and so forth. Punch the numbers in sequence moving down the first column of the matrix, then down the second, and so forth. If the numbers are not integers, decimal points must be punched at the appropriate places. If the numbers are integers, the decimal point is optional. However, if no decimal point is punched, the first number must be right adjusted to the tenth column, the second number right adjusted to the twentieth column, and so forth.

Following these directions, punch all the numbers in the first matrix. If there is only one matrix to be analyzed, this completes the data input. If there is a second matrix to be analyzed, punch R and C for the second matrix on the next card in the same fashion as was done for the first matrix. On the next card, begin punching the numbers for the second matrix, following the format given above. Continue in this fashion until all data for all matrices have been punched.

The *output format* includes the numbers T, chi square, E, and S for each matrix. T is printed on the first line and the other three numbers on the second line. All are clearly labeled.

If a matrix is input in which a row or column adds up to zero, the output for this matrix will be the single line; ERROR.   A ROW (OR COLUMN) ADDS UP TO ZERO. If this occurs, the analyses of subsequent matrices on the same run may not be correct. After correcting the input error, analysis of these matrices should be repeated.

If a matrix is input in which N equals 1, 2, or 3, the output will be a single line such as N EQUALS ONE.   INVALID INPUT.

The notation used above differs slightly from that used by Haldane. The FORTRAN symbols actually used in the program differ again, and the labels on the computer output also are slightly different. Table B.1 provides a complete translation among all these different notations.

Figure B.2 shows sample input and output for this program. Figure B.3 is the program listing.

TABLE B.1   Equivalent Notations for Program B.1

Text	Haldane (1939)	FORTRAN Program	Output Label
R or r	n	IR or FR	——
C or c	m	IC or FC	——
x_{ij}	a_{ij}	X(I,J)	——
s_i	s_i	S(I)	——
t_j	t_j	T(J)	——
N	N	N	——
chi square	chi square	CHISQ	CHI SQ
E	E	E	E
s	S	BS	——
t	T	BT	——
V	V	V	——
S	——	SS	S
T	——	TT	T
P_1	——	P(1)	——
P_2	——	P(2)	——
Q_1	——	Q(1)	——
Q_2	——	Q(2)	——
Number of matrices to be analyzed in one run	——	NJOBS	——

```
Sample Input

2
7 8
    1    3    4    1    1    0    0    0
    1    0    0    0    0    9    0    1
    4    1    2    2    0    0    0    0
    7    3    0    0    0    0    2    1
    0    1    6    0    1    0    1    0
    0    8    0    2    3    2    1    1
    0    0    1    3    3    0    1    2
12 9
    0    0    0    0    1    2    5    0
    0    4    2    1    0    1    1    1
    1    7    6    0    5    0    3    0
    0    0    1    0    3    8    6    3
    2    2    1    2    2    0    1    0
    0    3    2    1    3    1    1    0
    1    0    2    1    0    0    2    0
    0    1    1    0    1    2    1    1
    0    4    3    1    2    3    3    0
    0    0    0    0    1    0    0    0
    2    0    0    0   10    3    2    0
    1    7    6    0    0    1    4    1
    1    0    0    1    1    4    4    2
    2    0    2    1


Sample Output

T=          6.25366850
CHI SQ=    90.9250570     E=   42.5384610        7.7373138
T=          1.92030310
CHI SQ=   113.6792800     E=   88.5301200       13.0964530
```

FIG. B.2   Sample Input and Output for Program B.1

```
C     PROGRAM FOR HALDANE'S PROCEDURE TO COMPUTE STANDARD DEVIATION,
C     CHI SQUARE, E, AND T, WHEN EXPECTATIONS ARE SMALL.
      IMPLICIT REAL*8 (A-H,O-Z)
      DIMENSION X(40,40), S(40), T(40), P(11), Q(12)
      NID=5
      WRITE (6,1966)
      READ (NID,49) NJOBS
C     NJOBS= TOTAL NUMBER OF MATRICES TO BE ANALYZED IN ONE RUN.
C     NJOBS IS TO BE PUNCHED IN THE FIRST TWO COLUMNS OF THE VERY FIRST
C     CARD, RIGHT ADJUSTED, AND THE REST OF THE CARD LEFT BLANK.
      DO 500 IBLOB=1,NJOBS
      READ (NID,40) IR,IC
C     FOR EACH MATRIX, IR= NUMBER OF ROWS, IC= NUMBER OF COLUMNS.
      READ (NID,41) ((X(I,J),I=1,IR),J=1,IC)
C     IR IS TO BE PUNCHED IN THE FIRST 2 COLUMNS, RIGHT ADJUSTED,
C     IC IN THE NEXT 2, AND THE REST OF THE CARD LEFT BLANK.
C     THE MATRIX ELEMENTS ARE TO BE PUNCHED 8 OR FEWER TO A CARD, THE
C     FIRST BEING RIGHT ADJUSTED TO THE TENTH COLUMN, THE SECOND TO
C     THE TWENTIETH, THIRD TO THIRTIETH, AND SO ON. GO DOWN THE FIRST
C     COLUMN, THEN DOWN THE SECOND, AND SO ON.
      DO 1 I=1, IR
      S(I)=0.
    2 S(I)= S(I)+X(I,J)
      IF (S(I)) 1,3,1
    3 WRITE (6,42)
C     INVALID INPUT
      GO TO 500
    1 CONTINUE
      DO 4 J=1, IC
      T(J)=0.
    5 T(J)= T(J)+ X(I,J)
      IF(T(J)) 4,6,4
    6 WRITE (6,45)
C     INVALID INPUT
      GO TO 500
    4 CONTINUE
      XN=0.
      DO 7 I=1,IR
    7 XN=XN+S(I)
  650 IF (XN-1.) 651,600,651
  600 WRITE (6,610)
      GO TO 500
  651 IF (XN-2.) 652,601,652
  601 WRITE (6,611)
      GO TO 500
  652 IF (XN-3.) 700,602,700
  602 WRITE (6,612)
      GO TO 500

  700 SUMI =0.
      DO 8 I=1,IR
      SUM=0.
      DO 9 J=1,IC
    9 SUM=SUMJ+X(I,J)*X(I,J)/T(J)
    8 SUMI=SUMI+(SUMJ/S(I))
      CHI SQ=xN*(SUMI-1.)
      FC=IC
      FR=IR
      E=(FC-1.)*(FR-1.)*XN/(XN-1.)
      BS=0.
      DO 10 I=1,IR
   10 BS=BS+(1./S(I))
      BT=0.
      DO 11 J=1,IC
   11 BT= BT+(1./T(J))
      P(1)= XN/((XN-1.)*(XN-2.)*(XN-3.))
      P(2)=2.*(FR-1.)*(FC-1.)*XN*XN*XN
      P(3)=(FR*FR*FC*FC+2.*FR+2.*FC-4.)*XN*XN*XN
      P(4)=FR*FC*(FR-1.)*(FC-1.)
      P(5)=(FR+FC)*(FR+FC-2.)
      P(6)=FR*FC*(FR-2.)*(FC-2.)
      P(7)= (FR*FC+2.*FR-2.)*BT
      P(8)=(FR*FC+2.*FC-2.)*BS
      P(9)=FR*(FR-2.)*BT
      P(10)=FC*(FC-2.)*BS
      P(11)=BS*BT*XN*XN*(XN+1.)
      Q(1)=(P(2)+P(3)-2.*XN*(P(4)+P(5))-P(6))/(XN-1.)
      Q(2)=-XN*XN*(P(7)+P(8))+XN*(P(9)+P(10))+P(11)
      V=P(1)*(Q(1)+Q(2))
      SS=DSQRT(V)
      TT=(CHI SQ-E)/SS
      WRITE (6,43) TT
      WRITE (6,44) CHI SQ,E,SS
  500 CONTINUE
 1000 WRITE (6,1966)
   40 FORMAT (2I2)
   41 FORMAT (8F10.0)
   42 FORMAT (30H ERROR. A ROW ADDS UP TO ZERO,/)
   43 FORMAT (3H T=20,10)
   44 FORMAT (8H CHI SQ=,F14.7,6X,2HE=,F14.7,6X,F14.7,/)
   45 FORMAT (33H ERROR. A COLUMN ADDS UP TO ZERO,/)
   49 FORMAT (I2)
  610 FORMAT ( 30H N EQUALS ONE. INVALID INPUT.,/)
  611 FORMAT ( 30H N EQUALS TWO. INVALID INPUT.,/)
  612 FORMAT(32H N EQUALS THREE. INVALID INPUT.,/)
 1966 FORMAT(1H1)
      STOP
      END
```

FIG. B.3 Listing of Program B.1

PROGRAM B.2   Test for Normality with Provision for Standardization of Variables

It frequently is desirable to determine whether several separate groups of observations can be assumed, as a whole, to have a prescribed distribution. For example, it may be desirable—before performing an analysis of variance—to test whether the data as a whole can be assumed to be normally distributed.

This program has been written to perform the following functions: (1) to compute the means and unbiased estimates of the standard deviations of each of the groups separately; (2) to transform the original observations by subtracting its group mean from each datum and dividing this result by the standard deviation of the group—in other words, if x_{ij} is the ith observation in the jth group, the value of t_{ij} is computed for all i and j as follows:

$$t_{ij} = \frac{x_{ij} - \bar{x}_j}{\sigma_j},$$

where σ_j is the unbiased estimate of the group standard deviation; (3) to combine the values of t_{ij} into a single group, and to compute BETA1 and BETA2 for this group as a whole, where BETA1 is a measure of skewness given by

$$\text{BETA1} = \frac{m_3^2}{m_2^3} = \left(\frac{m_3}{\sqrt{m_2^3}}\right)^2$$

and BETA2 is a measure of kurtosis given by

$$\text{BETA2} = \frac{m_4}{m_2^2},$$

with m_k defined as

$$\sum_{i,j} (t_{ij.} - \bar{t})^k / N,$$

where N is the total number of observations; (4) to sort the values of t_{ij} in descending order and to list them (this list may be used to perform a *chi* square test for goodness of fit to any prescribed distribution after the user has grouped the data in any way that he feels is appropriate); and (5) to compute the mean deviate, given by the formula

$$A = \frac{\left(\sum_{i,j} |t_{ij} - \bar{t}|\right)/N}{m_2}.$$

The statistics BETA1 and BETA2 are discussed by Kendall and Stuart (1958, Vol. 1, pp. 85–86).

Any number of groups may be included for one job, and any number of jobs may be stacked together and run successively. For each group, at least two input cards must be punched: (1) the first card must contain in columns 1 through 4 an integer indicating the number of variables in that group; and (2) the second card contains the variables for the group, punched in floating point format, eight variables to a card, in successive ten-column fields. Further cards may be used as needed to include all of the variables. This pattern then is repeated for each group in the job. There is one important *restriction* on the input: the total number of variables for any one job may not be more than 4,000. To stack jobs, a blank card is inserted between the input cards for each job. After the input cards for the last job to be processed, a card with the integer 9999 punched in columns 1 through 4 is used, instead of a blank card.

The output includes (1) for each group, the number of variables, the mean, and the standard deviation; (2) for each job, BETA1, BETA2, and the mean deviate; and (3) the list of all the variables, after normalization, sorted into descending order.

An error message reading TOO MANY VARIABLES will be printed if any job contains more than 4,000 variables.

Figure B.4 shows sample input and output for this program. Figure B.5 is a listing of the program.

PROGRAM B.3   Linear Regression in Two Variables

This program carries out computations associated with fitting of a straight line to a set of observations, using the method of least squares. If the observations are denoted by (x_i, y_i) for $i = 1, 2, \ldots, n$, and if the line to be fitted is of the form $y = a + bx$, then

$$\hat{b} = \frac{n\Sigma x_i y_i - \Sigma x_i \Sigma y_i}{n\Sigma x_i^2 - (\Sigma x_i)^2},$$

$$\hat{a} = \frac{\Sigma y_i - \hat{b}\Sigma x_i}{n},$$

where all sums Σ are from $i = 1$ to n. This program also calculates and prints out the mean and standard deviation of y, the standard deviation of x, the correlation coefficient, the standard error of the estimate of y, the standard error of the estimate of b, and the ratio of $\hat{b}$ to the standard error of the estimate of b (this is called the statistic T). These statistics and the others calculated in this program are defined by Acton (1959).

The program offers three different kinds of output, specified as options 01, 10, or 00. Option 01 (see Figure B.7) gives only the basic statistics listed above and produces only a single page of output. Option 10 (see Figure B.8) gives—in addition to the basic statistics—a table listing x, y, $\hat{y}$, and $y - \hat{y}$, with an indication that the residual $(y - \hat{y})$ is unusually large if this is the case; this option

Sample Input

```
  5
3.0        1.0        5.0        2.0        4.0
  5
1.9        1.0        1.3        1.7        1.5

  9
   45.47     46.00      39.00      43.00      43.32      50.23      45.09      50.60
   46.50                                                                          1
  9
   52.30     41.25      44.00      36.97      44.00      48.59      48.64      45.07
   44.29                                                                          2
  9
   77.84     80.21      69.00      77.63      77.65      76.00      77.27      76.70
   75.35                                                                          3
9999
```

Sample Output

```
    N        MEAN          STD DEV
    5       3.000000      1.581138
    5       1.480000       .349284

A =      .846785


          B1              B2
          .010794       1.769544


    1.264    1.202     .632     .629     .057    0.000    -.515    -.632   -1.264   -1.374

    N        MEAN          STD DEV
    9      45.467777      3.588949
    9      45.012222      4.478792
    9      76.405555      3.092935

A =      .731381


          B1              B2
          .373206       3.384606


    1.627    1.430    1.326    1.230     .809     .798     .463     .402     .395     .28
     .279     .148     .095     .012    0.000    -.105    -.131    -.161    -.226    -.22
    -.341    -.598    -.687    -.840   -1.795   -1.802   -2.394
```

FIG. B.4   Sample Input and Output for Program B.2

```
C     NORMALITY PROGRAM
      DIMENSION T(4000)
1     IFR=1
      NID=5
      WRITE(6,1966)
      WRITE (6,905)
      N=0
      TLSM=0.0
2     READ (NID,901) NJ
      KD=1
      IF (NJ) 3,4,3
3     IF (NJ-9999) 18,19,18
19    KD=2
      GO TO 4
18    NL=IFR+NJ-1
      IF (NL-4000) 16,16,17
17    WRITE (6,909)
      WRITE (6,1966)
      STOP 7
16    N=N+NJ
      READ (NID,902) (T(K),K=IFR,NL)
      TSUM=0.0
      TSS=0.0
      DO 5 K=IFR,NL
      TK=T(K)
      TSUM=TSUM+TK
      TSS=TSS+TK*TK
5     CONTINUE
      AN=NJ
      SIG= SQRT((AN*TSS-TSUM*TSUM)/(AN*(AN-1.0)))
      AV=TSUM/AN
      WRITE (6,903) NJ,AV,SIG
      DO 6 K=IFR,NL
      TK=(T(K)-AV)/SIG
      IF (TK-100.0) 8,9,9
8     IF (TK+100.0) 15,15,10
15    TK=-99.999
      GO TO 10
9     TK=99.999
10    T(K)=TK
      TLSM=TLSM+TK
6     CONTINUE
      IFR=NL+1
      GO TO 2
4     AN=N
      TBR=TLSM/AN
      TMD=0.0
      TM2=0.0
      TM3=0.0
      TM4=0.0
      DO 7 K=1,N
      TK=T(K)-TBR
      TMD=TMD+ ABS(TK)
      TK2=TK*TK
      TM2=TM2+TK2
      TM3=TM3+TK2*TK
      TM4=TM4+TK2*TK2
7     CONTINUE
      TMD=TMD/(AN* SQRT(TM2/AN))
      WRITE (6,910) TMD
      TK2=TM2*TM2
      WRITE (6,906)
      B1=AN*TM3*TM3/(TM2*TK2)
      B2=AN*TM4/TK2
      WRITE (6,904) B1,B2
11    WRITE (6,908)
C     SHELL SORT
      M=N
24    M=M/2
      IF(M) 22,22,21
21    K=N-M
      DO 23 J=1,K
      II=J
27    IM=II+M
      IF (T(II)-T(IM)) 25,23,23
25    TLG=T(II)
      T(II)=T(IM)
      T(IM)=TLG
      II=II-M
      IF(II-1) 23,27,27
23    CONTINUE
      GO TO 24
22    WRITE (6,907) (T(K),K=1,N)
      WRITE (6,908)
20    GO TO (1,12),KD
12    WRITE (6,1966)
      STOP
901   FORMAT (I4)
902   FORMAT (8F10.4)
903   FORMAT ( 1H ,I5,2F15.6)
904   FORMAT ( 1H ,2F15.6)
905   FORMAT ( 1H ,3X,1HN,7X,4HMEAN,11X,7HSTD DEV)
906   FORMAT ( 1H ,8X,2HB1,13X,2HB2)
907   FORMAT(10F8.3)
908   FORMAT ( 1H )
909   FORMAT (19H TOO MANY VARIABLES)
910   FORMAT (4H0A =,F12.6)
911   FORMAT(2I5,3E15.8)
1966  FORMAT(1H1)
      END
```

FIG. B.5 Listing of Program B.2

produces two pages of output. Option 00 (see Figure B.9) gives—in addition to the basic statistics and the table produced by option 10—a measure of the tolerable error in $\hat{y}$ for each x, and an indication of unusual values for x or y or for the residual (these unusual values are denoted by BXD, BDY, and BDR, respectively).

The *input* for this program requires three cards that provide program control parameters, followed by the cards that make up the data deck. On the first card, the output option is specified in columns 1 and 2 as either 01, 00, or 10 (see preceding paragraph). On the second card, the total number of cases to be processed (KASE) is specified in columns 1 through 4. Any number of cases may be processed, one immediately following the other. This card appears only once, before the data deck, no matter how many cases are to be processed in a single run. A card of the third type must precede the observations data for each case to be run. In columns 1 through 4 of this third card is specified the total number of observations for the case being processed (N). In columns 5 through 8 of this card is specified the number of standard deviations (M) acceptable so that the sample data, when examined against sample statistics, falls within the desired confidence limits.

The three cards providing program control parameters are followed by the data deck, in which each observation (that is, both x and y values) is specified on a separate card. The x value (independent variable) is given in columns 1 through 10, and the y value (dependent variable) is given in columns 11 through 20. This information always is entered from the punched-card reader. Up to 1,000 observations may be processed at one time. The input data format is (2F10.3).

Figure B.6 shows a sample parameter and data deck; Figures B.7, B.8, and B.9 show sample output from the three available options; and Figure B.10 shows a listing of the program.

PROGRAM B.4   Nonlinear Least Squares

This program provides a method of fitting a nonlinear equation to data. The user specifies the function used in the equation, in the form of a FORTRAN function subprogram. The program then computes—for all possible combinations of parameters—the sums of the squares of the differences between values observed and calculated for such a specified function, for up to 7 variables, 6 parameters, and 400 observations.

If the user has a clear idea of the general form of the equation that is to describe the observed results and has some notion of the smallest and largest values to be obtained by each parameter, this program will indicate the best possible combination of parameters—relative, of course, to the mesh size (increments of the parametric values) chosen by the user. The algorithm proceeds in the fol-

```
01
  1
 25   1
  -25.    24.0
  -24.    28.3
  -23.    32.0
  -22.    28.8
  -21.    31.7
  -20.    29.9
  -19.    33.3
  -18.    35.2
  -17.    34.7
  -16.    36.8
  -15.    35.0
  -14.    30.9
  -13.    32.3
  -12.    33.3
  -11.    29.4
  -10.    32.8
   -9.    31.3
   -8.    33.5
   -7.    30.4
   -6.    33.3
   -5.    31.8
   -4.    34.6
   -3.    33.7
   -2.    33.9
   -1.    32.9
```

FIG. B.6   Sample Parameter and Data Deck for Program B.3

```
                              LEAST SQUARES FIT


         FOR    25   OBSERVATIONS

         FOR  THE  EQUATION  OF  THE  FORM   Y = A + B  X

                          Y  =   0.34170990E 02 + 0.15531546E 00   X

         FOR  THE  EQUATION  OF  THE  FORM   Y = C  X

                          Y  =  -.18547430E 01   X



         ADDITIONAL   INFORMATION

                                  MEAN = -.13000000E 02

                     STANDARD  DEVIATION  OF  X = 0.73597994E 01

                     STANDARD  DEVIATION  OF  Y = 0.26979265E 01

                      CORRELATION  COEFFICIENT = 0.42370427E 00

                   STANDARD  ERROR  OF  ESTIMATE = 0.24963465E 01

             STANDARD  ERROR  OF  COEFFICIENT,   B  = 0.69236219E-01

                             THE  STATISTIC   T = 0.22432680E 01



         CORRELATION  COEFFICIENT  AND  T  ARE  BOTH  ABSOLUTE

         TABLE SHOULD BE CHECKED     23. DEGREES OF FREEDOM
```

FIG. B.7   Sample Output for Program B.3 Using Output Option 01

LEAST SQUARES FIT

FOR   25   OBSERVATIONS

FOR THE EQUATION OF THE FORM Y = A + B X

$$Y = 0.34170990E\ 02 + 0.15531546E\ 00\ X$$

FOR THE EQUATION OF THE FORM Y = C X

$$Y = -.18547430E\ 01\ X$$

ADDITIONAL INFORMATION

MEAN = -.13000000E 02

STANDARD DEVIATION OF X = 0.73597994E 01

STANDARD DEVIATION OF Y = 0.26979265E 01

CORRELATION COEFFICIENT = 0.42370427E 00

STANDARD ERROR OF ESTIMATE = 0.24963465E 01

STANDARD ERROR OF COEFFICIENT, B = 0.69236219E-01

THE STATISTIC T = 0.22432680E 01

CORRELATION COEFFICIENT AND T ARE BOTH ABSOLUTE

TABLE SHOULD BE CHECKED   23. DEGREES OF FREEDOM

	Y	X	Y ESTIMATED	ACTUAL Y-YEST	
1	0.24000000E 02	-.25000000E 02	0.30288101E 02	-.62881012E 01	BAD
2	0.28299988E 02	-.24000000E 02	0.30443405E 02	-.21434174E 01	BAD
3	0.32000000E 02	-.23000000E 02	0.30598724E 02	0.14012756E 01	BAD
4	0.28799988E 02	-.22000000E 02	0.30754044E 02	-.19540558E 01	BAD
5	0.31699997E 02	-.21000000E 02	0.30909363E 02	0.79063416E 00	BAD
6	0.29899994E 02	-.20000000E 02	0.31064667E 02	-.11646729E 01	
7	0.33299988E 02	-.19000000E 02	0.31219986E 02	0.20800018E 01	
8	0.35199997E 02	-.18000000E 02	0.31375305E 02	0.38246918E 01	BAD
9	0.34699997E 02	-.17000000E 02	0.31530624E 02	0.31693726E 01	BAD
10	0.36799988E 02	-.16000000E 02	0.31685928E 02	0.51140594E 01	BAD
11	0.35000000E 02	-.15000000E 02	0.31841248E 02	0.31587524E 01	BAD
12	0.30899994E 02	-.14000000E 02	0.31996567E 02	-.10965729E 01	
13	0.32299988E 02	-.13000000E 02	0.32151886E 02	0.14810181E 00	
14	0.33299988E 02	-.12000000E 02	0.32307205E 02	0.99278259E 00	
15	0.29399994E 02	-.11000000E 02	0.32462509E 02	-.30625153E 01	BAD
16	0.32799988E 02	-.10000000E 02	0.32617828E 02	0.18215942E 00	
17	0.31299988E 02	-.90000000E 01	0.32773148E 02	-.14731598E 01	
18	0.33500000E 02	-.80000000E 01	0.32928467E 02	0.57153320E 00	
19	0.30399994E 02	-.70000000E 01	0.33083771E 02	-.26837769E 01	BAD
20	0.33299988E 02	-.60000000E 01	0.33239090E 02	0.60897827E-01	
21	0.31799988E 02	-.50000000E 01	0.33394409E 02	-.15944214E 01	BAD
22	0.34599991E 02	-.40000000E 01	0.33549728E 02	0.10502625E 01	BAD
23	0.33699997E 02	-.30000000E 01	0.33705032E 02	-.50354004E-02	BAD
24	0.33899994E 02	-.20000000E 01	0.33860352E 02	0.39642334E-01	BAD
25	0.32899994E 02	-.10000000E 01	0.34015671E 02	-.11156769E 01	BAD

FIG. B.8   Sample Output for Program B.3 Using Output Option 10

```
                              LEAST SQUARES FIT


FOR   25  OBSERVATIONS

FOR  THE  EQUATION  OF  THE  FORM  Y = A + B X

                    Y  =  0.34170990E 02 + 0.15531546E 00  X

FOR  THE  EQUATION  OF  THE  FORM  Y = C X

                    Y  =  -.18547430E 01  X



ADDITIONAL  INFORMATION

                              MEAN = -.13000000E 02

              STANDARD DEVIATION OF X = 0.73597994E 01

              STANDARD DEVIATION OF Y = 0.26979265E 01

              CORRELATION COEFFICIENT = 0.42370427E 00

          STANDARD ERROR OF ESTIMATE = 0.24963465E 01

    STANDARD ERROR OF COEFFICIENT,  B = 0.69236219E-01

                      THE STATISTIC  T = 0.22432680E 01


CORRELATION COEFFICIENT AND T ARE BOTH ABSOLUTE

TABLE SHOULD BE CHECKED    23. DEGREES OF FREEDOM


      ------X------ *****Y*****  Y------ESTIMAED  YACTUAL-YESTMD   M*ERROR OF EST
   1  -.25000E 02 0.24000E 02  0.30288101E 02   -.62881012E 01BDR  0.96930647E 00
   2  -.24000E 02 0.28300E 02  0.30443405E 02   -.21434174E 01BDX  0.91065967E 00
   3  -.23000E 02 0.32000E 02  0.30598724E 02   0.14012756E 01BDX  0.85360092E 00
   4  -.22000E 02 0.28800E 02  0.30754044E 02   -.19540558E 01BDX  0.79847062E 00
   5  -.21000E 02 0.31700E 02  0.30909363E 02   0.79063416E 00BDX  0.74569625E 00
   6  -.20000E 02 0.29900E 02  0.31064667E 02   -.11646729E 01     0.69581491E 00
   7  -.19000E 02 0.33300E 02  0.31219986E 02   0.20800018E 01     0.64949286E 00
   8  -.18000E 02 0.35200E 02  0.31375305E 02   0.38246918E 01BDR  0.60754502E 00
   9  -.17000E 02 0.34700E 02  0.31530624E 02   0.31693726E 01BDR  0.57093608E 00
  10  -.16000E 02 0.36800E 02  0.31685928E 02   0.51140594E 01BDR  0.54075193E 00
  11  -.15000E 02 0.35000E 02  0.31841248E 02   0.31587524E 01BDR  0.51811606E 00
  12  -.14000E 02 0.30900E 02  0.31996567E 02   -.10965729E 01     0.50404698E 00
  13  -.13000E 02 0.32300E 02  0.32151886E 02   0.14810181E 00     0.49926925E 00
  14  -.12000E 02 0.33300E 02  0.32307205E 02   0.99278259E 00     0.50404698E 00
  15  -.11000E 02 0.29400E 02  0.32462509E 02   -.30625153E 01BDR  0.51811606E 00
  16  -.10000E 02 0.32800E 02  0.32617828E 02   0.18215942E 00     0.54075193E 00
  17  -.90000E 01 0.31300E 02  0.32773148E 02   -.14731598E 01     0.57093608E 00
  18  -.80000E 01 0.33500E 02  0.32928467E 02   0.57153320E 00     0.60754502E 00
  19  -.70000E 01 0.30400E 02  0.33083771E 02   -.26837769E 01BDR  0.64949286E 00
  20  -.60000E 01 0.33300E 02  0.33239090E 02   0.60897827E-01     0.69581491E 00
  21  -.50000E 01 0.31800E 02  0.33394409E 02   -.15944214E 01BDX  0.74589625E 00
  22  -.40000E 01 0.34600E 02  0.33549728E 02   0.10502625E 01BDX  0.79847062E 00
  23  -.30000E 01 0.33700E 02  0.33705032E 02   -.50354004E-02BDX  0.85360092E 00
  24  -.20000E 01 0.33900E 02  0.33860352E 02   0.39642334E-01BDX  0.91065967E 00
  25  -.10000E 01 0.32900E 02  0.34015671E 02   -.11156769E 01BDX  0.96930647E 00
```

FIG. B.9   Sample Output for Program B.3 Using Output Option 00

```
        DIMENSION XX(1000),YY(1000)
        KASY=0
        WRITE (6,119)
        READ (5,51) ISEN2,ISEN3
   51 FORMAT (2I1)
    3 READ (5,101) KASE
   36 READ (5,101) N,M
    4 EN=N
        EM=M
        SX=0.
        SY=0.
        SXY=0.
        SX2=0.
        SY2=0.
        READ (5,102) (XX(I),YY(I),I=1,N)
        DO5I=1,N
        X=XX(I)
        Y=YY(I)
        SX=SX+X
        SY=SY+Y
        SXY=SXY+X*Y
        SX2=SX2+X*X
    5 SY2=SY2+Y*Y
        XBAR=SX/EN
        YBAR=SY/EN
        CX2=SX*SX/EN
        CXY=SX*SY/EN
        VX2=SX2-CX2
        VXY=SXY-CXY
        B=VXY/VX2
        A=YBAR-B*XBAR
        C=SXY/SX2
        R=(((EN*SXY-SX*SY)**2)/((EN*SX2-SX*SX)*(EN*SY2-SY*SY)))
        RA=SQRT (ABS (R))
    8 S2SX=(EN*SX2-SX*SX)/(EN*(EN-1.))
        S2SY=(EN*SY2-SY*SY)/(EN*(EN-1.))
        S2YGX=((EN-1.)/(EN-2.))*(S2SY-B*B*S2SX)
        SYGX=S2YGX**.5
        SB=SYGX/((S2SX*(EN-1.))**.5)
        IF(B)9,10,10
    9 BA=-B
        GO TO 11
   10 BA=B
   11 T=BA/SB
        IF(T)12,13,13
   12 TA=-T
        GO TO 14
   13 TA=T
   14 DF2=EN-2.
        SEX=((SX2-SX*SX/EN)/(EN-1.))**.5
        SEY=((SY2-SY*SY/EN)/(EN-1.))**.5
        WRITE (6,103)
        WRITE (6,104) N
        WRITE (6,105)
        WRITE (6,106) A,B
        WRITE (6,107)
        WRITE (6,108) C
        WRITE (6,109)
```

FIG. B.10   Listing of Program B.3

```
      WRITE (6,110) XBAR
      WRITE (6,117) SEX
      WRITE (6,118) SEY
      WRITE (6,111) RA
      WRITE (6,112) SYGX
      WRITE (6,113) SB
      WRITE (6,114) TA
      WRITE (6,115)
      WRITE (6,116) DF2
      WRITE (6,119)
      IF (ISEN3) 16,16,32
   16 IF (ISEN2) 60,60,70
   60 SEXM=SEX*EM
      SEYM=SEY*EM
      SGM=SYGX*EM
      SS=SGM
      WRITE (6,122)
      DO31I=1,N
      X=XX(I)
      Y=YY(I)
      SM=SS*(SQRT ((1./EN)+((X-XBAR)**2)/(SX2-(EN*(XBAR**2)))) )
      KW=1
      XD=XBAR-X
      YD=YBAR-Y
      YES=A+B*X
      SDO=Y-YES
      IF(XD)17,18,18
   17 XD=-XD
   18 IF(YD)19,20,20
   19 YD=-YD
   20 IF(XD-SEXM) 24,24,23
   23    KW=2
      GOTO26
   24 IF(YD-SEYM)26,26,25
   25 KW=3
   26    IF(ABS (SDO)-SGM)28,28,27
   27    KW=4
   28    GO TO (29,41,42,30),KW
   29    WRITE (6,120) I,X,Y,YES,SDO,SM
      GOTO31
   30 WRITE(6,121) I,X,Y,YES,SDO,SM
      GOTO31
   41 WRITE(6,124) I,X,Y,YES,SDO,SM
      GOTO31
   42 WRITE(6,125) I,X,Y,YES,SDO,SM
   31 CONTINUE
      GOTO32
   70    SEXM=SEX*EM
      SEYM=SEY*EM
      SGM=SYGX*EM
      WRITE (6,1220)
      DO 310 I=1,N
      X=XX(I)
      Y=YY(I)
      KW=0
      XD=XBAR-X
      YD=YBAR-Y
      YES=A+B*X
```

FIG. B.10—*Continued*

```
          SDO=Y-YES
          IF(XD)  170,180,180
170       XD=-XD
180       IF(YD)190,200,200
190       YD=-YD
200       IF(XD-SEXM)        240,240,230
230       KW=1
          GOTO280
240       IF(YD-SEYM)        260,260,250
250       KW=1
          GOTO280
260       IF(ABS (SDO)-SGM)        280,280,270
270       KW=1
280       IF(KW)        290,290,300
290       WRITE (6,1200) I,Y,X,YES,SDO
          GOTO310
300       WRITE (6,1210) I,Y,X,YES,SDO
 310  CONTINUE
   32 KASY=KASY+1
      WRITE (6,119)
      IF(KASY-KASE) 34,33,33
   34 GO TO 36
   33 WRITE    (6,119)
   99 STOP
  101 FORMAT (2I4)
  102 FORMAT (2F10.3)
  103 FORMAT  (1H0, 21X,21H  LEAST   SQUARES   FIT)
  104 FORMAT (//6H0 FOR  I4,14H  OBSERVATIONS)
  105 FORMAT ( 48H0 FOR  THE  EQUATION  OF  THE  FORM  Y = A + B X)
  106 FORMAT (1H0,26X,7H  Y  =  ,E14.8,3H + E14.8,3H   X)
  107 FORMAT (1H0,'FOR  THE  EQUATION  OF  THE  FORM Y = C X')
  108 FORMAT (  1H0,   26X,7H  Y  =  ,E14.8,3H   X)
  109 FORMAT(///25H  ADDITIONAL   INFORMATION)
  110 FORMAT    (1H0,35X,8H MEAN = ,        E14.8)
  111 FORMAT ( 1H0,   16X,27H CORRELATION COEFFICIENT = ,E14.8)
  112 FORMAT ( 1H0,13X,30H STANDARD ERROR OF ESTIMATE = ,E14.8)
  113 FORMAT ( 44H0        STANDARD ERROR OF COEFFICIENT,  B  = ,E14.8)
  114 FORMAT ( 1H0,23X,20H THE STATISTIC  T = ,E14.8)
  115 FORMAT (//49H0 CORRELATION COEFFICIENT AND T ARE BOTH ABSOLUTE)
  116 FORMAT(26H0 TABLE SHOULD BE CHECKED F6.0,19H DEGREES OF FREEDOM)
  117 FORMAT(1H0,16X,27H STANDARD DEVIATION OF X = ,E14.8)
  118 FORMAT(1H0,16X,27H STANDARD DEVIATION OF Y = ,E14.8)
  119 FORMAT (1H1)
  120 FORMAT (1H ,I4,1X,2(1X,E11.5),2(2X,E14.8),5X,E14.8)
  121 FORMAT (1H ,I4,1X,2(1X,E11.5),2(2X,E14.8),3HBDR,2X,E14.8)
  122 FORMAT  (1H ,6X,11H-----X-----,1X,11H*****Y*****,2X,14HY-----ESTIMAT
     1ED,2X,14HYACTUAL-YESTMD,5X,14HM*ERROR OF EST)
  123 FORMAT (4HCASE,I5,13H IS COMPLETED)
  124 FORMAT ( 1H ,I4,1X,2(1X,E11.5),2(2X,E14.8),3HBDX,2X,E14.8)
  125 FORMAT ( 1H ,I4,1X,2(1X,E11.5),2(2X,E14.8),3HBDX,2X,E14.8)
 1220 FORMAT (1H ,14X,1HY,17X,1HX,13X,11HY ESTIMATED,6X,13HACTUAL Y-YEST
     1)
 1200 FORMAT (1H ,I4,4(4X,E14.8))
 1210 FORMAT (1H ,I4,4(4X,E14.8),4H BAD)
      END
```

FIG. B.10—Continued

lowing steps: (1) all possible combinations of the parametric values are considered for the increments and ranges of each variable that the user has specified; (2) for each combination, all observations are compared with computed values, and these differences are squared; and (3) the sum of the squares is taken and printed in the output column headed DIFSQ, in the same row with the corresponding values of the parameters used. The user then selects the smallest entry in the DIFSQ column and chooses the corresponding combination of parameters.

If a better choice is desired, the user can refine his mesh on the basis of the information supplied by this program. He will simultaneously narrow the range of parametric values to be considered and will choose smaller increments of those values. In this manner, the user can obtain as close a fit of the function to the data as desired, if the correct general form of the equation has been selected. An example of the use of this program is given in Section 5.7.

The *input* for this program must include the function subprogram and data cards. Figure B.11 includes an example of the function subprogram, FCN. *Only* the fourth statement of this subprogram — the statement defining the function through an equation — can be changed by the user. For example, the statement

0001   FUNCTION FCN(Y,P1,P2,P3,P4,P5,P6,K)

cannot be changed, but must appear in exactly the same form in the input for every user, regardless of how many parameters the user actually includes in his function. The fourth statement, which may be changed by the user, has the general form,

0004   FCN=f(Y(K),Y(K+1), . . . , Y(K+NOVAR−1);P1,P2, . . . ,PNOPAR)

where f(. . .) is the user's function, with the first variable denoted by Y(K), the second variable by Y(K+1), and so forth, and the first parameter denoted by P1, the second parameter by P2, and so forth, and where NOVAR stands for the number of variables and NOPAR stands for the number of parameters that appear in the user's function.

In the sample input of Figure B.11, the function selected is

$$FCN = \frac{a_1 e^{-a_2 x} - a_2 e^{-a_1 x}}{a_1 - a_2}$$

The sample input clearly illustrates the necessary translation. The user's function may take any form, so long as it is called FCN and contains no more than 7 variables and 6 parameters. All other statements in the function subprogram must appear in exactly the same form as that used in the sample input of Figure B.11.

Following the function subprogram is the set of data cards, which must contain (1) the first card punched in columns 2 through 4 with an integer indicating

```
      FUNCTION FCN(Y,P1,P2,P3,P4,P5,P6,K,JSW)
      IMPLICIT REAL*8(A-H,O-Z)
      DIMENSION Y(1)
      FCN=(P1/DEXP(P2*Y(K))-P2/DEXP(P1*Y(K)))/(P1-P2)
      IF(JSW)1,2,1
    1 WRITE(6,66)FCN
   66 FORMAT(1H0,T15,'FCN=    ',D25.6)
    2 CONTINUE
      RETURN
      END
```

Listing of Sample Function Definition

```
   8    2    0
 0.0                                                                    1.0
 1.0                                                                    .6662
 2.0                                                                    .4450
 3.0                                                                    .2291
 4.0                                                                    .0805
 5.0                                                                    .0687
 6.0                                                                    .0576
 7.0                                                                    .0412
 1.5        3.0       0.5       0.5       0.8       0.1
```

Sample Input

```
 PARAM1       PARAM2      DIFSQ
   1.5000      0.5000    0.520956D-01
   1.5000      0.6000    0.174047D-01
   1.5000      0.7000    0.838289D-02
   1.5000      0.8000    0.124174D-01
   2.0000      0.5000    0.273096D-01
   2.0000      0.6000    0.726136D-02
   2.0000      0.7000    0.108240D-01
   2.0000      0.8000    0.257353D-01
   2.5000      0.5000    0.167880D-01
   2.5000      0.6000    0.607041D-02
   2.5000      0.7000    0.176672D-01
   2.5000      0.8000    0.395448D-01
   3.0000      0.5000    0.118047D-01
   3.0000      0.6000    0.751728D-02
   3.0000      0.7000    0.246506D-01
   3.0000      0.8000    0.513326D-01
```

Sample Output

FIG. B.11   Sample Input and Output for Program B.4

the number of observations, in column 8 with an integer indicating the number of parameters, and in column 12 with a zero if the values of the function are not to be printed in the output or a one if the values of the function are to be printed in the output; (2) next, one card for *each* observation, with values of the independent variables for the particular observation punched in columns 1 through 70 and the corresponding value of the dependent variable punched in columns 71 through 80—all entries must conform to the format F10.4; (3) next, one card for each *two* parameters, with the minimal value for a particular parameter punched in columns 1 through 10, the maximal value for the same parameter punched in columns 11 through 20, and the desired increment for the same parameter punched in columns 21 through 30; columns 31 through 60 may contain analogous information for a second parameter (if there is one); all entries must be in the format F10.4; columns 61 through 80 must be blank; parameters must appear in the data deck in the same order as they are designated in the user's function — that is, P1 appears first, then P2, and so forth; and (4) additional sets of data may be run, one after the other, with each set of data cards containing cards as described in 1, 2, and 3 above; a blank card must follow the last set of data to be run.

The *output* appears in NOPAR+1 columns of figures (where NOPAR is the number of parameters in the user's function). The headings of these columns are PARAM1, PARAM2, . . . , and DIFSQ. The final column contains the sum of the squares of the differences for the particular combination of parameters specified in the preceding columns. All entries are in format F10.4, except for DIFSQ, which is printed in E12.6 format.

In the sample problem (Figure B.11), eight observations were used as data, with the variable x moving successively through values of 0, 1, 2, . . . , 7. Two parameters are used in the function; the first takes a minimal value of 1.5 and a maximal value of 3.0, with increments of 0.5, and the second takes a minimal value of 0.5 and a maximal value of 0.8, with increments of 0.1.

Figure B.12 is a listing of the program.

PROGRAM B.5   Generation of Random Numbers

The generation of random numbers is discussed in Part Three. Producing a sequence of numbers by some algorithm obviously cannot result in generation of a truly random sequence. A truly random number or occurrence can be produced only by some physical phenomenon, such as white noise. The numbers produced by algorithms properly are called "pseudorandom numbers" if they meet certain tests for "randomness." However, it will be convenient in the following discussion to use the term "random numbers" to refer to these pseudorandom numbers.

The properties of a random number generator should include the following: (1) the numbers generated should have as nearly as possible a uniform distribution; (2) the generator should be fast; (3) the generator program should not require large amounts of core; (4) the generator should have a long period — that is, it should produce a long sequence of numbers before the sequence begins to repeat; (5) the generator should be able to produce different sequences of random numbers or to reproduce the same sequence, depending upon the needs of the user; and (6) the algorithm should never degenerate to produce a sequence of identical numbers. A number of generator programs are described below, using different algorithms to meet these objectives.

Figure B.13 is a listing of a program for a generator that uses a random method to generate uniform random numbers. A ten-digit number X is taken as a

```fortran
C        LEAST SQUARES PROBLEM
C     THIS PROBLEM COMPUTES THE SUM OF THE SQUARES OF THE DIFFERENCE
C     BETWEEN VALUES OBSERVED AND CALCULATED FOR A FUNCTION NOT NECESS-
C     ARILY LINEAR OF UP TO 7 VARIABLES, 6 PARAMETERS, 400 OBSERVATIONS.
      IMPLICIT REAL*8 (A-H,O-Z)
      READ(5,30) NOOBS,NOPAR,JSW
9     WRITE(6,1966)
1966  FORMAT(1H1)
7     IF(NOOBS)17,7,6
      WRITE(6,1966)
      CALL EXIT
6     M=8*NOOBS
      N=3*NOPAR
8     DIMENSION B(3200),A(18)
      READ(5,10) (B(J),J=1,M)
      READ(5,20) (A(L),L=1,N)
10    FORMAT(8F10.4)
20    FORMAT(6F10.4,20X)
30    FORMAT(3I4)
35    LIMOBS=1+(NOOBS-1)*8
      LIM1=1.0+((A(2)-A(1))/A(3))
      IF(NOPAR-1)40,130,40
40    LIM2=1.0+((A(5)-A(4))/A(6))
      IF(NOPAR-2)50,140,50
50    LIM3=1.0+((A(8)-A(7))/A(9))
      IF(NOPAR-3)60,150,60
60    LIM4=1.0+((A(11)-A(10))/A(12))
      IF(NOPAR-4)70,160,70
70    LIM5=1.0+((A(14)-A(13))/A(15))
      IF(NOPAR-5)80,170,80
80    LIM6=1.0+((A(17)-A(16))/A(18))
      GO TO 180
130   WRITE(6,230)
      GO TO 330
140   WRITE(6,240)
      GO TO 330
150   WRITE(6,250)
      GO TO 330
160   WRITE(6,260)
      GO TO 330
170   WRITE(6,270)
      GO TO 330
180   WRITE(6,280)
230   FORMAT(1H ,2X,6HPARAM1,6X,5HDIFSQ)
240   FORMAT (1H ,2X,6HPARAM1,6X,6HPARAM2,6X,5HDIFSQ)
250   FORMAT(1H ,2X,6HPARAM1,6X,6HPARAM2,6X,6HPARAM3,6X,5HDIFSQ)
260   FORMAT(1H ,2X,6HPARAM1,6X,6HPARAM2,6X,6HPARAM3,6X,6HPARAM4,6X,
     15HDIFSQ)
270   FORMAT(1H ,2X,6HPARAM1,6X,6HPARAM2,6X,6HPARAM3,6X,6HPARAM4,6X,
     16HPARAM5,6X,5HDIFSQ)
280   FORMAT(1H ,2X,6HPARAM1,6X,6HPARAM2,5X,6HPARAM3,5X,6HPARAM4,5X,
     16HPARAM5,5X,6HPARAM6,6X,5HDIFSQ)
330   DO 730 J1=1,LIM1
      D=J1-1
      PAR1=A(1)+D*A(3)
      IF(NOPAR-1)340,335,340
335   LIM2=1
      J2=LIM2
336   LIM3=1
      J3=LIM3
337   LIM4=1
      J4=LIM4
338   LIM5=1
      J5=LIM5
339   LIM6=1
      J6=LIM6
340   GO TO 430
      D=J2-1
      PAR2=A(4)+D*A(6)
      IF(NOPAR-2)350,336,350
350   DO 730 J3=1,LIM3
      PAR3=A(7)+D*A(9)
      IF(NOPAR-3)360,337,360
360   DO 730 J4=1,LIM4
      D=J4-1
      PAR4=A(10)+D*A(12)
      IF(NOPAR-4)370,338,370
370   DO 730 J5=1,LIM5
      D=J5-1
      PAR5=A(13)+D*A(15)
      IF(NOPAR-5)380,339,380
380   DO 730 J6=1,LIM6
      D=J6-1
      PAR6=A(16)+D*A(18)
430   DIFSQ=0.
      DO 440 I=1,LIMOBS,8
      OBSVAL=B(I+7)
      C=(FCN(B,PAR1,PAR2,PAR3,PAR4,PAR5,PAR6,I,JSW)-OBSVAL)**2
      DIFSQ=DIFSQ+C
440   IF(NOPAR-1)460,450,460
450   WRITE(6,630) PAR1,DIFSQ
      GO TO 730
460   IF(NOPAR-2)480,470,480
470   WRITE(6,640) PAR1,PAR2,DIFSQ
      GO TO 730
480   IF(NOPAR-3)500,490,500
490   WRITE(6,650) PAR1,PAR2,PAR3,DIFSQ
      GO TO 730
500   IF(NOPAR-4)520,510,520
510   WRITE(6,660) PAR1,PAR2,PAR3,PAR4,DIFSQ
      GO TO 730
520   IF(NOPAR-5)550,530,550
530   WRITE(6,670) PAR1,PAR2,PAR3,PAR4,PAR5,DIFSQ
      GO TO 730
550   WRITE(6,680) PAR1,PAR2,PAR3,PAR4,PAR5,PAR6,DIFSQ
630   FORMAT(1H ,F10.4,2X,D12.6)
640   FORMAT(1H ,2(F10.4,2X),D12.6)
650   FORMAT(1H ,3(F10.4,2X),D12.6)
660   FORMAT(1H ,4(F10.4,2X),D12.6)
670   FORMAT(1H ,5(F10.4,2X),D12.6)
680   FORMAT(1H ,6(F10.4,2X),D12.6)
730   CONTINUE
      GO TO 9
      END
```

FIG. B.12 Listing of Program B.4

```
        SUBROUTINE RAND(IX,RN,IFLAG)
C       IX=9876543210=ISEED(1)
        E8=1.E8
        E9=1.E9
        E10=1.E10
666     IY=ISEED/E9
        MM=Y+1
1       DO 113 I=1,MM
2       IZ=IX/E8
        IF(IZ.LT.10) GO TO 14
        IZZ=IZ/10
        IZ=IZ-IZZ*10
14      IJMP=3+IZ
        GO TO (1,2,3,4,5,6,7,8,9,10,11,12,13),IJMP
3       IF(IX.LT.5000000000) IX=IX+ 5000000000
4       IX=IX**2/E5
        IF(IX.LT.10) GO TO 5
        IXX = IX/10
        IX = IX - IXX*10
5       IX = 1001001001*IX
        IF(IX.LT.E10) GO TO 6
        IXX = IX/E10
        IX = IX - IXX*E10
6       IF(IX.LT.100000000) GO TO 16
        IX = E10-IX
        GO TO 7
16      IX = IX + 9814055677
7       IXT = IX
        IF(IXT.LT.E5) GO TO 17
        IXX = IXT/E5
        IXT=IXT-IXX*E5
17      IX = E5*IXT+IX/E5
8       IX = 1001001001*IX
        IF(IX.LT.E10) GO TO 9
        IXX = IX/E10
        IX = IX-IXX*E10
9       IXX = 0
        IXTEM = IX
19      IF(IXTEM.EQ.0) GO TO 10
        ISHI = IXTEM/10
        IDIG = IXTEM-ISHI*10
        IF(IDIG.EQ.0) GO TO 20
        IDIG = IDIG-1
20      IXX = IXX*10+IDIG
        IXTEM = ISHI
        GO TO 19
10      IX = IXX
        IF(IX.LT.E5) GO TO 101
        IX = IX-99999
        GO TO 11
101     IX = IX**2+99999
11      IF(IX.NE.0) GO TO 111
        IFLAG=1
        RETURN
111     DO 1112 J=1,2
        IF(IX.GE.E9) GO TO 112
        IX = 10*IX
112     CONTINUE
1112    CONTINUE
12      IX = IX*(IX-1)/E5
        IF(IX.LT.E10) GO TO 13
        IXX = IX/E10
        IX = IX-IXX*E10
13      CONTINUE
113     RNORMAL = 281474976710655
C       THIS RNORMAL = NORMALIZATION, IS FOR THE CDC-6500
        XXX = IX
        RN = XXX/RNORMAL
        RN = RN*10**4
        RETURN
        END
```

FIG. B.13 Listing of Program for Generator Using Random Method

seed. This number then is modified randomly by the program to give a new number, which is the next random number in the sequence. The process is repeated, each time using the new value of X as the seed. In the sample program listed here, statement 1 allows the new number to be computed a random number of times; statement 2 allows transfer of program control to a random step in the program.

Figure B.14 is a listing of a program for a generator using the midsquare technique. A four-digit integer seed is selected to initialize the generator. The first random number is obtained from the seed in the following manner: (1) the seed is squared and all digits of the result except the middle four are ignored; (2) this result then is normalized to give the first random number; and (3) this number subsequently is used as the new seed. The midsquare technique seldom is used today, because this algorithm has a tendency toward rapid degeneration. If the number zero ever is generated, all subsequent numbers generated also will have a zero value unless special steps are provided to handle this case. (No such provision has been made in the example program.) Furthermore, this technique is slow, because many multiplications and divisions are required to access the middle digits in a fixed-word binary computer.

Figure B.15 is a listing of a program for a generator using the midproduct technique, which is similar to the midsquare technique, except that each successive number is obtained by multiplying the current number by a constant K and taking the middle digits of the resulting product. This technique provides a longer period than the midsquare technique and results in numbers that are more nearly uniform in distribution than are the numbers produced by the midsquare technique, but this method also tends to degenerate.

Figure B.16 is a listing of a program for a generator based on the Fibonacci sequence. The method is represented by

$$X_{n+1} = (X_n + X_{n-1}) \bmod m$$

This method usually produces a period of length greater than m; however, the

```
          SUBROUTINE RANMID(ISEED,RN)
     C    FIRST SEED = ANY FOUR DIGIT NUMBER ( 1217 USED IN TESTS)
     C    RNORMAL WILL DEPEND ON WORD-LENGTH OF MACHINE USED.
          IRIGHT = ISEED**2/100
          ILEFT = IRIGHT/10000
          ISEED = IRIGHT - ILEFT*10000
          RN = ISEED
          RNORMAL = 10000
          RN = RN/RNORMAL
          RETURN
          END
```

FIG. B.14   Listing of Program for Generator Using Midsquare Technique

```
        SUBROUTINE MIDPROD(ISEED,RN)
C       FIRST SEED = ANY FOUR DIGIT NUMBER (1217 WAS USED IN TESTS)
C       RNORMAL WILL DEPEND ON WORDLENGTH OF MACHINE USED.
        K = 4093
        IRIGHT = ISEED*K/100
        ILEFT = IRIGHT / 10000
        ISEED = IRIGHT-ILEFT*10000
        RN = ISEED
        RNORMAL = 10000
        RN = RN/RNORMAL
        RETURN
        END
```

FIG. B.15   Listing of Program for Generator Using Midproduct Technique

```
        SUBROUTINE RANFIB(ISED1,ISED2,RN)
C       INITIAL ISED1 = 1, ISED2 = 0.
        SED1 = ISED1
        SED2 = ISED2
        ITEM = SED1 + SED2
        IRN = SED1 + SED2
        RN = IRN
C       2**48-1 = 281474976710655
        RNORMAL = 281474976710655
        RN = RN/RNORMAL
        ISED2 = ISED1
        ISED1 = ITEM
        RETURN
        END
```

FIG. B.16   Listing of Program for Generator Based on Fibonacci Sequence

numbers obtained using this method fail to pass many of the common tests for randomness. Consequently, this method must be regarded as unsatisfactory.

The congruential methods of random number generation have been studied extensively. These methods give numbers that are more uniformly distributed than those produced by any other method studied thus far. Generators based on congruential methods also have longer periods and can be faster, in general, than other methods. A congruential sequence, however, eventually will begin to cycle.

The general formula for the congruential method is

$$X_{n+1} = (cX_n + a) \bmod m, \text{ for } n \geq 0,$$

where a is an increment, c is the multiplier, m is the modulus, and X_0 is an arbitrarily chosen seed. The formula states that the quantity $(cX_n + a)$ is to be divided by m, and X_{n+1} is to be set equal to the remainder from this division.

There are several important rules for choosing the constants: (1) a should be an odd integer, not evenly divisible by either 3 or 5; (2) c usually can be taken as any desired constant; however, to assure good results, c should be chosen so that $c = 5$ mod 8 for a binary computer, or so that $c = 21$ mod 200 for a decimal computer; (3) a large value should be chosen for m; for convenience, m usually is set equal to the word size of the computer. The sample programs given here were written for a CDC-6500 computer with a word size of 60 bits. Because $2^{48} - 1$ is the value of the largest integer that can be represented in floating point form in this computer, this constant is used for m. Each number generated by these programs is normalized so that it can be represented as a fraction between zero and one.

Figure B.17 is a listing of a program for a generator using the mixed congruential method. This method uses the general formula above, with $c \neq 1$ and $a \neq 0$. If a is set equal to zero, the general formula reduces to the simpler form

$$X_{n+1} = cX_n \bmod m.$$

Figure B.18 is a listing of a program for a generator using this multiplicative congruential method.

The quadratic congruential method is a more complex variation on the general formula

$$X_{n+1} = (dX_n^2 + cX_n + a) \bmod m,$$

where d is a constant chosen by the same rules used in choosing c. If this method is to give satisfactory results, m must be a power of 2. Figure B.19 is a listing of a program for a generator using this method.

In some generators, two linear congruential methods may be combined to assure randomness in the numbers generated. This method requires generation of two sets of numbers using the congruential methods already mentioned — for example, according to the formulae

$$X_{n+1} = (cX_n + a) \bmod m,$$

and

$$Y_{n+1} = (gY_n + h) \bmod m.$$

```
SUBROUTINE RANMIX(ISEED,RN)
K = 31623
IADD = 2178281829
ISEED = ISEED*K+IADD
RN = ISEED
RNORMAL = 281474976710655
RN = RN/RNORMAL
RETURN
END
```

FIG. B.17   Listing of Program for Generator Using Mixed Congruential Method

```
         SUBROUTINE RANMUL(ISEED,RN)
         K = 31623
         ISEED = ISEED*K
         RN = ISEED
  C      2**48-1 = 281474976710655
         RNORMAL = 281474976710655
         RN = RN/RNORMAL
         RETURN
         END
```

FIG. B.18   Listing of Program for Generator Using
Multiplicative Congruential Method

```
         SUBROUTINE RANQUAD(ISEED,RN)
         IC = 31623
         ID = 42613
         IADD = 27181829
         ISEED = ID*ISEED**2+IC*ISEED+IADD
         RN = ISEED
  C      2**48-1 = 281474976710655
         RNORMAL = 281474976710655
         RN = RN/RNORMAL
         RETURN
         END
```

FIG. B.19   Listing of Program for Generator Using
Quadratic Congruential Method

Next, the sign bits of each of these numbers are set to zero, indicating positive numbers. The 47th through the 52nd bits of X_{n+1} are determined, and Y_{n+1} is subjected to a left circular shift by this amount. (The particular bits of X_{n+1} used here were chosen arbitrarily.) Then the sign bit (60th bit) of the shifted Y_{n+1} is set to zero, and the new Y_{n+1} is added to X_{n+1} with no carry. Finally, this sum is divided by 2^{59} to obtain the next random number in the sequence. Figure B.20 is a listing of a program for a generator using this combined congruential method.

```
        SUBROUTINE RNACOMB(ISEED,RN)
        ISEED1 = ISEED
        ISEED2 = ISEED+3634928
        CALL RANMUL(ISEED1,RAN1)
        CALL RANMUL(ISEED2,RAN2)
C       ANY ONE LINE CONGRUENTIAL GENERATOR MAY BE CALLED HERE.
C       IN FACT, TWO DIFFERENT ONE-LINE GENERATORS MAY BE CALLED.
        IHOLD = RAN1
        IHOLD2 = RAN2
        ITEM1 = IHOLD .AND. 377777777777777777777B
        ITEM2 = IHOLD2 .AND. 377777777777777777777B
        IMUL = (ITEM1/2**47) .AND.77B
        DO 15 I=1,IMUL
   15   ITEM2 = ITEM2+ITEM2
        ITEM2 = ITEM2 .AND. 377777777777777777777B
        ISEED = ITEM1 .AND..NOT.ITEM2.OR..NOT.ITEM1.AND.ITEM2
        RNORMAL = 281474976710655
        SEED = ISEED
        RN = SEED/RNORMAL
        RETURN
        END
```

FIG. B.20   Listing of Program for Generator Using
Combined Congruential Method

Appendix C

GPSS Characteristics

SECTION C.1   GPSS/360 Block Definition Cards
SECTION C.2   GPSS/360 Entity Definition Cards
SECTION C.3   GPSS/360 Control Cards
SECTION C.4   GPSS/360 Program Errors
SECTION C.5   GPSS/360 Block Types Not Discussed in the Text
SECTION C.6   Description of GPSS V

435

C.1 GPSS/360 Definition Cards

Each block definition card has three fields: (1) the *location* or LOC field in columns 2 through 7; (2) the OPERATION field in columns 8 through 18; and (3) the OPERANDS field in columns 19 through 72. The LOC field may contain any valid GPSS/360 symbolic name, which then can be used to reference the block. The OPERATION field must contain a code word that specifies the type of block being defined. The OPERANDS field may contain a series of operands appropriate to the type of block being defined. These operands must appear sequentially, separated by commas, and without intervening blank spaces. Any entries on the card following one or more blank spaces in the OPERANDS field will be regarded as comments and will be ignored by the compiler.

Table C.1 defines the OPERATION and OPERANDS fields for each of the possible GPSS/360 blocks. Section references are given for each block discussed in the text. Further discussion of the other blocks will be found in Section C.6 of this appendix and in the *General Purpose Simulation System 360 User's Manual*. The entries in the column titled "Allowed Types of Operands" are explained in Chapters 10 and 11 of the text. The "Standard" types are k, $*n$, SNAj, or SNA$*j$.

TABLE C.1   OPERATION and OPERANDS Fields for GPSS/360 Block Definition Cards

OPERATION Field	OPERANDS Field			
	Operand	Description	Allowed Types of Operands	Text Reference
ADVANCE	A	Mean	Standard	10.6
	B	Spread, or function modifier	Standard, or FNj, FN$*n$	
ALTER	A	Group number	Standard	——
	B	Count, or ALL	Standard, or ALL	
	C	Priority, or parameter number to be altered	PR, or Standard	
	D	Value of alteration	Standard	
	E	Transaction priority, or parameter numbers matching	PR, or Standard	
	F	Matching SNA	Standard	
	G	Alternate exit	Standard	
ASSEMBLE	A	Number of transactions to be assembled	Standard	——

TABLE C.1—*Continued*

OPERATION Field	OPERANDS Field			
	Operand	Description	Allowed Types of Operands	Text Reference
ASSIGN	A	Parameter number [operator]	Standard [±]	11.3
	B	SNA to be assigned	Standard	
	C	Number of function modifier	Standard	
BUFFER	——	——	——	——
CHANGE	A	"FROM" block number	Standard	——
	B	"TO" block number	Standard	
COUNT X	A	Parameter number in which to put count	Standard	——
	B	Lower limit of entity class to be examined	Standard	
	C	Upper limit	Standard	
	D	Comparison value, if the code X is a conditional operator	Standard	
	E	Entity attribute to be counted	Any SNA except matrix reference entities	
DEPART	A	Queue number	Standard	10.9
	B	Units	Standard	
ENTER	A	Storage number	Standard	10.8
	B	Units	Standard	
EXAMINE	A	Group number	Standard	——
	B	Numeric value, used only in numeric mode	Standard	
	C	Alternate exit block number	Standard	
EXECUTE	A	Block number of block to be executed	Standard	——
GATE X	A	Equipment entity number, or matching block number, depending on the code X	Standard	——
	B	Next block if condition is false	Standard	
GATHER	A	Number of transactions to be gathered	Standard	——

TABLE C.1 — *Continued*

OPERATION Field	OPERANDS Field			
	Operand	Description	Allowed Types of Operands	Text Reference
GENERATE	A	Mean time	k, FNj, Vj, Xj, XHj	10.6, 11.3
	B	Spread, or function modifier	k, Vj, Xj, XHj, FNj	
	C	Initialization interval	k, FNj, Vj, Xj, XHj	
	D	Creation limit	k, FNj, Vj, Xj, XHj	
	E	Priority	k, FNj, Vj, Xj, XHj	
	F	Number of parameters	k, FNj, Vj, Xj, XHj	
	G	Parameter type	F, H	
INDEX	A	Parameter number	Standard	——
	B	Increment	Standard	
JOIN	A	Group number	Standard	——
	B	Used in numeric mode for numeric value source	Standard	
LEAVE	A	Storage number	Standard	10.8
	B	Number of units	Standard	
LINK	A	Chain number	Standard	11.14
	B	Ordering of chain	LIFO, FIFO, Pj	
	C	Alternate block number exit	Standard	
LOGIC X	A	Logic switch number	Standard	——
LOOP	A	Parameter number	Standard	——
	B	Next block number	Standard	
MARK	A	Parameter number	Standard	——
MATCH	A	Conjugate block number	Standard	——
MSAVEVALUE	A	Matrix number [operator]	Standard [$\pm$]	11.5
	B	Row number	Standard	
	C	Column number	Standard	
	D	Value	Standard	
	E	Halfword indicator	H	
PREEMPT	A	Number of facility to be preempted	Standard	10.7
	B	Priority mode of operation	PR	
	C	Optional transfer block for preempted trans-action	Standard	

TABLE C.1—*Continued*

OPERATION Field	OPERANDS Field			
	Operand	Description	Allowed Types of Operands	Text Reference
	D	Parameter number of preempted transaction to contain scheduled time preempted	Standard	
	E	Option to remove pre-empted transaction from contention for facility	RE	
PRINT	A	Lower limit of range of entity numbers for entity to be printed	Standard	11.15
	B	Upper limit of range	Standard	
	C	Mnemonic code for entity	——	
	D	Optional paging indicator	Any nonblank character	
PRIORITY	A	Reset priority of trans-action to this value	Standard	——
	B	Buffering option to re-schedule movement of transaction according to new priority	BUFFER	
QUEUE	A	Number of queue to be entered	Standard	10.9
	B	Occupancy weight of new entry	Standard	
RELEASE	A	Number of facility to be freed	Standard	10.7
REMOVE	A	Group number	Standard	——
	B	Number of members to be removed	Standard	
	C	Numeric value to be removed	Standard	
	D	Transaction attributes for comparison in conditional removal	PR for priority, or parameter number given by Standard types	
	E	SNA for comparison	Standard	
	F	Alternate exit if nu-meric value not found	Standard	
RETURN	A	Number of facility to be returned	Standard	10.7

TABLE C.1—*Continued*

OPERATION Field	OPERANDS Field			
	Operand	Description	Allowed Types of Operands	Text Reference
SAVEVALUE	A	Savevalue number [operator]	Standard [±]	11.5
	B	SNA to calculate savevalue	Standard	
	C	Halfword indicator	H	
SCAN	A	Group number	Standard	—
	B	Transaction attribute for comparison	PR for priority, or Standard types for parameter number	
	C	Comparison value for transaction attribute	Standard	
	D	Attribute to be computed if match is successful	PR for priority, or Standard types for parameter number	
	E	Parameter number of parameter to receive computed attribute	Standard	
	F	Alternate exit if no match	Standard	
SEIZE	A	Facility number	Standard	10.7
SELECT X	A	Number of parameter to contain entity number selected	Standard	—
	B	Lower limit of numbers for entity type to be examined	Standard	
	C	Upper limit of numbers	Standard	
	D	Comparison value when X is a conditional operator	Standard	
	E	Entity attribute to be examined	Any SNA except matrix savevalues	
	F	Alternate exit if no entity satisfies conditions	Standard	
SPLIT	A	Number of copies of transaction	Standard	—
	B	Block for copies	Standard	
	C	Parameter number for serial numbering of copies	k	
	D	Number of parameters for copies	Standard	

TABLE C.1—*Continued*

OPERATION Field	OPERANDS Field			
	Operand	Description	Allowed Types of Operands	Text Reference
TABULATE	A	Table number	Standard	11.7
	B	Weighting units	Standard	
TEST X	A	First SNA for comparison	Standard	11.13
	B	Second SNA for comparison	Standard	
	C	Transfer block when comparison is false	Standard	
TERMINATE	A	Number of units by which termination count is to be decreased	Standard	10.6
TRANSFER	A	Selection mode	—	10.6
	B	Next block A	Standard, unless A is ALL, when direct specification of block must be made	
	C	Next block B	Same as for operand B	
	D	Indexing factor for ALL mode of selection	k	
TRACE	—	—	—	10.15
UNLINK	A	User chain number	Standard	11.14
	B	Next block for unlinked transaction	Standard	
	C	Transaction unlink count	Standard, or ALL	
	D	Type of removal	Standard, BACK, or BV*j*	
	E	Comparison value	Standard	
	F	Alternate exit	Standard	
UNTRACE	—	—	—	10.15
WRITE	A	Jobtape number	JOBTA1, JOBTA2, or JOBTA3	—

C.2 GPSS/360 Entity Definition Cards

Each entity definition card has three fields: (1) the location or LOC field in columns 2 through 7; (2) the OPERATION field in columns 8 through 18; and (3) the OPERANDS field in columns 19 through 72. Except for the INITIAL card (where it is not applicable), the LOC field may contain any valid GPSS/360 symbolic name or a number, which then may be used to reference the entity. Table C.2 defines the OPERATION and OPERANDS fields for the possible GPSS/360 entities. Entries in this table are of the same form as those in Table C.1.

TABLE C.2   OPERATION and OPERANDS Fields for GPSS/360 Entity Definition Cards

OPERATION Field	OPERANDS Field			
	Operand	Description	Allowed Types of Operands	Text Reference
BVARIABLE	A	Boolean statement	Expression involving Boolean variables and operators	——
FUNCTION	A	Function argument	Standard	11.10
	B	Function type	Cn, Dn, Ln, En, or Mn	
FVARIABLE	A	Arithmetic statement	Formula involving SNAs and arithmetic operators	11.11
INITIAL	A	Savevalue to be initialized	Xj, XHj, MX$j(m,n)$, MH$j(m,n)$	11.6
	B	Initial value	k	
MATRIX	A	Type of matrix save-values	X or H	11.5
	B	Number of rows	k	
	C	Number of columns	k	
STORAGE	A	Capacity	k	10.8
TABLE	A	Table argument	Standard [−], RT, IA	11.7
	B	Upper limit of lowest interval	k	
	C	Interval width	k	
	D	Number of intervals	k	
	E	Arrival time interval	k	
VARIABLE	A	Arithmetic statement	Formula involving SNAs and arithmetic operators	11.11

C.3 GPSS/360 Control Cards

Each control card requires at most two fields: (1) the OPERATION field in columns 8 through 18; and (2) the OPERANDS field in columns 19 through 72. Table C.3 defines these fields for each of the GPSS/360 control cards.

TABLE C.3   OPERATION and OPERANDS Fields for
GPSS/360 Control Cards

OPERATION Field	OPERANDS Field			
	Operand	Description	Allowed Types of Operands	Text Reference
CLEAR	A–Z	Optional list of fullword and halfword save-values not to be set to zero	Xj and XHj	10.10
END	——	——	——	10.10
JOB	——	——	——	10.10
JOBTAPE	A	Tape name	JOBTA1, JOBTA2, JOBTA3	——
	B	Next block for entering transactions	k	
	C	Offset time before first entry	k	
	D	Scaling factor for inter-arrival and transit time	k	
LIST	——	——	——	——
READ	A	Optional numeric value indicating number of files to skip on save tape	k	——
RESET	A–Z	List of entities not to be reset by card	Fj, Qj, Sj, CHj, and TBj	10.10
REWIND	A	Tape name to be re-wound	JOBTA1, JOBTA2, JOBTA3	——
RMULT	A	Initial multiplier for RN1	k	11.9
	B	Initial multiplier for RN2	k	
	.	.	.	
	.	.	.	
	.	.	.	
	H	Initial multiplier for RN8	k	

TABLE C.3—*Continued*

OPERATION Field	OPERANDS Field			
	Operand	Description	Allowed Types of Operands	Text Reference
SAVE	A	Optional indicator to start new file on save tape	Any nonblank character	——
SIMULATE	——	——	——	10.10
START	A	Run termination count	*k*	10.10
	B	Printout suppression	NP	
	C	Output snap interval	*k*	
	D	Optional indicator for standard transaction output	1 for printout; blank for no printout	
UNLIST	——	——	——	——

C.4 GPSS/360 Program Errors

Table C.4 explains the significance of each of the assembly program error reports that may appear in GPSS/360 program listings.

TABLE C.4　Significance of GPSS/360 Program Error Reports

Error Number	Significance
1 *through* 77	*Assembly Program Errors*
1	Illegal selection mode specified in operand A of TRANSFER block
2	Illegal operation field
3	Entity number to be reserved by EQU card has been reserved by previous EQU card
4	This block symbol has been used in an EQU card
5	Illegal TABLE argument
6	Fractional selection mode is more than a three-digit number
7	Syntax error in EQU or MATRIX card
8	Illegal entity indicator
9	Operand A of ASSIGN block is greater than 100
10	First operand in a MATRIX card is not X or H
11	Undefined block symbol
12	Illegal jobtape specified

TABLE C.4—*Continued*

Error Number	Significance
13	The number of rows and/or columns specified in a MATRIX card are/is not (a) constant(s)
14	Operand E of MSAVEVALUE block is illegal
15	TRANSFER block with ALL or PICK selection mode contains operand C whose value is less than operand B
16	TRANSFER block with ALL selection mode contains operand B and operand C range that is not divisible evenly by the operand D
17	Blank location field in card that must have an entry in location field
18	Illegal halfword matrix savevalue
19	Illegal mnemonic specified in operation field of GATE, LOGIC, TEST, COUNT, or SELECT block
20	Illegal operand B in PRIORITY block
21	A symbol in the above entity function follower card has been used in an EQU card or has been used as a block symbol or has been used in a previous entity function
22	Illegal Boolean variable number
23	Illegal report type specified in REPORT card
24	Above card type is not permitted within the report type specified
25	Storage defined with capacity greater than the maximal permissible value
26	The table must be specified numerically
27	Illegal symbol
28	Illegal function type
29	Modifier of GENERATE or ADVANCE block exceeds mean
30	Operand A omitted where it must be specified
31	Operand B omitted where it must be specified
32	Illegal facility number
33	Illegal storage number
34	Illegal queue number
35	Illegal logic switch number
36	Illegal chain number
37	Illegal table number
38	Illegal variable number
39	Illegal savevalue number
40	Illegal function number
41	Illegal symbol in location field, or no symbol where one is required
42	Illegal group number
43	Illegal symbol (too long)
44	Syntax error in above card

TABLE C.4—*Continued*

Error Number	Significance
45	Illegal SNA
46	Operand C omitted where it must be specified
47	Illegal matrix savevalue number
48	Operand D omitted where it must be specified
49	Maximal number of MACROs already defined
50	Undefined MACRO
51	Illegal MACRO argument; argument must be alphabetic A–J
52	MACRO card expanded past column 72
53	More than two MACROs nested within a MACRO
54	More than ten arguments specified in above MACRO card
55	Operand C of SAVEVALUE block is illegal
56	Illegal halfword savevalue
57	There is no legal entity number left to be assigned to the entity symbol
58	Operand field extends into column 72
59	There are more right parentheses than left parentheses in a VARIABLE card
60	There are more left parentheses than right parentheses in a VARIABLE card
61	An impossible modulo division has been specified in a VARI-ABLE card
62	Operand E omitted or illegal where it must be specified
63	EQU card or entity function specifies that illegal entity number be reserved
64	Graph cards out of order
65	Illegal operand A of statement request card
66	Illegal row request in statement card
67	Illegal operand B of statement request card
68	Too many columns requested in statement card
69	Decreasing row numbers requested in statement card
70	Illegal starting column requested for statement
71	Illegal SNA requested in graph card
72	Illegal entity range in graph request card
73	Illegal request in origin card
74	Illegal entity requested in title card
75	Illegal field in X request card
76	Illegal numeric operand in X or Y request card
77	Illegal request in Y card
201 *through* 299	*Input Errors*
201	Number of transactions exceeded

TABLE C.4—*Continued*

Error Number	Significance
202	Referenced transaction not inactive
203	Priority exceeds 127
205	Number of parameters exceeds 100
206	GENERATE block: operand F must be F, H, or blank
207	PREEMPT block: operand B must be PR
208	PREEMPT block: operand E must be RE
209	PREEMPT block: operand C not specified with D and/or C operands
210	Illegal mnemonic in operation field
211	Illegal storage number
212	Operand D not necessary if MAX or MIN mode specified
213	Illegal mnemonic in operand C of PRINT block
214	Illegal format in logic switch INITIAL card
215	Amount of available GPSS/360 common core exceeded
216	Modifier cannot exceed mean
217	Action time not $\geq$ zero
218	Illegal fullword matrix number
219	Illegal halfword matrix number
220	Illegal format for TRANSFER block in ALL mode
221	Illegal table number
222	Illegal function number
223	Function x values not in ascending order
224	UNLINK block: operand E must be blank if BACK specified
225	Illegal fullword savevalue number
226	Illegal halfword savevalue number
227	Illegal format in savevalue INITIAL card
228	Mnemonic other than X or XH used in savevalue INITIAL card
229	First index higher than second index in multi-INITIALization
230	Illegal logic switch number
231	Variable definition card: column 18 not blank
232	Variable definition card: illegal variable number
233	Variable definition card: number stated incorrectly
234	Variable definition card: improper number of parentheses
235	Variable definition card: too many sets of parentheses
236	Variable definition card: impossible modulo division
237	Variable definition card: illegal Boolean variable number
238	Variable definition card: modulo division in floating-point variable
239	No comma in matrix definition card

TABLE C.4—*Continued*

Error Number	Significance
240	Illegal Boolean operator
241	Illegal statement of operation in variable
242	Illegal SNA in variable definition card
243	Illegal matrix row number
244	Illegal matrix column number
245	Illegal matrix savevalue mnemonic
246	Illegal format in matrix INITIAL card
247	Illegal mnemonic in savevalue INITIAL card
248	Illegal halfword savevalue
249	Too many numeric digits in constant
250	Illegal SNA mnemonic
251	Missing operator in variable
252	Operand E not blank when BV specified in UNLINK block
253	Illegal mnemonic in operand A of TRANSFER block
254	Fraction in operand A of TRANSFER block is not three digits
255	Matrix INITIAL card: illegal index for rows
256	Matrix INITIAL card: illegal index for columns
257	Illegal queue number
258	Illegal jobtape number
259	Cyclic definition of variable
260	Variable not defined
261	Illegal variable number
262	Cyclic definition of function
263	Illegal function number
264	Undefined function
265	Illegal function type
266	Function must have more than one point
270	No operand C in EXAMINE block
271	Illegal entity number on RESET card
272	Illegal entity type requested on RESET card
273	Sequence error on RESET card
274	Illegal request on selective CLEAR card
275	Illegal savevalue number on CLEAR card
276	Illegal range of savevalues on CLEAR card
277	Illegal halfword savevalue on CLEAR card
278	Illegal range of halfword savevalues on CLEAR card
279	READ/SAVE identifier not found on specified READ device
280	Illegal allocation of entities on READ device
282	Error in block redefinition

TABLE C.4—*Continued*

Error Number	Significance
283	Illegal block number
284	Illegal transaction referenced in chaining routine (not a user's error)
285	Illegal frequency class designation on table definition card
290	Illegal reference to GPSS/360 common core (not a user's error)
291, 293	Illegal SNA referenced (not a user's error)
299	Illegal RMULT card specification
401 *through* 699	*Execution Errors*
401	No new event in the system
402, 403, 404	Illegal transaction in future events chain (normally not a user's error)
405	Number of parameters exceeded
406	Illegal priority computed for transaction being created at GENERATE block
413	Illegal entry to GENERATE block
415, 416	Facility RELEASEd by transaction that has not SEIZEd it
417	Interrupt count is minus (not a user's error)
421	Facility RETURNed by a transaction that has not PREEMPTed it
425	Transaction leaving by more than storage contents
428	Transaction that is leaving queue by more than queue contents
429	Operand A parameter zero before entering LOOP block
432	Illegal halfword savevalue number
433	Illegal fullword savevalue number
434	Weighting not specified in operand D of table definition card for table being referenced
435	Illegal table number
436	Table not defined by TABLE card
437	Illegal transaction number referred to under block condition (not a user's error)
438	Attempting to place a transaction on a delay chain when the transaction is on the delay chain (not a user's error)
442	No preempt count in transaction returned from preempt condition (normally not a user's error)
443	Number of transactions exceeded
453, 463, 466, 467	Attempting to remove transactions from illegal chains (not a user's error)
468, 469	Number of transactions exceeded
470, 471, 472, 475	Illegal transaction number being acted on (not a user's error)
474	Preempt interrupt count exceeds 127
476, 477	Attempting to remove an interrupt on a transaction that has not been interrupted (not a user's error)

TABLE C.4—*Continued*

Error Number	Significance
492	Illegal transaction parameter number
497	Illegal link chain referenced
498	Illegal facility number
499	Illegal storage number
500	Illegal queue number
501	Illegal logic switch number
505	Minus time-delay computation at GENERATE or ADVANCE block
506	Cyclic function definition
507	Illegal function number
508	Function not defined by FUNCTION card
509	Illegal index evaluated for list-type function
512	Entering undefined block
514	Illegal variable number
515	Arithmetic variable not defined by VARIABLE card
516	Cyclic definition of arithmetic variable
518	Too many levels of interrupt
530	Spread exceeds mean in time-delay computation at GENERATE or ADVANCE block
560	Illegal matrix savevalue
561	Illegal row in MSAVEVALUE card
562	Illegal column in MSAVEVALUE card
599	Limits of GPSS/360 common core exceeded
601	Next sequential block number is illegal
603	Illegal block number
604	Illegal table argument
607	Operand A assembly or gather count is zero at ASSEMBLE or GATHER block
609	Transaction of a one-member set is at MATCH, ASSEMBLE, GATHER, GATE-M-, or GATE-NM- block
610	Upper limit less than lower limit in COUNT or SELECT block
611	Illegal transaction parameter number
612	Illegal block number referenced in TRANSFER BOTH or ALL
613	Illegal user's chain
614	Priority exceeds maximum allowed (127)
615	Error in core assignment (not a user's error)

TABLE C.4—*Continued*

Error Number	Significance
616	Transaction parameter zero referenced
617	Illegal matrix number
618	Cyclic definition of matrix
619	Matrix not defined by MATRIX card
620	Illegal matrix column number
621	Illegal matrix row number
622	Illegal Boolean variable number
623	Boolean variable not defined by BVARIABLE card
624	Cyclic definition of Boolean variable
626	Illegal group number
627	Operand C less than operand B in TRANSFER PICK
644	Error in WRITE block operation
669, 670	Improper queue assignment (not a user's error)
698	Illegal change in CHANGE block
699	Illegal argument in EXECUTE block
702 through 769	*Output Errors*
702	Illegal facility number
704	Illegal user chain number
708	Illegal logic switch number
712	Illegal fullword savevalue number
713	Illegal halfword savevalue number
714	Illegal facility number
715	Illegal storage number
716	Illegal queue number
717	Illegal group number
718	Illegal user chain number
722	Illegal storage number
723	Illegal queue number
724	Illegal table number
726	Error in square root routine
727	Illegal halfword matrix savevalue number
728	Illegal fullword matrix savevalue number
729	Illegal entry to output (other than END, SNAP, PRINT, TRACE, or ERROR IN EXECUTION)
769	Illegal TITLE card

C.5 GPSS/360 Block Types Not Discussed in the Text

GPSS/360 provides many other block types in addition to those discussed in Chapters 10 and 11 of this text. Table C.5 indicates briefly how these blocks can be used. Full descriptions of each block are given in the *General Purpose Simulation System/360 User's Manual*.

TABLE C.5   GPSS/360 Block Types Not Discussed in the Text

Block Type	Brief Description of Use
ALTER	Modifies attributes of transactions that are members of a specified group entity
ASSEMBLE	Joins the indicated number of transactions belonging to an assembly set into a single transaction
BUFFER	Stops the processing of the entering transaction and forces the control program to restart the scan of the current events list
CHANGE	Changes the blocks in a model during the run
COUNT	Determines the number of items meeting a specified condition
EXAMINE	Alters the flow of transactions through the model, based on group membership
EXECUTE	Allows the execution of almost any other block type in the model without a transfer to that other block type
GATE	Blocks or alters the flow of transactions through a model, based on specified conditional or logical relationships
GATHER	Suspends the movement of transactions belonging to the same assembly set until a specified number of such transactions have been gathered at the block
INDEX	Allows the contents of parameter 1 to be adjusted, according to the value of any parameters in the entering transaction
JOIN	Places an element into the specified group
LOGIC	Sets, resets, or inverts the status of the specified logic switch
LOOP	Controls the number of times that a transaction will be transferred to a specified block, according to the value of the parameter specified
MARK	Reinitializes transaction or parameter mark time
MATCH	Synchronizes processing of transactions in the same assembly set
PRIORITY	Sets transaction priority
REMOVE	Removes members from the specified group
SCAN	Interrogates group membership
SELECT	Selects the first entity satisfying the specified condition
SPLIT	Creates a specified number of transactions belonging to the same assembly set as that of the entering transaction
WRITE	Records information about entering transactions onto external storage media, such as tapes, discs, and so forth

C.6 Description of GPSS V

GPSS V is a later version of the General Purpose Simulation System. It is compatible with GPSS/360 and contains several additional, useful features. A few of the more important of these features are discussed here. For a complete discussion, see the *General Purpose Simulation System V User's Manual* (IBM Publication No. SH20–0851).

GPSS V can process two new arithmetic types. The first type consists of byte values that deal with integral numbers in the range from $-(2^7 - 1)$ to $+(2^7 - 1)$. The use of byte arithmetic for smaller numbers results in significant savings of memory space. A more useful additional arithmetic type is floating point, which allows for the processing and storage of fractional as well as integral values. To accomodate these arithmetic types, several new SNAs have been added, and several of the existing SNAs have been modified. In addition, the definitions of many block types have been adjusted slightly to reflect these changes. Some of the more important effects include the addition of byte and floating point parameters to transactions, and that of byte and floating point savevalues and matrix savevalues.

Another important extension is the ability of transactions to carry up to 1,020 parameters (up to 255 of each of the four types allowed in GPSS V).

GPSS V provides several additional block types to facilitate the simulation of unavailable storages and facilities. For example, block types are available to facilitate the simulation of a teller window temporarily closed during the lunch hour. In addition, facility and storage statistics are adjusted automatically for the time periods when the entities are unavailable.

Indirect addressing has been extended in GPSS V, so that $SNA*SNAj$ is a valid expression. (In GPSS/360, the secondary reference must be a parameter number, as in $SNA*j$.)

A free format rule has been introduced in GPSS V, easing the stringent coding rules of GPSS/360 about the columns used for each field. In GPSS V, the LOC, OPERATION, and OPERANDS fields may begin in any column, with at least one blank column required to separate adjacent fields. For example, the OPERATION field may begin in column 5, 6, 8, or 10, or any other column, so long as at least one blank column separates it from the preceding LOC field. Another useful change in GPSS V is the printing of full-text error messages instead of the simple reference numbers printed in GPSS/360.

Perhaps the most important improvement in GPSS V is a provision that allows the analyst to store specified entity types on auxilliary storages such as discs. This feature permits the construction of much larger models in the same or in smaller memory partitions. With this feature, the capabilities of GPSS are greatly improved for the simulation of very large or complex systems. However, this new capability may result in significantly longer running times for simulations.

Bibliography

Acton, F. S. 1959. *Analysis of Straight-Line Data.* New York: John Wiley and Sons. [Paperback edition. New York: Dover Publications.]

Ainslie, T. 1968. *Ainslie's Complete Guide to Thoroughbred Racing.* New York: Trident Press.

Anscombe, F. J., and J. W. Tukey. 1963. "The examination and analysis of residuals." *Technometrics* 5(2):141–60.

Anscombe, F. J., C. Daniel, W. H. Kruskal, T. S. Ferguson, J. W. Tukey, and E. J. Gumbel. 1960. [Series of papers on outliers.] *Technometrics* 2(2):123–66.

Beyer, W. H., ed. 1966. *Handbook of Tables for Probability and Statistics.* Cleveland, Ohio: Chemical Rubber Co.

Bohl, M. 1971. *Flowcharting Techniques.* Chicago: Science Research Associates.

Bonini, C. P. 1963. *Simulation of Information and Decision Systems in the Firm.* Englewood Cliffs, N.J.: Prentice-Hall.

Bonner, A. J. 1969. "Using system monitoring output to improve performance." *IBM Systems Journal* 8(4):290–98.

Borko, H., ed. 1962. *Computer Applications in the Behavioral Sciences.* Englewood Cliffs, N.J.: Prentice-Hall.

Box, G. E. P. 1954. "Effect of inequality of variance in the one-way classification." *Annals of Mathematical Statistics* 25:290–302.

Box, G. E. P., and W. G. Hunter. 1962. "A useful method for model building." *Technometrics* 4(3):301–18.

Box, G. E. P., and M. E. Muller. 1958. "A note on the generation of normal deviates." *Annals of Mathematical Statistics* 28:610–11.

Bross, I. D. J. 1961. "Outliers in patterned experiments: a strategic appraisal." *Technometrics* 3(1):91–102.

Butler, E. L. 1970. "Algorithm 370, general random number generator [G5]." *Communications of the Association for Computing Machinery* 13:49–52.

Chorafas, D. N. 1965. *Systems and Simulation.* New York: Academic Press.

Cochran, W. G., and G. M. Cox. 1957. *Experimental Designs.* 2nd ed. New York: John Wiley and Sons.

Cohen, J. 1969. *Statistical Power Analysis for the Behavioral Sciences.* New York: Academic Press.

Coplin, W. D., ed. 1968. *Simulation in the Study of Politics.* Chicago: Markham Publishing Co.

Coveyou, R. L., and R. D. MacPherson. 1969. "Fourier analysis of uniform random number generators." *Journal of the Association for Computing Machinery* 14:100–19.

Cramer, H. 1946. *Mathematical Methods of Statistics.* Princeton, N.J.: Princeton University Press.

————. 1955. *Elements of Probability Theory and Some of Its Applications.* New York: John Wiley and Sons.

————. 1964. "Model building with the aid of stochastic processes." *Technometrics* 6(2):133–60.

Dahl, O. J. 1968. "Discrete event simulation languages." In *Programming Languages,* ed. F. Genuys, pp. 349–95. New York: Academic Press.

Dahl, O. J., and K. Nygaard. 1967. *SIMULA: A Language for Programming and Description of Discrete Event Systems: Introduction and User's Manual.* Oslo, Norway: Norwegian Computation Center.

de Sola Pool, I., R. P. Abelson, and S. L. Popkin. 1964. *Candidates, Issues and Strategies: A Computer Simulation of the 1960 and 1964 Presidential Elections.* Cambridge, Mass.: M.I.T. Press.

Dixon, W. J., and F. J. Massey, Jr. 1969. *Introduction to Statistical Analysis.* 3rd ed. New York: McGraw-Hill Book Co.

Domnauer, R. 1969. "Read-error ties up 360/30 under DOS for 95 seconds" [letter to the editor]. *Computerworld* (August 6, 1969).

Draper, N., and H. Smith. 1966. *Applied Regression Analysis.* New York: John Wiley and Sons.

Ehrenfeld, S., and S. B. Littauer. 1964. *Introduction to Statistical Methods.* New York: McGraw-Hill Book Co.

Feller, W. 1957, 1966. *An Introduction to Probability Theory and Its Applications.* 2 vols. New York: John Wiley and Sons.

Fischer, A. H. 1970. "System design via on-line simulation," *Software Age* 4(2):8–15.

Forsythe, G. E. 1951. "Generating and testing of random digits at the National Bureau of Standards." In *Monte Carlo Method,* National Bureau of Standards Applied Mathematics Series No. 12, pp. 34–35. Washington, D.C.

Freund, J. E. 1962. *Mathematical Statistics.* Englewood Cliffs, N.J.: Prentice-Hall.

Glock, C. Y., ed. 1967. *Survey Research in the Social Sciences.* New York: Russell Sage Foundation.

Goode, H. H. 1962. "Deferred decision theory." In *Recent Developments in Information and Decision Processes,* ed. R. E. Machol and P. Gray, pp. 71–91. New York: Macmillan Co.

Gordon, G. 1969. *System Simulation.* Englewood Cliffs, N.J.: Prentice-Hall.

Green, B. F., Jr. 1963. *Digital Computers in Research: An Introduction for Behavioral and Social Scientists.* New York: McGraw-Hill Book Co.

Green, B. F. W., J. F. K. Smith, and L. Klem. 1959. "Empirical tests of an additive random number generator." *Journal of the Association for Computing Machinery* 6:527–37.

Greenberger, M. 1961. "A prior determination of serial correlation in computer generated random numbers." *Mathematics of Computation* 15:383–89.

Greville, T. N. E. 1968. "Spline functions, interpolation and numerical quadrature." In *Mathematical Methods for Digital Computers,* ed. A. Ralston and H. Wilf, vol. 2, pp. 156–68. New York: John Wiley and Sons.

Guetzkow, H., C. F. Alger, R. A. Brody, R. C. Noel, and R. C. Snyder. 1963. *Simulation in International Relations: Developments for Research and Teaching.* Englewood Cliffs, N.J.: Prentice-Hall.

Haldane, J. B. S. 1939. "The mean and variance of chi square, when used as a test of homogeneity, when expectations are small." *Biometrika* 31:346–55.

Hansen, M. H., W. N. Hurwitz, and W. G. Madow. 1953. *Sample Survey Methods and Theory.* 2 vols. New York: John Wiley and Sons.

Harbaugh, J. W., and G. Bonham-Carter. 1970. *Computer Simulation in Geology.* New York: John Wiley and Sons.

Harman, H. H. 1967. *Modern Factor Analysis.* 2nd ed. Chicago: University of Chicago Press.

Hartley, H. O. 1961. "The modified Gauss-Newton method for the fitting of non-linear regression by least squares." *Technometrics* 3(2):269–80.

Haskins, B. S. 1968. *Use of a Factor Analysis Technique to Identify Influential Demographic and Office Characteristics That Affect Operations to Select a Representative Sample of Offices That Will Be Used to Predict Results of Change in a Multi-Office National Social Insurance System.* Report No. SSA–ORS–TP–9. Baltimore, Md.: Operations Research Staff, Social Security Administration.

————. 1969a. *Computer Simulation of the Queueing Characteristics of the Social Security Administration's Operations.* Publication No. SSA–ORS–SP–19. Woodlawn, Md.: Social Security Administration, U.S. Department of Health, Education and Welfare.

————. 1969b. *An Analysis of the Sources of In-Office Claims Workload on the Social Security Administration's District Offices.* Report No. SSA–ORS–SP–20. Baltimore, Md.: Operations Research Staff, Social Security Administration.

————. 1969c. *An Analysis of the Sources for In-Office SSA–1, SSA–2, SSA–8, and SSA–16 Claims in the Social Security Administration's District Offices.* Report No. SSA–ORS–SP–26. Baltimore, Md.: Operations Research Staff, Social Security Administration.

Hemmerle, W. J. 1967. *Statistical Computations on a Digital Computer.* Waltham, Mass.: Blaisdell Publishing Co.

Howell, J. R. 1969. "Algorithm 359, factorial analysis of variance." *Communications of the Association for Computing Machinery* 12:631–32.

International Business Machines Corporation. 1966. *Bibliography on Stimulation.* IBM Publication 320–0924–0. White Plains, N.Y.

Jaffray, G., and F. Gruenberger. 1965. *Problems for Computer Solution.* New York: John Wiley and Sons.

Johnson, N. L., and F. C. Leone. 1964. *Statistics and Experimental Design in Engineering and the Physical Sciences.* 2 vols. New York: John Wiley and Sons.

Juran, J. M. 1962. *Quality Control Handbook.* 2nd ed. New York: McGraw-Hill Book Co.

Katz, J. H. 1966. "Simulation of a multiprocessor computer system." *American Federation of Information Processing Societies Conference Proceedings* 28:127–39.

————. 1967. "An experimental model of the System/360." *Communications of the Association for Computing Machinery* 10(11):694–702.

Kendall, M. G., and A. Stuart. 1958. *The Advanced Theory of Statistics.* Vol. 1. London: C. Griffin Co.

Kiviat, P. J., R. Villanueva, and H. M. Markowitz. 1969. *The SIMSCRIPT II Programming Language.* Englewood Cliffs, N.J.: Prentice-Hall.

Knuth, D. E. 1968. *The Art of Computer Programming,* Vol. 1: *Fundamental Algorithms.* Reading, Mass.: Addison-Wesley Publishing Co.

————. 1969. *The Art of Computer Programming,* Vol. 2: *Seminumerical Algorithms.* Reading, Mass.: Addison-Wesley Publishing Co.

Krasnow, H. S. 1969. "Simulation languages." In *The Design of Computer Simulation Experiments,* ed. T. H. Naylor, pp. 320–46. Durham, N.C.: Duke University Press.

Leeds, H. D., and G. M. Weinberg. 1961. *Computer Programming Fundamentals*. New York: McGraw-Hill Book Co.

Lehmer, D. H. 1959. "Mathematical method in large-scale computing units." In *Proceedings of the Second Symposium on Large-Scale Digital Computing Machinery*, pp. 141–45. Cambridge, Mass.: Harvard University Press.

Lucas, H. C., Jr. 1971. "Performance evaluation and monitoring." *Association for Computing Machinery Computing Surveys* 3(3):79–91.

MacDougall, M. H. 1970. "Computer systems simulation: an introduction," *Computing Surveys* 2(3):191–209.

McLeod, J., ed. 1968. *Simulation*. New York: McGraw-Hill Book Co.

Maisel, H. 1966. "Best k of $2k - 1$ comparisons." *Journal of the American Statistical Association* 61(314):329–44.

————. 1969. *Introduction to Electronic Digital Computers*. New York: McGraw-Hill Book Co.

Maisel, H., J. Albertini, C. Roberts, and R. Mason. 1963. "The Centaur war game." In *Proceedings of the U.S. Army Operations Research Symposium*, pp. 107–28. Durham, N.C.

Marsaglia, G., and M. D. MacLaren. 1965. "Uniform random number generators." *Journal of the Association for Computing Machinery* 12:83–89.

Marsaglia, G., M. D. MacLaren, and T. A. Bray. 1964a. "A fast procedure for generating normal random variables." *Communications of the Association for Computing Machinery* 7:4–10.

————. 1964b. "A fast procedure for generating exponential random variables." *Communications of the Association for Computing Machinery* 7:298–300.

Martin, F. F. 1968. *Computer Modeling and Simulation*. New York: John Wiley and Sons.

Miller, G. A., E. Galanter, and K. H. Pribra. 1960. *Plans and the Structure of Behavior*. New York: Holt, Rinehart and Winston.

Muller, M. E. 1959. "A comparison of methods for generating normal deviates on a computer." *Journal of the Association for Computing Machinery* 6:376–83.

————. 1962. "Techniques and programming for sampling populations on magnetic tapes." In *Proceedings of the 1962 Middle Atlantic Conference of the American Society for Quality Control*, pp. 249–88. Milwaukee, Wisc.

National Bureau of Standards. 1964. *Handbook of Mathematical Functions with Formulas, Graphs and Mathematical Tables*. NBS Applied Mathematics Series No. 55. Washington, D.C.: U.S. Department of Commerce.

Naylor, T. H. 1969a. "Simulation and gaming, bibliography 19." *Computing Reviews* 10(1):61–69.

————, ed. 1969b. *The Design of Computer Simulation Experiments*. Durham, N.C.: Duke University Press.

Naylor, T. H., J. L. Balintfy, D. S. Burdick, and K. Chu. 1966. *Computer Simulation Techniques*. New York: John Wiley and Sons.

Nielsen, N. R. 1967. "The simulation of time-sharing systems." *Communications of the Association for Computing Machinery* 10(7):397–412.

Operations Research Staff. 1967. *BDOO/OA District Office Study Representative Instructions*. Baltimore, Md.: Operations Research Staff, Social Security Administration.

————. 1968. *BDOO/OA Initial Report: District Office Data Collection: Public Service Demands*. Baltimore, Md.: Operations Research Staff, Social Security Administration.

Orcutt, G. H., M. Greenberger, J. Korbel, and A. M. Rivlin. 1961. *Micro-Analysis of Socioeconomic Systems: A Simulation Study*. New York: Harper & Row.

Ozarowski, A. J., J. Enwright, and H. H. Holland. 1969. *BDOO/OA District Office Management Report*. Baltimore, Md.: Operations Research Staff, Social Security Administration.

Patrick, R. L. 1966. "Not-so-random discs." *Datamation* (June 1966):77–78.

Pritsker, A., and P. Kiviat. 1969. *Simulation with GASP II.* Englewood Cliffs, N.J.: Prentice-Hall.

Ralston, A., and H. S. Wilf, eds. 1960, 1967. *Mathematical Methods for Digital Computers.* 2 vols. New York: John Wiley and Sons.

Rosenfeld, J. L. 1969. "A case study in programming for parallel-processors." *Communications of the Association for Computing Machinery* 12:645–55.

Sakai, T., and M. Nagao. 1969. "Simulation of traffic flows in a network." *Communications of the Association for Computing Machinery* 12:311–18.

Sarhan, A. E., and B. G. Greenberg, eds. 1962. *Contributions to Order Statistics.* New York: John Wiley and Sons.

Scheffe, H. 1959. *The Analysis of Variance.* New York: John Wiley and Sons.

Schriber, T. J. 1970. *Fundamentals of Flowcharting.* New York: John Wiley and Sons.

Seaman, P. H., and R. C. Soucy. 1969. "Simulating operating systems." *IBM Systems Journal* 8(4):264–79.

Siegel, S. 1956. *Nonparametric Statistics for the Behavioral Sciences.* New York: McGraw-Hill Book Co.

Spang, H. A. 1962. "A review of minimization techniques for non-linear functions." *Society for Industrial and Applied Mathematics Review* 4:343–65.

Teichroew, D., and J. F. Lubin. 1966. "Computer simulation: Discussion of the technique and comparison of languages." *Communications of the Association for Computing Machinery* 9:723–41.

Thomson, W. E. 1958. "A modified congruence method of generating pseudo-random numbers." *The Computer Journal* 1(2):83–84.

Tompkins, S., and S. Messick, eds. 1963. *Computer Simulation of Personality.* New York: John Wiley and Sons.

United States Ordnance Corps. 1952. *Tables of the Cumulative Binomial Probabilities.* U.S. Ordnance Corps Pamphlet ORDP 20–1. Washington, D.C.: U.S. Government Printing Office.

Wadsworth, G. P., and J. G. Bryan. 1960. *Introduction to Probability and Random Variables.* New York: McGraw-Hill Book Co.

Wald, A. 1947. *Sequential Analysis.* New York: John Wiley and Sons.

Walsh, J. E. 1962, 1965, 1968. *Handbook of Nonparametric Statistics.* 3 vols. Princeton, N.J.: D. Van Nostrand Co.

Webster's Seventh New Collegiate Dictionary. 1967. Springfield, Mass.: G. and C. Merriam Co.

Weinert, A. E. 1967. "A SIMSCRIPT–FORTRAN case study." *Communications of the Association for Computing Machinery* 10(12):784–92.

Wilson, B. 1891. *Integral Calculus.* London.

Wolberg, J. R. 1967. *Prediction Analysis.* Princeton, N.J.: D. Van Nostrand Co.

Wood, D. C., and E. H. Forman. 1971. "Throughput measurement using a synthetic job stream." *American Federation of Information Processing Societies Conference Proceedings* 39:51–56.

Wyman, F. P. 1970. *Simulation Modeling: A Guide to Using SIMSCRIPT.* New York: John Wiley and Sons.

Index

Bold-faced entries indicate the page on which the indexed term is defined.

Absolute frequency, **42**

Activity, **17**, **163**

Additive congruential generator, **142**

Advantages of simulation, 5–6, 21

All possible regressions (combinations), **98**

Analog computer, **8**, 13

Analysis of variance, **114**–31

Arrival frequency at district offices, 62–65, 360–64

Arrivals, simulation of, 164–66, 360–64

Attributes, **16**–17, 27, **163**

Average contents, **181**–82

Average utilization, **181**–82

Backward elimination, **98**–99

Bank branch simulation, 213–18, 238–45, 251, 297–310, 314

Batch system, simulation of, 324–28

Binomial distribution, **48**–49, 61

Binomially distributed numbers, 155

Cell, **115**

Censored samples, 85

Central limit theorem, **52**, 61

Central moments, **48**

Chain, **170**

Chebyshev criterion for function-fitting, **90**

Chi square distribution, **59**, 398

Chi square test, 82–85, 86–87, 137–39, 398, 408–12

Choice of distribution, 56

Composite method, **153**

Computer jobs, data on, 83, 86, 128–31

Computers, simulation of, 26, 317–42

Confidence interval, **76**, 91

Confounded effects, **123**

Congruential method, 136, **140**–42, 430–33

Contingency tables, **82**–83

Continuous density and distribution, 46

Continuous system, **12**–13

Control group, **33**, 36, 389–90

Correlation coefficient, **93**

Covariance, analysis of, 125–26

Critical-event models, **15**, 19–21, 163

Critical value, **75**

Cross-over designs, 126

Cumulative time integral, **181**

461

Data sources, 27–29
Density, **45**–47
Deterministic system, **13**–14
Disadvantages of simulation, 6, 21
Discrete system, **12**–13
Distance (D^2) test, **138**–39
Distribution, 41, **46**–47
District office simulation, 9–12, 343–94

Empirical density, 45
Empirical distribution, **42**, 54–58
Empirically distributed numbers, 150–52, 156
Endogenous variables, **16**
Entity, **16**, 27, **162**
Equidistribution test, **137**
Erlang distribution, **157**–58
Error in regression, 91
Error in testing hypotheses, 68–69
Error reduction, 125–26
Event, 15, **163**
Exogenous variables, **16**
Expert opinion, 29, 35, 37
Explained sum of squares (SSE), **92**
Exponential distribution, **52**–53, 61, 406
Exponentially distributed numbers, 154–55

F distribution, 59–**60**, 399–402
F test, 75–76, 97, 114, 117, 399–402
Factorial designs, **115**–16
Field, **31**
Field study, 27–30, 37, 348–49, 351–56
FIFO queues, **169**
File, **31**
Flowchart, **27**, 38
FORTRAN, 166–69
FORTRAN scientific subroutines,
    AVCAL, 124
    AVDAT, 124
    KOLM1, 79
    KOLM2, 77
    MEANQ, 124
    MULTR, 95
    STPRG, 99
    UTEST, 82
Fractional factorial design, **123**
Frequency test, **137**

Gap test, **139**
Games, **16**, 19

Gamma distribution, 125, 157, **364**–66
Garbage collection, **173**
GASP, 162, 205–6
Gauss-Markov theorem, 91
Geometrically distributed numbers, 155
GPSS, 198–203, 206–8, 211–307
    ADVANCE, 200, **223–25**, 273, 436
    ALTER, 436, 452
    ASSEMBLE, 436, 452
    assembled form, **216–18**
    ASSIGN, **256**, 437
    average contents, 181, **237**
    average time per transaction, **235**, **237**, 238
    average utilization, 181, 234–**35**, **237**
    block count, **218**
    block definition cards, **220**, 436–41
    block diagram, 213
    block diagram shapes, 220
    block entities, **212**
    block name, **220**
    block types, 199, 212, 219–22
    BUFFER, 437, 452
    BVARIABLE, 442
    chain entity, **199**
    CHANGE, 437, 452
    CLEAR control card, 203, 231–32, 262, 443
    clock times, **218**
    comment request card, 291
    COMMENTS field, 220, 222
    control cards, **202**, 216, 230–32, 443–44
    COUNT X, 437, 452
    cumulative time integral, 181, **233–35**
    current contents, **237**
    debugging, 243–**46**
    definition cards, **202**, 442
    DEPART, 201, **229**, 437
    district office program, 384–85
    editing packet, **285**
    equipment entities, 213
    END, 230, 443
    endgraph request card, 297
    ENTER, 201, **227–28**, 437
    entity definition cards, 442
    error messages, 246, 444–51
    EXAMINE, 437, 452
    EXECUTE, 437, 452
    facility entity, 198, **225**
    facility statistics, 235
    floating point variable, **273**
    format request card, 290
    frequency classes, **264**
    frequency distribution table, 263
    function definition card, 269, 442
    function entity, 269
    function follower cards, 269
    functions, 269, 273
    FVARIABLE, 442
    GATE X, 437, 452
    GATHER, 437, 452
    GENERATE, 200, **223**–25, 273, 438
    graph request card, 292

GPSS,
  graphic output, 292
  graphing packet, **292**
  include request card, 288
  INDEX, 438, 452
  indirect addressing, **257**
  indirect specification, **257**–58
  INITIAL control card, **262**, 442
  initialize savevalues, 262
  input deck format, 232
  integer constants, **255**
  JOB, 443
  JOBTAPE, 443
  JOIN, 438, 452
  LEAVE, 438
  LINK, **281**–82, 438
  LIST, 443
  LOC field, 220, 222
  LOGIC X, 438, 452
  LOOP, 438, 452
  MARK, 438, 452
  MATCH, 438, 452
  matrix definition card, 260, 442
  matrix savevalue, 260
  maximum contents, **237**–38
  mean argument, 267
  MSAVEVALUE, **260–62**, 438
  number of entries, **235**
  offset time, **223**
  OPERANDS field, 220–21
  OPERATION field, 220–21
  output request card, 291
  origin request card, 293
  percent zeroes, **238**
  PREEMPT, **225–27**, 438–39
  PRINT, **284**–85, 439
  PRIORITY, 439, 452
  QUEUE, 201, **229**, 439
  queue entity, 199, 228
  queue statistics, 235
  queue table entity, **266**
  READ, 443
  random number generator, 144–45, 267–69
  redefining savevalues, 262
  relative clock, **219**, 255
  RELEASE, 201, **226**, 439
  REMOVE, 439, 452
  report request card, 285–86
  RESET control card, 202, **231**, 262, 443
  RETURN, **226**, 439
  REWIND, 443
  RMULT control card, **268**, 443
  SAVEVALUE, **259**, 440
  savevalues, **259**–62
  SCAN, 440, 452
  SEIZE, 201, 225–**26**, 440
  SELECT X, 440, 452
  SIMULATE control card, **230**, 444
  SNA, **254**–55
  source program, **216**
  special output, 285
  spill classes, **264**
  SPLIT, 440, 452

GPSS,
  standard deviation, 267
  standard numerical attributes (SNAs), **254**–55
  standard table output, 266
  START control card, **230**, 444
  statement request card, 297
  storage definition card, 227, 442
  storage entity, 227
  storage statistics, 235
  symbol tables, **216**
  symbolic names, **222**, 254
  table definition card, 264, 442
  table entity, 263
  TABULATE, 202, **265**, 441
  TERMINATE, 200, **223–25**, 441
  termination count, **224**, 230
  TEST, 202, **280**–81, 441
  title request card, 287
  TRACE, 246, 441
  transaction parameters, 255–56
  transactions, **198**, 213
  TRANSFER, 202, 223–**25**, 232, 441
  transit time, **264**
  UNLINK, 281–**83**, 441
  UNLIST, 444
  UNTRACE, 246, 441
  user chain link indicator, **282**
  user chain SNAs, 283
  user chains, 281–84
  utilization statistics, 232
  variables, 273–75, 442
  WRITE, 441, 452
  X request card, 293
  Y request card, 296
  zero entries, **238**
GPSS V, 453

Head pointer, **170**, 178

Hearings data, 95–96, 104–5, 108–9

Historical standard, 35, 37

Horse race data, 93–95, 100–102, 109–11, 117–18, 313

Hypergeometric distribution, 61

Homoscedasticity, **115**

Incomplete blocks, 126

Increment, **140**

Initialize, **21**

Interaction, 115, **119**–20

Interarrival times, 43–46, 53, 56–58, 80, 121–23, 128, **182**

Interview times, 78, 83–85, 87, 128, 364–66

Inverse transformation method, **150**–52, 154

Job generator, 319

Keyboard-to-tape devices, **31**
Keypunch, **30**
Kolmogorov-Smirnov test, 77–79, 137, 403
Kurtosis, **48**

Latin squares, 126
Lattice designs, 126
Least-squares, **90**–105, 414–26
Length of a generator, **136**
Level of significance, **68**–69
Levels of factors, **115**
LIFO queues, **169**
Linked lists, **170**
List processing in PL/I, 171–73, 177–79

Macro-level of computer simulation, **318**
Main effects, **123**
Man-machine simulations, **15**–16
Mann Whitney U test, 81–82
Marsaglia methods,
    exponentially distributed numbers, 155
    normally distributed numbers, 154
    uniformly distributed numbers, 143
Mean, **47**, 61
Mean square about regression, **92**
Mean square due to regression (SSE), **95**
Median, **80**
Micro-level of computer simulation, **318**
Microprogrammed system, simulation of,
    328–41
Mid-square method, **136**
Minimax criterion for function fitting, **70**
Mixed congruential generators, **141**
Mixed method, **153**
Model, **5**, 14–15, 21, 26–27, 37–38
Modulus, **140**
Moments, **47**–48
Multilinked lists, 170
Multinomial distribution, 61
Multiple linear regression (MLR), **95**–103
Multiplicative congruential generators, **141**
Multiplier, **140**
Multivariate distributions, 60

Negative binomial distribution, 61
Noncentral F distribution, 117
Noncentral t distribution, 73
Nonlinear regression, **103**–4, 417–26

Nonparametric one-way analysis of variance,
    118
Nonparametric tests, **70**, 77–85
Normal distribution, 51–52, 61, 396, 413–14
Normally distributed numbers, 153–54

One-tailed test, **72**
One-way analysis of variance, **116**–18
Oil port data, 72, 74–75, 81–82
Optical scanner, **31**
Order statistics, 85
Outliers, **102**–3

Paired samples, 86
Parameter, **35**
Parametric tests, **70**–77, 85
Period of a generator, **136**
Permutation test, **138**
Personnel requirements, 29, 33–37
PL/I, 173–80
Pointer, **170**
Poisson distributed numbers, 155–56
Poisson distribution, **49**–50, 61, 76–77
Poisson parameter, testing of, 76–77
Poker test, **138**
Postprocessor, 386–87
Power curve, **69**
Power of a test, **68**–69
Preprocessor, 366–69, 382–84
Problem formulation, 25–26
Pseudorandom numbers, **136**

Queues, **169**, 179, 180
Queueing disciplines, **169**

Random event, **42**
RANDOM queues, **169**
Random number generation, 50, **135**–58,
    405–6, 426–33
Random sample, **71**
Randomized blocks, 126
RANKED queues, **169**
Record, **31**
Regression, **90**–110, 126–27, 414–17
Rejection method, **152**–53, 155
Relative frequency, **42**
Relaxed forward stepwise MLR, 98–**99**
Reneges, 76–77
Replication, **115**

Residual variance, **92**
Residuals, **92**–95
    analysis of, 102–3
    fitting to, **98**–99
Robust, **116**
Run, computer, **18**–19
Run, statistical, **79**–81
Runs test, 79–81, 138, 404

Sample space, **42**
Screening, **123**
Seed of a generator, 141
Sequential test, 73
Serial test, **137**
SIMSCRIPT, 183–98, 206–8
    ACCUMULATE, 192
    CANCEL, 190
    CAUSE, 190
    COMPUTE, 192
    CREATE, 188
    definition section, **183**
    DESTROY, 188
    DO, 192–93
    endogenous routine, **185**
    event routine, **183**
    event routine list, **185**
    example, 194–98
    exogenous event list, **186**
    exogenous routine, **185**
    FIND, 193
    FILE, 191
    IF, 191
    initialization section, **186**
    permanent system variables, **183**
    REMOVE FIRST, 191
    report generator, **193**
    statements, 188–94
    statistics, 193
    temporary entities, **183**
SIMULA, 162, 205–**6**, 208
Simulation, **4**
Simulation clock, **164**
Sine function fitting, 104–7
Skewness, **48**
Software, **7**
Spectral test, **138**
Stagewise regression, **98**–99
Standard deviation, **48**, 61
Standard error of estimate, **92**
Standard normal distribution, **51**, 61
Standard uniform distribution, 50, 61
State of a system, **163**
Statistical regularity, **42**
Statistics gathering, 180

Status attribute, **17**
Stepwise regression, **98**–99
Stochastic system, **14**
Straight line, fitting a, 92–95, 414–17
Student's *t* distribution, **58**–59
Subsystem, **9**
Sum of squares of residuals (SSR), **92**
Survey techniques, 29, 38
Synthetic job streams, 320–21
System, **8**–10, 21, 163

t test, 71–75, 86, 397
Tail pointer, **170**, 178
Telephone booth simulation, 162–168,
    173–80, 194–98, 203–5
Tests, statistical,
    censored samples, 85
    dispersions, 75–76
    distributions, 77–79, 81–85
    levels, 71–75, 81–82, 86, 114–27
    linear regression, 93, 414–17
    MLR, 103
    order statistics, 85
    outliers, 102
    Poisson parameter, 76–77
    sample variance, 86
    sequences, 79–81
    summary, 70
3^n designs, **125**
Ticket counter simulation, 275–80
Time-slice models, **15**, 19–21
Total sum of squares (TSS), **92**
Traffic problems, 49–50
Transit time, **182**
Triangular distribution, **57**
2^n designs, **123**–24
Two-tailed *chi* square test, 86–87
Two-tailed test, **72**
Two-way analysis of variance, **118**–23
Type I error, **68**–69
Type II error, **68**–69

U statistic, **81**
Uniform distribution, **50**–51, 61

Validity, 19, 21, **33**–35, 105–8, 124, 388–90
Variance, **48**, 61
Verifier, **30**

Weibull distribution, 61

Z statistic, **82**

Sponsoring editor: Stephen Dennis Mitchell
Project editor: Larry McCombs
Designer: Michael Rogondino
Figures: Ayxa Art of Palo Alto, California.
Photographer: Ken Graves

The text of this book was set in Optima, a sans-serif face
designed in 1958 by Hermann Zapf. Major heads are set in Futura.
Helvetica was used for computer language within the text,
for subheads, and for figure legends and tables. Subscripts
and superscripts are set in Times Roman.

Composition was done on film by Applied Typographic Systems
of Mountain View, California.

The book was printed by Kingsport Press, Kingsport, Tennessee.